HD
7256
.U6
P74
1995

Principles And Practices Of Disability Management In Industry

Principles And Practices Of Disability Management In Industry

Editors

Donald E. Shrey, Ph.D., C.R.C.
Michel Lacerte, M.D.

GR PRESS, INC.

Copyright © 1995 by GR Press
Copyright © 1997 by CRC Press LLC

All rights reserved. No part of this publication may be reproduced, stored in a retrieval system or transmitted in any form or by any means, electronic, mechanical, photocopying, recording or otherwise, without the prior written permission of the publisher.

Printed and bound in the U.S.A. Printed on acid-free paper.

10 9 8 7 6 5 4 3 2

ISBN 1-878205-63-3

Library of Congress Card Number 94-073029

Opinions and views expressed in this book do not necessarily represent those of the publisher nor does it serve as an endorsement for those views or opinions.

This publication is designed to provide accurate and authoritative information in regard to the subject matter covered. It is sold with the understanding that the publisher is not engaged in rendering legal, accounting, or other professional service. If legal advice or other expert assistance is required, the services of a competent professional should be sought.

Direct all inquiries to CRC Press, 2000 Corporate Blvd., N.W., Boca Raton, Florida 33431. Phone (561) 994-0555.

TABLE OF CONTENTS

ABOUT THE EDITORS ix

CONTRIBUTING AUTHORS xi

ACKNOWLEDGMENTS xv

INTRODUCTION xvii

SECTION I: WORKSITE-BASED DISABILITY MANAGEMENT PRACTICE

1   Worksite Disability Management and Industrial Rehabilitation:
    An Overview 3
    Donald E. Shrey, Ph.D., C.R.C.

2   Disability Management Practice at the Worksite: Developing,
    Implementing, and Evaluating Transitional Work Programs 55
    Donald E. Shrey, Ph.D, C.R.C.

3   The Role of the Physical Therapist in Transitional
    Work Programs 107
    Joseph H. Daly, M.A., P.T.

4   Occupational Health Nurses in Disability Management 131
    Karen J. Martin, Ph.D., C.O.H.N.

5   Ergonomics, Injury Prevention, and Disability Management 157
    Anil Mital, Ph.D., P.E.

6   The Role of the Physician in Disability Management 175
    Steven Scheer, M.D.

7   Evaluation of Work Disability from a Worker—
    Work Environment Perspective 207
    Michel Lacerte, M.D., C.R.C.
    Lorraine Desjardins, C.R.C.

8   Building Joint Labor-Management Initiatives for
    Worksite Disability Management 225
    Debra L. Mills

9   Interdisciplinary Factors in the Management of
Cumulative Trauma-related Disability 249
Mark R. Stultz. M.S.I.E., P.T.

10   Functional Capacity Assessment, Worker Evaluation
Strategies, and the Disability Management Process 269
Lester A. Owens, D.O.
Rodney L. Buchholz, M.Ed.

11   Essential Competencies in Industrial Rehabilitation
and Disability Management Practice: A Skills-based
Training Model 303
Norman C. Hursh, Sc.D., C.R.C., C.V.E.

SECTION II: DISABILITY MANAGEMENT PERSPECTIVES AND TRENDS

12   Historical Perspectives on the Rehabilitation Counseling
Profession and Disability Management 355
Joseph E. Havranek, Ed.D., C.R.C.

13   Occupational Stress: A Disability Management Perspective 371
Robert G. Lasky, Ph.D.

14   Disability Management: A Family Perspective 411
Paul W. Power, Sc.D., C.R.C.
Arthur E. Dell Orto, Ph.D., C.R.C.

15   Legal Perspectives on Disability Resolution and
Industrial Rehabilitation 433
Luca E. Conte, Ph.D., C.R.C.
Mary K. Van Antwerp, J.D.

16   Integrated Disability Management and Claims
Management: An Employer-centered Alternative
to Costly Litigation 451
Steven Cantlon

17   A Canadian Perspective on Disability Management 465
Wolfgang Zimmermann

18   Health Insurance, Workers' Compensation, and the
Americans with Disabilities Act 479
Brian T. McMahon, Ph.D., C.R.C.

19   Protecting the Employability of the Working Elderly 499
Donald E. Shrey, Ph.D., C.R.C.
Norman G. Hursh, Sc.D., C.R.C., C.V.E.

20 Managed Care Concepts in the Delivery of Disability
    Management Services to Industry 519
    William J. DeMarco, C.M.C.
    Karen Wolfe, R.N., M.A., M.B.A.
21 An International View of Work Disability: Trends and
    Implications for Worker Rehabilitation 555
    Andrew Remenyi

GLOSSARY 603

INDEX 629

About The Editors

DONALD E. SHREY, PH. D., C.R.C.

Dr. Shrey is President of Advanced Transitions, Inc., an international consulting business, specializing in workers' compensation cost control. He is a pioneer in the development of employer-based transitional work programs and disability management systems for labor and industry. He has been a disability management researcher, training specialist, and human resource consultant to employers for 20 years.

Dr. Shrey has also served as Associate Professor in the Department of Physical Medicine and Rehabilitation at the University of Cincinnati Medical Center since 1987. He was Associate Professor for the Department of Rehabilitation Counseling at Boston University, and he has taught in the graduate school of Syracuse University, where he earned his doctorate degree in Rehabilitation Counseling. His career has included work as a psychologist and as a Certified Rehabilitation Counselor. For several years, he was a senior consultant to Liberty Mutual Medical Service Center in Boston, and he was a featured speaker at loss prevention seminars throughout the United States.

Dr. Shrey has consulted with industry, health care providers, insurance companies, and government in the United States, Canada, Australia and New Zealand. He has been a World Rehabilitation Fellow and World Institute on Disability Fellow, and he has studied disability management systems in Canada and Australia. He has been a Vocational Expert for the Social Security Administration in the United States since 1977. He currently serves on the International Advisory Board for Canada's National Institute on Disability Management and Research.

Dr. Shrey has developed disability management programs for Honda, Toyota, General Electric Aircraft Engines, Campbells, Schneider Trucking, TS Trim, Minster Machine Company, MacMillan-Bloedel, the City of Oregon, Ohio, and other employers. He specializes in developing joint labor-management sponsored industrial rehabilitation programs in industry.

Dr. Shrey received the 1991 national research award from the National Rehabilitation Association. He serves on the editorial board of the *Rehabilitation Counseling Bulletin*, the *Journal of Occupational Rehabilitation*, and *Work Injury Management*, and he has served on the Medical Advisory Board of the American Trucking Association. Dr. Shrey has published over 50 articles, book chapters, papers and reports related to disability management and industrial rehabilitation.

Disability Management Development Services

Employer Consultation to Develop On-site Disability Management Systems & Transitional Work Programs and Disability Management Training & Educational Services for Labor and Management

Contact Dr. Donald Shrey at:
Advanced Transitions, Inc.
2959 Perthwood Drive
Cincinnati, Ohio 45244
(513) 232-6592

MICHEL LACERTE, M.D.

Dr. Lacerte is Associate Director of the University of Western Ontario Faculty of Medicine, Office of Continuing Education. He is responsible for all matters related to disability issues. He is a specialist in Physical Medicine and Rehabilitation Medicine. His background includes medical training at McGill University, specialty training at the Mayo Clinic and research fellowship at the University of Washington in Seattle. His clinical activities are centered around the evaluation and treatment of musculoskeletal injuries and the rehabilitation of catastrophic injuries (spinal cord and head injuries).

Dr. Lacerte is involved as a disability management consultant with several insurance and rehabilitation agencies. He has developed the musculoskeletal system Impairment Evaluation Training Program for the Workers' Compensation Board of Ontario. He has been appointed by the Ontario Government as Medical Representative to the advisory board of the Office of the Employers Advisers. He has also had extensive involvement as a consultant to both employer and labor organizations.

Dr. Lacerte has published articles in a wide variety of journals and publications, and is currently on the editorial board of *Work Injury Management*, a national newsletter for rehabilitation professionals working in the field of workers' compensation rehabilitation. He is an international speaker on topics related to disability management and disability evaluation.

Contributing Authors

Chapter 10
RODNEY L. BUCHHOLZ, M.ED.
  Exercise Physiologist, Work Rehabilitation Specialist, Fit For Work Center, Theda Clark Regional Medical Center, Neenah, WI

Chapter 16
STEVE N. CANTLON
  Vice President, Cantlon and Associates, Columbus, OH

Chapter 15
LUCA E. CONTE, PH.D., C.R.C.
  Vice-President, Parker-Conte Associates, Louisville, KY

Chapter 3
JOSEPH H. DALY, M.A., P.T.
  Occupational Health Management, Inc., Columbus, OH

Chapter 14
ARTHUR E. DELL ORTO, PH.D., C.R.C.
Chairman and Professor, Department of Rehabilitation Counseling, Sargent College of Allied Health Professions, Boston University, Boston, MA

Chapter 20
WILLIAM J. DEMARCO, C.M.C.
  President, DeMarco & Associates, Inc., Rockford, IL

Chapter 7
LORRAINE DESJARDINS, C.R.C.
> Manager, London Disability Management Research Group, Inc., London, Ontario, Canada

Chapter 12
JOSEPH E. HAVRANEK, ED.D., C.R.C.
> Assistant Professor, Rehabilitation Counseling Program, Bowling Green State University, Bowling Green, OH

Chapters 11 and 19
NORMAN C. HURSH, SC.D., C.R.C., C.V.E.
> Director of Industrial Rehabilitation and Disability Management, Department of Rehabilitation Counseling, Boston University, Boston, MA

Chapter 13
ROBERT G. LASKY, PH.D.
> Vice President of Rehabilitation, Human Service Options, Inc., Braintree, MA

Chapter 7
MICHEL LACERTE, M.D.
> Associate Director, Office of Continuing Education, University of Western Ontario, London, Ontario; Canada

Chapter 4
KAREN J. MARTIN, PH.D., C.O.H.N.
Professor and Assistant Dean of Research, Department Head of Graduate Studies, College of Nursing, Valdosta State University, Valdosta, GA

Chapter 18
BRIAN T. MCMAHON, PH.D., C.R.C.
> Professor and Area Chair, Rehabilitation Counseling Program, Education Psychology Department, University of Wisconsin-Milwaukee, Milwaukee, WI

Chapter 8
DEBRA L. MILLS
Director; Vocational Rehabilitation and Service Effectiveness, Compensation Services Division, Workers' Compensation Board of British Columbia, Richmond, British Columbia, Canada

Chapter 5
ANIL MITAL, PH.D., P.E.
    Professor, Department of Mechanical, Industrial & Nuclear Engineering, University of Cincinnati, Cincinnati, OH

Chapter 10
LESTER A. OWENS, D.O.
    CEO, Rehabilitation Resource Group, Green Bay, WI

Chapter 14
PAUL W. POWER, SC.D., C.R.C.
    Director, Rehabilitation Counseling Program, Counseling and Personnel Services Department, University of Maryland, College Park, MD

Chapter 21
ANDREW G. REMENYI, M.A., A.I.E.
    Senior Lecturer, LaTrobe University, Department of Behavioural Health Sciences, Bundoora, Victoria, Australia

Chapter 6
STEVEN J. SCHEER, M.D.
    Director, Department of Physical Medicine and Rehabilitation, University of Cincinnati Medical Center; Director, Rehabilitation Medicine, The Drake Center, Inc., Cincinnati, OH

Chapters 1, 2, and 19
DONALD E. SHREY, PH.D., C.R.C.
    President, Advanced Transitions, Inc.; Associate Professor, Department of Physical Medicine and Rehabilitation, University of Cincinnati Medical Center, Cincinnati, OH

Chapter 9
MARK R. STULTZ, M.S.I.E., P.T.
   Senior Ergonomist, Manager of Corporate Development, The Saunders Groups, Inc., Chaska, MN

Chapter 15
MARY K. VAN ANTWERP, J.D.
   Workers' Compensation Claim Supervisor, Wausau Insurance Companies, Indianapolis, IN

Chapter 20
KAREN WOLFE, R.N., M.A., M.B.A.
   President/CEO, Health Management Technologies, Inc., Managed Disability Software, Moraga, CA

Chapter 17
WOLFGANG ZIMMERMANN
   Executive Director of the Disabled Forestry Workers' Foundation of Canada; Chairperson for the British Columbia Premier's Advisory Council for Persons with Disabilities, Port Alberni, British Columbia; Canada

Acknowledgments

There were many individuals who contributed time, ideas, and encouragement in the development of this book. Meaningful contributions take many forms. We wish to thank Dr. Paul Deutsch and Dr. Brian McMahon for their charisma regarding the need for this book, and the encouragement to begin the task of outlining the book's concepts during the initial "idea" stage. Several people assisted with the awesome task of editing the chapters to ensure accuracy and consistency. We thank Ann Groom for her perseverence throughout the editorial process. Special thanks also to Susan Shrey for her assistance in reviewing several chapters, and to Nancy Scott for her contributions regarding Canadian trends in workplace integration and disability management. A very special thanks to Patty Williams for coordinating correspondence among the many contributors to this book, and for her ability to organize challenging projects and to maintain accurate filing systems. We are grateful to Don Sanders, President of Workplace Innovations Network, for showing us how to measure the financial impact of transitional work programs and disability management systems. Also, Jim Bishop, President of American Workplace Consultants, who shared his perspectives on safety and loss prevention services, as a vital component of an optimal disability management system in industry. We are most appreciative of the assistance from Dave Radecke of the Ohio Bureau of Workers' Compensation – Rehabilitation Division, for his clinical perspectives on disability management. Thank you, Dave, for helping us design Ohio's first transitional work program at Malta Windows Division of Phillips Industries in 1990, and for your ongoing commitment to educate employers as effective disability managers. For his personal support and encouragement, we gratefully acknowledge Wolfgang Zimmermann and the staff of Canada's National Institute on Disability Management and Research. We would also like to thank the many employers who have given us the privilege of assisting them in the development of disability management systems and transitional work programs. Especially, we thank both labor and management representatives of MacMillan-Bloedel, Honda of America Manufacturing, Campbell's Fresh, the City of Oregon in Ohio, TS Trim, and Minster Machine Company. We also wish to recognize all the labor organizations that have actively participated in many of the disability management systems reviewed in this book. Particularly, we wish to thank the Communications, Energy, and Paper Workers Union (CEP) and the International Woodworkers of America/Canada (IWA). Acknowledgment is also made to Dean Robert McMurtry for recognizing the importance of disability issues and the need for a division of Continuing Education on Disability Issues at the University of Western Ontario. Finally, a personal thank you to Lorraine and Maria for their ongoing support and patience.

INTRODUCTION

This book is based on several interrelated principles. First, disability management is the proactive process of minimizing the impact of injury, disability, or disease on the worker's capacity to perform work. Second, the goal of disability management is to protect the employability of the worker, while preserving the financial interests of the employer. Third, disability management interventions, programs and services are most efficacious when provided (as much as possible) at the worksite. This third principle assumes the prominent role of labor and management in the coordination and provision of disability management services. Fourth, disability management is an interdisciplinary concept that includes physical, emotional, vocational, medical and organizational factors that impact on employment.

In order for the total book to retain high philosophical consistency, it was essential for all authors to integrate disability management themes, as described above, within their respective chapters. It was not the intent of the editors to unnecessarily restrict authors from developing chapters based on their areas of expertise. In fact, the selected authors represent professionals from a broad range of backgrounds, all of which reflect the multidimensional nature of disability management.

Many journal articles and publications have been written regarding disability management concepts and principles. However, we recognized a current need for a book that provides more specific information on the development of disability management programs, services, and interventions. Therefore, some chapters in this book address practical applications of concepts, as well as philosophies and principles. For example, many chapters begin with an overview of relevant concepts, existing models and current issues, followed by practical information, guidance and suggestions for the reader to develop and implement disability management interventions.

We also believe that many employers have relinquished control and responsibility for disability management to external third parties and service providers. This has been a costly error for employers and for injured workers. Employers need to acquire the knowledge and skills that are central to managing injury and disability problems. Business and industry must create its own infrastructure to support return to work programs for injured workers, and these programs must be responsibly managed by employers in collaboration with labor organizations. In large part, this book was written to encourage joint labor-management initiatives in disability management. Strategies are discussed to increase organizational effectiveness, without sacrificing the health, safety and employability of workers with disabilities.

In response to the changing socioeconomic environment, employers are pressured to integrate and accommodate people with disabilities. To accomplish legislatively mandated goals for reintegration, this book offers cohesive, comprehensive, and progressive worksite-based strategies to managing the complex needs of people with disabilities.

Section I of the book, *Worksite-based Disability Management Practice*, provides a comprehensive overview of optimal disability management and industrial rehabilitation services, and model programs in industry. The step-by-step process of developing a worksite-based transitional work program is presented, which offers an effective approach to reducing lost time and associated costs. The authors stress the importance of bringing rehabilitation interventions to the worksite, rather than extending rehabilitation activities in hospitals and clinics. The roles of physical therapists, occupational health nurses, ergonomists, physicians, and case managers, as members of the on-site disability management team, is discussed extensively in Section I. Current models of industry-based disability management programs are illustrated, including program features, operational policies, and measurable outcome criteria. Section I also underscores the importance of joint labor-management support for worksite-based disability management programs. Procedures for establishing joint labor-management initiatives are discussed. Finally, Section I identifies the essential competencies, including skills and knowledge, required for outcome-based disability management systems in industry.

Section II of the book offers the reader a comprehensive view of *Disability Management Perspectives and Trends*. Beginning with a historical perspective on the evolution of industrial rehabilitation and disability management services, the reader is offered viewpoints on disability management from various stakeholders, including: rehabilitation psychologists, the injured worker's family, the workers' compensation attorney, the claims manager, the health care provider, the advocate for the person with a disability, the older worker, and the managed care system. The reader is given an overview of current challenges to disability management, and a projection of trends for future disability management policy and practice. Included in Section II is a detailed discussion of national health insurance issues, workers' compensation, and the Americans with Disabilities Act. International perspectives and trends, with respect to occupational case management and reintegration, are extensively discussed in Section II.

Finally, our book was designed as resource text for employers, labor organizations, allied health professionals, physicians, occupational health nurses, human resource managers, and other disability management professionals. All chapter au-

Introduction

thors were invited to develop a Glossary of Terms, which has been included in this book. Also, hundreds of references were cited throughout the book, providing the reader with additional resources to explore and to research specific topics of interests. We are hopeful that the ideas and experiences shared in this book will provide our readers with a foundation for developing successful disability management and transitional work programs in industry.

                                  Donald E. Shrey, Ph.D., C.R.C
                                  Michel Lacerte, M.D.

Section I

Worksite-based Disability Management Practice

… — 1 —

Worksite Disability Management And Industrial Rehabilitation: An Overview

Donald E. Shrey, Ph.D., C.R.C.

INTRODUCTION TO DISABILITY MANAGEMENT

Employers are faced with increasing societal and legislative pressure to integrate and accommodate people with disabilities. Concurrently, escalating workers' compensation and health care costs are threatening the survival of business and draining resources otherwise allocated to future economic development. This chapter introduces worksite disability management and industrial rehabilitation principles, strategies, and practices. Disability management is given an operational definition in this chapter, which is examined at societal, clinical, management, and environmental levels. This chapter delineates the goals and objectives of disability management in the context of maintaining the "occupational bond" between employers and workers. The importance of the therapeutic work environment is examined.

Beginning at the societal level, an overview is presented on disability management economics, implications of the aging workforce, and the significance of the Americans with Disabilities Act. Disability management is also viewed from a labor relations perspective, and strategies to facilitate joint labor-management initiatives in injured worker rehabilitation are discussed. This chapter offers a strong focus on "early intervention" concepts, citing outcome studies, psycho-social issues, and proven strategies in promoting timely services to workers with injuries and disabilities.

The key principles of worksite disability management programs are outlined, with examples of model disability management programs and joint labor-management initiatives. The multiple roles of on-site and contractual disability managers are reviewed, including essential roles and functions suggested by experts in disability management research and practice. Finally, this chapter presents key organizational concepts in disability management that strengthen service delivery and successful outcome through rehabilitation planning and decision-making. Promoting respect and dignity between workers with disabilities and the professionals that serve them is emphasized.

DISABILITY MANAGEMENT DEFINITIONS AND KEY CONCEPTS

Disability management has been conceptualized at various levels (e.g., societal, clinical, administrative), and by many parties (e.g., medical providers, politicians, bureaucrats, claims managers, insurance carriers, rehabilitation professionals). Each discipline seems to have used the term *disability management* to promote its self-interests. As a result, disability management has become one of the most broadly defined (and often distorted) terms in health care. Disability management is an important concept that deserves clear definition. Disability management, being a highly interdisciplinary concept, requires an operational definition that includes goals, objectives, policies, and procedures.

> Disability management is the least understood, yet most important, mechanism for reducing risks and controlling the consequences of workplace injury and disability. In order to more fully understand disability management, it is helpful to clarify what disability management is not. It is _not_ claims management, a process coordinated through workers' compensation or disability insurance to distribute cash benefits and coordinate medical payments. It is _not_ the traditional vocational rehabilitation process. It is _not_ an expensive approach to controlling injury and disability costs. It is _not_ an approach that relies only on outside experts, such as safety consultants or loss control managers. It is _not_ a "faddish" health promotion and wellness program designed for employee health care risk reduction. Most important, disability management is _not_ an approach that excludes the employer. It is _not_ a "canned" approach or "packaged" process intended to work similarly for employers. It clearly is _not_ a passive response to injury and disability. Above all, disability management requires the active planning and coordination of labor, management, insurance carriers, health care providers, and vocational rehabilitation professionals. (Shrey, 1990, pp. 92-93)

OPERATIONAL DEFINITION

Disability management is operationally defined as "an active process of minimizing the impact of an impairment (resulting from injury, illness, or disease) on the individual's capacity to participate competitively in the work environment." The basic principles of disability management are as follows:

1. It is a proactive (not passive or reactive) process.
2. It is a process that enables labor and management to assume joint responsibility as proactive decision-makers, planners, and coordinators of workplace-based interventions and services.
3. It promotes disability prevention strategies, rehabilitation treatment concepts, and safe work-return programs designed to control the personal and economic costs of workplace injury and disability.

Disability management involves the use of services, people, and materials to minimize the impact and cost of disability to employers and employees and encourages return to work for employees with disabilities (Schwartz, Watson, Galvin, & Lippoff, 1989). When defining *disability management*, it is important to distinguish between the related concepts *impairment*, *disability*, and *handicap*, which the World Health Organization has defined as follows:

Impairment: any loss or abnormality of psychological, physiological, or anatomical structure or function.
Disability: any restriction or lack (resulting from an impairment) of ability to perform an activity in the manner or within the range considered normal for a human being.
Handicap: a disadvantage for a given individual, resulting from an impairment or a disability that limits or prevents the fulfillment of a role that is normal (depending on age, sex, social, and cultural factors) for that individual.

Based on these definitions, one needs to understand that not all impairments result in a disability; nor do all disabilities necessarily result in a handicap. To prevent impairments and subsequent disabilities from becoming handicaps, it is necessary to manage personal, environmental, and organizational factors that functionally compromise an individual's fulfillment of a specific role. That role, in the context of disability management, is competitive employment (Dell Orto & Marinelli, in press).

Successfully managing the consequences of illness, injury, and chronic disease in the work force requires an accurate understanding of the following:

- Types of injuries and illnesses that occur;
- The employer's timely response to the injury or illness;
- Clear administrative policies and procedures; and
- The effective utilization of health care and rehabilitation services.

Disability management practices are based on a comprehensive, cohesive, and progressive employer-based approach to managing the complex needs of people with disabilities within a given work and socioeconomic environment. Despite rapidly escalating costs of injury and disability, rehabilitation technologies, and disability management resources are available to facilitate immediate and recurrent savings among business and industry. Disability management policies, procedures, and strategies, when properly integrated within the employer's organization, provide the infrastructure which enables employers to effectively manage disability and continue to compete in a global environment.

Controlling the cost of disability in business and industry and its ultimate impact on employee productivity is not a simple task. Complex and conflicting relationships exist between employer goals, resources, and expectations, the needs and self-interests of workers, health care providers, labor unions and attorneys, and the services available in the community. The ability of the employer to participate actively and effectively in this relationship will contribute to the control of costs, as well as the protection of the worker's sustained employment.

DISABILITY MANAGEMENT OBJECTIVES

Employer policy and procedure, as well as disability management strategies and interventions should be designed to accomplish realistic and attainable objectives. Disability management programs at the worksite should enable the employer to:

- Facilitate employer control of disability issues;;
- Improve corporate competitiveness;
- Reduce work disruptions and unacceptable lost time;
- Decrease incidence of accidents and magnitude of disability;
- Reduce illness and disability duration (and costs);
- Promote early involvement and preventive interventions;
- Maximize use of internal (employer) resources;
- Improve management of external service providers;
- Reduce human cost of disability;
- Enhance morale by valuing employee physical and cultural diversity ;
- Protect the employability of the worker;
- Insure compliance with ADA and other legislation;
- Reduce adversarial nature of disability and litigation;

- Improve labor relations;
- Promote joint labor-management collaboration; and
- Facilitate direct worker involvement in planning.

OCCUPATIONAL BONDING

Traditionally, timely rehabilitation interventions have been characterized as services directed exclusively at the individual level. In most cases, the work environment was all but ignored. Little attention was paid to labor relations issues, concerns about the worker's job satisfaction, ergonomic job modifications, and the like. Employer-based disability management interventions recognize and utilize the therapeutic value of the physical, psychological, social, and environmental dimensions of the workplace. Workers, despite their impairments, must continue to perceive themselves as valued employees who remain attached to the workplace. Otherwise, the worker's disability will manifest itself in extended lost time and more severe occupational disability.

Occupational bonding refers to the "mutually beneficial relationship between the worker and the employer." For example, workers have bonds with co-workers, supervisors, work processes, and work environments. Workers are accustomed to a daily routine of going to work, producing, and socializing with others in the workplace. When injury or disability strikes, this bond may become "unglued," especially when the balance between the worker's expectations and the employer's intentions become confusing or unclear. When no system is in place to objectively evaluate and accommodate the worker with a disability, mutual distrust grows between workers and employers. This often leads to an adversarial relationship that promotes litigation and disability rather than productivity. As a result, injured workers often find themselves "bonded" to or dependent upon treatment providers, attorneys, and disability benefits.

While "early intervention" is a key factor in effective disability management, the principle of "early return to work" is essentially the second half of the formula for achieving successful rehabilitation outcome. The "occupational bond" between the worker with a disability and the work environment is also an important underlying factor related to "early return to work." Successful work adjustment requires worker adaptation to the routines and rhythms of work, as well as the development of compatible relationships among supervisors and co-workers (Shrey, 1993a, 1993b).

THE THERAPEUTIC WORK ENVIRONMENT

Traditional vocational rehabilitation approaches are insufficient for getting injured workers back on the job. Historically, there has been an over-emphasis on altering physical and psycho-social characteristics of individuals with impairments. Both medical and rehabilitation practitioners have neglected to acknowledge the importance of external environmental factors, such as worksite and labor relations influences. For example, the classic rehabilitation strategy is to examine and evaluate the worker, counsel the worker to influence appropriate behavioral change, provide treatment to the worker, teach the individual work adjustment and job-seeking skills, and place the worker into competitive employment (Shrey, 1992).

Once the injured worker moves beyond the acute stage of rehabilitation, the workplace should be considered the therapeutic environment of choice. At the worksite, the injured worker continues to interact with co-workers, supervisors, and union representatives. The work environment is an ideal site for teaching workers proper body mechanics, safe work practices, and appropriate pacing of work activities. The work environment provides opportunities to involve supervisors and others in job accommodation and ergonomic job modification processes.

It is neither in the psycho-social interests of the injured worker, nor the economic self-interests of the employer to delay a return to work until the worker has achieved a full physical recovery. In practical terms, it makes more sense to pay injured workers to be productive, than to provide them with disability benefits while remaining inactive. A systematic gradual work-return process allows the worker to experience therapeutic gains and proper work adjustments. Concurrently, by focusing on worker-work environment adaptations and accommodations, both injured workers and employers are actively engaged in the resolution of work disability, worker reintegration, and worker retention.

THE ECONOMICS OF DISABILITY MANAGEMENT

The economics of injuries and disabilities continue to deplete the financial assets of employers, insurance carriers, and persons with disabilities. This cost is often passed along to the consumer in the form of higher prices for goods and services and increased insurance premiums. In 1988, work accidents and injuries cost U.S. employers, workers, and society an estimated $47.1 billion. This represented a 35% increase from the $34.8 billion incurred in 1986 (Frieden, 1989). From 1980 to 1989, the average medical claim in workers' compensation rose from $1,741 to $5,370, while the average wage-loss claim increased from $4,522 to $10,735 (Thompson, 1991). According to the California Workers' Compensation Institute (1993), workers' compensation medical payments to California physicians in 1991 were 25% higher than in 1990, resulting in record payments of $1.55 billion.

Berkowitz (1990) suggested that America had experienced a 400% increase in workers' compensation and health care costs over the preceding 15 years. Hunt and Habeck (1993) reported the following, based on 1990 data from the Bureau of Labor Statistics, US Department of Labor, and other sources:

> ... 7 in every 100 workers suffer a nonfatal work injury every year, or 6.2 million injured workers in 1988. These injuries resulted in 2.9 million lost workday cases, which include an average of 19 lost workdays per case, or 55 million total lost workdays ... In 1989, nearly two million workers sustained injuries that resulted in disabilities. At that time, the cost of occupational injury was conservatively estimated at $83 billion (Hensler, 1991). Chelius, Galvin, and Owens (1992) found that total disability costs comprised slightly more than 8 percent of payroll in a small non-random sample of firms they studied. (p. 1)

As expenses for health care and insurance coverage continue to escalate, it becomes crucial that methods be developed for controlling these costs. Some experts suggest that employers can no longer rely on government or outside third parties (e.g., insurance carriers, claims management organizations) to manage uncontrolled workers' compensation costs. Wollner (1993) illustrates the role of private self-interests in the escalation of these costs to employers:

> Most people do not realize that the economic incentives for insurance companies differ from those of [employers]. In today's competitive business environment, insurance companies are looking for ways to maximize income while cutting expenses. Some may be tempted to trim their safety and claims management programs, providing services only to the extent required to keep the business. You may not get safety and claims management service enhancements unless you know what you need and ask for such services. Similarly, with workers' compensation losses charged back to the policy-holder through experience modifiers and other premium rating elements, the financially strapped insurance company may have little incentive to help the insured reduce costs. Consumer vigilance is critical in monitoring the premium rating system. (p. 34)

When employees experience work disruptions due to illness or disability, the employer must often bear the costs incurred as a result of wage loss, and medical and rehabilitation services. In addition to the insured costs of injury and disability, employers are significantly impacted by "hidden" costs, which include:

- hiring and training costs associated with replacing the injured worker.
- overtime payments to other workers to avoid lost production.
- reduced productivity among replacement workers during periods of training and orientation.
- increased demands on supervisors for production management and training of replacement workers (Miller, 1991).

Workers' compensation in most Western nations is best described as constantly changing, complex, confusing, expensive, adversarial, and bureaucratic. This can be illustrated by the increasingly complicated legislation, regulations, and policies addressing issues related to workers' compensation costs. These include 24-hour coverage, experience rating, reemployment obligations, and definitions of compensable injury, cumulative trauma, and occupational disease. Currently, compensable injuries and diseases may include conditions such as work-related stress, fibromyalgia, carpal tunnel syndrome, chronic pain, cancer, and other nontraumatic conditions.

Facing all these problems, it is not unusual for employers to engage in counterproductive behaviors often characterized as passive or reactive, rather than being facilitative or proactive. Frequently, employers avoid responsibility for managing injury and disability problems. They exhibit feelings of helplessness, often projecting blame on others for unmanaged workers' compensation problems. Too often, employers engage in self-defeating actions such as contesting all disability claims, maintaining rigid reemployment policies, being unwilling to accommodate, and resorting to aggressive litigation.

Despite trends reflecting highly escalating costs and employer apathy, the recent National Workers' Compensation Attitude Survey reflected surprising optimism among responding employers (Kentucky Self-insurers Reporter, 1993). The survey results indicated that concrete actions taken by employers could result in reduced costs. Ninety percent of respondents associated reduced injury costs with the manner in which an injured worker is treated at the time of injury. Confidence in safety programs as a loss-control strategy was reported by 86% of respondents. Sixty-five percent believed that employer efforts to control costs can have a positive impact on worker morale, productivity, and quality. Surprisingly, fraud was not considered a significant problem by the majority of respondents (e.g., considered less than 5% of the total workers' compensation problem by more than half of the respondents). Employer controls associated with feelings of optimism included: modified duty programs, establishing medical provider relationships, continued contact with injured employees, and maintaining active involvements on all open claims.

THE OLDER WORKER AND DISABILITY MANAGEMENT

Older workers with disabilities can be an imposing force impacting on disability costs and industry's economic survival. As the American work force ages, business and industry will be competing for a decreasing labor pool. According to the U.S. Bureau of the Census (1990), nearly 53 million Americans (21% of the population) were age 55 or older in 1990, and 32 million (12.6%) were age 65 or older. It is projected that, before the year 2010, 74 million people (26%) will be 55 or older, and 39 million (14%) will be 65 or older. The median age of the U.S. population will rise from 33 in 1990 to 39 in 2010. Cumulative trauma and other chronic disabling conditions, particularly compensable work-related impairments and occupational diseases, are likely to parallel the aging demographics of the work force. Longer time periods for rehabilitation among older workers translate into longer periods of work disruption and lost time from the work force. Consequently, the employer's financial liability for treatment and rehabilitation services will increase substantially. The health care cost and chronicity of short-term and long-term disability for older workers will, likewise, increase industry's economic burden.

Results from a three-year study funded by the National Institute on Disability and Rehabilitation Research (1991) indicated work disruption trends among 1,296 workers over the age of 45. Those having lost time due to industrial injuries or illnesses were more likely to work less than full-time for their employers, work another job 5 to 10 hours per week, and feel that powerful others control their health. As a group, they were indifferent to or disliked their jobs, rather than having higher levels of job satisfaction. Overall, the study revealed that seniority was a better injury/work disruption predictor than was age, and that job tasks and reported lifting requirements were not significant predictors of injury.

For an extensive view of disability management issues impacting older workers, employers, and society, the reader is referred to the chapter, "Protecting the Employability of the Working Elderly," by Hursh and Shrey.

THE ADA AND WORKERS WITH DISABILITIES

> Compliance with the ADA and controlling injury and disability costs are not mutually exclusive concepts. Unknowingly, many proactive employers have created an atmosphere of ADA compliance through the development of innovative and successful disability management programs. Effective disability management strategies and interventions typically include the development of "functional job descriptions," making "reasonable accommodations," and utilizing joint labor-management efforts in maintaining non-discriminatory practices. Indeed, the definition of disability management embraces the spirit of the ADA. (McMahon & Shrey, 1992, p. 20)

On July 26, 1992, the Americans with Disabilities Act (ADA) was signed into law by President Bush. The law is administered by the United States Equal Employment Opportunity Commission (EEOC), which is also responsible for administering the Age Discrimination in Employment Act, the Equal Pay Act, and the Rehabilitation Act. It is anticipated that many injured workers will come under the protection of the ADA (McMahon & Shrey, 1992).

American employers are most concerned with Title I of the ADA, which prohibits discrimination against people with disabilities in job application procedures, hiring, advancement, or discharge of employees, employee compensation, job training, and other employment terms, conditions, and privileges. As of April 30, 1993, only 8,505 ADA charges were filed with the EEOC, representing approximately one charge for every 1,000 employers covered by the ADA. Bell (1993) reported that, by January 31, 1993, over 80% of the ADA charges reported to the EEOC had been from current employees rather than job applicants with disabilities. The largest single disability category represented among those filing ADA violation charges was "back impairment" (16.8%), and 40% of this group had claimed ADA discrimination on the basis of discharge from work. This trend is expected to continue. Therefore, employers can no longer view injured workers only from a workers' compensation perspective.

Until recently, employers who questioned the aggressive enforcement of the ADA may have chosen to calculate the cost of compliance against the cost of prospective litigation. The Civil Rights Act of 1991, however, leaves no question as to the prospects for enforcement of the ADA for employers. Every compliance effort to achieve access and accommodation is well advised since the remedies for breach, or penalties for discrimination, were extended by this law in November 1992. These include compensatory and punitive damages up to $300,000 per incident IN ADDITION to corrective action and legal expenses (McMahon & Shrey, 1992).

Both employers and risk managers might consider that good faith efforts to re-employ the industrially injured worker not only reduce the risks of such litigation but also the length of lost work time and associated temporary total disability benefits paid to the injured worker. Such "good faith" compliance activity is also likely to be perceived positively by the state workers' compensation system (Blumenthal, 1992).

Every incident associated with workplace injury and disability must be considered a potential ADA issue from the beginning. As such, Morris (1993) offers the following ADA advice and guidelines to risk managers and other corporate representatives:

- Workers' comp and the ADA are two separate systems. A permanent disability award does not end the employer's obligation for ADA compliance.

- The employer no longer can require that the employee become 100 percent functional before returning to work, although the employee must be able to perform his or her essential job functions.
- Company-wide efforts to coordinate ADA requirements are essential, both to encourage compliance and to address possible conflicts with unions.
- The employer's administrators must become familiar with the ADA and be prepared to respond appropriately if an ADA issue begins to emerge.
- The employer must develop the expertise to objectively evaluate whether an employee can perform the essential job functions, with or without accommodations. Job descriptions should include statements regarding the essential functions of jobs and the company's written policy relating to return-to-work.

Legislation similar to the ADA is, at this writing, being considered as part of Canada's National Strategy for the Integration of Persons with Disabilities. This is occurring at a time when the cost of health-related absences in Canada accounts for nearly 16% of the country's $300 billion payroll. Similar to Germany and France, Canada is considering obliging employers to demonstrate that 6% of their work force is represented by people with disabilities. Current employment equity provisions prohibit discrimination of persons with disabilities in the work place. As with the ADA in the U.S., it is probable that Canada's National Strategy will dovetail with current workers' compensation statutes. For example, in Ontario, a company that fails to modify either the work or the work place in order to reinstate an injured worker may be subject to a fine the equivalent of a worker's annual salary and/or be required to pay compensation to the worker for one year. Alberta, on the other hand, offers incentives such as a 100% subsidy for a one-month work trial, and subsidies to cover the costs of necessary modifications to the work place (Rogers, 1993).

The reader is referred to McMahon's chapter, "Health Insurance, Workers' Compensation, and the Americans with Disabilities Act," for a detailed examination of injured worker issues, as relates to the ADA.

DISABILITY MANAGEMENT: A LABOR RELATIONS ISSUE

Relationships between workers and work environments are dynamic and complex. Compatible relationships often lead to job satisfaction, enhanced productivity, and positive labor relations, all of which are mutually rewarding for the worker and the employer. However, relationships characterized by unresolved conflicts can lead to mutually destructive consequences for workers and employers. Understanding the dynamics of person-environmental interactions in the work place is an important first step in resolving injury and disability claims.

Traditionally, worker injury and disability has been viewed as a *medical* problem, requiring medical interventions (e.g., impairment evaluations, treatments). Numerous cases of iatrogenic disability (treatment induced disability) indicate that the interventions may actually magnify the disability problem instead of resolving it (e.g., unnecessary surgery, prolonged therapeutic modalities, and over-extended treatment by psychologists, physicians, allied health professionals, and rehabilitation specialists). Unresolved issues of work disability typically become *legal* problems, requiring extensive litigation and additional medical interventions. When work-related "stress" becomes a compensable component of the worker's impairment, the disability claim becomes a *psychosocial* problem.

Over the past decade, it has become fashionable to "blame the system" for unresolved disability cases. As a result, the disability claim becomes a *bureaucratic* problem. Moreover, when workers are financially rewarded for being disabled, considerable attention is focused on the *financial disincentive to work* problem. To varying degrees, many of these "problems" are valid. They all contribute to work disruptions and increasing costs to employers. However, there is a tendency for all these problems to emerge "after" the initial occurrence of a work-related injury or disability.

Injury and disability in industry may be more of a "labor relations" problem than a "medical" problem. Negative labor relations can be a significant factor contributing to the actual disability claim. Poor relationships between workers and managers can also impact negatively on the resolution of a disability claim. The successful management of injury and disability in industry requires the employer to respond to impaired workers in a timely and "proactive" fashion. Unfortunately, many employers are more "reactive" to injury and disability problems, many of which could have been initially avoided through preventive and early intervention approaches.

> Most employers today treat workers' compensation as a cost of doing business—a painful cost. Painful because losses always seem to escalate, consuming a bigger and bigger chunk of operating costs. Yet unlike other business challenges, when it comes to workers' comp, employers commonly look to others - their insurance carriers and state legislators—for solutions. So far, results from these sources haven't been very encouraging. (Randall, August, 1992, p. 36)

Increasing evidence suggests that the ability to control workers' compensation and disability costs are, for the most part, within the employer's grasp. Habeck

(1993) reported the results of a survey of 124 Michigan firms, which supported the assumption that many factors causing unacceptable workers' compensation costs are internal to companies and within the employer's power to control. The study identified two distinct and equally weighted processes involved in disability management: processes involving injury prevention, and processes involving disability management after injury occurrence. Management philosophy, policies, and practices were found to be strongly related to successful claims outcome. Factors related to favorable claims experiences included: "an open management style, a human resource orientation, more rigorous adoption of safety and prevention interventions, and specific procedures to prevent and manage disabilities."

Further evidence supporting the relationship between employer policies and practices and disability management results was cited (Habeck, 1993). Factors related to successful disability management outcome included those associated with Safety Diligence (e.g., excellent housekeeping and continuous equipment maintenance; timely investigation of risks and accidents; constant safety policy compliance), Safety Training (e.g., dissemination of safety information among all employees; addressing all relevant hazards and applicable safe work practices), and Proactive Return-to-Work Programs (e.g., joint involvement of injured workers and supervisors in work-return planning; creative placement and accommodation options; timely utilization of external providers). Successful disability management outcome was measured in terms of lower incidence of lost workday cases, fewer workers' compensation wage loss claims, and lower total lost workday rates.

Injury and disability in the work place are commonly treated as medical-legal problems. However, negative labor relations can be the most pervasive barrier to resolving a worker's disability claim. Workers who dislike their jobs, their supervisors, and their co-workers are more likely to exaggerate medical problems and symptoms associated with an injury. Likewise, the supervisor who dislikes a particular worker may actively prevent that employee from returning to work after a lost-time injury. In either case, the results are similar—more lost time, extensive medical involvement and associated costs, and disability claims out of control. Consider the following case study:

> Bill is a 35-year-old machinist, who sustained a low back injury when he fell on a slippery floor at work. He had back surgery six months ago, and has been involved in physical therapy for the past four months. He attends therapy sessions three times per week. There is no indication that his condition has improved as a result of therapy. Bill complains that his treating physician gives him no indication of his prognosis for recovery.
>
> After the accident, Bill was hospitalized for several days, during which time he had no contact from his employer. He received three or four telephone calls from an insurance claims adjuster representing his employer, who seemed to be

more interested in investigating the details of his accident than with Bill's injury and treatment. Initially, Bill did not receive his first workers' compensation check until three months after his injury, due to a lengthy claims investigation process and administrative delays. Bill now receives workers' compensation benefits of $360 per week, as well as supplemental benefits from his employer ($45 per week).

Bill was a good, productive worker. However, it seemed that he could never please his supervisor, who was excessively demanding and unrealistic about production goals. Work was plentiful prior to Bill's accident, but Bill's employer recently lost a major production contract to a competitor and there have been rumors of anticipated lay-offs at the plant. Bill was concerned about his job security, lack of contact from his employer, unclear medical prognosis, and economic uncertainty. He recently retained the services of an aggressive workers' compensation attorney.

Bill's workers' compensation case is currently in litigation, and his attorney is seeking a significantly high settlement for permanent and total disability. Bill does not understand the legal process, but has put total trust in his attorney who has assured him of a major financial award. No one has suggested vocational rehabilitation to Bill, particularly in light of the poor prognosis cited in the most recent medical report from Dr. Jones, a physician recommended to Bill by his attorney.

Things look very bleak to Bill. He has lost all contact with his employer. Everything is in the hands of his attorney, the physicians, and the workers' compensation board. Bill's future depends upon the outcome of the litigation process. Anger, frustration, uncertainty and stress continue to mount. Things have also deteriorated at home. Bill's relationship with his wife seems to be one continuous argument—mostly about Bill's excessive drinking and complaining. Even the kids have lost respect for Bill, since all he does is sit around all day, "feeling sorry for himself."

CASE STUDY ANALYSIS: PREDICTORS OF WORK DISRUPTIONS AND DISABILITY

Upon examination of the above case study, several negative forces are impacting on work-return goals for the injured worker. Ineffective or prolonged therapy results in this worker's diminished hope for recovery. As the period of work disruption increases, the worker becomes "bonded" with treatment providers. Concurrently, communication between the worker and his employer has stopped, and the worker-employer "bond" has been broken. Lengthy claims investigation processes and delays in receiving benefits creates a deeper adversarial climate between the worker and his employer. Many workers, after having reached this point, choose to punish their employers by becoming uncooperative and continuing to draw weekly compensation benefits at the employer's expense.

Disabled worker and employer relationships typically deteriorate during the claims investigation process, when the impaired worker experiences delays in claims processing and fails to receive his or her due benefits. Claims adjusters lacking empathy, understanding, and sensitivity often create additional stress for the worker. Conflicts arise when the worker's interest in economic self-sufficiency becomes challenged by the insurance carrier's (or third-party administrator's) self-interests in controlling the costs of questionable disability claims. The result is often extended work disruption, litigation, and greater personal and economic costs for the employer and the worker.

In the case study, labor relations appears to have played a major role in this employee's potential for returning to work. The marginal relationship with his supervisor, the threat of a reduction in the work force, and the risk of losing economic security have a significant impact on the worker's loyalty to the employer. The worker's self-interest in controlling the negative impact of the work environment conflicts with the employer's self-interest in reduced lost time and increased productivity.

Litigation activity becomes the battleground where worker-employer adversity is played out. Independent medical examiners become mercenaries, while attorneys draw up the battle plans. Once the war has ended, the generals claim their victories measured in legal fees, while injured workers are counted among the casualties.

Corporate attorneys may try to gather and present evidence that minimizes the disabled worker's functional impairment and work disability. By reducing the extent and consequences of disability, the cash settlement is reduced and the short-term self-interest of the employer is satisfied. However, the attorney's failure to recognize the subjective nature of the worker's disability often competes with the injured worker's self-interest of securing financial independence due to a significant disabling condition. Litigation, by its adversarial nature, causes further animosity. Labor relations between the employer and the worker (including some sympathetic co-workers) is often irreversibly damaged.

The injured worker's attorney uses a different strategy, hoping to offer evidence that maximizes the client's impairments and disabilities. More extensive impairments translate into larger settlements (and larger attorney fees). The disabled worker may be discouraged from participating in vocational rehabilitation and work-return activities during the litigation process. Therefore, the self-interest of the attorney is often financial in nature, rather than rehabilitation in spirit. As time passes, the injured worker's general health often deteriorates, the family structure is frequently disrupted, and psychological, stress and social problems begin to dominate.

Battles involving injured worker issues are fought in the home as well as the courtroom. As the previous case study revealed, secondary psychosocial problems typically emerge as lost work time increases. Relationships with family members often deteriorate rapidly, under the strain of excessive drinking and learned helplessness. Maladaptive behaviors resulting from work disruption are common. However, when other family members are affected by the "fall out" of a litigated disability claim, pathological relationships within the family emerge. The disabled worker undergoes "role changes." Family members experience "role change reactions." The once independent, self-supporting worker now takes on a role of passive dependency. Resentment abounds when the family is disrupted by the presence of an ever-demanding, sometimes angry, and often depressed individual. This is a typical outcome of unresolved labor relations problems, fueled by stress, and ignited by litigation activity and intense adversarial proceedings. Although the relationship among these forces is not always understood, the damage is usually profound.

THE RESPONSIBLE EMPLOYER

Poor labor relations can translate into increased disability claims and associated costs. Contrary to the belief of many employers, workers' compensation and disability insurance premiums are not simply "the cost of doing business." They are "the cost of not taking care of business." Skeptical employers often feel powerless and unable to change "the system." This skepticism turns to cynicism, leaving many managers and supervisors feeling angry, frustrated, and victimized by the "comp system."

Management's attitudes, policies, and procedures are critical to the success of an effective disability management program in industry. Good labor relations means "paying positive attention" to employees. Once the relationship between the employee and the work environment is understood, forces impacting on stress and resulting work disruption can be reduced or eliminated. Positive labor relations and a pro-active corporate disability management program are not mutually exclusive.

DISABILITY MANAGEMENT STRATEGIES THAT PROMOTE POSITIVE LABOR RELATIONS

Trends suggest that effective disability management strategies and interventions can be jointly developed and implemented by labor and management (examples of joint labor-management initiatives are described later in this chapter). Both labor and management have vested interests in protecting the employability of workers, while controlling industry's injury and disability costs. Labor unions want to protect the employability of the workers they represent. Management wants to avoid costly worker turnover, while retaining productive, reliable, and experienced employees.

The following disability management strategies have been demonstrated to impact positively on labor relations:

- Know your organization's strengths and weaknesses, as well as the resources available to properly manage the injured worker's safe and timely return to work;
- Understand the corporate culture, including the attitudes, motivations, and self-interests of labor and management regarding injury prevention, worksite accommodation, and injured worker rehabilitation;
- Recognize the unique patterns of injury and disability in the employer's workforce, including types of impairments, ages of workers, lost-time statistics, accident data and costs associated with disability claims;
- Promote early interventions and the systematic monitoring of injured workers;
- Design benefit plans to reward disabled workers for returning to work and remaining healthy and productive;
- Develop flexible and creative work-return transition options and reasonable accommodations for disabled workers;
- Support positive labor relations that promote job satisfaction and worker involvement in decision-making;
- Be sensitive to the psychological and social consequences of injury and disability and the overall impact of work disruption on the worker's family;
- Actively promote accident prevention and risk-reduction programs by encouraging employee input;
- Do not relinquish all company control and responsibility to "outside" third parties, such as insurance carriers, claims administrators, and attorneys. Rather, develop functional alliances between quality resources and the employer-based disability management system;
- Understand the value of securing vocational rehabilitation and effective case management services for workers with restrictions;
- Create expectations among employees, with respect to policies and procedures to follow from the point of injury to the safe return to work;
- Provide treating physicians with information regarding the physical demands of the injured worker's job, and invite them to visit production sites and work areas;
- Get directly involved by identifying, utilizing, and evaluating effective medical and rehabilitation services in the community;

- "Internalize" these external resources, making them part of the employer's disability management infrastructure. Then, guide injured workers to responsible service providers;
- Seek independent medical and physical capacity evaluations when evaluating questionable claims or when reviewing medical reports that fail to objectively substantiate the worker's alleged impairments and medical restrictions;
- Create labor-management agreements that protect the employability of the worker by identifying alternatives to costly work disruptions and chronic absenteeism; and
- Analyze jobs that cause injuries and develop effective ergonomic modifications that prevent future work disabilities

EARLY INTERVENTION: KEY TO SUCCESSFUL DISABILITY MANAGEMENT

Perhaps the most important principle of disability management is "early intervention." Rehabilitation policy and practice among most disability benefit systems recognize the value of early intervention, in light of compelling empirical evidence resulting from disability management research over the past decade. From a historical perspective, there is strong evidence that "early intervention" has attained broad acceptance among various disability benefits systems, especially workers' compensation and long-term disability insurance carriers. More recently, the Social Security Administration in the U.S. conducted a series of research and demonstration projects to test various early intervention and rehabilitation approaches. Preliminary results from these studies suggest that at least 20% of disability beneficiaries would participate in rehabilitation and work-return programs if they were provided access to timely services (Shrey, Bangs, Mark, Hursh, & Kues, 1991). New initiatives, with respect to early intervention services from the private sector, are expected to emerge with more progressive Social Security policy changes.

Research evidence from the U.S. and international studies on disability management strongly support the early intervention approach to rehabilitation as a practical alternative to a delayed service delivery approach. Galvin (1985) studied international and U.S. disability management systems, and concluded:

> At the outset it is important to recognize that to delay rehabilitation is to jeopardize rehabilitation. All too often disability intervention, management and rehabilitation services are delayed or absent, the employee's health condition becomes increasingly severe, the employee begins to accept the "sick role," and disability benefits

> become an attractive alternative to continued, but problematic, employment. Unfortunately even when the initial signs of chronic illness, functional limitation and reduced productivity are apparent little provision for disability management and rehabilitation is made until absolute disaster has struck the employee and he/she begins to consider the "security" offered via disability benefits. Much of this travail can be avoided. Through planning and creative, coordinated intervention we could substantially avoid one of our most vexing problems—the reemployment of individuals who are receiving workers' compensation, social security or disability insurance benefits. (p.57)

Generally, empirical evidence and widely held convictions among medical and rehabilitation professionals, support the belief that "early intervention" is the key to rehabilitation outcome. Indeed, countless studies have documented the importance of "early intervention," in terms of cost-effectiveness of rehabilitation service delivery; cost-savings to insurance carriers, employers, and persons with disabilities; and important psycho-social benefits experienced by patients and their families.

According to Hood and Downs (1985), historical support was noted for an early intervention philosophy among state workers' compensation programs and policies. Lewis (1973) urged consideration for comprehensive rehabilitation efforts to return injured workers to their pre-injury physical and economic status. Stout Vocational Rehabilitation Institute (1983) highlighted the "early warning systems" among insurance carriers' home offices, that respond to catastrophic injuries, as well as the "prompt contact programs" for noncatastrophic cases, both under workers' compensation and automobile insurance systems. Referring to the "early intervention" concept, the following was noted:

> This concept provided positive results regardless of what law was applicable or what type of policy was in effect that covered the injury and resulting disability. Most private rehabilitation specialists have accepted these concepts and have geared their approach to comply with these prompt contact programs. They do not wait for the end of the "healing period" to make contact as do some state rehabilitation programs. It behooves the private rehabilitation specialist to zero in on replacement and the preservation of the employee's job when possible. Because this model, and its flexibility, have shown positive results, it has also been adopted by many non-profit agencies, self-insurers, and in some state rehabilitation programs....(Chapter V, p. 23)

TIME: THE NEMESIS OF REHABILITATION

Successful rehabilitation generally depends on a number of factors, which include: (1) a prompt initiation of rehabilitation interventions, (2) a rehabilitation team familiar with the multifaceted needs of the individual, and (3) the relationship between access to benefits and active involvement in rehabilitation activities (Sunshine, 1979). An immediate multidisciplinary response to the rehabilitation needs of the individual prevents the person from feeling powerless and not responsible for recovery (Andrews, 1981).

A commonly held view is that an inverse relationship exists between the length of a work disruption due to injury/disability, and work-return potential. For example, Weiler (1986) reported on return-to-work rates among workers' compensation beneficiaries in the U.S. and persons with injuries and illnesses in the United Kingdom. Approximately one-third of the individuals studied returned to work within one month. Another third became re-employed between the second and sixth month post-injury/illness. Approximately 17% returned to work between month seven and twelve. The remaining 16% of these individuals were unemployed at the end of the first year. Rundle (1983) reported work-return and cost-savings statistics, as relates to the timing of rehabilitation intervention, on a sample of 5,620 workers' compensation beneficiaries. There was a 47% return-to-work rate among workers referred for rehabilitation services within three months post-injury, resulting in a 71% cost-savings. For those referred between months four through six, return-to-work rates and cost-savings dropped to 33% and 61%, respectively. Only 18% of the injured workers referred for services beyond 12 months post-injury returned to work, and corresponding cost-savings dropped to 51%.

Pati (1985) found that "the best predictor of successful rehabilitation potential is the amount of time that has elapsed from time of injury to referral." Gardner (1987) noted, "vocational intervention at an early stage of the rehabilitation process is more likely to secure a timely return to work at a salary rate that is comparable to the pre-injury wage level." According to Scheer (1990), the cost-effectiveness of early intervention with the physically or cognitively injured worker should not be underestimated. He concluded that vocational counselor involvement in the early stages of rehabilitation is prudent from medical, humanistic, and financial perspectives. Giarrantano (1989) reported that significant cost-savings can be demonstrated when quality case management and vocational rehabilitation services are coupled with early referral.

EARLY INTERVENTION: COST-EFFECTIVENESS AND COST-SAVINGS

During the mid-1980s General Electric Company developed, implemented, and evaluated the Convalescent Assistance to Recovering Employees (CARE) Program. According to Stempien (1989), the mission of this program was to provide quality health care to injured or ill workers in a timely and coordinated fashion. Early intervention services, coordinated by occupational health nurses, yielded highly significant results. At one GE plant, the cost per employee consistently decreased each year, over a three-year period, in the areas of short-term disability (33% decrease), salary continuance and hourly sick pay (23% decrease), and workers' compensation (35% decrease). General Electric's CARE program is more fully described in the chapter "Occupational Health Nurses in Disability Management" by Martin.

The Insurance Bureau of the State of Michigan reported that "estimates have shown that for every dollar spent on rehabilitation $9 are returned through increased productivity and for every rehabilitated spinal cord injury, $60,000 in future medical and nursing home costs are saved." The Bureau further concluded that these cost-savings are possible only when appropriate post-accident rehabilitation interventions are made as soon as possible (Giarrantano, 1989).

According to a report in the *National Underwriter* (1989), education about the rehabilitation process and early involvement of rehabilitation professionals are the keys to solving system-related problems. This report, based on the 1989 Workers' Compensation Congress, called for legislators, injured workers, insurers, attorneys, employers, physicians, and others to be educated about "redirecting their primary attention to equitably resolving rehabilitation issues in a realistic fashion that eliminates the adversarial (litigious) approach." The report stressed the importance of "early, prompt and realistic determinations of employee rehabilitation potential" and concluded that evaluation for rehabilitation potential among the state's injured workers within six months of injury could save the employers and insurers nearly $6 million per year, while possibly increasing the earnings of workers with disabilities by $9 million per year.

Boschen (1989) provided one of the most extensive critiques of "early intervention" research. She summarized a study by the California Workers' Compensation Institute (1985), which reported statistically significant determinants of vocational rehabilitation costs for injured workers. In the study, there was a $76 cost for each month of delay in referral for vocational rehabilitation services. Once referred, there was a $369 cost associated with each additional month of delay in the start of a rehabilitation plan. Each additional month of rehabilitation plan duration cost $726. Early identification of potential rehabilitation candidates, and early rehabilitation and work-return interventions were significantly related to rehabilitation success, based on a regression analysis.

The following is a summary of typical reasons for initiating early rehabilitation interventions (Boschen, 1989):

1. Intervention with the disabled person and the family can help prevent the development of psychosocial problems that could interfere with successful outcomes of rehabilitation.
2. Availability of guidance can ease the process of coping and adjustment.
3. Early rehabilitation assists the individual in making a personal commitment to reestablish a sense of order in his or her life.
4. Feelings of loneliness and abandonment can be decreased or prevented.
5. The person's level of motivation to recover can be stimulated and maintained.
6. Family members can be immediately enlisted to provide positive reinforcement to the person with a disability.
7. The waiting period can be avoided during which individuals often begin to build up resentment toward the family, the medical profession, and the rehabilitation agency or employer for delays in service.
8. The individual avoids the "runaround" or the feeling of being shuffled from one professional to another.
9. Secondary gains of being disabled can be minimized or kept in perspective.
10. Early intervention prevents the individual from settling into the sick role, with the disability becoming a way of life.

Overall, there is compelling evidence that "early intervention" is required to ensure successful rehabilitation outcome. Despite critiques of empirical research methodologies associated with early intervention studies, there is virtually no basis for initiating rehabilitation services other than in a timely fashion.

PSYCHO-SOCIAL IMPACT OF EARLY INTERVENTION

To understand the importance of early intervention in the rehabilitation process, one must consider more than statistics related to cost-analyses, incidence reports, and medical data. Accidents are, by their very nature, sudden in onset. Most individuals who sustain significant injuries are unprepared to deal with the physical, social, psychological, vocational, and financial implications imposed by such an event (Riggar, Maki, & Wolf, 1986). Access to timely rehabilitation resources and support services are critical to the individual's psycho-social adjustment. Any unnecessary delays in meeting the individual's psycho-social needs typically results in secondary disabilities, which are often characterized by feelings of hopelessness, depression, isolation, and further physical deterioration.

The theoretical rationale for "early intervention" generally parallels widely accepted typologies of the stages of adjustment (e.g., stages of denial, anger, bargaining, depression, and acceptance) (Kubler-Ross, 1969). Similarly, Hartman and Burgess (1985) theorized the adjustment phases following heart attack to include the crisis phase, immediate post-crisis, the transition phase, and total integration at home and work. Regardless of the benefit system, a period of adjustment is experienced among most, if not all, individuals whose life expectations and functional capacities have become compromised by an injury or disability. As suggested by Linveh (1986), the initial impact of disability is characterized by shock and anxiety. Denial, internalized anger, and depression often follow. Energy spent in retaliation or externalized aggression, among persons with disabilities, often needs to be "rechanneled" productively through appropriate rehabilitation intervention strategies. Supportive interventions, as posed by the learned helplessness model (Engberg & Welker, 1973; Seligman, 1991, 1975), are necessary to prevent the onset of depression, feelings of helplessness, and passivity. Walker (1992) offered an "injured worker helplessness" paradigm for explaining motivational problems during the recovery process among workers' compensation beneficiaries. He suggests that "the non-contingent rewards and the uncontrollable dynamics characteristic of workers' compensation systems lead to claimants' learning helplessness." A total quality management (TQM) prevention system was suggested as an organization's best approach to reducing the likelihood of learned helplessness. A summary of the key components to TQM of disability, as suggested by Walker, include:

- Top management commitment
- Team approach, including the injured worker
- Effective communications
  * Exposing hidden agendas
  * Revealing self-interests
  * Problem identification
  * Problem-solving
  * Extension of corporate commitment to optimum use of all human resources

The importance of early intervention among injured and disabled persons cannot be underestimated. Disability is a complex phenomena that cannot be holistically addressed by medical interventions alone. The multidisciplinary nature of disability requires timely medical, psychosocial, economic, and vocational interventions, with case management coordination. Delays in providing medical interventions to persons with impairments result in loss of function and reduced potential for physical restoration. Likewise, the failure to address the individual's multidimensional needs, through early interventions, significantly jeopardizes rehabilitation success.

Indeed, "time" is the nemesis of rehabilitation. Lost time translates into increased medical and rehabilitation costs. Early rehabilitation interventions have consistently contained the personal and economic costs of injury and disability. Timely rehabilitation services benefit the government by turning "tax users" into "tax payers." They benefit the insurance industry by reducing the liabilities otherwise associated with secondary disabilities, which often emerge when primary disabilities are not fully addressed. Early intervention benefits employers and labor organizations by protecting the employability of experienced workers. More important, early rehabilitation interventions preserve the integrity and economic security of the individuals whose lives, and families' lives, have become compromised by the consequences of injury and disability.

WORKSITE DISABILITY MANAGEMENT PROGRAMS: KEY PRINCIPLES

In response to rapidly escalating workers' compensation costs and mandated disability program benefits, many employers have initiated disability management programs at the worksite. The following principles are central to an effective disability management program in business and industry:

JOINT LABOR-MANAGEMENT INVOLVEMENT, SUPPORT, AND ACCOUNTABILITY

Disability management requires employer and union involvement, support, and accountability. Both are key contributors in the disability management process, participating actively as decision-makers, planners, and coordinators of interventions and services. Many unionized employers have successfully developed and implemented on-site disability management programs under the guidance and support of joint labor-management committees. Bruyere & Shrey (1991) reviewed joint labor-management supported programs in the *Rehabilitation Counseling Bulletin*'s special issue on "Disability Management and Industrial Rehabilitation."

EARLY INTERVENTION—EARLY RETURN TO WORK

Early intervention strategies and early return to work programs result in decreased lost time, increased employer productivity, and decreased workers' compensation and disability costs. Regardless of origin of disability (e.g., work or nonwork-related), "early intervention" is considered to be the primary factor upon which the foundation of medical, psycho-social, and vocational rehabilitation is established (Lucas, 1987; Pati, 1985; Scheer, 1990; Wright, 1980). However, the successful management of disability also requires "early return-to-work" opportunities, accommodations and supports (Habeck, Leahy, Hunt, Chan, & Welch, 1991; Shrey & Olsheski, 1992). Typical "early return-to-work" programs in industry include a combination of disability management interventions, facilitated by an employer-based multidisciplinary team, and coordinated by a skilled case manager.

PROACTIVE INTERVENTIONS AT INDIVIDUAL AND WORK ENVIRONMENT LEVELS

Disability management interventions must be directed at both the individual and the work environment. The traditional approach to rehabilitation often ignores the fact that occupational disability may originate as much from environmental barriers as from the worker's personal traits. Workers dissatisfied with their jobs, supervisor-worker conflicts, and poorly designed work stations rank high among the many environmental barriers to disability management. In short, to maximize rehabilitation outcomes among injured workers, an equally balanced focus on the individual and the work environment is needed. Job accommodations, as required under the Americans with Disabilities Act, often expand the range of transitional work options for an injured worker. Redesigned tools, ergonomically correct work stations, adaptive devices, and work schedule modifications are all effective disability management methods that enable the worker to perform essential job tasks (Gross, 1988). These same interventions can be utilized in a preventive manner to identify and redesign jobs which are likely to cause future injuries.

Disability management is a proactive (preventive) process—the early prevention or resolution of a disability requires the timely utilization of employer-based resources and community-based services and interventions. The following interventions have been demonstrated as effective in the control of employer costs and in the protection of employability among workers with disabilities:

- functional job analyses;
- physical capacity evaluations;
- physical reconditioning;
- job coaching;
- ergonomic job modifications;
- work station modifications;
- safe work practices monitoring;
- modified duty work assignments;
- gradual return-to-work transitioning;
- supportive counseling and employee assistance services;
- medical management services; and
- worker retraining.

INTERDISCIPLINARY DISABILITY MANAGEMENT TEAM

Disability management requires an interdisciplinary disability management team. Members of this team often include employer representatives (e.g., safety managers, occupational health nurses, risk managers, human resources personnel, operations managers), labor union representatives, the worker's treating physician, a rehabilitation case manager, an on-site physical/occupational therapist, and the worker with a disability. (See chapter on Evaluation of Work Disability from a Worker-Work Environment Perspective by Lacerte and Desjardins.)

CASE MANAGEMENT SERVICES

Case management services are necessary to facilitate the development and implementation of disability management strategies and return-to-work plans for workers with disabilities. The case manager serves as a central disability management team member by functioning as a liaison between employers, labor representatives, injured workers, community health care providers, and others. (See section on *Contractual Disability Management Services* in this chapter for discussion of case management roles and functions).

OCCUPATIONAL BONDING

"Occupational Bonding," described earlier in this chapter, is the fundamental principle to creating an effective return-to-work program for employees with work restrictions (Bruyere & Shrey, 1991). Disability management interventions introduced within the ecological context of the workplace strengthen the bond between the worker with functional restrictions and the employer (Shrey, 1992).

EMPLOYER-BASED TRANSITIONAL WORK PROGRAMS

Disability management is perhaps best characterized through employer-based transitional work programs. Transitional work is generally developed by integrating any combination of job tasks and functions which may be performed safely and with remuneration by an employee whose physical capacity to perform functional job demands has been compromised. Such programs are designed to encourage and support an injured employee's safe and timely return to work. They provide the worker with accommodations and an opportunity to gradually "transition" back to work through conditioning, safe work practices education, and work re-adjustment. Essential components of on-site programs include:

- objective worker evaluations;
- an analysis of job tasks and physical functions;
- designated jobs or work transition units;
- on-site clinical supervision; and
- a gradual work-return plan that increases the worker's capacity to return to full-duty;

(See chapter on Disability Management Practice at the Worksite: Developing, Implementing and Evaluating Transitional Work Programs by Shrey, for a comprehensive overview of on-site transitional work programs).

MODEL DISABILITY MANAGEMENT PROGRAMS

Disability management programs are typically designed to protect the employability of workers, whether they have job related or nonjob-related disabilities. Shrey and Breslin (1992) reviewed the rehabilitation and business literature, which described model disability management programs, all of which feature early intervention strategies. Taulbee (1991) described several disability management programs in business and industry, including important economic outcomes attributed to early rehabilitation involvement. For example, Consumer Power Company's program resulted in a 48% decrease in the number of work days lost due to recordable lost-time injuries. Safeway Stores saved $8 for each dollar spent, and reduced back injuries and related costs by 50%. Marriott, with 20,000 employees in 50 states, reduced the number of workers' compensation cases by 30 to 50%, saved $4 for every dollar spent, and reduced litigated workers' compensation cases by 50%. Patenaude (1989) described the disability management program of Lockheed Missile and Space Company, which reduced worker visits for physical therapy and associated costs by 50% during the first year of its operation.

Habeck (1991) reported on the features and outcomes of several on-site disability management programs. Both public and private employers were cited, including the City of Lansing, Steelcase Corporation, Walbro Corporation, Walt Disney World, Herman Miller Corporation, and Federal Express. The following elements have been found to be common among most successful disability management programs:

- Early intervention and early return-to-work philosophy;
- Joint labor-management commitment and involvement;
- Multidisciplinary interventions (e.g., medical, vocational, psychological, ergonomics, engineering);
- Case management/case coordination;

- Effective disability prevention strategies;
- Employee education and involvement;
- Utilization of employer-based and community resources;
- Supportive policies and procedures to facilitate accommodations and jobsite modifications;
- System that ensures accountability of all parties; and
- Management information system for program evaluation

A functional alliance between the employer, the insurance carrier, and community medical services can yield high dividends to employers, in terms of cost-containment. For example, Travelers Insurance Company revitalized its claims management and injured worker monitoring services in 1988 through a program of increased utilization review, medical bill audits, and an expanded nursing staff for medical management. The new approach included a managed care network specific to workers' compensation. Within three years, an automated information system facilitated early referrals of injured workers to preferred providers. Program results included a reduction in median injury reporting time from 15 to 4 days, a 50% reduction in attorney involvement, and a 24% reduction in median closure time with reduced administrative costs. Overall claims costs were reduced by 31% (WCRI Research Brief, 1993).

Employers often use a blend of disability management interventions to produce desirable results. For example, the Long Island Railroad combined modified duty jobs, wellness programs, and early intervention strategies to produce annual savings of more than $6 million. Four years into the program, the railroad had only eight of its 7,000 employees with more than one year of lost time. Prior to instituting the disability management program, 244 employees had remained out of work for a year or more (Fruen, 1992).

Steelcase, Inc., a world leader in office furniture manufacturing, was voted *Risk & Insurance's* "Best Program" for 1993, in the workers' compensation category. With 11,000 plus employees, Steelcase estimated savings of $24 million between 1986 and 1993, by creating a comprehensive worksite disability management system. The company's disability management board recommends policies and procedures to support a range of interventions from injury prevention to a work return transition program. Workers with restrictions perform modified, productive work. Services provided by on-site medical and physical therapy centers are blended into the daily routines of injured workers. Case management is offered immediately following a lost-time injury, and participating workers are informed of their legal rights and responsibilities. Employees with more lengthy work disruptions are typically invited back to the company for lunch or coffee, as an effort to maintain the worker-employer bond. The program's success has been measured in terms of reduced lost time and associated costs. The average claim has gone from approximately $1,550 in 1983 to $1,250 in 1992, despite escalating health care costs. Less than 5% of cases are litigated. Lost time for back injuries resulting in surgery, which averaged 9 to 12 months in the early 1980s, now averages only six to eight weeks. Steelcase attributes much of its disability management success to a shift from assembly-line production to the concept of "work cells," or work units where employee teams complete entire products. By cross-training injured workers to perform other team tasks, creative options are easily made available for modified work. Also, subtle pressure from other team members to return to full duty plays a crucial role in shaping the injured worker's attitudes and behaviors (Wasserman, 1993).

The Foxboro Company, in Massachusetts, reported similar results from their worksite-based disability management program. The company's Total Loss Containment program represents a strong sports medicine approach to managing injuries, integrated with modified duty or transitional work options. After two years, the program boasts a 74% reduction in lost work days, with an injury severity rate that is half the industry average (Weinstein, 1993).

Exemplary worksite disability management programs are prominently being featured in the rehabilitation, business, and insurance literature. These emerging models of disability management, and their cost-containment results, are giving employers good reason to be cautiously optimistic. Enthusiasm was also reflected among two surveys which polled executives on issues related to future workers' compensation costs and effective management interventions. Flax (1993) reported on the results of these surveys by Johnson and Higgins and Towers Perrin:

- The average cost per workers' compensation claim increased 35% (from $3,842 to $5,197 per claim) from 1989 to 1991.
- The average number of claims per 100 employees decreased from 10.9 to 10.1 from 1989 to 1991.
- Eighty percent of employers polled identified medical costs as the leading cost factor. Medical costs accounted for one-third of the total workers' compensation claims cost in the early 1980s; they accounted for nearly half the costs in 1993.
- The cost of "medical only" claims increased by more than 43% between 1989 and 1991.
- Only 20% of 1,050 surveyed companies believe workers' compensation costs will be out of control in five years (down from 30% polled two years earlier).
- Managed care techniques were identified as effective in controlling workers' compensation costs (utilization review and use of managed care networks increased 150% between 1989 and 1991).
- Practices reflecting the coordination of workers' compensation and group health programs increased 129% over two years.

- Use of case management services among polled employers increased 180% over a two-year period.
- Respondent utilization of precertification for medical treatment increased by 300% over two years.
- Other cost-control measures cited among these surveys included:
    * early return-to-work programs
    * vocational rehabilitation
    * claims administration audits
    * fee schedule compliance checks
    * medical bill audits
    * health care provider profiling

JOINT LABOR-MANAGEMENT INITIATIVES

A BRIEF HISTORICAL PERSPECTIVE

During the late 1970s through the early 1980s, Akabas, Fine, and Yasser (1982) conducted several research projects featuring joint labor-management collaboration. One such study was designed to assess a preventive rehabilitation service's cost and potential for reducing the negative impact of disability. The study included high and moderate risk disability claimants who were participants in the health plan of a large urban union. The study's early intervention and preventive services resulted in cost savings for the union's insurance carrier and prevented unnecessary expenditures of time and money. An earlier study by Akabas, Gottlieb, and Yasser (1979) included evaluations on the impact of early intervention and coordination of rehabilitation resources on members of AFSCME, a member union of the AFL-CIO. The results of this study supported the value of preventive rehabilitation, and found that early intervention resulted in reduced incidence of recurrent disability, an easier return to work, and better health outcomes among workers who returned to their jobs after a period of work disruption associated with disability.

A similar program, which was jointly supported by labor and management was conducted among textile workers with disabilities (Enteen, Tramm, & Herman, 1979; Tate, Hockett, & Starkman, 1985). The Amalgamated Clothing and Textile Workers Union (ACTWU) developed a model disability management program with the cooperative efforts of the union, employers, and rehabilitation agencies. Although this program yielded significant rehabilitation benefits to union members, labor realized additional benefits, which included:

- having input into policies and procedures having an impact on employment patterns;
- fulfillment of the union's indirect legal obligation to conform with federal requirements;
- providing additional services to union members;
- maintaining valuable workers;
- reducing workplace problems and insurance and pension costs through rehabilitation efforts;
- improving public perception of labor; and
- increasing the power and potential for goal achievement of both labor and the disabled community.

RECENT LABOR-MANAGEMENT TRENDS

Current trends in disability management research suggest significant growth in joint labor-management supported rehabilitation programs. Typically, the mission of such joint initiatives is to protect the employability of the worker, while reducing the employer's financial liability for the consequences of disability. A recent example of exemplary disability management practices resulting from joint labor-management collaboration (WCRI Research Brief, 1993) is reflected in a variety of positive practices among the Electrical Employers Self Insurance Safety Plan (EESISP). The EESISP provides supplemental benefits for members of the International Brotherhood of Electrical Workers in New York City - Local 3 for both work-related and nonwork-related disabilities. Defying all expectations, in 1991 the plan provided benefits 44% higher than maximum workers' compensation would allow, yet the resulting costs of workers' compensation were only 70% of the industry's scheduled rates for electrical workers. These positive results were attributed to the following factors:

- Joint labor-management focus on safety;
- Supplemental benefits for workers, which are created as a result of reduced costs.;
- Peer pressure to avoid unnecessary litigation, poor or partisan medical providers, and unwarranted medical treatment;
- Managed care relationships among quality medical care providers at discounted fees, and a medical clinic specifically for union members, which discourages "doctor shopping";
- Work return networking among multiple employers participating in the plan, which expands job options for workers with restrictions beyond the pre-injury employer; and
- Reduced litigation and corresponding adversarial climate by using "benefit counselors" who ensure prompt payments when claims are made.

A joint labor-management initiative between Cominco Metals, Trail Operations of British Columbia, Canada and the United Steelworkers of America resulted in the development of the Selective Work Program (Zimmermann, 1992). The intent of the worksite-based disability management program is to provide meaningful work, where possible, for the permanently disabled employee, while not prejudicing any participant in receiving rights negotiated under the collective agreement.

This program had its roots in the 1970s as a relatively informal program offering trivial "light duty" jobs to a small number of workers with restrictions. During the 1980s the program was expanded to company operations in the tailor shop, pallet building, and bicycle repair. However, the program was only responsive to workers with temporary disabilities, and the program length was limited to 90 days. Shortfalls of the program included employees being removed from their normal worksites, inconsistent management of disabilities, and poor support from other levels of management.

An aging workforce, drastic increases in repetitive motion claims, and a policy of contesting claims contributed to increases in benefit costs. Undeveloped relationships between the company and health care providers in the community also contributed to poorly managed claims. The 1990s brought a series of program changes, including the creation of the union benefits coordinator position, an employer-paid full-time position for Local 480. Disability management concepts and multidisciplinary approaches were implemented to integrate return-to-work plans, and case management and occupational therapy services were utilized. A separate seniority unit was established for permanently disabled workers, a new Selective Work Policy Statement was jointly endorsed by labor and management, and the costs associated with disability and lost time were charged back to the corresponding work unit to ensure program accountability among supervisors (Zimmermann, 1992).

Employees disabled as a result of workplace and non-workplace injury or illness are eligible to participate in the program. Both temporary and permanent positions are made available to workers with restrictions, based on the employee's physical capacities and compatible work tasks. A listing of all jobs, including physical requirements, facilitates appropriate placements and fosters workplace rehabilitation and reintegration. The company's medical consultant, who collaborates with treating physicians, the Workers' Compensation Board medical advisor and the vocational rehabilitation consultant, specifies the types of work to be included in an employee's return-to-work plan (Zimmermann, 1992).

The program's placement committee includes the union benefits coordinator, the company claims management representative, the medical consultant, and the Workers' Compensation Board rehabilitation consultant. This committee regularly reviews employee progress toward rehabilitation and reintegration, with ongoing communications with line management, union officials, members of the human resources group, the employee's physicians, and Workers' Compensation Board representatives. Prior to participating in the Selective Work Program, both the worker and the supervisor consult with the program's placement committee, and a progressive return-to-work plan is initiated. Where appropriate, skill upgrading is provided to employees to facilitate their reintegration to the workplace. The company medical consultant monitors the employee's progress, with ongoing communication with the worker and the supervisor (Zimmermann, 1992).

The program also features a steering committee consisting of senior union and management representatives. This committee formulates and maintains operational policies and procedures for the program, with support from the union benefits coordinator, union and company safety representatives, company claims management personnel, and the company medical consultant. As needed, the steering committee seeks input from representatives of the Workers' Compensation Board Adjudication and Rehabilitation Departments (Zimmermann, 1992).

Zimmermann (1992) offered primary reasons for employers and unions to jointly implement disability management programs, and the expected results:

- Efficiency–increased organizational productivity.
- Economy–coordinate a return to work and simply minimize the costs and impact of disabilities on employers and workers alike.
- Social Responsibility–concern with employee welfare and reflection of organizational values i.e., one recent US report indicated that union executives spend up to 50% of their time being troubled by and working with workers who have disabilities.
- Legislative Obligations–compliance with many private sector employment equity, human rights, affirmative action, and legislative statutes.
- For rehabilitation to be effective, it is essential that intervention take place at the earliest possible time and be workplace oriented. To accomplish this, disability managers are required. They should be people who are currently part of the employer's workforce and who work in cooperation with union benefits coordinators.

CONTRACTUAL DISABILITY MANAGEMENT SERVICES

Frequently, employers have neither the time nor the expertise to provide ongoing case management, medical management, and injured worker monitoring services. A contractual disability manager, positioned within the employer's organization, can be an effective alternative management support system for controlling injury and disability problems. This is a particularly attractive alternative for smaller employers with few management resources, or for companies having a limited need (e.g., few lost-time injuries) for an on-site disability manager. Contractual arrangements with a community-based provider may be developed for specific blocks of time (e.g., from one day per week to full-time), or the service may be utilized on a case-by-case basis (i.e., to develop a work-return transition plan for an injured worker).

When an employer decides to contract for an on-site disability manager, a planning meeting is typically convened to outline the designated disability manager's specific roles and functions. Once these duties and responsibilities have been delineated and a supervising employer representative has been identified, a mutually acceptable contract is developed between the community-based organization and the employer. On the designated start date, the disability manager initiates the contractual services on-site, and functions as a representative of the contracting employer. The disability manager may also receive ongoing supervision from a senior staff member of the community-based service.

The defined duties of the disability manager are based on the specific interventions, programs, and services required to facilitate the employer's management of workers with disabilities. The following services are typically associated with on-site disability management services, whether provided under contract or by an employer representative.

DISABILITY RESOLUTION SERVICES

Multidisciplinary evaluations of impaired workers are obtained to resolve any questions or issues involving the relationship between the employee's physical/mental job demands and his/her capacities to successfully perform competitive employment. These include: job analyses, independent medical examinations, functional capacity evaluations, vocational evaluations, and psychological assessments. Both overestimation and underestimation of the worker's capabilities can result in unnecessary prolongation of disability and subsequent costs. If the physician overestimates the worker's physical capabilities, premature return-to-work may result in re-injury. More commonly, the physician conservatively sets return to work restrictions which greatly underestimate a patient's physical capabilities, thus delaying the restoration of function. Consolidation of information from the functional capacity evaluation, medical/psychological impairment evaluation, and vocational assessment helps substantiate the disabled person's medical impairment, disability, and job handicap.

The outcome of Disability Resolution Services is the identification of realistic and attainable options for resolving disability and work performance problems among workers with disabilities. Such options may include job-site redesign, reasonable accommodations, rehabilitation engineering, ergonomic job restructuring, worker assignment to temporary modified duty, permanent job reassignment, worker referral to treatment or rehabilitation programs, out-placement services, litigation/case closure services, or award of disability benefits. Whether provided by contractual or on-site basis, the disability manager must be able to translate the evaluation outcomes into a prediction of rehabilitation potential, including projections of wage loss resulting from a medical or psychological impairment.

Disability Resolution Services are provided using a coordinated, interdisciplinary process. This process is initiated by the disability manager, in collaboration with employer representatives. Evaluation reports resulting from the overall disability evaluation and resolution process can often facilitate employer compliance with ADA accommodation requirements, since they typically include the following information:

- A statement that clearly defines the employee's problem performance criteria, medical diagnosis, degree of impairment, medical prognosis, worker physical capacities, and projected work-return date.
- A statement of physical demands of the worker's job, resulting from the job analysis and ergonomics assessment (this information is often requested to resolve temporary total workers' compensation claims or long-term disability claims).
- Identification of differences between the worker's job demands and the worker's physical capacity to perform specific job tasks.
- Identification of the range of options available to the impaired worker (e.g., physical restoration, treatment, job site accommodation, transitional work assignment, outplacement services, vocational rehabilitation and retraining) and the documented cost for each option.
- A ranking of each recommendation with respect to its respective potential for success.
- Identification of resources available to implement work return, worker retention, rehabilitation and treatment options.
- Description of specific action steps required to implement the recommendations.
- Description of follow-up and evaluation procedures.

JOB ANALYSIS SERVICES

A formal analysis of tasks associated with a specific job or group of jobs is completed, to identify what the worker does. The analysis includes: the purpose of performing each job task; the tools, equipment and processes used in the performance of the job; physical demands required of the worker performing essential job functions; knowledge, skill, and experience level required to safely and accurately perform the job; and other measurable and descriptive information. The job analysis report serves as an accurate written job description to be made available to treating physicians when determining work-return dates. Also, the analysis may be used when developing on-site transitional work and modified duty options for disabled workers, as well as for ADA compliance or other disability management purposes.

DEVELOPMENT OF WORK-RETURN TRANSITION/WORKER RETENTION PROGRAMS

The worksite disability manager, depending on skills and experience, may facilitate the development, implementation, and evaluation of an on-site transitional work or worker retention program. It may be desirable for an employer to develop and implement such programs to: (1) prevent work disruptions among employees with medical impairments that effect work performance, and (2) promote a safe and timely return to work among impaired workers on medical leave, workers' compensation, or long-term disability. In the administration of an on-site transitional work program, the disability manager may take on direct clinical responsibilities, such as: (1) objective worker evaluations, (2) classification of the physical job demands, (3) medical surveillance and follow-up, and (4) planning for placement in an acceptable permanent modified duty option.

DEVELOPMENT OF LABOR-MANAGEMENT DISABILITY MANAGEMENT COMMITTEES

It is always desirable to initiate on-site disability management programs with joint labor-management support. This requires a collaborative problem-solving, decision-making, and planning effort. The disability manager often serves as a catalyst in the development of labor-management disability management committees, bringing to bear considerable resources and experience in resolving work disability. Guidance provided by the disability manager promotes objective evaluation and planning activities, and assures that disability management objectives are met in a timely fashion. A contractual or employer-based disability manager can be instrumental in developing policy, procedure, and protocol, as relates to work-return transition planning.

VOCATIONAL EVALUATION & VOCATIONAL REHABILITATION SERVICES

Many disability management consultants are trained and experienced in providing the full range of vocational assessment and vocational rehabilitation services. Most required testing can be conducted on-site. Assessment services may include a transferability of skills analysis of the worker with restrictions, and a profiling of the worker's qualifications to perform alternate job duties. Testing may also be conducted to determine the worker's aptitude for training or placement in another job.

MEDICAL MANAGEMENT SERVICES

Disability managers may provide medical management services for impaired employees to ensure quality rehabilitation and treatment outcomes. Duties may include visits to physicians and treatment programs, and functioning as a liaison between the employer, other community treatment providers, and the impaired worker. The disability manager may accompany impaired workers during physician office visits and for independent medical evaluations. Likewise, the disability manager may conduct visits to "home-bound" impaired workers to monitor the recovery process and to facilitate work-return planning activities.

WORKSITE DISABILITY MANAGER: ROLES AND FUNCTIONS

Many employers initiate disability management services by delegating cost-containment and worker-monitoring responsibilities to human resource personnel and other managers within their organizations (e.g., safety managers, risk managers, occupational health nurses, insurance managers, benefit coordinators, operations managers). Some employers recruit disability managers from the private rehabilitation, nursing, and allied health sectors. The specific roles and functions of these individuals may vary, depending upon their skills, experience, and training. Likewise, the strengths and weaknesses of an employer's disability management program is often reflective of the disability manager's orientation (i.e., financial vs. clinical; medical vs. vocational; human resource management vs. rehabilitation).

Various opinions abound regarding the essential roles and functions of the worksite disability manager, as well as the professional qualifications necessary for performing this important role. Buys (1993) suggested a possible duty statement for in-house rehabilitation counselors in the performance of disability management functions:

Duty Statement for In-House Rehabilitation Counselor

1. Contact injured workers as soon as possible following injury to determine their rehabilitation needs, and advise them about the vocational rehabilitation program, including their rights and responsibilities.

2. Arrange for appropriate assessments to determine injured workers' functional limitations and capacities.

3. Identify appropriate return to work duties which match workers' functional capacities in consultation with workers, treating specialists, line management, and labor organizations.

4. Organize for worksite modifications as required.

5. Arrange for vocational evaluation if workers are unable to return to their previous jobs. Develop suitable retraining programs in consultation with workers, management and claims agents.

6. Arrange and coordinate external rehabilitation services necessary to assist workers to return to work and to their communities.

7. Develop and document a Return to Work Plan in consultation with workers, their families, line management, treating specialists, labor representatives and claims agents.

8. Provide support to workers and their families while workers are away from work, during the transition back to normal or alternative duties or during the retraining process.

9. Prepare and distribute progress reports, and convene case conferences to ensure all parties are involved in and informed of workers' progress in the rehabilitation program. Modify the return to work program as required in consultation with relevant parties.

10. Develop and conduct education programs for all company employees about workers' compensation laws and regulations, the rehabilitation process and company policies and schemes covering these areas (p. 9).

Buys (1993) suggested that the in-house rehabilitation counselor hold a Master's Degree in Rehabilitation Counseling or closely related degree, and be a Certified Rehabilitation Counselor (CRC). Recommended skills and qualifications include a working knowledge of vocational rehabilitation, workers' compensation statutes, industrial relations, human resource management policies, insurance principles, and claims administration. Communication and negotiation skills are recommended as essential to coordinating information and services among injured workers, families, management, physicians, union representatives, claims managers, and others. Research and training skills are also identified as important to policy development, program evaluation, and educational program development.

Habeck and Munrowd (1987) identified the following skills, knowledge, and abilities relevant and important to disability management:

- Clinical & Direct Service Skills
    * Counseling
    * Case Management
    * Vocational Evaluation and Planning
    * Labor Market Assessment
    * Services Coordination
    * Job Placement
    * Knowledge of Medical, Psychological and Social Consequences of Disability
- Administrative Skills
    * Program Development
    * Program Management
    * Planning and Policy Development
    * Data Gathering and Analysis
- Organizational Development and Consultation Skills
    * Systems Analysis
    * Analytical and Communications Skills
    * Group Dynamics
    * Leadership

Pape and Tarvydas (1993) outlined functional hierarchies for training, with respect to providing ADA implementation services. Many of the core knowledge, principles, and functions related to ADA consultation may be considered important components of the disability manager's responsibilities. Included among these are:

- Interdisciplinary Team Building and Facilitation
- Interpretation of Laws and Regulations related to Rights of Persons with Disabilities

- Resolution of Ethical Issues in Rehabilitation Decision-making and Practice
- Identification and Integration of Multidisciplinary Factors (e.g., psychological, social, cultural, economic, environmental, physical) to Facilitate Disability Management Program Implementation
- Selection and Administration of Evaluative Tests and Techniques to Determine Work Abilities
- Conducting Job Analyses and Recommending Job Modifications/ Reasonable Accommodations
- Vocational Counseling and Work Adjustment Services
- Facilitator/Advisor to ADA Task Force

Based on the author's personal experience as a disability management consultant and researcher, the following skills and knowledge are necessary when maintaining a corporate infrastructure supportive of disability management interventions and services:

ESSENTIAL WORKSITE DISABILITY MANAGEMENT SKILLS/ KNOWLEDGE

DISABILITY CLAIM AND CASE MANAGEMENT SKILLS/KNOWLEDGE
- Information Management Systems
- Rehabilitation and Work-Return Program Monitoring
- Interpersonal Communication and Leadership
- Multidisciplinary Rehabilitation Services
- Time Management
- Early Intervention Strategies and Concepts

EVALUATION SKILLS/KNOWLEDGE
- Medical Terminology
- Medical Diagnosis and Treatment
- Functional Capacity Evaluation Methods
- Psychosocial Assessment
- Computer-assisted Evaluation Procedures
- Ergonomic Job Analysis and Accommodation Assessment
- Vocational Evaluation Methods

ANALYSIS AND PLANNING SKILLS/KNOWLEDGE
- Organizational Development and Human Resource Management
- Parameters of Injury Healing Periods
- Determinants of Disability Duration
- Interpretation of Vocational Evaluation Results
- Transferability of Skills Analysis and Concepts
- Labor Market Trends and Analysis
- Nature and Needs of Persons with Various Types of Disabilities

- Rehabilitation Plan Development
- Career Plan Development Concepts
- Occupational, Vocational, and Technical Education Programs

INTERVENTION SKILLS/KNOWLEDGE
- Clinical Treatment Approaches (Work Conditioning, Transitional Work)
- Uses of Prosthetics and Orthotics
- Injury Prevention Approaches (Safety, EAPs, Work Practices Education)
- Behavioral Management Concepts (Pain/Stress Management)
- Drug/Alcohol Issues and Treatment Resources
- Work Adjustment Services
- Ergonomics, Rehabilitation Engineering, and Job Site Accommodations
- Community Service Networking
- Community Resource Development

CASE RESOLUTION SKILLS/KNOWLEDGE
- Work Retention/Work Adjustment Strategies and Services
- Labor Relations Issues and Dispute Resolution Strategies
- Job Development and Placement
- Financial Dynamics—Work-Return Disincentives

For a more thorough review of essential skills and competencies in worksite disability management, the reader is referred to the following two chapters in this book: "Essential Competencies in Industrial Rehabilitation and Disability Management Practice: A Skills-based Training Model" by Hursh; and "Occupational Health Nurses in Disability Management" by Martin.

KEY ORGANIZATIONAL CONCEPTS IN DISABILITY MANAGEMENT

PARTNERSHIPS

Managing the personal and economic costs of injury and disability in the workplace requires an active partnership. This partnership includes all those participating in the development, implementation, and evaluation of the injured worker's rehabilitation plan. Relationships among workers, unions, employers, insurers, treating physicians, and other health care providers are dynamic and complex. Compatible relationships among these parties often lead to the resolution of workplace disability. However, when workers become injured, relationships characterized by unresolved conflicts can lead to mutually destructive consequences for all those involved, especially workers and employers.

An active partnership is essential to the achievement of rehabilitation objectives for the injured worker. This partnership must be client-centered, and the injured worker must be enabled to access the multidisciplinary resources and services available through other rehabilitation team partners. Such a partnership greatly facilitates an injured worker's active participation in developing realistic and attainable goals, objectives, and time frames, associated with the rehabilitation plan.

GOAL-ORIENTED REHABILITATION PLAN

Frequently, goals, objectives, and plans are not developed for employees who could benefit from rehabilitation services. There are often extended time periods between disease onset or injury and the initiation of rehabilitation programming for impaired workers. Even when such plans are developed, the injured worker may not be directly involved in the development of his or her own rehabilitation plan.

The Rehabilitation Plan serves as the key instrument in the coordination of disability management activities for impaired workers. For employees with prolonged work disruptions (e.g., greater than three months projected time loss), or for employees having hospitalizations in excess of two weeks, case management and medical management activities should be immediately assigned and closely monitored. Concurrently, a written rehabilitation plan should be developed by the rehabilitation team or a designated "disability manager." In such cases, the utilization of specialists in the community may be justified (i.e., rehabilitation nurse, rehabilitation counselor).

The rehabilitation team, or designated "disability manager," when establishing the rehabilitation plan, will need to obtain and coordinate the information necessary to complete and continuously update this plan. The rehabilitation plan may be developed using a variety of sources: 1) the insurance carrier's claims supervisor or rehabilitation nurse, 2) the treating physician and other medical, allied health, and rehabilitation service providers, 3) the employee's supervisor, and 4) the injured worker.

The completed rehabilitation plan should identify the following key variables and components:

- Specific impairments allowed in the claim
- Impact the impairments may have on the employee's ability to perform the job
- Services, interventions, or treatments to be provided
- Barriers to work return
- Specific rehabilitation and work-return transition steps:
    * Objectives
    * Time frames

- * Responsibilities of the claims supervisor, rehabilitation nurse, medical personnel, employee supervisor, impaired worker, and others
  * Resources to be used
  * Resources needed
  * Service costs
- Alternatives to work return if employee is at high risk for not returning to work due to age, severity of injury, emotional or labor-relations problems
- Monitoring schedule
- Evaluation of overall rehabilitation activities, outcomes, and projected costs

Rehabilitation plans enhance communication and service coordination through clearly defined goals, objectives, and responsibilities. The rehabilitation plan also serves as a tool to evaluate the progress of the injured worker, as well as the quality of services provided by insurance, medical, and rehabilitation providers.

In formulating a rehabilitation plan for the injured worker, three important tasks are accomplished. The first is to determine what obstacles prevent work return or work retention, and what must be done to remove barriers to sustained employment. To make this determination, knowledge of the injured worker's capabilities, physical job demands, and the relationship between these two factors is critical. Second, the injured worker and the employer must be made aware of any incongruence between job demands and worker functional capacities, and the available options for remediating these differences. The third step is setting up a schedule that provides for evaluation of success at definite points. This helps the injured worker to pace his or her own progress, making adjustments as needed.

Once the rehabilitation plan has been developed, the insurer or employer authorizes the expenditures and the disability manager implements and monitors the various phases of the plan. The overall goal of the plan is to approximate the injured worker's return to his or her pre-injury physical and economic status. Therefore, any activity, treatment, or rehabilitation intervention aimed at meeting this goal defines the injured worker's rehabilitation objectives. For example, activities and services such as vocational evaluation, counseling, training, job analysis, and job site accommodation may be necessary for the injured worker to accomplish goals compatible with his or her pre-injury status.

SEPARATION OF DECISION-MAKING FUNCTIONS REGARDING ENTITLEMENT VERSUS REHABILITATION PLAN APPROVAL AND FUNDING

Functions related to rehabilitation and work-return plan approval and funding must be separated from benefit entitlement decisions. Claims adjusting and rehabilitation planning decisions should be independent functions, in order to maintain the highest level of objectivity and integrity, with respect to injured-worker rehabilitation. Every attempt should be made to remove the potential for competing and conflicting self-interests to interfere with effective and equitable rehabilitation practice.

Claims adjusters are trained to make entitlement decisions. Disability managers, if properly trained, are skilled at developing objective rehabilitation and work-return plans. A separation of these functions ensures the fair and equitable resolution of disability among all injured workers served by the rehabilitation team.

Funding is a prominent issue related to rehabilitation plan approval. To maintain consistency among rehabilitation service providers, the rehabilitation and work-return plan should include designated diagnostic related groups (DRGs) for authorized services reflected in the plan. In this manner, a fixed funding amount is assigned to the overall plan. Reasonable and appropriate DRG rates are typically based on the past experiences of other boards and commissions. Once funding of the plan's services has been determined and approved, it is the disability manager's responsibility to monitor the utilization of these funds to successfully meet the goals and objectives reflected in the plan.

ACCESSIBLE, TIMELY, AND PRO-ACTIVE SERVICES

Rehabilitation services are neither beneficial to the worker nor cost-effective unless the services are accessible and offered in a timely fashion. The key to rehabilitation success is early intervention and early return to work. Unnecessary delays in the provision of rehabilitation services result in the worker's loss of confidence, lengthier periods of lost time, and the emergence of secondary disability problems (e.g., psycho-social problems, gradual physical deconditioning, and labor relations problems).

It is imperative that a functional alliance be developed with community treatment and rehabilitation services. When services are unavailable, they must be developed. If services are undeveloped or nonexistent, incentives and supports should be established to create or attract accessible services.

RESPECT AND DIGNITY

Providers of individualized rehabilitation services should be sensitive to any cultural, social, racial, or ethnic differences among injured workers. Attitudes of respect and dignity must be conveyed to the injured worker throughout the various phases of work-return plan development and implementation. The "client-centered" approach to rehabilitation is an important way to communicate to the injured worker an attitude of respect for individual differences and needs. Dignity is conveyed through both the timeliness of service provision, as well as the extent to which the injured worker is empowered to participate actively in all phases of the rehabilitation and work-return process. Ultimate respect and dignity for an injured worker is conveyed when the benefits of full employment are enjoyed by the injured worker.

Mutual respect among disability management team members is also important. Such respect is typically communicated when each member values all disciplines represented within the interdisciplinary team. It is necessary to delineate the roles, functions, and responsibilities of team members to avoid unnecessary service duplication and conflict. Mutual respect can be greatly facilitated through the establishment of clearly defined policies, procedures, and service protocol.

TOTAL QUALITY ASSURANCE

Internal and external controls are necessary to assure the quality of the injured worker's case management services and associated rehabilitation interventions. Quality assurance methods should be compatible with the established standards of the insurance industry or workers' compensation statutes.

Internal controls address the quality of relationships among claims representatives, rehabilitation professionals, disability managers, and other primary members of the interdisciplinary team. Such controls focus specifically on the quality of internal communication, as required during the development, implementation, and evaluation of the injured worker's rehabilitation plan. The quality and timeliness of service provision, service access, reporting standards, and other administrative functions must be assured, in order to modify and continuously improve rehabilitation service delivery.

Likewise, external controls are important for assessing and monitoring community-based services, which include medical services, allied health services, vocational rehabilitation services, psychosocial services, and other contractual service providers. Just as the internal disability manager is evaluated, so are providers of those services delineated in the rehabilitation and work-return plan. Typical criteria to consider for service provider quality assurance includes: credentials, experience level, skill, and expertise in injured worker rehabilitation, and relationships with employers and workers. Performance level criteria may include quality of: written reports, rehabilitation plans, vocational assessments, service coordination, utilization of multidisciplinary services, counseling effectiveness, job development and placement, communication with rehabilitation team members, fee documentation, and service cost-effectiveness. External controls should include active injured worker representation, either through direct quality assurance involvement, or through the use of objective and valid assessment techniques (e.g., service satisfaction questionnaires).

The overall quality assurance methodology should focus on the quality of employment options developed for the injured worker, as well as the level of satisfaction among injured workers, supervisors, and employers. Likewise, research on the efficacy of disability management interventions and cost-savings to the employer is an important measure of rehabilitation service quality assurance. Linkages with university-based and foundation-based research programs often facilitate such research efforts.

Education and training is an essential component of disability management activities involving workers, labor organizations, and employers. The attitudes, behaviors, and policies of business and industry are shaped through training initiatives as well as research dissemination. Active affiliations with educational institutions and professional organizations are important when accessing educational and research resources.

CONCLUSIONS

The purpose of this chapter was to provide a comprehensive overview of worksite disability management and industrial rehabilitation interventions. The economics of disability in industry establishes the importance of disability management program development, implementation, and evaluation. Worker demographics is a parallel force in escalating disability costs, particularly those demographics associated with an aging workforce in America. A brief overview of the Americans with Disabilities Act (ADA) was presented. Disability management principles and practices should be viewed as an important strategy for employers to reintegrate and accommodate persons with disabilities, as mandated under the ADA. The ADA is given extensive coverage in the chapter, "Health Insurance, Workers' Compensation, and the Americans with Disabilities Act," by McMahon.

Early intervention is one key to successful disability management outcome. This chapter presented a lengthy discussion of this topic, including a historical perspective of early intervention programs, current research on cost-effectiveness and cost-savings, and the psycho-social importance of timely disability management interventions.

This chapter offered a focused definition of disability management, based on some of the most prominent researchers and writers of the topic, including representatives from industry, labor, and the rehabilitation profession.

Philosophically, this chapter and others in this book emphasize the importance of *worksite* disability management, and the critical need for responsible employer involvement and accountability. Joint labor-management commitment and responsibility is essential to worksite disability management. The utilization of proactive interventions, at individual and work environment levels, and the importance of the interdisciplinary disability management team, were reviewed in this chapter. Concepts such as on-site case management, occupational bonding, and employer-based transitional work programs were discussed.

Model disability management programs, including joint labor-management initiatives, were reviewed in this chapter. Model employer-based programs are given more detailed coverage among other chapters in this book. This chapter examined the option of contractual disability management services for those employers having neither the time nor the current expertise to provide ongoing and quality services to workers with disabilities. An overview of contractual services was provided, followed by a comprehensive overview of essential disability manager roles and functions.

Disability management operating policy guidelines were suggested, with an emphasis on partnership development, rehabilitation, and work-return plan development, and the importance of separating decision-making functions regarding benefit entitlement from rehabilitation and work-return plan approval and funding. The respect and dignity of workers with disabilities, as well as mutual respect among disability management team members was stressed. Finally, essential criteria for total quality assurance and performance level criteria for disability management program evaluation and improvement was reviewed.

For a more detailed framework for designing worksite disability management programs, including on-site transitional work services, the reader is referred to the chapter, "Disability Management at the Worksite: Developing, Implementing and Evaluating Transitional Work Programs" by Shrey.

REFERENCES

Akabas, S. H., Fine, M., & Yasser, R. (1982). Putting secondary prevention to the test: A study of an early intervention strategy with disabled workers. *Journal of Primary Prevention, 2*(3), 165-187.

Akabas, S., Gates, L., & Galvin (1992). *Disability management.* New York: Amacom.

Akabas, S. H., Gottlieb, A., & Yasser, R. (1979). Preventive rehabilitation: Untapped horizon for VR agencies. *American Rehabilitation, 5*(2), 20-24.

Andrews, H. B. (1981). Holistic approach to rehabilitation. *Journal of Rehabilitation*, April-June, 28-31.

National Underwriter. (1989). Report finds rehab crucial to WC system. *Author*, Oct. 9, p. 40.

Avers, L. (1989). Hard at work. *Ohio Monitor.* Dec., 5-10.

Bell, C. (1993). The Americans with Disabilities Act and injured workers: Implications for rehabilitation professionals and the workers' compensation system. *Rehabilitation Psychology, 38*(2), 103-114.

Berkowitz, M. (1990). Should rehabilitation be mandatory in workers' compensation programs? *Journal of Disability Policy Studies, 1*(1), 63-80.

Blumenthal, S. (1992). Impact of the ADA on the vocational rehabilitation of industrial injured workers under workers' compensation. *In the Mainstream, 17*(1), 19-22.

Boschen, K. A. (1989). Early intervention in vocational rehabilitation. *Rehabilitation Counseling Bulletin, 32,* 34-45.

Bruyere, S., & Shrey, D. (1991). Disability management in industry: A joint labor-management process. *Rehabilitation Counseling Bulletin, 34*(3), 227-242.

Bureau of Labor Statistics. (1990). *Occupational injuries and illnesses in the United States by industry,* 1988. U.S. Department of Labor, Bulletin 2366. Washington, DC: BLS.

Buys, N. (1993). Management in the 1990's: A time for employer-based rehabilitation. *Journal of Rehabilitation Administration*, February, 1993, 7-11.

California Workers' Compensation Institute Research Update. (May, 1993). Physical Medicine in California Workers' Compensation (pp. 1-2), San Francisco: Author

California Workers' Compensation Institute (1985). VR: 1985 costs and results. *CWCI Research Notes* (pp.2-3). San Francisco: Author.

Chelius, J., Galvin, D., & Owens, P. (1992). Disability: It's more expensive than you think. *Business and Health, 11*(4), 78-84.

Davis, D. H. (1983). Bridging the claims dollar gap through rehabilitation. *Risk Management, 30*(3), 1-6.

Dell Orto, A., & Marinelli, R. (in press). Encyclopedia of disability and rehabilitation. New York: MacMillan.

Engberg, H., & Welker, T. (1973). *Acquisition of keypecking via autoshaping as a function of prior experience: Learned Laziness?* Psychonomics Society.

Enteen, R., Tramm, M., & Herman, R. (1979). Unions and affirmative action for handicapped individuals. *Rehabilitation Literature, 40,* 196-206,

Flax, P. (1993). Medical costs continue to drive comp expenses. *Risk & Insurance, 4*(9), 13.

Frieden, J. (1989). Cost-containment strategies for workers compensation. *Business and Health, 7*(10), 48-54.

Fruen, M. (1992). Disability management focuses on prevention. *Business & Health, 10*(10), 27-29.

Galvin, D. (1985). Employer-based disability management and rehabilitation programs. In Pan, Newman et al. (Eds.), Annual review of rehabilitation (Vol. 5). New York: Springer.

Gardner, J. (1987). Vocational rehabilitation: Lessons for employers. *Business and Health, 5*(20), 20-24.

Giarrantano, M. (1989). No-fault auto insurance: Cost-containment is necessary. *Forum, 14*(1), 15-17.

Habeck, R. (1993). Work injury management. *Achieving Quality and Value in Service to the Workplace, 2*(3), 1, 3-5.

Habeck, R. (1991). Managing disability in industry. NARPPS Journal and News, 6(3&4), 141-146.

Habeck, R., & Munrowd, D. (1987). Employer-based rehabilitation practice: An educational perspective. *Rehabilitation Education, 1*(3), 1-13.

Habeck, R., Leahy, M., Hunt, H., Chan, F., & Welch, E. (1991). Employer factors related to workers' compensation claims and disability management. *Rehabilitation Counseling Bulletin, 34*(3), 210-226.

Hartman, C. R., & Burgess, A. W. (1985). Illness-related post-traumatic stress disorder: A cognitive-behavioral model of intervention with heart attack victims. In C. R. Figley (Ed.), *Trauma and its wake* (pp. 338-355). New York: Brunner/Mazel.

Hensler, D. R. (1991). *Compensation for accident injuries in the United States*. Santa Monica, CA: RAND Institute for Civil Justice.

Hood, L. E., & Downs, M. A. (1985). *Return to work: A literature review*. Topeka, KS: The Menninger Foundation.

Hunt, H., & Habeck, R. (1993). *The Michigan disability prevention study*. W. E. Kalamazoo, MI: Upjohn Institute for Employment Research.

Kentucky Self-Insurers Reporter. (1993). *National WC survey shows surprising optimism*. Frankfort, KY: Kentucky Self-Insurers Association, 5(2), 1,3.

Kubler-Ross, E. (1969). *On death and dying*. New York: Macmillan.

Kurlander, H., Miller, W., & Seligman, M. (1978). Learned helplessness in humans: Critique and reformulation. *Journal of Abnormal Psychology, 87*, 49-74.

Lewis, J. H. (1973). A workman's restoration system. In M. Berkowitz (Ed.), *Supplemental studies for the national commission on state workman's compensation laws* (pp. 499-516). Washington, DC: National Commission on State Workman's Compensation Laws, 499-516.

Linveh, H. (1986). A unified approach to existing models of adaptation to disability: Part I - A model adaptation. *Journal of Applied Rehabilitation Counseling, 17*(1), 5-16, 56.

Lucas, S. (1987). Putting a lid on disability costs. *Management Solutions*, April, 16-19.

McMahon, B., & Shrey, D. (1992) The Americans with Disabilities Act, disability management, and the injured worker. *Journal of Workers Compensation, 1*(4), 9-29.

Matkin, R. E. (1986). Employers, insurers, and vocational rehabilitation: The need for cooperation. *Forum, 13*(2), 10-11.

Miller, T. (1991, Nov.). Tracking the true cost of accidents. *Safety and Health Magazine*.

Morris, B. (1993). Meshing worker' comp with the ADA. *Risk & Insurance*, August, 26, 28-30.

National Institute on Disability and Rehabilitation Research. (1991). Special issue in disability management. *Rehab Brief, 13*(7), 1-4, Washington: Author.

National Underwriter. (1989). Report finds rehab crucial to WC system. *National Underwriter*, Oct. 9, 40.

Pape, D., & Tarvydas, V. (1993). Responsible and responsive rehabilitation consultation on the ADA: The importance of training for psychologists. *Rehabilitation Psychology, 38*(2), 117-131.

Patenaude, S. (1989). Promoting functional ability in industry. *Industrial Rehabilitation Quarterly, 2*(1), 34, 40-41.

Pati, G. C. (1985). Economics of rehabilitation in the workplace. *Journal of Rehabilitation,* Oct./Nov./Dec., 22-30.

Randall, R. (1992). Comp costs can be reduced. *Risk & Insurance, 3*(7).

Riggar, T. F., Maki, D. R., & Wolf, A. W. (1986). *Applied rehabilitation counseling*. Springer Publishing Co.

Rogers, M. (1993). OH&S Canada's buyers' guide. *Disability Management: Getting by with a Little Help*, 1-5.

Rundle, R. L. (1983). Move fast if you want to rehabilitate worker. *Business Insurance*, May 2, 10-12.

Scheer, S. J. (1990). *Multidisciplinary perspectives in vocational assessment of impaired workers.* Rockville, MD: Aspen.

Schwartz, G., Watson, S., Galvin, D., & Lippoff, E. (1989). *The disability management sourcebook.* Washington, DC: Washington Business Group on Health.

Seligman, M. E. P. (1975). *Helplessness: On depression, development, and death.* San Francisco: W. H. Freeman.

Seligman, M. (1991). *Learned optimism.* New York: Alfred A. Knopf.

Shrey, D. (1993a). *Workplace-based disability management: Challenges & opportunities for joint employer-rehabilitation professional initiatives.* Paper presented at the Second National Rehabilitation Conference on Rehabilitation: Reducing the cost of injury & disability (May 12-14, 1993), Sydney, New South Wales, Australia.

Shrey, D. (1993b). Disability management at the worksite: Proactive concepts in rehabilitation practice. *Bulletin of the Australian Society of Rehabilitation Counselors, 4*(3), 22-25.

Shrey, D. (1992). Employer-based work return transition programs and the deinstitutionalization of America's injured workers." *Work Injury Management, 1*(4), 4-6.

Shrey, D., & Breslin, R. (1992). Disability management in industry: Accommodating workers with disabilities. *International Journal of Industrial Ergonomics, 9*(2), 183-190.

Shrey, D., & Breslin, R. (1992). The Americans with Disabilities Act, employer-based disability management strategies and work return transition programs. In *The Americans with Disabilities Act: Access and Accommodations.* B. McMahon & N. Hablutzel (Eds.), Winter Park, FL: GR Press.

Shrey, D., & Olsheski, J. (1992). Disability management & industry-based work return transition programs. In *Physical medicine & rehabilitation: State of the art review.* Gordon & P. E. Kaplan (Eds.). Philadelphia: Hanley & Belfus, Inc., 6(2), 303-314.

Shrey, D. (1991). Disability management, occupational bonding, and the industrially injured worker. In *Work injury management 1991: Industry and healthcare: Building a Coalition* (pp. 104-113). (Proceedings). Center for the Advancement of Industrial Rehabilitation and Evaluation. Eugene, OR.

Shrey, D., Bangs, S., Mark, L., Hursh, N., & Kues, J. (1991). Returning Social Security beneficiaries to the work force: A proactive disability management model. *Rehabilitation Counseling Bulletin, 34*(3), 257-273.

Shrey, D. (1990). *Disability management, occupational bonding and the injured worker.* Paper presented at the National Issues Forum on Medical Roles in Disability Management at the Workplace, sponsored by the National Institute for Disability and Rehabilitation Research, Washington, DC, September 13.

Shrey, D. (1990). Disability management: An employer-based rehabilitation concept. In *Assessing the vocational capacity of the impaired worker.* Aspen, CO: Aspen Publisher.

Stempien, D. (1989). *CARE Program: Executive summary.* Fairfield, CT: General Electric Company.

Stout Vocational Rehabilitation Institute. (1983). *Private-public rehabilitation: A better understanding.* Menomonie, WI: University of Wisconsin-Stout, Research and Training Center.

Sunshine, J. (1979). *Disability.* Washington, DC: OMB (Staff Technical Paper).

Tate, D., Hockett, C., & Starkman, J. (1985). *Disability management and health promotion: An annotated bibliography.* Disability Management Project. Lansing, MI: Michigan State University.

Taulbee, P. (1991). Corralling runaway workers' comp costs. *Business & Health, 9*(4), 46-55.

Thompson, R. (November 1991). *Putting the brakes on workers' comp.* Nation's Business.

U.S. Bureau of the Census. (1990). U.S. population estimates by age, sex, race, and hispanic origin: 1989. *Current Population Reports.* Series P-25. March 1990: No. 1057.

WCRI Research Brief (July, 1993). *Workers' compensation success stories, 9*(7), 1-3.

Walker, J. M. (1992). Injured worker helplessness: Critical relationships and systems level approach for intervention. *Journal of Occupational Rehabilitation, 2*(4), 201-209.

Wasserman, L. (1993). Risk & Insurance's best programs 1993. *Risk & Insurance, 4*(4), 1, 23-24.

Weiler, P. C. (1986). *Permanent partial disability: Alternative models for compensation.* A report submitted to William Wrye, Minister of Labour.

Weinstein, M. (1993). Proactive prevention. *Risk & Insurance, 4*(2), 1, 12-13.

Wollner, K. (1993). How to reduce workers' comp premium. *Risk & Insurance,* (4)8, 34-35.

Wright, G. N. (1980). *Total rehabilitation.* New York: Little Brown and Company.

Zimmermann, W. (1992). *Industrial disability management: An effective economic and human resource strategy.* Disabled Forestry Workers Foundation of Canada.

— 2 —

Disability Management Practice At The Worksite: Developing, Implementing, And Evaluating Transitional Work Programs

Donald E. Shrey, Ph.D., C.R.C.

The previous chapter and other chapters in this book describe various models of disability management systems. The features of these systems typically include early intervention services, injured worker monitoring strategies, medical and case management, and a variety of interdisciplinary approaches. This chapter features the transitional work program (TWP) model of disability management. The TWP model encompasses many features of exemplary disability management practice, including joint labor-management involvement, early intervention strategies, job site accommodation, occupational bonding, safe work practices education, and direct therapeutic involvement at the worksite.

The purpose of this chapter is to offer a structured process for creating formal transitional work programs at the worksite. Program development consists of three phases: 1) Foundation Development, 2) Program Establishment, and 3) Program Enhancements. It is important to recognize that disability management programs should be designed to address the unique characteristics and needs of the employer organization. Therefore, variations in program design characteristics are, without exception, quite common. Program development phases described in this chapter will reflect a liberal design, providing the reader with a systematic approach to developing a comprehensive disability management systems.

PHASE I: FOUNDATION DEVELOPMENT

A. THE DISABILITY MANAGEMENT ANALYSIS

Prior to creating a disability management program, it is necessary to properly assess the employer's current culture, resources, and capabilities. The Disability Management Analysis is an auditing tool for examining the patterns of influence that contribute to work disruptions and unacceptable costs related to worker injuries and impairments. Information is collected from six specific sources (Fig. 1), in order to diagnose both positive forces and negative disability management influences:

1. KEY INTERVIEWS

The first source of information in developing a foundation for a disability management program is key interviews. To gain first-hand insight into an employer's culture, attitudes, policies, practices, and resources, interviews are conducted with key individuals having direct involvement or indirect influence in disability management activities. Pre-arranged interviews are scheduled with labor and management representatives, employees, and rehabilitation professionals who have had involvement with, or are currently responsible for, various aspects of injury and disability management. Such individuals typically include the following:

- Human Resource Personnel
- Safety Managers
- Risk Managers
- Occupational Health Nurses
- Workers' Compensation Managers
- Union Representatives
- Third Party Administrators/Insurance Representatives
- Supervisors and Middle Managers
- Current and Past Injured Workers
- Corporate and Community Medical Service Providers
- Rehabilitation Professionals and Case Managers

The interview serves as an information-gathering tool, allowing the disability management program developer to assess the employer's capacity to manage injuries and disabilities. It also aids in understanding the roles, functions, and responsibilities of those currently involved in disability management activities. The interview process offers an opportunity to explore employer-based and community resources that will strengthen the disability management program operations. The

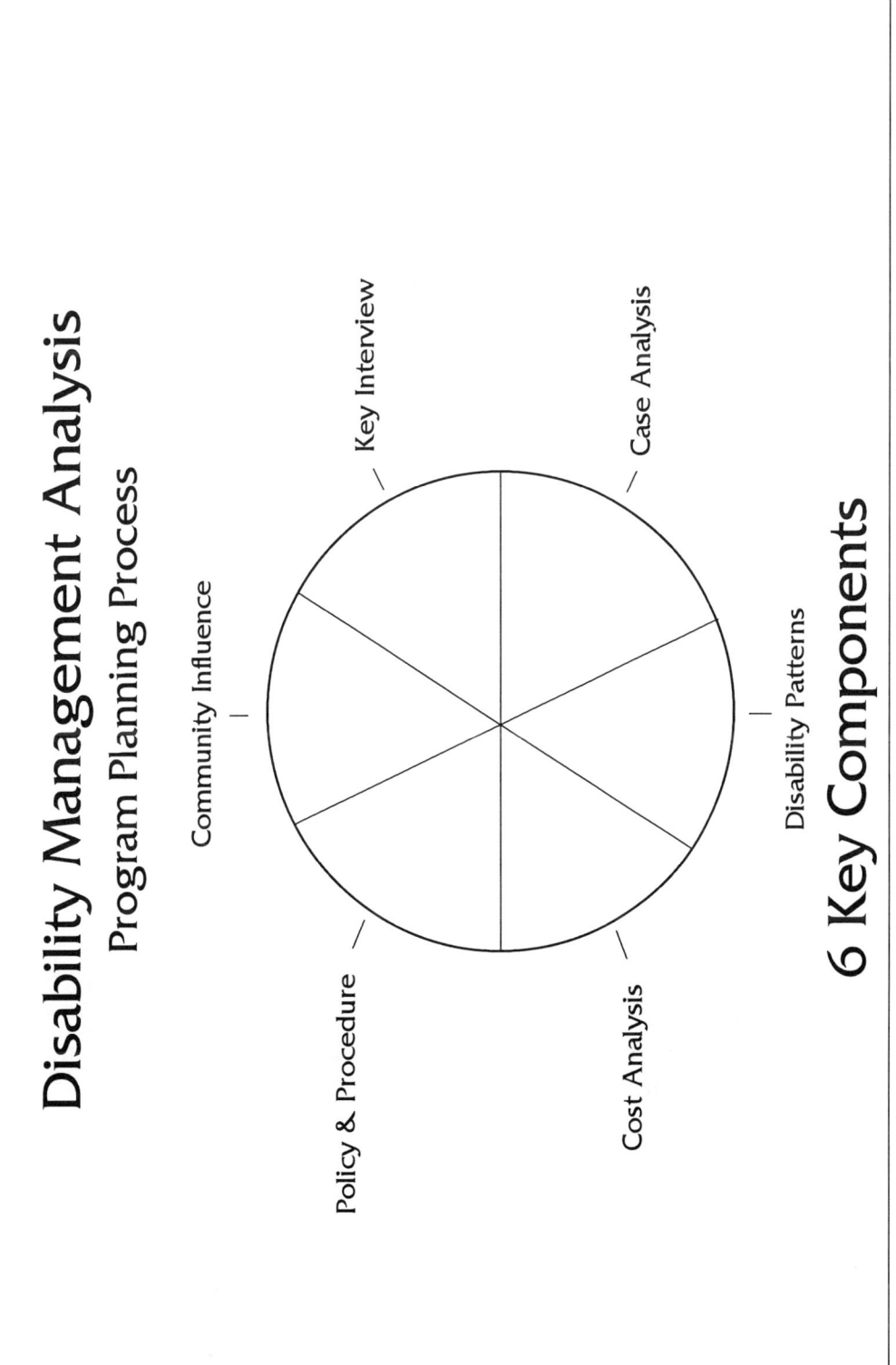

Figure 1. Disability Management Analysis

Disability Management Interview Form offers a structured guide for gathering information relevant to disability management program development. In addition to information addressed on the interview form, the interviewer should develop additional questions to direct at the interviewee, depending upon his or her area of expertise.

For example, a Safety Manager might be asked to describe the employer's safety practices and safety record, as well as the role of the joint labor-management safety committee in safety surveillance and accident prevention. Such an interview might be followed by conducting an ergonomic analysis of "high risk" jobs. This analysis is designed to identify current and potential environmental risk factors for overexertion injuries and cumulative trauma claims (e.g., carpal tunnel syndrome, chronic back pain). The results of this assessment will help determine the need for modifications of the work processes and environment, training of workers and supervisors, and policy changes regarding breaks, work practices, and administrative controls.

An occupational health nurse might be asked to discuss medical management issues and relationships with treating physicians in the community. Injured workers interviewed may be asked to describe their personal experiences during the injury, rehabilitation, and return-to-work processes. Treatment providers in the community should be specifically asked to describe the features of their services, outcomes, and communication linkages with employer representatives.

The information-gathering format of the structured interview should be designed to access useful facts and details that can be synthesized by the disability management program developer. In many cases, the information gathered serves as the raw material for developing consultation progress reports for management. This information is typically summarized in terms of employer strengths, weaknesses, resources available, and resources needed. Once gaps in personnel roles and functions have been identified, management can make effective decisions in delegating important disability management responsibilities to others within the organization. The overall interview process also enables the interviewer to "pre-screen" labor and management representatives who may later be selected to serve on the employer's Disability Management/Transitional Work Program Committee. The roles and functions of committee members are outlined later in this chapter.

2. CASE ANALYSIS

The second source of information related to developing a foundation for the disability management program is the case analysis. This involves a retrospective review of information within the records of individual injured/disabled workers. By analyzing information within the records, the disability management program developer is able to assess the level of employer involvement and respective outcomes in response to work disruptions caused by illness or injury. This information can be supplemented by gathering additional details from treating physicians, the worker's supervisor, and others. The purpose of the case analysis is to review the chronology of events which occurred from the worker's disability onset to the present. The goals of this process are:

- To evaluate the effectiveness of the employer and/or other third parties (e.g., insurance claims adjuster, private rehabilitation provider, medical and allied health providers) in resolving work disruptions due to illness or injury
- To distinguish between those impaired workers having little or no potential for work-return, and those who may benefit from aggressive case management and work return planning activities
- To evaluate the quality of information available to the employer to facilitate effective disability management planning for individuals with disabilities
- To assess the existence and quality of communications between external service providers and the employer, as relates to implementing effective strategies to resolve work disabilities

Table 1 reflects the factors typically identified during the case analysis process. They are explored by completing a thorough review of the impaired employee's case file and by interviewing the impaired worker, the supervisor, treating physicians, claims representatives, and other involved parties. This information and data is analyzed, with the objective of reviewing: (1) the past case management of the impaired worker, (2) identification of previous work-return/retention barriers, (3) negative forces influencing rehabilitation and work-return/retention failure, and (4) positive forces influencing rehabilitation and work-return/retention success. An extensive case analysis of unresolved disability problems provides the disability management program developer with insight into the employer's injury claims process, referral procedures, and treatment/rehabilitation interventions.

After a review of multiple cases, case management trends often emerge, revealing patterns of influence on successful and unsuccessful outcomes. A microanalysis of an unresolved disability case enables the disability management program developer to delineate specific case resolution recommendations (e.g., return-to-work strategy, claims investigation, utilization review). From a macro level, the analysis of multiple cases helps the program developer to shape corporate disability management policy and procedure to resolve disability problems through early intervention and proactive disability management practice.

Table 1
Information And Data Analyzed In The Case Analysis Process

- Nature of Disability (Severity, Functional Impairments, Prognosis)
- Course of Medical Management (Treatments, Therapy, Medical Evaluations)
- Time from Initial Work Disruption to Present
- Age of Impaired Worker
- Length of Service with Employer
- Current Disability Benefits
- Additional Financial Disincentives to Employment
- Attorney Involvement and Litigation Activities
- Impaired Worker's History of Disability Claims
- Labor Relations Issues
- Employee Work Performance Ratings
- Employee Job Satisfaction
- Employer Satisfaction of Worker
- Potential Risks of Reinjury to the Employee
- Work Return/Retention Options Available (Work Adjustment Services, Vocational Rehabilitation, Retraining, Alternate Job Placement, Part-time Employment, Transitional Work, Reasonable Accommodations)
- Nature and Quality of Employer Follow-up Activities
- Employer's Willingness to Accommodate the Worker
- Employer's Policy and Expectations Regarding Work Return/Retention and Disability Employment
- Psychosocial Aspects of Disability
- Marriage and Family Status
- Secondary Disability or Health Problems

3. DISABILITY PATTERNS

The third source of information related to developing a foundation for the disability management program involves the establishment of disability patterns. Most employers (or their workers' compensation claims representatives) maintain statistical information on the incidence and magnitude of "lost-time" and "medical-only" injuries. The Occupational Health and Safety Administration requires employers to maintain injury logs (e.g., OHSA-200 logs). Division and departmental managers within corporations may also maintain injury and disability statistics. Unfortunately, business and industry does not have a uniform database system reflecting injury and disability demographics. To complicate matters, data regarding workers receiving sickness/accident and long-term disability benefits is rarely combined with workers' compensation data. The extent to which any data is maintained by employers varies considerably. Yet, data establishing the unique disability patterns within any employer organization is necessary. Quality data is needed to design a customized disability management system that is responsive to types of injuries among workers within various age groups, who are employed within different work categories.

There is no "canned" or "packaged" disability management system that works well for all employers. The interventions and services that characterize an employer's disability management system should be based upon carefully diagnosed problems and factors specific to the employer's workforce. Otherwise, the interventions used by the employer may fail to resolve the problems. For example, an employer offering "back schools" to all employees may be unpleasantly surprised to find that when this information is made available to the general workforce, claims for back injuries increase. A prior analysis of the employer's disability patterns may have revealed that the employer had relatively few, but costly, back injuries. This problem is not necessarily resolved by implementing a back injury prevention program. The proper solution may well have been to implement an aggressive medical management program to monitor treatments and costs among the expensive back injury claims. Conversely, if 10% of the employer's workforce had experienced lost time back injuries over the past year, the "back school" may have proven to be the intervention of choice. Likewise, aggressive medical management services may have also been an appropriate intervention to control costs among those cases associated with prolonged, and perhaps unnecessary treatment.

Not only do employers differ in terms of worker demographics, variations also occur in corporate culture, the availability of resources, community services, and management commitment. Many of these factors were addressed in the previous chapter. For the purposes of the Disability Management Analysis, Table 2 lists information to establish an employer's disability patterns.

Patterns tend to repeat themselves, unless interventions are used to breach them. Once an employer's unique patterns of injury and disability have been established, the interventions required to alter them may be simple or complex. A careful analysis of the above factors may suggest any combination of interventions, including safe work practices education, ergonomic job modification, job site accommodation, transitional work, medical management, and worker reassignment.

Table 2
Information To Establish Disability Patterns

- High Risk Jobs by Work Unit
- Lost Time Days by Work Unit
- Age Group Patterns (e.g., incidence of injury and magnitude of lost time among younger vs. older workers)
- Ergonomic Job Modification Needs
- Types of Injuries by Age, Sex, Work Units, and Jobs (e.g., strains, sprains, cuts, soft tissue injuries, repetitive motion disorders)
- Body Parts Affected (e.g., shoulder, arm, wrist, leg, knee, hand, foot, back, neck, head, eye)
- Cause of Injury (e.g., slip, fall, safety violation, driving accident, fallen object, weight overload, improper use of tool, poorly designed work station)
- Repeat Claims Patterns (e.g., multiple claims among individual workers within the same work unit)
- Other Absenteeism/Lost Time Patterns (e.g., higher incidence of injuries during holiday seasons, increased lost time associated with anticipated lay-offs)

4. COST ANALYSIS

The fourth source of information related to developing a foundation for the disability management program involves cost analysis. An employer's total cost of injury can be elusive, since the hidden costs of disability have been calculated to exceed those costs that are more easily ascertained. Hidden costs, for example, often represent all the costs of replacing a non-productive injured worker. These hidden costs may include recruitment costs, administrative costs, orientation costs, lost productivity costs, overtime payments to other workers, and loss of use of idle equipment.

More traditionally, it is important to assess an employer's disability costs, with respect to wage replacement benefits, medical costs, fees for case management and rehabilitation services, administrative costs, claims reserves, and costs associated with workers' compensation premium ratings. New managed care developments in workers' compensation are creating options for employers to pool their risks with other low-risk employers (e.g., group plans). Other options include self-insurance, self-administration of claims, state-fund administration, and private insurance coverage. Management is unable to make informed choices among these financially driven options without a clear understanding of injury/disability and associated cost patterns. A wrong choice at the wrong time may result in dramatic increases in ratings and premium structures within two or three years. Those employers considering the self-insurance option must be able to manage current claims to reduce future reserve rates. Once self-insured, they must be able to maintain cost-controls into the future.

Many employers fail to realize that controlling costs begins at the individual case level. For example, one catastrophic injury within a small company can have a devastating effect on future workers' compensation premiums. Multiple claims, even within a large organization, can impact adversely on future premium ratings. Early interventions and transitional work programs are among the many effective solutions to cost-control problems.

An analysis of an employer's costs will typically reveal patterns that require both internal and external cost controls. Internal controls include those interventions that are directly within the employer's grasp (e.g., such as introducing effective injured worker monitoring systems, creating modified duty options, offering employee assistance services, making worksite accommodations). External controls include the development of partnerships with managed care systems, influencing employee utilization of quality and responsive health care systems, and creating functional alliances with rehabilitation services in the community.

The analysis of disability patterns and their associated costs are essential to building the employer's foundation for disability management. The success of a disability management program is measured in reduced expenditures. Therefore, it is important to achieve a baseline measure of an employer's cost patterns from the beginning. Cost patterns associated with community treatment providers and service outcomes also allow an employer to survey the market and compare for cost-effectiveness.

5. POLICY AND PROCEDURE

The fifth source of information related to foundation development of the disability management program involves an analysis of corporate policy and procedure. Both formal and informal policies and procedures for managing claims and coordinating services for impaired workers are examined by the disability management program developer. Through discussions and interviews with management and others, operating relationships with insurance carriers and third-party administrators are identified. Benefits coordinators and labor relations personnel are identified and consulted regarding their involvements, contributions, and influences in managing corporate disability problems.

The impact of insurance plans, compensation laws, benefit plans, and labor-management agreements is critiqued with respect to work-return barriers, locus of control issues, and legal implications of corporate practices and interventions. Management's attitudes and knowledge of disability management strategies and interventions are assessed. The roles, functions, and influences of top, middle, and line management are delineated, to assess corporate accountability, with respect to managing workers with disabilities.

This component of the Disability Management Analysis also addresses the employer's policies and procedures related to physician selection methods and health care utilization practices. Injury reporting and referral processes are noted and levels of communication between medical care providers and management are identified, as relates to the employer's established policies, procedures, and protocol.

Corporate policies and procedures often reflect distinct management attitudes and values, with respect to disability management. For example, policy that dictates the aggressive denial of all claims reflects management values that may have been shaped by ongoing frustration and an over-dependence upon litigation as a means to resolve unacceptable disability costs. Such "reactive" policies generally have an adverse impact on labor relations, and often result in extensive litigation and increased costs to the employer. Corporate policies and procedures that reflect an emphasis on safety, prevention, and early intervention strategies are often developed by an enlightened management team. Such "proactive" policies tend to facilitate positive labor relations and have significant implications for cost-containment.

Written labor-management agreements often contain language establishing the parameters of disability management practice. Seniority and job classification issues may limit the employer's flexibility when designing transitional work options for injured workers. Conversely, language that reflects special conditions and creative work-return options may result in an expanded range of accommodations for workers with restrictions. For more concrete examples of proactive labor-management agreements, the reader is referred to the chapter "Building Joint Labor-Management Initiatives for Worksite Disability Management."

6. COMMUNITY INFLUENCE

The sixth source of information relevant to developing the foundation for a disability management program involves an analysis of community influence. An effective disability management program cannot rely exclusively on the internal resources of the employer. The rehabilitation and return-to-work processes for injured workers are strongly influenced by community treatment providers, external case management services, and legal practice patterns. These community influences are often strong forces in the shaping of injured workers' attitudes and behaviors. Unfortunately, the self-interests of those in the community are not always compatible with the self-interests of the employer.

The involvement of multiple parties in the disability management process creates highly political tensions. The self-interests of these parties contribute to the complexity and subsequent costs of workers' compensation and disability claims.

The Insurance Carrier

The insurance carrier recognizes "profit" as an ultimate self-interest. However, this self-interest may be a negative community influence on disability management success, when insurance carrier profits are taken at the expense of the employer. For example, when the cost of injury and disability increases, the employer's workers' compensation premiums and reserves increase, and the insurance carrier experiences increased revenue from higher premiums. Claims management fees are sometimes based on claims volume. In both cases, an economic disincentive may exist for the insurance carrier to efficiently manage claims. A reduction in the employer's exposure to disability may translate into reduced profits. Also, the extent to which insurance carriers allocate their resources will have an impact on the resolution of disability problems. Many employers do not exercise the full benefits of their premium dollars, when they fail to take advantage of loss prevention and safety consultation services offered through their policies.

Insurance carriers and third-party claims administrators can also be a positive community influence among employers faced with workers' compensation problems. Many offer excellent loss prevention services, including management safety training, ergonomic technical assistance, and disability management consultation services. The disability management program developer should clarify the range and quality of services provided to the employer by the insurance carrier. These services may also include case management, medical management, vocational rehabilitation and legal representation services. Once the services promoted by the insurance carrier or third-party administrator are clarified, the service agency should be held accountable for providing quality services on a timely basis.

The Medical Profession

In most of the U.S., medical costs account for more than half the total cost of workers' compensation. The medical profession is highly motivated by profits, and this self-interest often conflicts with work-return goals associated with disability management programs. Workers with disabilities are often subjected to prolonged treatment, unnecessary medical services, and questionable surgical interventions. In many communities, treating physicians often acquire reputations as being "company-oriented" or "worker-oriented." Likewise, some physicians are viewed as "hired guns" for plaintiff attorneys, while others tend to be linked with defense attorneys. These medical-legal influences in the community will have important implications for disability resolution, particularly after injured worker claims escalate to the litigation stage.

Someone influences where injured workers go for treatment. They may be influenced by co-workers, union representatives, neighbors, relatives, or attorneys. In any event, the employer should consider the opportunity to exert a strong influence in the worker's choice of treatment providers. This, however, will require the employer to become familiar with community treatment providers and to establish collaborative working relationships. The disability management program developer may facilitate this process during the initial Disability Management Analysis by conducting surveys and interviews with these providers and the individuals that have received treatment.

The Workers' Compensation Attorney

Defense attorneys representing the insurance carrier or employer try to gather and present evidence that minimizes the injured worker's functional impairment and work disability. By reducing the extent and consequences of disability, the settlement is reduced and the self-interest of the insurance carrier/employer is satisfied. However, the attorney's failure to recognize the subjective nature of the worker's disability often competes with the worker's self-interest of securing financial independence due to a significant disabling condition.

The self-interests of plaintiff attorneys are primarily to secure the best possible settlement award for their clients. When representing the injured worker, these attorneys typically hope to offer evidence that maximizes their client's impairments and disabilities. In other words, the greater the disability, the larger the settlement from the insurance carrier.

This process often works to the disadvantage of the injured worker and competes with his or her self-interests of financial and vocational independence. For example, the injured worker may be either actively or passively discouraged from participating in a transitional work program during the litigation process. The legal process itself is often lengthy and it may take months before a hearing date is established by the courts. During this prolonged period, the injured worker often becomes more dependent on workers' compensation benefits and loses the motivation to return to employment. Also, secondary disabilities begin to emerge, such as physical deconditioning, weight gain, disruptions in the family, and other psychosocial problems.

As consumers of community-based services, employers must learn to take both control and responsibility for managing medical and rehabilitation services for their employees. The focus of control is often relinquished to an external third party that has little vested interest in service accountability and cost-containment. Many employers have successfully demonstrated a positive impact on managing community influences. Employer-based injured worker monitoring programs, utilization review services, managed care systems, and transitional work programs are typical examples.

Information obtained as a result of the Disability Management Analysis provides a wealth of material from which a comprehensive disability management system may be structured. This data and information serve as a blueprint for management to develop interventions and allocate necessary resources to resolve unacceptable costs and improve disability management practices. Corporate planning activities, based on information established through the analysis, are responsive to the identified organizational barriers to effective disability management. Once appropriate disability management goals and planning objectives have been established, the next step in developing a corporate disability management program is to clarify specific roles, functions, and responsibilities among managers and supervisors.

B. MANAGEMENT ORIENTATION AND AWARENESS

Education is a powerful tool when establishing the foundation for a disability management program in industry. Early in the development of a program, it is essential to provide labor and management representatives with a proper orientation. The goal of this orientation is to present an overview of disability management goals, objectives and processes. It is often helpful to share information from optimal models of exemplary disability management programs, including special features and measurable outcomes. Both labor and management representatives need to become familiar with the steps to developing the program, how the program is expected to operate, and the benefits to both the worker and the employer (see Table 3).

Employers often use divergent and contradictory methods of managing worker injury and disability. Effective monitoring and disability management activities are central to protecting the employability of the worker. One component of disability management involves facilitating the movement of injured workers through sequential procedures. Although managers and supervisors are often in the best position to respond to work disruptions, they may not have the necessary skills, knowledge, and resources to coordinate disability management activities for employees with injuries and disabilities.

The orientation should be responsive to the knowledge and skill deficits among managers, supervisors, and union representatives who make decisions involving absenteeism, illness, injury, and other forms of employee work disruptions. Orga-

Table 3
BENEFITS TO PARTICIPATING EMPLOYERS AND INJURED WORKERS

- Protects the employability of injured workers through the development and implementation of a work transition program, including modified duty options and accommodations.
- Sustains optimal work performance among impaired workers through jobsite accommodations and modifications.
- Increases independence among injured workers with respect to health care and rehabilitation service utilization.
- Promotes more efficient use of employer-based disability management resources.
- Demonstrates the cost-effectiveness of a worksite-based disability management system for injured workers whose performance is compromised.
  Demonstrates Joint-management collaboration in developing, implementing, and evaluating an on-site disability management system.
- Increases involvement of injured/disabled workers in the development of policies, procedures, and practices potentially impacting safe and timely return to work.

nizational development objectives in disability management training should target all personnel who are responsible for human resource functions, production, labor relations, insurance issues, safety, risk reduction, and benefits coordination.

The content and methodology for management training in "Disability Management" interventions, practices and strategies may take many forms. A variety of training methods, such as structured experiential tasks, case studies, "expert" presenters, audiovisual presentations, problem-solving sessions, and lecture formats may be used to address core topics, including those listed in Table 4.

Case studies used in an orientation program may be extrapolated and modified from the existing injured/disabled worker files (e.g., information resulting from the case analysis process). Specific training and awareness modules should address the unique orientation needs of managers, supervisors, and labor representatives, as relates to their existing roles and functions in managing worker injuries and disabilities. One of the primary goals of the orientation is to encourage the active involvement of labor and management representatives. An awareness seminar should

Table 4
Disability Management Training Topics

- Principles of Disability Management
- Cost-effective Disability Management Interventions
- Barriers to Work Return or Worker Retention
- Medical Management and Claims Management
- Psychosocial Aspects of Injury/Disability
- Health Promotion, Risk Reduction, and Disability Prevention Programs
- Labor Relations Impact on Disability Claims
- Occupational Medicine Resources and Interventions
- Vocational Rehabilitation Services
- Disability Management Program Development
- Disability Management Program Evaluation
- Transitional Work Program Design
- Resolving Work Performance and Disability Problems
- The Americans with Disabilities Act and the Injured Worker

allow opportunities for open discussion regarding obstacles to program success, while encouraging an atmosphere of active decision-making and problem-solving.

The orientation includes a philosophical overview of work-return transition programs, including the detailed process of program development, implementation, and evaluation. Participants are also oriented to roles and functions of the case manager, and other processes important to successful program operations. During the management orientation, participants may be provided informational packets, outlines, and supplemental materials describing disability management program features and interventions. Table 5 offers a suggested orientation outline, which can be modified according to the time limits and priorities of the employer.

Table 5
Labor/Management Orientation Outline: Transitional Work Program Development for Injured Workers

MODULE I: Understanding Return-to-Work Issues

Topics: Types of work-return barriers among injured workers
Upper extremity cumulative trauma and low back injury: Implications for injured workers
Principles of disability management
Characteristics of disability in the workplace
Economic impact of injury and disability
Competing self-interests in managing disability
The role of ergonomics in work return and worker retention

Objectives: Explain the need for and goals of transitional work programs
Explain the essential components of transitional work programs
Outline the cost factors related to injury/disability in the workplace
Identify the conflicting self-interests of all parties involved when workers become injured/disabled
Define transitional work in operational terms
Define ergonomics and, using case studies, describe the impact of ergonomic job analysis and job site redesign on the resolution of work disability

MODULE II: Disability Management Analysis Process

Topics: Steps to performing a Disability Management Analysis and injured worker case analysis procedures
Disability management policy analysis

Objectives: Identify patterns of injury and illness
Identify patterns of medical and rehabilitation treatments and related costs

(Continued on next page)

Describe linkages between employer and medical treatment facilities

Define employer characteristics, as they relate to illness and injury onset, health care utilization and work-return

Identify influences of union contracts on work-return processes for injured workers

Identify patterns of worksite and community influence on health care and rehabilitation services

Identify significant barriers to work return:
Medical management problems
Claims management problems
Economic disincentives
Psychological/Social problems
Labor relations/Worksite problems
Secondary disability/Health problems

MODULE III: Case Management Strategies

Topics: Employee identification
Program steps
Policies and procedures
Service areas
Management responsibilities
Implementation plan

Objectives: Review screening criteria for identifying rehabilitation potential of injured workers

Understand case management process, goals, and objectives

Specify policy and protocol for implementing case management activities

Clarify roles and functions of labor/management in the injured worker case management process

Identify the essential components of developing an individualized modified reemployment plan for the injured workers

(Continued on next page)

(Continued from previous page)

MODULE IV: Selection and Utilization of Internal and External Disability Management Resources

Topics: Essential criteria for selecting community service providers
Identification and utilization of internal resources
Procedures for evaluating service outcomes
Model work adjustment and work-transition programs
Specific methods to facilitate re-employment efforts

Objectives: Select and evaluate internal/external resources
Understand modified duty concepts and the needs among injured workers for job site accommodations
Identify cost-effective in-house and community resources for resolving the disability and work performance problems of injured workers, including work conditioning programs, job analysis procedures, functional and work capacity evaluations.

MODULE V: Disability Management Program Performance Audit

Topics: Data collection procedures
Referral outcomes
Service outcomes
Cost/service assessments
Injured/disabled worker service satisfaction
Supervisor/Manager satisfaction with workers

Objectives: Identify critical variables related to program outcome
Evaluate overall cost-effectiveness of Disability Management System
Assess levels of consumer satisfaction with case management and re-employment planning
Evaluate supervisor/manager satisfaction with program features and outcomes

Disability Management Practice at the Worksite

C. ACCESSING CASE MANAGEMENT RESOURCES

Case management is the nucleus of a disability management system. The previous chapter included an extensive discussion of the roles and functions of case managers in disability management programs. Case managers may be selected from the ranks of "internal" human resource personnel. They may be recruited and hired to complement an employer's internal "disability management team." Case managers may also be accessed on a consultation basis from private rehabilitation vendors in the community.

Establishing the foundation for the worksite disability management program requires direct access to case management services. Case management services, interventions, and coordinated activities are included in Table 6.

Table 6
Case Management Services, Interventions And Activities

- Coordination and monitoring of medical and rehabilitation services.
- Development of disability management planning and case coordination activities among employees, managers/supervisors, labor union representatives, human resource personnel, treating physicians, and on-site therapists.
- Development of transitional work plans.
- Facilitating employee and physician understanding of work-return options.
- Coordination of independent medical examinations and functional capacity evaluations.
- Securing job analysis information for examining physicians to understand the type of work the employee is able to perform.
- Performance of vocational evaluations to determine transferable skills to perform alternate work.

Case managers are needed to coordinate multidisciplinary prevention, rehabilitation, and treatment activities for workers. They collaborate with medical and health care providers, public and private rehabilitation providers, and key labor-management members of the disability management team. A formalized disability management program requires a systematic effort to coordinate information and implement work-return and worker-retention plans. Case managers coordinate the employer's response to injury and disability through the development and implementation of rehabilitation plans and work-return/work- transition programs. Along with this major responsibility should come management's support for the case manager to recommend corporate policy and procedure in this important role. Therefore, it is important that the roles and functions of the case manager be clearly delineated, supported by management, and thoroughly communicated to other active participants in the disability management process (e.g., labor representatives, claims representatives, employee supervisors).

Perhaps the most significant level of communication in the disability management process will be between the case manager and employee supervisors. Injuries, subsequent disabilities and work disruptions originate, for the most part, within the work environment. The work supervisor is generally most familiar with his or her employees, work demands, and the circumstances surrounding the alleged injury or disability onset. Thus, the case manager will play a key role, both in communicating vital information to the disabled worker's supervisor and in implementing work-return options for the employee with work restrictions.

DEVELOPMENT OF REHABILITATION PLANS

The case manager, when establishing the work-return transition/worker-retention plan, will need to obtain and coordinate the information necessary to complete and continuously update this plan. This plan may be developed using a variety of sources: (1) The occupational health nurse, (2) the treating physician and other medical and allied health personnel, (3) community rehabilitation service providers, (4) the employee's supervisor, (5) the labor representative, and (6) the employee with work restrictions. The completed work-return transition/worker-retention plan will identify the key variables reflected in Table 7.

Through the development of work-return transition/worker-retention plans, the case manager will enhance communication and service coordination. The plan will delineate clearly defined goals, objectives, and responsibilities. The plan will also serve as a tool to evaluate the progress of the impaired worker, as well as the quality of services provided by medical and rehabilitation providers.

In formulating this plan for the impaired worker, the case manager accomplishes three important tasks. The first is to determine what obstacles prevent employee work return or worker retention, and what must be done to remove these barriers. To make this determination, knowledge of the impaired worker's capabilities, physical job demands, and the relationship between these two factors will be critical. Second, the impaired worker and management must be made aware of any incongruence between job demands and worker functional capacities, and the available options for remediating these differences. The third step completed by the case

Table 7
Key Variables of the Work-Return Transition Plan

- Specific impairments allowed in the claim
- Impact the impairments may have on the employee's ability to perform the job
- Services or treatments to be provided
- Barriers to work return
- Specific work-return transition steps:
  * Objectives
  * Time frames
  * Responsibilities of the claims supervisor, rehabilitation nurse, medical personnel, employee supervisor, impaired worker, and others
  * Resources to be used
  * Resources needed
- Alternatives to work return if employee is at high risk for not returning to work due to age, severity of injury, and emotional or labor-relations problems
- Monitoring schedule
- Evaluation of overall rehabilitation activities and projected costs

manager is to formulate a schedule that provides for evaluation of success at definite points. This will help impaired workers to pace their own progress, making adjustments as needed.

The case manager's role is to coordinate Case Resolution Services, Prevention Services, Medical Treatment and Rehabilitation Services, and Evaluation Services through direct linkages with internal employer resources and external services in the community. The case manager often works in collaboration with employer-based occupational health nurses to coordinate third-party insurance payments for services (e.g., health and accident, long-term disability, workers' compensation).

Case managers with medical management skills and experience often provide services for injured workers to ensure quality rehabilitation and treatment outcomes. These individuals may also conduct utilization reviews to ensure the accuracy and integrity of medical treatment and rehabilitation service billings.

For employees with prolonged work disruptions (e.g., greater than three months projected time loss), or for employees having hospitalizations in excess of two weeks, rehabilitation services and medical management activities should be closely monitored by the case manager. Case managers may be assigned responsibilities for making visits to rehabilitation and treatment programs, functioning as a liaison between the employer, community treatment providers, and the impaired worker. The case manager may accompany injured workers during physician office visits and during independent medical evaluations. Likewise, the case manager may make visits to "home-bound" workers to monitor the recovery process and to facilitate work-return planning activities.

The nature of case management and medical management activities will vary considerably, according to the acuity, chronicity, and other mediating circumstances among injured workers. Most injured workers will return to work after short periods of work disruption. This is greatly facilitated by a consistent monitoring process, which may be the responsibility of the case manager or another member of the internal disability management team (e.g., occupational health nurse). However, when illnesses and injuries result in work disruptions expected to last beyond 10 days, there becomes a greater need for aggressive medical management activity. Here the role of the case manager often expands beyond basic monitoring, into areas such as utilization review, evaluation of treatment plans, and the promotion of second medical opinions. The goal of this process is to reduce lost time by promoting effective health care services and coordinating realistic and attainable work-return options. The disability management process during the sub-acute phase often becomes a coordinated effort between the case manager and the occupational health nurse. Work-return expectations will be determined by the relationship between the worker's functional capacities and the physical demands of the job. Early rehabilitation interventions among sub-acute workers are critical to a successful work-return transition.

The relationship between the case manager and the occupational health nurse may intensify when responding to workers in the chronic phase of disability. A variety of resources are typically coordinated to facilitate evaluation, treatment, and rehabilitation activities to protect the employability of the worker. The case manager and the occupational health nurse may jointly develop a disability management plan that identifies treatment goals, objectives, resources, and timeframes. Through a series of well-coordinated activities, the impaired employee may undergo a functional capacity evaluation, independent medical examination, and vocational evaluation. Concurrently, the employee's job is analyzed to determine specific functional demands, and recommendations are developed to implement ergonomic changes, if necessary, to facilitate work-return activities. The case manager establishes the necessary lines of communication among placement personnel, labor representatives, safety managers, medical department staff, and others.

The case manager and the occupational health nurse share an important role in returning the employee to work. This role often will require counseling with the impaired worker regarding anticipated adjustments necessary to facilitate a successful work-return transition. Work-return options may include changes in the work schedule, job functions, or environmental changes. Temporary light duty assignments may be necessary to facilitate the worker's transition to his or her regular job. This will require ongoing monitoring and evaluation, with expectations of removing temporary work restrictions.

PLANNING FOR PROGRAM ESTABLISHMENT

In summary, laying the foundation for disability management program establishment requires an initial disability analysis, a labor-management orientation, and accessing case management services. During this initial stage of program development, a wealth of information is gathered, analyzed, and organized to facilitate planning for program establishment. This information serves as the "blueprint" for management, and expert guidance from the disability management program developer should address immediate, short-term, and long-term recommendations and targeted interventions. The developer's guidance should also respond to specific problems identified in the Disability Management Analysis that may not have been known previously. Specific employee characteristics, as well as illness and disability trends should be delineated. Recommended strategies should then be outlined to offer management the appropriate controls to maintain maximum worker productivity, while ensuring the worker a safe and supportive work environment. Specific targeted objectives of the worksite disability management program are found in Table 8.

Table 8
Targeted Objectives of the Disability Management Program

- Decrease the incidence of illness and accidents.
- Reduction of time between the onset of an injury or illness and the worker's return to employment.
- Better utilization of local medical and rehabilitation providers.
- More effective screening, treatment, and referral programs that are specific to the existing problems.
- Better informed management and work force related to the development of accurate and reasonable work-return expectations.
- Creation of greater work-return alternatives for workers with restrictions.

PHASE II: PROGRAM ESTABLISHMENT: THE TRANSITIONAL WORK PROGRAM

TRANSITIONAL WORK: AN OPERATIONAL DEFINITION

Transitional work is not an occupational goal. It is an interim step in the physical recovery and conditioning of a worker with restrictions. Transitional work represents an opportunity for the employer to protect the employability of the worker with restrictions, while reducing workers' compensation liability associated with work restrictions and unnecessary lost time. Transitional work is any job, task, function, or combination of tasks or functions that a worker with work restrictions may perform safely, for remuneration, and without risk of reinjury or risk to the worker or other employees.

TRANSITIONAL WORK PROGRAMS: THERAPEUTIC ADVANTAGES

The purpose of this section is to provide a detailed overview of the steps required to establish an employer-based transitional work program. Shrey and Olsheski (1992) reviewed several important advantages of on-site transitional work programs (TWPs) over traditional work hardening services. For example, in TWPs workers are less likely to experience extensive lost time from work when early work-return options are offered by the employer. On-site programs keep injured workers involved in the day-to-day routine of going to work and interacting with co-workers and supervisors. Also, the worker is more likely to perform real work for pay, as opposed to simulated work without pay. TWPs bring the treatment team (i.e., therapist, vocational rehabilitation specialist, and ergonomics expert) to the worksite, rather than taking the injured worker to an off-site clinic. Both labor and management have direct involvement in the operation of an on-site program, where the employee is treated as a valued worker — not as a disabled patient. The development of on-site TWPs represents a disability management approach that relies primarily on the internal resources of the employer, the work environment, and the workers themselves.

Work hardening programs attempt to simulate real work activities in a clinical setting. However, realistic work simulation is difficult to achieve. Since many facilities lack sufficient space and resources, they usually rely on numerous work simulation devices as the primary method of simulation. One obvious deficit of the simulation approach is the inability to create a realistic work environment and deal effectively with work adjustment and labor relations issues. Workers may actually increase their physical capacities to perform work but fail to relate such physiological gains to actual job performance.

Treatment staff rarely have an opportunity to observe the performance of the worker's actual job duties and the conditions in the work environment. Likewise, there is often questionable validity regarding job descriptions and the physical demands of job tasks, as reported to treatment staff by injured workers. Although clinicians may occasionally visit the worksite, they are rarely afforded sufficient time to assess the work environment, work culture, labor relations, and technological processes. These factors play a vital role in the development and implementation of effective work-return plans.

Transitional work, if implemented appropriately, is of mutual benefit to the worker and the employer. Employers that provide transitional work opportunities for impaired workers demonstrate a commitment to the continued labor force participation of these workers while simultaneously reducing the financial liabilities associated with work-related disabilities. Impaired workers who participate in transitional work are able to minimize the economic, physical, psychological, social, and domestic losses related to work disruptions caused by injury or illness.

TRANSITIONAL WORK VERSUS LIGHT DUTY

It is important to distinguish transitional work from traditional light duty programs. Light duty elicits many negative reactions from employers and unions, particularly since these programs have achieved limited success and popularity among labor and management. Perhaps the most common problem associated with the traditional light duty model is that the period of light duty work is typically open-ended (i.e., many workers remain in light duty work assignments for an indefinite time, often resulting in permanent placements). The open-ended nature of many light duty programs usually results from a lack of therapeutic supervision and monitoring of the injured worker by an experienced and skilled therapist. Other problems related to light duty arise out of conflicts with collective bargaining agreements which make it possible for a more senior employee to bump an injured worker out of a light duty job. This problem stems from ineffective coordination with the union and a lack of formal policy responsive to such issues.

The Transitional Work Program model is preferable to the limited light duty model. The former emphasizes real work activities as an interim step in the expeditious reemployment of the impaired worker, facilitating a transition. One major difference between open-ended periods of light duty assignments and transitional work lies in the latter's use of clinical skills to monitor and progressively upgrade the level of real work activities which gradually result in returning the worker to full duty (the original job). Light duty programs typically rely on inexperienced work supervisors to attempt this objective. However, this approach risks failure since supervisors may not have the required clinical skills to achieve the worker's successful transition. Time spent in a light duty program is sometimes insufficient to enable a worker to return to full duty. By bringing clinical expertise to the actual worksite, it is possible to use work activities as therapeutic modalities and progressively condition the worker to resume usual job duties. Important features of Transitional Work Programs are characterized in Table 9.

Table 9
Important Features of Transitional Work Programs

- Transitional work represents a proactive disability management strategy which formalizes the work-return process by providing organization, structure, and accountability.
- Transitional work is a company-wide plan which recognizes the employer's and union's (or employees') responsibilities and active participation in the rehabilitation of its injured or ill employees.
- Transitional work assignments must be meaningful and productive; these assignments must contribute to the company's operations and provide a returning worker with a worthwhile job. Creating senseless jobs for the sole purpose of getting the person back to work insults the worker's integrity and undermines the therapeutic value of transitional work.
- Transitional work must have a therapeutic component and focus on removing or minimizing the worker's residual limitations. The first objective is always to return the worker to full duty or the original job. On-site clinical supervision is essential in the work task progression process designed to recondition the worker to perform original job duties.
- Transitional work programs encourage the use of environmentally focused interventions including ergonomic job modification and accommodation strategies.

JOINT LABOR-MANAGEMENT COMMITTEE ON TRANSITIONAL WORK

Joint labor-management committees are extremely important, particularly among unionized labor forces. In general, the committee should be composed of an equal number of management and labor representatives. One individual can be appointed as the program manager or the chairperson of the joint committee. Committee members typically have some type of involvement in work-related disability issues on behalf of either management or labor. Committee members representing management's interests may include compensation managers, risk managers, safety directors, medical directors, or human resources personnel. Labor representatives ordinarily include workers' compensation representatives, safety committee members, or other elected union officials. The purpose of the joint labor-management committee includes program policy development, formulating a program mission statement, dispute resolution, identification of transitional work opportunities, program evaluation, and continuous improvement. Direct consultation and guidance to the committee is offered by the disability management program developer through the pilot phase, with concurrent development of the TWP's operational policy and procedure.

The committee closely monitors the initial program participants to identify problems, making necessary policy revisions. It is recommended that instruments to assess the worker's and supervisor's satisfaction with the program be developed and used. This information is generally developed in collaboration with committee members. Program evaluation instruments and questionnaires are helpful in evaluating the success of the program and they give those who participate the opportunity to provide input for improvements in the program's operation.

ROLES AND FUNCTIONS OF TWP COMMITTEE MEMBERS

TWP committee members are responsible for attending regularly scheduled and special committee meetings. Members are responsible for developing and implementing fair and equitable procedures related to the overall mission of the TWP. Specific committee functions often include the resolution of work disability among employees with work restrictions, through the development and implementation of individualized transitional work plans. Members participate actively in the process of identifying modified duty and other work-return transition options for workers. Recommendations regarding reasonable accommodations for workers with restrictions are also identified by committee members. TWP committee members are expected to facilitate open communication among workers, unions, and management, with respect to the purpose, goals, and benefits associated with active participation within the TWP. Program information dissemination is also the responsibility of committee members.

Frequency of Meetings

TWP committee meetings are held regularly during the initial pilot stages of the program. It is anticipated that once the TWP is fully operational, the committee may meet on a regular bi-monthly or monthly basis. Meetings are convened by the TWP Manager, who establishes an agenda in advance. Committee members may request a meeting at any time, and members are responsible for submitting agenda items to the TWP Manager prior to the meeting. However, every effort should be made to resolve issues on an informal basis, rather than calling unnecessary meetings.

TWP OPERATIONAL POLICY AND PROCEDURE

The program's policy and procedure is designed to address such issues as program eligibility; scope of the program; resolution of potential collective bargaining conflicts; identification of roles and responsibilities; development of forms to be used in the program; establishment of methods for accommodating permanently disabled workers; development of program evaluation criteria, and development of program dissemination methods.

The initial TWP committee meetings should focus on the development of a program mission statement and the guiding parameters of the program's operations. Encouraging decision-making and policy formulation among committee members ensures joint labor-management ownership of the TWP. This process requires the skills of a resourceful and facilitative Program Manager, who may be initially supported by the disability management program developer.

Mission Statement

This brief statement should capture the essence of the TWP's purpose and goals. In unionized companies, the mission statement will typically reflect the self-interests of labor and management. It is often helpful to provide committee members with sample mission statements from other TWPs as a guide. The following mission statement was developed by Campbell's Fresh Mushroom Farm in Jackson, Ohio.

Campbell's Fresh
TWP Mission Statement

It is the mission of the Transitional Work Program (TWP) of Campbell's Fresh to make every reasonable effort to provide suitable alternate employment or make reasonable accommodations to any employee who is unable to perform his/her normal job duties as a consequence of a work-related industrial accident, injury, or illness. The TWP serves as both a benefit and as a resource to Campbell's Fresh injured workers, by facilitating their safe and timely return to full employment. Through early intervention, structured rehabilitation activities and accommodations, sustained employment will be promoted among employees at Campbell's Fresh. The TWP at

Campbell's Fresh represents an interdisciplinary team approach. Campbell's Fresh will attempt to accommodate injured workers who cannot perform the essential duties of their regular jobs, by utilizing the skills, experiences and resources of the TWP Committee at Campbell's Fresh. Members of this committee will collectively facilitate the development, implementation and evaluation of work return and worker retention activities for injured workers at Campbell's Fresh. Ultimately, the goal of the TWP at Campbell's Fresh is to promote the best interest and employability of injured workers. The TWP will minimize injuries, worker disability and lost time, in order to control the personal and economic costs of injury and disability. As much as possible, alternative productive work will be explored for injured workers who require a gradual transition to work. The employees are recognized as Campbell's Fresh's most important asset, and the dignity of the worker will be supported during involvement in the TWP.

Referral Process

Referrals to the TWP are typically initiated by the company representative responsible for coordinating early rehabilitation interventions. This may be the Program Manager, corporate medical director, an occupational health nurse, or a workers' compensation administrator. In TWPs, referrals are made in collaboration with the designated case manager. Other TWP committee members may recommend referrals to the TWP Program Manager at any time, provided they meet program eligibility criteria and there is a reasonable expectation that the referred worker can benefit from active participation in the program.

Program Eligibility Criteria

TWP participation is generally voluntary, although some state workers' compensation statutes include mandatory rehabilitation requirements. The benefits of participating actively in the TWP should be made available to any employee having a lost-time workers' compensation claim that is likely to result in work restrictions and/or further lost time. Employees with non-work-related injuries may also be eligible for participation in the TWP, although this is a policy decision that must be addressed by management.

Some TWPs classify employees with work restrictions, who are eligible for the TWP, as either *acute* or *chronic*. Each of these classifications requires different entrance criteria into the TWP and varying levels of services and interventions to ensure a successful transition of the worker to full employment.

Acute restrictions are generally defined as those in which the worker's condition is readily apparent, extent of work restrictions is fairly obvious, physical limitations are easily ascertained by the attending physician, and the duration of the work restriction is expected to be less than 14 days before the worker can return to normal duties with or without restrictions. The worker's physician of record determines if the condition can be classified as acute and makes any necessary recommendations for restricted work activity and the expected duration of such restrictions. These recommendations can be outlined on a Work Abilities Report (see Fig. 2). This form is returned to the TWP Program Manager (or other personnel responsible for TWP coordination). The Program Manager and the worker's supervisor then explore suitable work which is in the scope of the worker's restrictions.

WORK ABILITIES REPORT

Employee: _____

Diagnosis: _____

*Note to Examining Physician: We (the employer) are actively engaged in a transitional work program where workers with restriction can return to work with accommodations. For purposes of this program, workers are classified as either acute or chronic. We are committed to providing meaningful employment opportunities to workers who return to work in either category.

Acute: is defined as any condition which is usually short-term and of a less serious nature; the extent of work restrictions is fairly obvious, the worker's physical limitations are easily ascertained by the physician, and the duration of lost time from work is expected to be less that (2) two weeks before the worker can return to work with or without restrictions.

Chronic: is defined as any condition in which the extent of work restrictions is not readily apparent, the worker may not be medically stable, physical limitations are not easily ascertained by the physician, and the duration of lost time from work is expected to exceed (2) weeks.

Please complete the following information which will be used by the employer to make reasonable accommodations for our workers by providing transitional work opportunities, if required:

_____ Condition is ACUTE
A. _____ Worker can return to finish current work shift without restrictions.
B. _____ Worker can return to finish current work shift with the following restrictions: (e.g., lifting limited to 50 lbs.; limited walking or standing)
_____

C. _____ Worker can return to work next shift with no restrictions.
D. _____ See Attending Physician before returning to work.

TO BE COMPLETED BY ATTENDING PHYSICIAN

_____ Condition is Acute
_____ Condition is Chronic. Please evaluate for transitional work based on the following restrictions.
_____
_____

PHYSICIAN'S SIGNATURE: _____
TIME: _____ DATE: _____

Figure 2. Work Abilities Report

The following criteria should be considered when assigning the worker to suitable work within the limitations outlined by his or her physician:

- Return the worker to his or her regular job with no restrictions for that particular job (e.g., the restriction may be that the worker should not lift 50 lbs., but the job does not require this amount of lifting).
- Return the worker to his or her regular job with restrictions as specified by the physician. This may involve making accommodations.
- Return the worker to accommodated work that is compatible with the worker's restrictions or limitations. This could involve a move to another job which the worker may be able to perform without restrictions.

A worker who is classified as *acute* and participates in the TWP is generally expected to transition to normal duties in a two-to-three-week period, unless the disability is of such a nature that this period is not realistic (e.g., a worker with a broken arm may be in a cast for four to six weeks and may not be able to perform normal duties within a three-week period). If significant progress is not made for any worker initially classified as having an acute injury, and the restrictions become less obvious (e.g., a back injury which exceeds the expected recovery time), consideration should be given to providing more extensive services available to those workers, who may be classified as having a chronic condition.

Chronic conditions are defined as those conditions in which the extent of the worker's functional capacities are not readily apparent, the worker may not be medically stable, and physical limitations are not functionally defined in relation to the worker's job demands (e.g., the worker's work restrictions are unknown or unclear). Such workers are not expected to return to work with or without restrictions in less than 14 days. Workers classified as having a *chronic* ailment will require more extensive services which may include a functional capacity evaluation, job analysis, case management, and therapeutic monitoring by the on-site therapist.

EVALUATION OF WORKER WITH RESTRICTIONS AND JOB ANALYSIS

Workers referred to the TWP are evaluated to determine their readiness to safely and productively participate in the program. All workers participating in the TWP must have the consent of their respective physician of record. This is obtained by the Case Manager, who discusses TWP operations with the physician of record, and provides information regarding the worker's individualized transitional work plan.

An analysis of the worker's job, identifying essential job tasks and functional job demands is then performed by the on-site therapist. When appropriate, workers with restrictions participate in a functional capacity evaluation under the prescription of the attending physician or another physician designated by the TWP Program Manager. This evaluation is conducted by the on-site therapist, to determine the worker's physical restrictions, work capacities, and readiness to enter the TWP.

As much as possible, the therapist provides training in conditioning and related interventions to the injured worker when he or she is not scheduled for 40 hours/week in the on-site TWP. The goal is to integrate external therapeutic interventions (e.g., home exercise) with the on-site therapist's program for the worker.

REHABILITATION PLANNING PROCESS

The on-site therapist documents the relationship between the worker's job demands and his or her functional capacity to perform the essential job duties. The therapist then develops a written Transitional Work Plan for the worker, delineating conditioning activities, safe work practices education, program objectives, and timeframes for making a transition to full employment. This plan is then reviewed by the Case Manager.

The Case Manager incorporates the Transitional Work Plan into the overall Rehabilitation Plan, which is submitted to the claims manager (e.g., insurance carrier, third-party administrator, workers' compensation adjudicator) for approval. The Transitional Work Plan is made available for review by the worker, corporate medical personnel, the treating physician, the worker's supervisor, and other TWP committee members. If transitional work opportunities cannot be identified by the worker's supervisor, the therapist, or others charged with this responsibility, a TWP committee meeting may be called to explore realistic and attainable options for transitional work.

ON-SITE MONITORING OF WORKERS IN THE TWP

The TWP's therapist establishes a schedule of on-site sessions to provide therapeutic conditioning, safe work practices education, job coaching, and ongoing evaluation services to the worker with restrictions. The therapist also provides clinical supervision to any therapy assistants, as necessary, to promote safe work practices and worker conditioning activities while involved in the transitional work process. The therapist provides instruction and supervision to the worker's supervisor, to ensure safe work practices that are consistent with the worker's restrictions.

TIME PARAMETERS OF THE TWP

The expected duration of the TWP is eight weeks or less. This is largely determined by the on-site therapist, in collaboration with the case manager, the physician of record, and other members of the worksite disability management team. Under extenuating circumstances, the TWP may be extended, pending the review of the on-site therapist, the attending physician, and other TWP committee members. Criteria for program extension beyond eight weeks may include the following:

1. The worker has demonstrated significant progress with respect to strength and endurance, and is expected to make a successful transition to work within the additional time period.
2. The nature and severity of the worker's restrictions requires a maximum transitional period that is expected to exceed eight weeks, but no longer than a maximum 12-week period.
3. Due to an aggravation of the worker's impairment, the worker's involvement in the TWP is temporarily disrupted, limited, or modified.

Many employers have established a policy that workers must be able to participate in the TWP a minimum of 12 hours per week, but not less than four hours per day. An injured worker's time involvement in the TWP should parallel the worker's targeted work week for his or her work group (e.g., 30, 40, 50 hours per week)

PLACEMENT OF WORKERS IN PERMANENT MODIFIED DUTY WORK

In the event the worker is unable to return to the original job (full duty) after completion of 12 weeks in the TWP, the TWP committee may consider the therapist's evaluation of the worker when identifying permanent placement options.

RESPONSIBILITIES OF TWP PARTICIPANTS

The TWP Manager is responsible for the overall administration of the TWP, and coordinates activities with the case manager, company nurse, and other TWP committee members. He or she serves as chairperson of the TWP committee, and works jointly with human resource personnel and the claims administrator to assume all budgetary responsibilities regarding the fiscal management of the TWP.

The TWP Manager may delegate program management responsibilities to the occupational health nurse, the case manager, the worker's supervisor, TWP committee members, or other appropriate parties.

CASE MANAGER RESPONSIBILITIES

The case manager is responsible for the following:
1. Establishing communication among key program participants, including:
    - the worker with restrictions
    - the physician of record
    - the worker's supervisor
    - the on-site therapist
    - the occupational health nurse
    - the TWP Manager
    - other committee members
2. Meeting with the worker with restrictions to explain TWP activities, and to develop an individualized return-to-work plan, in collaboration with the on-site therapist, the worker's supervisor, and the occupational health nurse.
3. Developing a worker-retention plan to ensure that the worker will maintain safe work performance and productivity.
4. Conducting staff meetings with the TWP Manager, the worker with restrictions, the worker's supervisor, the on-site therapist, and other TWP team members, to establish the basis for an individualized return-to-work transition plan. Also, when appropriate, the case manager meets with the TWP committee to explore realistic and attainable return-to-work transition options, including accommodations.
5. Monitoring the progress of the worker in the TWP and providing details of program outcomes to the supervisor, the TWP Program Manager, the company nurse, the physician of record, and other TWP team members.
6. Coordinating the worker's discharge from the TWP through collaboration with the on-site therapist, the company nurse, and other TWP committee members.
7. Providing follow-up on the worker's adjustment to the original job or alternate job, coordinating additional interventions, as needed.
8. Facilitating the collection of data regarding TWP cost-effectiveness and related outcomes, in collaboration with other committee members, and reporting those outcomes to the TWP Manager.

RESPONSIBILITIES OF THE INJURED/DISABLED WORKER

Workers with restrictions participating in the TWP are responsible for maintaining regular attendance in the on-site work and rehabilitation components of the program, as outlined in the TWP Plan. Workers are also responsible for performing only those work tasks recommended by the on-site therapist, while observing safe work practices. Workers experiencing acute pain or discomfort are expected to immediately notify the company nurse, the physical therapist, and/or the supervisor, so that appropriate therapeutic interventions, job modifications or accommodations can be made.

RESPONSIBILITIES OF THE WORKER'S SUPERVISOR

Immediate Supervisors are responsible for monitoring the safe work practices of workers participating in the TWP, as delineated in the worker's TWP Plan. Supervisors also take an active role in the TWP by identifying work-return transition options, and nontraditional options, as necessary. Supervisors inform the TWP Manager of perceived progress as well as potential obstacles to the successful operation of the program.

PROGRAM EVALUATION

The TWP Manager is ultimately responsible for establishing the criteria for overall program evaluation, in collaboration with other designated members of the TWP committee, and the claims administrator. Baseline comparisons may be established, using cost and experience factors from previous periods. The following factors may be considered in evaluating the program:

1. *Cost-effectiveness:* as measured by the ratio of expenditures for program costs to employer savings (e.g., reduction of medical costs and other appropriate criteria).
2. *Reduction of Lost Time Days:* as measured by comparisons between TWP outcomes and baseline data from previous periods.
3. *Retention of Workers:* based on a database that will describe demographics and work-related characteristics of workers participating in the TWP (e.g., age, job code, disability type, benefit type, TWP option used).
4. *Worker, Supervisor and Treating Physician Satisfaction with Program:* based on responses to questionnaire completed by the respondents.

PILOT TESTING THE TWP

It is recommended that an on-site TWP begin with an informal *pilot* testing of program interventions and activities. This process begins with an initial referral of an injured worker to a case manager for the development of a transitional work plan. The case manager works collaboratively with the worker's supervisor and the on-site therapist to analyze the worker's job, and to evaluate the worker's physical capacities to perform his or her actual job. The TWP for the worker may involve a gradual return to work, and the utilization of other job tasks within that worker's physical capacities. Program duration is generally eight weeks or less. During this time, the therapist continuously upgrades the worker's tasks, while increasing the worker's physical capacities through conditioning activities.

Pilot testing of the program allows for the identification and resolution of potential barriers to the development of a formal TWP. It also allows the TWP team to demonstrate the success of this program on a gradual basis, prior to introducing the program formally to workers and supervisors.

It is critically important during the pilot phase to identify workers who are cooperative and motivated to return to work through transitional work activities. The selection of a willing and cooperative supervisor is equally important during the pilot phase. Remember, the goal of the pilot is to demonstrate the success of the program, which can then be expanded and replicated among other work units. Table 10 summarizes typical TWP procedural steps.

Table 10
Transitional Work Program Procedural Steps

The Company Nurse determines the expected duration of the employee's work restrictions, which are indicated on the Work Abilities Form, as completed by worker's physician.

For work restrictions expected to last less than 14 days:

1. Worker is returned to regular job within the 14-day period, with no accommodations, once restrictions are lifted.
2. Nurse, Worker's Supervisor, and Safety Coordinator explore suitable work which is within the scope of the worker's restrictions. Worker is returned to regular job with restrictions (as specified on the Work Abilities Form), utilizing accommodations as suggested by the above individuals.
3. Worker is returned to accommodated work that is compatible with restrictions, which may involve temporarily working in a different job within the same area. Injured worker then returns to regular job, with or without accommodations, within the 14-day period, once restrictions are lessened or lifted.

For work restrictions expecting to last longer than 14 days:

1. Nurse contacts TWP Manager and Human Resources Manager to review worker's candidacy for involvement in the Transitional Work Program.
2. Worker's Work Abilities Form is reviewed by Company Nurse, along with other relevant information.

(Table 10 continued on next page)

(Continued from previous page)

3. Nurse, in collaboration with Case Manager, initiates worker referral to the TWP Case Manager. Case Manager is provided with medical file information.
4. Case Manager makes telephone contact with injured worker, and schedules an immediate appointment to meet with worker to begin the development of the rehabilitation plan.
5. TWP Case Manager provides worker with detailed information regarding the TWP, and obtains worker's voluntary agreement to participate in the TWP.
6. TWP Case Manager contacts (or meets with) worker's attending physician, to obtain consent and approval for worker's participation in the TWP. (Physician is provided written information regarding the TWP and the worker's job analysis information).
7. TWP Case Manager obtains prescription from worker's physician for a functional capacity evaluation, to determine the relationship between the worker's residual functional capacities and his or her physical job demands.
8. Therapist performs a job analysis and functional capacity evaluation at the worksite.
9. Therapist designs an individualized TWP for the worker, indicating the specific tasks to be performed and the hours of participation in work/conditioning activities. The Therapist and the worker's Supervisor collaborate to identify accommodations, as necessary.
10. TWP Case Manager obtains approval from worker's treating physician for worker's active participation in the TWP.
11. TWP Case Manager completes overall rehabilitation plan, which is submitted to the insurance carrier/claims administrator Funding approval is secured for services provided by the Therapist, and other services required to return the injured employee to work.
12. Worker begins TWP at the worksite, with therapeutic monitoring, safe work practices education, job coaching and conditioning activities provided by the on-site Therapist.
13. Worker's progress in TWP is monitored by the Company Nurse. Repeat functional capacity evaluations are performed at two-week intervals to upgrade the worker's work tasks and time involvement in the TWP.
14. Within the eight-week TWP period, the worker is transitioned to his or her regular job, with or without accommodations.
15. Follow-up TWP satisfaction questionnaires are completed by the worker, the supervisor, and the treating physician.

PROCEDURES FOR WORKERS UNABLE TO TRANSITION TO REGULAR WORK

Workers unable to make a complete transition back to their regular jobs within the eight-week TWP timeframes are generally reviewed by the TWP Committee. The following hierarchy of options is then explored by the committee:

1. Evaluate the worker's need for a time extension to complete the TWP, not to exceed a total of 12 weeks in the program.
2. Identify alternative work, with or without accommodations, within the worker's department.
3. Identify alternative work, with or without accommodations, within the company.
4. Consider the worker's candidacy for involvement in a vocational rehabilitation program, for vocational evaluation, vocational retraining, or other rehabilitative services.

TWP PROGRAM DEVELOPMENT: AN EMPLOYER STUDY

The purpose of this section is to share the author's early experience in TWP program development and consultation. This particular employer study represents a typical program development process, which closely parallels the phases of program development described earlier in this chapter.

The employer represented in this study is a rural family-owned manufacturer of industrial equipment. The company employs approximately 900 workers, who are represented by two labor unions. The employer's labor relations manager began to recognize that the company's workers' compensation costs were getting out of control. Injury-related lost time days had been gradually increasing from year to year. Many injured worker cases were being resolved, at significant expense, through litigation. Safety programs implemented at the company were helpful in preventing injuries, but once injuries occurred, no significant interventions were available to promote a safe and timely return to work for the employer's injured workers. Case management services were accessed sporadically. However, the case manager was not an integrated participant of a worksite disability management team.

The company's profits continued to erode, as a result of escalating medical and wage replacement costs associated with injuries. In short, this company was in trouble and needed help. The first step in designing a disability management program for this company included interviews with labor and management representatives, as well as with workers having had lost time injuries over the previous year.

The interviews were followed by disability management orientation seminars for management and labor representatives. The orientation provided the program developer an opportunity to define the program development process, and to discuss the program's benefits to the unions, management, and workers with restrictions.

THE JOINT LABOR-MANAGEMENT COMMITTEE

The next step in developing an on-site disability management program was to develop a joint labor-management committee. The original committee of eight individuals consisted of representatives from the two unions, management, and the disability management consultant. The goal of this committee was to design, implement, and evaluate an on-site transitional work program for workers with restrictions. Committee members were oriented as to the transitional work process for injured workers. The roles and functions of the committee members were reviewed. The program consultant discussed eligibility criteria for worker referral into the transitional work program. Program operations were reviewed, including worker and job evaluations, rehabilitation planning processes, on-site monitoring of workers, time parameters of the program, and dispute resolution processes. Responsibilities of transitional work program participants (e.g., program manager, case manager, injured worker, immediate supervisor, physical therapist, treating physician, and others) were explained. The committee developed procedures for identifying modified duty work options that could be used for workers involved in the program, as well as strategies for ensuring early interventions, job site accommodations, and ergonomic services. The program evaluation process and the timeframes for initiating a pilot project within the company were established.

Early in the planning stages, the committee agreed upon the TWP's mission statement, which featured the following components:

EMPLOYER'S TRANSITIONAL WORK PROGRAM MISSION STATEMENT: KEY COMPONENTS

- To provide suitable alternate employment
- To make reasonable accommodations
- To serve employees unable to perform normal job duties
- Available to employees with work restrictions, whether work related or not
- Each department is accountable for accommodations of workers unable to perform the basic duties of their former positions
- Joint labor-management responsibility for locating suitable alternative employment
- Goals are to reduce costs, while promoting the employability of the worker

It is important to note that both labor and management agreed that the TWP would be available to employees with restrictions, whether work-related or not. Within three weeks, the program consultant guided the committee in the design of an operations manual, which fully described the policies, procedures, and protocols for a formalized on-site TWP. Concurrently, forms were developed for initiating referrals, describing the functional demands of jobs, and delineating the physical capacities of workers. Program satisfaction forms were developed for participating injured workers, supervisors, and treating physicians.

It was agreed that the program would last no longer than eight weeks. Past negative experiences with light-duty programs at this company reflected that, when injured workers were placed in light-duty positions, it was often difficult to have their restrictions lifted. As a result, many light-duty assignments became permanent placements. Therefore, it was imperative to establish realistic time parameters for program participation, thereby creating expectations among injured workers that they will return to their regular jobs within the prescribed time period. With program policies, procedures, protocol, and timeframes properly established, the stage had been fully set for the pilot testing of the program.

THE PILOT PROGRAM

Four injured workers were selected to participate in the pilot TWP. These four workers, two male and two female, had experienced lost time ranging from two to 16 months. Injuries included back strains, shoulder injuries, and carpal tunnel syndrome. The case manager met individually with each worker and discussed the goals and objectives of the TWP. The program was presented as an employee benefit, created to protect the employability of workers with restrictions. All four workers volunteered to participate in the pilot program.

Each of the four worker's jobs was analyzed to determined its respective functional demands. With the approval of each worker's attending physician, all workers participated in an on-site physical capacity evaluation. The physical therapist was thus able to determine the various degrees of compatibility between the worker's physical capacities and the corresponding physical demands of the worker's actual job tasks. Individualized task progression plans were developed for the workers. Some workers began a gradual return to work, beginning with participation as little as four hours per day and a total of 12 hours per week. Others participated more extensively, depending on their predetermined tolerances for the assigned work tasks.

The therapist provided all workers with safe work practices education (e.g., safe lifting techniques, proper posturing and pacing). Supervisors were taught by the therapist not to exceed the workers' prescribed limits of physical activity, and they were made aware of the work restrictions imposed by the treating physicians. The therapist, in some cases, recommended specific job accommodations and modifications. The workers were involved in conditioning activities and were assigned home exercises, which were monitored by the therapist. Considerable on-site job coaching was provided throughout each worker's program. Additional job tasks were added to the workers' daily programs, and time at the worksite was gradually increased from week to week. Concurrently, the workers began interacting positively with co-workers and supervisors. They began to behave and act like workers, rather than patients.

All workers in the pilot program were gradually transitioned back to their regular jobs within the eight-week program. The pilot program was an immediate success, and other referrals began to follow. The program gained wide acceptance among labor and management representatives, and it eventually became incorporated into the employer's corporate culture. At the end of the first year of operations, the employer's TWP had reduced the company's workers' compensation costs by half. One female employee, who had previously failed in a hospital-based work hardening program, agreed to participate in the on-site transitional work program. Within 40 days she had successfully returned to her former job. At six months follow-up, she continued to work at acceptable productivity standards, with no lost time.

This employer has successfully returned to work more than 60 injured workers over a three-year period. The program served as a prototype TWP, from which many additional programs have since been developed and implemented. Variations of this TWP model resulted in a 50% reduction in lost time and associated workers' compensation costs within a unionized beverage bottling and ice cream plant. TWPs based on this prototype were established within a major shoe manufacturer, a glass company, a sign manufacturing company, two major auto manufacturing companies, an insulation manufacturing company, an air conditioning and heating company, a major metropolitan hospital, a mushroom farm, several automobile parts supplier companies, a bakery, a major regional hospital, and over 25 other employers of various industrial classifications and diverse demographics.

The overall costs of these programs have consistently been less than half the costs of traditional hospital-based work hardening programs. Early return-to-work outcomes have exceeded those of traditional work hardening and facility-based work conditioning services. This is simply due to the fact that the therapeutic program *begins* with a return to work, either full-time with accommodations or on a gradual basis. With interventions to facilitate work adjustment and increased functional capacities, nearly all workers involved in TWPs return to and retain their regular jobs or modified jobs with the same employer.

PHASE III: PROGRAM ENHANCEMENTS

Once the TWP has been successfully pilot-tested, modifications and adjustments can be made to ensure long-range program stability. Program enhancements may include "streamlining" program operations, and eliminating unnecessary steps that delay work-return outcome. Program evaluation questionnaires are helpful when constructive ideas for program enhancements are shared by injured workers, supervisors, and treating physicians. Once a TWP has been launched at the worksite, it becomes integrated into the corporate culture. Workers begin to view the TWP as an expected benefit. Supervisors and managers perceive the TWP as standard operating procedure. Eventually, the TWP Committee finds that regular meetings are unnecessary, and that issues regarding program operations can be handled on a relatively informal basis.

The proactive employer does not become complacent, but always strives for a greater margin of success. The purpose of the Program Enhancement phase in program development is to expand and strengthen the impact of worksite disability management interventions and services. Consider the following illustrations:

CONDUCT PHYSICIAN TOURS OF WORKSITE

Relationships with treating physicians are important to the success of a TWP. Physicians in the community must be convinced that the TWP's objectives are consistent with the best interests of their patients. Therefore, ongoing communication between the treating physician and the employer must be maintained. This is greatly facilitated by the case manager, who establishes regular contact with the worker's physician and keeps him or her informed of the worker's functional gains during TWP participation. However, an additional strategy to strengthen the employer-physician relationship is to conduct physician tours of the worksite. Most physicians have little knowledge of the "world of work." They frequently impose work restrictions on their patients based on inaccurate assumptions of jobs and work environments. Often the sole source of information on jobs is the subjective report of the patient. Stoic patients may describe their heavy jobs as relatively easy, in an effort to secure an earlier return to work. Workers avoiding a return to work may exaggerate the physical demands of their jobs. Guided tours of work production areas can be an enlightening experience for physicians, who otherwise make work-return judgments without the benefit of observing actual jobs as they are performed.

DEVELOP LINKAGES WITH COMMUNITY OCCUPATIONAL HEALTH SERVICES

Employers often discover that their injured workers are utilizing a variety of health care services in the community, none of which is familiar with the company's operations. Many community occupational health services are aggressively seeking new markets for their services. Concurrently, many employers are exploring affiliations with effective and responsive service providers. Linkages with multidisciplinary agencies expand the continuity of services within an employer's disability management program.

EXPAND TWP TO ALL WORKERS WITH RESTRICTIONS

Frequently, TWPs are designed for employees with lost time workers' compensation claims. However, these programs work equally well for employees receiving short-term and long-term disability benefits. Many TWPs are designed for all workers with restrictions, regardless of their benefit program. Workers eligible to participate in such programs often include older employees with work performance problems, pregnant workers, employees with sports injuries, and auto accident victims. TWPs are effective in closing the window on lost time. Since lost time translates into lost productivity and reduced profits, TWPs are viewed as the disability management strategy of choice.

CREATE A DISPUTE RESOLUTION TASK FORCE

Litigation activity is costly to an employer. In many cases, it is more costly to an injured worker. Injured worker disputes that escalate to litigation result in increased costs for legal services and for representation by third-party claims management firms. Litigation prolongs lost time, particularly if the worker's attorney is creating delays to strengthen his or her case for severe disability. Employers also face fines, court costs, back pay, and job reinstatements for workers who are successful in filing discriminatory charges under the Americans with Disabilities Act. It is in the best interests of employers to create a dispute resolution process to informally settle disagreements before they escalate to the courts. Dispute resolution processes can be easily delegated to a joint labor-management TWP Committee. This enhances the disability management process, and it helps to create a balance between the intentions of the employer and the expectations of workers.

USE THE TWP AS A PLACEMENT MECHANISM TO DETERMINE IF WORKERS CAN PERFORM ESSENTIAL JOB FUNCTIONS

The TWP model represents an excellent mechanism to conduct placement evaluations. Once the essential functions of jobs have been clearly defined, workers with disabilities can be more easily evaluated to determine their functional capacities to perform the corresponding job tasks. This is particularly important for workers who are unable to return to their regular jobs due to severe injury.

DEVELOP A BANK OF JOB TASKS TO BE USED BY THE THERAPIST IN CREATING ALTERNATIVE WORK OPTIONS FOR PARTICIPATING WORKERS

As time passes and more injured workers participate in the TWP, more jobs become analyzed. Also, supervisors continue to identify alternative job tasks that are assigned to workers participating in the TWP. This accumulation of tasks creates a reservoir of options to be considered by the therapist when designing an individualized transitional work plan. This "bank" of job tasks enhances the TWP by offering the injured worker with more choices of alternative productive job tasks.

DEVELOP TEMPORARY, NONTRADITIONAL JOBS TO EXPAND TWP OPTIONS FOR WORKERS

Smaller employers are often limited in terms of available TWP options for workers with restrictions. In fact, many employers may argue that it is not possible to develop a TWP because of limited alternative duty options. This is not necessarily a barrier to developing a TWP. Many employers with limited options have created temporary, nontraditional jobs. Such jobs have included recycling of waste, inventory work, grounds improvement, painting, customer mailings, and jobs otherwise outsourced to subcontractors and vendors. It is important for employers to recognize the therapeutic value of creating temporary, nontraditional work options, as an effective alternative to community-based therapy programs (or as an alternative for the worker who remains homebound until fully released to return to work by the physician of record). By offering nontraditional temporary jobs to injured workers, the employer receives productivity in return, the worker receives pay for work and experiences feelings of productivity, and the worker-employer bond is maintained and strengthened. The involvement of an on-site therapist ensures a smoother transition of the worker to his or her regular job.

DEVELOP DEPARTMENTAL AND CORPORATE-WIDE DATA SYSTEMS TO EVALUATE PROGRAM OUTCOMES

TWPs can be enhanced by creating uniform data systems that promote program accountability and outcome evaluation. TWP management requires continuous access to worker and job data within specific departments. Such data may be used to create lost time and cost profiles for departments, as well as injured worker profiles within departments (e.g., worker demographics, job classification, treatment interventions, costs, accommodations). Corporate-wide data systems can be designed to integrate health and accident claims with workers' compensation claims. Profiles of reduced disability costs can be helpful in negotiating lower premium ratings and in evaluating the cost-effectiveness of community treatment and rehabilitation services.

CREATE TWP OPTIONS FOR WORKERS WITH PSYCHIATRIC DISABILITIES

TWP concepts and models can be enhanced by developing interventions and accommodations for workers with psychiatric disabilities. The focus of transitional work planning for such workers will require an analysis of worker traits such as temperament, ability to withstand day-to-day work stresses, capacity to interact with supervisors and co-workers, tolerance for decision-making and problem-solving, reliability, and the ability to concentrate and function independently in the work setting. Such traits must be evaluated in relation to the mental and psychosocial demands of the worker's job and work environment. The degree of compatibility between the worker's non-exertional capacities and corresponding job tasks will determine the worker's level of involvement in transitional work. Accommodations may focus on eliminating high stress tasks, reducing pressures associated with decision-making, and temporarily lowering production standards to facilitate work readjustment. Physically impaired workers are often impacted by pain and stress, particularly back injured workers with chronic disabling conditions. Therefore, TWP enhancements that address psychosocial needs and corresponding job site accommodations will benefit these workers as well.

USE EAP (EMPLOYEE ASSISTANCE PROGRAM) AND HEALTH PROMOTION RESOURCES

The integration of EAPs with TWPs provides a greater continuity of services and interventions to workers with disabilities. Injured workers experiencing family relationship concerns and financial problems should be encouraged to access EAP services. EAPs are also helpful to injured workers experiencing substance and/or alcohol abuse problems, as well as medication dependency difficulties. Worksite health promotion activities benefiting injured workers may include smoking cessation programs, health risk assessments, back care education, stress management classes, aerobic exercise sessions, nutrition counseling, blood pressure monitoring programs, and weight reduction groups. The organizational aspects of not addressing the behavioral consequences of injury and disability include increased absenteeism, repeat injuries, job turnover, and reduced productivity (Scofield, 1990).

USE TWP MODEL TO FACILITATE PLACEMENT AND REINTEGRATION OF DISABLED PERSONS IN THE COMMUNITY

The Americans with Disabilities Act and other reintegration legislation is designed to provide employment and training opportunities for persons with disabilities. New legislative mandates encourage joint labor-management initiatives to promote long-term integration in the workforce, and to implement new directions in employment equity policy. These new and revitalized approaches to employment integration include recruitment, promotion and retention of employees with disabilities. TWPs include many program features supportive of employment integration (e.g., pre-placement evaluation, job accommodation, job coaching).

WORKSITE DISABILITY MANAGEMENT SERVICES AND ENHANCEMENT TRENDS

The 1993 report, *Regaining Control of Workers' Compensation Costs: The Second Biennial Towers Perrin Report* (Towers Perrin, 1993), describes disability management initiatives currently being implemented by employers. This report was based on survey responses from over 1,000 organizations representing approximately 8.2 million employees and $4.7 billion of direct workers' compensation costs. A report summary (Devlin, 1993) indicated that 50% of employers reported using managed care networks, representing a 150% increase in utilization over a two-year period. Eighty-four percent of surveyed employers use case management services, representing a dramatic increase from the 30% utilization reported in 1991.

Other disability management initiatives and interventions on the rise include those reported in Figure 2.

Table 11
Employer Trends in the Use of Disability Management Initiatives and Interventions

Initiative/Intervention	% of Employers Using Initiative/Intervention	
	1991	1993
♦ *Pre-certification of Medical Treatment	19%	57%
♦ *Case Management	30%	84%
♦ Negotiated Provider Discounts	18%	46%
♦ *Utilization Review	28%	70%
♦ Use of Managed Care Networks	20%	50%
♦ *Coordination of Workers' Comp with Group Health Plan	17%	39%
♦ *Fee Schedule Compliance Checks	34%	50%
♦ *Medical Bill Audits	48%	68%
♦ *Claim Administration Audits	45%	61%
♦ *Return-to-work Program	62%	78%
♦ Vocational Rehabilitation	54%	66%
♦ *Safety Initiatives/Injury Prevention	84%	85%

* Eighty percent or more of the employers surveyed found these cost control measures effective in managing injury and disability problems.

Additional initiatives found to be highly effective included: accident evaluation to identify/implement safety measures; communication of workers' compensation benefits to injured workers; loss preparedness training, and healthcare provider profiling.

The Florida Workers' Compensation Managed Care Pilot Program, created by the Florida legislature in 1990, was designed to measure the impact of a managed care initiative in controlling workers' compensation costs (Appel & Borba, 1993). Two pilot programs were initiated in 1991, the first of which focused on injured workers among over 17,000 south Florida government employees. Half of the employees (control group) received traditional fee-for-service medical care, and the other half (experimental group) received medical care from a health maintenance organization (CAC-Ramsay). The average direct workers' compensation claims costs for injured workers in the HMO were 57.5% less than those of the control group, with the exclusion of administrative costs. With administrative costs included in the study's calculations, the majority of the differential costs (48.5%) were associated with the following:

- fewer treatments for claimants
- price discounting
- greater efficiency in delivering medical care

The remaining 9% differential in costs was associated with differences in demographic and injury characteristics among the claimants. Administrative costs were estimated to account for about 10% of the 48.5% cost differential. Therefore, the study concluded that the managed care program had reduced total workers' compensation claims costs by 38.5%. Further analysis revealed that the experimental group was subjected to fewer treatments, with lower prices, and that the injured workers were treated with a simpler and less costly mix of services.

The second pilot program focused on injured workers among approximately 7,500 private sector employees. Medical services to some injured workers (experimental group) were provided by Travelers' preferred provider organization (PPO). The control or comparison group claimants were treated by medical treatment providers outside the PPO network. Cost savings among the experimental (PPO) group only amounted to 3% to 4% less than the control group costs. Treatment costs for the experimental group claimants employed by self-insured firms were approximately 30% less than costs associated with the control group. However, most of this difference was associated with the much higher severity of injuries among control group claimants.

This study is replete with limitations in research design, including geographical differences in treatment patterns, the lack of controls in analyzing costs, and Travelers' economic interests in cost savings. This study was reviewed in *John Burton's Workers' Compensation Monitor* (July/August, 1993), and the study's merits and limitations were thoroughly discussed. Despite the limitations, this study represents one of few isolated attempts to document cost savings associated with managed care systems. Other controlled studies are needed to support the perceptions of employers (per the Towers Perrin 1993 report) regarding the true cost savings benefits associated with managed care initiatives in the workers' compensation arena.

SUMMARY

This chapter introduced the three-phase process of developing a worksite disability management program, with a focus on transitional work programs. The Foundation Development phase began with an initial Disability Management Analysis. A six-component program planning process was outlined, which included (1) Key Interviews, (2) Case Analysis, (3) Disability Patterns, (4) Cost Analysis, (5) Policy and Procedures, and (6) Community Influences.

Foundation development processes included Management Orientation and Awareness. A labor-management orientation program was outlined, which included modular topics and objectives.

A third component of foundation development included Accessing Case Management Resources. This chapter outlined case management services, interventions and activities. The process for developing rehabilitation plans was reviewed, including key variables to consider in the work-return transition plan.

A description of the Program Establishment phase of transitional work programs began with an operational definition of transitional work, therapeutic advantages, and a discussion of transitional work versus traditional light duty. The important features of TWPs were delineated. A discussion of joint labor-management TWP committees featured the essential roles and functions of committee members, with respect to operational procedures and program policy. The committee's role in designing the TWP included the design of a program mission statement, the referral process, and program eligibility criteria. Other program procedures established by the committee included worker evaluation, job analysis, and rehabilitation planning processes. Program time parameters were outlined. The responsibilities of supervisors, injured workers, case managers and others were reviewed. Finally, program evaluation approaches were discussed, including the elements of TWP satisfaction among supervisors, injured workers, and treating physicians.

A suggested process was introduced to facilitate the development and implementation of a TWP Pilot Program. Fifteen procedural steps for TWP operations were outlined. An employer study was shared, reflecting consultation experiences in designing and implementing a worksite-based TWP.

The final phase of disability management program development discussed was Program Enhancements. Suggested enhancements included physician tours of worksites, establishment of linkages with community occupational health programs, program expansion to include all workers with restrictions, and the development of dispute resolution procedures. The use of TWPs as effective placement mechanisms was suggested, particularly as relates to the integration of persons with disabilities. Other enhancements included the development of a job task bank to expand alternative work options for workers with restrictions, development of temporary nontraditional transitional jobs, and data systems for program evaluation.

Potential TWP implications for persons with psychiatric disabilities were reviewed, as was the importance of TWP linkages with EAPs and health promotion programs in industry. Finally, this chapter discussed recent trends in managed care and employer perceptions of effective initiatives to facilitate workers' compensation cost containment.

CONCLUSIONS

Workplace disability management and transitional work programs have heralded an era of transformation in rehabilitation practice. Clinical interventions are being taken to the worksite. Joint labor-management initiatives in disability management are creating both challenges and opportunities for rehabilitation professionals, union leaders, and human resource specialists.

The interdisciplinary members of the disability management team are learning to harness existing technologies and resources within the work environment. Employers are limited only by their creativity, imagination, and flexibility to adapt disability management interventions to the work environment. Job accommodations and temporary nontraditional job options expand the range of transitional work alternatives for workers with restrictions. Redesigned tools, ergonomically correct work stations, adaptive devices, and work schedule modifications are all effective disability management methods that enable the worker to perform essential job tasks (Gross, 1988). These same interventions can be utilized in a preventive manner to identify and redesign jobs which are likely to cause future injuries.

Protecting the rights of injured workers is an important component of disability management. Every year thousands of workers become disabled through industrial accidents and occupational disease. Without transitional work options and accommodations, workers with disabilities risk similar discrimination as other individuals with disabilities. Thus, disability management is an effective advocate tool, whether advocating for the employer or the person with a disability. Disability management interventions protect the employability of the worker, as well as the economic interests of the employer.

The profound impact of rapidly escalating workers' compensation costs will be experienced world-wide by business and industry throughout the next decade. Just as this crisis offers a challenge to industry, disability management interventions and transitional work programs create an opportunity. With a decreasing labor pool, an aging workforce, and increased worldwide competition, employers in industrialized societies must seize the opportunities to control the personal and economic costs of injury and disability. An employer's success will be determined by the extent to which it is able to shape positive attitudes among labor and management representatives, while creating an infrastructure supportive of disability management systems.

REFERENCES

Appel, D., & Borba, P. (1993). *Florida's managed care pilot program: Second interim report. Prepared for the Florida Department of Insurance.* Milliman & Robertson, Inc.

Devlin, P. (1993). Employers take action to control worker' comp costs. *Work Injury Management, 2*(5), 1, 3-7.

Gross, C. (1988). Ergonomic workplace assessments are the first step in injury treatment. *Occupational Safety and Health*, May 16-19, 84.

John Burton's Workers' Compensation Monitor. (July/August 1993). Horsham, PA: LRP Publications.

Scofield, M. (1990). *Occupational medicine: Worksite health promotion.* Philadelphia: Hanley & Belfus, Inc., *5*(4).

Shrey, D., & Olsheski, J. (1992). *Disability management & industry-based work return transition programs.* In *Physical Medicine & Rehabilitation: State of the Art Review, 6*(2), 303-314.

Towers Perrin. (1993). *Regaining control of workers' compensation costs: The second biannual Towers Perrin survey report.* New York: Author.

The Role Of The Physical Therapist In Transitional Work Programs

Joseph H. Daly, M.A., P.T.

INTRODUCTION

Physical therapists are in a unique position to significantly impact health care in industry because of their clinical expertise in musculoskeletal disorders, biomechanical dysfunction and pathokinesiology (DeRosa & Porterfield, 1992; Hochanadel & Conrad, 1993). This body of knowledge allows physical therapists to provide proactive education and conditioning programs, reactive acute/subacute treatment, rehabilitation and re-conditioning programs and return-to-work transitional work programs.

The evolving industrial health care paradigm is disability management. Disability management is "an active, planful process of coordinating the activities of labor, management, insurance carriers, health care providers and vocational rehabilitation professionals for the purpose of minimizing the impact of injury, disability or disease on a worker's capacity to successfully perform his or her job" (Shrey & Breslin, 1992). The success of disability management programs depends on early case intervention, forward case velocity through aggressive case management and timely case closure. In this model, the worker, once injured, would proceed through the following disability management steps: a thorough evaluation to establish a definitive diagnosis, acute and/or subacute treatment that specifically addresses the diagnosis, re-evaluation to assess the effectiveness of the current treatment and/or to plan further treatment such as rehabilitation, return to work (RTW) through a Transitional Work program (TWP), and finally, case closure through successful RTW or other statutory mechanism, such as litigation and settlement (see Table 1).

Table 1
Disability Management Model

Evaluation of Injury
- Definitive diagnosis
- Diagnostic tests
- Specialist consultations

Treatment
- Acute – Specific to injury
- Subacute – Further remediation

Re-evaluation
- Assess treatment to present
- Address secondary changes (e.g., chronicity)
- Further diagnostic testing
- Specialist consultations
- Further treatment – rehabilitation

RTW
- Transitional work
- Vocational assessment
- Functional work capacity assessments

Case Closure
- Return to work
- Retraining
- Maximum medical improvement
- Litigation & settlement

The physical therapist plays an integral part in all phases of the disability management model. However, it is in the TWP that physical therapists can make the most significant impact. Transitional work is "any job or combination of tasks and functions that may be performed safely and with remuneration by a worker whose physical capacity to perform functional job demands has been compromised" (Shrey & Olsheski, 1992). The role of the physical therapist in TWP is significantly different from that in traditional work hardening programs. The physical therapist must now assume greater flexibility in performing the duties of a negotiator, manager, facilitator, coach, and therapist. Initially, the physical therapist must obtain all referral information (e.g., demographic data, diagnostic test results) and perform an initial evaluation to determine the current status of the injury and the worker's safe work capacities. This information is then utilized to plan the TWP. These same initial steps are followed in the traditional work hardening program, but after the evaluation phase, the two programs diverge.

The primary focus for transitional work becomes the worksite instead of the clinic. In the TWP the physical therapist and the worker become actively involved in the work environment. This means interacting with the worker's co-workers, supervisors, work environment, and job. The physical therapist must develop a working knowledge of the worker's job demands. This is best accomplished by performing the job to become familiar with pacing, quotas, work processes, equipment, and tools. The physical therapist can integrate the evaluation information more effectively, while establishing greater credibility with the worker.

The physical therapist must also establish a positive relationship with the employer. As an "invited guest" at the worksite, the physical therapist may be viewed less than enthusiastically by co-workers and supervisors. To establish a working relationship with the employer, the physical therapist must develop an understanding of the corporate culture and the employer's attitudes and practices regarding disability management. It is imperative that early in the TWP, ownership of the injury and the investment in the RTW process is accepted by both the employer and the worker. Workers must view themselves as workers with injuries, rather than as "injured" workers. The RTW process is facilitated by an employer through an integration of corporate policy and procedure, in the context of the workers' compensation statutes, and in compliance with the Americans with Disabilities Act (U.S. Department of Justice, 1990).

The TWP physical therapist is entrusted to forge a balance between worker expectations and employer intentions. To accomplish this, all members of the transitional work team need to be identified and included in the RTW decision-making process. Communication channels must be established so that all team members can be informed in a timely manner. Transitional team members may include the worker, occupational nurse, company physician, physician of record, safety coordinator, team/section leader, co-workers, union representative, legal counsel (worker's and company's), human resource personnel, worksite physical therapist, rehabilitation consultant, worker's family, and any other entity that might have a vested interest. The TWP physical therapist may become a leading participant of this team as a result of skills in determining work-job site functional compatibility, and by maintaining a presence at the worksite. As a TWP team member, it is important for the therapist to network with other team members to maintain the focus on RTW goals, worker responsibilities, and employer accountability. This requires extreme flexibility on the part of the TWP physical therapist.

TWP OVERVIEW

Transitional Work Programs have evolved over the past several years in response to the shortcomings of traditional work hardening programs (e.g., high cost, narrow clinic-based focus) (Shrey, 1991; Shrey & Olsheski, 1992). The functional match of the worker with an injury to the job is the fundamental basis for TWP. Throughout the worker's individualized RTW plan, there is a continual re-evaluation of the employee's safe work capacities, so that incremental advances in work performance can be attained. The ultimate end point of the TWP is RTW to the same job, with the same employer through a process that increases the worker's strength and endurance and focuses on safe work capacities and work adjustment.

QUALIFICATIONS OF THE TWP PHYSICAL THERAPIST

To effectively implement the various roles required of the TWP physical therapist, an integrated clinical and industrial knowledge base is needed.

Clinical Qualifications. Clinical expertise in the orthopedic/sports medicine approach to work injuries is desirable, as functional gains take precedence over pain complaints and active exercise is emphasized over passive modalities (Mayer & Gatchel, 1988). Clinical knowledge should be founded in the scientific basis of treatment with the utilization of outcome-based treatment goals (DeRosa & Porterfield, 1992; Spitzer, 1987).

Industrial Qualifications. A working knowledge of industrial processes, tools, norms, and standards is necessary. This knowledge is best obtained through federal agency publications, international standards publications, industrial health publications, and hands-on experience.

FEDERAL AGENCY PUBLICATIONS

- The National Institute for Occupational Safety and Health (NIOSH) has published documents that contain information regarding manual material handling and cumulative trauma of the upper extremities (National Institute for Occupational Safety and Health, 1981; Putz-Anderson, 1988).

   The Work Practices Guide for Manual Lifting (NIOSH, 1981) establishes criteria for lifting, testing and ergonomics to address the effects of manual material handling on the workforce. In 1985, NIOSH (Walters, Putz-Anderson, Garg, & Fine, 1985) convened an ad hoc committee that reviewed the current research on lifting. New criteria has been recommended for defining lifting capacity and, in 1991, NIOSH published a revised lifting equation based on bio-mechanical, physiological, and psychophysical criteria (Walters et al., 1985). The revised lifting equation provides methods for evaluating asymmetrical lifting tasks and objects with less than optimal hand-container couplings. It offers new procedures for evaluating a larger range of work durations and lifting frequencies. It also introduced the lifting index (the ratio of the load lifted to the recommended weight limit) which supersedes the action limit and the maximum permissible limit equations.

The cumulative trauma disorders (CTD) manual for musculoskeletal diseases of the upper limb (Putz-Anderson, 1988) provides an overview of CTDs, specifies a set of procedures for identifying and analyzing records and jobs for stressors of cumulative trauma, outlines strategies for actively managing CTDs, and provides a series of ergonomic-based guidelines for modifying high-risk jobs.

- The Occupational Safety and Health Act of 1970 was enacted to protect all workers in all workplaces (Hopf, 1975). It charged the Secretary of Labor with establishing standards and enforcement guidelines. It also established NIOSH for research purposes, and the act established an independent quasi-judicial body to review citations and penalties and encouraged the states to assume full responsibility for their own occupational safety and health laws.

The TWP physical therapist should be familiar with the OSHA 200 work injury logs that are required by OSHA for workplaces with at least 11 workers. These logs are used to record work-related worker deaths, illnesses, and injuries that result in lost workdays, or require medical treatment (Hans, 1993). They can be utilized to identify trends in the company's work injury profile and to give insights into the company's philosophy toward work injuries. At this writing, the OSHA injury and illness records and guidelines are being reviewed with changes to be implemented by 1996.

- The U.S. Department of Labor (DOL) publishes the *Dictionary of Occupational Titles* (DOT) and the *Guide for Occupational Exploration* (GOE) (U.S. Department of Labor, 1979, 1982, 1991). The DOT identifies the occupational code number, the occupational title, the industry designation, the job description, the GOE code, the physical demands, the educational requirements, and the training requirements for over 18,000 jobs in U.S. industry. The DOT defines and standardizes strength categories, lifting frequencies by repetitions and percentages, and physical demands (see Table 2).

Table 2
Strength Categories, Lifting Frequencies, Physical Demands

Strength Categories	Physical Demands	
sedentary	walking	hearing
light	stooping	depth perception
medium	bending	finger manipulation
heavy	lifting	sitting
very heavy	reaching	standing
	handling	climbing
	crawling	balancing
Lifting Frequencies	carrying	kneeling
	pushing	crouching
occasional	pulling	feeling
frequent	vision	talking
constant		

The GOE is a companion guide to the DOT and provides additional information regarding the interests, aptitudes, and temperaments of jobs.

The physical therapist is cautioned that DOT information is generic and that a worksite analysis should be performed to correlate with the DOT information (see WSA section).

- The Americans with Disabilities Act (ADA) became law in 1990 (U.S. Department of Justice). This act guarantees equal opportunity for those individuals with disabilities in employment and in access to state and local government services, places of accommodation, public transportation, privately owned transportation services available to the general public, and telephone services available to the general public.

  The TWP physical therapist interacts with ADA under the equal opportunity in employment section when reintegrating the worker with an injury into the workforce. Factors that have been introduced through the ADA, as a result of providing employment access, include reasonable accommodation, essential job functions, and undue hardship. These factors significantly affect pre-placement testing, TWP, and labor/management issues.

INTERNATIONAL STANDARDS PUBLICATIONS

♦ Methods-Time Measurement standards (MTMs) were established in the 1950s and are recognized internationally (MTM Association for Standards and Research, 1988; Work Recovery, Inc., 1991). The MTM process analyzes manual work methods and delineates the basic motions required to perform them. It then assigns to each motion a predetermined time standard according to the nature of the motion and the conditions under which it is made.

The times assigned to the basic motions by MTM are normal (i.e., the time required for an average operator having average skill and experience and working at a normal pace to perform a given work task). The basic MTM motions are: reach (5 cases), move (3 cases), grasp (11 cases), position (3 classes of fit plus symmetry, and whether easy or difficult to handle), apply pressure (2 cases), wrist turns (15 increments), release (2 cases), disengage (3 types), eye travel and eye focus, body/leg/foot motions (e.g., bending, stooping, standing), and simultaneous motions.

The implementation of job modifications/accommodations and safe work practices can be effected by MTMs. The MTM Association in Fair Lawn, NJ publishes its own journal dedicated to the technical aspects and application development for the advancement of MTM.

INDUSTRIAL HEALTH PUBLICATIONS

♦ The TWP physical therapist needs to be aware of other related issues such as worksite design, worksite modifications, worksite material containers/equipment, tool design, and environmental considerations. Journals of specific interest include: *Ergonomics* (published in London), *Human Factors* (published in Santa Monica, CA), *Work Study* (published in Birmingham, AL), and *International Journal of Ergonomics* (published in Amsterdam).

PHYSICAL THERAPY PROGRAM COMPONENTS

History and Records Review ♦ Physical Therapy Evaluation
Functional Work Capacities Assessment ♦ Worksite Analysis
Non-Physical Factors Assessment ♦ Worker Profile ♦ Goal Setting
Program Development ♦ Independent Exercise Program
Program Updates ♦ Discharge Summary ♦ Program Evaluation

History and Records Review. To establish the entry level status of the worker into the TWP, information to be assessed includes: reports of diagnostic tests (e.g., MRI, CAT, EMG), physician of record reports, acute therapy and/or rehabilitation program discharge summaries, psychosocial reports and consultant reports (particularly if they are performed by specialists with specific expertise in the worker's pathology or performed as an independent medical examination). The history and records review justifies the TWP, reassesses the accuracy of the diagnosis in terms of the worker's response to the injury, validates the management of the worker's injury prior to the TWP, and determines how aggressive the TWP can be in terms of short- and long-term expectations (e.g., chronic changes, complications). The history and records review also establishes other factors impacting RTW, such as additional injuries, unrelated/pending surgeries or unrelated conditions (e.g., hypertension).

Physical Therapy Evaluation. This includes standard physical therapy clinical assessments that are tailored to the worker's specific pathology and guided by symptoms/complaints, diagnostic test results and/or physical therapy evaluation algorithms (DeRosa & Porterfield, 1992). The physical therapy evaluation includes:

- *subjective report* — the worker's account of the injury and the subsequent injury management
- *range of motion/flexibility tests* — comparison of major joint movements to established standards; assessment of involved and uninvolved joints
- *neurological/manual muscle tests* — grading of muscle strength against established standards; screening for nerve root involvement; assessment of involved and uninvolved muscle groups
- *gait/posture* — assessment of balance points and center of gravity alignment
- *specialized tests* — manual spinal and/or extremity orthopedic tests, and joint provocation tests.
- *musculo-skeletal examination* — palpation and inspection of the injured area, measurements such as muscle circumference or leg length.
- *non-organic signs tests* — correlates subjective complaints with evaluation data and diagnostic test results (e.g., pain drawings/questionnaires, Waddell's panel) (Hayes, Solyom, Wing, & Berkowitz, 1993).

By taking into account the critical job demands and the age and gender of the worker, the data collected in the physical therapy evaluation can be used retrospectively and/or prospectively to initiate the TWP or to identify the need for other consultant evaluations prior to the TWP (e.g., vocational and psychological assessments).

Functional Work Capacities Assessment (FWCA). An FWCA is an objective measurement of the worker's strength, endurance, positional tolerance, psychophysical status and kinesiophysical status. The goal of an FWCA is to document the worker's capacity to perform competitive work through a comprehensive assessment of entire body motions, safe work practices, kinesiophysical responses, metabolic responses, psychophysical responses and work behavior responses (U.S. Department of Health and Human Services, 1981). In the TWP, the FWCA is used initially to assess the match between the worker's capabilities and the critical demands of a specific job (Committee on Accreditation of Rehabilitation Facilities Manual, 1990). It is also used throughout the TWP to update the worker's work capacities so that adjustments in his or her work performance levels can be made.

FWCA data is generated through specific testing protocols that utilize generic work task tests (static and dynamic modes), specific worksite tests, or a combination of the two protocols. FWCA protocols should incorporate DOL standards and meet the scientific criteria of predictiveness, validity and reliability (Isernhagen, 1989; U.S. Department of Health and Human Services, 1981).

The physical therapist has specific training in kinesiology (the study of physical movement) and therefore can use the kinesiophysical approach to FWCA testing objectively (Isernhagen, 1989). Kinesiophysical criteria includes primary muscle movement, accessory muscle movement, body mechanics changes, fatigue patterns, and dysfunctional movements.

Physiological criteria (e.g., heart rate) have also been shown to be important measures in work performance ratings obtained through FWCA testing (Herrin, Chaffin, Andersson, & Pope, 1984; U.S. Department of Health and Human Services, 1981; Walters, et al., 1993). The inclusion of heart rate monitoring and the rating of perceived exertion scale in the FWCA tests can measure work characteristics such as total work load, peak work load, heat and humidity load, specific muscle load, and work/rest pattern.

Worksite Analysis (WSA). The physical therapist collects data regarding the job from three sources: the worker, the company, and the worksite. Objective data in the following categories is collected:

- company function,
- work schedules,
- work pace,
- work postures/methods,
- physical demands,
- vocational training/certification,
- equipment/vehicles/tools,
- environmental conditions,
- vision and hearing,
- psychological demands,
- physiological demands,

- essential job functions,
- reasonable accommodations,
- marginal job functions, and critical job demands.

The influence of ADA on the WSA is recognized in the categories of essential job functions and reasonable accommodations. The physical therapist utilizes the WSA to make the initial functional match of the worker to the job or to specific components of the job and to assess and implement appropriate job modifications. Throughout the TWP, the WSA information is utilized to direct job placement as work performance levels improve (see "FWCA" and "Worker Profile").

Nonphysical Factors Assessment. The psychosocial issues involved in TWP have become increasingly apparent. Their negative impact on RTW has been thoroughly documented (Bigos et al., 1992; Kreider, 1993; Mayer & Gatchel, 1988; Stultz, 1994). Issues such as job satisfaction, worker attitude toward employer, depression, hysterical personality, aging, dependent/immature personality, substance abuse, secondary gains and sociopathy are identified early through assessment tools such as the Modified Work Apgar (Bigos et al., 1992), RTW Forcefield Analysis (Lowe & Daly, 1993), or the North American Spine Society's Outcome Questionnaire (Deyo, 1993), so that their impact on the TWP and the RTW process can be measured. If these issues are treated as normal injury-labor-management issues, appropriate areas of responsibility can be assigned among the disability management team members, and incorporated into the TWP goal-setting process (see "Goal Setting").

Worker Profile. This is the integration of the data obtained from the physical therapy evaluation, the FWCA, the WSA, and the Nonphysical Factor Assessment. The Worker Profile compares the initial FWCA of the worker with the current WSA of the job. Matching components between the worker and the job(s) are identified, and then utilized to establish the entry level of work performance. The Worker Profile is modified throughout the TWP to reflect the changes in strength, endurance, and safe work capacities.

Goal Setting. Before implementing the TWP, the transitional work team members need an acceptable and realistic direction for the RTW process. This is accomplished through goal setting so that areas of responsibility can be assigned to the appropriate team members. During this process, an active TWP team member is identified as the program manager. As the goal-setting process evolves, ownership of the TWP is jointly assumed by the employer and the worker.

Program Development. As a result of the goal-setting process, an action plan to address the identified TWP goals for each transitional team member is developed. Action plans are then implemented, modified, and monitored throughout the TWP. Examples of action plans are:

- *worker* — a rehabilitation program to remediate specific deficits resulting from an injury; work conditioning to improve overall strength, endurance, flexibility, and safe work capacities; education
- *physician of record* — further diagnostic testing; TWP rechecks
- *worksite* — an ergonomic analysis to assess the feasibility of adaptive work equipment (e.g., padded gloves, rubber mats) or work station redesign (e.g., raise work height, job rotation schedule)
- *employer* — an ergonomics program that is functional and cost effective; education regarding disability management and its relationship to TWP.

Independent Exercise Programs. These are necessary due to the departure from clinic-based programming. They require maximum participation by the worker, thereby establishing ownership of the injury management process with the worker. During the initial weeks of the TWP, the worker may be working reduced hours per day and/or reduced days per week. This allows time to incorporate independent exercise programs. It is emphasized to the worker that the independent exercise program is a part of the employee's workday and, as a result of the gradual RTW process, there is a sufficient amount of time to exercise during the week. The independent exercise program involves a general work-conditioning program (e.g., aerobics, machine weights) and an injury-specific exercise program. It can be implemented at a local exercise facility, at the employer fitness facility if available, at home, or at all three places in combination. Creativity and resourcefulness, on the physical therapist's part, is the key to success when implementing an independent exercise program.

Program Updates. On-going assessment of TWP goals is done through staffings and progress reports. In this way RTW status is known at all times. Staffings are held at least bi-weekly. They should involve as many team members as feasible (e.g., physician of record, occupational nurse, rehabilitation consultant, worker, team leader, management, safety coordinators). The goal for each staffing is to assess program participation and to develop an action plan for the upcoming weeks, with well-defined areas of responsibility for all team members. In addition to formal staffings, many impromptu staffings are held at the worksite (e.g., discussing with the team leader a specific job task) or via phone calls to the rehabilitation consultant. Data collected from the staffings is summarized, at least on a monthly basis, in a progress report. This report is directed to the physician of record and includes TWP information on subjective comments, clinical examinations, work performance, independent exercise, goal assessment, and team action plan. The worker is given the opportunity to review and sign off on the progress report before it is sent to the physician of record. Two copies are sent to the physician of record, along with a self-addressed, stamped envelope to encourage a response. The progress report includes a separate section for the physician of record to agree/disagree with the team action plan and to comment on the status of the overall program. Progress reports provide a mechanism for the physician of record to interact knowledgeably with the TWP team members and it reassures the worker that the physician of record has ownership in the worker's TWP.

Discharge Summary. At the end of the TWP, resolution of the TWP team goals are assessed. All team members provide recommendations for the long-term success of sustained RTW. The physical therapist reevaluates the physical therapy evaluation and the FWCA (and summarizes program development), the independent exercise program, and the program updates to determine the discharge Worker Profile. Recommendations regarding future job placement and injury prognosis are made by the TWP team. If the TWP has been successful, the employer and the worker assume complete ownership of the long-term RTW process at the time of discharge.

Program Evaluation. In order for the TWP to establish its effectiveness in terms of an adjunct or a stand-alone alternative to work-hardening programs, its accountability in a disability management model must be established. This is done through the collection of outcome-based objective data. Methods for the collection of TWP data include:

- *goal sheets* — identify action plan objectives and include pre- and post-ratings
- *exercise parameters* — includes heart rates, aerobic points, lifting repetitions, weights, joint range of motion, performance quotas, etc.
- *satisfaction questionnaires* — provides outcome information from the employer, the supervisor, the worker, and the physician of record
- *staffings and progress reports* — measures functional outcomes and goal attainment

This data is then used to determine such factors as cost-effectiveness, impact on reduction of lost time, worker retention, employer/worker satisfaction, effect of case velocity, and programmatic content of the TWP.

ADVANTAGES OF TRANSITIONAL WORK PROGRAMS

The physical therapist's goal in a TWP is to create a balance between the employer (whose concerns are productivity, safety, and health compliance) and worker (whose concerns are how they are treated by the employer and their ability to do their job). Transitional Work Programs provide a mechanism to create this balance by assigning ownership of the injury and its consequences to the appropriate team members for remediation. There are many factors affecting the ability to obtain a working balance between the employer and the worker.

- *Early intervention* — the physical therapist should reintroduce the worker with an injury to the worksite as soon as the injury has stabilized and the worker exhibits safe work capacities. Transitional work is the logical continuum of the disability management model, as it prevents chronic problems that often result from slow case velocity.
- *Appropriate job placement* — the physical therapist can facilitate the placement of the worker into a job that is compatible with safe work capacities through clinical and functional testing. This will address the fears of both the employer and the worker concerning work expectations.
- *ADA compliance* — the TWP provides a mechanism for returning a worker with an injury to a job that meets the "reasonable accommodation" criteria of the ADA.
- *Employee benefit* — the physical therapist is available to the employer and to co-workers as an additional source of information, such as job modifications, job coaching, and safe work practices education. The TWP can be added to the list of "benefits" that the employer offers the worker.
- *Worksite "clinic"* — the physical therapist utilizes the worksite to implement the TWP. In this way, the work environment is effective in identifying the strengths and weaknesses of the RTW process and there is no guesswork regarding the job demands and the work performance ratings.
- *New team members* — the physical therapist interacts with management, team leaders, safety personnel, and co-workers at the worksite. This opens direct channels of communication with team members that have ownership in TWP issues that are specific to the worksite.

ADDITIONAL CONSIDERATIONS

There are other factors of importance to the physical therapist when implementing the TWP. The management of these factors determines their contribution to the working balance between the employer and the worker.

- *Travel* — this can impact the physical therapist greatly as in most cases more than one employer is visited per day. Travel time need not be "down time" as dictations or phone communications can be accomplished. A lease/purchase of a company car may make business sense.
- *Scheduling* — the physical therapist's work schedule needs to be flexible. When scheduling two workers at the same employer, it is important that

work schedules do not conflict so that the workers are available to the therapist. Work shifts can pose problems if worker A works days and worker B works nights. An office coordinator can monitor the scheduling from the home office when the physical therapist is at the worksite.

- *The "Office" Car* — worksite-based programming makes it necessary for the physical therapist to use a car as a mobile office. All necessary work clothes, exercise equipment, worksite analysis equipment, reference books, program paperwork, and health charts must be available at all times. Anticipation of daily/weekly clinical and consultant needs will alleviate the guesswork of what to bring.
- *The "Hail Mary" Therapist* — in many cases, employers are unable to implement a disability management program. They may look at TWP as a means to address their work injuries as a stand-alone entity. Such employers may look to the physical therapist to provide the answers. Through education and a thorough implementation of the TWP, ownership is established with the appropriate team members. Realistic goals and action plans are defined for remediation. Objective case closure is often desired by the employer through the TWP.
- *Customized Programs* — each employer and worker with an injury has unique goals. A TWP recognizes these individual goals and incorporates them into the RTW process.
- *Existing Networks* — the employer and/or the worker with an injury often have relationships with established health care systems that they wish to maintain. The physical therapist must make every effort to include these entities in the TWP. This includes physicians, hospitals, physical therapy clinics and local exercise facilities.
- *"Foreign" Environment* — the uniqueness of the TWP is the worksite. The physical therapist is given a fair amount of independence within this environment. Interactions within the work environment can significantly impact the ultimate success or failure of the TWP. The physical therapist must be as comfortable in an industrial worksite as in a PT clinic.

FUTURE CONSIDERATIONS

The TWP is an integral component of an optimal disability management system. For the physical therapist, it is an entry-level mechanism for the coordination of other disability management services that can be provided to the employer. Post-offer and/or pre-placement testing can be performed. There are existing protocols to do these tests. However, testing protocols that are employer-specific can be utilized. Job coaching for new hires or for workers who have returned to work from short-term disability, vacations, or are transferring jobs can be performed. Many of the concepts of the TWP can be used in job coaching, such as gradual RTW, identification of the functional worker-to-job match, and education in safe work practices. Physical therapists can also provide consulting services to the parent and/or sister companies. Successful networking improves the delivery of services.

On a more sophisticated scale, the physical therapist can be an integral part in the development of an occupational health management program that is employer-based by establishing a physical therapy clinic at the employer's facility. Through the managed care team, comprised of the occupational health nurse, the physician, and the physical therapist, immediate evaluation, treatment and follow-through to the worksite after a work injury can be provided. Occupational health care management programs can also be established within an industrial complex that houses multiple medium- to small-size companies that are in close proximity to one another. In this way, the managed care concept can be offered more cost-effectively to a number of employers through the pooling of their resources.

The TWP needs to establish validity, reliability, and predictiveness through research. The formulation of standard protocols and terminology will make it easier for comparative studies.

SUMMARY

Transitional work is *not* light duty. It is alternative, productive work that is performed for pay. It accommodates workers with injuries by allowing them to gradually return to work within their safe work capacities. Objective data is utilized to provide information regarding clinical and injury status, job options and demands, safe work capacities, and RTW goals and barriers. The worksite physical therapist facilitates the TWP by establishing ownership of the RTW goals and by implementing decisions based on the analysis of the objective data.

The success of the TWP depends on the flexibility and the acceptance of ownership by all team members. Transitional work programs provide an early return-to-work strategy through interdisciplinary intervention and TWPs are an integral part of an optimal employer-based disability management system.

Acknowledgements

For help with chapter review. Beal D. Lowe, Ph.D. and Wallace Linville, P.T.

CASE HISTORY

HISTORY AND RECORDS REVIEW

M.S. is a 45-year-old, right-hand-dominant female who was seen at her place of employment. Her job classification is Packer at a mushroom farm. She has been an employee of the farm for 11 years. She began noticing pain and numbness in her right and left wrists and hands approximately three years ago. These symptoms gradually worsened and resulted in carpal tunnel releases (bilateral) within the past 18 months. Within this same time, she also developed left elbow pain which resulted in surgery for ulnar nerve transplant. Diagnostic testing consisted of EMGs which were positive for carpal tunnel syndrome, bilateral. She attended a modality-oriented acute physical therapy program intermittently over a five-month period within the past year. Previous to the carpal tunnel syndrome releases, she also had a right trigger finger release.

She has had lost time in the past due to work injuries, but has had no significant time off from work within the past year. Currently, she is on an eight-hour work day restriction per her physician of record. This is significant because, due to the nature of mushroom farming, workdays can range from six to 10+ hours per day. M.S. was placed in the TWP by request of her employer so that an accurate identification of her functional work capacities could be obtained in lieu of her current restrictions.

PHYSICAL THERAPY EVALUATION

This was performed on-site in an area that the company had designated for the TWP test room.

> **Subjective Report.** M.S. complained of pain, tingling, and loss of strength in the left shoulder, elbow, and thumb. She also complained of right elbow pain. She stated that, by the end of the workday, she was "completely exhausted." She stated that she had particular difficulty with reach/handle work tasks above shoulder level, that required gripping two 5# lugs and with pulling boxes apart.
> **Manual Muscle Testing/Neurological.** She exhibited grade three strength for the left upper extremity. She exhibited specific weakness in the left shoulder girdle musculature and in the upper trunk postural muscle groups. Neurological testing for upper extremity motor reflexes and sensory deficits was unremarkable.
> **Range of Motion/Flexibility.** She exhibited bilateral normal shoulder motion in all planes except for internal rotation which exhibited a 50% defi-

cit bilaterally. Elbow, wrist, and finger motions were all within normal range, bilaterally. There was a significant decrease in the scapulo-thoracic rhythm, bilaterally.

Musculo skeletal Examination. Left shoulder-capsular tests and an orthopedic screening were negative.

Left elbow — The ulnar collateral stress test was positive. There was tenderness to palpation on the olecranon process, medially and posteriorly. There was a medial scar from her previous surgery.

Left wrist — There was a z-plasty scar from her previous surgery. There was tenderness to palpation at the base of the wrist. Carpal tunnel screen was moderately positive.

Right wrist — There was a z-plasty from her previous surgery. Carpal tunnel screen was negative.

Left thumb — There was rigidity in the distal phalanx.

Gait/Posture. She exhibited a forward head with protracted shoulders. She exhibited an increased carrying angle on the left. Gait cycle was normal.

FUNCTIONAL WORK CAPACITIES ASSESSMENT

The FWCA was performed using a combination of static and dynamic tests. The static tests were performed with a push/pull dynamometer and a hand-held Jamar dynamometer using standard protocols. The dynamic tests were performed with mushroom farm work materials using an acceptable maximal effort kinesiophysical protocol. M.S. exhibited light strength for carry, stoop/bend and push/pull work tasks. She exhibited sedentary strength for reach/handle work tasks. Fatigue symptoms were observed with increased repetitions of all tested work tasks as defined by the breakdown of safe body mechanics. There was obvious protection of the left upper extremity. Grip strength testing indicated strength in the 15th percentile for the left hand and 30th percentile for the right hand when compared to age and gender standards.

WORKSITE ANALYSIS

Her job classification is Packer. She works a rotating five-day work schedule. There is a requirement to work shifts that are longer than eight hours on any given day. Some of the work is self-paced, some is on a quota system. There are 10 to 12 different jobs that a packer must be able to perform. Work materials utilized includes lugs, pallet jacks, step ladders, packing boxes (assorted sizes), pallets and scales. She is exposed to temperatures ranging from 38 to 70. The work is performed 100% inside. There is exposure to moving objects, slippery surfaces, and dampness. The work is performed in confined spaces. Near and far vision is necessary.

The strength level of Packer is light plus with a weight range of 10-35 pounds. Work tasks are performed from floor level to above shoulder level. Work methods include: standing in place (constantly), grasping/finger manipulation (constantly), walking (frequently), stooping/bending (frequently), trunk turning/ twisting (frequently), climbing (occasionally), reaching up/out (constantly), wrist/forearm turning (constantly), hand controls (occasionally), and neck bending/turning (constantly). Physiological demands are 2.2 to 3.5 METS. Psychological demands are working as part of a team and working under stress. Critical job demands are: repetitive upper extremity motions, reaching up/out, static positioning of trunk, and repetitive lumbo-pelvic motions.

NONPHYSICAL FACTORS ASSESSMENT

This was performed through the use of the RTW Forcefield Analysis questionnaire to determine other factors affecting the RTW process. It was identified that M.S. had only three years to retirement and she needed to work to help pay off farm debts before retiring. She had concerns regarding her ability to work over eight hours per day on a weekly basis. She also had concerns regarding how her employer would treat her if she had continued working with restrictions.

WORKER PROFILE

This was outlined in chart format for the packing supervisor (see Table 3). M.S.'s safe work capacities were compared to the required work capacities of each job in packing. Each job was ranked according to the number of hours for safe competitive performance. A job rotation schedule was established in conjunction with the packing supervisor. Her workday was capped at eight hours. The profile was updated on a weekly basis and finalized at the time of discharge.

GOAL SETTING

Program goals were identified at a team meeting that included the worker, physical therapist, occupational nurse, packing supervisor, employer manager, and rehabilitation consultant. The employer's goal was to identify current safe work capacities. M.S.'s goals were to improve her overall strength and endurance, learn more effective pain management techniques, and to identify the packing jobs that were within her safe work capacities. The physical therapist's goals were to establish the safe work capacities of M.S., implement her worker profile, and remediate her pain complaints through an exercise program and the use of a dynamic left forearm strap.

Table 3
Worker Profile

Worker: M.S.
Effective Date: 1 June 1993
Company: Mushroom Farm
Restrictions: 8-hour workday
Lifting — 5# constantly, 10# frequently, 20# occasionally

Slicer		10# Line				High-speed Line				24-oz. Line
			3#	5#	10#	8 oz.	12 oz.	14 oz.	1#	
Dumper	0	Putting On	2	2	0	2	1	1	0	
Shaker	2	Weighing	2	2	2	2	2	2	2	
Catcher	3	Case Up	2	2	0	2	1	0	0	
Runner	1									

Basket Washer		Stacking Soup		Box Making, Manual	
Front	2	Stack	0	3#	2
Back	0	Dump	0	5#	2
		Weighing	0	10#	2
				24 oz.	1
				Slice	1

Box Making, Machine		Clean up	
8 oz.	3	All stations	1
12 oz.	3		
1#	3		

Job Rating
0 = unable to do
1 = up to 1 hour
2 = up to 2 hours
3 = 2+ hours

Job Modifications
Forearm
Ladder
Pallet jack
Rotate jobs every 2 hours

Critical Work Methods
Reaching/lifting up/out
High reps/forces with forearms/hands
Static positioning of trunk
Stooping/bending

PROGRAM DEVELOPMENT

Strengths for the TWP were:

1. Cooperative employer,
2. Long-term employee,
3. Currently working although with restrictions, and
4. M.S.'s motivation to improve work capacities.

Barriers for the TWP were:

1. Multiple injuries with multiple surgeries,
2. Low physical reserve of M.S., and
3. Expectation of employer for M.S. to attain previous functional work capacities.

An action plan for addressing each team member's goals included:

1. Education directed at the packing supervisor, M.S., and co-workers for safe work practices in relationship to the upper extremities;
2. Utilize dynamic forearm strap;
3. Initiate adaptive strengthening program, emphasizing upper extremities and postural muscle groups at the YMCA;
4. Aerobic walking program;
5. Identify safe work capacities;
6. Continue to work an eight-hour day, and
7. Establish worker profile.

INDEPENDENT EXERCISE PROGRAM

Through the help of the employer, a working relationship with the local YMCA was established. The employer allowed up to one hour per day on company time to participate in a supervised adaptive strengthening program. This was performed three times per week. In addition M.S. was given specific upper extremity exercises to do at home (e.g., hand grips, pendulum exercises).

PROGRAM UPDATES

Bi-weekly staffings involving the occupational nurse, packing supervisor, M.S., and the physical therapist were held. Progress reports to the physician of record and the rehabilitation consultant were written every three to four weeks. The worker profile was implemented in week three after all packer positions were analyzed and ranked for compatibility with M.S.'s safe work capacities. A left forearm strap was obtained in week four for pain management. Individual and group education regarding upper extremity and trunk safe work capacities was initiated in week two and was continued throughout the program. By the sixth week there was significant reduction in the pain complaints regarding the left elbow and M.S. stated that she was not as fatigued at the end of her work day. There were two episodes of increased pain complaints in the left elbow/wrist as well as new pain complaints in the right elbow. These were remediated by M.S. through medications, ice, use of dynamic forearm strap, and alteration of her Worker Profile.

DISCHARGE SUMMARY

M.S. was discharged after 11 weeks in the TWP. Goals achieved were:

1. Effective pain management techniques for the left and right elbow — ice, dynamic forearm strap;
2. Increased grip strength, left greater than right;
3. Increased endurance and strength — improved tolerance to repetition of work tasks;
4. Incorporation of safe work practices at the worksite;
5. Identification of long term, safe work capacities, and;
6. Implementation of Worker Profile.

M.S. was not able to significantly improve her safe work capacities so that she could perform all of the packer positions. Her employer was willing to accept an eight-hour work day cap, to adhere to the discharge Worker Profile and to allow M.S. to continue with the YMCA program, two to three times per week for an additional three to six months.

PROGRAM EVALUATION

Questionnaires were sent to the physician of record, the employer, M.S., and the rehabilitation consultant regarding the TWP. Pre- and post-test scores in grip strength, subjective pain reports, and lifting capabilities in the FWCA were compared. Pre- and post-data for sets, weights, and repetitions in the adaptive strengthening program, and walking times and exercise heart rates in the aerobic program were also compared. A six-month and one-year status-post discharge follow-up call to the occupational nurse confirmed that M.S. was still competitively employed per her Worker Profile and that she was continuing with her YMCA program.

REFERENCES

Bigos, S. J., Battie, M. C., Spengler, L. D., Fisher, L. D., Fordyce, W. E., Hansson, T., Nachemson, A. L., & Zeh, j. (1992). A longitudinal prospective study of industrial back injury reporting. *Clinical Orthopedics and Related Research, 279*, 21-34.

Committee on accreditation of rehabilitation facilities manual. Tucson, Arizona. 1990.

DeRosa, C. P., & Porterfield, J. A. (1992). A physical therapy model for the treatment of low back pain. *Physical Therapist, 72,* 261-272.

Deyo, R. A. (1993). Practice variations, treatment fads, rising disability. *Spine, 18*, 2153-2162.

ERGOS reference manual. (1991). Work Recovery, Inc. Tucson, Arizona.

Hans, M. (1993). OSHA recordkeeping : Is it time for a change? *Safety & Health,* Nov: 50-54.

Hayes, B. H., Solyom, C. A., Wing, P. C., & Berkowitz, J. (1993). Use of psychometric measures and monorganic signs testing in detecting nomogenic disorders in low back pain patients. *Spine, 18,* 1254-1262.

Herrin, G. D., Chaffin, D. B., Andersson, G. B. J., & Pope, M. H. (1984). Workplace evaluation. In M. H. Pope, J. M. Frymoyer, & G. Andersson (Eds.), *Occupational low back pain.* New York: Praeger.

Hochanadel, C. D., & Conrad, D. E. (1993). Evolution of an on-site industrial physical therapy program. *Journal of Occupational Medicine, 35,* 1011-1016.

Hopf, P. S. (1975). *Designer's guide to OSHA.* New York, NY : McGraw-Hill

Isernhagen, S. J. (1989). *Functional capacity evaluation.* Isernhagen Work Systems, Duluth MN.

Isernhagen, S. J. (1992). The evaluation standard for the 90s. *Industrial Rehabilitation Quarterly,* Summer, 58-59.

Kreider, J. R. (1993). The need for redefining chronic pain programs for the injured worker population. *Journal of Back and Musculoskeletal Rehabilitation, 3,* 83-87.

Lowe, B. D., & Daly, J. H. (1993). *RTW forcefield analysis.* Unpublished.

Mayer, T. G., & Gatchel, R. J. (1988). *Functional restoration for spinal disorders: The sports medicine approach.* Philadelphia, PA: Lea and Febiger.

Mayer, T. G., & Gatchel, R. J. (1988). An overview of functional restoration treatment : The basic issues and the therapeutic team approach. In T. G. Mayer, & R. J. Gatchel (Eds.), *Functional restoration for spinal disorders: The sports medicine approach.* Philadelphia, PA: Lea and Febiger.

Gatchel, R. J. (1991). Psychosocial assessment and disability management in the rehabilitation of painful spinal disorders. In T. G. Mayer, V. Mooney, & R. J. Gatchel (Eds.), *Contemporary conservative care for painful spinal disorders.* Philadelphia, PA: Lea and Febiger.

MTM Association for Standards and Research, 1988.

Putz-Anderson, V. (Ed.). (1988). *Cumulative trauma disorders: A manual for Musculoskeletal diseases of the upper limbs.* (Monograph) from NIOSH/DHHS/CDC/DBBS in Cincinnati. New York: Taylor and Francis.

Shrey, D. E., & Breslin, R. E. (1992) Employer-based disability management strategies and work return transition programs. In N. Hablutzel, & B. McMahon (Eds.), *The Americans with Disabilities Act: Access and accommodations* (pp. 139-154). Winter Park, FL: GR Press, Inc.

Shrey, D. E., & Olsheski, J. A. (1992). Disability management and industry-based work return transition programs. *Physical Medicine and Rehabilitation, State of the Art Reviews, 6,* 303-314.

Shrey, D. E. (1991). Get injured workers back on the job with on-site help. In *Building a healthy work force.* Supplement to the Greater Cincinnati Business Record. July 1-7, 5B.

Spitzer, W. O. (1987). Quebec task force on spinal disorders : Scientific approach to the assessment and management of activity-related spinal disorders. *Spine, 12, S1-S58.*

Stultz, M. R. (1994). Interdisciplinary factors in the management of cumulative trauma related disability. In Donald Shrey (Ed.), *Principles and practices of disability management in industry.* Winter Park, FL: G. R. Press, Inc.

U.S. Dept. of Justice. (1990). *Information bulletin.* Americans with Disabilities Act. Washington DC: Civil Rights Division, Coordinator and Review Section.

U.S. Dept. of Health and Human Services. (1981). *Work practices guide for manual lifting.* (NIOSH Technical Report 81-122.) Cincinnati, OH: National Institute for Occupational Safety and Health.

U.S. Dept. of Labor. (1982). *A guide to job analysis.* Washington, DC.

U.S. Dept. of Labor. (Rev. 1991). *Dictionary of occupational titles* (4th ed.). Washington, DC.

U.S. Dept. of Labor. (1979). *Guide for occupational exploration.* Washington, DC.

Walters, T. R., Putz-Anderson, V., Garg, A., & Fine, L. J. (1993) Revised NIOSH equation for the design and evaluation of manual lifting tasks. *Ergonomics, 36,* 749-776.

Occupational Health Nurses In Disability Management

Karen J. Martin, Ph.D., C.O.H.N.

INTRODUCTION

Managing employees with disabilities in the workplace is not a new concept. Nor is it new that much of this disability management is being done by more than 23,000 occupational health nurses. What is new is the expanded definition of disability and improved accommodations of persons with disabilities. Disabled persons are no longer defined in terms of injuries, illnesses, or limitations. Rather they are viewed as whole individuals with special physical, psychological, and social needs (Kaminshine, 1991). Consequently, managing disability requires a team approach.

Occupational health nurses (OHNs), as members of the safety and health team, are in a unique position to coordinate disability management because they function as the vital link between the worker with a disability, the employer, the health care community, and claims representatives. OHNs have valuable information about workers, their families, and their jobs; they are members of the management team; they serve as liaisons with health providers; and they facilitate the disability management process with insurance and third-party representatives. Because of this unique position, OHNs have the opportunity and responsibility to assist workers with disabilities to reach maximum productivity, both short- and long-term.

This chapter discusses the perspective of occupational health nursing in disability management, presents a nursing model for performing disability management, illustrates the application of disability management at four specific worksites, and discusses the challenges of the work return process among employees with disabilities.

PERSPECTIVE OF OCCUPATIONAL HEALTH NURSES IN DISABILITY MANAGEMENT

HISTORICAL PERSPECTIVE

Occupational health nurses have been assisting workers with disabilities since the industrial revolution. The first industrial nurse, Ada Mayo Stewart, was hired by the Vermont Marble Company in 1895 to make home visits to workers with disabilities to promote early return to work (Rogers, 1988). In 1909, Metropolitan Life Insurance offered home nursing to industrial policy holders, which proved very successful in returning workers to work and reducing long-term disability payments (Parker-Conrad, 1988). A sharp increase in the number of OHNs occurred when companies were compelled by workers' compensation legislation in 1911 to take responsibility for workplace safety and health; by 1914, 60 companies employed nurses (Parker-Conrad, 1988). Through the 1900s increases in OHNs have been associated with growth in industry, with surges during war years and times of economic prosperity. OHNs represent the largest health professional group involved in the health and safety of workers. As previously mentioned, there are presently about 23,000 occupational health nurses; and, although the degree of involvement varies by company, all of them participate in monitoring the progress of absent workers.

CONTEMPORARY PERSPECTIVE

Many factors enable OHNs to be effective in the management of workers with disabilities. They are employee advocates who have knowledge and expertise in workplace conditions, medical treatment, and claims processing. As of 1996, a four-year college degree in nursing will become the basic preparation for certification in OHN (American Board for Occupational Health Nurses, 1992). The education process for OHNs includes interactions with multidisciplinary teams, including industrial hygienists, safety engineers, occupational physicians, biostatisticians, and toxicologists, and the OHN curriculum has courses specific to disability management. Five years of experience is also required for certification; there are presently more than 5,000 certified OHNs.

In addition to academic preparation and experience, OHNs are the most visible and approachable health professionals in the workplace and, by nature of their work, OHNs spend the most time with employees. Employees become acquainted with the nurse during preplacement examinations, periodic physicals, and episodes of minor illness and injury. Employees recognize and regard nurses as advocates for their health and safety; therefore, they confide information about their personal lives and health problems (Burgel, 1991). The nurse learns about the worker's home life, life style, and major life events. The nurse knows the employee's stressors, both inside and outside of the workplace, and knows the resources the family has to draw upon. In other words, in many situations, OHNs are the only health professionals with prior knowledge of workers' personal stressors, which is a clear advantage when resolving the complex issues associated with workplace disability.

OHNs also are knowledgeable about the worksite and job processes. Nurses conduct frequent plant walk-throughs, evaluating job stations and processes, identifying potential for injuries and need for job modifications. Knowledge of the workplace is essential in designing alternate-duty programs and preparing job accommodations for early return to work.

Another reason for the effectiveness of OHNs in disability management is the influence within the company, especially regarding prevention of disability. As a member of the management team, OHNs work closely with safety and other personnel to influence management decisions about safety and health (Benner, Schilling, & Klein, 1987). Because of close association with the workers, nurses are able to present workers' perspectives when discussing issues of safety education, health promotion programs, and return to work.

Early return to work requires great skill in organizing, directing, and controlling a large cast of characters (Randolph & Dalton, 1989). OHNs serve as liaisons between employees and the health provider community in several ways. One way is to assist employees with decisions about treatment choices while working with providers on the treatment and rehabilitation plans. Another way is by interpreting diagnostic and treatment procedures to employees while explaining company policies and alternate-duty jobs to providers. The nurse speaks the language of medical and health professionals and has easy access to the complex health care system.

The complexity of the health care system is, in part, due to insurance procedures and protocols of third-party administrators. OHNs direct the processing of paperwork to assure uninterrupted medical care and wage payments. The nurse, who remains in close contact with the off-work employee, is in a position to identify the appropriate time for changes in treatment plans and make recommendations to the third-party administrator. Timely referral is also an important factor in return to work.

Figure 1 summarizes the unique position of OHNs in disability management. OHNs are effective in managing workers with disabilities because they are employee advocates who have knowledge and expertise in workplace conditions, connections with the medical community, and communication with the claims industry.

1. **Knowledgeable About Worker And Family**

    - Preplacement exams and periodic physicals
    - Health education/screening programs
    - Episodic care of minor illnesses/injuries
    - Familiarity with job assignments/job tasks
    - Understanding personal and job stressors
    - Information about personal and family resources

2. **Informed About Worksite And Job Processes**

    - Conduct plant walk-throughs
    - Familiarity with job assignments/job tasks
    - Evaluation of ergonomic conditions
    - Understanding of job modification

3. **Management Team Member Representing Workers**

    - Accident and illness prevention programs
    - Health promotion programs
    - Health and safety education
    - Ability to recommend job modifications

4. **Liaison Between Health Care Community/Employee**

    - Assist employee with treatment choices
    - Collaboration on treatment/rehabilitation plans
    - Interpret procedures to employees
    - Access to health care professionals
    - Explain job policies/alternate duty to providers

5. **Facilitator for insurance processing**

    - Uninterrupted medical/wage benefits
    - Documentation of progress
    - Recommend changes as progress indicates

Figure 1. Unique Position of Occupational Health Nurses in Disability Management

MANAGING DISABILITY

The concept of disability management is one of professional facilitation and individual empowerment within a work situation to ensure worker employability while limiting financial losses of the employer. The OHN assists the employee with decisions to promote rehabilitation and work return processes. There are four premises within the concept of disability management; these four Ps are: prevention, planning, process, and productivity. Disability management begins with prevention, emphasizes planning, prescribes a process, and leads to productivity (see Figure 2).

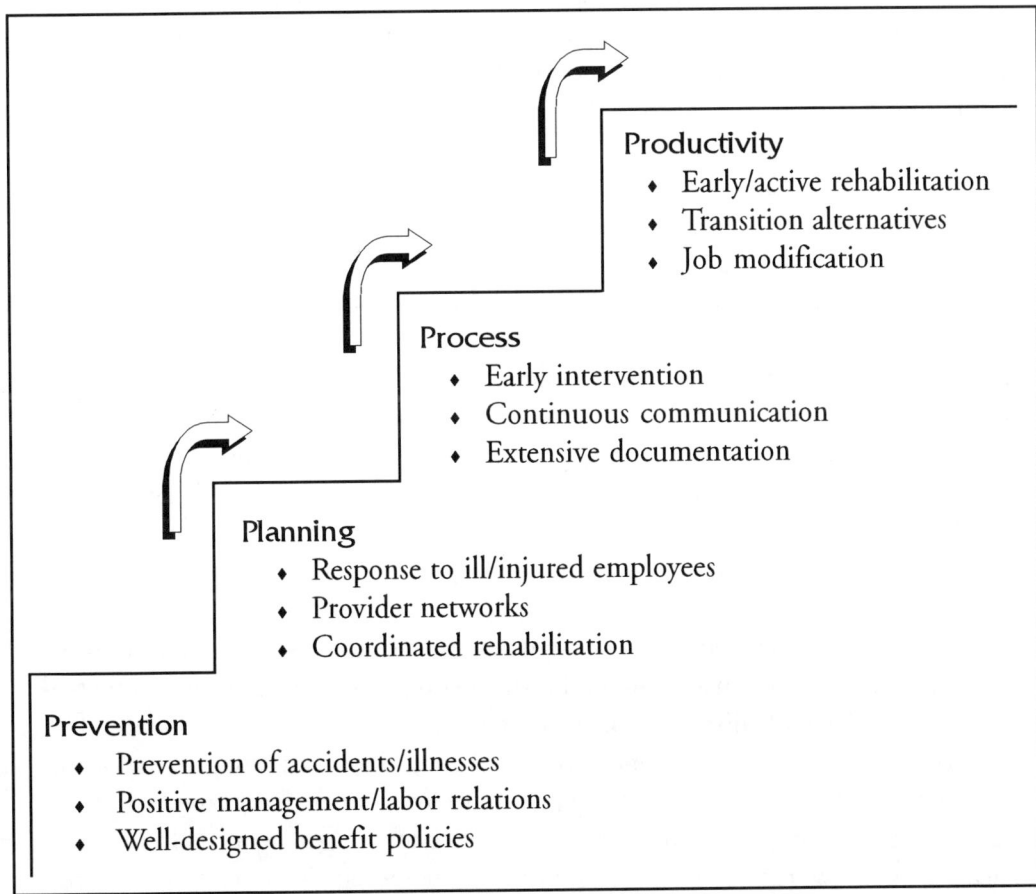

Figure 2. Martin's Model of Occupational Health Nursing Disability Management

As facilitator, the OHN can empower the worker to gain control of the work environment and life styles to prevent disabling illnesses or injuries (Burgel, 1991). In the event of an illness or injury episode, the OHN can coordinate worker progression from injury (illness) through rehabilitation to productivity.

PREVENTION

Disability management begins with creating a safe and healthy environment. Three components are essential in preventing disability: prevention of accidents and illnesses, positive management/labor relations, and design of benefits policies. The OHN plays a key role in all three of these areas. Safety and wellness form the foundation for avoiding disabilities, and the nurse shares responsibility for safety education and directs the health promotion efforts of the company (Pilon & Renfroe, 1990; Tate, Habeck, & Schwartz, 1986). For example, the nurse may conduct a back education program focused on proper lifting and may conduct a cholesterol screening to detect early cardiovascular warnings. In these ways, nursing interventions help prevent back injuries and heart disease emergencies.

The second way to prevent disability is to establish good management/labor relations; thereby creating an environment of joint labor/management collaboration, emphasizing the importance of every job and every employee (Bruyere & Shrey, 1991). It is well known that employees who enjoy their work come back to work earlier following an injury. Company nurses are in a unique position to foster positive employee relations by bringing workers' views to the management conference table. The OHN, as both an advocate for the employee and a colleague of the supervisor, inspires confidence that nursing recommendations will assure the best rehabilitation for the employee, while striving to maintain productivity for the employer.

A third prevention strategy is to design benefit packages that encourage prevention and discourage absence from work. Many companies are beginning to reward healthy lifestyles with discounts on insurance premiums and to recognize safety practices with bonuses or dividends (Galvin, 1986). Short- and long-term disability policies can be modified to discourage absence from work. For example, in most states, workers' compensation is not paid until one week of work is lost, which encourages the worker to miss a minimum of two weeks in order to collect full payment. But a company could pay wages for the first week of an injury; then, perhaps, the employee would be back in 7 or 8 days instead of staying off 15 in order to collect the first and second weeks of wages. The company could also pay the difference in wages if the employee is able to remain employed but in a lower-wage job. OHNs can be an employer resource for decision-making regarding benefits because they have knowledge of the rules and regulations of workers' compensation and disability insurance.

PLANNING

Disability management planning is a necessary step to assure early work return. OHNs frequently have responsibility for three major aspects in disability planning: responding to ill and injured employees, establishing provider networks, and coordinating rehabilitation. As members of health and safety teams, nurses are directly involved in designing the system to respond to ill and injured workers. This system includes medical treatment as well as accident investigation. Most company nurses have responsibility for first aid training and the first aid log, and may be the designated person to conduct the accident investigation.

A second step in planning anticipates serious injuries or illnesses which may require the care of medical specialists. Planning for this possibility results in a referral network, including the nearest hospital emergency department. The nurse contacts quality providers and invites them to tour the plant to observe production processes and safety measures. The OHN educates providers about company job descriptions and return-to-work policies. A close working relationship promotes communication when medical services are needed.

Making arrangements for early rehabilitation is a third planning step in disability management. OHNs can work with third-party administrators to develop procedures for the employee's transition back to work as soon as medically feasible (Burgel, 1991). If off-site rehabilitation programs are to be used, these facilities are reviewed by the OHN for appropriateness and quality of care.

When planning for return to work, timing is the most critical element for success. The nurse first considers the time that elapses from the injury or illness until initial response or first intervention. Second, attention is focused on the time it takes to get the employee to the appropriate specialist for proper diagnosis and treatment. Then the nurse prepares the groundwork for early rehabilitation. Proper disability management planning will shorten the time between injury/illness and return to work. OHNs expedite the process because nurses are involved from the point of injury/illness through complete rehabilitation to return to work.

PROCESS

The process of disability management is demanding and time-consuming because it requires early intervention, continuous communication, and extensive documentation (Burgel, 1991; Conti, 1989; Yeater, 1987). Early intervention means attention to the employee as soon as the injury or illness occurs. In large companies, the notification process may require the employee to notify the supervisor and the supervisor to report the incident to the nurse within 24 hours. The nurse then contacts the employee to obtain the health status and begin the process of guiding the employee through the complexities of the disability system. Referrals are made and claims forms are initiated. Early intervention is important to assure the best possible medical care and to prevent the employee from being off work without an income (Hayes & Carroll, 1986; Peters, 1990).

From the day of the incident the OHN maintains close contact with the employee, the supervisor, the treating physician, other health professionals, the third-party administrator, and the insurance carrier. There are certain "red-flags" which alert the nurse to a complicated case. Some of these are: unusual number of visits to the physician, unusual number of prescriptions for pain medication, unusual number or type of referrals, proposed surgery without diagnostic work-up, and cases extending beyond the expected resolution date (Zal, 1985). The nurse who is alert to anxious, frustrated, or angry communications from the employee or spouse is often able to resolve the difficulty and maintain positive progress.

The Cox nursing model of interaction describing client health behavior (Cox, 1982) is particularly useful when the OHN is dealing with delayed progress. There are four components that define interaction, which vary according to the needs and individuality of the client. The first aspect of interaction is the provision of health information, which is necessary to influence behavior change. The second mode of interaction is supportive, which addresses the client's need for affective or emotional support. The third factor of the client-nurse relationship is structuring the balance of decisional control, attempting to increase the client's sense of self-efficacy and enhancing behavior that is self-determined. The final role of the nurse is the provision of technical skills as required. Cox's model depicts a relationship between client and nurse that involves continuous reciprocal interaction between aspects of client singularity, the nurse-client interaction, and the health outcome (see Figure 3), which in this discussion is return to work.

Paperwork is a significant part of the process. There are a multitude of forms and procedures for processing claims that require careful attention. Often the entire work return process is halted due to an incomplete form. OHNs coordinate the completion of the proper forms by assisting employees, physicians, and rehabilitation professionals in a timely manner. The nurse's knowledge of the paperwork requirements can assure uninterrupted medical treatment, wage compensation, and early rehabilitation.

PRODUCTIVITY

Return to productivity is, in most cases, a shared goal of the employee with a disability and the employer. It is not always possible to return to full productivity while recovering from an injury or illness, but partial capability may be sufficient to return to a modified job. The nurse and the employee evaluate many alternatives for transition back to work. Conditioning and work hardening programs provide a structured way of progressing from disability to full employability (Deacon &

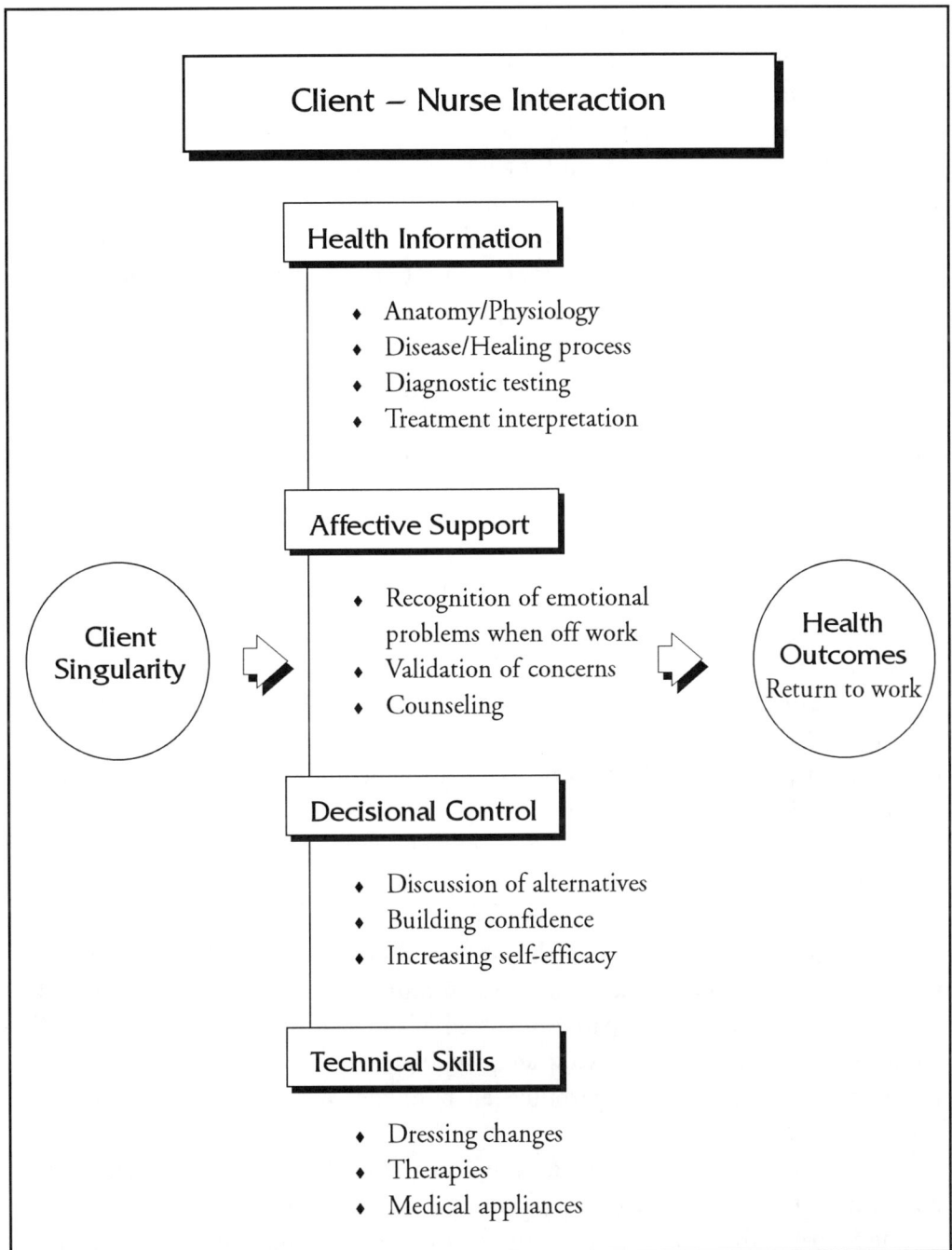

Figure 3. Using the Cox Nursing Model of Interaction in Disability Management

Congdon, 1984; Habeck, Williams, Dugan, & Ewing, 1989; Smith, 1991). Work hardening programs consist of physical strengthening exercises and workplace simulation tasks which can be performed on-site or off-site. Many employers combine on-site and off-site options into formal alternate-duty programs with the benefit of both professional supervision and actual job tasks.

Availability of transitional work or job-site accommodation is a requirement for successful early return to work, and the nurse has an essential role in developing the transition program. The nurse has both the knowledge of the job and the expertise regarding the physical conditions causing the limitations to be able to recommend appropriate job tasks and the progression to full duty.

A potential interference to a successful transition program may be reluctance on the part of the worker. Reasons for resisting return to work are complex and have been described as the disability syndrome (Burgel, 1986; Fitzler, 1983; Hanson-Mayer, 1984; Headley, 1989). It is known that the longer an employee is away from work, the less chance the worker has of ever returning. OHNs may be the first member of the rehabilitation team to observe this phenomenon of the disability syndrome because they are in such close communication with the off-work employee. The major characteristics of the syndrome are preoccupation with the injury and exaggerated subjective symptoms, usually pain, without a physiological basis (Zal, 1985). Depression and drug/alcohol abuse also are associated with delayed recovery (Burgel, 1986; Fitzler, 1983). Although there is no sure way to predict delayed recovery, there are some signs OHNs will recognize. Examples are continued use of pain medication six weeks after the injury date, physician orders which move backward to more rest, rather than forward to more exercise; unexpected orders for additional testing or surgery; and difficulties in relationships with treatment specialists (Fitzler, 1983; Hanson-Mayer, 1984). Once detected, steps can be taken to avert the negative patterns.

Prevention of the disability syndrome requires creating a work atmosphere in which both management and labor are committed to safety and health, plus a coordinated effort among all parties involved in the treatment of the injured or ill employee. Early intervention, as a strategy in disability management, assures attention to the signals of impending trouble, enabling the OHN to offer timely professional assistance.

The occupational health nursing conceptual model of disability management emphasizes four Ps: prevention, planning, process, and productivity. When operationalizing the concept, the OHN focuses on client individuality in the process of client-nurse interaction to direct nursing interventions and enable client decisions for health outcomes. The specific activities of OHNs in disability management are depicted in Figure 4. This diagram shows coordination and communication activities of the OHN with the employee, the supervisor/manager, health care providers, and claims representatives.

THE APPLICATION OF DISABILITY MANAGEMENT

In the previous section, an overview of OHNs in disability management was presented conceptually. This section illustrates the OHN role by describing four programs with national reputations for success.

GENERAL ELECTRIC

General Electric, a Fortune 500 international company, consists of 14 major businesses including aircraft engines, aerospace, appliances, plastics, utilities, medical

Employee
- Convey concern about injury/illness
- Answer questions about treatments/providers
- Facilitate employee decisions
- Intrepret progress
- Discuss target return to work

Supervisor/Manager
- Accident investigation
- Accident prevention, evaluate safety needs
- Promote wellness programs
- Explore job modifications
- Monitor restricted duty

Occupational Health Nurse

Health Care Providers
- Establish rapport, arrange plant tour
- Collaborate for treatment and rehabilitation
- Discuss target return to work
- Provide information on modified, light-duty jobs
- Facilitate referrals

Claims Representatives
- Initiate claims activity
- Assure uninterrupted medical/wage benefits
- Facilitate claims process
- Discuss rehabilitation timing and options

Figure 4. Coordination and Communication Activities of Occupational Health Nurses in Disability Management

equipment, transportation, communications, lighting, and finance. GE employs over 280,000 employees internationally.

At GE, OHNs are coordinators of an interdisciplinary health program called Convalescent Assistance to Recovering Employees (CARE). CARE is a health care management initiative to provide assistance to ill or injured employees who are absent from work or anticipate being absent from work for medical reasons. Armed with the knowledge that delayed recovery is medically and psychologically unsound, the goal of CARE is timely return to work. CARE was developed as a pilot study in 1986, and was so effective both in meeting employee needs and reducing disability costs that, in 1988, it was copyrighted by GE for companywide implementation. Today, more than 100 GE locations administer CARE.

CARE was a response to three needs: the need to provide caring support to employees facing a stressful medical period; the need to assure timely disability benefits to off-work employees; and the need to control disability absenteeism costs. Better management of lost-time illnesses and injuries was accomplished through utilization of GE's 270 OHNs who have professional expertise, knowledge and trust of employees, knowledge of job tasks, and working relationships with community health care providers. CARE coordinators are also trained in disability management and the CARE process. The CARE process is depicted in Figure 5.

The program has a strong component of cooperation between nurse, supervisor, and employee. Supervisors are trained in early identification of potential lost time and instructed to notify the nurse if a worker expects to be absent more than five days for medical reasons. The OHN immediately contacts the employee to express concern, and sends a "CARE package," which includes disability information and benefit forms. OHNs work closely with claims administrators for both personal and work-related disability cases to assure the benefit payment cycle is as short as possible. Continued communication with the employee throughout the absence maintains an important link to the workplace culture.

The anticipated return-to-work date is discussed with the physician, employee, and supervisor. Concerns about progress are directed to the physician by the OHN or the employee, who has been encouraged to ask questions. Temporary restrictions are accommodated, when possible, through job modification to facilitate early return to work. The OHN coordinates the transition, clarifying expectations, and monitors adherence to work restrictions during the transition back to full duty.

In the workplace, GE medical clinics provide follow-up nursing and medical treatments, and several GE locations have on-site physical therapy services. The OHN remains in contact with the returned employee to support continuing needs such as on-site or off-site therapies, including chemotherapy, cardiac care, and physical therapy. GE rarely uses external rehabilitation services because the CARE coordinators are fulfilling this role. Injured and ill employees continue in the CARE process until they are fully recovered.

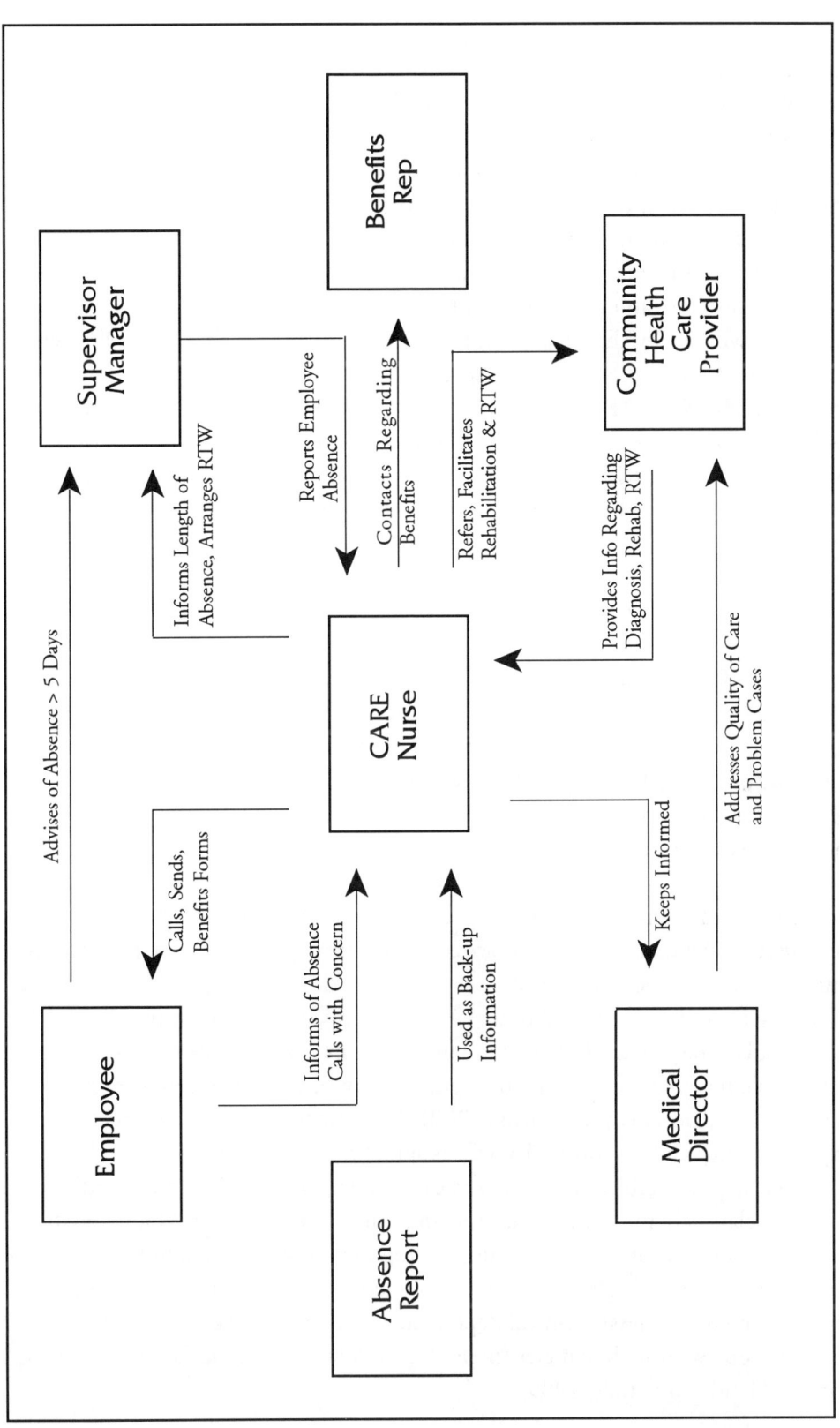

Figure 5. General Electric: Disability Management Process
Copyright © CARE Process General Electric Company

Support for the program is widespread among community health care providers, union leadership, and management. Health care providers willingly cooperate with the well-supervised transition program. They appreciate consistent management of disabled workers, whether from work or nonwork conditions. Union leadership has been supportive of the program, knowing restricted duty is short-term and that, in most cases, the employee is returned to the same job. Union leaders clearly recognize the financial and physical benefits of timely return to work. Management gains a motivated, productive employee as soon as medically feasible, and experiences reductions in costs of disability.

In plants where CARE has been implemented, early identification of absent employees has dramatically reduced the cycle time from disability to receipt of benefits. In addition, CARE sites have typically decreased costs of disability absences by 15% to 20% in the first year. Employee acceptance and appreciation of the program combined with the positive effect CARE has on productivity, absenteeism, and cost control have proven beneficial for both GE employees and GE businesses.

HONEYWELL CORPORATION

Honeywell Corporation is a national manufacturer of space and aviation systems, industrial automation and control systems, and homes and buildings. Honeywell employs 60,500 workers in 55 locations.

Occupational health nurses at Honeywell, designated as health services advisors, function as managers of high-cost health system users. Honeywell's corporate strategy for medical case management is to focus on a small number of individuals who account for a large proportion of health care spending with the dual purpose of improving treatment and containing costs. The program is a total disability management model that includes employees and their dependents. The program is voluntary for the disabled employee.

Planning for the program began in 1986 when health care costs for 3% of the insured population generated 54% of the health claims costs. Utilization data indicated multiple hospitalizations and an average of six physicians for each high-cost user (Henderson, Bergman, & Burns, 1989). Coordination of care was identified as a major priority and responsibility was assigned to occupational nurses.

The first step in establishing a focused case management program is identification of high claim charges, including information on demographic characteristics of high-cost users, diagnoses accounting for high costs, and type and site of care delivery. At Honeywell, high-cost users are divided into three groups: catastrophic, chronic, and mental illness/chemical dependency. Experience has shown high-cost cases are persons with malignancies, mental disorders, and circulatory diseases, in that order (Henderson et al., 1989).

There are four phases in the medical case management process at Honeywell: identification and referral, screening and assessment, active case management, and case closure (Widtfeldt, Rumpsa, & Bey, 1992). The four phases of case management are shown in Figure 6. Referral is most frequently made by the company hired to conduct utilization review, but can be made through the employee assistance program or by the health services advisor. Automatic referral into the program occurs if hospital length of stay is greater than five days or cost of the case reaches $10,000.

Screening by the company supplying case management services begins with an assessment of appropriateness for case management. The decision to manage the case initiates plan development, with recommendations for alternative treatment plans when appropriate. The external case manager actively monitors the case, keeping in close touch with the client, health care providers, and the health services advisor to alter the treatment program as the client progresses. The case is closed when there is no longer a need for case management.

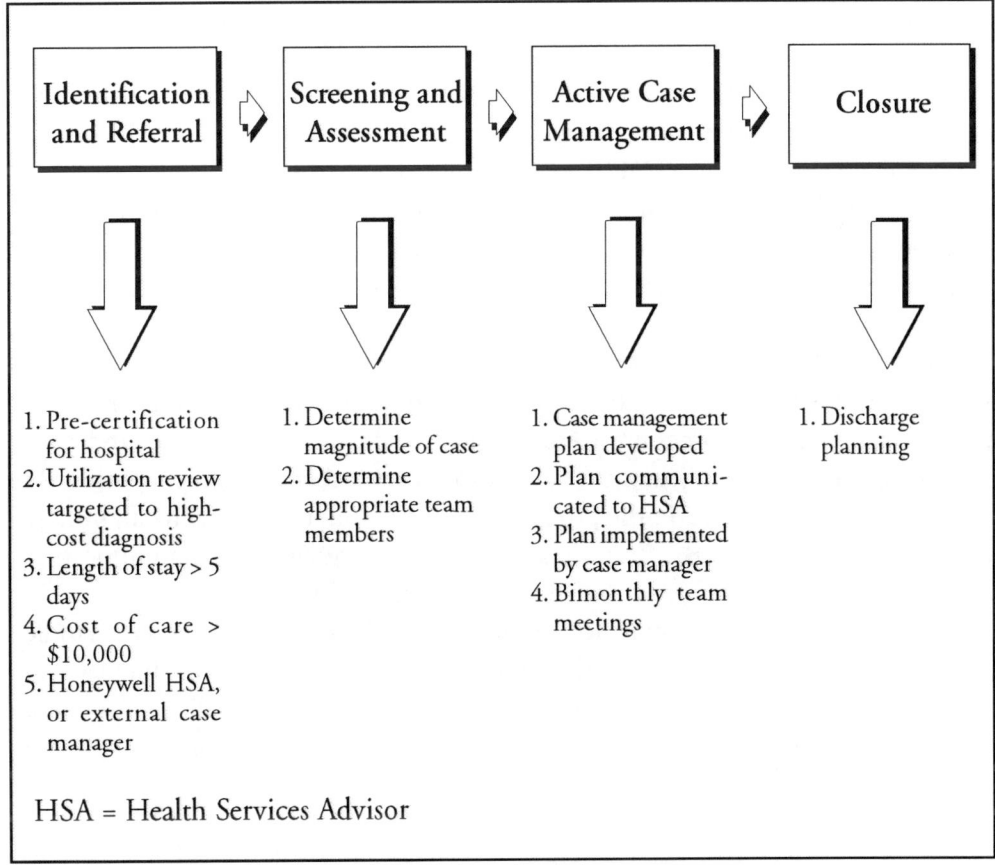

Figure 6. HONEYWELL: Case Management Process

Throughout the process, the health services advisor (OHN) acts as advocate for the client, reviewing treatment plans proposed by the case manager and assuring access to appropriate care. Since the program was implemented four years ago, client satisfaction and cost data are both positive. More than 80% of the clients expressed satisfaction with disability management and Honeywell has seen a 3:1 return on investment (Bey, Widtfeldt, & Burns, 1990).

MARRIOTT CORPORATION

Marriott Corporation owns 628 hotels, Host Travel Services, and retirement residences. Half of Marriott's businesses consist of Marriott Management Services, which includes food services to educational institutions, businesses, and hospitals. Marriott has more than 200,000 employees throughout the United States.

Marriott's occupational health nurses operate through the risk management division with emphasis on loss prevention from work-related injuries. The mission of the occupational health services department reflects Marriott's motto: "Take care of your employees and they will take care of your customers."

Marriott spent $60 million in 1990 on workers' compensation claims. Claims costs have decreased significantly where nurses have established formal case management programs. The first step was to identify losses, which was done through analysis of workers' compensation data.

There are three levels of OHN case management at Marriott (Ebert, 1992a). The three levels of actions are depicted in Figure 7. The first is primary care in which the on-site nurse at the hotel has responsibility for prevention, immediate care, referral, follow-up, return to work, and job accommodation. Ten hotels have on-site nurses.

The second level of lost-time management is called C.A.R.E., Coordinated Action Response to Employees, staffed by three nurses located in regional offices. A major function of this program is establishing local provider networks and contracts with local claims adjustors. These nurses are notified of injuries within 24 hours and immediately begin the process of coordinating treatment through these local contacts. The C.A.R.E. nurses act as employee advocates, communicating with all parties involved from acute care through rehabilitation.

The final level of management is claims review. These corporate nurses handle red-flag cases, conduct three-month medical reviews, and act as consultants and educational resources on medical issues, cost containment, and utilization review. Nurses review treatment reports, approve rehabilitation plans, arrange for special needs, negotiate prices, and audit bills.

**Level 3: Nurse Review Specialists
Casualty Claims Offices**

1. Health resource
2. Utilization review
3. Bill audits
4. Price negotiation
5. Independent medical examination panels

**Level 2: C.A.R.E. Nurse Managers
Regional Telephone Management**

1. Employee advocate
2. Provider networks
3. Communication among all parties
4. Coordination of activities

**Level 1: On-site Nurse Managers,
Primary Care**

1. Prevention, health promotion
2. Immediate care
3. Follow-up
4. Return to work
5. Job accommodation

Figure 7. MARRIOTT: Levels of Disability Management

The critical aspect of all three program components is the extensive communication between the OHN, the client, the provider network, and rehabilitation specialists. OHNs provide essential coordination to facilitate appropriate treatment and to decrease workers' compensation costs.

All three levels of nursing management have demonstrated financial success. In hotels with primary care nurses, lost-time injuries are down 30% to 40%, workers' compensation costs are down 20% to 30%, and employee morale and productivity have increased. The C.A.R.E. program has decreased litigated cases by 30% to 50%. In one year of operation, the nurse review specialists at the corporate level have saved Marriott over $600,000 (Ebert, 1992b). Marriott has plans to expand all three components of the occupational health services.

QUAKER OATS

Quaker Oats is a worldwide marketer of consumer grocery products with $5.6 billion in sales. Quaker Oats is a major producer of cereals, mixes, grain products, snacks, syrups, oils, beverages, and pet foods. Quaker Oats has plants in 16 states, as well as in Western Europe, Canada, and Latin America.

In the early 1980s, Quaker Oats took the offensive against rising health care costs, making a major commitment to health promotion, accident prevention, and managed workers' compensation cases. The message was: "Quaker Oats cares about the health and wellness of its employees."

Occupational health nurses at Quaker Oats advocate the best medical treatment and nursing care for injured employees with emphasis on early rehabilitation and return to work. There are now OHNs in 14 of Quaker Oats' 36 locations providing wellness education, safety instruction, and case management for employees with lost-time injuries.

The process of injury management begins at the time of the accident and ends when the worker is fully rehabilitated. The continuum of care is shown in Figure 8. Injury management starts with careful analysis of the circumstances of the accident and recommendations for prevention in the future. Injury treatment is provided on-site by the nurse and, if necessary, the employee is referred to a community physician. Establishing rapport with the treating physician is viewed as the key to the success of Quaker Oats' return-to-work program. In many locations physician networks have been established, assuring physician knowledge of job requirements and familiarity with company policies. Physicians are invited to tour the plant and are informed about workers' compensation, Occupational Safety and Health (OSHA), and Food and Drug (FDA) regulations are integrated with disability management procedures, as they apply to Quaker Oats. The physician, the employee, the supervisor, and the nurse work together to initiate early rehabilitation through work hardening and alternate-duty jobs.

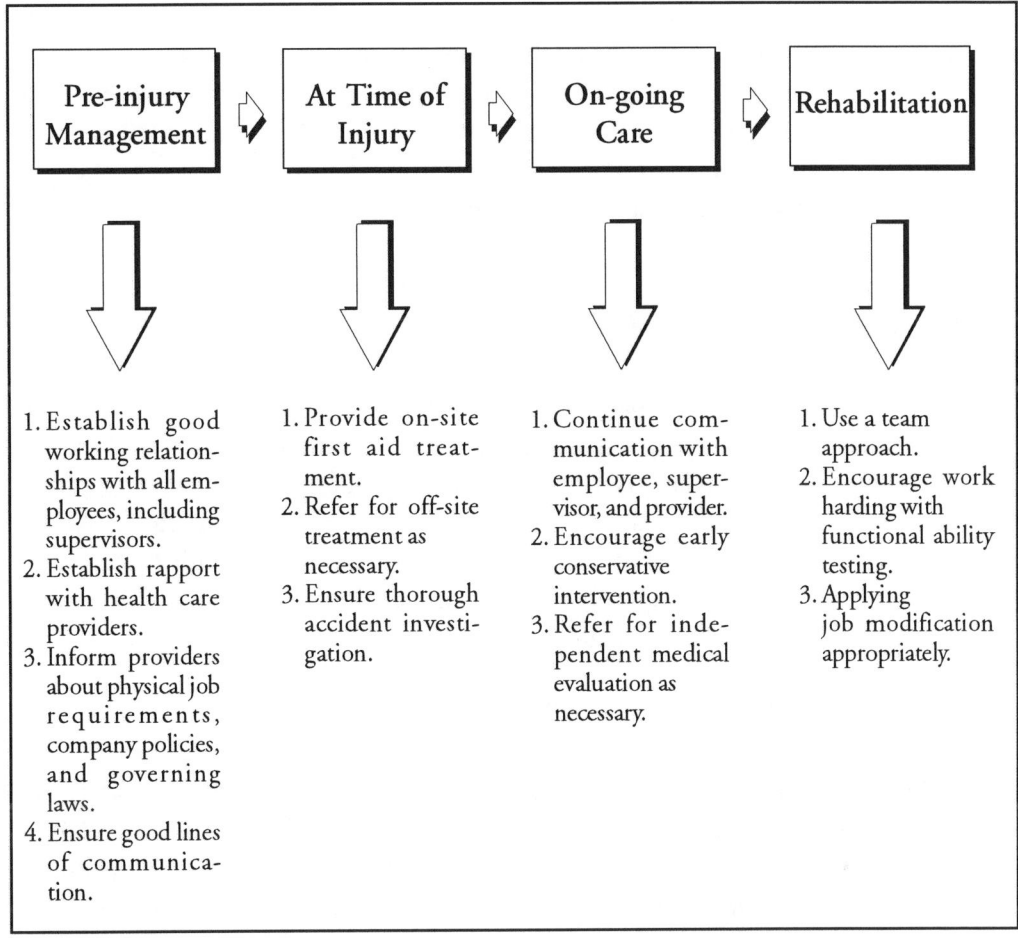

Figure 8. QUAKER OATS: Workers' Compensation Management Process

Several Quaker Oats plants have on-site work hardening programs under the direction of physical therapists. Job modifications and light-duty jobs are available in every plant, consistent with union contracts, to accommodate early return to work. Nurses work with supervisors to assist with adherence to medical restrictions during recovery.

Other strategies for early return to work used by Quaker Oats' nurses are: facilitating additional referrals to specialists, seeking independent medical examinations, and arranging physical capacities evaluations. Knowledge about state workers' compensation is critical and Quaker Oats encourages nurses to establish links with attorneys involved in the process and to attend claims hearings.

OHNs at Quaker Oats work in collaboration with third-party administrators to monitor the progress of injured workers and develop rehabilitation plans. Scheduled meetings are formally held on a quarterly basis and informal conferences are held on an individual case basis. Contracting for these services allows the nurse to function as employee advocate throughout the return-to-work process.

Effective disability management results from the valuable knowledge the nurse has about the employee, the family situation, and the job assignment. Nurses at Quaker Oats are guided by the principle that injured employees deserve the best possible care in the most timely way to promote early return to work.

THE CHALLENGES OF DISABILITY MANAGEMENT

The reality of disability management is that some employees never return to work. Failure to return to work is associated with individual factors as well as situational factors. Individual factors include personal and lifestyle characteristics, physical aspects of the injury or illness, and psychological aspects. Situational factors include job opportunities, cooperation of health care providers, insurance policy provisions, and economics. OHNs use this information to prioritize action plans for disabled workers and to set realistic goals for return to work.

WHICH EMPLOYEES DO NOT RETURN TO WORK?

Client profiles of older persons, without dependents or living alone, and who have little education and unskilled jobs have been found to have reduced probability of return to work (Gay & Wong, 1988; Foldspang, 1987). Severity of the injury or illness is also a significant determinant of return to work, but not to the extent of psychological and workplace factors.

Gay and Wong (1988) found a positive association between worker motivation and cooperation and successful return to work. Job satisfaction and perceptions of employer support have also been found to be significant indicators of positive rehabilitation outcomes (Brewin, Robson, & Shapiro, 1983; Williams, 1991). Williams (1991) found light-duty programs successful when job satisfaction was high and workers perceived support from the company.

Wage replacement has been shown to have an inverse relationship to return to work; and research indicates that persons injured on the job who receive workers' compensation remain disabled longer than those who suffer personal injuries (Brewin et al., 1983; Gay & Wong, 1988; Foldspang, 1987; Walsh & Dumitru, 1988).

These predictors for delayed recovery are valuable to OHNs who use a high-risk approach to case management. By using these findings OHNs can predict and place emphasis on difficult cases with potential for large losses for the company.

IMPORTANCE OF JOB AVAILABILITY

Is the job waiting for the off-work employee? Sometimes job availability is controlled by union contracts, other times by the size of the company or the nature of the job the employee held. Can the recovered employee perform the job as it has been in the past or will modifications be needed? Throughout recovery, the OHN acquires information from the employee, the supervisor, and the health provider to understand the capability of the employee and the opportunities in the work-place.

Gradual return to full capacity work is necessary if the disability has immobilized or severely limited physical activity. Strength, flexibility, and endurance are lost quickly when activity is restricted. Regaining the stamina to bend and lift for eight hours a day takes a structured program of progression. This can be accomplished in both on-site or off-site rehabilitation programs (Shrey & Olsheski, 1992). The advantages to staying within the plant are: the worker can perform the light-duty tasks with actual equipment, machinery, and processes of the job; and the employer receives the output from the effort. The main advantage of work hardening off-site is close supervision with a team of therapy professionals. Off-site programs generally provide education classes and counseling sessions. However, such support systems can be integrated into an on-site program.

An ideal combination is using therapy professionals to manage a worksite rehabilitation program. Structuring the gradual return to full capacity is a team effort, with the OHN playing a key role in monitoring the physical progress of the worker, advising the physician and rehabilitation specialist, and assisting the supervisor to modify the job as changes are indicated.

COORDINATING TREATMENT AND REHABILITATION

The major challenge in returning workers to productivity is continuous coordination, which is necessary for disability management (refer to Figure 4). Basic components of an effective treatment plan are: having the resources available at the company or within the community, gaining trust of the employee and the supervisor, gaining cooperation of the health care providers, and pursuing creative coverage with the insurance carriers.

When the provider network is established, specialty treatment centers and local rehabilitation programs are part of the referral system. Knowledge of these resources is essential for the OHN to direct the employee to the best treatment option at each step of progress. Making arrangements for the use of these resources requires flexible light-duty programs. For example, an employee in a transition program may need to leave during the day for physical therapy or chemotherapy treatments.

Often the difficulty is not with lack of resources, but reluctance on the part of the primary provider to refer to rehabilitation or transition programs. This hesitancy may be the fear that the employer will push the employee beyond his capabilities and reinjury will occur (Strasser, 1987). If the provider is fully informed by the OHN about the company's transition program, including detailed job descriptions, there is reassurance that the level of activity matches the level of ability. A collaborative relationship between the OHN and the vocational rehabilitation provider is important to assure appropriate services such as counseling, vocational evaluation, analysis of transferable skills, job analysis, and development of a comprehensive rehabilitation plan.

Sometimes a creative approach is necessary to bring an injured employee back to work. This could require special medical treatment or equipment not customarily covered by insurance. Progressive insurance companies will weigh the merits of the nurse's proposed plan against the continued pay-out of disability benefits, often allowing the new treatment.

Coordinating treatment, rehabilitation, and transition back into the workplace is a demanding task requiring extensive communication among the parties. The OHN has responsibility for determining available resources, gaining cooperation of the health care providers, and pursuing creative coverage with the insurance carriers to influence early return to work.

SUMMARY

When the issue is return to work, the OHN is one member of a large team dedicated to the task. The employee, the employer, the safety engineer, health care providers, rehabilitation specialists, third-party administrators, and insurance representatives interact with the nurse to create a system providing the best possible health care while assuring the earliest possible return to productivity.

The OHN holds a unique position in disability coordination because the nurse has the knowledge, the capability, and the trust to serve as both employee advocate and employer agent in communications. The information and expertise of the nurse in terms of employee health status, demands of the worksite, medical community resources, and insurance provisions delineate the nurse as key liaison among the involved parties.

The concept of disability management has four elements: prevention, planning, process, and productivity. As facilitator, the OHN empowers the client to gain control of the work environment and life styles to prevent disabling illnesses or injuries. In the event of an illness or injury episode, the OHN coordinates client progression from injury/illness through rehabilitation to productivity.

Nurse-managed disability programs such as the ones at General Electric, Honeywell, Marriott, and Quaker Oats all function under the basic principles of early intervention, timely referral to appropriate treatment, rehabilitation as soon as medically feasible, and transition jobs in the workplace. The programs demonstrate the disability management role of OHNs and cost savings for companies that utilize OHNs in this capacity.

The reality of disability management is recognizing that there are obstacles to returning employees to work. These are individual characteristics, the extent and type of illness or injury, and factors associated with the work situation. Management/labor relations and job satisfaction play a significant role in return to work. The challenge for the OHN is assuming responsibility for communication among all members of the team, keeping all involved parties fully informed in order to motivate and facilitate progress toward return to work.

PROJECTIONS FOR THE FUTURE

Although prevention strategies may decrease the consequences of illnesses and the incidence of injuries, ill and injured workers will continue to require attention during periods of work disability. Employees and employers have difficulty understanding a health care system that continues to become more complex and health care costs that continue to rise faster than other consumer services. OHNs are beginning to play a significant role in clarifying health care issues by organizing, planning, and managing company disability programs.

Many employers now recognize OHN expertise and capabilities in health promotion, accident prevention, and disability management and are shifting OHN activities from minor first aid to encompass much greater responsibility for total health services management. Health services will include prevention as well as treatment. A significant aspect of health services management is coordination of the many professional services involved in assisting disabled employees. In the future, OHNs will be directors of disability management, responsible for establishing complete systems of prevention, provider networks, case management, and rehabilitation. OHNs have a unique role in managing disabled workers because they are employee advocates who have knowledge and expertise in workplace conditions, connections in the medical and rehabilitation community, and interaction with the claims industry.

The author is grateful to the following people for their assistance: Rachel Ebert; Julie E. Hanson; Marie R. Ross; and Anne K. Widtfeldt.

REFERENCES

American Board for Occupational Health Nurses, Inc. (1992). *Board Certification in Occupational Health Nursing.* Madison, WI: University of Wisconsin.

Benner, C. L., Schilling, A. D., & Klein, L. (1987). Coordinated teamwork in California industrial rehabilitation. *The Journal of Hand Surgery, 12A*(2 Pt 2), 936-939.

Bey, J. M., Widtfeldt, A. K., & Burns, J. M. (1990). The nurse as health manager. *Business and Health, 8*(10), 24-31.

Brewin, C. R., Robson, M. J., & Shapiro, D. A. (1983). Social and psychological determinants of recovery from industrial injuries. *Injury: The British Journal of Accident Surgery, 14,* 451-455.

Bruyere, S. M., & Shrey, D. E. (1991). Disability management in industry: A joint labor-management process. *Rehabilitation Counseling Bulletin, 34,* 227-242.

Burgel, B. J. (1991). Case management: A system of care delivery for the future. *American Association of Occupational Health Nurses Update Series, 4*(13).

Burgel, B. J. (1986). Disability behavior: Delayed recovery in employees with work compensable injuries. *American Association of Occupational Health Nurses Journal, 34,* 26-30.

Conti, R. (1989). The nurse as case manager. *Nursing Connections, 2,* 55-58.

Cox, C. L. (1982). An interaction model of client health behavior: Theoretical prescription for nursing. *Advances in Nursing Science, 5,* 41-56.

Deacon, S. P., & Congdon, G. J. (1984). Rehabilitation after illness and injury — A study of temporary alternative work arrangements. *Journal of Sociological Occupational Medicine, 34,* 46-49.

Ebert, R. (1992a). Lowering costs through occupational health. *Journal of Workers Compensation, 1,* 59-63.

Ebert, R. (1992b). Risk management: The road to effectiveness in the workplace. *American Occupational Health Conference,* Washington, DC, May 6, 1992.

Fitzler, S. L. (1983). The disabled employee: Physical, psychological, and social changes. *Occupational Health Nursing, 31,* 9-15.

Foldspang, A. (1987). Standardized performance tests and their impact on the decisions determining the type of rehabilitation program. *Scandinavian Journal of Social Medicine, 15,* 253-60.

Galvin, D. E. (1986). Health promotion, disability management, and rehabilitation in the workplace. *Rehabilitation Literature, 47,* 218-223.

Gay, D. A., & Wong, D. W. (1988). Predicting rehabilitation outcomes from clinical and statistical data: A probability model. *International Journal of Rehabilitation Research, 11,* 11-19.

Habeck, R. V., Williams, C. L., Dugan, K. E., & Ewing, M. E. (1989). Balancing human and economic costs in disability management. *Journal of Rehabilitation, 55*(4), 16-19.

Hanson-Mayer, T. P. (1984). The worker's disability syndrome. *Journal of Rehabilitation, 50*(3), 50-54.

Hayes, S. H., & Carroll, S. R. (1986). Early intervention care in the acute stroke patient. *Archives of Physical Medicine and Rehabilitation, 67,* 319-321.

Headley, B. J. (1989). Delayed recovery: Taking another look. *Journal of Rehabilitation, 55,* 61-66.

Henderson, M. G., Bergman, A., & Burns, J. M. (1989). A guide to setting up a case management program. *Business & Health, 7*(3), 26-30.

Kaminshine, S. J. (1991). New rights for the disabled. *American Association of Occupational Health Nurses Journal, 39,* 249.

Parker-Conrad, J. E. (1988). A century of practice. *American Association of Occupational Health Nursing Journal, 36,* 156-161.

Peters, P. (1990). Successful return to work following a musculoskeletal injury. *American Association of Occupational Health Nurses Journal, 38,* 264-269.

Pilon, B. A., & Renfroe, D. (1990). Evaluation of an employee health risk appraisal program. *American Association of Occupational Health Nurses Journal, 38,* 230-234.

Randolph, S. A., & Dalton, P. C. (1989). Limited duty work: An innovative approach to early return to work. *American Association of Occupational Health Nurses Journal, 37,* 446-452.

Rogers, B. (1988). Perspectives in occupational health nursing. *American Association of Occupational Health Nurses Journal, 36,* 151-155.

Shrey, D. E., & Olsheski, J. A. (1992). Disability management and industry-based work return transition programs. *Physical Medicine and Rehabilitation, 6,* 233-244.

Smith, S. L. (1991). Returning to health: Getting injured workers back on the job. *Occupational Hazards,* February, 37-40.

Strasser, A. L. (1987). Setting a return-to-work date difficult task for attending physician. *Occupational Health & Safety, 56*(6), 18.

Tate, D. G., Habeck, R. V., & Schwartz, G. (1986). Disability management: A comprehensive framework for prevention and rehabilitation in the workplace. *Rehabilitation Literature, 47,* 230-235.

Walsh, N. E., & Dumitro, D. (1988). The influence of compensation on recovery from low back pain. *Occupational Medicine, 3,* 109-121.

Widtfeldt, A. K., Rumpsa, B., & Bey, J. M. (1992). Medical case management. *Twin Cities Personnel Association,* Minneapolis February 20, 1992.

Williams, J. R. (1991). Employee experiences with early return to work programs. *American Association of Occupational Health Journal, 39,* 64-69.

Yeater, D. C. (1987). The occupational health nurse as disability manager. *American Association of Occupational Health Nursing, 35,* 116-118.

Zal, H. A. (1985). The OHN's influence on employee attitude and ability to return to work. *Occupational Health Nursing,* December, 600-602.

Ergonomics, Injury Prevention, And Disability Management

Anil Mital, Ph.D, P.E.

INTRODUCTION

Ergonomics is the name given to an interdisciplinary field involving industrial and production engineers, work physiologists, medical and occupational health and safety professionals, design engineers, industrial hygienists and all those who are concerned with the performance of humans at work, how they cope with the working environment, how they interact with machines and, in general, how they deal with their surroundings. The term *ergonomics* is coined from two Greek words: *ergon*, meaning work, and *nomos*, meaning natural laws. In essence, ergonomics may be defined as a scientific discipline primarily concerned with the application of natural laws governing human work.

Ergonomics may also been defined in other ways. For instance, Singleton (1972) defines ergonomics as the technology of work design. The author defines ergonomics as the application of technology to assist the human element in manual work.

Ergonomics is also known by several other names, such as *Human Factors* and *Human-Machine Systems*. In the United States, the term *human factors* is more widely used. When ergonomics is applied to occupational settings, as opposed to nonoccupational settings, such as homes, it is generally referred to as *industrial ergonomics*.

Even though the terms *ergonomics* and *human factors* are generally considered synonymous, many individuals prefer to make a distinction. These individuals associate the term *human factors* with the behavioral aspects of human performance and the term *ergonomics* with the quantitative and/or health and safety aspects of humans at work in occupational and nonoccupational settings. In fact, lately, more people working in this interdisciplinary field have started associating themselves with the term *ergonomics* than with *human factors*. This reality was also reflected when the Human Factors Society of America recently changed its name to Human Factors and Ergonomics Society.

Regardless of the name, the overall objective of ergonomics is to fit the task to humans to enhance their effectiveness in the workplace. This means that ergonomics aims at:

- Eliminating or minimizing injuries, strains and sprains
- Minimizing fatigue and overexertion
- Minimizing absenteeism and labor turnover
- Improving quality and quantity of output
- Minimizing lost time and costs associated with injuries and accidents
- Maximizing safety, efficiency, comfort, and productivity

Ergonomics is based on biological (natural) sciences. The main components of ergonomics are anatomy, physiology, psychology, medicine, and engineering. Anatomy is concerned with the structure of the human body and involves the study of the human body size (anthropometry) and how the body responds when subjected to various internal and external forces (biomechanics). Physiology is mainly concerned with how the body functions when performing work (work physiology) or when subjected to different climatological factors (environmental physiology). Psychology is concerned with the behavioral responses of humans to work and environment and includes information processing and decision making (skill psychology) and training, effort perception, and individual worker factors (occupational psychology). Medicine is concerned with the diagnosis, including developing invasive and noninvasive tests, and treatment of injuries (acute and chronic). Engineering provides information about machinery and assists in adapting equipment for human use. Engineering knowledge also assists in designing and developing equipment and devices that fit humans.

EVOLUTION OF ERGONOMICS

Even though the word *ergonomics* was first introduced by Polish professor Wojciech Bogumil Jastrzebowski in an article published in the Poznan Weekly, *Przyroda i Przemysl,* in 1857 (Jastrzebowski, 1957), as pointed out by Seminara (1979), it came into being as a modern discipline in July 1949 (Murrell, 1965). Subsequently, the interest of a diverse group of professionals led to the formation of the Ergonomics Research Society in the United Kingdom. In 1957, the Human Factors Society was formed in the United States. In the same year, the Ergonomics Research Society started publication of its journal *Ergonomics* and the Human Factors Society started publication of *Human Factors*. In 1959, the International Ergonomics Association (IEA) was formed to link the various human factors and ergonomics societies around the world. The first meeting of the IEA was held in 1961 in Stockholm, Sweden. The Ergonomics Research Society later changed its name to Ergonomics Society. In 1992, the Human Factors Society also changed its name to Human Factors and Ergonomics Society.

In 1986, the author founded the International Foundation for Industrial Ergonomics and Safety Research. This organization is primarily concerned with the promotion of industrial ergonomics and occupational safety and organizes the Annual International Industrial Ergonomics and Safety Conferences. The first journal devoted to industrial ergonomics, *The International Journal of Industrial Ergonomics*, was started in 1986. Over the last 45 years, ergonomics as a discipline has grown tremendously. It is now an integral part of Industrial Engineering and Experimental Psychology curricula. Many schools in the United States, Europe, and the Far East offer advanced degrees in ergonomics/human factors through their Industrial Engineering or Psychology departments. Besides the growth in educational programs, ergonomics now has several dedicated research and application journals. Among the most prominent ones are: *Ergonomics, Human Factors, International Journal of Industrial Ergonomics, Applied Ergonomics,* the *Journal of Human Ergology*. Some of the basic resources are listed in the appendix.

Besides introducing the reader to ergonomics and explaining what ergonomics is, this chapter has several other objectives:

(a) to outline the scope of ergonomics, specifically its role in improving workers' safety and health and cost containment;
(b) to propose a comprehensive model that outlines the role of ergonomics in injury prevention and management; and
(c) to explain to the readers how ergonomics can aid employers in complying with many of the ADA (Americans with Disabilities Act) requirements.

SCOPE OF ERGONOMICS

As stated earlier, ergonomics has several distinct, but related, goals. The overall goal of ergonomics is to maximize workers' capabilities while, at the same time, ensuring their safety, comfort, efficiency, and effectiveness. During World War II and adolescent years of its growth, ergonomics was primarily concerned with ensuring that human operators were able to get the "best" out of their equipment. The drive to increase efficiency lead designers to know more about human capabilities, their limitations, and responses to things and the environment. The study of human performance became the central issue. *Designing for humans* and *human use* became the primary expressions ergonomists and human factors specialists started using in describing their activities.

As ergonomics evolved, it became clear that job satisfaction, quality of life, operator comfort, safety, injury control, stress, and productivity and efficiency were all related. The role of ergonomics in containing costs, particularly the costs directly resulting from and attributable to injuries, such as absenteeism, retraining new hires, increased medical costs and liability insurance and punitive damages, started getting wide recognition. Today, insuring maximum long-term health and safety of workers by preventing and/or controlling occupational injuries and illnesses is an important and prominent goal of ergonomics. The role of ergonomics in controlling cumulative trauma disorders (CTD) of the upper and lower extremities and the costs associated with these disorders is an appropriate example of this relatively new emphasis.

ROLE OF ERGONOMICS IN CONTROLLING OCCUPATIONAL INJURIES AND ASSOCIATED COSTS

Low back injuries and cumulative trauma disorders of the upper extremities, particularly those of the wrist, are two most prevalent categories of occupational injuries currently inflicting the industrial workforce. Back injuries account for one of every four workers' compensation claims (Klein, Roger, Jensen, & Sanderson, 1984). The direct and indirect costs of these back injuries have been estimated to be approximately $100 billion, annually (Mital, 1991). However, there is good reason to believe that this figure may represent a severe underestimate. For instance, Helms (1985) estimates that the costs of surgical procedures alone is $12 billion per year. If the cost of lost workdays, retraining new hires, increased insurance, and other costs are added to this number, the real cost may very well be far in excess of the $100 billion per year estimate.

The injuries resulting from the CTDs of the upper extremities form the second most expensive category of injuries. While the proportion of all overexertion injuries CTDs of the upper extremities constitute and how much they cost are not exactly known, some related injuries and costs are known. Aghazadeh and Mital (1987) conducted a survey of injuries resulting from the use of various powered and nonpowered hand tools. The results indicated that in the United States hand tool injuries constitute approximately 9% of all overexertion injuries. The cost of these injuries was estimated to be approximately $10 billion per year. Clearly, the proportion and cost of upper extremity CTDs will increase when other causes of CTDs are added to the list.

Given the cost and prevalence of back and wrist injuries, it is only logical that efforts be made to prevent such injuries. The following discussion focuses on ergonomics efforts to reduce the severity and frequency of back and upper extremity injuries.

Back Injuries

The ergonomics efforts to control back injuries date back to the early 1950s. Over the past four decades, ergonomics research has led to identifying the various occupational and personal risk factors associated with the occurrence of back injuries. Procedures have been developed to modify the psychophysical, physiological, and mechanical factors to prevent and eliminate back injuries. Equally important, procedures have been developed to determine the capabilities of individual workers to perform manual materials handling activities (Ayoub & Mital, 1989; Mital, Nicholson, & Ayoub, 1993).

Using epidemiology as an information base and ergonomic design as potential strategy, it has been proclaimed that up to one-third of back injuries can be prevented (Snook, 1978). In a survey carried out by the Liberty Mutual Insurance Company, it was found that up to a quarter of the jobs required manual materials handling of a magnitude acceptable to less than 75% of the workers. These jobs were responsible for half the back injuries reported, thus indicating a threefold increase in susceptibility when the tasks require such exertion. This implies that two-thirds of all back injuries associated with manual materials handling can be prevented if the jobs are ergonomically designed so as to fit at least 75% of the workforce (Kumar & Mital, 1992). Kumar and Mital further provide evidence that ergonomic intervention can provide at least a 30% margin of safety for the human back. Similar conclusions have been reached by others (Ayoub & Mital, 1989; Mital et al., 1993). Naturally, if the severity and frequency of injuries are reduced, the associated costs will also decline. Unfortunately, there is little publicly available data to prove this point (A case study by Dalton and Smitten [1991] provides some evidence). However, injury cost containment has been used as an ergonomics selling point and there are numerous companies in the United States, such as General Motors, Ford Motor Company, IBM, and Dupont, that now have well-established ergonomics/human factors departments.

Injuries of the Upper Extremities

As in the case of back injuries, ergonomics research has identified various risk factors that lead to upper extremity CTDs. Besides identifying the CTD risk factors, ergonomics has provided unique ways to prevent and control injuries (Konz & Mital, 1990; Mital & Kilbom, 1992a, b; Putz-Anderson, 1988). In addition to specifying design modifications, ergonomics provides procedures for work practice modifications. Ergonomics focuses on preventing CTDs by eliminating the causes (risk factors) through design and work practice modifications; whereas, physicians only cure the symptoms. Unless the root causes of CTDs are eliminated, which is what ergonomics accomplishes, the problem and symptoms recur.

As in the case of back injuries, little published data are available to prove that ergonomic interventions reduce the number and cost of upper extremity CTDs. However, the author's personal experience and unpublished evidence strongly suggest that poor equipment, tool and workplace designs, and work practices that cause fatigue and discomfort are frequently among the major causes of upper extremity CTDs. Ergonomics can eliminate or rectify these causes to bring the job demands within the capabilities of the workforce. The author's experience in many companies, such as the Ford Motor Company and Cinpac, has shown that in such cases both the frequency and cost of upper extremity CTDs are significantly reduced.

A MODEL FOR INJURY PREVENTION AND MANAGEMENT

One of the objectives of this chapter is to provide a generalized model for controlling injuries in the workplace and, when injuries happen, managing them effectively. Figure 1 shows the conceptual model.

Ergonomics aims at fitting the task to individuals and represents a proactive approach to injury control. It ensures that the tasks are designed such that the demands imposed upon individuals are within their capabilities. If this is accomplished, the risk of injury will be greatly reduced. It should also be realized that, even if work, workplaces, equipment, and tools are ergonomically designed, some injuries will still happen. The injured workers then need to be accommodated in the workplace. The role of ergonomics is not simply making job accommodations to integrate the injured, as some people believe. Rather, it involves determining residual work capacity of the injured, developing ergonomically designed physical training programs to enhance their capabilities, designing work and schedules during the transition from injured to recovered status, and finally making changes in the workplace, if needed, to accommodate the individual.

As this discussion points out, ergonomics is the central scientific discipline in injury or disability management. It not only aims at preventing injuries in general, but also plays a key role in returning the injured worker, or workers with any other limitations, to work.

The generalized injury management model depicted in Figure 1 can be broken down into several steps:

1. **Formation of an interdisciplinary injury management team.**
   Prevention and control of injuries requires input from professionals with a varied background. Specifically, specialists from the following areas play a major role:

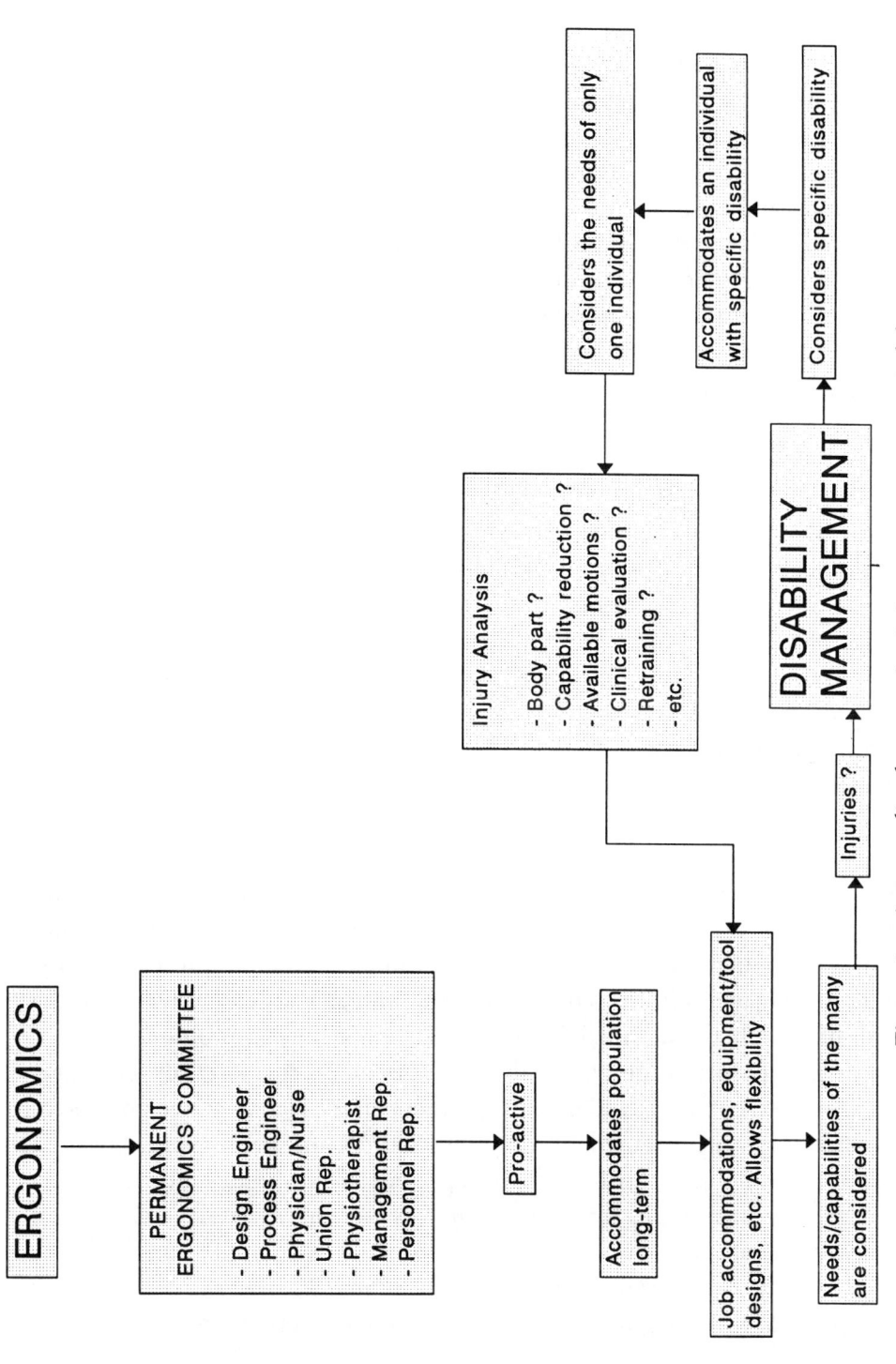

Figure 1. A generalized pro-active injury management model.

ergonomics, process engineering, product design, safety engineering, occupational health (nurse/physician), and workers' claims management. In addition, cooperation of the union, management, and line workers is essential. The interdisciplinary team not only provides insight into the different aspects of injury, it also becomes the driving force that changes the culture of the company—from a reactive participant to a proactive partner.

2. **Education and training of the injury management team.**

To accomplish the desired goal, reduction and control of injuries and related costs, it is essential that the team be educated in the philosophy and benefits of a proactive injury control program. The team must also receive training in ergonomics and the role it plays in preventing and controlling injuries, worker capacity determination, and design and development of training and transitional work programs. Without such education and training, no realistic gains in controlling injuries are possible.

3. **An in-depth review of injury records and costs.**

A thorough review of injury records, associated costs, and remedial measures taken is essential for several reasons, including: (a) to establish an injury-cost profile of the company; (b) to separate severe, frequent, and expensive injuries from other kinds of injuries; (c) to rank jobs in terms of physical demands, injury potential, and severity, to establish remediation priorities; (d) to determine which preventive measures, if any, were successful and to what degree; (e) to establish goals and intervention strategies; and (f) to compare future gains.

4. **Physical capacity assessment of the affected workforce.**

The simple injury avoidance principle is: ensure that job demands are within workers' physical capacities. The goal of an ergonomist is to ensure that worker capacity matches the assigned job's demands. If the job demands exceed capacity, an injury is likely to result. In comparison, if the worker's capacity well exceeds the demands of the job, the productivity of the system may be compromised.

Since workers vary from job-to-job and come in assorted sizes, differ in age, vary in physical capabilities, and belong to either gender, it may not be possible to utilize worker capacity knowledge from other sources and populations. From an ergonomics standpoint, at least the following kinds of capabilities must be determined: (a) body size (reach, etc.); (b) strength (static and dynamic); (c) physical work capacity (aerobic capacity, endurance time or stamina, etc.); (d) joint flexibility; and (e) gross body coordination. Various scientific techniques are available to quantify workers' physical abilities and should be utilized if one is serious about preventing injuries.

5. **Determination of physical demands (job analysis).**

    How well a worker performs a given job largely depends upon the physical demands of that job. Just as it is important to know workers' physical capabilities, all jobs must also be analyzed by applying ergonomic and engineering principles of physical demands analysis. At the very least, information must be gathered about the following: (a) the object (material, shape, size, weight, etc.); (b) the equipment (force needed to operate, types of controls, tools, frequency, etc.); and (c) the workplace (posture, reach, climate, work flow, etc.). Once the above information is gathered, it would become possible to quantify job demands. The demands of the job may be compared to workers' physical capacities to establish a particular job's injury risk potential.

6. **Ranking of jobs by severity, frequency, and cost of injuries and determination of shift, gender, age, and other effects.**

    Once the injury and cost data have been analyzed and job demands and workforce capabilities have been determined, all potentially risky jobs should be ranked by severity, frequency, and cost of injuries. This would establish a priority for future interventions. The injury data must also be systematically analyzed to determine if any age group, gender, or work group is at more risk than others.

7. **Review of work, workstation, equipment, tool and other designs, and workpractices.**

    Once the priority for ergonomics and engineering intervention is established, each task, associated equipment and tools, workstation design, and workpractices must be subjected to ergonomics analysis. The outcome will be identification of elements that contribute to workers' injuries.

8. **Job, workplace, equipment and tool redesign, and classroom training of workers and management in ergonomics.**

    All undesirable elements must either be eliminated or redesigned with the aim to minimizing injuries. Established ergonomics and engineering design procedures should be used. It is critical that attention be paid to the cost of the "solution." Usually, there are several ways to redesign a job. However, most people are satisfied with only one solution. There is no guarantee that the chosen solution is the most economical one. Therefore, it is very important that ergonomists and engineers, or others responsible for design changes, pay attention not only to changes but associated costs as well.

    It is also important that workers and managers receive training in ergonomics. Only when everyone involved is educated in ergonomics and its role in injury prevention and control, would it be possible to effectively control injuries and reduce costs.

9. **Monitoring the ergonomics program for future injuries.**

Once the first eight steps have been carried out, efforts should be directed towards monitoring the program for future injuries. It should be realized that, in spite of all ergonomics and engineering controls, some injuries, most likely the acute kind (resulting from accidents), will happen. According to Snook (1978), one-third of the injuries will occur despite any design effort. At least the following injury data must be recorded: (a) nature of injury (acute vs. chronic); (b) body part injured; (c) type of treatment; (d) cost; (e) job description; (f) details of object(s), equipment and tool involved; (g) age and gender of the injured worker; (h) prior injury history at the present job and other jobs; (i) description of the task (posture, forces involved, frequency, etc.); (j) records of other workers injured on the same job; (k) shift in which the injury happened; and (l) any other details that can help in describing and analyzing the incident.

10. **Review and analysis of injury data for trends.**

The injury data must be analyzed to determine trends, if any. An ergonomic analysis should be carried out and task demands should be established once again. These demands should be related to capacity data to eliminate the possibility of an oversight during initial analyses. Solutions, such as reducing the task demands further to accommodate the weaker members of the workforce and redesigning the workplace, should be considered. Job matching procedures should also be instituted and job content tests should be considered.

11. **Determination of injured worker residual capacities.**

The injured worker must eventually be integrated in the workforce. However, it is very likely that some time may elapse before the injured worker fully recovers from the injury. It is also possible that the injury may leave him or her permanently disabled. Furthermore, the injured worker will most likely need to undergo some kind of physical therapy not only to accelerate the recovery process but to regain the pre-injury physical capacities. This means that the injured worker's residual capacities must be known at different points in time. Knowledge of the injured worker's residual capacities at the following junctures is important:

(a) before designing and implementing a physical training program for therapeutic purposes, and
(b) at the end of the recovery period to determine the extent of recovery so that:
  (i) job, equipment, tool, and other design changes may be made to allow the worker with a disability to return to his or her previous job, or
  (ii) job matching procedures may be implemented and the disabled worker may be assigned a job within his or her physical abilities.

At least the following must be done to determine the residual capabilities of the injured worker prior to starting physical training or returning the worker to full-time employment:

(a) development of available motions inventory,
(b) assessment of the strength of various muscle groups, particularly those of the back, shoulder, arm, leg, and grip,
(c) determination of reach profiles,
(d) determination of physical work capacity and stamina,
(e) determination of hearing and vision,
(f) determination of lung capacity, and
(g) determination of general physical fitness.

There are well-established ergonomics and rehabilitation engineering procedures to accomplish the above evaluation.

In addition to ergonomic and physical evaluations, medical, vocational, and psychological evaluations are also necessary before a determination about initiating transitional training or returning to work, full-time, can be made (Lacerte & Wright, 1992).

12a. Design and development of a physical training program to enhance the injured worker's affected capacities.

The primary goal of a physical training program is to enhance a worker's physical capabilities, particularly strength and joint flexibility. Several studies have shown that physical training enhances a person's strength and joint flexibility (Asfour, Ayoub, & Mital, 1987; Hilyer, Brown, Sirles, & Peoples, 1990). Physical training is also known to reduce absenteeism (Baun, Bernacki, & Tsai, 1986; Lynch, Golaszewski, Clearle, Snow, & Vickery, 1990), improve psychological perception of work (Dehlin, Berg, Andersson, & Grimby, 1981) and reduce cost (Baun et al., 1986).

Simulating those physical elements of the job that are critical to performing the task satisfactorily in the training program is critical. In fact, it has been observed that if job motions and resistance are simulated, even without a formal physical training program, the improvement in physical capabilities is almost as much as it might be in a formal training program (Mital & Ayoub, 1981). The use of simulated job strengths for job matching has also been reported by the author (Mital, Channaveeraiah, Fard, & Khaledi, 1986; Mital, Wang, & Fard, 1987).

12b. Design and development of a transitional work program that not only takes into consideration the available capacities but also accounts for the training effects.

A transitional work program, in conjunction with a physical training program, is essential in restoring, to whatever extent possible, the physical abilities of the injured worker. The key consideration in designing transitional work is **residual capacity of the injured worker**. Transitional work that simulates physical elements of the job are important as their inclusion accelerates the injured worker's psychological outlook and acceptance, while concurrently improving those abilities needed to perform the job.

13. Making changes in the work, workplace, and equipment to accommodate the affected worker.

In the event the injured worker suffers from a permanent disability (partial or total) or the recovery is not complete, it becomes necessary that changes in the workplace and/or equipment be made to accommodate the worker. Knowledge of worker residual abilities and ergonomics and engineering design principles is essential in job restructuring, modifying the worksite, designing or procuring adaptive aids, and, if necessary, specifying work restrictions. In general, the goal is to individualize the accommodation.

14. Injury and cost audit.

Continuous monitoring of future injuries and cost audit are essential features of the proposed injury prevention and management model. It is important to realize that injury prevention and cost containment are dynamic processes and a one-time attention will not achieve the desired goals.

ERGONOMICS AND ADA

The provisions of the Americans with Disabilities Act (ADA) impacted on all employers with 25 or more workers, beginning July 26, 1992. Beginning July 26, 1994, the ADA covered all employers with 15 or more workers. The ADA and its implications are discussed in detail in other chapters in this book, and no attempt will be made to discuss its provisions further in this chapter. However, the role of ergonomics in assisting employers in meeting the requirements of ADA are appropriate for discussion here.

In general, ADA requires employers to: (1) have nondiscriminatory application procedures, qualification standards, and selection criteria and all other terms and conditions of employment and (2) make reasonable accommodation to the known limitations of a qualified applicant or employee unless to do so would cause undue hardship. Ergonomics has a vital role to play in meeting both these requirements. Specifically, ergonomics can assist employers in:

(1) designing and developing job content tests to determine if a potential employee can perform the job;
(2) quantifying the extent of a potential employee's limitations and developing reasonable accommodations through design modifications covering all relevant aspects of work and equipment;
(3) analyzing injury and cost data to focus on those jobs that are potentially more dangerous;
(4) performing ergonomic and engineering analyses of potentially risky jobs and redesigning them so that job demands are within workers' capabilities;
(5) accurately assessing the abilities of qualified applicants with limitations or those employees who, as a result of an injury, have developed a functional disability;
(6) developing a physical training program to restore, to whatever degree possible, the abilities of an injured worker;
(7) developing transitional work options at the worksite to accelerate the return of the worker with a disability to work; and
(8) individualizing accommodations and job site modifications in general.

SUMMARY

This chapter provides a brief introduction to ergonomics. Besides defining the term ergonomics, a brief history of the evolution of ergonomics is presented. Sources of ergonomics information are also provided. A 14-step generalized pro-active injury management model is presented and the role ergonomics plays in implementing this model is described in detail. It is reasoned that ergonomics is the pivotal discipline in managing injuries and resulting disabilities. The philosophy that ergonomics is central to accommodating the person with a disability in the workplace and controlling injury-related costs is justified. The role of ergonomics in identifying residual capacities of the persons with disabilities and ways to integrate them effectively in the workplace, in the context of ADA, is also outlined.

REFERENCES

Aghazadeh, F., & Mital, A. (1987). Injuries due to handtools. *Applied Ergonomics, 18,* 273-278.

Asfour, S. S., Ayoub, M. M., & Mital, A. (1984). Effects of an endurance and strength training program on lifting capacity of males. *Ergonomics, 27,* 435-442.

Ayoub, M. M., & Mital, A. (1989). *Manual materials handling.* London: Taylor & Francis, Ltd.

Baun, W. B., Bernacki, E. J., & Tsai, S. P. (1986): A preliminary investigation: Effect of a corporate fitness program on absenteeism and health care cost. *Journal of Occupational Medicine, 28,* 18-22.

Dalton, J. M., & Smitten, N. (1991). Cost reduction through modification of a heavy physical task. In B. M. Pulat & D. C. Alexander (Eds.): *Industrial Ergonomics* (pp. 75-84). Atlanta, GA: Industrial Engineering and Management Press.

Dehlin, O., Berg, S., Andersson, G.B.J., & Grimby, G. (1981). Effect of physical training and ergonomic counseling on the psychological perception of work and on the subjective assessment of low-back insufficiency. *Scandinavian Journal of Rehabilitation Medicine, 13,* 1-9.

Helms, C. T. (1985). CT of spine: An overview. In *Low Back Pain: Solving the Clinical Challenge* (pp. 5-12). Secaucus, NJ: The Network for Medical Education Publication, 467.

Hilyer, J. C., Brown, K. C., Sirles, A. T., & Peoples, L. (1990). A flexibility intervention to reduce the incidence and severity of joint injuries among municipal firefighters. *Journal of Occupational Medicine, 32,* 631-637.

Jastrzebowski, W. B. (1957). Rys ergonomji czyli nauki o pracy, opartej na prawdach poczerpniet z nauki przyrody (An outline of ergonomics or science of work based upon the truths drawn from natural science). *Przyroda i przemysl* (Poznan weekly).

Klein, B. P., Roger, M. A., Jensen, R. C., & Sanderson, L.M. (1984). Assessment of workers' compensation claims for back sprain/strains. *Journal of Occupational Medicine, 26,* 443-448.

Konz, S., & Mital, A. (1990). Guidelines: Carpal tunnel syndrome. *International Journal of Industrial Ergonomics, 5,* 175-180.

Kumar, S., & Mital, A. (1992). Margin of safety for the human back: A probable consensus based on published studies. *Ergonomics, 35,* 769-781.

Lacerte, M., & Wright, G. R. (1992). Return to work determination. *Physical Medicine and Rehabilitation, 6,* 283-302.

Lynch, W. D., Golaszewski, T. J., Clearle, A. F., Snow, D., & Vickery, D. M. (1990). Impact of a facility-based corporate fitness program on the number of absences from work due to illness. *Journal of Occupational Medicine, 32,* 9-12.

Mital, A. (1991). Design and analysis of multiple activity manual materials handling tasks. In B. M. Pulat & D. C. Alexander (Eds.): *Industrial Ergonomics* (pp. 29-40). Atlanta, GA: Industrial Engineering and Management Press.

Mital, A., & Ayoub, M. M. (1981). Effects of task variables and their interactions in lifting and lowering. *American Industrial Hygiene Association Journal, 42,* 134-142.

Mital, A., & Kilbom, A. (1992a). Design, selection, and use of handtools to alleviate trauma of the upper extremities: Part I – guidelines for the practitioner. *International Journal of Industrial Ergonomics, 10,* 1-5.

Mital, A., & Kilbom, A. (1992b). Design, selection, and use of handtools to alleviate trauma of the upper extremities: Part II – the scientific basis. *International Journal of Industrial Ergonomics, 10,* 7-21.

Mital, A., Channaveeraiah, C., Fard, H. F., & Khaledi, H. (1986). Reliability of repetitive dynamic strengths as a screening tool for manual lifting tasks. *Clinical Biomechanics, 1,* 125-129.

Mital, A., Wang, L. W., & Fard, H.F. (1987). Boundary line between the strength and endurance regions in manual lifting. *Clinical Biomechanics, 2,* 220-222.

Mital, A., Nicholson, A. S., & Ayoub, M. M. (1993). *A guide for manual materials handling.* London: Taylor & Francis, Ltd.

Murrell, K. F. H. (1965). *Ergonomics: Man in his working environment.* London: Chapman and Hall.

Putz-Anderson, V. (1988). *Cumulative trauma disorders.* London: Taylor & Francis, Ltd.

Seminara, J. L. (1979). A survey of ergonomics in Poland. *Ergonomics, 22,* 479-505.

Singleton, W. T. (1972). *Introduction to ergonomics.* Geneva: World Health Organization.

Snook, S. H. (1978). The design of manual handling tasks. *Ergonomics, 21,* 963-985.

APPENDIX: SELECTED RESOURCES

ORGANIZATIONS

Human Factors and Ergonomics Society
P.O. Box 1369
Santa Monica, CA 90406
Phone: (310) 394-1811

International Foundation for Industrial Ergonomics and Safety Research
Dr. S. Dutta, Secretary
Dept. of Industrial Engineering
University of Windsor
Windsor, Ontario N9B 3P4
Canada
Phone: (519) 253-4232 (Ext. 2607)

International Labour Organization
4 route des Morillons
CH 1211 Geneva
Switzerland
Phone: 22 996111

National Safety Council
444 North Michigan Ave.
Chicago, IL 60611
Phone: (312) 527-4800

World Health Organization
Avenue Appia
CH 1211 Geneva 27
Switzerland
Phone: 22 912111

JOURNALS

Applied Ergonomics
Butterworths
P.O. Box 63
Westbury House, Bury Street
Guildford, Surrey GU2 5BH
United Kingdom
Phone: +44 483-31261

Ergonomics and **Ergonomics Abstracts**
Taylor & Francis Ltd.
4 John Street
London WC1N 2ET
United Kingdom
Phone: +44 71-4052237

Human Factors
Human Factors and Ergonomics Society (see above)

International Journal of Industrial Ergonomics
Elsevier Science Publishers
P.O. Box 211
1000 AE Amsterdam
The Netherlands
Phone: +31 20 5803642

Journal of Human Ergology
Center for Academic Publications Japan
4-16 Yayoi 2-chome
Bunkyo-ku, Tokyo 113
Japan

Journal of Safety Research
National Safety Council (see above) *Books*

A Guide for Manual Materials Handling
A. Mital, A. S. Nicholson, and M. M. Ayoub
Taylor & Francis Ltd., 1993

Applied Ergonomics Handbook
Ian Galer, 2nd Ed.
Butterworths (see above), 1987

Encyclopedia of Occupational Health and Safety
International Labour Office, 1983

Ergonomics in Rehabilitation
A. Mital and W. Karwowski (Eds.)
Taylor & Francis Ltd., 1988

Evaluation of Human Work: A Practical Ergonomics Methodology
J. R. Wilson and E. N. Corlett (Eds.)
Taylor & Francis Ltd., 1990

Fitting the Task to the Man
E. Grandjean
Taylor & Francis Ltd., 4th Ed., 1986

Handbook of Human Factors
G. Salvendy (Ed.)
John Wiley & Son, 1987

Human Factors in Engineering and Design
M. S. Sanders and E. J. McCormick
McGraw-Hill, 6th Ed., 1987

Occupational Biomechanics
D. B. Chaffin and G. B. J. Andersson
John Wiley & Son, 2nd Ed., 1991

The Ergonomics of Workspaces and Machines: A Design Manual
T. S. Clark and E. N. Corlett
Taylor & Francis Ltd., 1984

Work Design: Industrial Ergonomics
S. Konz
Publications Horizon, 1990

Workspace, Equipment and Tool Design
A. Mital and W. Karwowski (Eds.)
Elsevier Science Publishers, 1991

CONFERENCES

Annual International Industrial Ergonomics and Safety Conference
International Foundation for Industrial Ergonomics and Safety Research
Second Week in June
Write to the Secretary (see above)

Annual Meeting of the Human Factors and Ergonomics Society
Human Factors and Ergonomics Society (see above)
September/October

The Role Of The Physician In Disability Management

Steven Scheer, M.D.

"Occupational illnesses are not biologically different, just socially different."
Sigerist (1936)

INTRODUCTION

Trends in the evolution of industrial disability management necessitate that physicians receive a proper education in a number of concepts which at present are not necessarily found in the standard undergraduate or graduate medical curriculum. The curriculum of most medical and osteopathic training programs includes little mention of assessment of ability or restoration of function (Symington, 1984). By the time they graduate, many medical students entering residencies have not received training in mobility, self-care, and home safety. According to Rosenstock (1981), there is also insufficient training during these early formative years in such vocational issues as workplace hazards, protective measures against toxic exposures, or effects of medical problems on work performance. In a journal symposium on the status of workers' compensation insurance in the United States and Canada, Elling (1990) and fellow discussants commented that few medical schools incorporate many of these concepts in physician training.

There is cause for optimism. Estep, Mitchell, and DeHart (1992) conducted a phone survey among representatives of all allopathic (126) and osteopathic (15) schools of medicine in the U.S. and Puerto Rico. Half (71) of the schools allotted a median number of five hours of lecture time for occupational topics. Only 46 schools (32%), however, offered an elective clerkship in Occupational and Environmental Medicine, and on average, less than two students (at each school) per year were taking advantage of the rotation.

There is such limited exposure to clinical issues of the workplace for many medical students, that one might hope specialty training would offer graduate physicians a better appreciation for workplace issues and work capacity. Residency training in such fields as occupational medicine, physical medicine and rehabilitation, and orthopaedics, generally includes variable exposure to work function issues. Formal training in occupational medical assessment is unusual, however, for the majority of family medicine physicians and internists trained on this continent (Institute of Medicine, 1988). These primary care physicians are often in a decision-making capacity for their patients' work fitness since more than three-fourths of the U.S. work force is employed by small companies that do not have on-site health services (Rothstein, 1984). Thus, family physicians and internists will likely continue to serve as medical monitors and primary decision makers to determine work readiness of most injured workers, and yet lack an opportunity to receive formal training in occupational medical assessment prior to establishing a practice.

The use of a traditional medical model to assess workers results in physicians' tendencies to try to treat injured workers as any other patients: there is pathology which, once diagnosed, treated, and eliminated, will allow the patient's return to activity. Unfortunately, a number of medical conditions commonly seen in the industrial clinic are not so easily diagnosed with certainty. Low back pain and a host of disorders now referred to as *cumulative trauma* or *repetitive strain injuries* are identified generically, but their true pathologic descriptions may remain elusive in spite of the availability of the most sophisticated anatomic imaging and neurophysiologic tests (Armstrong & Silverstein, 1987; Frymoyer & Howe, 1984). Fortunately, the majority of these conditions seem to be self-limited; for 80% of workers with minor injuries, no time is lost from work (President's Commission, 1972). For many others, healing generally occurs with rest and a brief program of conservative measures (Andersson, 1981; Svensson & Andersson, 1983). When recovery does not occur so readily, however, or when apparent healing does not lead to work return, many physicians are troubled by the lack of apparent solutions and controls (Louis, 1987; Nachemson, 1983).

This chapter provides information physicians should receive during training to develop an appreciation for the broader context of work injury, treatment efficacy, and worker-employer relationships. The final section describes the typical types of physician involvement in work injury management.

CONTEMPORARY TRAINING IN OCCUPATIONAL MEDICAL ASSESSMENT

WORK — A SEARCH FOR MEANING

The great French author and playwright, Albert Camus, is commonly attributed the comment that without work, all life goes rotten, and that when work is soulless, life is stifled as a result. In *Civilization and its Discontents*, Freud (1961) attempts to unravel the purpose of human existence. He describes that work, more than any other life construct, helps to attach common man to reality, and states that its value is "something indispensable to the preservation and justification of existence in society." So important is an occupation to one's appreciation for life that psychiatrists describe a Sunday neurosis, a kind of depression afflicting people who see a total lack of fulfillment coming from their lives when the week of work is over. Suicide has been linked, in some percentage of cases, to this phenomenon (Frankl, 1984).

The importance of work in the lives of Americans is portrayed well in Terkel's (1974) best-selling book, *Working: People Talk About What They Do All Day and How They Feel About What They Do*. Terkel captures the minds and spirit of countless workers who comment about the role of work in their lives. For most, work was important as a means to be remembered, a way to immortality. Sadly, precious few work was savored as an ultimate pleasure; the stone mason, the piano tuner, the bookbinder, and the fireman were exceptional in enjoying their professional lives. Some were searching for a sense of pride, as, for example, the waitress in a fashionable restaurant who explained, "When I put the plate down, you don't hear a sound...When someone says, 'How come you're just a waitress?' I say, 'Don't you think you deserve being served by me?'" There are those who practice their professions wherever they go. Actress Geraldine Page told Terkel about a dentist who, after seeing her portrayal in "Sweet Bird of Youth" from the front row of the theater, came backstage to ask what poor excuse of a dentist had been doing her fillings.

In view of the importance many people ascribe to the role of work in their lives, physicians' involvement in determining work potential is not to be taken for granted. Occupational medical assessment ought to have a place in the curriculum of every medical school.

IMPAIRMENT, DISABILITY, AND HANDICAP

A conceptual basis for understanding differences between impairment, disability and handicap has been developed by Wood (1980) in the internationally distributed *International Classification of Impairments, Disabilities, and Handicaps*. The book is a taxonomy which categorizes disablement as follows:

1. **Impairment:** a health defect at the level of the organ or body system (e.g., coronary artery disease);
2. **Disability:** a bodily dysfunction caused by impairment (e.g., inability to climb a flight of stairs); and
3. **Handicap:** a deficit in role fulfillment reflecting societal disadvantages not accommodated in the environment (e.g., loss of a job due to employer's unwillingness to move an office to the ground floor).

Physicians involved in determinations of work capacity need to appreciate the difference between a pathologic process (disease or impairment); its functional ramifications (disability); and the handicapping environment of the disabled person. As an example, a 30-year-old construction worker with a recently diagnosed muscular low back pain is unable to lift a 40-pound box of tools or to bend forward to hammer. However, she is not vocationally handicapped since her boss will allow her to continue working in inventory control at the main office of the company rather than on the construction site.

One can also easily understand how a worker can be deconditioned functionally to the point of being disabled but no longer have an impairment. The same construction worker may have noted diminished back pain, but if the process of healing took six or more weeks, the loss of ability to lift loads or bend agilely (a disability) may have necessitated some work rehabilitation for return to the original job tasks. Determining whether or not there is functional disability is a matter of ascertaining job and home living requirements and comparing these to the measured abilities of the worker, regardless of present diagnosis.

EPIDEMIOLOGY AND PATHOPHYSIOLOGY OF WORKPLACE INJURY/DISEASE

A major treatise on diseases and injuries associated with the workplace is well beyond the possible scope of this chapter. It will suffice to say that three principles must be incorporated into training curricula for those receiving a medical education.

There are many potentially toxic exposures existing in the workplace (Zenz, 1988) and there are, for example, known cancer risks (Dodson & Zenz, 1988). The physical work environment may contain such stressors as lifting hazards, dangerous work surfaces, excessive noise or vibration, extremes of temperature, prolonged or awkward postures, or air pressure changes (Zenz, 1988). Therefore, the first principle is that evaluating physicians should have some index of suspicion about chemical solvents, pesticides, or other toxins that may cause the worker to have dermatologic, respiratory, visual, or work performance difficulties (Rosenstock, 1981). At times a search for an explanation of how and whether the workplace is involved in a worker's illness is made easy by the worker mentioning that similar maladies have been described by co-workers.

A second principle relates to the fact that many medical conditions with putative work-relatedness may, in fact, have little or no etiologic association to the workplace (Armstrong & Silverstein, 1987; Scheer, 1991b). The worker's attribution of the disorder to the workplace is encouraged by the hope for secondary gain in the form of more lucrative workers' compensation insurance benefits (health care plus wage replacement). Development of carpal tunnel syndrome in a worker with rheumatoid arthritis, for example, could be ascribed to the stresses of the job. An examining physician may suspect that the condition could have occurred whether or not the worker was employed. In most jurisdictions, any role, however minor, which the job has played in causation of injury or disease is sufficient reason to allow workers' compensation coverage (Hadler, 1984). Even more distressing to employers, particularly those self-insured, is the situation of a worker known to be an avid golfer coming to work Monday morning with a lumbar strain induced by his hobby but claiming a lifting episode at work was responsible for the back pain. This situation may become a legal causality dispute (see causality discussion below).

The third principle relating to pathophysiology relates to the frequency with which job-related physical overuse may lead to musculoskeletal injury (Andersson, 1981; Armstrong & Silverstein, 1987; Kelsey & White, 1980; National Institute for Occupational Safety and Health, 1981; Silverstein, Fine, & Armstrong, 1986). The pathomechanical risk factors leading to occupational overuse syndromes are by now well documented. For low back pain (LBP), the most expensive single ailment to affect the workplace, the major predisposing work tasks are those with prolonged or awkward postures; frequent bending and twisting; repetitive lifting; heavy work; vibration exposure; and sudden unexpected movements (Andersson, 1981; Biering-Sorensen, 1983; Frymoyer et al., 1983; Magora & Taustein, 1969; Svensson & Andersson, 1983). Overuse of spinal structures may result in muscular or ligamentous strain, end-plate fracture, torsional stress and inflammation of the facet joints, or multilevel degenerative disc disease (Frymoyer & Howe, 1984). In spite of our long-standing awareness of low back pain as a continuing legacy of human uprightness, the incidence and prevalence of the disorder have shown no decline in industrialized society (Nachemson, 1983). Each year, 2 to 3% of the work force will experience lost time due to LBP (Kelsey & White, 1980). The actual incidence of the disorder is much higher than recorded, in part from the fact that many people accept working with back pain: LBP is not included in company health statistics when work is not missed (Biering-Sorensen, 1983; Carey & Hadler, 1986; Frymoyer & Howe, 1984; Frymoyer et al., 1983; Scheer, 1991b; Svensson & Andersson, 1983).

For upper extremity work, pathomechanical risk factors for overuse include repetition of movement; sustained awkward postures, particularly with the wrist; forcefully held objects or tools; mechanical stress; vibration exposure; and low temperatures (Armstrong & Silverstein, 1987; Joseph, 1989; Mital, 1991). Examples of cumulative trauma disorders from upper extremity work include carpal tunnel syndrome, tendonitis and tendon sheath inflammation, finger and wrist joint arthritis, and epicondylitis ("tennis elbow") (Joseph, 1989). Previous uncertainty by the lay public as to how workplace activities might cause these conditions has been replaced in recent days by considerably increased awareness on the part of many workers about the potential for workplace overuse syndromes (Drewczynski, 1986).

CAUSALITY AND WORKERS' COMPENSATION INSURANCE

Physicians in training do not generally learn to worry about insurance difficulties. In the resolution of work injury cases, our American system of workers' compensation insurance has evolved into a complex network of perplexing legalities. The original intent of this system's developers was to provide individuals disabled by work-related conditions with replacement income as well as expenses for medical care to "cure and relieve the effects of injury" (Berkowitz & Berkowitz, 1991). Each state in the U.S., and each Canadian province, has its own set of laws governing these payments. Federal laws cover civilian employees, longshoremen, railroad workers, and coal miners as well (Rothstein, 1990).

The laws established that, in exchange for a guaranteed financial arrangement, usually two-thirds of a worker's pre-disability wages (Richman, 1982), the worker will not hold the employer at fault for the injury; neither can the employer accuse the worker of contributory negligence (Hadler, 1984; Rothstein, 1990). In actuality, there are a few instances when the employee retains the right to sue, as in a wanton act of the employer (Blankenship v. Cincinnati Milacron Chemicals, Inc., 1982); or when a disease results from the worker's use, in his job, of a defective product marketed by the employer (Birnbaum & Wrubel, 1982). Physicians who deal with workers must be intimately aware of the intricacies of this insurance in their particular jurisdictions. With each relocation to a new state or province, physicians must become familiar with a new set of policies.

The question of causality, or work-relatedness of an injury or disease claim, is often the first one posed to the physician in order to establish which insurance — workers' compensation or personal health — will cover evaluation and treatment (Scheer, 1991a). So long as the worker can identify that the injury or disease arises out of and in the course of employment, workers' compensation insurance is in effect. The latter is more favorable for the worker than personal health coverage which compensates for medical costs but not wages. The worker need only prove this work association for coverage through workers' compensation. Frequently, the particular exposure is not observed by another worker, and there is no one to attest to a worker's assertion of a work association. As a result, the occupational or family physician may be put in the middle of this dispute.

By providing less than the full salary, the wage replacement with workers' compensation was theoretically meant to be a less than adequate incentive to remain out of work (Richman, 1982). A disincentive to return to work does exist, however, since workers' compensation benefits are not taxable. For a number of reasons, the workers' compensation system has become increasingly litigious in direct proportion to the period of time a worker remains out of work (Berkowitz & Berkowitz, 1991; Leavitt, Johnston, & Beyer, 1971). Therefore, the role that physicians involved in occupational assessment can play in this process, and it is a crucial one, is to advocate for expeditious implementation of a therapeutic program of work-directed rehabilitation care. The program should occur before the worker loses the desire to work, the inevitable result of internalized feelings of disability and a need to maintain benefits.

Interestingly enough, there is some evidence that even the time for healing is tied to work causality. Sander and Meyers (1986) found that railroad workers who had back injuries on the job took over twice as long to recover compared to those with substantially the same injury while off work. The authors related the difference in healing time to the far more satisfying financial support obtained by workers who could implicate the workplace. Hester (1990) listed a number of additional disincentives to work return which are tied to the entire disability support system for injured workers.

It might seem prudent to combine mandated rehabilitation programs with the workers' compensation system. Unfortunately, for many states, rehabilitation is not inherently a part of the statutes requiring payment of insurance benefits (Berkowitz & Berkowitz, 1991). In the 1980s, some states added provisions for rehabilitation evaluations at 60 to 120 days post-injury, and a few have provided for mandatory rehabilitation. In general, there has been a state-by-state retreat, however, from requiring rehabilitation as part of workers' compensation benefits. Some legislators may have had difficulties in justifying the added expense without proven efficacy (Berkowitz & Berkowitz, 1991). By the time a few months have passed following a work injury, the chances of ever returning the worker to the job may have lessened to the extent that it is no longer cost-effective to rehabilitate (McGill, 1968; Nachemson, 1983).

All of these factors related to causality and workers' compensation make for great difficulty, particularly with inexperienced physicians. Welter (1988) suggests that the evaluating physician ask the following questions in determining work-relatedness:

1. Are the symptoms consistent with the diagnosis?
2. Are the signs consistent with the diagnosis?
3. Is the temporal relationship of exposure and disease clear?
4. Do fellow workers with similar exposure have similar problems?
5. Is workplace monitoring data available and indicative of suspected exposure?
6. Is the condition biologically plausible and confirmed?
7. Is there a lack of nonoccupational exposure to the toxic agent?

Whenever there is doubt as to causality, a situation which may delay start of treatment, an adversarial situation may develop during which the worker may seek legal representation. The longer the disagreement lasts, the greater is the distrust between worker and employer, and the greater is the worker's investment in building a case for work-related disability (Scheer, 1991a). Along with this worker internalization of disability comes decreasing likelihood that he or she will ever work again. McGill (1968) found that patients out of work for low back pain more than six months had only a 50% chance of working again. After two years of work absence, the chance that the back-injured worker would return were almost zero.

Another complexity relating to causality is the courts' establishment of legal precedence for the work-relatedness of cardiac illness and psychologic stress (Battista v. Chrysler, 1986). Physicians could thus find themselves in a position to decide on the likelihood that a work connection can be made to pathophysiologic processes whose true etiologies are unclear.

FURTHER DEFINITION OF THE PHYSICIAN'S ROLE

There are several ways a physician may participate in determining work capacity. In some such situations the assessment can be performed by the worker's own private physician. At other times, however, the typical physician-patient relationship does not exist, as when a company hires its own medical personnel. The company physician or nurse is frequently perceived by the worker as a representative of management, a situation which creates an apparent conflict of interest (Rothstein, 1984). Recognizing the inherent difficulties of physicians making decisions in the best interests of both workers and employers, the American Occupational Medicine Association (1976) developed an extensive code of ethics. The code "accords the highest priority to the health and safety of the individual in the workplace" and encourages occupational physicians to avoid allowing medical judgements to be influenced by conflict.

Yet conflict is inherent to the practice of occupational medicine. According highest priority to the worker's health may at times seem burdensome to the patient/worker who expects quicker return to work. Withholding information from an employer at the express wishes of a patient may have a detrimental impact on the patient's or co-workers' health, creating an ethical dilemma for the occupational physician (Welter, 1988). Finally, conflict occurs when a physician reports health risks identified in a work injury case to the company management. Risks associated with particular job exposures could result in a number of sequelae: retribution directed at the employee (whistle-blower effect); loss of occupational referrals from the company; and plant closure or strike.

A common situation in which the physician-patient relationship is altered involves the seeking of expert opinions. The circumstances may follow a disagreement regarding the returning worker's fitness to perform the job, pitting the private physician against the company physician. Alternatively, there may be a state mandate to require an independent examination of any injured workers not able to return to work after a delimited recovery period, often 60, 90, or 120 days (Bureau of Workers' Compensation, 1991). In any such involvement, when a worker is required by legal or administrative policy to be evaluated by an impartial physician, the atmosphere of the evaluation may at times be awkward and uncomfortable. The feeling may translate into the worker's distrust of the physician's motives and opinions. Whether made by family physicians or company representatives, by generalists or specialists, judgments regarding a worker's capacity have not always been made using objective criteria (Brewerton & Daniel, 1971; Kuh & Hanman, 1944). Lumbar spine X-rays have been used, for example, to screen out workers from employment. The practice has been singled out as unreasonable; X-rays are not a valid indicator of future back pain since findings are rarely of prognostic value (American College of Radiology, 1973). Moreover, the Americans with Disabilities Act (ADA, 1990), prohibits such practices among most employers. Even if a positive finding on an X-ray indicates a high likelihood of future medical difficulties, the finding cannot be used to screen out the worker who can physically perform the essential tasks of the job in question.

When fitness to work is simply a medical question, most physicians can provide broad medical guidelines for work readiness or will know when to call in a medical specialist who can make the purely medical decision. Fitness to work is often not simply a medical matter, however, particularly for a very demanding job or after a prolonged rehabilitation. Occupationally involved physicians must, therefore, be aware of the need to compare functional capacity of a prospective worker to details of required job duties. The old practice of making a decision about work capacity merely on the basis of a physical examination and laboratory studies will often be insufficient for a physically or otherwise demanding job (Hanman, 1958).

Functional capacity testing based on an accurate job description generally involves direct observation of the prospective worker performing the tasks actually required at the job site (see Fig. 1). The testing is overseen by one or more allied

Functional Capacity/Job Requirement Compatibility Analysis
For Journeyman Ironworker (Recovering)

Client Name: _____

Job Requirement	Current Level of Physical Capacities	Compatibility	Intervention and Recommendations
Strength	**Strength**	**Strength**	**Strength**

Very heavy work. Client is required to occasionally lift 100 lbs. from the floor, 50 lbs. from waist or above; frequently to push and pull up to 150 lbs.; frequently carry up to 50 lbs.	Floor to Waist
	  occasional 93 lbs.
	  frequent 63 lbs.
	  constant 32 lbs.
		Moderate	Client has 93 lbs. maximum lift from floor to waist. For objects that weigh more than 93 lbs he will have to use a mechanical device or have assistance from another employee. I believe his strength could improve to the point where he could lift up to 150 lbs. if his employer would allow him to gradually build up to that level. I believe he would benefit from further education on home program for his back strength and abdominal strength. He would also benefit from further education on body mechanics.

	Waist to Shoulder
	  occasional 70 lbs.
	  frequent 45 lbs.
	  constant 30 lbs.
		Moderate	

	Shoulders or Overhead
	  occasional 45 lbs.
	  frequent 25 lbs.
	  constant 15 lbs.
		Moderate	

	Carry
	  2 hand 75 lbs.
	  right or left hand 45 lbs.		

	Push or Pull Sled 150 lbs.		

Figure 1. Functional Capacity/Job Requirement Compatibility Analysis *(continued on next page)*

Job Requirement	Current Level of Physical Capacities	Compatibility	Intervention and Recommendations
Balance	Balance	Balance	Balance
He has to maintain his balance in awkward positions on the ground and in the air on 4" beams.	He has satisfactory balance when he has a normal or widened base of support. However, his balance is impaired moderately when he has a decreased base of support.	Satisfactory on the ground except with a narrow base of support or on 4" beams in the air.	The deficit will prevent the client from working on small beams in the air. I believe he has sufficient balance to work on the ground.
Frequently stoops, kneels, and crouches	Client is able to perform these activities safely on a stable surface.	High	Client has no limitations with stooping, crouching, crawling, or kneeling.
Occasionally crawls	Client is able to crawl normally	High	
Climbing	Climbing	Climbing	Climbing
Occasionally he ascends and descends ladders, stairs, and scaffolding.	He was able to ascend and descend 100 steps safely; he could safely climb a scaffold or ladder if he had access for good upper extremity support.	Moderate	He requires a ladder or scaffold that provides good upper extremity and lower extremity support. I do not believe he would be safe climbing a beam.

Figure 1. Functional Capacity/Job Requirement Compatibility Analysis *(continued on next page)*

Job Requirement	Current Level of Physical Capacities	Compatibility	Intervention and Recommendations
Reaching	Reaching	Reaching	Reaching
Extending hands and arms in all directions is required.	Normal	High	No limitations with reaching.
Handling	Handling	Handling	Handling
He is required to seize, hold and grasp various hand tools and welding equipment.	Handgrip and finger strength is sufficient to perform his job. He appears to have no limitation in finger coordination.	High	No intervention needed.

Summary: The client has satisfactory physical capacity to substantially perform the job tasks. However, climbing onto beans above ground would be ill-advised. The client will need some additional body mechanics instruction and a home strengthening program.

Figure 1. Functional Capacity/Job Requirement Compatibility Analysis

health specialists. It should be safe, repeatable between testers, valid and job-relevant (Wickstrom, 1990). The physician involved in occupational assessment needs to know when to refer for functional testing.

Job-specific awareness is not only the province of the treating therapists who perform functional testing of workers. Physicians practicing occupational medicine, whether as a full-time profession or as a result of primary physician relationships with patients, can and should learn the benefits of job-site visitation also (Rosenstock, 1981; Welter, 1988). It can be argued, in fact, that the physician cannot fully appreciate the nature of work-injury relationships and the return-to-work goal of a worker-patient without a visualization of the workplace.

CIRCUMSTANCES OF WORK-RELATED DECISIONS BY PHYSICIANS

There are a variety of ways physicians have been involved in decisions about medical fitness to work (Scheer, 1991a), including (1) pre-employment examinations; (2) post-injury or -illness return-to-work letter; (3) evaluation after lengthier treatment; (4) medical surveillance screening; (5) impairment rating; (6) Social Security disability evaluation; (7) impartial medical evaluation; and (8) medical testimony. These processes are described in the next section.

PRE-EMPLOYMENT EXAMINATION

Many companies have historically required some form of pre-employment assessment, usually performed by the work candidate's primary (family) physician. Previous knowledge of the work candidate's history had always expedited this process. The ADA (1990) has now disallowed pre-employment inquiry and screening physical exams. It is now considered discriminatory to <u>not</u> hire an individual with a particular disease or disability merely out of fear that the worker is at increased risk to put forward an injury claim. However, the law does allow incorporation of a post-job offer, pre-placement functional assessment which can include specific, job-relevant activities. The exam cannot be used selectively on risky prospective workers, but must be universally utilized. This functional capacity testing is now required on an increasing basis, and will become increasingly rigorous for essential job tasks as a result of the ADA. Use of functional testing will help to appropriately match workers with jobs they can physically perform. If functional testing is not performed, workers may initially tolerate overburdening job hazards with confidence that workers' compensation will eventually cover any injury incurred (Armstrong & Silverstein, 1987).

RETURN-TO-WORK LETTER AFTER SHORT-LIVED INJURY/ILLNESS

Patients and employers may commonly call upon physicians to substantiate a worker's ability to return to work after a self-limited disease or minor injury. Generally, these determinations require only a physical examination supplemented by laboratory testing.

EVALUATION AFTER LENGTHIER TREATMENT

The commitment of the workers' compensation carrier is to medically remedy the worker to the point of "maximum medical improvement": the best health status after treatment that can be expected with regard to the work injury (Berkowitz & Berkowitz, 1991). The worker is not entitled to care for medical problems which existed prior to the work-related condition and bear no relation to it. If the worker is left with some permanent impairment, a cash benefit may be settled upon as partial compensation (Berkowitz & Berkowitz, 1991).

The workers' compensation system establishes, in effect, that treatment after a work injury should be job-relevant. Whether the therapeutic program is conservative or surgical, acute or requiring a comprehensive multidisciplinary program over many weeks or months, the treatment should ideally be work-directed. When treatment of a more substantial nature is necessary, proper timing for safe work return is at times a difficult decision, and may require functional capacity assessment (Scheer, 1991a; Wickstrom, 1990). Assessment of the worker may become difficult when psychosocial or vocational variables complicate the medical recovery. These variables will most likely overwhelm the medical recovery process when delays in making a definitive diagnosis, worker/employer disagreements about work-related causality, or lag time in insurance processing or treatment implementation have occurred (Leavitt et al., 1971) or (see Table 1).

The physician plays a crucial role in implementing appropriate treatment in a timely fashion. Whenever recovery appears to be delayed, the attentive physician should bear the responsibility of either expediting a search for medical solutions or seeking a case manager (from the involved company or private sources) to address and overcome potential vocational and psychosocial difficulties. This process of case facilitation is a major component of disability management, described elsewhere in this book.

In work-related injury supported by workers' compensation insurance, it is not always necessary for a healing worker to have complete recovery before returning to work so long as a determination that the worker can perform the essential job duties has been made (Gardner, 1991). This fact is not always understood by the worker.

MEDICAL SURVEILLANCE SCREENING AND EXAMINATION

Medical surveillance screening is a proactive process of injury or disease prevention in which a medically trained person observes and analyzes a job in an attempt to eliminate medical hazards which are the proverbial "accidents waiting to hap-

Table 1
Factors Associated With Early Return To Work After Industrial Injury

	ENABLERS	CONFOUNDERS
Worker	Strong work ethic; acute need of $; sufficient functional capacity for job demands	Bad pathology; previous injury history; prevailing psychosocial issues; drug dependence
Insurance	Seen as facilitating; work comp doesn't apply	Slow work comp start-up; lag in Rx authorization
Physician	Communicative; advocating; competent; confidence-restoring	RTW urged too soon (or late); unempathic; proposes unnecessary treatment
Treatment	Expeditiously started; including necessary education; work-directed	No exercise; job functions not addressed
Employer-Union	Showing concern; advocating; flexible	Indifferent; maintains job unchanged; demands full-duty return immediately
Job site	Adapted easily, enticing; allowing job autonomy	No light-duty; job trauma expected to continue; supervisor conflict maintained
Attorney	Job discrimination averted	Litigation

pen." By determining potentially harmful effects within the work environment, whether acute or chronic, the physician can greatly contribute to the well-being of both worker and employer (Welter, 1988). For the worker, there is the realization that the physician cared enough to make the extra effort and studied the work sufficiently to know whether risk factors for disease or injury truly existed. The employer, too, is often satisfied to know that the physician cares about the effects on employees of the work environment. On occasion, the employer may be threatened by the intrusion of a physician who may make a costly discovery, another source of conflict for the occupationally involved physician.

IMPAIRMENT RATING

A legalistic system was devised over 20 years ago to compensate workers for anatomic impairment after a work injury or disease. In the U.S., the most commonly used system is that described in the *Guides to the Evaluation of Permanent Impairment* produced by the American Medical Association (AMA) specialty panels (1984). The book contains more than 200 charts and graphs, and was developed to assist physicians in enumerating the extent of anatomic impairment as a percentage of the whole body. Amputation of a right arm, for example, is listed as a 60% impairment; a lumbar dissectomy and fusion after disc herniation is equivalent to a 5% of whole body impairment (AMA, 1984). The system can be used to assist a person in receiving a cash settlement after a permanent injury, but it has been subject to abuse.

Physicians are warned in the preface of the text to avoid allowing decisions of impairment to be influenced by consideration of education, employment opportunity, or psychosocial factors. Physician behavior is known to be highly variable, however, in making impairment decisions (Brand & Lehman, 1983; Gloss & Wardle, 1982). An administrative decision over the extent of impairment will often be an average of two or more physicians' ratings. Depending on the extent to which employment variables and other individual biases are included by the physician doing the evaluation, a wide variety of numerical calculations can be seen in the same patient (Workers' Compensation Research Institute, 1987).

It is important for physicians asked to make impairment ratings to be aware that the system is not an evaluation of employability or vocational capacity (Scheer, 1991a). However, the results of ratings are used to compensate a worker for altered ability to work. It would seem that a flaw in this system awards benefits on the basis of anatomic alteration rather than functional incapacity.

SOCIAL SECURITY DISABILITY EVALUATION

A trust fund was established by the Social Security Administration in 1954 to compensate persons who become unable to work. To be eligible a person must a) have a severe disability which has lasted or is expected to last for at least a year or result in death; and b) have worked and paid a tax into the system for a required period (Bruyere & Shrey, 1991). Breakdown of the roughly 400,000 new SSDI recipients in 1984 is indicated in Table 2.

The steps of the application and appeals process are complicated and burdensome. Most applicants can ask their personal physicians to submit medical information from office records and discharge summaries in support of applications. In

Table 2
Distribution Of Major Diagnostic Groups Among New SSDI Beneficiaries In 1981 And 1984

Diagnostic Group	Percentage 1984
Circulatory System Disorders	19.8
Mental Disorders	17.9
Neoplasms	16.5
Musculoskeletal System Disorders	12.8
Nervous System and Sense Organs Disorders	7.9
Respiratory System Disorders	5.3
Other	19.8
Total	100.0

Source: Derived from the Social Security Bulletin, Annual Statistical Supplements, 1983 and 1986, U. S. Government Printing Office, Washington, DC.

about one-third of the cases, a consultative examination is done by an independent physician at the request of Social Security (Carey & Hadler, 1986). Physicians are asked to evaluate history, physical findings, test results, and severity indicators. The employability and degree of disability are not to be considered or mentioned in the report. The physician is then supposed to identify whether or not an applicant meets the criteria of impairment described in the Disability Evaluation under Social Security handbook, a listing of tables for the physician (U.S. Department of Health Education & Welfare, 1979).

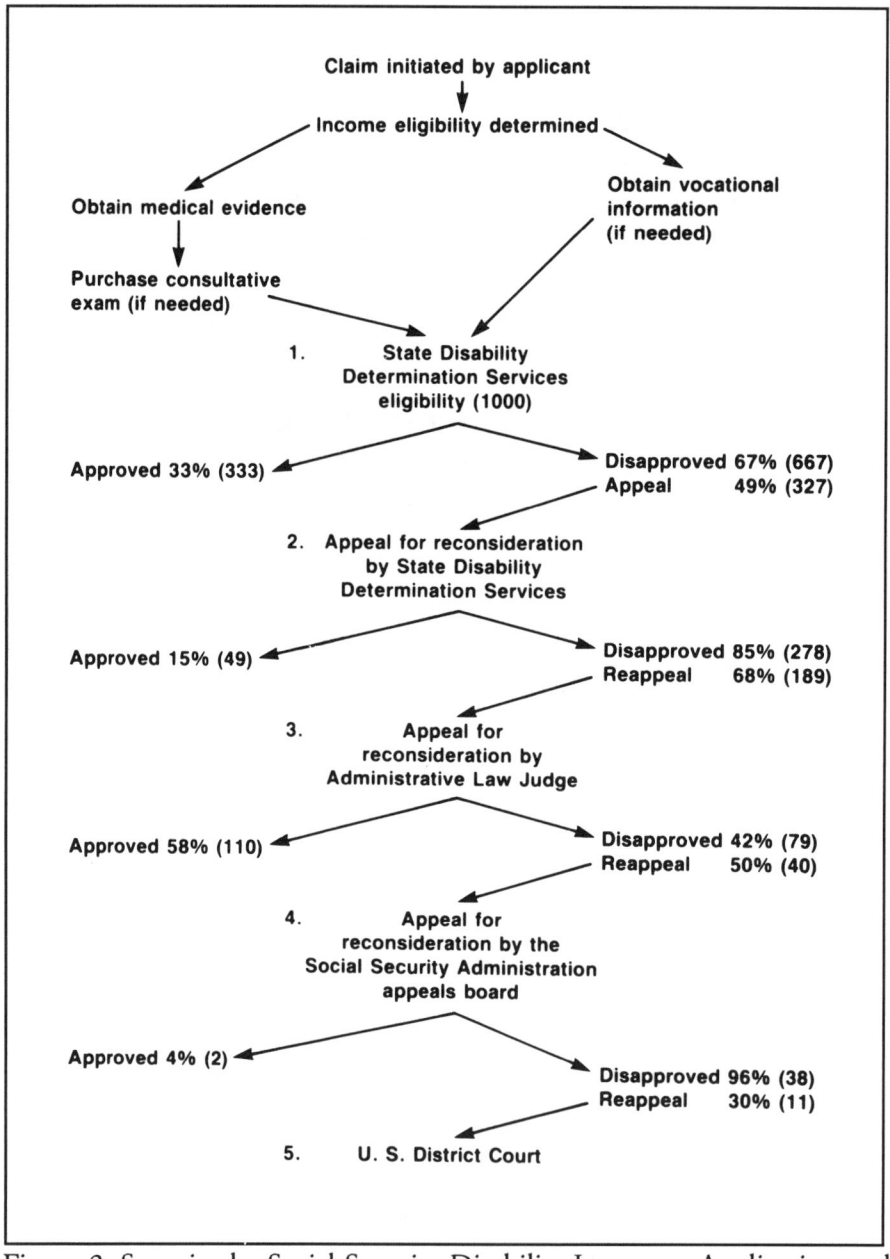

Figure 2. Steps in the Social Security Disability Insurance Application and Appeals Process. A total of 495 of 1,000 applications (49.5%) are approved. Number in parentheses correspond to 1,000 initial applicants.

Reproduced, with permission, from T. S. Carey & N. M. Hadler, The Role of the Primary Physician in Disability Determination for Social Security Insurance and Workers' Compensation, Annals of Internal Medicine. 1986; 104:706-710.

After information is submitted in support of the applicant, a physician and administrator employed by the state's disability determinations agency will make the initial determination (Carey & Hadler, 1986). As shown in Figure 2, a number of possible pathways can then be taken. Ultimately, approximately one-half of those who apply will be awarded Social Security Disability insurance benefits.

During the waiting period, while attempting to prove the extent of disability, persons with disabilities may lose any motivation for recovery and avoid vocational rehabilitation for fear it will affect the application. In actuality, the original legislation for SSDI was supposed to have included vocational rehabilitation as a component (Berkowitz, 1985). Unfortunately, few SSDI beneficiaries ever return to work again: less than 1% of insurance beneficiaries returned in spite of at least 10 to 15% of beneficiaries who demonstrated the potential to work (General Accounting Office, 1987). Even if initially refused the insurance, the lengthy process of applying, lasting a minimum of five and more often 12 months, inevitably scars the applicant with internalized disability (Hester, 1990).

IMPARTIAL (OR INDEPENDENT) MEDICAL EVALUATIONS

Occasionally, a specializing physician will be asked to perform an Independent Medical Evaluation (IME). Such a report is generally a formal and quite thorough assessment of a variety of issues relating to a disability or impairment. The IME is often an independent opinion sought to settle a dispute between physicians, employer and patient, the workers' compensation system and patient, or opposing attorneys. The independent physician will be asked to review one or more physicians' medical records, test results, operative reports, the company records, therapy services, and job description. Such examinations frequently last much longer than the usual doctor visit time, and IME reports may be quite lengthy. Because of their role in legal disputes, IMEs have become a lucrative source of revenue for some physicians (Scheer, 1991a).

While an IME may be used for a number of medicolegal issues, one of the most common is in the situation of a work-related injury. When an injured worker, cared for by a private physician, continues to require treatment beyond what the company physician considers is reasonable, the employer or the worker's attorney may call for an IME to decide if further treatment is truly indicated. The state of Ohio, which manages its own workers' compensation system, has recently instituted a system of mandatory IMEs to be performed by board-certified physicians on any injured workers still out of work after 90 days. To the usual fee for these IMEs ($280), an additional $50 is awarded to physicians who elect to contact the treating physician for questions about diagnosis, causality, and treatment (Bureau of Workers' Compensation, 1991). It has been shown that the physician "ombudsman" can cut down work injury costs by continually challenging unnecessary procedures and by expediting the flow of services (Wiesel, Feffer, & Rosthman, 1984).

The physician may be asked to consider causality questions, since these are at times a source of dispute. It is increasingly common to hear of the more insidious types of work injury, such as carpal tunnel syndrome and other cumulative trauma disorders, or stress disorders, being implicated in work injuries (Armstrong & Silverstein, 1987; Bonfiglio & Bonfiglio, 1992; Silverstein et al., 1986). There may be difficulty in attributing an ongoing medical problem to the workplace. An aging worker may have a number of medical conditions to distinguish between (comorbidity), promoting questions of whether work is causal in a particular symptomatology (Bonfiglio & Bonfiglio, 1992). In all such cases, an IME may be requested of an independent expert.

Figure 3 is a list of typical questions commonly posed for expert physicians who perform IMEs. The helpfulness of the exam is in direct proportion to the degree of specificity indicated by the requesting party.

MEDICAL TESTIMONY

Physicians are rarely prepared in medical school, to the extent necessary, for participation in legal work. The workers' compensation system continues to be litigious, and so long as it is, physicians who assist workers will be asked to testify sooner or later. Medical testimony can be given in or outside the courtroom. Be-

---

Ten Questions Commonly Posed To The Physician Performing an IME

1. What is the condition and the extent of severity?
2. What is the cause of that condition?
3. Have the necessary tests been performed?
4. Is treatment being rendered appropriately?
5. Might additional recommendations improve the outcome or hasten recovery?
6. Has maximum medical improvement (MMI) been reached?
7. Can the worker return to the former job, and if so, how soon?
8. Will there be residual disability, and if so, to what extent?
9. What is the permanent impairment rating, if any?
10. What activity and work limitations are recommended?

Source: Physician' Group to the Independent Medical Examination; Ohio Bureau of Workers' Compensation; Medical Services Division; 1990.

Figure 3. Ten Questions Commonly Posed To The Physician Performing An IME

cause of the difficulty of accommodating busy schedules, a physician will frequently be asked to provide formal testimony in a deposition performed in the doctor's or attorney's office. Preparation for testimony is accomplished by thoroughly reviewing the available case records. All documents prepared by the physician, or those utilized by the physician in formulating opinions are admissible evidence for either side to examine. A particular focus of opposing counsel will clearly be the areas of disagreements in the various reports of physicians and treatment sites.

One of the most crucial elements to understand in legal treatment of a medical issue is that the written word is sacred. "The best physician strategy for dealing with workers' compensation testimony is to provide adequate ongoing patient medical record documentation, thereby significantly reducing the need for testimony" (Bonfiglio & Bonfiglio, 1992). Physicians asked to render medical testimony will generally have examined the injured worker, but the examination may have been performed many months or years before testimony. Thus, reports should be thorough so as to easily call to mind the many facts in consideration. Reports should be inclusive of all medical opinions generated and treatments attempted. The interjecting of unsubstantiated claims and inflammatory language can be detrimental to the credibility of the reporter and is an obvious target for the attorney.

The legal concept of the phrase, "within a reasonable degree of medical probability" to establish a proximate and direct cause for injury is a tricky concept for the medical mind. When the physician's response is that the work incident "could have been," "might have been," or "possibly was" the cause of injury, the response is of no legal value for counsel. The physician will inevitably be pushed for a more unequivocal answer (Johnston, 1992). Johnston (1992) cites six recommendations for the physician's survival in a legal world:

1. Always know your file.
    The physician must be aware of material found not only in the patient's file but also in relevant literature written by leading experts in the field (typical practice), including the physician's own professional writing in the medical area.

2. Listen to the question: answer only the question asked.

3. Always elaborate on the foundational questions.
    Foundational questions go to the heart of a case. These issues must be consistently and clearly stated. Obviously, preparation and proper instruction by an attorney will lead the physician to understand what the crucial issues are.

4. Always concede the weak points.
    It is best to be completely frank in owning up to what cannot be known.

5. Never concede foundational points.
    Unless new evidence presents itself to completely reverse the medical opinion, the physician should attempt to not back down on the crucial issues.

6. Always read what you write.

EFFICACY OF A RETURN-TO-WORK OUTCOME

It is well beyond the scope of this chapter to describe the proper treatment for the many types of work injury. There is, however, one important and timely principle relating to treatment which bears mentioning here. The extent to which an employer participates in the treatment recommendations, including the actual rehabilitation program, can make a great difference in the return-to-work outcome (Bruyere & Shrey, 1991; Wiesel et al., 1984; Yelin, Henke, & Epstein, 1986). On-site work return transition programs, as discussed elsewhere in the book, are a potent way for employers to not only show their eagerness to return the worker to the job site, but also to retain some control in the rehabilitation activities and thus effect a treatment result mutually favorable to the employer and the worker. During the program, any needs to utilize ergonomic solutions should be addressed. The injured worker is receiving the nurturing support of co-workers, and feeling the work environment closely. For these on-site transition programs to work, there must have been a previous agreement with any involved union organizations.

The origin of this phenomenon of employer involvement effecting a positive return-to-work outcome is known as "occupational bonding" (Shrey, 1992), and should ideally have pre-dated the work injury. Occupational bonding is a concept physicians can readily appreciate: that a previously established and mutually satisfying relationship had existed between worker and employer will undoubtedly bolster the chance of work return after a work-related injury or illness. Both employers and workers benefit when occupational bonding is strong, as for example when the employer actively protects the employability of the worker after injury, and the worker responds positively by attempting to return to work as expeditiously as possible (Shrey, 1992). Such a relationship must be nurtured, however, and can be threatened at just the time when it should be sustained if the employer does not continue to show concern for the injured worker. To sustain the relationship, a balance must be maintained between the expectations of workers and the intentions of employers (Shrey & Breslin, 1992).

There is a limit as to how far employers will go with occupational bonding. A 1988 study by Hester, Planek, & Decelles, revealed that 77% of U.S. employers did not believe that every employee who became disabled should be guaranteed a job. Some American employers may not feel a moral obligation to support disabled workers who will become, in their perception, a financial burden. That feeling has become less relevant, however, as awareness of the Americans with Disabilities Act (1990) Title I, (affecting employment practices) is spread. In this legislation, the disabled employee who can still perform the essential functions of the job should be accommodated by the employer for nonessential aspects of the job so long as to do so will not pose an economic hardship for the company. The legislation does not define what "financial hardship" means, which will no doubt be determined by case-made law on this subject (McMahon & Shrey, 1992).

The physician must understand that the longer a worker remains out of work due to a work-related injury, the greater the likelihood that a relationship with the employer will be jeopardized. The need for prompt attention to diagnosis and treatment, with a functional approach that ensures return to work as one of the treatment goals, is an important concept for physicians to grasp. Once occupational bonding is diminished, it becomes increasingly difficult for the worker to ever view the employer with trust.

The development of unions has led to a need for physicians to understand both their important contributions and their limitations toward the settlement of worker injury disputes. Historically, organized labor has been responsible for establishing many on-the-job rights, including health, safety, and job retention rights, for previously unprotected workers (Akabas, 1986). In the U.S., 12.6% of the labor force belongs to labor organizations. In situations of union involvement, its representation may give the worker confidence. A sense of belonging generally makes the worker feel less insignificant facing the employer. However, this notion is at times naive, since organized labor is often relatively uninvolved with injured workers (Bruyere & Shrey, 1991). The time when this involvement materializes may be closer to the planned return to work. At this point, the union may facilitate this process, as in a situation where the steward allows a light-duty return to compensate for the worker's slow recovery. But the labor union may also pose an obstacle to early return, as in a situation where restrictive language has been negotiated into the collective bargaining agreements between labor and management. In this case, seniority rights might not allow an easier job to go to a less senior, recovering worker (Bruyere & Shrey, 1991).

Labor-management conflict can be an obstacle to securing the injured worker's expeditious return to work. There is a perception that such conflicts often exist. According to a survey by Hester et al., (1988), 42% of employers believed that most union contracts make it impossible to shift job assignments. Union leadership may harbor suspicions of poor motivation among the plant management as well. A failure to involve both parties in the rehabilitation plan may often result in unnecessary delay of work return (Bruyere & Shrey, 1991). The Long Island Railroad reformed its poor record of work return in 1986 into a highly successful program in 1987 merely by instituting more flexible restricted duty placements of recovering workers, a policy which labor and management negotiated through collective bargaining (Cohen, Parrinello, & Kelliher, 1990). Cooperation between General Motors and the United Auto Workers resulted in a highly improved rehabilitation program (Tate et al., 1987).

Job satisfaction is extremely important in determining a worker's post-treatment destination. A study by Yelin et al., (1986) revealed two factors distinguishing arthritic workers who were disabled but still working from those similarly disabled and out of work. The factors were the job desirability and the opportunity to have task choices at the job. It is common to hear chronic pain patients complain about their jobs. It is difficult to know, however, if they became so critical and angry before their work injuries or during the prolonged period of disability internalization after the injury (Leavitt et al., 1972). Physicians involved in evaluation of chronically disabled workers should know to ask them the seemingly naive, open-ended question, "How do you feel about your job?" during the history-taking.

Once treatment, of whatever type, has been administered, the directing physician must utilize a knowledge of prognosis to advise the worker on future precautions and speed of return to maximum capacity. This advice may, with permission of the worker, be passed on to the employer. Because there are few documented guiding principles known to assist the physician in determining the speed of reentry (Carey & Hadler, 1986), it will often be necessary to use judgment and an awareness of the extent to which the employer or union can be flexible. The reader is again referred to Table 1 for some of the enabling and confounding factors affecting the rapidity of return to capacity.

CASE STUDY

The following case study is useful in demonstrating some of the many issues encountered by physicians involved in work injury resolution:

J.M. is a 31-year-old construction worker who sustained an apparent low back injury at work, his fourth claim in the three years he has worked for Ready Made Homes. The company, which had recently become self-insured for workers' compensation, is a large construction company designing pre-fab, low-cost two-level homes in the New England area.

As he had explained to his family doctor three days later, after a period of bedrest with only slight improvement, he had noted back pain immediately after easing a piece of dry-wall to the ground, and because the pain was sharp and associated with referral into his right leg, he reported it to the foreman and came home. He noted to his physician that this foreman had insisted he carry the dry-wall section by himself across an apparently slippery construction site since a co-worker was unavailable at that moment. J.M. further mentioned that he did not get along particularly well with this foreman under whom he had twice before had work-related injuries. On the last episode, he had missed a step while bringing tools to the foreman, and the resultant fall had led to a lumbar strain with a subsequent four-month work absence. J.M. had been back at work six months since that incident.

The family physician was familiar with this history. J.M. was a high school graduate with two years of apprenticeship to learn carpentry and electronics. He had a wife and two small children, and owned his own home. There was a history of smoking a pack a day for 14 years, and he was an occasional beer drinker. There were no other health problems.

On examination, J.M. was reasonably mobile and of essentially normal strength, but did demonstrate a diminished right Achilles reflex and mildly diminished pinprick sensation on the bottom of the foot, both new findings. His straight-kneed hip flexion (straight-leg-raising) on the right was half what it was on the left (40° compared to 80°). The physician explained the possibility of a nerve root injury, recommended anti-inflammatory and muscle relaxant medications, and suggested one more week of rest with slow resumption of household activity.

By the next week, J.M. reported that his back pain and leg referral were unchanged. However, he had been active, in fact quite a bit more active than the physician had hoped: he had finished the paneling of a basement family room and admitted doing some light yard work. His clothes bore the distinct odor of freshly cut grass. The physician renewed his request for prudence in limiting activity and decided to refer J.M. for physical therapy to instruct him in body mechanics and a more judicious exercise program.

Having reported the work injury claim to his employer on the day of the last visit, J.M. had gotten no subsequent response. Now the physician's billing clerk reported that J.M.'s employer had spoken to her and refused to accept the work-relatedness of the back injury since J.M. had been seen by the foreman hobbling out of his car early on the day of the alleged back injury. The employer advised the billing clerk that J.M. obviously had already hurt himself prior to work, and should use his personal health insurance for physician and allied health needs. The billing clerk informed J.M., causing immediate anger and defiance. He did not carry personal health coverage, this being a financial burden he felt the need to forego.

J.M.'s attorney fought the contested claim for almost four months before the employer was finally forced to accept it as a work-related injury. The back pay through workers' compensation just barely saved J.M.'s mortgage foreclosure, although his wife had two weeks earlier taken a part-time job to help make ends meet. Four weeks of physical therapy were not helpful, being a very passive approach. The family physician referred J.M. to a local orthopedist, who tried a course of three epidural steroid injections over three weeks, to no avail.

By this time, J.M. was still showing hypesthesia and positive straight-leg-raising limitation, moderate general weakness, and a very depressed affect had replaced his usually confident nature. Because of J.M.'s pain, the orthopedist prescribed a narcotic pain reliever, giving him brief periods of pain relief. In the entire period, J.M. had not once heard from his employer except through his attorney.

The family physician felt an expert in chronic pain was needed, and referred him to a physiatrist. An electrophysiologic study (EMG) performed by the physiatrist showed continuation of the nerve root impingement, but no acute process was identified. The physiatrist's recommendation for a chronic pain inpatient program was denied by the employer, who asked for his own IME by an independent orthopedist. After examination, the latter physician felt that all findings except the pinprick change could be explained by deconditioning, and suggested that maximum medical improvement had been reached. He rated J.M. as having a 2% of whole body impairment. J.M.'s attorney referred him to still another physician for a second IME to determine the extent of impairment. The results of this second assessment, rating J.M. at 20% of whole body impairment, were reassuring to J.M. that he was indeed quite disabled. For unrelated reasons, Ready Made Homes now went bankrupt; no settlement for damages could be awarded to J.M.

At this point, 19 months after the current back pain had begun, J.M. was separated from his family. He was addicted to codeine, drinking a six-pack of beer virtually every day for anxiety relief. He applied for Social Security disability benefits, was initially turned down and subsequently had the denial overturned at the administrative law judge level when he made a personal appearance with his attorney. He continues to live on SSDI.

This case study exemplifies a number of common problems which are instructive for the physician who handles industrial injury cases. Rehabilitation efforts can be sabotaged by employer-employee relations problems quite commonly (Bruyere & Shrey, 1991). A history of repeated work injuries and prolonged work absence is a bad prognostic sign for similar future occurrences (Andersson, 1981). The passing of time before institution of proper treatment, whether due to delays in case claim acceptance, difference of medical opinion, or otherwise, is often a harbinger of a drawn out case settlement and frequently leads to attorney involvement (Leavitt et al., 1972). Most importantly, physicians must realize that a patient's decision to apply for Social Security disability insurance is a very important one; practically every applicant who goes through the lengthy process to its conclusion will never work again (General Accounting Office, 1987). It is therefore not a temporary state of income restoration in almost all circumstances. Physicians who support their patients in receiving SSDI must be aware, then, of how important the decision to apply is.

CLOSING

The continuing escalation of health care costs, including costs to pay for disability in the workforce, will inevitably force employers to search for cost-cutting measures. A greater involvement of these employers in the process of worker rehabilitation, including their active advocacy in the choosing of workers' physicians, will put an onus of accountability on physicians to provide responsive services as never before. On-site work return transition programs will become increasingly commonplace, and physicians involved in industrial rehabilitation will therefore need a greater knowledge of the workplace. They will need to practice good communication skills with case managers from within the company and from the private sector. Without such interactions, the process of expediting the worker's return to work will be disrupted.

Some companies, particularly the larger ones, have taken on occupational physicians (Rothstein, 1984). Others have purchased the services of physician ombudsmen to facilitate communication with the family doctor. The physician-physician contact may take the form of a simple call to ask about the need for delayed work return or a request to allow the worker to come in for a light duty assignment. On certain occasions, the recommendation to reconsider a surgical referral is made to the family doctor. A simple call indicating that someone else with medical knowledge is concerned about the treatment and follow-up can make a great deal of difference in improving the quality and lowering the cost of care.

Physicians play an extremely important role in the process of assisting injured workers to return to their jobs. They can be "gate openers or gate slammers," as Norman Cousins (1983) has been quoted as saying, in their use of words of encouragement or alternative pessimistic language. The involvement with injured workers should be objective, expeditious, and considerate. Physicians must be ever-mindful that much depends on their approach to those whose very livelihoods are at stake.

REFERENCES

Akabas, S. (1986). Disability management: A long-standing trade union mission with some new initiatives. *Journal of Applied Rehabilitation Counseling, 17*(3), 33-37.

American College of Radiology. (1973). Conference on low-back X-rays in pre-employment physical examinations (Contract NO. HSM-00-72-153). Tucson, AZ: *Proceedings of Meeting, National Institute of Occupational Safety and Health.*

American Medical Association. (1984). Guides to the evaluation of permanent impairment (2nd ed.). Chicago: Author.

Americans with Disabilities Act of 1990. Washington, DC: *U. S. House of Representatives Conference Report 101-596.*

Andersson, G. B. J. (1981). Epidemiologic aspects of low back pain in industry. *Spine, 6,* 53-60.

Armstrong, T. J., & Silverstein, B. A. (1987). Upper extremity pain in the workplace—role of usage in causality. In N. M. Hadler (Ed.), *Clinical concepts in regional musculoskeletal illness* (pp. 333-354). Orlando, FL: Grune & Stratton.

Battista v. Chrysler Corp. (1986). *Super. Court of Delaware, and (1986) Nix v. City Houma, Sup. Court of Louisiana.*

Berkowitz, M. (1985). Government initiatives: Reactor's comments. In R. V. Habeck, D. E. Galvin, W. D. Frey, et al (Eds.), *Economics and equity in employment of people with disabilities* (pp. 132-135). Lansing, MI: Michigan State University, pp. 132-135.

Berkowitz, M., & Berkowitz, E. D. (1991). Rehabilitation in the work injury program. *Rehabilitation Counseling Bulletin, 34,* 182-196.

Biering-Sorensen, F. (1983). A prospective study of LBP in a general population: I. occurrence, recurrence, etiology. *Scandinavian Journal of Rehabilitation Medicine, 15,* 71-79.

Birnbaum, S. L., & Wrubel, B. (1982). California Supreme Court adopts a "manufacturer" liability exception to the exclusive remedy provisions of workers' compensation. *The Forum, 17,* 939-946.

Blankenship v. Cincinnati Milacvon Chemicals, Inc. (1982). *Northeast Reporter, 2nd series, 433,* 572, Ohio.

Bonfiglio, R. P., & Bonfiglio, R. L. (1992). Medical testimony in workers' compensation matters. *Physical Medicine and Rehabilitation Clinics of North America, 3,* 665-676.

Brand, R. A., & Lehman, T. H. (1983). Low-back impairment rating practices of orthopedic surgeons. *Spine, 8,* 75-78.

Brewerton, D. A. & Daniel, J. W. (1971). Factors influencing return to work. *British Medical Journal, 4,* 277-281.

Bruyere, S. M., & Shrey, D. E. (1991). Disability management in industry: A joint labor-management process. *Rehabilitation Counseling Bulletin, 34,* 227-242.

Bureau of Workers' Compensation. (1991). *Request and criteria for provider network for independent medical examinations.*

Carey, T. S., & Hadler, N. M. (1986). The role of the primary physician in disability determination for social security insurance and workers' compensation. *Annals of Internal Medicine, 104,* 706-710.

American Occupational Medicine Association. (1976). Code of ethical conduct for physicians providing occupational medical services. *Journal of Occupational Medicine, 18,* cover.

Cohen, D., Parrinello, A., & Kelliher, T. (1990). Disability management on the Long Island Railroad. *Worklife, 3*(1), 29-39.

Cousins, N. (1983). *The healing heart: Antidotes to panic helplessness.* New York: W. W. Norton & Company.

Dodson, V. N., & Zenz, C. (1988). Occupational cancer risks. In C. Zenz (Ed.), *Occupational medicine: Principles and practical applications* (2nd Ed.) (pp. 815-833). Chicago: Year Book Medical Publishers.

Drewczynski, A. (1986). Ergonomics — what is requested and what is needed to satisfy the occupational community. In *Proceedings of the 19th annual conference*. The human factors association of Canada, Vancouver.

Elling, R. H. (1990). Workers' health, safety, and compensation in historical and cross-national perspective; an overview. *Annals of the New York Academy of Sciences, 572*, 240-255, 1989.

Estep, D. A., Mitchell, L. V., & DeHart, R. L. (1992). *Teaching OEM in United States medical schools*. Oklahoma City, Oklahoma: Division of Occupational & Environmental Medicine, University of Oklahoma Health Sciences Center.

Frankl, V. E. (1984). *Man's search for meaning*. New York: Washington Square Press.

Freud, S. (1961). *Civilization and its discontent*. New York: W. W. Norton & Company.

Frymoyer, J., & Howe, J. (1984). Clinical classification. In M. H. Pope, J. W. Frymoyer, & G. B. J. Andersson (Eds.), *Occupational low back pain* (pp. 71-98). New York: Praeger.

Frymoyer, J. W., Pope, M. H., Clements, J. H., et al. (1983). Risk factors for low back pain. *Journal of Bone and Joint Surgery, 65A*, 213-218.

Gardner, J. A. (1991). Early referral and other factors affecting vocational rehabilitation outcome for the workers' compensation client. *Rehabilitation Counseling Bulletin, 34*, 197-209.

Gloss, D. S., & Wardle, M. G. (1982). Reliability and validity of AMA's guides to rating of impairment. *Journal of the American Medical Association, 248*, 2292-2296.

General Accounting Office. (1987). *Social security: Little success achieved in rehabilitating disabled beneficiaries* (Report No. GAO/HRD 88-11). Washington, DC: Author.

Hadler, N. M. (1984). Occupational illness: The issue of causality. *Journal of Occupational Medicine, 26*, 587-593.

Hanman, B. (1958). The evaluation of physical ability. *New England Journal of Medicine, 258*, 986-993.

Hester, E. J. (1990). Disability and disincentives: Prospective models for change. In S. J. Scheer (Ed.), *Multidisciplinary perspectives in vocational assessment of impaired workers* (pp. 205-218). Rockville, MD: Aspen Publishers, Inc.

Hester, E. J., Planek, T., & Decelles, P. G. (1988). *Attitudes of employers and rehabilitation professionals toward employees who become disabled*. Topeka, KS: The Menninger Foundation.

Institute of Medicine. (1988). *Role of the primary care physician in occupational and environmental medicine*. Division of Health Promotion and Disease Prevention. Washington, DC: National Academy Press.

World Health Organization. (1980). *International Classification of Impairments, Disabilities and Handicaps*. Geneva, Switzerland: Author.

Johnston, W. (1992). Importance of communication between physician and attorney. In E. W. Johnson (Ed.) *Physical medicine and rehabilitation clinics of North America, 3*, 677-694.

Joseph, B. S. (1989). Ergonomic considerations and job design in upper extremity disorders. *Occupational Medicine, 4*, 547.

Kelsey, J. L., & White, A. A. (1980). Epidemiology and impact of low back pain. *Spine, 5*, 133-142.

Kuh, C., & Hanman, B. (1944). Current development affecting the physician's role in manpower development. *New England Journal of Medicine, 125*, 265-270.

Leavitt, S. S., Johnston, T. L., & Beyer, R. D. (1971 & 1972). The process of recovery patterns in industrial back injury. Part I (costs) and Part IV (mapping the health-care process). *Industrial Medicine & Surgery, 40*, 7-12; *41*, 5-9.

Louis, D. S. (1987). Cumulative trauma disorders. *Journal of Hand Surgery, 12A*, 823-825.

Magora, A., & Taustein, I. (1969). An investigation of the problem of sick-leave in the patient suffering from low back pain. *Industrial Medicine & Surgery, 38,* 398-408.

McGill, C. M. (1968). Industrial back problems. A control program. *Journal of Occupational Medicine, 10,* 174-178.

McMahon, B. T., & Shrey, D. E. (1992). The Americans with Disabilities Act, disability management, and the injured worker. *Journal of Workers' Compensation, 1,* 9-28.

Mital, A. (in press). Hand tools: injuries, illnesses, design, and usage. In A. Mital & W. Karwowski (Eds.), *Workplace, equipment, and tool design.* Amsterdam: Elsevier.

Nachemson, A. (1983). Work for all-for those with LBP as well. *Clinical Orthopedics & Related Research, 179,* 77-85.

National Institute for Occupational Safety and Health. (1981). *Work practices guide for manual lifting* (PB82). Washington, DC: National Technical Information Service.

Ohio Bureau of Workers' Compensation; Medical Services Division. (1990). Physician's guide to the independent medical examination. Columbus, OH: Author.

President's Commission on State Workmen's Compensation Laws. (1972). *The report of the national commission on state workmen's compensation laws.* (Y3.W89/3:1/972). Washington, DC: U.S. Government Printing Office.

Richman S. I. (1982). Why change? A look at the current system of disability determination and worker's compensation for occupational lung disease. *Annals of Internal Medicine, 97,* 908-914.

Rosenstock, L. (1981). Occupational medicine—too long neglected. *Annals of Internal Medicine, 95,* 774-776.

Rothstein, M. A. (1990). Legal issues related vocational capacity. In S. J. Scheer (Ed.). *Multidisciplinary perspectives in vocational assessment of impaired workers* (pp. 219-227). Rockville, MD: Aspen Publishers, Inc.

Rothstein, M. A. (1984). Role of occupational medicine. In *Medical screening of workers* (pp. 1-13). Washington, DC: Bureau of National Affairs.

Sander, R. A., & Meyers, J. E. (1986). The relationship of disability to compensation status in railroad workers. *Spine, 11,* 141-143.

Scheer, S. J. (1991a). The physician' responsibility in assessing vocational capacity. In S. J. Scheer (Ed.) *Medical perspectives in vocational assessment of impaired workers* (pp. 1-18). Gaithersburg, MD: Aspen Publishers.

Scheer, S. J. (1991b). Vocational capacity with low back pain impairment. In S. J. Scheer (Ed.), *Medical perspectives in vocational assessment of impaired workers* (pp. 19-63). Gaithersburg, MD: Aspen Publishers.

Shrey, D. E. (1992). Employer-based work return transition programs and the deinstitutionalization of America's injured workers. *Work Injury Management* (pp. 4-6). Eugene, OR: Center for the Advancement of Industrial Rehabilitation and Evaluation.

Shrey, D. E., & Breslin, R. E. (1992). Employer-based disability management strategies and work return transition programs. In N. Hablutzel & B. T. McMahon (Eds.), *The Americans with Disabilities Act: Access and accommodation* (pp. 139-154). Winter Park, FL: G. R. Press.

Sigerist, H. E. (1936). Historical background industrial and occupational diseases. *Bulletin of the NY Academy of Medicine, 12,* 597-609.

Silverstein, B. A., Fine, L. J., & Armstrong, T. J. (1986). Carpal tunnel syndrome: Causes and a preventive strategy. *Seminars in Occupational Medicine, 1,* 213.

Svensson, H. O., & Andersson, G. B. J. (1983). Low back pain in forty to forty-seven year old men: Work history and work environmental factors. *Spine, 8,* 272-276.

Symington, D. C., (1984). Vocational rehabilitation — how everybody benefits. *Rehabilitation Digest, 15,* 2-3.

Tate, D., Munrowd, D., Habeck, R., Kasim, R., Adams, L., & Shepard, D. (1987). *Disability management and rehabilitation outcomes: The Buick-Oldsmobile-Cadillac Lansing Product Team Report.* East Lansing, MI: Michigan State University, School of Health Education, Counseling, Psychology, and Human Performance, Disability Management Project.

Terkel, S. (1974). *Working.* New York: Pantheon Books.

U. S. Department of Health, Education, & Welfare. (1979). Disability evaluation under social security: A handbook for physicians. (1979) Washington, DC: Author.

Welter, E. S. (1988). The role of the primary care physician in Occupational Medicine: Practical observations, and recommendations. In C. Zenz (Ed.), *Occupational medicine: Principles and practical applications* (2nd ed.) (pp. 62-73). Chicago: Year Book Medical Publisher.

Wickstrom, R. J. (1990). Functional capacity testing, In S. J. Scheer (Ed.) *Multidisciplinary perspectives in vocational assessment of impaired workers* (pp. 73-88). Rockville, MD: Aspen Publishers.

Wiesel, S. W., Feffer, H., & Rothman, R. (1984). Industrial LBP—prospective evaluation of a standardized diagnostic and treatment protocol. *Spine, 9,* 199-204.

Workers' Compensation Research Institute. (1987). *Use of medical evidence—low back permanent partial disability claims in New Jersey.* WCRI Research Brief. *Use of medical evidence — low back permanent partial disability claims in New Jersey. 3,* 10.

Yelin, E. H., Henke, C. J., & Epstein, W. V. (1986). Work disability among persons with musculoskeletal conditions. *Arthritis and Rheumatism, 29,* 1322-1333.

Zenz, C. (1988). *Occupational medicine: Principles and practical applications* (2nd ed.). Chicago: Year Book Medical Publisher.

Evaluation Of Work Disability From A Worker-Work Environment Perspective

Michel Lacerte, M.D., C.R.C.
Lorraine Desjardins, C.R.C.

SCOPE

The concept of occupational handicap assessment is introduced in this chapter as an essential element of the disability management process. This requires an interdisciplinary approach and joint effort from labor and management. The process by which occupational handicap is established must be defined within the context of corporate disability management principles and practices. Rehabilitation interventions derived from the occupational handicap assessment make maximum use of existing resources within the employer organization. Considerations of work demands and environmental factors specific to a given organization are critical. Such a process minimizes the impact of disability, maximizes residual abilities, protects the employability of the worker and reduces financial hardship to the employer. A case summary is presented to illustrate how occupational handicap assessment is used in the individualized disability management process.

INTRODUCTION

During the 1990s, employers will face increasing legislative pressure to integrate and accommodate people with disabilities, due to the passage of the Americans with Disabilities Act. It is also expected that employers will have higher workers' compensation and health care costs within an ever-changing labor market and economic environment.

In response to these challenges, the concept of disability management has arisen. Disability management practices are based on a comprehensive and cohesive employer-based approach to managing the complex needs of people with disabilities (Bruyère & Shrey, 1991). The term *worker* in this chapter refers to both the injured worker (work or non-work-related injury) and the person with a disability attempting to enter the work force.

Disability management policies and practices must be responsive to and compatible with corporate culture. Corporate disability management policies and procedures should be designed to strengthen the occupational bond between the worker and the work environment (Shrey, 1990). As such, rehabilitation interventions should take place within the work environment and should make maximal use of its resources.

The goals of an employer-based disability management program are to minimize the impact of disability, maximize residual abilities, facilitate communication, protect employability, and reduce associated costs. Disability management requires an interdisciplinary approach and joint labor-management coordinated effort to address the complex nature of disability, individual worker characteristics and the worker-work environment relationship (Shrey, 1990).

The evaluation of work disability from a worker-work environment perspective is accomplished through an occupational handicap assessment (OHA). The OHA provides the necessary information to formulate the individualized disability management plan (IDMP).

OCCUPATIONAL HANDICAP ASSESSMENT DEFINITIONS

Evaluating work disability from a worker-work environment perspective is an essential step in the disability management process. Unfortunately, the terms *impairment, disability,* and *handicap* are commonly used interchangeably. This situation has brought about much confusion which may be resolved by adopting the World Health Organization's definitions (see Table 1).

OCCUPATIONAL ABILITY

Occupational ability is defined as the worker's ability to perform, to standards, all the essential tasks of a job without safety or health hazards to self or others. Standards set by legislation, collective bargaining agreements and trade, workplace or regulating bodies will have a major bearing on determining occupational ability.

Table 1	
World Health Organization's Definitions	
Impairment:	Any loss or abnormality of psychological, physiological, or anatomical structure or function.
Disability:	Any restriction or lack (resulting from an impairment) of ability to perform an activity in the manner or within the range considered normal for a human being.
Handicap:	A disadvantage for an individual resulting from an impairment or a disability that limits or prevents the fulfillment of a role that is normal for that individual.

OCCUPATIONAL FITNESS

Occupational fitness refers to the degree to which an individual's work capacity matches the demands or standards of the job. Metabolic and biomechanical demands must be taken into account to prevent excessive fatigue and strain (Lacerte & Wright, 1992). Health care professionals play a key role in evaluating the degree to which an individual's work capacities are compatible with the demands specific to a given job.

OCCUPATIONAL HANDICAP

Occupational handicap is the individual's ability to perform within a given work environment. Environmental disadvantages or barriers may be cultural, social, economic, or organizational. Handicap encompasses the interaction between an individual's disability and the environment. Thus, when defining occupational handicap, an individual's lack of ability to fulfill all essential tasks of a job including knowledge, skills, interests, personality, physical, and emotional requirements specific to the workplace is addressed.

OCCUPATIONAL HANDICAP ASSESSMENT

The OHA requires the coordination of multidisciplinary services, as provided by a disability management intervention team (DMIT) which develops the IDMP. An OHA is the interaction between the medical disability, work capacity, job analysis, and vocational rehabilitation evaluations within the context of an individual's work environment. The purpose of this assessment is to determine the extent of occupational handicap and to make use of this information in the development of the IDMP (see Appendix A at end of chapter).

The DMIT includes the worker, union representative, direct supervisor, case coordinator, physician(s), ergonomist, and other health care professionals. Staff should be selected for team membership based on their experience, training, and potential contributions to the IDMP.

The IDMP is a written plan delineating the terms, conditions, rights, and remedies under which the services are provided. This plan should reflect intermediate and long-range goals. Any information regarding the implementation of the plan should be communicated in a timely fashion to the worker and affected team members by the DMIT coordinator.

The OHA should be initiated when the worker is at risk of or has developed a disability. The OHA provides the information necessary to analyze and plan preventive interventions, treatment and restorative services or physical accommodations essential to sustaining occupational ability. Achieving maximum medical outcome is not a prerequisite for initiating the OHA or rehabilitation efforts.

The OHA consists of four sets of evaluation components: 1) Medical Disability, 2) Work Capacity, 3) Ergonomic Job Analysis, and 4) Vocational Rehabilitation (see Figure 1). All evaluations are performed within the context of the work environment. Each evaluation may require the specialized expertise of one or more DMIT members.

OCCUPATIONAL HANDICAP ASSESSMENT METHODOLOGY

The OHA forms the structure of the Work Ability Box (WAB) (Lacerte & Wright, 1992). The WAB is a decision-making model which may be used to facilitate the analysis and planning of the IDMP. The different elements composing the WAB are illustrated in Figure 1.

MEDICAL DISABILITY EVALUATION

Medical disability evaluation plays an important role in the planning of both the OHA and IDMP. It provides the information necessary to determine the appropriateness, timeliness, and extent to which a person with a disability can engage in the OHA process and any subsequent interventions. Medical disability evaluation referrals must clearly outline their intended purpose(s) within the OHA. Referrals may have several purposes, as discussed below (Guidotti, Cowell, & Jamieson, 1989).

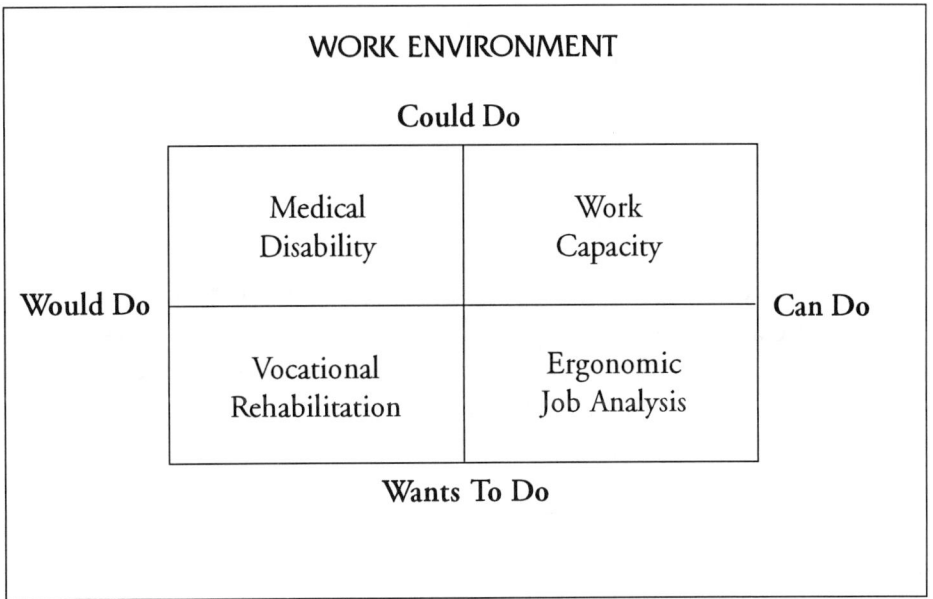

Figure 1. Work Ability Box

Evaluation of the Presence of a Medical Condition

A typical referral consists of a medical evaluation for the purpose of a pre-placement assessment. This type of evaluation is conducted to screen for the presence of medical condition(s) or risk factor(s) that may preclude the performance of tasks specific and essential to the individual's targeted job. Subsequent annual checkups ensure that employees continue to have the attributes necessary to satisfactorily perform job tasks. Specific issues to address when conducting a pre-placement evaluation include past medical history, current medications, the presence of risk factors and medical condition necessary to meet the job demands.

Establishment of Diagnosis and Medical Treatment Plan

The nature and extent of a medical condition, once recognized and documented, leads to the establishment of a diagnosis and an appropriate treatment plan. The relationship of the medical conditions and the associated disability, along with the expected duration, are addressed.

Evaluation of Residual Work Abilities

Another reason for referral for a medical disability evaluation is to determine the extent to which an individual can return to previous employment. To evaluate residual work abilities, the physician must be provided with a job description delineating essential tasks. The physician's role is to assess occupational fitness based on the knowledge of work demands in relation to a worker's medical condition and current functional capacities.

Work Restrictions and Precautions

It is necessary for the physician to make judgements regarding the worker's capacity to tolerate various working conditions (temperature, humidity, illumination, noise level, air quality, etc.). The physician must indicate the precautions, work restrictions, or the degree of supervision required to ensure the safety of the worker and other employees.

Medical Condition and Disability Prognosis

The medical disability evaluation must provide sufficient information to establish the extent and anticipated consequences of the injury or disease process. The physician must make reference to time frames in which the recovery or deterioration is most likely to occur. Restrictions and precautions must be identified as permanent or temporary.

Role of the DMIT Physician

The involvement of the physician on the DMIT is important. Functions of the DMIT physician are:

1. Be familiar with the work environment and disability management general principles.
2. Understand the importance of the OHA as a basis of the IDMP.
3. Be able to perform basic disability evaluation.
4. Advise on the need for and referrals required to complete the medical disability evaluation (e.g., orthopaedic specialist consultation).
5. Help formulate specific questions directed to the treating physician, specialist, or other health care providers.
6. Insure that necessary background information is provided to the consultant(s).
7. Review, analyze, and interpret information contained in the consultation reports.
8. Act as the link between the DMIT and outside health care providers.
9. Participate in the elaboration of a medically sound IDMP by assuring the appropriateness and timeliness of medical and rehabilitation interventions.

10. Emphasize that reaching maximal medical recovery does not preclude the initiation of vocational rehabilitation efforts and that medical management can be done concurrently with vocational rehabilitation interventions. A worker may participate in a transitional return to work program while taking part in a physiotherapy program.
11. Convey genuine interest in the worker's integration into a suitable and safe work environment.

A clarification of the physician's role and function in the DMIT is illustrated in the case summary.

WORK CAPACITY EVALUATION

Most physicians complete a worker's physical capacity report with some degree of reluctance. This is partly related to the fact that the physician often lacks tools to perform direct observations of the tasks required of the worker in the workplace (Lacerte & Wright, 1992). The physician must, in most cases, resort to medical judgement when completing work capacity reports. Consequently, the injured worker may be prematurely returned to work, unable to physically perform all essential job tasks. In other cases, the physician's conservative judgement may result in unnecessary return to work delays.

The WCE attempts to measure, as objectively as possible, an individual's capacity to dependably perform the work demands specific to the job (Matheson, 1983). The WCE is most appropriately performed by an occupational or physiotherapist, rather than the physician who has neither the tools nor the time. A WCE is best performed at the worker's job site. This ensures validity since it takes into account environmental factors and barriers that might not be identified through job simulation approaches common in rehabilitation facilities. Allowing the therapist to perform the evaluation in collaboration with the worker's supervisor facilitates the identification of job modification or accommodation options.

The WCE should be performed early in the development of the IDMP. This information is required in the planning of a work-return transition program, or when considering vocational alternatives.

To provide face validity and concurrent validity, WCE criterion-referenced measurement items must be based on an analysis of the specific job being considered. A typical job analysis may be performed by a rehabilitation professional, occupational therapist, or physical therapist, depending upon training and experience. A specific analysis of essential versus nonessential job tasks is required. In complex cases, where job modifications are indicated (e.g., jobs causing definite symptoms of carpal tunnel syndrome), an in-depth ergonomic evaluation may be required.

ERGONOMIC JOB ANALYSIS

The purpose of an ergonomic job analysis is to identify hazards, evaluate risks, and recommend modifications (Lacerte & Wright, 1992). The ergonomist uses techniques for analyzing, designing, and/or predicting interactions that arise between people, processes, and environments (Wilson, 1990). These same interactions are of paramount importance to both the physician and the ergonomist when matching the individual's work capacity with specific job demands.

Three main components are analyzed by an ergonomist or job analyst: 1) general information about the company, the worker, and the work station; 2) a job analysis (description of tasks, work station layout, physical environment, and risk factors); and 3) minimum requirements for successful performance of the job (Lacerte & Wright, 1992).

The integration of work capacity and job analysis data provides the basis and standards needed to evaluate occupational handicap, job modifications/accommodation, pre-placement criteria, and health and safety training needs.

It is in the employer's best interests to develop and maintain a database, cataloging all ergonomic job analyses. When the DMIT is exploring employment options and possible jobs for a worker, the information can be quickly accessed from this database. An informed decision about medical restrictions can be made when the physician is provided with both a list of the essential job requirements and data from the WCE.

VOCATIONAL REHABILITATION EVALUATION

The purpose of the vocational rehabilitation evaluation is to determine an individual's work potential based on aptitudes, interests, skills, and abilities (Athelstan, 1982). The presence of psychosocial barriers affecting vocational potential is also evaluated. A general vocational assessment determines vocational and financial consequences of a disability by reviewing the factors listed in Table 2.

Formal standardized vocational testing may be used to assess vocational aptitudes, vocational interests, work personality, psychosocial factors, intelligence, self-concept, and adjustment to disability. The vocational rehabilitation evaluation is best performed by a vocational rehabilitation counselor. As a member of the DMIT, the rehabilitation counselor is knowledgeable about corporate disability management policies and procedures. The counselor is familiar with the workplace and the jobs available. Thus, results of the general vocational assessment and formal vocational testing can then be interpreted within the context of the work environment.

Table 2 **General Vocational Factors**
• Educational history • Vocational history • Transferable skills (sports, hobbies, social groups) • Work interests • Work behaviors • Financial situations • Funding agency involvement • Interest group involvement

To be successful, the OHA must take into consideration the information gathered during the vocational rehabilitation evaluation. For example, if an individual has limited clerical aptitude, clerical work might not be realistic as a transitional work program option. It is therefore necessary for the DMIT to have such information available to appropriately analyze and formulate the IDMP. Without consideration of these factors, the chances of success for the IDMP would be greatly reduced.

INDIVIDUALIZED DISABILITY MANAGEMENT PROGRAM DEVELOPMENT

The information gathered during the OHA makes up the four basic elements forming the structure of the WAB (Figure 1). The role of the WAB is to facilitate the analysis and development of the IDMP. The relationship between the elements of the WAB will provide the information necessary to establish what the individual can, wants to, could, would, and should do.

To develop the IDMP, it is essential that the information gathered be shared among the DMIT members. The case coordinator ensures that relevant information circulates in a timely fashion to and from each DMIT member and service provider. It is essential that the return-to-work process be established in collaboration with the worker.

Realistic vocational options are identified by comparing the vocational rehabilitation and medical disability evaluations. What the worker "would do" is determined by verifying that the worker's aptitudes, interests, skills, and abilities are within the work restrictions and precautions.

What the worker "can do" (occupational fitness), is determined by the relationship between the individual's work capacity and the ergonomic job analysis. If the individual's work capacity is incompatible with specific job demands, rehabilitation interventions may be considered. These may include physical conditioning, job accommodation or modifications to reach occupational ability (threshold). Combining results of the medical disability and work capacity evaluation provides better insight into what the worker "could do" dependably and safely.

The determination of what the worker "wants to do" can be estimated by assessing the relationship between worker's vocational interests, aptitudes, and values, and the job description, as obtained through the ergonomic job analysis (Lacerte & Wright, 1992).

It is only when one considers all four elements within the context of the work environment that a realistic IDMP can be developed. The IDMP defines operationally what the worker ultimately "should do." Rehabilitation interventions identified in the IDMP should bridge the gap between the worker's current status and what is required to meet the standards of the targeted job.

Multiple intervention possibilities are available to the DMIT. These interventions can be directed toward the worker, job, work environment, and employer organization. The provision of such involves a host of professionals skilled in different fields such as health care, engineering, and management. These interventions might be evaluative, preventive, or restorative.

Rehabilitation interventions derived from the OHA should make maximum use of existing resources within the organization to protect occupational bonding between worker, employer, and work environment (Shrey, 1990). Therefore, interventions such as transitional work programs or modified work placements are preferred.

Selection, Utilization, and Evaluation of External Resources

It is sometimes necessary to select external resources that best meet the requirements of the IDMP. It must be ensured that service providers are meeting standards (external control) established by the corporate disability management policies and the IDMP. To ensure that these requirements are met, a set of internal and external controls must be put into place (Leek & Cowles, 1983).

When first deciding to deal with external agencies, the DMIT selects the type of service(s) required and establishes service delivery quality standards. Once it has been established that an agency is capable of meeting standards that follow disability management principles, a service contract can be negotiated.

This contract should specify the nature of the services, time frames, and reporting requirements specific to the IDMP. Details concerning responsibility, accountability, and financial remuneration should also be stipulated (Leek & Cowles, 1983).

The DMIT case coordinator monitors services provided as part of the utilization control. Contract requirements are compared with the services rendered. The DMIT determines, on an ongoing basis, if there is any need for alteration(s) in the service contract, approved providers or service expectations.

When internal resources are used, the DMIT monitors each department to ensure that it meets the requirements of the IDMP. Corporate disability management policies and procedures take the place of service contracts. The utilization control process is performed on an ongoing basis by the DMIT following corporate goals and objectives (Leek & Cowles, 1983).

CASE SUMMARY

John Doe, a 26-year-old man employed as a laborer, sustained an industrial injury on June 24, 1992. He injured his low back while lifting a 60-pound box from floor to waist height. He experienced immediate low back pain and was unable to complete his work shift. He reported to the plant Occupational Health and Safety Nurse.

The occupational nurse completed an accident report. The nurse contacted the shipping/receiving area supervisor to obtain details of the incident and job information. Arrangements were made to have John Doe see a physician at the contracted walk-in emergency care clinic.

A diagnosis of acute lumbar strain was made. The emergency care physician gave him reassurance and provided around the clock analgesics with the advice to take two days off work. The worker's supervisor contacted John Doe to express his concern and support.

The next day, the DMIT physician reviewed the accident report and the medical assessment from the walk-in clinic. The DMIT physician arranged to assess the worker on the third day following the accident. The DMIT physician concurred with the diagnosis and contacted Mr. Doe's treating physician to discuss the medical intervention plan. The company's disability management philosophy and available rehabilitation services were offered to the treating physician. During that time, the case coordinator familiarized the worker with the company's disability management program.

An active physiotherapy program aimed at preventing loss of flexibility and maintaining aerobic fitness was initiated. Biweekly physiotherapy reports were sent to the treating physician and the DMIT case coordinator. As Mr. Doe had not returned to work by July 24, 1992 (one month post-accident), the case coordinator added his name on the agenda of the DMIT's weekly meeting.

For the initial meeting, the case coordinator brought together the worker, his supervisor, his labor representative, the DMIT physician, and nurse. The team members came prepared to fulfill their specific roles, as outlined in Table 3.

Table 3 DMIT Roles	
Chair	Monitor and Facilitate DM
Case Coordinator	IDMP Coordination
Worker	Active Participant
Supervisor	Job Possibilities
Rehabilitation Counselor	General Vocational Assessment Job Analysis IDMP Preparation
Labor Representative	Labor Concerns
Occupational Physician	Medical Advisor
Others: PT, OT, EAP	Special Reports As Needed Work Capacity Evaluations
Psychology, ergonomics	Interventions

A member of the joint labor-management Disability Management Implementation Committee chaired the meeting. Department heads and labor leaders make up this committee. It's function is to develop, implement, and monitor the company's disability management program.

The occupational nurse presented a summary of the accident. She also reported that the Health and Safety ergonomic committee was asked to review the accident and report on the need for corrective intervention such as job redesign. The DMIT physician then provided a brief review of the available medical information. This included the medical assessment, diagnosis, prognosis, and planned interventions, whether diagnostic, therapeutic, or rehabilitative. The DMIT physician paid special attention to the current medical disability status and necessary medical restrictions and precautions.

The occupational physician determined that Mr. Doe's current functional capacity, as reported in the last physical therapy report, allows him to participate in a modified return to work program. The temporary (3 months) medical restrictions are to avoid bending, lifting, and twisting. Lifting and carrying should be no greater than 20 pounds on a continuous basis and be limited between waist to shoulder height. Attempts to alternate standing and sitting on a 30-minute basis should be made when designing the modified work program. The restrictions should be reviewed for their appropriateness early during the return to work process.

The worker and worker's supervisor informed the team on the nature of the job by providing copies of the job profile obtained from the ergonomic database. In addition, the supervisor indicated that a modified work program would be impossible to implement in the shipping/receiving area since bending, lifting, and twisting from floor to shoulder height loads greater than 20 pounds constitute essential tasks of this worker's pre-injury job. Job alternatives or modifications are not available in his area.

The rehabilitation counselor presented the details about Mr. Doe's work experience, seniority, transferrable skills, education, and vocational history, as obtained from the vocational evaluation.

The case coordinator recorded the key points presented by the team members using the work ability box as the analysis tool. The chair in turn acted as the neutral facilitator to the meeting and, when required, provided clarification to disability management policies and procedural issues.

The WAB illustrated that John Doe cannot do the essential tasks of his usual job for at least the next three months. Alternatives and/or accommodations are not available within the shipping and receiving area. Suitable short-term alternate job placement is required. More information about the present work capacity was lacking but was needed for job placement. The chair reaffirmed the company's policy and present bargaining agreement concerning short-term job placement. Placements no longer than six months have no adverse effects to job seniority or union status.

The DMIT agreed to the IDMP outlined in Table 4.

This intervention plan is revised and updated by the case coordinator on a bimonthly basis for the DMIT review. As soon as medically appropriate, arrangements are made for Mr. Doe to return to his pre-injury job.

Table 4
Individualized Disability Management Plan – John Doe

Goals (as established at DMIT meeting of July 31, 1992):

1. Increase or maintain work capacity by active rehabilitation.
2. Secure modified work, short-term placement
3. Return to pre-injury job on November 7, 1992.
4. Post-employment services following case resolution.

Interventions	Responsibility	Start	End
1. Short-term job placement (3 mos.) based on current medical restrictions	WCE Team	August 4	August 5
2. Work capacity evaluation (specific to previous job)	Case Coordinator	August 6	November 5
3. Active physical conditioning	Physical Therapist	August 6	To Be Determined
4. Biweekly meeting with worker	Case Coordinator	August 3	
5. Biweekly contact with area supervisor	Case Coordinator and Worker	August 3	
6. Monthly DMIT review	Case Coordinator	August 3	

CONCLUSION

To perform work disability assessments from a worker-work environment perspective, it is essential that the concept of occupational bonding be reinforced and that the principles of disability management be respected. To do this, employers must establish internal and external controls through a joint labor-management process.

This can be accomplished by the establishment of the DMIT. Individual needs of each worker should be reflected during the OHA and formulation and implementation of the IDMP. Resources, both internal and external must be identified and monitored on an ongoing basis to ensure that organizational needs and corporate disability management principles and policies are being met.

If employers and labor are to meet the challenges related to injury and disability, it is necessary that "disability management" become an integral part of the corporate structure. Only then will employers be empowered to meet the requirements of the ADA and protect the employability of workers.

REFERENCES

Athelstan, G. T. (1982). Vocational assessment and management. In F. J. Kottke, G. K. Skillfully, & J. L. Lehmann (Eds.). *Krusen's handbook of physical medicine and rehabilitation, 3rd edition* (pp. 163-189). Philadelphia: WB Saunders Co.

Bruyère, S. M., & Shrey, D .E. (1991). Disability management in industry: A joint labor-management process. *Rehabilitation Counseling Bulletin, 34*(3), 227-273.

Guidotti, T. L., Cowell, J. W. & Jamieson, G. G. (1989). *Occupational health services: A practical approach* (pp. 210-212). Chicago, Ill.: American Medical Association.

Lacerte, M., & Wright, G. (1992). Return to work determination. In C. Gordon (Ed.), *Physical medicine & rehabilitation: State of the art reviews. 6*(2), 213-232. Philadelphia: Hanley & Belfus, Inc. 6(2), June 1992, p. 213-232.

Leek, J. W., & Cowles, R. S. (1983). Quality management. In R. G. Brandenburg (Ed.), *What every manager needs to know about manufacturing* (pp. 107-117). New York, NY: American Management Association.

Matheson, L. N. (1983). *Work capacity evaluation: An interdisciplinary approach to industrial rehabilitation.* Anaheim, CA: Employment and Rehabilitation Institute of California.

Shrey, D. E. (1990). Disability management: An employer-based rehabilitation concept. In S. J. Scheer (Ed.). *Multidisciplinary perspectives in vocational assessment of impaired workers* (pp. 89 - 106). Rockville, MD: Aspen Publications.

Wilson, J. R. (1990). A framework and a context for ergonomics methodology. In J. R. Wilson & E. N. Corlett (Eds.), *Evaluation of Human Work* (pp. 1-29). London: Taylor & Francis.

World Health Organization. (1980). *International classification of impairments, disabilities, and handicaps.* Geneva, World Health Organization.

Wright, G. N. (1980). *Total rehabilitation* (pg. 116). Boston: Little, Brown and Company.

APPENDIX

DISABILITY MANAGEMENT STRATEGY

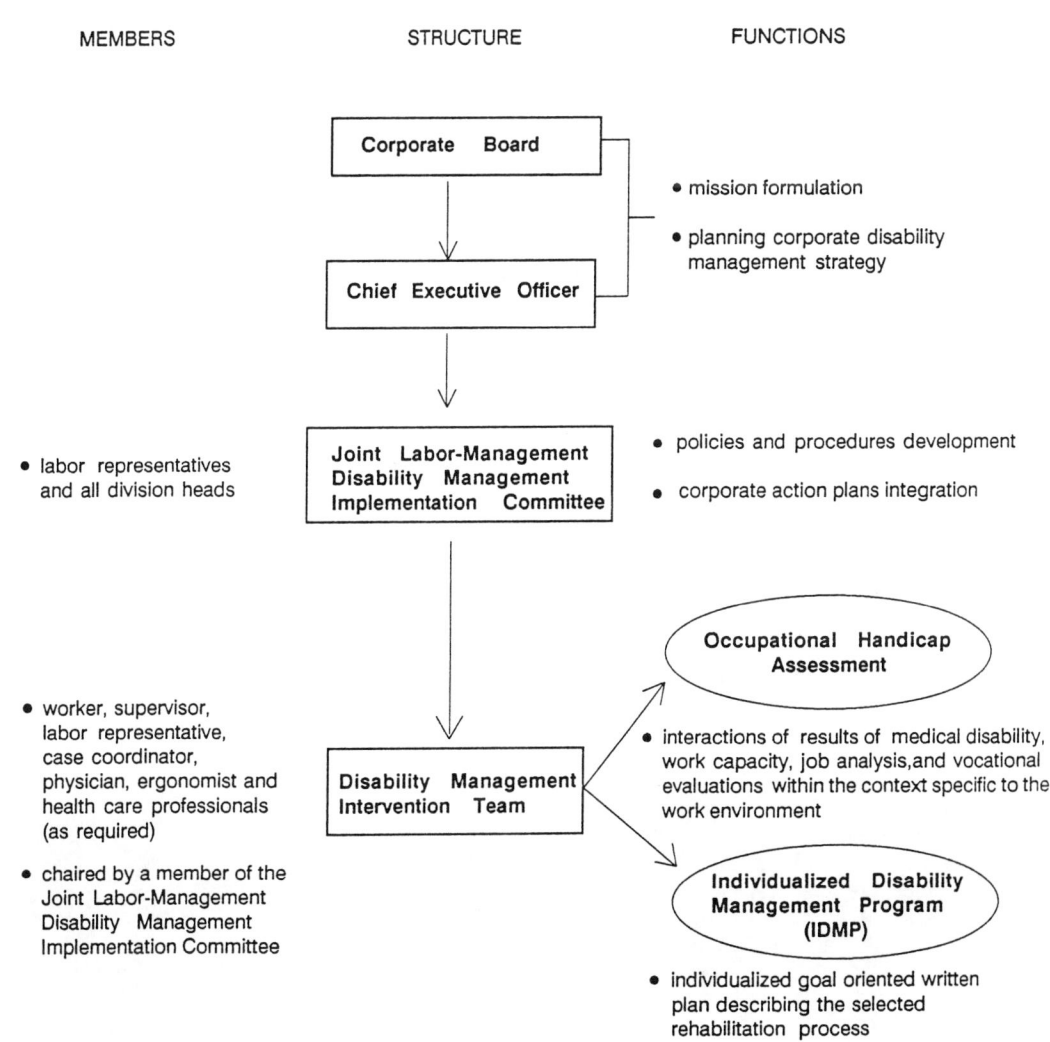

8

BUILDING JOINT LABOR-MANAGEMENT INITIATIVES FOR WORKSITE DISABILITY MANAGEMENT

Debra L. Mills

INTRODUCTION

Employers are restructuring in an effort to increase profits and stabilize their market share in a highly competitive world economy. Concurrently, unions are striving for collective agreements that represent the needs and interests of workers. Joint labor-management negotiations and agreements define the parameters of employer-worker relationships. Maintaining a balance among such relationships ensures worker productivity, safety, and economic security.

This chapter explores the relationship between workers and employers in the context of workplace disability management. The roles of labor unions and employers are reviewed, with respect to the resolution and management of workplace injury and disability. Despite inevitable labor-management conflicts and potentially adversarial relationships, employers and unions often find "common ground" in disability management programs. The development of such programs are often facilitated by the Return to Work Pact, which serves as the blueprint of disability management policy and procedure. This chapter offers an example of the Return to Work Pact, and the subsequent benefits of disability management for labor and industry. The challenges of establishing joint labor-management disability management programs are discussed and a 10 point summary reviews the key elements of successful program development.

THE ROLE OF LABOR UNIONS

Unions have existed for nearly 200 years. They have evolved as organizations, ensuring that workers receive fair wages, that attention is paid to health and safety conditions at the worksite, and that workers are treated equitably with respect to job duties, promotions, and job security. Unions are the collective voice of workers.

Unions have played a significant role in improving conditions for all workers. They have been instrumental in reducing the work week from 60 or more hours to 40 or fewer hours, promoting a healthier balance between leisure and work. Vacation pay and other health care benefits for workers have also evolved as a result of representation from labor organizations.

Despite improvements made for workers through the efforts of labor organizations, many negative union perceptions exist. The idea that unions want to strike and "bully" employers has been well publicized and reinforced during embittered labor disputes. In reality, less than 3% of all collective bargaining results in a strike (United Way of the Lower Mainland, 1991). When the issues are significant enough, the voting power of unions can bring a workplace to a grinding halt.

WORKERS WITH DISABILITIES

Unions have become increasingly concerned about the needs of their members with disabilities. Unions support full worker participation in all aspects of society — political, social, and economic. Unions view the benefits of employment as a right to be enjoyed by all, including workers with disabilities. Union involvement in emerging reintegration programs for persons with disabilities is a prime example of the labor movement's commitment in this area.

In addressing the Canadian Labour Congress' "Bridging Rehabilitation and Work" conference in 1986, Guy Adam spoke of the labor movement's responsibility to promote human rights and to fundamentally oppose discrimination against workers on many grounds, including disability (Adam, 1986). He stated that "such clauses appear in our collective agreements because we have included them in our bargaining demands. Employers have agreed because we have insisted...." He reflected on the labor movement's past focus "... demanding that workers who were injured not be fired; that their service (or seniority) be honored; that they be transferred to jobs that they felt they were capable of performing; and that they receive re-training if necessary."

Unions are not strangers to the issues faced by workers with disabilities. The British Columbia Federation of Labour, along with other labor federations and local unions, have adopted policy statements on the employment of people with disabilities. Although this has been a phenomenon primarily of the last decade, the statements speak to the labor movement's frustration with its own slow progress in this area and to its ongoing commitment to improve access and integration into the work force (employment equity) for people with disabilities.

Despite the gradual change process, labor has made significant gains for their members with disabilities. They continue to tackle problematic workers' compensation issues. Unions have attained short- and long-term disability benefits for their members who are displaced from the workplace due to accident or disability. Labor organizations have also promoted adequate accommodation and retraining for those unable to return to their pre-injury or pre-disability jobs.

One of the most direct ways unions can effect these changes is through progressive collective bargaining that specifies the rights and, in some cases, the exceptions that will be made to accommodate the special needs of their injured or disabled members. Several exemplary provisions for persons with disabilities, as reflected within negotiated agreements, are cited at the end of this chapter. Also, a sample memorandum of understanding, outlining the details in a negotiated return to work program within the health care industry is offered.

Many clauses in labor-management contracts deal with exceptions to the application of seniority. Seniority is probably the most frequently encountered hurdle in accommodating people with disabilities in organized worksites. It is a fundamental union right of membership which affords certain privileges to members in accordance with such factors as their length of service to a company or long-standing union membership. These may be combined with attributes such as superior ability or specialized skills which may, for example, provide the employee with a 10% margin of advantage in job competitions. Seniority provides a means of relating one member's ranking to another. Greater seniority may offer advantageous bidding on promotional opportunities, vacation entitlement, and rights during times of layoff.

No matter what legislative provisions or moral motivation exists, persons with disabilities can only work when jobs are made available to them. For those who are employed at the time of their injury or at the onset of a disability, the ultimate aim is to maintain the worker's occupational bond with the current employer. Research has shown only a 48% return-to-work rate among people entering benefit systems due to disabilities and work disruptions (Gottlieb, 1988). Not only does this represent a significant loss of productivity, it further burdens insurance and tax-based safety nets. These consequences are significant for both workers and employers, as well as society.

THE ROLE OF EMPLOYERS

Although the information age and advanced technology are changing the traditional workplace, employers need human resources. As the steel manufacturer Dofasco, Inc. boasts, "Our product is steel, our strength is people." Employers invest inordinate amounts of energy and dollars on recruiting, hiring, and training. Companies may spend tens of thousands of dollars on a single hire, supported and maintained through the provision of benefits, including: unemployment insurance and workers' compensation insurance, vacation pay, sick pay, and medical and dental plans. A major investment has been made by the employer through all phases of the employment process. Losing the productivity of skilled and experienced employees is costly.

Employers often find it difficult to understand the advantages of returning injured workers to the workplace. This shortsightedness may be reinforced by a fear of additional costs such as purchasing special adaptive equipment, making ergonomic adjustments to the workplace, or absorbing the loss due to reduced productivity. These concerns are understandably heightened in difficult economic times.

Most people with disabilities do not require any special accommodation. Two-thirds of job modifications, including adaptive equipment, cost less than $500. However, persons with disabilities usually face employment discrimination largely because of the misconception that accommodation is prohibitively expensive (Job Accommodation Network, 1993).

Small employers tend to be the most concerned with an inability to make special accommodations for people with disabilities. Smaller employers are less likely to have the resources to allocate to a reintegration program. They frequently have no alternate jobs available for injured workers who cannot return to their pre-injury jobs. The pool of expertise tends to be small and specifically focused on the nature of the business itself, rather than issues related to workplace disability. Research has shown that small employers typically provide fewer accommodations and, not surprisingly, employ proportionally fewer people with disabilities than do medium and large employers (Vencill, 1982). A 1987 survey confirmed that only one-third of small employers reported making accommodations for employees with disabilities, as compared to 59% of large employers and about 33% of medium-sized companies (International Center for the Disabled, 1987). For small employers, accommodation seems to be an overwhelming challenge.

Middle-sized employers may not have in-house expertise to promote work-return interventions and programs. Such employers typically have human resources departments, but such departments focus almost exclusively on the administration of payroll and benefits. As a result, only about one-third of medium-sized employers make accommodations for people with disabilities (International Center for the Disabled, 1987).

Large employers often have a greater range of resources and specialized expertise to respond to workplace disability problems. For example, large companies often have either on-site or externally contracted employee assistance programs. Such programs have a range of depth, with most dealing with worker alcohol problems, and some designed to respond to "broad brush" physical, psychological, family, and financial issues. The International Center for the Disabled (1987) found that the majority of large employers have reported making accommodations for employees with disabilities. In Canada, however, the 1991 Health and Activity Limitation Survey (HALS) (Statistics Canada, 1991) reported that accommodations had been made for only 2% of people with more than one year of disability-related absence from the work force.

Given that companies with fewer than 100 employees employ over one-third of the work force and that employers with fewer than 500 workers employ half of all workers in the United States, demystifying disability management and making it a workable business strategy are challenges that must be met (U.S. Small Business Administration, 1989). Companies of all sizes have their advantages and disadvantages with respect to being proactive and effective disability managers. Small and medium employers often enjoy closer relationships within their work forces due to smaller size and greater length of employee tenure. They may also be more flexible and are sometimes perceived as having a more compassionate attitude toward the needs of their employees. Larger employers, on the other hand, may have significantly greater resources. However, they may be much more bureaucratic and rigid in their structure and less receptive to making accommodations, with employees being viewed as small cogs in a big wheel. Convincing large employers that they already have most of the tools at hand to establish disability management programs is often a challenge. Demonstrating that accommodations will result in significant savings is a realistic and attainable goal (Lucas, 1987).

LABOR-MANAGEMENT CONFLICT

There is an adage in the labor movement that "employers get the union they deserve." This saying refers to the origins of the labor movement and its focus on protecting workers from potential exploitation by employers. It speaks to the distrust that unfortunately still plagues many labor-management relationships.

Some industries have particularly harsh reputations for wearing out their employees over time due to the nature of the work and the disproportionate health and safety hazards of many types of jobs. Critics accuse employers of expending their "people" resource much as they would any other resource, simply as a cost of doing business, and discarding workers when they are no longer able to produce at a competitive level. Many workers with disabilities have access to benefit systems which provide at least temporary financial support. However, their personal losses and the loss of any remaining productivity to the economy, are wasteful and morally questionable.

Unfortunately, both unions and employers deceive themselves by believing that workers with disabilities will be accommodated by existing benefit systems and rehabilitation services. Unions may also, unwittingly, encourage workers with disabilities to aggressively pursue available disability benefits. This is often viewed as a means through which union members may achieve financial security through income replacement schemes such as long-term disability benefits or compensation pension plans. Although the worker's financial future may appear to be more secure with this approach, it entirely ignores the spirit of rehabilitation and worksite accommodation.

Losing a job means losing a part of one's identity or self-concept. It means losing relationships with co-workers and the psychosocial rewards attained through the routines and rhythms of work. Neither workers nor their families are adequately prepared to deal with the ultimate consequences of lengthy work disruptions. Nor can employers afford to lose trained and experienced employees who, despite an injury or illness, remain employable and potentially productive.

DISABILITY MANAGEMENT: JOINT LABOR-MANAGEMENT RESPONSIBILITY

There are mutual advantages to labor and management, with respect to disability management initiatives. However, successful outcomes require mutual trust and commitment. Disability management programs in business and industry are initiated by identifying the common ground upon which constructive and mutually beneficial relationships can be built. Labor must overcome cynicism toward what they perceive to be another new "management idea." Poor past experiences and tough economic environments may be fueling strained tensions. Workplace disability management strategies must fully address and integrate the interests, needs, and goals of all parties. They must be sensitive to the anxieties of workers and employers, must overcome the disincentives within our disability systems and must focus on the *economic, psychological,* and *social benefits of return to work*. The common ground between labor and management is often rooted in the concept of "protecting the employability of the worker."

There are multiple competing and conflicting self-interests that impact the success or failure of a disability management program. It is important for both labor and management to recognize the nature of forces that influence worker and employer behaviors, with respect to work-return goals. For example, a major force influencing work-return outcome is worker fear of reinjury, particularly when expected to return to work at full productivity without the benefit of a gradual return-to-work transition process. This usually intensifies as the worker approaches the point at which the injury has stabilized and return to work is imminent.

Injured worker deconditioning often occurs rapidly when an individual becomes physically inactive. Resulting stiffness, associated with the worker's transition to low-intensity activities, may be interpreted as re-injury rather than the body's physical readjustment. Although this is particularly the case among workers with high physical demand jobs, similar responses are typical among workers re-entering relatively low physical demand positions.

There is a critical need to differentiate activities that harm versus those that hurt. Physicians are particularly helpful in educating and reassuring their patients, in advance of return to work, by cautioning them to expect initial discomfort that comes with reactivation. Physicians are in the best position to encourage workers to maintain activation throughout the healing process, in order to minimize the effects of deconditioning. Simply prescribing mild activation throughout almost every healing process will result in much less discomfort when activities are increased. Unfortunately, many physicians continue to recommend deactivation and rest rather than carefully prescribed exercise and conditioning, with worker integration into transitional work activity.

Another significant fear among workers, as they approach return to work, is the loss of financial security. Although most employees are motivated to return to work, some worry about their ability to return to full productivity. Worker concerns are often focused on the potential loss of job security, particularly when the employer views the worker as being less capable or valuable as a result of an injury or disability. These concerns may be further magnified by employer reluctance to accommodate workers' needs or to modify their jobs.

The level and duration of benefits may be an additional factor influencing return to work. Research has shown that recovery time increases significantly and return to work decreases when benefits are too lucrative (Leavitt, 1992; McGill, 1968). If lucrative benefit levels or the opportunity to "stack" compensation, pension, or debt coverage benefits exist, the financial disadvantages of returning to work may far outweigh any perceived benefits.

This does not mean that workers entitled to benefits should not receive them. Benefits exist to ensure that workers have income protection if an accident or injury precludes them from maintaining pre-incident employment. Aside from workers' compensation benefits, most benefit plans require contributions from workers through payroll deductions. Depending upon the employment contract, some benefits may be taxable. This results in the expectation that one should be able to draw upon such safety nets especially when one has invested in them.

Care should be taken in establishing compensation plans to ensure that the true intent and usage of the coverage delivers the anticipated results. Ensuring that workers have a financial bridge to maintain income continuity while recovering from an injury or illness offers one perspective on benefits. Creating the expectation that a workplace injury or recreational accident is financially lucrative is another perspective. With these two opposing perspectives in mind, the very plan that is intended to support workers while they get back on their feet and back to work, may in fact be the biggest reason they don't!

Psychosocially adaptive responses to time off work may become maladaptive, quickly establishing new and often rigid behavior patterns that adversely affect the individual's likelihood of return to work. Workers tend to receive "secondary gains" such as attention from their families, friends, and sometimes their employer and/or benefits carrier. Not all of the attention is positive but it is attention, nevertheless. Settling into this "cared for" role is not difficult and breaking out of it can be awkward for a worker. Sometimes, the worker's partner may return to work part-time or shift the work schedule to spend more time at home. This, in turn, may mean that child care or other family obligations fall back on the worker who is off work due to injury or illness. Such role reversals or adaptations may establish new family dynamics that can be extremely resistant to change when the employee is faced with imminent return to work. These complicated psychosocial factors are disproportionately present in the most challenging cases. Due to the delays in resolving such cases and the reinforcement of these elements over time, overcoming them can become an almost insurmountable challenge. Focusing on early and safe return to work will minimize the chance of such patterns developing and facilitate a return to normalcy.

Employers often have a different perspective regarding work-return barriers for employees with disabilities. A frequent reason given by employers, for not returning injured employees to work, is that they cannot afford to pay for less than full productivity. Many maintain that having someone back at "half strength" costs them money, sets a bad example for other employees, and is simply poor business practice.

In reality, an off-work employee offers the employer no productivity. Employers pay for this when workers receive benefits of some kind as part of their employment contract or in the form of workers' compensation payments. Depending on the benefit structure and insurance scheme, often both premiums and the employer's experience factor will be adversely affected by such claims. Yet, many employers are willing to forego partial productivity from disabled workers, even on a temporary basis, under the premise that paying for less than 100% productivity is an unacceptable proposition. In other words, there is a preference among many employers to pay the worker with a disability to remain idle, rather than paying the employee to work.

Along with the short-term loss of productivity, employers run the risk of bearing even more extensive costs if their employees fall into the expanding pool of displaced employees with disabilities. Such workers will often receive loss of earnings awards to make up for their economic loss, even if they still are capable of employment. It is widely accepted that the most significant disability costs are those incurred to support workers in the long-term, such as permanent pension benefits through workers' compensation systems or long-term disability plans. These are usually lifelong benefits with substantial financial liability for the employer. In British Columbia, for example, a workers' compensation total economic loss pension for a young, high wage earner easily approaches a half million dollars with the charges being assessed to employers who fund the system. Again, depending on the particular plans, employers may determine that after a certain point, recouping costs is a lost cause, as they have reached the maximum premium rate or maximum demerit penalty. They often conclude that, since the situation cannot be any more financially punitive than it is, there is no sense in expending any more effort or dollars to reintegrate a worker.

Another consideration for employers is potential future liability for a worker's reinjury or aggravation to an existing injury. When the injury originally occurred at work and is part of an existing workers' compensation claim, employers are concerned enough about the costs they will bear from the initial claim. They do not want any part of making matters worse and being held responsible for additional damages.

These are often valid concerns for employers and, if an adversarial labor relations climate exists, there is sometimes the urge to cut losses on both sides. This can be a significant source of employer resistance to the reintegration of people with disabilities and serves to further antagonize labor relations. Most compensation systems have "relief of costs" provisions or "second injury funds" that protect employers from additional costs arising from a reinjury or aggravation to a preexisting condition. This may apply to situations involving claims originating at their worksite or in cases of new employees who have preexisting disabilities or conditions. In either case, the intent is to encourage reintegration and accommodation of those with disabilities.

It is clear that many factors impact the return-to-work scenario. Some employers reap the benefits of reduced lost time and increased productivity. Others shoulder the burden of costs for practices that preclude reintegration. Where the will exists, both labor and management must work hard to capture and sustain the spirit of the return to work strategies. Reintegration programs for workers with disabilities must not be viewed as a temporary phenomenon, or they will not be fully accepted. Disability management must be seen as a practical, sound, and effective way of demonstrating commitment to the interests of both the worker and the employer. Disability management is a long-term investment.

THE RETURN TO WORK PACT

Roger Fisher and William Ury's (1991) well-known book *Getting To Yes: Negotiating Agreement Without Giving In* gives valuable advice for developing a Return to Work Pact. This book clearly describes the process required to identify interests, find common ground, and establish joint strategies that do not compromise the principles to which the parties subscribe. Effective negotiation and problem solving is an important platform from which solutions to disability management challenges may be launched. Therefore, this book should be fundamental reading for joint labor-management representatives of the disability management team.

The following process is suggested in developing the Return to Work Pact, beginning with the pact's mission or purpose statement:

PURPOSE STATEMENT

Intended to express the shared values and spirit of the Return to Work Pact, this statement forms the foundation for the entire Disability Management policy and program. Its development is dependent on the ability of all parties to honestly and candidly put their interests on the table. These are then translated into a series of value statements that focus on joint labor-management activities.

Example

The workers and management of Widgets Company value and mutually benefit from the contribution of all employees and believe that a compassionate workplace will benefit all. In this spirit, a joint disability management program has been established to ensure that early and safe return-to-work options are provided to employees who become temporarily or permanently disabled. When the injury or disability requires special consideration, reasonable accommodation will be made to facilitate reintegration into the original job or into a suitable alternate job. Return to work focuses on returning employees to their previous jobs unless short-term transitional work, permanently modified employment, or alternate, on-site employment is required by virtue of the physical restrictions caused by the temporary or permanent disability. All workers, regardless of the origin of their disability and entitlement to any benefits will be treated in a "seamless" fashion ensuring that consistent return-to-work expectations and provisions exist for all.

PRINCIPLES

Intended to guide the development and use of the Return to Work Pact, principles combine the critical elements of the policy and set expectations for its implementation. They hold parties accountable for their commitment to the agreement. Principles refocus the energy required to invigorate the initiative.

Example

- A safe and healthy work-place is a good work-place.
- Early and safe return to work promotes proactive and healthy rehabilitation.
- Partnerships mean mutual commitment to common values and goals.
- Return to work is everyone's responsibility.
- Success equals return to work.
- Disability management promotes and protects the right to work for all employees.

OBJECTIVES

Objectives serve as the benchmarks of program operation and effectiveness in meeting the needs of all parties involved, by clearly establishing specific goals of the Return to Work Pact and setting a framework for evaluation.

Example

- To promote effective early intervention and a coordinated response to incidents of injury.
- To facilitate positive reintegration attitudes and practices among workers, co-workers, and supervisors.
- To return workers to the familiarity of previous jobs whenever possible.
- To reduce the number of workers off the job due to disability.
- To decrease the impact of injury/disability on one's ability to work.
- To minimize the costs of disability.
- To minimize disability-related attrition.

THE PARTNERS

The need to establish disability management strategies in partnership with workers and organized labor has been emphasized in this chapter. Regardless of employer size, there must be absolute, unequivocal support from senior management and the union executive. If this does not *visibly* exist, no effort will be successful. Inconsistency in the operations of a disability management system will jeopardize early intervention and work-return initiatives. For example, if a supervisor and a manager conspire to avoid reintegrating an unpopular employee, the noted inconsistency will undermine the program. Similarly, a shop steward operating from a nonreturn-to-work agenda will disrupt work-return efforts. A lack of good faith in the process will quickly displace the trust that the must be fostered and maintained. Without a "top down" commitment from senior management and union executives, middle managers and the rank and file are likely to resist program implementation or abandon their support for the disability management initiative.

Assuming senior union and management support exists, consider the following example of a medium-sized company with an employee work force of 250 employees. Typically, companies this size have a human resources department as well as a variety of others who fulfill "quasi-specialists" roles in key related areas such as safety, first aid, or labor relations. These responsibilities usually fall to management but such areas often have special union committees or designated employee representatives.

Members of disability management teams must clearly delineate their competencies and responsibilities at the onset. They must be willing to acknowledge their strengths, weaknesses, and their commitment to seek additional expertise, as required. Tapping technical expertise from within the organization and from acceptable external resources to design, build, or install required modifications and to provide specialized assistance will facilitate successful program operations. Sharing the disability management program's goals with all involved in the process is imperative.

Most disability management committee members become involved as motivated and committed union and employer representatives who are there to facilitate the reintegration strategies. They are there to get things done, to remove barriers, and to ensure that the joint policies and interventions are implemented fairly and consistently. They keep things on track and ensure that all interests are represented throughout the return-to-work process.

Although composition of the disability management team is largely dependent on the resources at hand, the role of case manager should remain constant. The dedicated involvement of a case manager ensures that there is one individual throughout the process responsible for collecting all information, and facilitating and monitoring return-to-work plans.

Aside from being the central contact person for the worker and supervisor, the case manager has the responsibility for establishing and maintaining working relationships with outside sources: physicians, community agencies, and benefits carriers. The maintenance of this role makes the process more efficient, consistent, and less onerous on the team members and more effective in its results.

Many other less obvious, but often equally important resources are likely to exist within the company. Departments staffed with mechanics, engineers, draftspeople, welders, and computer programmers can be sources of easily accessible expertise and can contribute technical knowledge to design and install required job or worksite modifications. Too often line staff are overlooked when their contributions may be invaluable to removing workplace barriers.

Employee participation and the acknowledgement of it may be the most influential internal public relations vehicle available to the disability management initiative. Focus on involvement helps reduce the mystery and will likely enhance the receptivity of co-workers as it dispels false rumors, and alleviates fears and anxieties. As one person with a disability stated: "The more people know about the difference, the less difference it makes" (B.C. Ministries,1992).

DISPUTE RESOLUTION

There will invariably be times when even effective and long-standing disability management programs falter. Establishing acceptable dispute resolution protocol *before it is needed* is the key to weathering conflict. Having acknowledged the possibility in advance allows the parties to deal proactively with problems as they emerge.

Dispute resolution can take many forms. However, simple processes that facilitate expedient problem solving, negotiation, and active interventions are preferable to complex multistep processes that collapse under their sheer weight. The appointment of ad hoc union and employer representatives may allow issues to be resolved outside of the regular committee structure. Depending on the nature of the dispute, it may be prudent to refer a medical question to an independent physician who is pre-approved by both labor and management. Handling the issue quickly, with common sense, and according to an established protocol are the keys to success.

To minimize later conflict, the joint committee should try to anticipate the most likely areas of dispute when establishing policies and programs. Some areas of dispute are predictable, but vary with the size and type of company or industry, the labor relations climate, and the general receptivity of the workers. In heavy industry, for example, physical compatibility is often the most contentious issue. Anticipating the potential for conflict in this area may require agreeing in advance to seek an independent medical opinion of the individual's physical limitations in conjunction with a functional capacity evaluation to resolve the impasse with minimal disruption or delay. Agreeing to mutually acceptable resources in advance also avoids adding more complications to the dispute resolution process. "Preferred providers"

PREPARATION

The concept of disability management is likely to be foreign to most, if not all, participants in the process. In order to equip the key players with the attitudes, expectations, and skills that are likely to make the venture successful, appropriate preparation is required. Although preparation does not need to be elaborate, it must address the most common questions and issues likely to arise in establishing a new policy and program.

Preparation includes many of the features previously discussed (e.g., the context of disability; an overview of what promotes and hinders return to work; the interests of workers [often represented by unions] and employers; common disincentives for the worker and employer; exemplary joint disability management programs and policies). Basic training in team-building and negotiation is also valuable for the disability management partners.

Establishing a reading list which covers these topics or contracting with specialists to function as information resource specialists in these areas will help fill the gaps. The aims are to reduce future conflicts and to establish acceptable protocol to resolve disputes that will undoubtedly arise from time to time no matter how carefully disability management policies are designed. The process of disability management, however, need not be complicated or intimidating. It is a logical process with clear, mutual goals. The challenge is to maintain focus and achieve results.

THE PROCESS

The obvious purpose of disability management programs is to put people back to work and to minimize displacement from the job and the worksite. The first objective is to establish the parameters of the worker's physical restrictions arising from the injury or disability. This requires a thorough physical evaluation and is usually conducted by the individual's personal physician. Other examinations by specialists or by benefits carriers may also be required. The goal is to clearly identify *specific physical restrictions* that will limit the worker's ability to perform *actual job duties.*

A specific job analysis describes the duties that comprise the work day: their frequency, physical requirements (e.g., lifting, bending, stooping, sitting, standing, walking), and the related tolerances of each, usually described as duration and physical demand (e.g., weight lifted from waist to shoulder; distance carried). Job analysis information may be collected from a *detailed job description* and from *direct observation of the job tasks, as typically performed.*

A *job site analysis* should be simultaneously conducted. This includes an analysis of the work station (i.e., the specific setting within which the work is performed), identifying work space dimensions, and equipment and machinery used. In addition, an analysis is made of the general work environment (i.e., the overall conditions), including such factors as temperature, lighting, humidity, air quality, indoor/outdoor setting, and social situations.

This information is summarized in a comprehensive job site analysis used to assist a physician to determine the *potential work limitations imposed by specific physical restrictions* of a very detailed and well-defined job. The physician should provide an opinion *only on the specific physical restrictions affecting the performance of well-detailed job tasks.* It is the responsibility of the vocational rehabilitation specialist, or other skilled member of the disability management team, to interpret the restrictions in the context of the overall job and to determine what modifications, if any, are required in response to the identified restrictions. It is strongly advisable for the physician to visit the worksite to view the job firsthand. The more information that is available, the better the planning and decision-making will be. This, in turn, will add precision to the return-to-work strategy and increase its chances for success.

Only after comparison of the physical restrictions with the job site analysis can the development of a suitable return-to-work plan begin. It is the role of the joint labor-management disability management team to develop and implement the plan. The suitability of specific job duties and any requisite accommodations will be identified.

The best scenario is one in which a direct return to the pre-injury job is possible. The individual is able to perform all of the duties and is able to work a regular schedule. No adjustments or modifications are required. The only reason this type of case would reach the disability management team would be to record the incident and circumstances that led to the individual's injury or accident. If it occurred at the workplace, the team would initiate an investigation of potential health and safety risks in order to prevent such incidents in the future. These cases are generally easy to resolve, and require no intervention by the team other than a commitment of further involvement if any unforeseen problems arise.

For employees unable to make a full return to their pre-injury job, various return-to-work options may be provided. *Transitional return to work* or *transitional modified return to work plans* are temporary alterations to pre-injury working conditions. Full-time employment at the pre-injury job is the ultimate goal. If permanent medical restrictions prevent the worker from returning to the pre-injury job, permanent *alternative employment* is considered. Successful full-time employment in a different job, with the same employer, is the goal for these individuals. Once comprehensive evaluations of the individual's needs and the job requirements have been undertaken, each option is carefully considered.

Transitional return to work is the *temporary* strategy of choice. The worker is able to perform the essential functions of the pre-injury job but, consistent with physical restrictions, may not be able to sustain activity for a full work shift and/or for the full work week. Fewer hours in each shift, fewer shifts and/or an altered work week may be necessary to accommodate the worker's gradual return to full-time employment.

Some workers with disabilities may be able to return to their previous employment but are unable to assume the full scope of their previous duties. Their physical restrictions may require a paring down of job duties to eliminate heavy lifting or driving, for example. They may or may not be able to work full time. By re-arranging job tasks or by swapping certain job activities with co-workers (previously negotiated by the labor-management committee), a safe and appropriate return-to-work plan can be tailored to arrive at suitable temporary modified transitional employment.

When a temporary transitional work-return plan is required, a specified predefined gradual reintroduction of remaining job tasks over a specific time period is established at the onset to clarify expectations and to set goals for achievement. The disability management team and injured worker must realistically develop, communicate, and fulfill their respective responsibilities as outlined in the plan.

Permanent modifications to the worker's pre-injury job may be required to facilitate a safe and timely return to work. For example, adaptive equipment can be installed or physical changes to the work station can be made if indicated by a job site analysis and physical restriction evaluation. Other temporary jobs may be utilized in the transitional work-return plan as a stepping stone approach to achieving pre-injury employment. These jobs may or may not be modified but they must maximally utilize the returning worker's skills and abilities without posing further risk of re-injury or increased disability. Once again, strict time designations for gradual reintroduction to the pre-injury job are delineated.

In contrast to transitional work, alternative employment is a permanent solution for injured workers unable to return to previous jobs due to significant permanent restrictions. This option considers other jobs that exist at the workplace, the re-engineering of existing jobs or the creation of new jobs to provide a compatible employment opportunity for the worker by accommodating permanent restrictions.

Whenever possible, return to work activities should occur at the workplace rather than in a simulated setting. Regular starting time should be maintained to reinforce the work routine, even if the shift itself is shortened. This ensures that the worker returns to the familiar work environment, works with regular co-workers, experiences the same work expectations, and reintegrates as realistically as possible.

Sometimes, the team will need to draw upon the expertise of in-house or contract job site evaluators, therapists, and ergonomists to finalize details, specify modifications to the job duties, and suggest environmental/physical accommodations assisting the worker to reintegrate safely and appropriately. The use of an ergonomist is prudent when injury patterns among several workers in a given worksite emerge. An ergonomic analysis and implementation of appropriate modifications to work stations may prevent future injuries and contribute to a decrease in disability costs. The ultimate goal is to prevent injuries. The need to ensure that preventive and rehabilitative measures are linked is paramount in achieving these goals.

ESTABLISHING THE PROGRAM

In order to support a worksite disability management program, both labor and management must create the infrastructure to support the program's operations. The following 10-point summary reviews key elements to establishing the worksite disability management program:

1. Be explicit about the roles of senior management and labor. A statement on the accountability of supervisors and the expectation of front line ownership of the reintegration strategy must be prepared and disseminated.
2. Take stock of your resources. Identify key players from labor (workers or union representatives in an organized worksite) and management. Representation is usually drawn from departments such as Human Resources, Labor Relations, Occupational Health and Safety, and specialized functions (which will vary according to the type of work environment) such as engineering, computer programming, or mechanical. Assign the participants to the disability management team.
    - Be prepared to honestly evaluate the committee's strengths and weaknesses and anticipate the need for specialized expertise (see point 4 below).
    - Select a case manager. This may be a team member or an external resource but the individual will carry the greatest responsibility for program implementation so must be competent and capable of engendering labor/management trust and confidence.
3. Define Disability Management policy. Establish a Return To Work Pact including a Purpose Statement, Principles and Objectives. Specify Referral and Discharge Criteria for program participants and their responsibilities during program participation. These will focus program activities and provide consistency to the process.

4. Agree on complementary resources that will support team resources and facilitate the reintegration process. Specialized vocational rehabilitation, ergonomic, therapy or functional capacity evaluation resources should be identified and agreed to by all parties from the start. A combination of internal and external resources may be required.
5. Establish Dispute Resolution protocol at the outset.
6. Orient the workplace. Prepare and present a basic disability education program, disability management goals, and establish supervisory/shop steward support and accountability.
7. Establish performance measures and set program targets. Initially there may be the need to measure program performance against a preprogram base line of return-to-work rates and disability costs.
8. Implement the program. The case manager takes the lead role, utilizing team expertise and appropriate external resources to facilitate the return-to-work process.
9. Monitor and evaluate the program. Measure the outcome against the target, identify snags and gaps, negotiate and implement refinements.
10. Reinforce the program's success by frequently acknowledging staff, union, and management efforts. An award system may provide a more tangible means of recognition.

CONCLUSION

The needless waste of human and economic potential must be reversed by direct labor-management responsibility for disability management policies and interventions. Society can no longer afford the tremendous costs associated with such restrictive attitudes or behaviors. Taking responsibility means being proactive and innovative in integrating a customized disability management program within the workplace. It means integrating the interests and perspectives of labor and management to ensure that the disability management program meets the expectations of employers and workers, building joint commitment to the process.

This chapter provided an overview of the issues and interests of labor and management, with respect to the resolution of disability in the workplace. Procedures were offered to establish dispute resolution processes, accommodation strategies, and work-return alternatives for persons with temporary and permanent work restrictions. For a more detailed framework for designing worksite disability management programs, including on-site transitional work services, the reader is referred to the chapter, "Disability Management at the Worksite: Developing, Implementing, and Evaluating Transitional Work Programs."

REFERENCES

Adam, G. (1986). *Address to "Bridging Rehabilitation and Work" Conference.* Canadian Labour Congress. Vancouver, BC.

B.C. Ministries of Advanced Education, Training and Technology; Education; Finance, Health, Social Services; and the Premier's Advisory Council for Persons With Disabilities. (1992). *A closer look – A profile of people with disabilities in British Columbia*, p. 29. Victoria, BC: Author.

Dofasco, Inc., Hamilton, Ontario.

Fisher, R., & Ury, W. (1991). *Getting to yes: Negotiating agreement without giving in.* New York: Penguin Books.

Gottlieb, A., Vandergoot, D., & Lutsky, L. (1988). Directions of disability: From neglect to priority. *Business and Health*, (11), 26-29.

International Center for the Disabled (ICD), and Louis Harris Associates. (1987). *The ICD Survey II: Employing disabled Americans.* New York: Louis Harris Associates.

Job Accommodation Network. (1993). Morgantown, WV.

Leavitt, F. (1992). The physical exertion factor in compensable work injuries: A hidden flaw in previous research, *Spine, 17* (3), 307-310.

Lucas, A. (1987). Putting a lid on disability costs. *Management Solutions, 32* (4), 16-18.

McGill, C. (1968). Industrial back problems : A control program. *Journal of Occupational Medicine, 10*(2), 174-178.

Statistics Canada. (1991). *Health and activity limitation survey: Users' guide.* Ottawa, Ontario: Author.

United Way of the Lower Mainland, Labour Participation Advisory Committee on the Disabled. (1991) . *Building bridges: A resource for the employment of people with disabilities.* Vancouver, BC: Author.

U.S. Small Business Administration. (1989). *The state of small business: A report to the president.* Washington, DC: U.S. Government Printing Office.

Vencill, M., Vencill, M., Barker, L., & Collignon, F. (1982). *A study of accommodations provided to handicapped employees by federal contractors: Final report to the U.S. Department of Labor – Volume 1, study findings.* Berkeley, CA: Berkeley Planning Associates.

APPENDIX

SAMPLES OF COLLECTIVE AGREEMENT PROVISIONS

Provision:

Lists of permanent and temporary job designations for disabled workers. Job list approved by both union and employer.

Negotiated between Canada Packers Inc. (employer) and the United Food and Commercial Workers International Union (U.F.C.W.), not dated, Article 15.8.

Provision:

Exception of seniority rights at layoff.

Negotiated between Canadian Fabricated Products Ltd. and the International Union, United Automobile, Aerospace, Agricultural Implement Workers of America (U.A.W.), Local 1325, December 1980, Article 18.

Provision:

Bidding preference for employees who have sustained a major compensable injury with the employer.

Negotiated between Hayes-Dana Inc., Ontario, and International Union of the United Automobile Workers (U.A.W.), Local 676, June 1, 1980 - May 31, 1983, Article 9.19.

Provision:

Provision of suitable employment upon receipt of qualified medical opinion. Exception of seniority rights but cannot bump existing incumbent.

Negotiated between Inca Metals Co. (INCA) and United Steelworkers of America (U.S.W.A.), June, 1979, Ontario Division, Sudbury District Operations, Article 11.23.

Provision:

Preference for light duties assignment.

Negotiated between Arrowhead Metals Ltd. and International Union, United Automobile, Aerospace and Agricultural Implement Workers of America, Local 399, February, 1981, Schedule D.

Provision:

Transfer to suitable alternate job or eligibility for early retirement (at age 61) with record of long and faithful service.

Negotiated between Halifax Industries Ltd. and Industrial Union of Marine and Shipbuilding Workers of Canada, Local 1 and 13, 1980-1982, Articles 5.09, 11.25 and 11.28.

SAMPLE GUIDELINES FOR NEGOTIATED EARLY SAFE RETURN-TO-WORK PROGRAMS

Negotiated between Health Labour Relations Association of British Columbia (employer) and the British Columbia Nurses' Union, April 1991 - March 1994, Master Collective Agreement, Appendix "D."

The Union and the HLRA agree that ill or injured employees may benefit from involvement in Early Safe Return-to-Work Programs which may involve a number of initiatives such as a gradual increase in hours of work-up to full shift hours, modified work, workplace modifications, a work-hardening program or, if necessary, a change in work assignment.

Participation in such a program shall be voluntary for both the employee and the employer and contingent upon the written consent of the employee's physician. The program shall be considered as part of the treatment/rehabilitation process. All employees engaged in a rehabilitation/treatment shall be supernumerary.

The employee, an employer designate responsible for the Early Safe Return-to-Work Program, the Union steward and the employee's immediate supervisor will meet to agree on a suitable program.

A written program for the employee will include:
1. An overview of the employee's program plan, including its expected outcome and end date. (Programs shall not exceed six months).
2. The number of phases in the program, their duration, and the number of hours to be worked per shift in each phase.
3. A detailed outline of employer and employee responsibilities under the program.
4. A schedule of evaluations to determine progress toward the program outcome. As a result of an evaluation, a program may be modified or discontinued by mutual consent of the parties.

Employees engaged in an Early Safe Return-to-Work Program shall be provided with a copy of the written program.

The employer designate, in conjunction with the immediate supervisor, shall be responsible for making all necessary arrangements for the employee's return to the workplace. The Union steward shall be allowed time away from the usual assigned duties to meet with Union members at the worksite to familiarize them with the terms and conditions of their co-worker's return to work and to ensure co-worker support and encouragement.

The Union and the employer agree that employees participating in an Early Safe Return-to-Work Program for 15 hours or more per week are entitled to all the benefits of the agreement, on a proportionate basis, except medical, extended health, dental plan coverage, group life, and LTD which shall be paid in accordance with Article 46. It is further agreed that participation in the program will not delay LTD entitlement.

Employees engaged in an Early Safe Return-to-Work Program will fall into one of four groups, although on occasion an employee may, depending on changed circumstances, move from one group to another. Wage and benefit entitlements, when participating in the program will be consistent with the terms of the agreement and are outlined below:

Group 1 – Employees suffering an occupational illness or injury who are in receipt of WCB payments.

Receive full wages and benefits. (Article 42.07 Leave – Workers' Compensation).

Group 2 – Employees suffering a nonoccupational illness or injury or who are awaiting acceptance of a WCB claim; who have accumulated sick time and/or who choose to utilize accumulated vacation time.

Receive pay and appropriate premiums for all hours worked at the workplace and receive sick pay/vacation pay for all hours not worked. All benefits continue uninterrupted.

Group 3 - Employees suffering a nonoccupational illness or injury or who are awaiting acceptance of a WCB claim, who have no accumulated sick time and/or do not choose to utilize accumulated vacation time.

Receive pay and appropriate premiums for all hours worked at the workplace and receive UIC (Unemployment Insurance) sick benefits for the balance, subject to their entitlement. Medical, dental, extended health, LTD, group life insurance, and superannuation coverage are reinstated on commencement of the program and all other benefits are reinstated when working 15 hours or more per week as outlined in Article 11.03(B).

Group 4 - Employees in receipt of LTD benefits.

These employees are considered disabled and under treatment.
These employees receive pay for all hours worked. The LTD plan will pay for hours not worked at two-thirds of basic monthly earnings at the date of disability. Ben-

efits will be reinstated in the same manner as for Group 3, excepting LTD. Employees shall have their group life insurance premiums waived.

The cap in Appendix B, Section 3(D) is waived for the duration of the employee's participation in an Early Safe Return-to-Work Program.

Therapy or functional capacity evaluation resources should be identified and agreed to by all parties at the outset. A combination of internal and external resources may be required.

Interdisciplinary Factors In The Management Of Cumulative Trauma-related Disability

Mark R. Stultz, M.S.I.E., P.T.

INTRODUCTION

Employers, insurers, and government are greatly concerned about the incidence and severity of occupationally related cumulative trauma disorders in the United States. Staggering statistics abound regarding the personal and economic cost to industry and society due to these maladies, as well as the incalculable human suffering and stress they produce. Although low back pain is the most common of these disorders, upper extremity cumulative trauma disorders have increased more than tenfold over the past decade, accounting for nearly 60% of workplace illnesses.

Low back pain serves as both the leading cause of activity limitation in individuals under age 45, and as one of the leading causes of office visits to physicians (Deyo, 1983). Since low back pain episodes comprise 25% of all occupational injuries and account for 90% of the total costs associated with these injuries (Snook, 1983), they provide a means through which we can explore valid and effective injury and disability management. Although most of the information available to us regarding the management of occupational illnesses and injuries is related to low back pain, most of this information is applicable to other types of cumulative trauma as well.

CURRENT INTERVENTION STRATEGIES

Traditionally, employers have applied several interventions to control the incidence, magnitude, and consequences of cumulative trauma. Typical strategies have included the utilization of ergonomic interventions, pre-placement selection and screening strategies, and safe work practices education.

When used exclusively as an approach to injury prevention, none of these interventions address the nonphysical factors that affect the reporting and severity of occupationally related pain disorders. In addition to recognizing and addressing the physical stressors present at the worksite, there is also a need to understand the coexistence and effect of psychological variables and mental stressors. Of the physical and psychological variables evaluated in a study by Svensson and Andersson (1989), only dissatisfaction with the work environment, a higher degree of worry, and fatigue at the end of the work day, were directly related to onset of low back pain. Given these findings, it is interesting to note that most of the literature dealing with low back pain causation focuses only on the presence of physical factors. The fact that occupational stressors are associated with psychological, behavioral, and physiological outcomes is well documented (Smith, 1987). Although a direct correlation between occupational stress and complaint of pain due to cumulative trauma has not been well established, a less direct relationship appears appropriate for analysis and discussion.

Research prior to the Americans with Disabilities Act of 1990 revealed that only 50% of those individuals unable to return to work within six months of injury, ever returned to productive employment. For injured employees absent from work for one year, the likelihood of returning to work was 25%, while for those workers unable to return to work within two years from the date of injury, the possibility of returning was almost nil (McGill, 1968). Kelsey (1982) reported that the highest work-related injury costs are attributable to the 7% of workers who continue to complain of pain for more than six months following onset. Although incidence rates for low back pain have been stable, the disability rate continues to increase (Waddell, 1987). Since total prevention of cumulative trauma disorders is unlikely, the priority in treating these types of disorders must be management of disability, rather than the prevention of injury (Rowe, 1983; Snook, 1988a).

Katz and Kahn (1978) have pointed out that unacceptable injury rates should be viewed as organizational, rather than individual problems, thus requiring organizational solutions (Dwyer, 1987; Isernhagen, 1988, Snook, 1988; Dwyer, 1987). The level of occupational stress, as a contributor to pain severity, is certainly a factor which can be manipulated and affected by organizational culture and management initiatives.

The following disability management model addresses:

- factors affecting the report of occupationally related pain
- cumulative trauma disability and its accompanying stress
- the role of management in reducing these stressors

Intervention strategies, which facilitate a reduction in occupationally and disability-related stress, will also be reviewed within the context of factors which are under management's control. The role of worker stress, as a sole cause of occupationally related pain will not be considered here, but rather those factors which are functions of stress and which are likely to result in disability.

AN ERGONOMIC MODEL OF OCCUPATIONALLY RELATED PAIN REPORT

There are three primary and interactive factors which impinge upon the likelihood that an employee will experience occupationally related pain (see Fig. 1). The first of these includes the physical stressors present in the task, such as aerobic

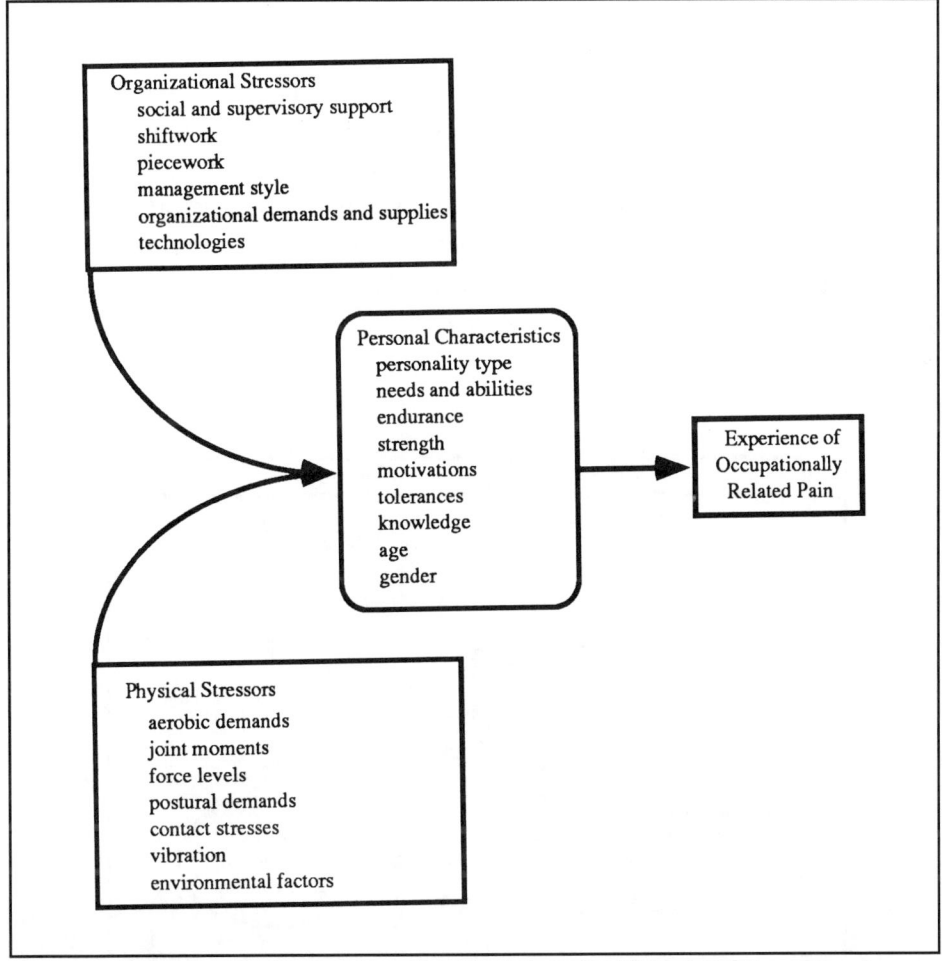

Figure 1. Interactive Factors Involved In The Likelihood Of Experiencing Occupationally Related Pain

demands, joint movements, force levels, repetition rates, postural demands, contact stresses, vibration, and various environmental factors. Second, organizational stressors associated with job satisfaction, shiftwork, incentive pay systems, supervisory and social support, organizational demands and supplies, job control, monotony, and limited growth potential also play a role. In addition to these worksite factors, individual worker characteristics must also be considered. These may include the employee's gender, age, endurance, strength, personality type, needs and abilities, motivations, tolerances, intelligence, family history, and support system, among others. The interaction between these occupational demands and personal attributes will determine the likelihood of occupationally related pain.

While Figure 1 reflects some of the factors predictive of experiencing occupationally related pain, other factors impact the likelihood of simply reporting the pain to management or supervisory personnel (see Fig. 2). It is obvious that the personal characteristics and past and present performance of the worker impact, to a great extent, management's perception of the employee. The reporting of pain or injury, of itself, also has a profound effect upon management's perception of that particular worker (Fordyce, 1987). Because of the concern over the potential for negative alteration of the supervisor's or employer's perception of and relationship with the worker following onset of pain, some employees may be reluctant to report the pain. Indeed, the factors which facilitate a reduction in reporting may be, in large part, responsible for the increases observed in injury severity rates (Fitzler & Berger, 1982, 1983; Melton, 1983; Tomer, Olson, & Lepore, 1984). If disability prevention is to become a priority, then early reporting of symptoms is imperative to enable effective and timely interventions.

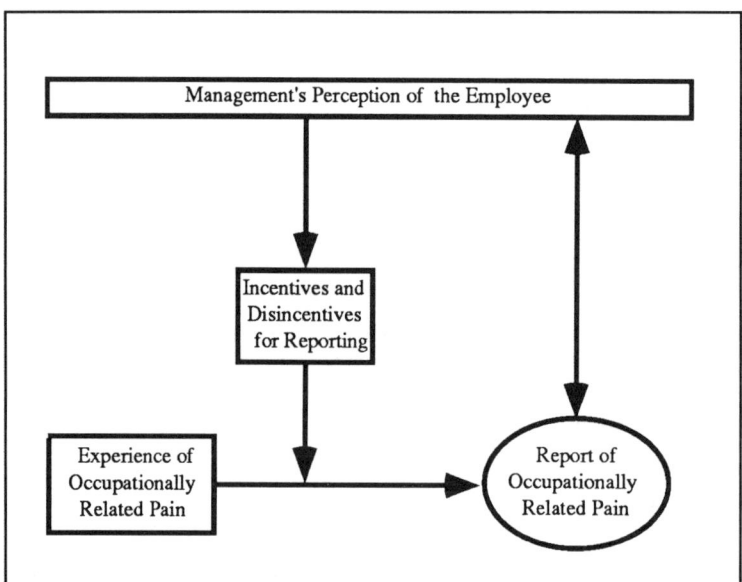

Figure 2. Interactive Factors Involved In The Likelihood Of Reporting Occupationally Related Pain

Worker perceptions of management's attitudes and management's support of disability management programs are central factors with respect to successful rehabilitation outcomes. Fitzler and Berger (1982, 1983) reported that employees must feel comfortable in reporting injuries to management without fear of derision or dispute. In fear of being labeled as complainers, many employees do not report symptoms which, if understood, may be appropriately addressed, thus preventing disability. Instead, many workers become conditioned to disregard the cumulative nature of these disorders secondary to management's past negative attitudes and prior adverse consequences. When pain or injury is not reported at the time the first symptoms of a problem become evident, reporting the pain as occupationally related often becomes difficult for the worker.

Many employees are viewed as malingerers by their employers when they awake with severe pain on the morning following what had been considered an "inconsequential incident." The employee in this situation is required to make the difficult decision of either proving disability (furthering the concept that he is "faking") or pretending to be well (potentially fostering additional tissue strain) (Lehmann, Frymoyer, & Milhous, 1984). Neither option serves the employer or employee well. In this situation, denial may be used as a coping mechanism by the worker with occupationally related pain. The worker copes with the event by anticipating the probable negative outcome of reporting the incident and takes steps to avoid the conflict. That is, the worker avoids reporting the injury because the threat, negatively biasing management's perception of the worker, is perceived to be less desirable than the worker's own discomfort. The employee has been pressured into making a very poor and costly decision.

EMPIRICAL THEORETICAL SUPPORT

Three years after introducing "Attitudinal Change," a management training program at American Biltrite, Fitzler and Berger (1982, 1983) reported a 90% reduction in back injury claims, a 50% reduction in lost workdays and a tenfold reduction in workers' compensation costs, from $200,000 per year to $20,000 per year. The primary thrust of this intervention strategy involved the facilitation of positively accepting pain reports. Employees were no longer "second guessed" when they indicated the development of a problematic or painful condition.

Although similar statistical examples may be found among other industries, many research methodologies are confounded by the fact that multiple interventions were utilized to help control the development and progression of disability. Melton (1983), for example, reported a 40% decrease in lost workdays with associated reductions in medical insurance premiums in her study of eight different industries. Although there was an increase noted in the reporting (or incidence) of pain, those who did report showed an 86% reduction in lost time days. Tomer et al. (1984), also reported that, although incidence rates may increase somewhat, lost-time injuries can show marked reductions. In Tomer's study, for example, incidence rates rose approximately 8% while lost-time injuries decreased from 63% to 19% among those employees who reported painful incidents.

These authors have concluded that the increases in reporting are probably due to the change in management's perception and acceptance of pain or injury reporting and the concomitant willingness on the part of the employee to report these incidents without the fear of rejection or negative consequences. One of the primary methods utilized in their intervention with these employers was management- and supervisory-level training. Before management can be expected to receive pain complaints without prejudice, however, they need to understand and accept cumulative trauma disorders for what they are. In the case of low back pain, for example, it must be perceived as a disorder of unknown origin that affects almost everyone, develops insidiously, is not always due to strenuous activity, recurs frequently, and is usually self-limiting over several days or weeks (Snook, 1988a).

Management's attitude that occupationally related pain is significantly related to malingering, and that malingering is prevalent in industry requires alteration as well. Indeed, in an assessment of 2,500 workers, only seven were felt to be true malingerers, accounting for less than 0.3% of the sample (Braverman, 1978). It is only after management has an understanding of how cumulative trauma disorders manifest themselves, that they will be capable of providing the support required of them by the injured employees.

THE ROLE OF MANAGEMENT IN DISABILITY PREVENTION

In a nationwide study of 28,000 employees conducted by the St. Paul Fire and Marine Insurance Company, poor supervisory practices ranked as one of the top workplace stressors leading to problems in one's personal life (Kohler, 1992). In addition to a strong relationship between supervision and health problems, individuals who did not rank their supervisor as good were more likely to feel fatigued at the end of the day. Indeed, job factors were found to be more likely to result in poorer work performance and health problems even more than such profound personal problems as the death of a family member.

Management's role may be expanded to providing and fostering support mechanisms for employees in an attempt to reduce or prevent occupational stress. According to House (1981), "Support must be central in any comprehensive effort to control stress (or its adverse effects) in blue collar work." Additionally, LaRocco, and Jones (1980) supported the notion that, in the case of work-related strain, such as cumulative trauma disorders, support from work-related sources may even be more relevant than nonwork-related sources of support.

James House (1981) in *Work Stress and Social Support,* proposed three mechanisms by which support may be effective. The first of these involves direct alteration of the stressor. This effect may be observed in the case where simple lack of social support is the cause of the stress. Once support is finally offered, the stress is abated. Another of the positive effects of social support, described by House, is its ability to enhance the nonwork-related aspects of life. This, however, does not represent a primary goal for the prevention of cumulative trauma-related disability. The manner in which support appears to be most effective, in the case of pain reporting and disability prevention, is in its buffering effect. Supervisory support was demonstrated to produce a buffering effect between health and perceived occupational stress in 36% of the cases evaluated (House, 1981). This buffering effect may be particularly important, especially among those cases where other intervention strategies are impossible or cost-prohibitive.

PROACTIVE VERSUS REACTIVE DISABILITY MANAGEMENT

Managers and supervisors need to maintain continuous monitoring of workers, encouraging early reporting of pain before expensive or unnecessary medical, surgical, or legal intervention is required. When problems are identified during the monitoring phase, there are several options available to manage disability and prevent escalation of symptoms. These options include ergonomic redesign, worker rotation, modified duty, rest breaks, position reversal or circulation stimulation exercises, and training, to name a few.

Injury is an advanced stage in the continuum which extends from fatigue to disability. (see Fig. 3). Management personnel need to pay close attention to the presence of early warning signs in an attempt to control the precursors to injury. In many cases, fatigue is the first recognizable symptom of occupationally related cumulative trauma and musculoskeletal problems. While fatigue will not be present in cases of acute injury, many occupationally related pain disorders appear to be due to the accumulation of stresses while sensations of fatigue are discounted or ignored. Fatigue can usually be controlled by the properly trained employee, by altering the technique or equipment used, performing position reversal or circulation stimulation exercises, or rotating between significantly different tasks.

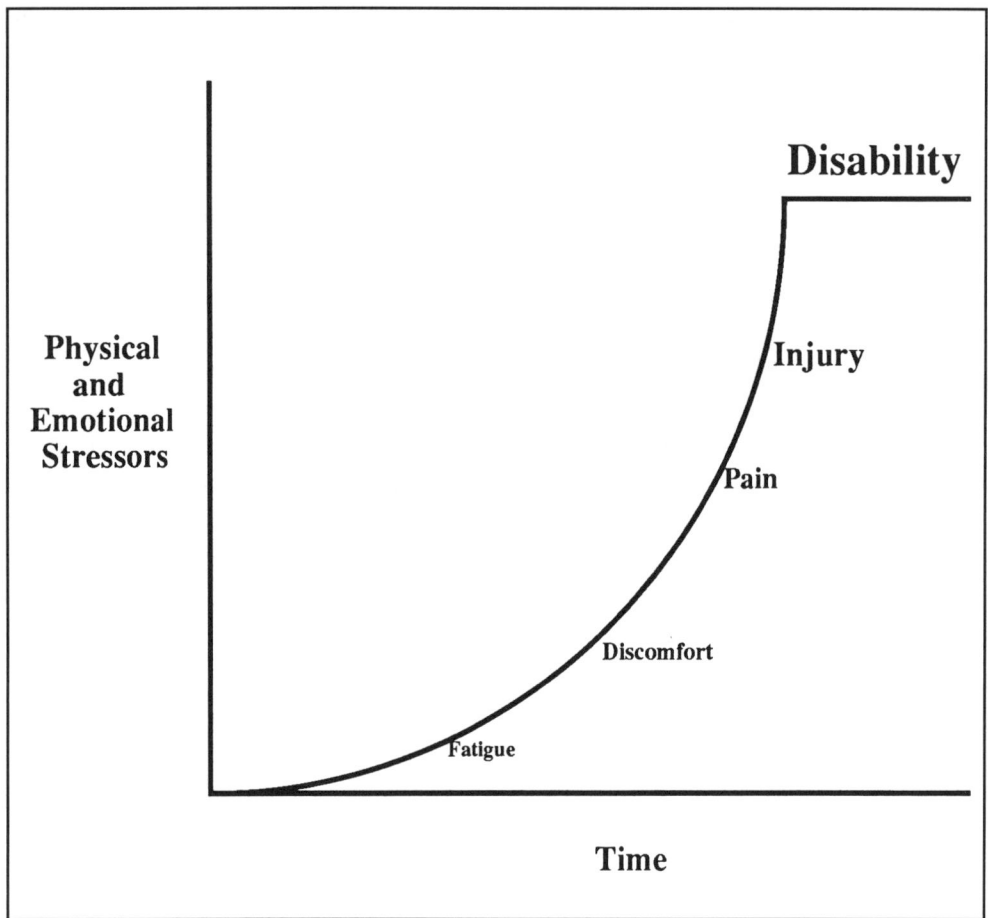

Figure 3. The Fatigue To Disability Continuum

When this progression through the continuum is not checked, what had started as fatigue may eventually lead to discomfort as nutritional support to the tissues diminishes and microtrauma advances within the affected body parts. At this point in the process, the options narrow and the employee may need to be transferred to another job or the work station may require more substantial ergonomic analysis and modification. None of these changes, of course, can occur if management has not been apprised of the symptoms.

Although preventive (proactive) health care has been a widely accepted concept, support for proactive injury management has not been as popular. Through various safety incentive programs, many employers unwittingly reward employees for not reporting pain and injury when a predetermined amount of time has passed without a lost time injury. Frequently, such practices may reinforce under-reporting of pain, as well as the fatigue and discomfort which preceded it. When pain is eventually reported, at which point it is referred to "as injury," the singular interventions, which earlier could have reversed the process, are no longer sufficient to manage the injury and subsequent disability. For these individuals, medical and disability management becomes the reactive alternative to proactive reporting. More aggressive, expensive, and extensive strategies will thus be necessary to return these injured employees to work.

When injury or pain has progressed to the point of work disability and lost time, management can still play an important role in expediting the employee's safe and timely return to work. Whereas control of physical fatigue is perhaps the best means of preventing cumulative tissue injury, minimization of emotional fatigue or psychological stress may be the treatment of choice in preventing the injury from becoming a disability. Although the relationship between social support, stress, and return to gainful employment is less clear in the prevention of disability, as compared to the prevention of lost time, there are several options available to management which are likely to reduce worker stress and expedite return to work.

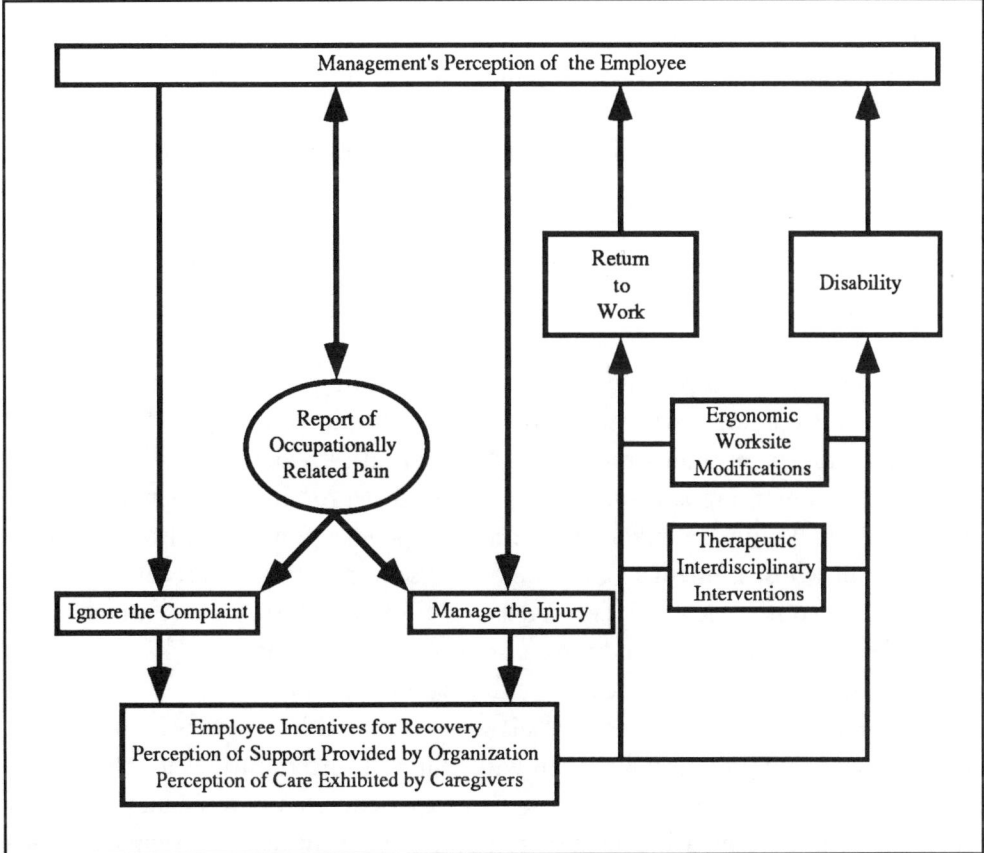

Figure 4. Management Options And Outcomes In Responding To The Report Of Occupationally Related Pain

The remainder of this chapter addresses those options and provides an understanding of how those interventions can have stress-reducing qualities.

There appear to be two primary interventions at management's disposal when interceding responsibly after the report of occupationally related pain by an employee (see Fig. 4). Those two interventions are organizational management and medical management. A third option, ignoring the complaint, is likely to lead toward more severe symptoms over time, eventually requiring lost time and, potentially, disability. Since the focus is to understand those interventions which affect stress reduction, and therefore are likely to reduce the potential for disability, ignoring the complaint is neither responsible nor an option which deserves consideration.

THE DILEMMA

Preventing disability, following pain report, requires management to understand both the injured employee's plight, as well as those factors which affect the progression from pain to injury and from injury to disability. There are incentives for returning to work and incentives for being "sick" which need to be managed and manipulated. Once accepted and understood, those which increase the likelihood of returning an employee to work can be fostered, while those which tend to potentiate disability, can be minimized. Not until the employer understands the interaction of all these factors can effective intervention be made on the employee's behalf.

Given the current workers' compensation system, in order for the employee to receive disability income benefits for medically advised time off work, disability must be proven. Since the physician is in part responsible for the continuation of disability benefits and is partially in control of determining when and under which restrictions the employee will return to work, the employee is required to play out two apparently incongruous roles with the medical provider. According to Nagi (1969), "... something is wrong with a system that produces conflicts of interest on the part of an injured worker whose future depends upon maximum restoration of health but whose immediate attention is focused upon financial recovery." This apparent role conflict can be identified as a stressor which surfaces relatively early within the disability process and must also be considered when establishing protocols to minimize the stress associated with disabling injury.

The employee who requires time off work is placed in an awkward and novel situation; a setting undoubtedly laden with fear and uncertainty. With the uncertainty and lack of clarity surrounding this experience, employees may be overwhelmed. The perceived inability to respond effectively to these vague circumstances may amplify fears and increase the injured employee's stress level. Many negative consequences, such as loss of income, reduction in social status, lower levels of job performance, and strained family, sexual, and co-worker relationships, accompany this fear of failure to respond appropriately, and even higher levels of stress are likely. These emotions may be accounted for, in large part, by a lack of information regarding this new situation. Information is, according to information theory, simply the reduction of uncertainty. The fear and stress related to these uncertainties is readily alleviated by the simple provision of information by a knowledgeable party, the employer.

Employees need to know how and through whom assistance in overcoming these barriers will occur. When the information available tells them that a planned response is in place to facilitate their eventual return to work, certainty replaces uncertainty, and a perceived ability to respond effectively replaces the previously perceived inability to respond effectively.

THE TIME FACTOR IN DISABILITY PREVENTION

Time is another factor which management should consider in implementing a strategy to reduce disability. As the duration of time from injury increases, the likelihood of ever returning the employee to the worksite decreases (McGill, 1968). Physical condition, behaviors, motivations, desires, expectations, and even neurophysiological processes tend to change following lost time injury. In the absence of appropriate disability management, the direction of these changes rarely fosters return to work.

Effective early intervention is perhaps the management strategy which affords the greatest benefit (McElligot, Miscovich, & Fielding, 1989). "Early," in this sense, does not simply imply that rapid referral is provided to rehabilitation facilities, but that disability prevention strategies are set in motion and far precede the need to rehabilitate. Early intervention implies that the employee is guided toward resolution of symptoms from first complaint of fatigue, discomfort, pain, or injury. Stress can be prevented or reduced simply by exposing the employee to the fact that there is a planned protocol or schedule to follow. Plans and schedules are designed to reduce uncertainty and enable prediction which, as has been discussed earlier, can facilitate a reduction in stress.

ORGANIZATIONAL RESPONSIVENESS TO THE WORKER WITH PAIN

The planned response for intervention begins with a company representative such as the first line supervisor. Based upon the findings of LaRocco, and Jones

(1978), the person who can best support the employee during a period of work-associated strain should themselves be affiliated with the work environment.

Second, because supervisors are already involved within the chain of command, they are in a unique situation to offer social support, exert influence on behalf of the employee, and assist in coordinating the efforts of those who will aid in returning the employee back to pre-injury status (House, 1981). In this sense, disability prevention, as in the case of proactive injury prevention, is a function of the relationship between the supervisor and employee prior to the pain-provoking incident or events. Early intervention thus serves as both an antecedent, and a response, to the incident.

Third, research has revealed that when safety and health administration is under the control of lower level management, the severity and frequency of accidents is reduced (McIntosh, 1986). Assuming that this strategy is accepted within industry, it makes sense for the supervisor (lower level manager) to be involved with health and safety administration, as well as disability prevention and management. Currently, separation of employee safety, health and disability management is all too common. If more safety personnel can be made aware of the impact they can have in facilitating proactive, rather than reactive measures, the need for disability management could be markedly reduced.

According to Martin (1975), the supervisor is a veteran of the system, intimately associated with the environment in which the employee must work. The supervisor has credibility with the employee and insights into the requirements of various tasks within the organization. In an analogy regarding the importance of putting teams of people together who have similar backgrounds, education, and experiences, Martin states that "two G.I.s make it better together on a battlefield than a Colonel and a G.I." For these reasons, it appears that the supervisors are well suited to provide the social support, education, and coordination of services required by the injured employee.

The chosen company representative performs several critical functions soon after an employee reports injury. Their primary role is to educate and support the afflicted worker during this stressful period, while helping to facilitate a "return-to-work" orientation and discourage the acquisition of disability behaviors and characteristics. The effectiveness of these interactions is related to the immediacy with which the company representative is able to act, not react. The effective execution of a planned response is imperative. The worker should be contacted immediately after the report of pain or authorization for time off work. This early personal interaction serves to potentiate the employee's belief that return to work is not only possible, but imminent. When the perceived threat and fear of inability to return to work is reduced, more energies may be expended in healthful manners.

This interface with the employee serves to alleviate any fears that the employer is no longer desirous of maintaining a relationship with the worker. Until the employee's future role is understood and reinforced, this ambiguity can also provide an additional source of stress (Kahn, 1964). Immediate employee contact communicates the employer's commitment to protecting the health and employability of the worker. The mere statement that the employer is willing to hold the job until the employee is able to return to work results in an enormous reduction in stress and may motivate the employee to improve. Although the Americans with Disabilities Act of 1990 may alter the status quo as it relates to returning employees to the workplace following injury, the fact remains that "the injured worker who has a job to return to gets well—the injured worker without a job cannot afford to get well" (Cheit,1961).

Of course, none of these interventions will be viewed as sincere if the relationship with the worker has been adversarial or less than facilitative. The importance of proactive interventions and pre-injury relationships should not be underestimated when facilitating an effective, planned response to injury. The company representative must be seen, literally, as a visual supporter of injury prevention efforts. If the company representative has exhibited no observable effort toward reducing the likelihood of pain and injury, how can the employee believe that this person is sincere after the fact? These efforts may be as relatively simple as taking short stretch breaks with workers, participating in pre-work exercise and flexibility programs, or serving as a member of the safety team.

WORKER EDUCATION AS A STRESS-REDUCING FACTOR

Early employee support which communicates the employer's desire to return the employee to work can reduce the stress experienced by the injured worker. However, worker education also serves to reduce stress and uncertainty. The injured employee's lack of knowledge or understanding regarding rights under workers' compensation law, can result in fear and in behaviors which are counter-productive to the return-to-work process. Thirty years ago, 90% of injured or disabled workers were found reluctant to participate in rehabilitation. This reluctance was based on an unfounded fear that they would experience a reduction in or loss of disability benefits (Cheit, 1961). There continues to be considerable misunderstanding regarding worker rights following injury. It is difficult to know what unsubstantiated fears and beliefs workers may still hold that could disrupt the rehabilitative process. Fear based upon a lack of clear understanding of rights under workers' compensation law, is easily quelled by an effective interaction initiated by the company representative.

Fears, based on ignorance and left unchecked, may progress to isolation and worry, emerging as an adversarial worker-employer relationship (Martin, 1975). Within an adversarial setting there is a nonproductive focus on rights, rather than recovery and return to work. If this adversarial stance progresses to the point that litigation ensues, the cost of the reported incident increases significantly. Andersson (1992) reports that when low back injury claims involve legal consultation, the cost of the claim increases an average of $26,000.

Stress also increases as separation from work-related sources of support grows. Indeed, prolonged isolation from the employer and co-workers is the primary cause of disability-related emotional problems (O'Connor & Anderson, 1989). Timely, simple, and frequent contact with the employee, communicating the message that the employee is remembered and continues to be important to the organization, can serve to prevent these types of occurrences.

This concept of an employee contact, support, and follow-up system is very similar to the type of intervention strategy implemented by Wood (1987). In this particular health care setting, the director of personnel became the company representative responsible for managing disability. A process was initiated whereby the injured employee received immediate contact following the report of symptoms. Regular 10-day follow-up telephone contact was scheduled to communicate the message that "you are an important part of the team" and "your work is important and your job is waiting for you." The director of personnel also served as a liaison between the workers' compensation board and the employee's supervisor to facilitate communication and to encourage early return to work. The proportion of high hour claims at this facility (those over 1,000 hours) dropped from 7.1% of those individuals requiring lost time, to 1.7% within the first four months of the program.

THE EFFECT OF CHOOSING APPROPRIATE MEDICAL CARE

Another less direct means of providing support to the disabled worker involves the selection of appropriate health care professionals. The preferred providers chosen by the organization determine to a great extent both the stress experienced by the worker and the final ability/disability outcome. The ideal provider should possess and endorse attitudes which fit within the organizational injury management philosophy. Namely, the providers chosen should be aware of the stressors experienced by the disabled workers and be willing and able to take the measures necessary to diminish their intensity.

The provider should be able to formulate a treatment plan, while providing some indication of the anticipated progression of symptoms. This plan and progression provides a basis for expectations while facilitating a sense of control over the incident and the concept that symptoms will eventually terminate. LaCroix et al. (1990) have made it clear that patient understanding is critical to successful injury and disability management. In their study, 94% of patients possessing good understanding of their problem returned to work, while only 33% of patients with poor understanding of their problem returned to work. Additionally, this increased understanding may result in improved medical and therapeutic compliance assuming the relationship between intervention and outcome has been established through education.

Likewise, if stress is to be minimized, the provider must be willing to generate prompt and proper reports for the workers' compensation provider to insure timely payment of benefits to the worker. The fact that 68% of workers are in financial trouble after only 14 days of disability, serves as an indicator of the importance of timely report generation (Martin, 1975). When expected, warranted, and required disability benefit payments do not arrive on time, stress and the likelihood of an adversarial relationship increases.

The terminology used by the care provider should preferably be free of medical jargon that may imply chronic disease or illness. Haynes, Sackett, and Taylor (1978) reported increased sick role behaviors, such as absenteeism, when asymptomatic individuals have been diagnosed or given a disease label. Resembling a self-fulfilling prophecy, of sorts, these individuals altered their behavior to accommodate the "disease." Hadler (1987) has gone to the extent of advocating that the term "injury" not be applied in cases of cumulative trauma as it may connote a concept of violent tissue disruption and potentiate an already adversarial stance. Terms or phrases which imply "degeneration" may foster the concept of long-term ill health and do little in the way of facilitating self-responsibility and empowerment for recovery.

Finally, the provider should function in such a manner as to be consistently available to patients such that continuity of care, and the employee's perception of care may be maximized. Even when the care is appropriate, if the employee somehow gets the stereotypical "company doctor" impression, a defensive posture may be assumed and the stress may again increase. The employee's perception of the employer is also blemished when the chosen provider does not care enough about the patient as an individual to provide personal and consistent care throughout the rehabilitative process.

The provider should desire to facilitate a rehabilitation orientation among workers with lost time injuries, while making them aware that the primary goal is a safe and timely return to the worksite. When early return to work is indicated, the provider should become familiar with the jobsite so the options available in returning the employee to modified duty are clear. That this provider is willing to be visible to the employees and take the time to perform this function may provide an indication of "philosophical fit" with the organization.

MANAGEMENT'S FACILITATION OF EARLY RETURN TO WORK

The final factor to be considered in management's role in stress reduction and disability prevention involves the development of an early return to modified duty plan. Facilitating the employee's return to work before healing is complete and pain is abolished promotes a focus on abilities rather than disabilities (Stelter, 1989). It also allows continued co-worker socialization and maintenance of support structures which are extremely important when dealing with work-related sources of stress. Early return to work may also be related to reduced depression and maintenance of self-worth (McElligot et al., 1989). The prevention of disability-related behaviors, learned helplessness, and physical deconditioning should also be considered as some of the advantages of incorporating a modified duty plan into an organizational disability and stress management framework.

SUMMARY AND CONCLUSIONS

A comprehensive disability model has been presented which considers both the antecedents and resultants of pain and injury within the framework of disability management (see Fig. 5). An appropriate organizational response to occupationally related pain disorders, both in terms of facilitating the early reporting of symptoms and in executing a plan for managing the process following pain report, can have significant positive effects. These effects include a reduction in the stress one experiences during such an incident and the diminished likelihood of the pain to extend to long-term disability. In many cases, work environments or processes cannot be effectively modified to facilitate optimal levels of employee comfort and health. Managing the fatigue to disability process, through these organizational and less tangible means, may be the only option available to employers in reducing the long-term cost and effect of injury to individuals, organizations, and to society at large.

Management of Cumulative Trauma-related Disability 265

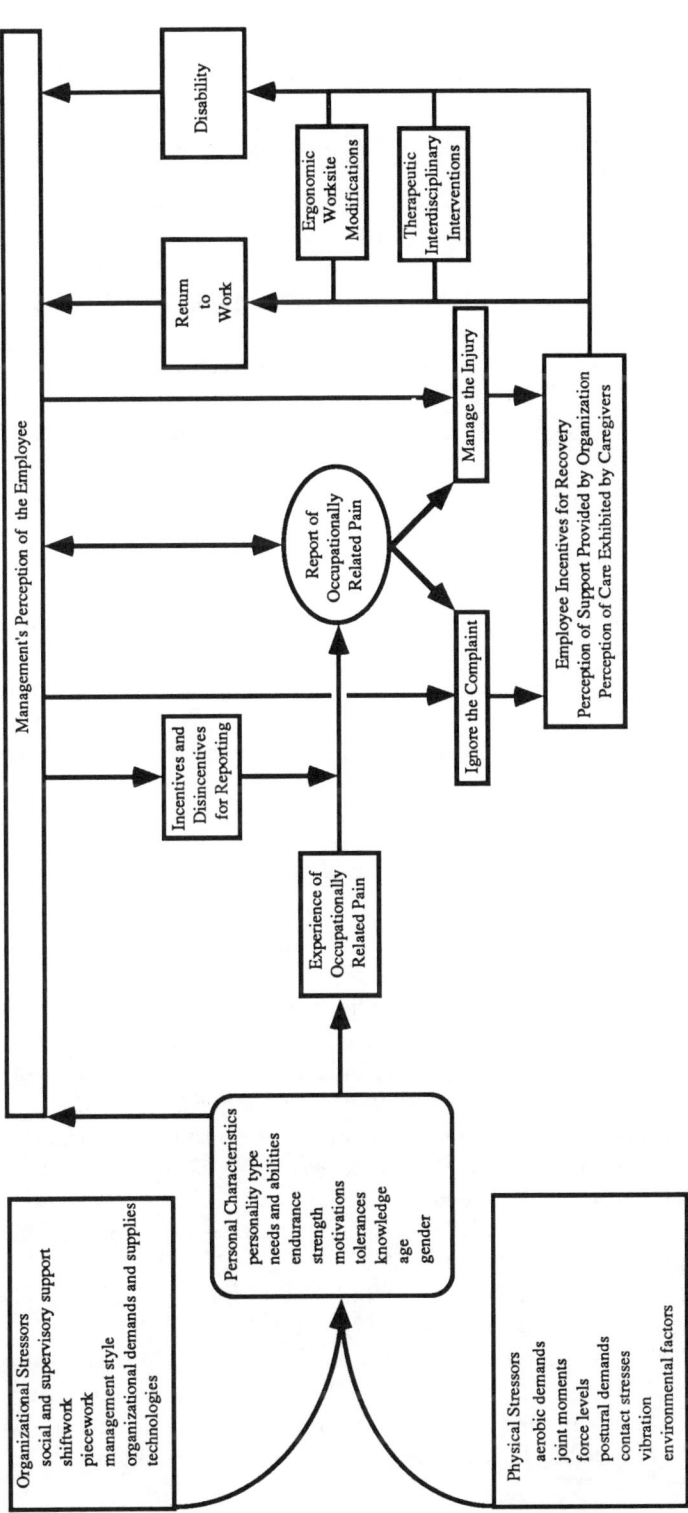

Figure 5. The Disability Model

REFERENCES

Andersson, G. B. J. (1992). Assessing the costs: Leg pain, lawyers, and abnormal scans. *The Back Letter, 7*(5), 3.

Braverman, M. (1978). Malingering: Post injury malingering is seldom a calculated ploy. *Occupational Health and Safety, 47,* 36-48.

Cheit, E. F. (1961). *Injury and recovery in the course of employment.* New York: John Wiley and Sons, Inc.

Deyo, R. A. (1983). Conservative therapy for low back pain. *Journal of the American Medical Association, 250*(8), 1057-1062.

Dwyer, A. P. (1987). Backache and its prevention. *Clinical Orthopaedics and Related Research, 222,* 35-43.

Fitzler, S. L., & Berger, R. A. (1982). Attitudinal change: The Chelsea back program. *Occupational Health and Safety, February,* 24-26.

Fitzler, S. L., Berger, R. A. (1983). Chelsea back program: One year later. *Occupational Health and Safety, July,* 52-54.

Fordyce, W. E. (1987). Prevention of reinjury. *Ergonomics, 30*(2), 457-462.

Hadler, N. M. (1987). *To be a patient or a claimant with a musculoskeletal illness.* Orlando, FL: Grune and Stratton.

Haynes, R. B., Sackett, D L, & Taylor, D W (1978). Increased absenteeism from work after detection and labeling of hypertensive patients. *New England Journal of Medicine, 299*(14), 741-744.

House, J. S. (1981). *Work, stress and social support.* Reading, MA: Addison-Wesley.

Isernhagen, S. J. (1988). *Work injury: Management and prevention.* Rockville, MD: Aspen Publishers, Inc.

Kahn, R. L., Wolfe, D. M., Quinn, R. P., Snoek, J. D., & Rosenthal, R. A. (1964). *Organizational stress: Studies in role conflict and ambiguity.* New York: Wiley.

Katz, D., Kahn, R. L. (1978). *The social psychology of organizations* (2nd ed.). New York: John Wiley and Sons.

Kelsey, J. L. (1982). *Epidemiology of musculoskeletal pain.* New York: Oxford University Press Publishers.

Kohler, S. (1992). *American workers under pressure* October 13. The Saint Paul Companies. St. Paul, MN.

LaCroix, J. M., Powell, J., Lloyd, G., Doxey, N., Mitson, G. L., & Aldam, C. F. (1990). Low back pain—factors of value in predicting outcome. *Spine, 15*(6), 495-499.

LaRocco, J. M., & Jones, A. P. (1978). Co-worker and leader support as moderators of stress strain relationships in work situations. *Journal of Applied Psychology, 63,* 629-634.

Lehmann, T. R., John Frymoyer, & Raymond Milhous. (1984). Treatment, education and rehabilitation. In M. H. Pope, J. Frymoyer, & G. Andersson (Eds.), *Occupational low back pain* (pp. 185-208). Philadelphia: Praeger Scientific.

Martin, R. A. (1975). *Occupational disability: Causes, prediction, prevention.* Springfield, IL: Charles C. Thomas, Publisher.

McElligot, J., Miscovich, S., & Fielding, P. (1989). Low back injury in industry: The value of a recovery program. *Connecticut Medicine, 53*(12), 711-715.

McGill, C., M. (1968). Industrial back problems: A control program. *Journal of Occupational Medicine, 10*(4), 174-178.

McIntosh, B. (1986). Accident compensation as a factor in influencing managerial perceptions and behavior in New Zealand. In J. Chelins (Ed.), *Current Issues in Workers' Compensation* (pp. 347-372).

Melton, B. (1983). Back injury prevention means education. *Occupational Health and Safety, July,* 20-23.

Nagi, S. Z. (1969). *Disability and rehabilitation: Legal, clinical and self concepts and measurements*. Columbus, OH: Ohio State University Press.

O'Connor, S., & Anderson, N. (1989). Early rehabilitation intervention in workers' compensation claims. *Michigan Hospitals, August*, 11-19.

Rowe, M. L. (1983). *Backache at work*. New York: Perinton Press.

Smith, M. J. (1987). Occupational stress. In G. Salvendy (Ed.), *Handbook of human factors* (pp. 844-860). New York: John Wiley and Sons.

Snook, S. H. (1983). Low back pain in industry. In A. A. White & S. L. Gordon (Eds.), *Procedings workshop idiopathic low back pain* (pp. 23-38). St. Louis, MO: C. V. Mosby.

Snook, S. H. (1988a). Approaches to the control of back pain in industry: Job design, job placement, and education/training. *Occupational Medicine: State of the Art Reviews, 3*(1), 45-59.

Snook, S. H. (1988b). *The control of low back disability: The role of management* (pp. 97-101). San Francisco, CA: American Industrial Hygiene Association.

Stelter, B. (1989). Return to work program involves employee/employer cooperation. *Michigan Hospitals, August*.

Svensson, H. O., Andersson, & G. B. J., Gunnar B. J. (1989). The relationship of low-back pain, work history, work environment, and stress: A retrospective cross sectional study of 38- to 64-year-old women. *Spine, 14*(5), 517-522.

Tomer, G. M., Olson, C., & Lepore, B. (1984). Back injury prevention training makes dollars and sense. *National Safety News*, (January), 36-39.

Waddell, G. (1987). A new clinical model for the treatment of low back pain. *Spine, 12*, 632-644.

Wood, D. J. (1987). Design and evaluation of a back injury prevention program within a geriatric hospital. *Spine, 12*(2), 77-82.

—10—

FUNCTIONAL CAPACITY ASSESSMENT, WORKER EVALUATION STRATEGIES, AND THE DISABILITY MANAGEMENT PROCESS

Lester A. Owens, D.O.
Rodney L. Buchholz, M.Ed.

INTRODUCTION

The Functional Capacity Assessment (FCA) is a tool used to assess an individual's abilities to perform work-related tasks. Traditionally, health care providers review an individual's medical history, perform a physical examination, listen to the worker's subjective reports of pain, and study the findings of various diagnostic tests including x-ray, CAT scan, MRI, EMG, and various laboratory data to determine an individual's diagnosis, the extent of injury, the cause of pain, and the degree of physical impairment. Using this information, the physician or health care provider *indirectly* assesses physical disability and functional ability. However, these traditional methods do not quantify the functional effects of injury or one's ability to perform specific work tasks. In contrast, the FCA consists of a battery of tasks specifically designed to directly measure an individual's functional ability to perform specific tasks. This assessment allows the health care provider to determine an individual's work ability based on physical performance, rather than the extrapolation of an individual's abilities based on the methods of traditional medical diagnostics.

THE GOAL OF THE FUNCTIONAL CAPACITY ASSESSMENT

The primary goal of the FCA is to determine the working capabilities of an individual and, when possible, compare this with the physical demands of the job.

These capabilities include high-force, nonrepetitious tasks such as lifting, pushing, and pulling; low-force tasks such as repetitive movements; precision tasks such as finger dexterity; and static and dynamic posture tolerances such as sitting, standing, and walking. The specific tasks performed in the FCA will be determined by the purpose of the assessment (i.e., pre-placement or return-to-work post-injury). The tasks may be specific to the job to which the employee will be returning, or the tasks may encompass a variety of physical abilities that can be applied to many jobs.

A secondary goal of the FCA is to enable the evaluator to make legally defensible conclusions regarding the physical capabilities of an individual. Of concern is the validity of the assessment tasks and the credibility of the information derived from the assessment. The fundamental credibility issue is whether or not an individual is putting forth a best, honest effort. The evaluator must design an assessment that answers the questions for which the assessment is being conducted, with the highest possible degree of legal certainty.

WHEN IS AN FCA INDICATED?

An injured worker may not be able to return to the pre-injury job in situations involving permanent disability. The FCA can be designed with nonspecific job tasks to help determine "the general type of work tasks" the individual can perform. This type of FCA would include tasks that are common to a broad range of jobs and can help the vocational rehabilitation specialist guide the worker to appropriate job options.

The FCA can be used to monitor the rehabilitation progress of an injured worker. Job-specific work tasks can be simulated in the rehabilitation clinic and periodically performed by the injured worker to determine the improvement in functional ability. Although traditional performance assessments such as range-of-motion testing and isokinetic testing can measure physical improvement and impairment, these do not measure the functional ability to perform a specific job task.

Functional testing in rehabilitation is also useful when the physical demands of the job are known and can be used as a goal for the rehabilitation program. In this role, the FCA can help determine when the worker is ready to safely return to work. The FCA can provide the health care provider with objective data from which to base safe return-to-work recommendations. The employer can reduce the risk of re-injury to the injured worker by following the recommendations.

Only 50% of individuals off work due to low back pain for six continuous months will ever become employed again; only 25% return after one year; and after two years, only a negligible number return (Kelsey & White, 1988). The FCA can be useful in situations where an injured worker's safe functional capabilities fall below the physical demands required of the worker's job. By using the information from the FCA, the employer can provide modified duty, alternate duty, or gradual return-to-work options, enabling the injured worker to safely return to work sooner than would have been possible if only the pre-injury job was available. Earlier return-to-work benefits both the injured worker and the employer by reducing workers' compensation costs (Maxfield, 1989) and allowing the convalescing worker to continue to recover from injury while safely returning to the pre-injury job or one of the options (American Health Consultants, Inc., 1992).

The enactment of the Americans with Disabilities Act (ADA) in July, 1992, created a need for a method employers can use for assessing whether prospective employees can perform the essential functions of a job as presented in the job description. A carefully designed FCA that utilizes appropriate testing methods can be employed to provide the necessary information.

With the exception of performing an FCA for vocational rehabilitation purposes, all the indications for conducting the assessment relate to the worker's ability to perform a specific job involving specific job tasks. The test administrator must have a clear and precise understanding of the physical demands for each of the tasks that are crucial to the successful performance of the job. Once the crucial demands are identified, the FCA tasks must assess the individual's ability to perform the work tasks.

JOB ANALYSIS

Establishing the demands of the job can be accomplished through several methods:

1. Interview the worker being tested

In a return-to-work situation, the person actually doing the job probably knows the job best. This person knows all the tasks of the job, including the infrequent ones. The worker also knows the most difficult tasks. However, the worker may not give an accurate job description, especially regarding the weight of objects and push and pull forces. Workers tend to overestimate the weight of material.

2. Obtain a job description from the employer

Written job descriptions provide an overview of the worker requirements. Usually, these descriptions do not contain enough detail from which to base an accurate assessment. They may not include some of the infrequent tasks and may not provide weights, heights, and the frequencies of repetitive tasks.

3. Obtain a videotape of the job

If filmed correctly, videotapes can provide the assessment designer with a relatively complete analysis of a job. This approach is especially useful if accompanied with a written description or if viewed with either the worker or the worker's supervisor.

4. Perform a job-site assessment

The job assessment is an objective, systematic procedure for determining the physical requirements and demands of a specific job, as well as determining the exposure to generic risk factors (Keyserling, Armstrong, & Punnett, 1991) (see Table 1). Included in the job assessment are the work objectives of the job, the production rate, the equipment and tools used to perform the job, a description of any materials or products that are handled, and the work methods employed. Work methods consist of the weights and forces required to move material and equipment, distances the materials are carried, and time durations of any sustained forces and postures.

Unlike the first three methods, completing a job assessment requires the actual measurement of any materials that are handled, including the weight and the physical dimensions. These measurements are critical for obtaining an unbiased job demand. These measurements are important when designing the FCA: the physical demands of lifting a 30-lb. tool box with handles are much different than the demands of lifting a 30-lb. sheet of plywood.

Although performing a job assessment is the best approach to determine job demands, this approach requires the greatest amount of time and effort. However, this information can be used for writing a job description that meets the employer's need for ADA compliance.

Table 1
Generic Risk Factors

- Forceful Exertions
- Awkward Postures
- Localized Contact Stresses
- Vibration
- Temperature Extremes
- Repetitive Motions or Prolonged Activities

NIOSH developed an equation to evaluate lifting demands and for computing a weight limit for manual lifting in a specific task (Waters et al., 1993). The equation uses biomechanical, physiological, and psychophysical criteria because each lifting task places different requirements on the worker. The equation is based on a 23 kg (51 lbs.) Load Constant (i.e., "the maximum recommended weight for lifting at the standard lifting location under optimal conditions"). This load is acceptable to 99% of male workers and 75% of female workers. Six multipliers or modifiers are then used in the equation to account for less than ideal lifting circumstances. The result of the equation is a Recommended Weight Limit (RWL) that is a reduction of the Load Constant.

The influence the biomechanical, physiological, and psychophysical criteria have on lifting are reflected by the six multipliers:

Horizontal Location of the hands forward of the midpoint between the ankles at the beginning of the lift, up to a maximum of 25 inches.

Vertical Location of the hands above the floor at the origin of the lift.

Vertical Travel Distance of the hands between the destination and the origin of the lift.

Asymmetric Angle - The angle of the sagittal plane with the load plane (i.e., the angle of twist in the body).

Coupling of the Hands with the load, either good, fair, or poor.

Frequency or Number of Lifts per minute compared to the duration of the activity: less than one hour, less than two hours, less than eight hours.

By recording the above measurements, one can determine the RWL for a specific task. This analysis will establish lifting limits that 99% of the general male population and 75% of the female population can perform with minimal risk to the back.

The Lifting Index is the ratio between the load weight and the RWL. A value of 1.0 indicates that the job demand is equal to the RWL; a value less than 1.0 indicates that the job demand is less than the RWL and that the risk for back injury is low; a value greater than 1.0 indicates that the job demand is greater than the RWL, the load is greater than what 99% of the males and 75% of the females can safely lift, and that this job task should be modified.

The Lifting Index can also be used to compare the relative risk of two or more tasks. The tasks with the highest indices are the ones with the greatest risks. However, a task with Lifting Index of 3.0 does not have twice the risk of a task with an Index of 1.5. Only a relative comparison can be made.

Specific components of the NIOSH (1993) equation can be analyzed in greater detail. A biomechanical analysis of the lifting task can be conducted to estimate the compression force at the L5/S1 disc. Lifting tasks that result in compression forces at this joint that are in excess of 770 lbs. are considered by NIOSH to be unsafe. Musculoskeletal injury incidence rates increase in workers lifting in excess of this limit.

With a two-dimensional static model, a photograph of the individual performing the lift is used to determine the body joint angles. Based on the forces and torques acting on the musculoskeletal system, the compression force at the L5/S1 disc can be calculated. The two-dimensional analysis only considers movement in the sagittal plane (as viewed from the side of the individual). The three-dimensional model enables a more realistic analysis of the task by allowing the input of torso twists and bends and more complex hand forces, thereby depicting a greater variety of lifting positions and postures. Both static models assume the effects of acceleration to be zero.

Use of a dynamic biomechanical model to calculate the back compression forces at the L5/S1 disc can result in a more accurate lumbosacral compression force estimation than a static model because the speed and acceleration of the lift is taken into account. In a comparison of static and dynamic modeling, the lumbosacral compression force was, on average, 45% greater in the dynamic model (Leskinen, 1985). The difference will be less at slow lifting rates and greater at fast lifting rates. The collection of the necessary data require the use of commercially available computer equipment that can digitally record body segment movements and load acceleration. Although using a dynamic model can provide an accurate measure of back compression force, this value cannot be compared with the NIOSH (1991) recommendation of 770 lbs. The NIOSH recommendation is based on studies involving static loads placed on the spine segments of cadavers, and a valid comparison cannot be made between these studies and dynamic measurements.

Cardiovascular endurance can be assessed to determine if the individual has the aerobic capacity to meet the demands of a job. Typical endurance demands for each of the work classifications published in the *Dictionary of Occupational Titles* have been calculated (Matheson, Anzai, & Niemeyer, 1991):

Sedentary:	1.5 - 2.1 METs
Light:	2.2 - 3.5 METs
Medium:	3.6 - 6.3 METs
Heavy:	6.4 - 7.5 METs
Very Heavy:	Over 7.5 METs

One MET, or metabolic equivalent, is equal to the oxygen consumption of an individual at rest. The endurance demands of a job can also be estimated from tables of similar jobs (*Eastman Kodak Company*, 1986; Wenger & Hellerstein, 1978). These two approaches provide, at best, an approximation of the actual cardiovascular requirements of a specific individual's job. Analyzing the specific tasks of the job can provide a more accurate analysis of the endurance requirement (Ayoub, 1982; Drury, 1983). Commercial computer software is available that simplifies the calculations.

The motivation status of the worker being evaluated will also influence the FCA design. The worker being assessed for pre-placement may have a much higher level of motivation than a worker being assessed for return-to-work recommendations. In the case of the former, the potential for dispute lies in the validity of the test (i.e., does the test truly represent the actual job task and does it accurately differentiate between those who can and cannot perform the task). These are the questions likely to arise if an individual is denied employment due to not being able to perform the pre-determined job tasks. Performance credibility becomes the issue of potential dispute for the case involving return-to-work readiness: Did the individual perform below the job demand because of a true lack of ability, or because of a submaximum performance?

LEGITIMACY ISSUES

The second goal of the FCA is to produce legally defensible assessment results regarding an individual's ability to work. The procedures and equipment incorporated into the FCA must be chosen carefully to ensure that basic testing criteria are satisfied. The issues essential to the FCA are safety, standardization, objectivity, validity, reliability, and performance credibility.

SAFETY

The safety of the individual must be of primary concern to the assessment administrator. Equipment and procedures must not place undue risk of injury or re-injury on the individual. The assessment administrator must take into account the specific condition or injury of the individual; a procedure that is safe for one person may not be safe for another. Disgruntled injured workers who may be looking for ways to "get back at the system" require caution. Such individuals may look for opportunities to claim the testing procedure caused an injury and, therefore, are entitled to additional compensation.

ASSESSMENT STANDARDIZATION

Assessment standardization deals with the uniformity of the assessment procedure from one assessment to another. The oral instructions, task demonstrations, subject placement, and data collection and analysis should be documented and followed each time the assessment is administered, and should not change regardless of the individual administering the assessment.

The application of standardization procedures is dependent on the purpose and the setting of the assessment. Tasks with standardized procedures and equipment may be used in which there is normative data available for performance comparisons. The amount of deviation from the average can be determined and indicate the relative degree to which the worker's performance is above or below normal. Standardized tasks may not exist for job-specific tasks. However, the method for determining the specific job tasks to be incorporated into the FCA, the design of the task assessment, the method of instructing the worker to perform the task, and how the data is collected and interpreted needs to be standardized. Although the job tasks may be different from one FCA to another, there needs to be consistency in the methods for designing and conducting the assessment.

OBJECTIVE AND SUBJECTIVE DATA

One of the greatest strengths of the properly designed FCA is its ability to provide legally defensible results. Legal defensibility is enhanced by conclusions based on objective rather than subjective data. Objective findings are unbiased, impartial, and not influenced by the assessment administrator. These data include various measurements such as weight of a lifted object, force of an exertion, variation between repeated trials, and changes in heart rate. This information is measurable and reproducible.

The collection of subjective data can also be of significant value. Subjective data, such as rating scales and open-ended questions, are open to the bias and interpretation of the assessment evaluator as well as the worker, and great care must be taken in providing guidelines for the collection and interpretation of this data.

VALIDITY

Internal and external test validity issues must be identified and resolved when designing the FCA battery. Internal validity deals with whether the assessment measures what it is intended to measure. To achieve strong internal validity, the testing procedure must have sufficient controls so that influencing factors are eliminated. For example, a static (isometric) lifting test can have a high level of internal validity because many of the variables involved in the lift can be controlled: the speed of the movement (i.e., no speed), the lifting posture, and the lift duration. A dynamic lifting test may have a much lower degree of internal validity since the above variables cannot be controlled.

External validity concerns the generalization of the test results to a larger population or application. To achieve strong external validity, the test needs to have a close resemblance or approximation to the actual work task. The FCA task with the highest degree of external validity is the work task itself. For this reason, FCAs conducted at the worksite may be more valid and defensible than simulated clinic-based FCAs.

Matheson et al. (1991) suggest using "content validity" procedures, which is "a professional judgment as to the degree to which the test measures the job's demands and is based on the thorough and systematic job analysis." The isometric test has a low degree of external validity because most, if not all, work-related lifting tasks have movement associated with them. The dynamic lifting test performed on-site, using the actual job material, has a very high degree of external validity.

It is difficult to design a test that has both strong internal as well as external validity. As control of the task increases, external validity decreases. The assessment administrator needs to decide which factor is more important and design the test accordingly.

Performance validity, as opposed to test validity, is a measure of an individual's ability to complete a task within specific guidelines. In order for a performance to be valid, the individual must attempt, though not necessarily complete, the task as instructed by the evaluator. An individual who is unable to complete a task because of pain or a physical limitation will be deemed to have given a valid performance. However, an invalid performance will result when an individual does not attempt or alters the method of performing a task.

RELIABILITY

Statistical reliability is a measure of consistency. Assessment reliability deals with the ability of the equipment and testing procedure to consistently reproduce a given measurement. There should not be any statistical difference in the outcome of multiple trials or testings if an individual provided consistent effort on a given piece of equipment. Equipment reliability is usually demonstrated through studies using motivated subjects who are assumed to give consistent, maximum efforts.

Performance reliability deals with the consistency of a performance of a given task. An objective method of analyzing the consistency of multiple-trial outcomes is the determination of the coefficient of variation (CV) (Matheson et al., 1991). The CV is derived by dividing the standard deviation for a set of values by the average, expressed as a percentage[1]. A CV of 15 or less is generally considered reflective of a consistent effort; a CV greater than 15 indicates the effort was not consistent.

PERFORMANCE CREDIBILITY

Many times performance reliability is used to determine performance credibility based on the assumption that an individual will produce similar outcomes in a series of *maximal* trials (Matheson, 1988b). Studies have found force CVs to range from 8.6% to 15.4% when measuring isometric lift performances (Kroemer, 1983; Owens & Buchholz, 1993). However, performance inconsistency can have several possible causes other than a submaximal performance (Blankenship, 1986):

1. A learning effect took place in which the first trial was submaximal because the individual did not know what to expect, and the subsequent trials were performed at a maximum effort. This can be avoided by performing four trials and dropping the first.
2. Pain on one or two trials resulted in an inconsistent effort. This should correlate with pain reports and observed pain behaviors.
3. The assessment procedure or equipment lacks standardization or is poorly designed.
4. Inconsistent effort due to the individual not understanding the procedure.

Data analysis performed by the authors suggest that some injured individuals can perform isometric tasks at a submaximum level and still be consistent.

Several additional methods have been developed to measure performance credibility. Objective measures include the increase in the heart rate during and immediately following the performance of a strenuous task, indicating the relative level of exertion. Performing whole-body isometric activities will elicit a cardiac response that can be measured and compared to task-specific norms. Several studies have shown that a large exercising muscle mass will elicit a greater increase in heart rate than a smaller muscle mass, regardless of whether the activity is dynamic or static in nature (Pollock & Wilmore, 1990). However, drury and Spitz (1976) state that the heart rate increase is independent of which muscle groups are contracting, and that rates can rise by over 30 beats per minute during contractions approaching the limit of endurance. The cardiac response to the isometric lift task may provide an

---

[1] The correct formula for the standard deviation utilizes the population size of "n" rather than the population size of "n-1." The statistical method indicates the variability of all the scores of a task, not a sample of the scores. Use of the inappropriate formula will result in an inflated CV (Matheson, 1988).

indication for the level of exertion: increases of 15 beats per minute can be expected when the assessment is performed with significant effort.

Surface EMG signals may also lend insight to the amount of effort exhibited in isometric performances. Signal amplitude and shifts in the median frequency of the EMG signal are being studied as a valid indicator of maximum effort, as well as the determination of muscle impairment and fatigue (DeLuca & Knaflitz). Physiological criteria for determining performance reliability are task-specific; the responses are unique to specific activities and cannot be inferred to other activities. The expected physiological responses from the specific tasks should be based on norms derived from populations representative of the users (Anastasi, 1982).

The Horizontal Strength Change test is another method of determining performance credibility of lifting tasks (Staats, 1990). The premise is that an individual standing further from a load cannot generate as great a lifting force as when standing close to the load. To administer the test during a series of isometric lift tests, the individual is positioned 10 inches either further or closer to the handles of the lifting device and asked to perform an additional lift. This is done at each lift level. Performance credibility must be questioned if the individual's outcomes do not change by at least 33% in two or more of the lift positions (Berryhill et al., 1993).

Performance credibility can also be subjectively determined by looking for consistencies and incongruity between task performances. For example, posture and position should influence lifting ability. An individual will not have the same maximum lifting ability for a shoulder-level lift as for a mid-level lift; a two-finger pinch should not be as strong as a key-type pinch. Performances that do not follow normal or expected patterns can indicate a less than sincere effort. Reports of pain and observed pain behaviors should also be specific to the type of tasks performed and correlate with the individual's injury. An individual with an upper extremity injury would not be expected to have reports of pain when performing lower extremity tasks. However, one would expect an individual to demonstrate pain behaviors, such as rubbing the injured area, grimacing, groaning, and moving relatively slow and guarded, and/or state that it hurts when using an impaired body part to perform specific job tasks. Pain reports and pain behaviors that are not task-specific may indicate an undiagnosed condition, psychophysical limitations, or a worker who is not being cooperative.

An astute evaluator may find discrepancies between a worker's pain reports and pain behaviors. The stoic person or the motivated worker who fears having restrictions placed on him/her may not express any reports of pain. However, this person may unknowingly demonstrate pain behaviors. Inconsistencies may also be found in the injured worker who does not want to return to work. The worker may give frequent pain reports but have few, if any, pain behaviors.

Care must be taken when interpreting pain reports and pain behavior. An individual can develop pain as a result of assuming an uncomfortable body posture while performing a task of a seemingly noninjured body part or function. If the worker with a low back injury has difficulty sitting, then performing the grip strength test in a sitting position may produce reports of pain even though the worker is performing a seemingly unrelated task. A well-designed battery can include two or more tasks that assess the same key job function to help determine legitimate reports of pain and performance capability.

The worker's rating of pain can also lend insight to the likelihood of obtaining a reliable performance. Using a scale of 0 to 10 (zero indicating the absence of pain), the evaluator can record the person's perceived level of pain at the beginning and end of the assessment session. One would expect an injured individual's perceived level of pain to correlate with the evaluator's observations of the perfor-

Table 2 Subjectively Reported Pain Level Scale		
Reported Pain Level	Clinical Categorization	Description
1-3	Low	– Probably no pain medication – Normal function with all but moderate heavy activities
4-6	Moderate	– Probably on pain medication – Reasonably normal function with self-limited activities – Substitution movement patterns – Slowing of some movements – Refusal to perform some activities
7-9	High	– Taking regular pain medication, muscle relaxants, and anti-inflammatory drugs – Very limited activities – Grossly altered and slowed movement patterns – Obvious pain-induced facial expressions
10	Emergency	– Only concern is to reduce pain – Individual needs immediate care

mance and pain behavior. Blankenship (1986) devised a scheme of associating an individual's reported pain perception with the expected clinical observations (see Table 2). An exaggerated pain rating may help identify a "symptom magnifier."[2] Symptom magnifiers will often report pain in the 7 to 10 range which does not correlate with their movement patterns, activity level, body posture, or facial expressions. Even though symptom magnifiers claim they are in extreme pain, they are still able to proceed with the FCA. These exaggerated and amplified pain behaviors indicate the pain is perceived to be much more severe than it really is. This type of performance can be differentiated from a credible performance by the specificity of the pain reports and behaviors.

Another subjective credibility measure is the individual's perceived physical strain (effort). Borg (1982) designed a scale that quantifies an individual's subjective symptoms in an attempt to measure the degree of perceived physical strain by an individual when exerting an effort. The individual chooses a descriptive word or phrase that best represents the level of difficulty of performing the task. The descriptive words and phrases correspond to a number. This Rating of Perceived Exertion enables the evaluator to better understand the individual's perception of the degree of difficulty in performing a specific task.

Table 3
Rating of Perceived Exertion

6	
7	very, very light
8	
9	very light
10	
11	fairly light
12	
13	somewhat hard
14	
15	hard
16	
17	very hard
18	
19	very, very hard

---

[2] As defined by Matheson (1988a), Symptom Magnification Syndrome is defined as "a conscious or unconscious self-destructive socially reinforced behavioral response pattern consisting of reports or displays of symptoms which function to control the life circumstances of the sufferer."

The first of two scales was designed to increase linearly with the exercise intensity of work on the cycle ergometer (see Table 3). Values of the scale range from 6 to 20 with correlations of 0.80 to 0.90 to heart rates, ranging from 60 to 200 beats per minute. This scale may work best with activities that require a relatively long, sustained effort and are limited by cardiovascular factors, such as walking, running, climbing stairs, or prolonged repetitive work activity.

The second scale has a different number and wording system (see Table 4). The scale ranges from 0 to 10 and the expressions are located on the scale according to their quantitative meaning; each word or phrase is a ratio of the adjacent word or phrase. This perceived exertion scale may best be used with short duration activities that are limited by muscular strength and pain.

Table 4
Rating of Perceived Exertion

0	Nothing at all	
0.5	Very, very weak	(just noticeable)
1	Very weak	
2	Weak	(light)
3	Moderate	
4	Somewhat strong	
5	Strong	(heavy)
6		
7	Very strong	
8		
9		
10	Very, very strong	(almost maximum)

The authors developed a scale called the Rating of Perceived Ability (RPA) (see Table 5). At the completion of a task, the individual is asked to rate how much better the task could have been performed in the pre-injury state (i.e., if the injury had not occurred). A rating of 10 indicates that the worker felt that the pain severely limited performance of the activity. A rating of 0 indicates that the performance was not influenced by pain. The response gives insight to the individual's perception of the injury as well as the congruency of current pain behaviors, pain reports, and the statistical reliability of performance as it compares to the physical and physiological data.

Table 5
Rating of Perceived Ability (RPA)

10	very, very much better
9	
8	very much better
7	
6	much better
5	
4	little better
3	
2	very little better
1	
0	none . . . . no pain present

GRIP STRENGTH ASSESSMENT

The purpose of the grip strength assessment in the FCA is two-fold: first, to assess hand grip strength; second, to document the individual's proclivity to perform maximum voluntary efforts. The Jamar® hand dynamometer is frequently used because it has been shown to be valid and reliable, and it can measure static grip strength at five grip spans.

Three trials of one or more grip spans is performed. Alternating hands for each trial should provide enough recovery time to avoid fatigue. The initial grip span may be the widest setting or the smallest setting. The force variability of multiple trials, expressed as the CV, has been demonstrated to range from 9.01% to 5.48% (Matheson et al., 1988c). Values greater than this might indicate a noncredible performance.

The use of a multi-position device enables the collection of additional data that can be used to determine performance credibility. A graphical representation of the forces at each of the five grip positions should reveal a "biomechanical curve," with the lowest force values occurring in positions one and five and the highest values in position two, three, or four. The failure to produce this bell-shaped curve would cast doubt on the individual's tendency to perform at a maximum level.

The Jamar® hand dynamometer can also be interfaced with the desktop computer, enabling the collection of average as well as peak force values. It has been suggested that sincerity of effort can be determined when the peak force is compared to the average force. When instructed to "jerk" the handle to their maximum grip force as rapidly as possible and to hold that force for five seconds, subjects providing a sincere effort had an average force to peak force ratio not less than 0.90 (Gilbert & Knowlton, 1983).

STRENGTH ASSESSMENTS

Determining muscular strength capacities can generally be performed using one of three types of assessments: isometric, isokinetic, and isoinertial.

Isometric: Isometric assessments require a force exerted against an object that does not move; there is muscle contraction without any joint movement. In its simplest form, a handle is attached to a strain gauge or computerized load cell via a chain or cable. This method of assessment is relatively simple, quick, and inexpensive to administer. In a study of over 1,000 volunteers, Zeh et al. (1986) found that 5% of the subjects discontinued the lift test because of pain, and 0.5% developed an injury. Sontag and Oliveri (1993) state that, overall, isometric testing is safe if the number of exertions are not too great. Normative data is available for many isometric tasks, including lifting, pushing, pulling, and hand grip, and normative data is available for many tasks, including lifting, pushing, pulling, and hand grip.

Chaffin (1975) described the guidelines for performing an isometric lift test; these guidelines can be used for administering any isometric assessment:

> The isometric exertion should be maintained for a period of four to six seconds to provide adequate time for the person to assume a steady state of exertion.
>
> The measuring device should be capable of time averaging the force during the steady state. Only a three-second, time-averaged value of the steady state exertion should be used as the static strength value. This averaging method avoids the errors induced by tremor and motion dynamics.
>
> The force measuring device should not influence a worker's exertion by causing hand discomfort. Handles used should allow a full, wrap around finger grip.
>
> Adequate rest periods between repeated exertions are necessary to avoid fatigue. Two minutes appear to be adequate if more than 15 trials are taken in one test session. A minimum of 30 seconds should be given if only a few measurements are to be made.
>
> Since body position can influence strength, good control and specificity of body positions chosen for testing are essential to produce valid strength values.

Although a great deal of control can be applied to the isometric testing procedure, estimating maximum dynamic performance from isometric testing may not be appropriate, or possible, because of differences in the way the body responds to the work (Kishino et al., 1985; Kroemer, 1970, 1983; Langrana, & Lee, 1984). It may be even more difficult to estimate submaximal, repetitive, dynamic abilities from the maximum isometric test result. Because maximum isometric contractions are held for the relatively short time of 5 to 10 seconds, cardiovascular limits, which can be a factor in a deconditioned person performing repetitive lifts, cannot be assessed.

Isokinetic: Isokinetic testing is a dynamic test that restricts the movement to a specific speed. A sophisticated machine enables an individual to apply a maximal effort against a device that will allow movement at a pre-determined velocity while the machine records the amount of force exerted throughout the movement. A relatively simple design is a set of handles attached to a rope that is wound around a drum. The velocity that the drum rotates determines the velocity of a lift against the handles. The force applied to the handles is continuously monitored and recorded.

This type of testing may have a greater degree of test validity than does isometric testing since there is movement involved in the assessment. However, Hazard et al. (1988) found that observations of the subject performing the isokinetic test is more accurate than analyzing curve variability because of difficulties in discriminating between submaximal effort due to pain, fatigue, or malingering. The area in the range of the lift movement where the greatest and least force is exerted should be consistent over several trials. "Hitch points" or areas of decreased strength that could be caused by pain or lack of neuromuscular coordination can be detected since the actual force output at each moment of the lift is recorded (Kishino et al., 1985). For these reasons, this type of testing is usually limited to muscle testing rather than task performance assessments. Performance credibility can be assessed through force curve variability. However, test validity may be questioned since actual task performance is usually not performed at a constant velocity. This type of testing is usually limited to muscle testing rather than task performance assessments.

Isoinertial: Isoinertial assessments require the individual to perform a task without any constraints. Through a series of increases and/or partial decreases, the difficulty of the task is increased until either a predetermined endpoint is reached or the individual states that he/she cannot continue. Depending on the termination criterion, the assessment can establish the maximal performance of the individual. This method of assessment holds a high degree of test validity since the assessment task can be designed to closely replicate the job task. However, this method requires more time to administer than the isometric or the isokinetic methods. There may also be a greater risk for injury since more repetitions are performed before an endpoint is reached. The standardization and the degree of internal validity of the assessment may be questioned since the individual is not under any constraints when performing the lift.

All methods of lifting assessment incorporates psychophysical limits. The individual will limit the performance because of a conscious or unconscious fear of injury or re-injury, pain, or the motivation limit is reached. This fact must be taken into account when studying the results of any assessment task.

CARDIOVASCULAR ENDURANCE

Several procedures are available to determine an individual's cardiovascular endurance. Submaximal protocols, which have predetermined termination points based on a percentage of the individual's estimated maximum heart rate, is the preferred method, since the assessment involves less risk to the individual and requires less time and expense to administer. In general, this method is used for healthy (free of metabolic- and cardiovascular-related diseases) individuals, and does not require the presence of a physician nor the collection of ECG and blood pressure data (Pollock & Wilmore, 1990). There are situations in which a maximal aerobic stress test may be desired, as in testing an individual with a known cardiopulmonary condition or when testing for an aerobically stressful occupation such as a fire fighter or lumberjack. However, adequate procedures and precautions must be followed.

The endurance test is commonly performed on a treadmill or a bicycle ergometer. Step tests, running tests, and walking tests are other methods of submaximal testing but may not be desirable for orthopedically injured individuals. The treadmill is the most frequently used mode of testing and will give the most accurate results since most individuals are very comfortable with the walking movement. However, the treadmill is relatively expensive and very difficult to transport. The bicycle ergometer offers greater mobility and is less expensive, but the American population is generally not accustomed to cycling and the results may be underestimated. The arm ergometer is a method of assessing cardiovascular fitness in cases were the lower extremities cannot be used or when repetitive arm work is being assessed. The equipment of choice is the one that is most similar to the worker's job. The details of the administration of these assessments are documented elsewhere (American College of Sports Medicine, 1986; Pollock & Wilmore, 1990).

The result of the assessment is the estimated maximum quantity of oxygen (measured in milliliters) that can be utilized per kilogram of body weight per minute (VO_2max), written as ml/kg/min. The oxygen uptake at rest is approximately 3.5 ml/kg/min, which is equivalent to one metabolic unit (MET). Maximum oxygen uptake capacity for upper-body work is approximately 70% of the treadmill-derived value (Rodgers, 1988).

MOBILITY AND POSTURE TASKS

Mobility and posture tasks are performed to determine the movements and postures that the individual either has difficulty or is unable to perform. The choice of movements to assess is dependent on the area of injury and the demands of the job. Mobility tasks commonly incorporated into the FCA include bending, squatting, crawling, reaching, and twisting.

There are several methods available to conduct this evaluation. The individual may be asked to perform a given number of repetitions of the movement or be asked to perform the movement for a specified length of time. Another method is to incorporate the movements into a predesigned work station. For example, several movements can be assessed by working on a work station as illustrated in Figure 1. The individual may bend or squat to retrieve an object, such as a bolt or nut, from the floor, and/or stand and twist to attach the hardware to a panel located overhead. Evaluated in this manner, the work station can be designed to duplicate the actual job and, thereby, ensure greater test validity.

Figure 1. Work Station

The benefit of using a work station is that the purpose of the test can be disguised. The same sequence of tasks can be used for measuring the ability to bend, stoop, twist, and reach; work at a single station in a standing position; or perform repetitive hand movements. If asked, the test administrator can distract the individual by stating an alternate purpose for the test while pursuing an ulterior intent.

WORK RECOMMENDATIONS

The frequency and duration of the lifting can be difficult to define and measure. The *Dictionary of Occupational Titles* (U.S Dept. of Labor, 1991) classifies lifting only by duration of the activity or the length of time the condition exists:

Occasional: lifting a given weight up to one-third of the time
Frequent: lifting a given weight from one-third to two-thirds of the time
Continuous: lifting a given weight two-thirds or more of the time

The authors' method of classification is based on the frequency of the lifting task for a duration of up to eight hours:

Occasional: one lift per five minutes or less
Frequent: no more than four lifts per minute
Continuous: five or more lifts per minute

The *Revised NIOSH Equation for the Design and Evaluation of Manual Lifting Tasks* (1991) describes the frequency as the number of lifts per minute, ranging from 0.2 lifts per minute (one lift per five minutes) to 15 lifts per minute. The duration of lifting task is described as less than one hour, less than two hours, or less than eight hours.

There does not seem to be a consensus on how to define lifting frequency. This situation increases the difficulty in communicating with an employer the results and work restrictions of an employee.

Descriptions of classifications for the strength demands of work, taking into account the frequency and the weight of the lifting, has been published in the *Dictionary of Occupational Titles*, Volume II (U.S. Dept. of Labor, 1991). Table 6 lists the forces applied to lift, carry, push, pull, or otherwise move objects for each of the categories. In addition to the strength demands, sedentary work involves sitting most of the time, but can involve walking or standing for brief periods of time. Light work includes jobs requiring lifting negligible amounts of weight and significant walking and standing, pushing and/or pulling of arm or leg controls or materials of negligible weight while sitting.

Table 6
Strength Demands of Work as Defined by the Dictionary of Occupational Titles

Strength Rating	AMOUNT OF TIME THE ACTIVITY OR CONDITION EXIST		
	Occasional (up to 1/3)	Frequently (1/3 to 2/3)	Constantly (over 2/3)
Sedentary	10 lbs.	negligible	negligible
Light	20 lbs.	10 lbs.	negligible
Medium	20-50 lbs.	10-25 lbs.	10 lbs.
Heavy	50-100 lbs.	25-50 lbs.	10-20 lbs.
Very Heavy	100 lbs. +	50-100 lbs.	20-50 lbs.

Frequency of activity, stated previously, is described in percentages of the work shift that the activity is performed: 0 to 33% is Occasional; 34 to 66% is Frequent; and 67 to 100 % is Constant.

ORDER OF TASKS

The general sequencing of tasks is to perform the easier tasks first and progress to the more demanding tasks. The purpose of this is two-fold. First, the individual will not be overly fatigued and hampered from completing the easier tasks in the assessment battery. Second, the easier tasks become a warm-up for the more demanding tasks, thereby reducing the chance of injury. An individual with a low back injury, for example, may first perform a mid-level lift assessment before performing the shoulder- or low-level tasks.

One must also consider the possibility that the consequences of one task performance may mask the performance of another. The discomfort resulting from a maximum strength performance may prevent the individual from performing subsequent tasks that would otherwise be within normal capabilities. Although the initial task may be a part of the job, the individual may not be required to perform the task to a level that would preclude the performance of other tasks.

THE FCA AT THE WORKSITE

The procedures for conducting the FCA at the place of employment are essentially the same as for conducting the assessment in a clinical setting. An accurate assessment of the essential functions of the job is needed so that appropriate tasks are assessed. The purpose of the assessment must be identified and the method of assessment determined.

It can be very difficult to simulate some jobs due to the unique nature of the job or the type of material handled by the employee. These tasks might not be adequately simulated to provide information on which to make valid job competency determinations. The primary benefits of conducting the FCA at the worksite is the access to the actual work tasks rather than designing a potentially unreliable and invalid simulated task.

A secondary benefit is the convenience. Employee travel is eliminated and the tests can be scheduled at times best for the employer and employee rather than the clinic. The injured worker actively participating in an on-site transitional work program can be tested more frequently during the rehabilitation process and be placed back into the pre-injury job as soon as the physical abilities are restored.

When performed on-site, the individual tasks of the FCA can performed with "low tech" equipment (i.e., using the material of the actual job, boxes, barrels, and bags). Establishing performance credibility can be done by comparing pain behaviors and pain reports and relative levels of ability between the assessment tasks and looking for a pattern that is consistent with the injury. Standardized tasks can be added to the assessment to aid in establishing performance credibility, such as the multiposition grip or a static lift test.

A less structured FCA is to have the employee simply perform the pre-injury job for a portion of the workday. If the employee can successfully do the job for an hour or two over several days, the work time can be increased. Appropriate physical testing can be periodically performed to document strength gains, as the worker progresses toward a full eight-hour workday.

EQUIPMENT

The equipment needs for conducting functional capacity assessments varies, depending on the number of different jobs that will be assessed and the degree of sophistication that is desired. However, the two basic goals of the assessment must be addressed: determining the safe working capabilities of an individual and enabling the evaluator to make legally defensible conclusions regarding the physical capabilities of an individual.

As was previously discussed, a primary legal conclusion encountered is deciding if the individual has performed to the best of his or her ability (i.e., the credibility of the individual's performance.) The simplest technique to measure this is to statistically determine the consistency of repeated trials of a task. In most situations the only practical assessment method for doing repeated trials is static or isometric tasks. Fortunately, this equipment is relatively inexpensive and simple to operate. Systems that use a chain or a cable to link the handle to the load cell work fine for lifting measurements. A rigid connection that swivels can be used for lifting, pushing, and pulling. The equipment should be computerized to enable the collection and averaging of exertional forces during the last three seconds of a five-second effort. Isometric grip testing can also be used to assess performance credibility at a very low cost in both expense of equipment and floor space. Additional credibility documentation can be recorded by noting pain reports and pain behaviors throughout the assessment and looking for patterns that are either consistent or inconsistent with the injury.

EQUIPMENT FOR ON-SITE ASSESSMENTS

Job-specific task assessment at the place of employment may not require the purchase of any additional equipment or, at most, very inexpensive equipment. Many times the material used in the job can be used in the assessment. For example, assessing a material handler's lifting ability may entail initially lifting empty boxes and progress to the full boxes that are lifted on the job; pushing/pulling may involve using an empty cart and progressing to a full one.

Obviously, some jobs do not have tasks that can be taken from the work station for testing or the tasks in question occurs infrequently. In these situations a simulation may be required. For example, an individual with low back pain may be required to frequently bend/stoop. By designing a work station that necessitates frequent bending/stooping and having the individual perform the simulated task for an extended time, the observation of pain reports and pain behaviors can help determine if the individual is capable of performing the work task. The ability to perform a variety of repetitive tasks can be assessed in this fashion. Repetitive twisting, lifting, lowering, reaching in any direction, grasping, and pinching, among others, can be assessed with proper design of the work station. A basic frame may accept a variety of attachments such as shelves or a nuts and bolts panel for supination and pronation.

While much of the equipment needed for conducting the functional capacity assessment is relatively inexpensive, computerized versions of the tasks can be purchased; the costs of these can reach the six-figure range. The best (and usually most expensive) pieces allow the user to closely simulate a given task with recording and performance printout features. The greatest benefit of using this type of equipment is the collection of data that could not otherwise be recorded. However, the cost of such equipment will limit its use in on-site assessment facilities, especially when the additional data that it can provide may not provide additional insight as to the ability of the individual to perform a given task.

CASE STUDIES

The following case studies illustrate the functional assessment process, as it relates to work-return objectives:

CASE STUDY 1

Mrs. Smith is a 26-year-old laundry worker employed for two years at a retirement community. She indicates that she was loading approximately 20 to 25 pounds of wet laundry into the clothes dryer when she felt pain in the left side of her mid- and lower back. She indicates that she went to the nurse's station and took aspirin but did not report an injury at that time. She felt that the pain would go away after a night's rest. When the pain persisted the next morning, she reported the incident to her employer.

Medical treatment was first sought at a local chiropractor two days after the incident. The chiropractor had three x-rays taken of Mrs. Smith's back and has been treating her daily since that time. The employer has expressed concern regarding Mrs. Smith's treatment with this particular chiropractor.

Mrs. Smith states that she picks up dirty linen from the nurses' areas, places it in a cart, and pushes the cart to the laundry room. She sorts the laundry, places it in a front-loading washing machine, transfers it to a front-loading dryer when washing is completed, folds and stacks the clean linen on a waist-high counter, places it into the cart and delivers it back to the nurses' stations. Mrs. Smith states that she works five hours per day, five days per week. She is required to stand and walk continuously for up to three hours before she gets a break. She frequently bends and stoops. She is occasionally required to kneel, reach above her shoulders, lift from a low level and carry up to 25 pounds, lift up to 15 pounds to the shoulder level, and push a wheeled cart loaded with 100 pounds of laundry. A telephone call to the employer verified her job description; a job-site analysis was not performed, since there was agreement between the employee and the employer as to the specific job functions and physical demand requirements.

The attending physician referred Mrs. Smith for a functional capacity assessment for the purpose of determining if Mrs. Smith is capable of returning to work on full or modified duty; and if modified duty is indicated, an assessment regarding the work restrictions under which she can safely work was requested.

A functional assessment was designed to determine if Mrs. Smith was able to perform the essential functions of her job; namely, frequently lifting from floor-to-waist height, frequently bending/stooping and squatting, occasionally pushing and twisting, and continuously standing/walking. To objectively establish her propensity to provide a credible performance, static lifting tests at a low level (16 inches) and at a mid level (elbow height), and static pushing and pulling were performed on the Isometric Strength Testing Unit. A multiposition grip strength test was also performed. Performance credibility in the lifts, push, and pull were determined by the force consistency between three, five-second trials (CV), and the surface EMG activity and the increase in the heart rate measured during and immediately after each lift trial, respectively. Grip performance credibility was determined by the force consistency between three trials and by the force relationship of the various grip positions.

The results of this analysis showed that Mrs. Smith's performance was marginally credible due to lifting, pushing, and pulling force inconsistencies. These inconsistencies were likely due to her overexerting behavior (i.e., she exerted more force on her initial trials of lifting, pushing, and pulling than with subsequent trials), thus showing a fatigue-type pattern. Her heart rate and EMG activity were within the expected ranges.

Job-specific tasks were performed to determine her ability to perform during the most difficult moments of her job. A dynamic, repetitive, low-level lift was performed, lifting a small box to a shelf four times per minute for 10 minutes. Mobility tasks were performed for 20 minutes at a work station that required her to bend and twist to reach small parts on the floor and attach them to a panel located at waist level (see Fig. 1).

Walking and standing tolerance was assessed during the performance of the various tasks as well as during more strenuous movements such as climbing stairs and carrying weighted trays. The time of occurrence of pain reports, pain behaviors, and the use of substitution movements were documented for each task. Additional performance credibility was assessed by documenting pain behaviors and pain reports during the assessment and looking for injury-specific patterns. For example, Mrs. Smith stated that she felt pain in her low back when performing the isometric low level lift, the dynamic lifts, and during the repetitive bending/stooping task. There were also pain behaviors observed during these tasks, including wincing and grimacing during the lifting, and stretching movements during the bending/stooping. She did not have these behaviors or reports during the mid-level isometric lifts or when walking and climbing stairs, which indicate that her behavior was selective and specific to her injury.

The following table and narrative was included in the report to the employer's insurance carrier:

Table 7
Results and Recommendations — Table Codes

The subject's performance was inconsistent and represents either an under-exerted or an over-exerted, but safe, functional capability. This performance is influenced by behavioral factors such as pain, fear, anxiety, and motivational level.

Tasks	Code	PERFORMANCE CAPACITIES				JOB DEMANDS			
		Occas. lbs.	Freq. lbs.	Cont. lbs.	Not at all	Occas. lbs.	Freq. lbs.	Cont. lbs.	Not at all
LIFTING									
Knuckle to Breast Level		58	31	8		25			
Floor to Knuckle Level		81	43	11		15			
CARRY									
Two Hand		45	24	6		15			
PUSH									
Waist Level		72	39	10		X			
PULL									
Waist Level		79	42	10		X			
MOBILITY TASKS									
Bending and Stooping		X				X			
Squatting		X				X			
Kneeling/Walking on Knees			X			X			
Reaching Above Shoulders				X			X		
HAND FUNCTIONS									
Right Hand Grip Strength		83% of Normal							
Left hand Grip Strength		95% of Normal							
Climbing Stairs		5 Flights, Nonstop						None	
Standing		No Restriction						3 Hours, Continuous	
Walking		Restricted to 45 to 60 minute duration, 6 to 8 hours per day (frequent).						3 Hours, Continuous	

The overall performance was inconsistent and represented an overexerted effort. Mrs. Smith was able to perform all of the physical demands of the job; there is not a mismatch between her evaluation performance and the demands of a laundry worker. Mrs. Smith had difficulty performing the bend/stoop and squat tasks, but is still able to perform these tasks as required on the job. Pain reports and pain behaviors were selective, correlating with her described injury.

SECONDARY RECOMMENDATIONS

Based on observations made during the performance of the various tasks, a general physical conditioning program is recommended for Mrs. Smith.

CASE STUDY 2

Ms. Jones is a 32-year-old waitress who was involved in a motor vehicle accident. She has a chief complaint of pain over the posterior neck and shoulder-girdle area extending into the right upper extremity. She states that her arm feels fatigued whenever she uses it, though she denies any numbness or tingling. She was referred for a functional capacity assessment 15 months post-accident, to determine if she can now perform her job. She had not returned to work since the accident.

An analysis of Ms. Jones' job as a food and beverage waitress at a ski slope restaurant revealed that she must be able to occasionally carry 30 pounds on her shoulder, carry 30 pounds at waist level, and lift 50 pounds from the floor; occasionally exert 55 pounds of force to push a wheeled cart; frequently reach above the shoulders, bend/stoop, and squat; and continually stand and walk for four hours. The functional assessment was designed to establish her performance credibility as well as her ability to meet the lifting, carrying, and standing/walking requirements.

Three trials of the five-position grip test was performed along with three trials of bilateral isometric lifting at mid- and high-levels. An increasing weight, dynamic lifting sequence from the floor to a shelf positioned at waist height was used to assess low-level lifting ability. A tray and small sand bags were used to determine Ms. Jones' ability to lift and carry a tray on her shoulder; a tote pan was used to measure bilateral carrying ability. Reaching was assessed by setting up the work station to necessitate reaching forward and above the shoulder in order to place small parts in their proper location. Performance credibility was further documented by looking for consistency in the similar tasks: the overhead reach and the high-level reach, the dynamic low-level bilateral lift and the bilateral carry.

The following was included in the report to the employer's insurance carrier:
> A reliable performance was demonstrated in the Functional Capacity Assessment. The results of this assessment are indicative of her safe and functional capabilities.

Table 8
Results — Table Codes

The subject's performance was inconsistent and represents either an under-exerted, but safe, functional capability. This performance is influenced by behavioral factors such as pain, fear, anxiety, and motivational level.

Tasks	Code	PERFORMANCE CAPACITIES				JOB DEMANDS			
		Occas. lbs.	Freq. lbs.	Cont. lbs.	Not at all	Occas. lbs.	Freq. lbs.	Cont. lbs.	Not at all
LIFTING									
Breast To Over-Head Level		45	12	3		30			
Right Hand		34				30			
Left Hand		38							
Knuckle To Breast Level		56	28	7		30	50		
Floor To Knuckle Level		89	48	12		50			
CARRY									
Two Hand		60	45	11		50			
PUSH									
Waist Level		74				55			
MOBILITY TASKS									
Bending and Stooping				X			X		
Squatting				X			X		
Reaching Above Shoulders			X				X		
HAND FUNCTIONS									
Right Hand Grip Strength			Above Normal						
Left Hand Grip Strength			Above Normal						
Right Hand Grip Capacity				X					
Left Hand Grip Capacity				X					
Climbing Stair			No Restrictions						
Sitting			Continuous			Breaks Only			
Standing			Continuous			4 Hours, Continuous			
Walking			Continuous			4 Hours, Continuous			

Ms. Jones is able to perform all of the physical demands of the job; there is not a mismatch between her evaluation performance and the demands of a waitress. Pain reports and pain behaviors were selective.

THE FUTURE OF THE FUNCTIONAL CAPACITY ASSESSMENT (FCA)

The FCA has assisted the health care professional by objectively measuring and quantifying an injured worker's safe return-to-work abilities. The future of the FCA lies in making the individual assessments valid, objective, reliable, and reproducible. The FCA must also be cost-effective to administer.

There are several issues with which the FCA can help the employer with hiring and job placement. A well-designed FCA will aid employers in determining if new hirees have the functional abilities for performing specific job tasks. The employer will be able to identify specific individuals who are at high risk or who are physically unable to perform specific job tasks. This will assist in maintaining compliance with the ADA by enabling the employer to make hiring decisions based on valid and objective performance assessments that are legally defensible. Obtaining functional assessments on new employees will also provide baseline work abilities that can later be used for comparison of the worker's pre-injury functional abilities to post-injury abilities. The FCA can also be used in post-placement job situations when an employee wishes to change from one job to another job requiring different physical demands.

It has been shown that returning an injured employee to work as soon as he or she is physically capable can reduce workers' compensation losses. The results of the FCA can objectively identify the employee's ability to return to a previous job, or to modified duty. The FCA can be used to develop recommendations for job modifications, accommodations, or work-station redesign. With the information obtained from the FCA, the employer can develop meaningful, productive, and profitable return-to-work duties, that can also bolster the self-esteem of the injured worker. However, many employers and their representatives, including shop foremen and on-line supervisors, do not know how to interpret the work-restriction reports. The development of job-specific FCA reports will assist everyone involved in the return-to-work process. It can help the employer, supervisors, insurance company representatives, and health care providers to identify and understand the injured worker's abilities to perform specific job tasks.

The FCA is a useful tool for implementing a return-to-work program into the day-to-day work operations. In the future, employers will have their injured workers conduct their work-conditioning on-site through a structured return-to-work program. This program will be based upon objective assessments of the injured worker's safe functional capabilities as determined by the FCA. The employer, with the help of the ergonomist, physical or occupational therapist, exercise physiologist, or physician, can assess which jobs an injured employee can do, then progress them to more difficult job tasks. The job tasks will accommodate the worker's injury. This will eliminate some of the costly off-site work conditioning programs that are currently performed at hospitals and other medical facilities.

SUMMARY

The FCA is a process that is used to assess one's ability to perform work tasks. If the essential demands of the job are determined, a properly designed assessment will provide a valid conclusion of a worker's ability to perform a given job within a reasonable degree of certainty. The assessment can utilize isometric, isokinetic, or isoinertial testing methods, depending on the type of equipment used. Conducting the FCA at the job-site can allow the use of the actual job tools and material, thereby increasing the validity of the assessment.

The FCA is an important aspect of disability management and work-return programming. On-site functional capacity assessments engage direct labor and management collaboration, and involve the injured worker within the familiar work environment. As such, transitional work programs at the worksite are generally developed by integrating any combination of job tasks and functions which may be performed safely and with remuneration by an employee whose physical capacity to perform functional job demands has been compromised.

Such programs are designed to encourage and support an injured employee's safe and timely return-to-work. They provide the worker with accommodations and an opportunity to gradually make the transition back to work through conditioning, safe work practices education, and work re-adjustment. Essential components of on-site programs include objective worker evaluations, an analysis of job tasks and physical functions, designated jobs or work transition units, on-site clinical supervision, and a gradual work-return plan that increases the worker's capacity to return to full-duty.

Many of the functional capacity assessment strategies discussed in this chapter have traditionally been performed in clinical environments, rather than at the worksite. However, recently demonstrated programs, described elsewhere in this book, provide strong evidence of the evolution of such clinical practices within real work settings. Rehabilitation at the worksite is rapidly becoming an internationally accepted concept, as employers are assuming more responsibility for managing rapidly escalating costs. In the United States, the ADA has become an important catalyst for the emergence of worksite programs. In many ways, the spirit of the ADA has become operationalized through assessment procedures that determine worker-work environment compatibility. Such practical assessment strategies protect the employability of persons with disabilities, while concurrently protecting the financial interests of employers.

REFERENCES

American College of Sports Medicine. (1986). *Guidelines for exercise testing and prescription.* (3rd ed.). Philadelphia: Lea & Febiger.

American Health Consultants, Inc. (1992). Restricted duty programs get people working quicker. *Back Pain Monitor, 10*(2). Atlanta, GA: Author.

Anastasi, A. (1982). *Psychological testing* (5th ed.). New York: McMillan Publishing Co., Inc.

Ayoub, M. A. (1982). Control of manual lifting hazards: III. Pre-employment screening. *Journal of Occupational Medicine, 24,* 751.

Berryhill, B. H., Osborne, P., Staats, T. E., Brooks, F. W., & Skarina, J. M. (1993). Horizontal strength changes: An ergometric measure for determining validity of effort in impairment evaluations — A preliminary report. *Journal of Disability, 3,* 143-148.

Blankenship, K. L. (1986). *Functional capacity evaluation: The procedure manual.* American Therapeutics, P. O. Box 5084, Macon, GA 31208-5084.

Borg, Gunnar A. V. (1982). Psychophysical bases of perceived exertion. *Medicine in Science, Sports and Exercise, 14*(5), 377-381.

Chaffin, D. B. (1975). Ergonomics guide for the assessment of human static strength. *American Industrial Hygiene Association Journal, July,* 505-511.

DeLuca, C. J., & Knaflitz, M. ( ). *Surface electromyography: What's new?* Boston, MA: NeuroMuscular Research Center, Boston University.

Drury, C. G., & Spitz, G. (1976). Strength, duration, and recovery mechanisms. In *Safety in manual materials handling* (pp.46-51). Cincinnati, OH: National Institute for Occupational Safety and Health.

Eastman Kodak. (1986). *Eastman Kodak Company ergonomics group: Ergonomic design for people at work, Vol 2,* pp. 162, 175, 480. New York: Van Nostrand Reinhold.

Gilbert, J. C., & Knowlton, R. G. (1983) Simple method to determine sincerity of effort during a maximal isometric test of grip strength. *American Journal of Physical Medicine, 62,* 135-144.

Hazard, R. G., Reid, S., Senwick, J., & Reeves, V. (1988). Isokinetic truck and lifting strength measurements: Variability as an indicator of efforts. *Spine, 13,* 54-57.

Kelsey, J. L., & White, A. A. (1988). Epidemiology and impact of low back pain. *Spine, 5,* 133-134.

Keyserling, W. M., Armstrong, T. J., & Punnett, L. (1991). Ergonomic job analysis: A structured approach for identifying risk factors associated with overexertion injuries and disorders. *Applied Occupational and Environmental Hygiene, 65,* 353-363.

Kishino, N. D., Mayer, T. G., Gatchel, R. J., McCrate Parrish, M., Anderson, C., Gustin, L., & Mooney, V. (1985). Quantification of lumbar function: Part 4: Isometric and isokinetic lifting simulation in normal subjects and low-back dysfunction patients. *Spine, 10*(10), 921-927.

Kroemer, K. H. E. (1970) Human strength: Terminology, measurement, and interpretation of data. *Human Factors, 12,*3, pp. 297-313.

Kroemer, K. H. E. (1983). An isoinertial technique to assess individual lifting capability. *Human Factors, 25*(5), 493-506.

Langrana, N. A., & Lee, C. K. (1984) Isokinetic evaluation of trunk muscles. *Spine, 9,* 171-175.

Leskinen, T. (1985). Comparison of static and dynamic biomechanical models. *Ergonomics, 28,* 285-291.

Matheson, L. N. (1988a, October). *Symptom magnification syndrome.* Presented at Industrial Medicine: An Introductory Course for Therapists. Boston, MA.

Matheson, L. N. (1988b). "How do you know that he tried his best?" The reliability crisis in industrial rehabilitation. *Industrial Rehabilitation Quarterly, 1.*

Matheson, L. N., Anzai, D., & Niemeyer, L.O. (1991). LIDO workset cookbook: A tasty collection of testing protocols and procedures for the serious connoisseur of functional activity simulation, evaluation and training. Employment and Rehabilitation Institute of California in collaboration with Loredan Biomedical, West Sacramento, CA.

Matheson, L., Carlton, R., & Niemeyer, L. (1988c). Grip strength in the disabled sample: Reliability and normative standards. *Industrial Rehabilitation Quarterly, 1*, No. 3.

Maxfield, J. (1989). Injury treatment services. In Newdirk, W. L. & Jones, L. D. (Eds.), *Occupational health services: A guide to program planning and management* (p. 48). American Hospital Publishing, Inc.

Owens, L., & Buchholz, R. (1993). Assessing reliability of performance in the functional capacity assessment. *Journal of Disability, 3,* 149-160.

Pollock, M. L., & Wilmore, J. H. (1990). *Exercise in health and disease: Evaluation and prescription for prevention and rehabilitation.* Philadelphia: W. B. Saunders Company.

Rodgers, S. H. (1988). Job evaluation in worker fitness determination. In *Occupational Medicine: State of the Art Reviews 3,* (2), pp. 219-239.

Sontag, M., & Oliveri, D. (1993). Strength testing in the evaluation of low-back pain. *Journal of Disability, 3,* 17-25.

Staats, T. E. (1990). *Stress — effect on disability: Psychological testing applied to disability evaluation.* Presented at the American Academy Of Disability Evaluating Physicians - Clinical Training Program. Chicago, IL September 1990.

U. S. Department of Labor. (1991). *Dictionary of occupational titles.* 4th ed. Rev. Supplement. U.S. Dept. of Labor, Employment and Training Administration. Appendix C.

Waters, T., Putz-Anderson, V., Garg, A., & Fine, L. (1993). Revised NIOSH equation for the design and evaluation of manual lifting tasks. *Ergonomics, 36*(7), 746-776.

Wenger, N. K., & Hellerstein, H. (Eds.). (1978). *Rehabilitation of the coronary patient.* (pp. 203-241). New York: John Wiley.

Zeh, J. Hansson, T., Bigos, S., Spengler, D., Battie, M., & Wortley, M. (1986). Isometric strength testing: Recommendations based on statistical analysis of the procedure. *Spine, 11,* 43-44.

Essential Competencies In Industrial Rehabilitation And Disability Management Practice: A Skills-based Training Model

Norman C. Hursh, Sc.D., C.R.C., C.V.E.

INTRODUCTION

Vocational rehabilitation and rehabilitation counselor education training programs have developed from a significant federal commitment to provide rehabilitation services to individuals with a disability. The goal of vocational rehabilitation has long been to assist individuals in returning to work and becoming productive members of society. While initially only serving individuals who had physical disabilities, the program now serves individuals who have emotional, cognitive, behavioral, physical, and developmental disabilities.

The development of graduate level rehabilitation counselor education programs was initiated in 1954 through extensive training grants to colleges and universities. The purpose of the federal support was, and continues to be, to develop professional rehabilitation counselors who could provide quality vocational rehabilitation services in the state-federal programs. Initially, rehabilitation counselor education curriculum focused on rehabilitation counseling and case management skills. As federal priorities shifted and vocational rehabilitation programs grew, rehabilitation counselor education programs began to train specialists who could function in specific roles (e.g., vocational evaluator, job placement specialist, rehabilitation psychologist) or in specific settings (e.g., rehabilitation administrators).

In the United States, the provision of vocational rehabilitation services for individuals with a disability has been supported and delivered largely through the public sector, primarily the state-federal vocational rehabilitation system. In contrast, vocational rehabilitation services provided to injured workers have been coordinated primarily through a state legislated workers' compensation system. With the exception of a few monopolistic state-administered workers' compensation programs, most programs are administered by an insurance company or third-party administrator (TPA). Vocational rehabilitation services, where provided, have been generally provided through contractual arrangements with private vocational rehabilitation agencies. However, driven by the escalating economic and personal costs of work-related injury and disability, several proactive employers have developed and implemented innovative rehabilitation programs that emphasize internal or worksite rehabilitation approaches. Examples of representative programs and their impact on industry and injured workers are detailed throughout this book.

Although employer-based disability management program models have been reported in the literature and described throughout this book, the role and function of the employer-based disability manager who coordinates such programs has received relatively little attention. Often disability management responsibility is assigned to an occupational health nurse, an employee assistance program (EAP) professional, or a representative from the employer benefits, personnel, safety, risk management, or human resources department.

The provision of rehabilitation services at the worksite is a natural extension and logical application of the role and function of the rehabilitation counseling professional. With the continuing need to contain the costs of work-related injury, to comply with employment-related disability legislation, to accommodate qualified individuals on the job, and to project the shifting labor needs within a rapidly changing labor market, rehabilitation professionals have become important resources to the employer.

The skills and expertise of the vocational rehabilitation counselor can be utilized directly in the workplace to provide direct services to the injured worker. However, the disability management professional in industrial rehabilitation also requires additional specialized skills, competencies, and a unique knowledge base to understand business practices and legislation, and to be effective in addressing the multiple concerns of labor, management, health care, rehabilitation, and the individual with a disability. The challenge for rehabilitation counselor education is to develop and adapt curriculum objectives to meet the market needs and service priorities required in disability management and that are consistent with rehabilitation philosophy and practice.

This chapter identifies the issues and trends that are influencing rehabilitation practice in the work place and the roles and functions of the rehabilitation counselor in industrial rehabilitation and disability management. Specific industrial rehabilitation skills, competencies, experiences, and disability management strategies will be presented. Also, this chapter will review essential disability management training objectives, that can be integrated into a core masters degree program in rehabilitation counseling. This chapter includes a model industrial rehabilitation and disability management curriculum that has been developed at Boston University and that lends itself to modification for the skills-based training of other human resource professionals, as well as graduate-level rehabilitation counselor students.

ECONOMIC, BUSINESS, AND REHABILITATION TRENDS IN INDUSTRIAL REHABILITATION

Industrial rehabilitation and disability management is influenced by the relative stability and health of the economy, by the characteristics of the work force and work-related injuries, by business and labor practices, and by advances in rehabilitation practices and technologies. To be effective, disability managers must recognize and understand the characteristics and trends of these systems and how each must be integrated into disability management programs and practices. To a large degree, these characteristics define the unique skills, competencies, and knowledge base that disability managers must utilize throughout their practice.

Similarly, if rehabilitation counselor education programs are to train effective disability managers, there must be a shift from a curriculum development process that often relies on priorities established by federal funding resources to a market-driven model that is responsive to the needs of individuals with a disabilities and the employer, labor, and health care constituencies that are involved in disability management services (Gilbride, Connolly, & Stensrud, 1990; Kilbury, Benshoff, & Riggar, 1990; Rasch, 1992).

The following sections examine present economic, business and labor, disability, and rehabilitation trends and how each may impact the roles and functions of the disability manager and the evolution of disability management practice.

ECONOMIC AND LABOR MARKET TRENDS INFLUENCING INDUSTRIAL REHABILITATION

To succeed in developing disability management opportunities in the work place, it is necessary to understand the economic, labor market, and business trends that shape and influence the present workplace as well as future employment opportunities.

Economic and Employment Trends

Between 1990 and 2005, the United States economy is expected to grow more slowly than it has in past decades. Economic growth will be only 75% of the growth rate of the previous 15-years. The slowdown in the economy is primarily attributed to a decrease in the number of younger people entering the work force (Bogue, 1985). Labor force growth during the 15-year period between 1990 and 2005 will be slower than in any similar period over the past 30 years.

The lack of younger people entering the work force has created a concern by employers that there would be a lack of workers for entry level jobs. However, current projections appear to indicate that toward the end of the 1990s the number of younger workers will gradually increase (Kutscher, 1992). Despite the economic and work force trends, the labor force is expected to grow from 124 million workers in 1990 to over 150 million by 2005, an increase of 21% (Fullerton, 1992).

At a time when growth in the economy will be relatively slow, the labor force will experience a noted shift in age, race, and sex composition. In 1985, white males comprised about one-half (47%) of the labor force in the United States. By the year 2000, white males will make up only 15% of the labor force (Hudson Institute, 1987). The shift across the labor force will be reflected by increases in the numbers of women, minority members, and older workers.

The number of blacks in the labor force is expected to increase by 32%. Hispanics are projected to increase by 75% by 2005 and will represent almost 16% of all new workers. Older workers will continue to experience growth at twice the rate of increase of the total labor force (Fullerton, 1992). The increasing numbers of minority and aging workers has significance for disability management, as the incidence of disability across these groups is higher. The implications for industrial rehabilitation is examined in more detail later.

Employment opportunities. While the labor force will change in size and composition, the profile of job and employment opportunities will also shift. Influenced by rapidly changing technologies, a more competitive and open world market, and increased demands for goods and services, the United States labor market will shift from a strong manufacturing and industrial market to a service and information technology market (Berman & Cosca, 1992; Kutscher, 1992). The most significant growth will be in the service producing industries which will account for 90% of all new jobs by 1995 (Williams & Rice, 1987).

Within the service industry, health services and business services opportunities will demonstrate significant growth, accounting for about one-quarter of the total growth in actual numbers of jobs. Within the service industry, retail trade, government, and finance, insurance and real estate will also contribute a substantial number of new jobs (Carey & Franklin, 1992). Conversely, construction and manufacturing jobs are projected to decline, although there will be selective and fluctuating opportunities that will continue to show modest growth. For example, government is expected to support improvements in the nation's infrastructure. Construction projects such as bridge and road work will, therefore, experience consistent growth over the next decade.

Table 1 identifies many of the occupations reflecting the greatest growth potential over the next 15 years.

Table 1
Job Outlook for 1990 – 2005
Positions with Strong Growth Projections

<u>Executive and Managerial Occupations</u>
    Accountants and auditors
    Health services managers
    Marketing advertising and PR managers

<u>Computer, Mathematical and Operations Research Occupations</u>
    Computer systems analyst
    Computer programmers
    Operations research analyst

<u>Teachers and Counselors</u>
    Kindergarten and Elementary school teacher
    Secondary school teachers
    Teacher's Aide
    Pre-school workers

<u>Health Assessment and Treating Occupations</u>
    Registered nurses
    Respiratory therapists
    EKG technologist
    Licensed practical nurse
    Medical record technologist
    Radiological technologist
    Surgical technologist

<u>Marketing and Sales</u>
    Cashiers
    Manufacturer's and service and sales representative
    Retail sales workers

<u>Administrative Support Occupations</u>
    Receptionists and information clerk
    General office clerk

<u>Service Occupations</u>
    Protective services
    Food and beverage preparation and service
    Health service
    Nursing aides and psychiatric aides
    Medical assistants

Adapted from U.S. Department of Labor, Bureau of Labor Statistics. (1992). *The job outlook in brief: 1990-2005.* Occupational Outlook Quarterly, Spring, pp. 12-40.

Implications. The shift in employment by occupation and the relative education and skill requirement of new jobs, has significance for both injured workers and industrial rehabilitation practice. Occupations projecting faster than average growth also require higher levels of education and training. Two-thirds of the fastest growing occupations, and one-half of the 30 jobs with the largest number of actual new jobs, require education or training beyond high school (Silvestri & Lukasiewicz, 1992). Occupations that are experiencing decline require less formal education, training, or skill. Significantly, blacks and Hispanics, who will represent approximately 25% of all workers in the labor market, are represented in occupations that project slow or declining growth. They also are typically less educated, have more limited skills, and fewer opportunities to access education. Employers fear a shortfall of skilled workers and an overrepresentation of unskilled workers who are not prepared for tomorrow's jobs.

BUSINESS TRENDS

Industrial rehabilitation opportunities for injured workers are influenced both positively and negatively by trends in business, management, and technological advances that injured workers are able to access.

Advances in technology in the work place create both opportunities and challenges for today's workers. Jobs automation displaces many workers and changes the nature of the job for others. Examples of technological advances are even evident in occupations that experience significant decline, such as jobs in manufacturing and industrial production. Computerized control of machinery, such as in tool and die casting redefines how the job is performed and creates demand for workers with more skill and a higher level of training.

Application of computer technologies may also change a job from one requiring physical and manual skills, to one that relies on decision-making, interpersonal, or problem-solving skills. For example, voice command work stations control robotics, computers, communications, and information retrieval and dissemination activities (Leung, 1988).

Technology, through high and low tech applications, also assists workers who may experience loss of function, impairment, or disability. Through creative use of worksite modifications, utilization of assistance devices, or application of rehabilitation engineering resources, a disability can be accommodated to allow the worker to perform a job function that previously was not within his or her capabilities. Examples of assistive technologies in the workplace may range from computer keyboard overlays, computer access aids, structural aids such as tool and work station design, or access aids such as TTYs (Brandt & Rice, 1990; McCray, 1987). Common sense modifications such as raising or lowering work spaces, using carts to carry excessive loads, or utilizing a Velcro® fastener to hold material represent creative low tech applications.

Industries are also exploring innovative business practices that maximize productivity and satisfaction in the workplace. Programs such as flex time, job sharing, task rotation, total quality management, wellness programs, and increased worker input recognize that when employees' needs are acknowledged, production may be maximized. The same creative applications of accommodated work scheduling and task performance requirements can be key to work-return transition planning for an injured worker.

Implications. Today's work force must be ready to adapt to rapidly changing jobs and work activity, be receptive to retraining, and be accepting of technological changes that occur at the workplace.

Implications for Rehabilitation Counselors

The economy and employment market will experience important changes over the next 15 years. Traditional jobs will be replaced by new jobs, and the new jobs will require better trained and more highly skilled workers. Employers have a valid concern that there will be a shortfall of skilled workers. Qualified workers with a disability represent a potential labor force resource for the projected 24 million new jobs.

In the past, counselors have responded slowly and inadequately to changes in the economy (Roessler, 1987). If rehabilitation counselors are to be effective in developing employment opportunities in industry, they must be skilled in areas as:

- Performing labor market trend analysis.
- Performing job and worksite analysis to identify skill and knowledge requirements of job market and/or employment demands.
- Assisting injured workers to assess how present skills transfer to future jobs.
- Developing and utilizing rehabilitation technologies to accommodate functional loss and disability.
- Working with industry to develop nontraditional training resources that are responsive to technological advances and the training needs of the work force.
- Working with industry to explore incentives to hire or retain qualified workers with disabilities.

TRENDS IN WORKPLACE INJURY AND DISABILITY

The economic and personal costs of work- related injury and disability described throughout this book are staggering. More compelling and difficult to understand is that the incidence and costs are increasing at an unacceptably high rate and with seemingly uncontrollable consistency.

In 1987, the government and private sector paid an estimated $120 billion in overall disability claims benefits, with $27.4 billion paid in workers' compensation benefits alone (Drury, 1991; Nelson, 1990). Since the early 1980s, disability and health care costs have increased approximately 16% per year, with a 400% increase in workers' compensation costs over the past 15 years (Berkowitz, 1990; Shrey, 1990). Unchecked and runaway disability and health care costs have resulted in many employers turning to creative means to address illness, injury, and disability incidence.

Issues in Injured Worker Rehabilitation

Typically, when workers become injured, employers rely on medical and rehabilitation professionals, insurance claims managers, and third-party administrators to manage the injury. During this time, the employer has little involvement and less interaction with the worker. As the length of time the person remains away from work increases, work activity patterns, worker role identity, and the occupational bond between the worker and co-worker/employer/and worksite are replaced with sedentary patterns of inactivity (often with secondary gains), identification with the disability role, legal involvement, adversarial relationships with employers, and financial disincentives to return to work. The longer the worker is away from work, the more formidable the labor, legal, medical, and rehabilitation barriers to return to work become.

Industrial Rehabilitation Trends

Recently, employers have developed on-site disability management programs to regain control over escalating disability costs and assume responsibility for planning and coordinating return-to-work interventions. Disability management programs are developed to provide early intervention after injury or disability, as well as safe and timely return to full-time work. Successful disability management programs also develop methods to monitor and control medical and health care costs.

Program characteristics that are common to successful disability management programs cited in the literature (Galvin, 1992; Habeck, 1989; Shrey, 1990) include the following:

1. Senior management support and identified commitment to disability management programs and policies.
2. Corporate policy that emphasizes the value of the employee.
3. Early and regular disability management interventions.

4. Case management interventions for effective use of interdisciplinary health care and rehabilitation services.
5. Modified job opportunities to promote early return to work.
6. Supervisors and front line managers who encourage early return to work.
7. Employee education and involvement in prevention and rehabilitation program development.
8. Union participation at outset of disability management program development and planning.
9. Monitoring of incidence, benefit utilization, program costs, and return-to-work outcomes.

Examples of proactive disability management interventions, programs, and policies are described in more detail throughout this book.

Implication for Rehabilitation Educators

For the rehabilitation counselor, many of the core rehabilitation skills and knowledge areas are transferable to industrial rehabilitation practice. However, there is also a range of new skills and an expanded knowledge base that is needed to work with injured workers, labor and management, and occupational health care professionals.

In the rehabilitation counseling program at Boston University, the following skill-based components comprise the core areas of the industrial rehabilitation and disability management specialization:

- **Direct Service Skills**
  Direct service skills include assessment, counseling, job and worksite analysis, prevention and early intervention strategies, case monitoring of transition planning, employee training and marketing.
- **Labor/Management Coordination Skills**
  Performing industry and disability analysis, policy analysis and development, and labor/management coordination.
- **Disability Programs and Disability Characteristics in Industry**
  Information on worker compensation and disability income systems (LTD, SSDI), disability characteristics that are common to industry (e.g. cumulative trauma disorders, cardiac disabilities, AIDS and work place issues).

DISABILITY CHARACTERISTICS AND TRENDS IN THE WORKPLACE

Types of impairments and disability characteristics among industrially injured populations often differ from those found among persons with disabilities within the public-sector rehabilitation program. For example, the most frequent injury in the work force involves back injury with associated acute and chronic pain. In addition, repetitive motion and cumulative trauma disorders constitute over 56% of all occupational impairments and are increasing in incidence and costs for both blue and white collar workers.

Along with specific medical features associated with workplace disabilities, the disability manager must recognize and respond to the adjustment factors that are present in the process of developing and providing work-return interventions.

The following sections identify characteristics of disabilities that are specific to industrial rehabilitation. In addition, emerging issues associated with groups of workers as a whole, specifically aging and minority workers, are discussed.

Repetitive Motion Disorders

Repetitive motion, or cumulative trauma disorders, represent a significant cause of lost productivity, lost work time, escalating health care costs, and chronic personal suffering. As a disability category, repetitive motion disorders include impairments such as low back pain, cervical strain, degenerative disc disease, carpal tunnel syndrome, tendinitis, rotator cuff injury, and epicondylitis (commonly called *tennis elbow*). It is estimated that over 25% of all workers in the United States will experience such disabling conditions at one point in their work life (Morris, 1984). With 40% of all recorded absences from the workplace resulting from back pain, it is second only to the common cold as a reason for absenteeism (Kelsey & White, 1980).

The incidence, rate, and impact of Carpal Tunnel Syndrome (CTS) has risen to such an extent that researchers have labeled CTS as an "industrial epidemic." The incidence of CTS has risen from 20,000 cases in 1983 to over 74,000 in 1987 (Mallory & Bradford, 1989). Carpal tunnel syndrome among employees in the computer field alone has escalated 538% from 1981 to 1991 (Martin, 1992). While work-related back injuries comprise approximately 25% of all worker compensation claims (Klein, Jensen, & Sanderson, 1984), it is estimated that cumulative trauma disorders, as a whole, will constitute over 50% of claims by the year 2000 (Mallory & Bradford, 1989).

Repetitive motion disorders not only represent a significant number of work-related injuries, but also a significant and increasing cost to employers. It is estimated that back injury treatment costs and compensation payments are over $14 billion annually, with one insurance company reporting payments in excess of

$800,000 each day (Tabor, 1982; Wakefield, 1985; White, 1982). A typical carpal tunnel syndrome claim cost $3,500 in rehabilitation and benefit costs, escalating to between $30,000 and $70,000 if surgery is required (Joyce, 1988). These figures do not include costs related to decreased productivity, absenteeism related to a progressive impairment, and costs incurred through increased supervision and retraining.

Despite recognition of the enormity of the problem in terms of personal and economic costs, medical management, and physical rehabilitation, interventions have demonstrated less than satisfactory outcomes in returning injured workers to work and retaining them. Most controlled studies reveal that, even when reemployment occurs, upon completion of physical rehabilitation, workers with cumulative trauma impairments are unable to sustain employment. Moreover, such workers demonstrate little differences with control groups at 12 month follow-up (Millin, Jarvikoski, & Verkasalo, 1984; Smith & Crisler, 1985). It is clear that medical intervention and physical rehabilitation alone is insufficient to respond to the multiple effects of repetitive motions disorders.

With increasing incidence and escalating costs, repetitive motion disorders will play a more prominent increasing role in both industry-based and general rehabilitation counselor caseloads (Greer, Jenkins, & Roberts, 1992). The disability manager must be familiar with the signs, symptoms, and characteristics of repetitive motion disorders, as well as program strategies that reduce work disruption and promote productivity for workers who are involved in repetitive motion activity.

If the incidence and impact of repetitive motion disorders is to be reduced, disability managers must be able to develop and implement prevention, early identification, and early intervention programs as a proactive disability management approach. Preventive disability management interventions include ergonomic evaluation, job modification, rehabilitation engineering, and worksite accommodations. These interventions are critical at the early indications of a repetitive motion disorder, but also continue as case management strategies if the worker continues or returns to the repetitive work activity.

Employers and insurance companies are not always receptive to prevention efforts and question methods to evaluate cost-effectiveness. The disability manager must develop case monitoring methods and negotiating skills to demonstrate the need and benefits of prevention efforts.

When workers experience advanced stages of repetitive motion disorders, or when the work activity is unable to be modified or accommodated to their residual capacities, alternative jobs or work activities must be identified. Disability managers must be competent in performing a transferable skill analysis to provide for the worker who experiences a repetitive motion disorder and must change jobs or alter work functions.

CARDIAC DISABILITIES AND REHABILITATION IN THE WORKPLACE

The effectiveness of medical interventions in cardiac impairments has had a dramatic impact on the lifespan and quality of life for cardiac patients. Symptomatic coronary artery disease impacts over 5 million people in the United States, with over 800,000 incidents of myocardial infarction and nearly 250,000 coronary artery bypass surgeries yearly (American Heart Association, 1990). With advances in medical care and increased functional outcomes for individuals with cardiac involvement, the cardiac impairment is increasingly being viewed as a vocational, as well as a medical disability.

Although the medical costs for cardiac care are high – approximately $85 billion in 1986 – they are small compared to the personal costs experienced by the individual and family unit. Additionally, many individuals view options such as disability retirement, or access to income maintenance programs such as long-term disability (LTD) or Social Security disability insurance (SSDI) benefits, as the only available alternatives to work. The results are a loss of productivity at the workplace, and a drain on the disability or health benefit system.

While the medical field has made strides in diagnosis and treatment with cardiac patients (Stewart & Gregor, 1984), employment and reemployment outcomes have not reflected similar success (Dennis, 1991). In fact, Dennis (1991) concludes that decisions and planning around vocational rehabilitation remains largely a subjective process, with little objective information to develop vocational protocols or to guide the vocational rehabilitation process.

While a major factor influencing return-to-work planning is the medical status of the individual, including the presence or absence of angina, the involvement of the nonmedical factors of cardiac impairment contributes significantly to return-to-work outcomes. Factors such as family influence, patient perception of the impairment, employer attitudes, the availability of income benefit options such as LTD, SSDI, or disability retirement benefits, as well as the functional capacity, work demands, and availability of accommodations interact significantly with return-to-work efforts.

Research into treatment and case management interventions in vocational rehabilitation is only a recent practice. Vocational planning with cardiac patients has not been studied extensively and there is little objective knowledge about the impact of return-to-work interventions. Preliminary studies show that, where rehabilitation efforts emphasize early return to work, there is improved perception of health, that medical costs are lower, and that patients earn over $2,000 per person more than patients in a control group at 6 months follow up (Picard, Dennis, & Schwartz, 1989).

Recent efforts utilizing rehabilitation technology in assessment, as part of total return to work planning, have demonstrated positive vocational outcomes. Hiatt,

Nawaz, Regensteiner, and Hossack (1988) and Hiatt Regensteiner, Hargarten, Wolfel, and Brass (1990) have developed a functional capacity measure to accurately assess the individual's physical capacity in relation to the demands of the person's specific job. When capacity has been below job demand requirements, capacity has been increased through exercise rehabilitation along with additional treatment interventions.

Rehabilitation and health care providers must study interventions such as physical capacity evaluations, on-site work transition programs, worksite modifications, and how nonmedical factors impact vocational outcomes. Education for patients, physicians, and health care providers about measuring functional capacity, conditioning programs, and worksite interventions must be developed.

Vocational rehabilitation efforts with cardiac patients have only recently being accepted as a critical component of cardiac care. However, increased involvement of vocational rehabilitation will contribute to the psychological and physical well-being of the individual, as well as the economic health, production, and stability of a business or industry.

Job-Simulated Cardiac Rehabilitation: Emerging Research

In June 1993, a three-year Field Initiated Research study, entitled *Development and Evaluation of a Job-Simulated Cardiac Rehabilitation Program* was funded by the National Institute on Disability Research (U.S. Department of Education). This study, directed by Donald Shrey, Ph.D. and Anil Mital, Ph.D. at the University of Cincinnati, is integrating job simulations within the cardiac rehabilitation program at Cincinnati's Christ Hospital. The project provides transitional work programming for 200 cardiac rehabilitation patients.

These researchers are developing and evaluating a job-simulated cardiac rehabilitation program and transitional work-return planning. At present, there is no cardiac rehabilitation program that includes the active participation of the employer in developing return-to-work options. The project will develop the necessary protocol for rehabilitating cardiac rehabilitation patients, using a physical training program based on actual job requirements and using a patient's transferable work skills for placement in jobs within their physical and psychological capabilities. Such a cardiac rehabilitation program is currently unavailable to cardiac patients and, once developed and evaluated, it is expected to shorten work disruption periods significantly. The project will identify the program protocals and disability management interventions to promote early return-to-work for cardiac patients.

Acquired Immune Deficiency Syndrome (AIDS) and the Workplace

The human immunodeficiency virus (HIV) and Acquired Immune Deficiency Syndrome (AIDS) represent a chronic and progressive disease process that is rapidly reaching epidemic proportions in the United States. It is estimated that between 1 million and 1.5 million people in the United States test HIV positive and as of June 1992, over 230,100 have been diagnosed with AIDS (Center for Disease Control, 1992). Current projections reveal that by 1995, there will be between 60,000 and 75,000 new cases of AIDS per year (Brookmeyer, 1991).

Although initially linked to specific population groups or lifestyles, AIDS now involves men, women, and children of all races, socioeconomic levels, and all education and occupation levels. Most disturbing is that the incidence of AIDS in adolescents and young adults is increasing at an alarming rate (Douce, 1993).

Due to the high mortality rate of AIDS victims, the apparent lack of medical remedy, and the misinformation about contracting AIDS, there is often an unfounded fear and almost a "collective paranoia" associated with the disease and the people who have contracted the disease. In the workplace this fear is manifest through both overt and covert discrimination against the workers with AIDS or HIV, and those regarded as having potential to acquire AIDS.

Although the incidence of AIDS in the workplace has been low, AIDS is now becoming a major issue for employers. The expected AIDS-related cost to employers through health care claims, absenteeism, and lost productivity was estimated to have totaled $55 billion by 1991 (Backer, 1987). As understanding and medical knowledge of the disability increases, AIDS is becoming less of an acute disease and more of a chronic, although still deadly, disability. Consequently, workers may be able to remain on the job and extend their worklife for far longer than in the past (Bollman, Ray, & Emener, 1990; Keeling, 1993).

The social, medical, legal, and ethical implications of AIDS in the workplace are highly complex and unquestionably more emotionally charged than with any other disease, impairment, or disability type. Employers, workers, and the public raise questions about the rights of workers with AIDS, the rights of co-workers who work side-by-side workers with AIDS, and the rights of customers who may be served by workers with AIDS. Employers ask bottom-line questions concerning the obligation to accommodate workers with AIDS and to pay for the increasing health care costs associated with AIDS.

Although it is clear that employers must develop policies, procedures, and worksite programs to manage AIDS in the workplace, few have taken even first steps to acknowledge the problem and accept responsibility for their obligations (Cohen & Cohen, 1989). In one study of over 2000 firms, only 8% of employers reported having a written AIDS policy (Zilig, 1989). With increasing incidence of AIDS in the workplace, employers and occupational health care professionals must become more involved with health care, benefit, employment, and labor issues created by the disability.

The Americans with Disability Act (ADA) has recognized AIDS as a disability, and provides legal protection from discrimination for qualified workers with AIDS. Employers must not discriminate against workers with AIDS in any employment practice and must make accommodations in the workplace so that these workers may perform the essential functions of their jobs. However, more than actual implementation of a law will be needed to overcome the medical, employment, and attitudinal concerns related to AIDS. Rehabilitation counselors have a considerable role in working with employers, co-workers, and workers with AIDS.

Employer interventions. Rehabilitation counselors have an education, policy, and program development role in helping industry respond to AIDS in the workplace. Employers and co-workers need current and accurate information about the nature and course of HIV and AIDS as the stigma associated with AIDS is often the most significant vocational issue for disability managers to address in vocational planning (Reichert and MacGuffie, 1988). Management and co-workers need the opportunity to discuss their attitudes and reactions to individuals with AIDS and a forum to discuss unfounded fears about casual transmission (Darling & Lonnguist, 1988). Co-workers need to understand the legal issues and responsibilities of employers who must accommodate workers who contract HIV.

Rehabilitation counselors can also assist employers in developing clear and written policy that reflects the industry's position on employing individuals with AIDS. Policy should be broad-based in discussing equal employment opportunities, confidentiality, AIDS testing and screening, reasonable accommodations for workers, employer education efforts, and medical benefit coverage (Schiller & Myers, 1987). Programmatically, rehabilitation counselors can assist in developing worksite interventions that consider accommodations, modifications, or reassignment as the disease progresses and the individual experiences increasing functional losses.

Workers with AIDS. In addition to working with employer and employment problems, rehabilitation counselors can assist the worker with AIDS to understand and cope with the disease (Winiarski, 1991). Fear of stigma, potential discrimination, and concern for job security often prevent workers from asking for assistance. Counselors must be aware of the rapidly developing medical knowledge resulting from AIDS research, the physical signs and symptomatology related to the disease, as well as adjustment issues commonly experienced by individuals with AIDS. Counselors must be prepared to discuss the nature of HIV and AIDS disease progression and to provide additional resource information, such as the availability of AIDS support groups, if the individual wishes to utilize them.

Beyond the role of worker-educator, the counselor must be skilled in responding to themes and issues experiences by individuals with AIDS. These issues may include adjustment to the rejection by friends, family, and co-workers, concerns about transmitting the disease to others, suicide, fears about progressive pain, disability, and eventual death (Dworkin & Pincu, 1993).

The rehabilitation counselor also plays a consulting and case management role, especially as the disease progresses. The counselor should develop and coordinate home-based case management programs instead of utilizing costly and unnecessary inpatient services (Thorn, 1990). The potential reaction and concerns of the health care team members may hamper or limit planning and must be confronted, responded to, and facilitated.

Professional issues. The counselor must also be aware of his or her own feelings, attitudes, and reactions to individuals with AIDS. The counselor faces significant competency issues surrounding the level of skill needed to work with AIDS counseling, adjustment, case management, and program development interventions in the workplace. While little graduate training related to AIDS rehabilitation practice is available, the counselor is bound by professional and ethical tenets to develop options and resources that improve practice and provide effective services.

AGING WORKER TRENDS

One of the significant demographic trends in the U.S. work force is the dramatic increase over the next decade in the number of older workers. Between the years 1982 and 2000, the number of workers between 18 and 34 years of age will decrease by 12%. However, individuals between 35 and 54 years of age will increase 53% (Morrison, 1984). With a decrease in the number of individuals entering the work force, older workers represent a potentially valuable resource to employers. This is particularly true in light of projected economic expansion resulting in approximately 18 million new jobs by the year 2005.

While demographic trends are quite clear, the impact of an aging work force on business and industry is highly complex and far less understood. What is clear is that, as the work force ages, the incidence of disability increases. Two-thirds of all individuals with work disability are over 40 (Blake, 1981). Older workers experience disability and impairments that include chronic disabilities, such as heart disease, anteriosclerosis, and hypertension; progressive and cumulative trauma disorders (e.g., degenerative disc disease, carpal tunnel disorders), and functional decline (e.g., diminished hearing, vision, or motor speed).

Older workers and older workers with a disability experience stereotyping and discrimination on the part of employers and the health care system because of their age. Older people are conceptualized as a homogenous group with similar characteristics. They may be seen as having poor memory, faulty judgement, reduced reaction time, or inability to learn or to adjust to new situations. Attitudes toward older workers, and decisions that are made, are often based on these stereotypes.

In reality, older individuals are highly heterogeneous with far greater differences than similarities. However, "ageism" is so pervasive that the older worker often internalizes society's stereotypes and devalues his or her abilities and potentials.

Recently, business and industry has developed programs to respond to the impact on the aging process on the worker. These programs utilize the potential of the worker in the work force. Several of the programs are described in detail elsewhere in this book.

To work effectively with older workers, rehabilitation counselors and health care professionals must first reassess their own attitudes towards older individuals with a disability. Research has shown that rehabilitation and health care professionals demonstrate a high degree of age bias and view older persons more negatively than they do younger persons (Benedict & Ganikos, 1981; Myers, 1983). Rehabilitation counselors must understand certain older workers' reluctance to change, to accept and report declining function, to work with new technologies and to participate in retraining efforts. Concurrently, continued participation in the work force after disability for an older worker is not the right choice for all workers. The rehabilitation counselor must be skilled in early intervention and assessment, adjustment counseling, and understanding of functional losses among older workers, as well as the impact of aging and chronic impairment on individuals and their family. The role of the counselor and disability management team is to ensure that the older worker experiencing disability is aware that there are many options other than disability retirement, early retirement, Long-Term Disability, or reliance on Social Security disability insurance benefits.

CROSS-CULTURAL PARTICIPATION IN THE WORK FORCE

Minority participation in the work force on the part of black, Asian, and Hispanic individuals is expected to increase significantly by the year 2005 (Fullerton, 1992). This increase impacts both large and small employers, as well as rehabilitation service providers.

Employers. At a time when fewer individuals are leaving the workforce and the economy is shifting from manufacturing to service and information technology, the minority population is one of the fastest growing segments of the work force. Minority workers generally are less educated and unskilled, typically perform manual labor, and work in manufacturing or production positions. They are overrepresented in areas and levels of the economy with the slowest projected growth, and underrepresented in occupations projecting greatest growth (Kutscher, 1992).

By virtue of their minority status, they often do not have skills or training to access the jobs of the future. New jobs in the business services, health services, and information technology will require specialized training and education. Even for skilled minority workers, lack of education limits them from transferring skills or learning new skills easily.

Often the lack of basic academic foundations or language and communication skills hinders attempts at retraining through internal industry education programs. Conversely, ethnic minority groups often choose to maintain their language as part of their unique cultural identity, further limiting their ability to access the range of training or retraining opportunities available.

Rehabilitation Counselors. As a large proportion of the minority population is of working age, they represent a potential pool of clients for rehabilitation. This is supported by the fact that minority workers are overrepresented in manual labor jobs that are physically demanding and have high incidence of injury. It is not surprising that minority workers experience higher incidence of disability and greater utilization of health and benefit systems.

Disability status compounds the effects of both minority status and socioeconomic level, resulting in lowered ability to access jobs, reduced ability to obtain and take advantage of training, increased utilization of health care resources, and reduced economic resources. As the number of minority members in the population grows it can be expected that there will be an increased demand on health care and rehabilitation services.

However, depending on cultural influences, minority workers may or may not be able to utilize health care and rehabilitation resources effectively. Brown (1990) reports that only 20% of rehabilitation caseloads consists of individuals from ethnic and minority backgrounds. Effective utilization is highly dependent on cultural expectations of the individual and the structure of the medical and rehabilitation systems (Fitzgerald, 1992).

While minority workers demonstrate greater utilization of health care services and higher incidents of injury and disability, health care providers and rehabilitation practitioners often lack understanding of cultural issues and exhibit both overt and covert discrimination against minority clients (Acosta, Yamamoto, Evans, & Skilbeck, 1983; Leong, 1986). This may result in denial of the individual for services, in delivery of different training, employment services, and referral to only limited employment settings.

CROSS-CULTURE REHABILITATION COUNSELOR TRAINING NEEDS FOR THE WORKPLACE

Few rehabilitation counselor education programs have courses in multicultural rehabilitation practice and fewer programs address the challenges presented by minority workers who are disabled on the job. Recently the Council On Rehabilitation Education (CORE) guidelines have emphasized that cross-cultural rehabilitation strategies must be incorporated in course work throughout rehabilitation education curricula. There are several knowledge and skill areas that rehabilitation counselor education should address for practitioners who work with multicultural workers who become injured or disabled.

First, curriculum must develop an understanding of individual differences between and within different minority groups (Smart & Smart, 1992). The rehabilitation counselor must learn how his or her culture, as well as the culture and customs of the workplace and the medical/rehabilitation service influence or interact with the cultural roles, values, and expectations of the worker (Fitzgerald, 1992). Disability is often viewed differently across different cultures. One culture may devalue the person who becomes injured, another may feel that it is a sign of weakness to notify a supervisor of an advancing loss of function. Another culture may magnify or catastrophize a minor impairment. It is necessary to understand disability, and how the individual may or may not seek health care services, from the cultural reference point.

Rehabilitation education curricula should make practitioners aware of culturally relevant services and how workers may access them. Examples may include English language skill development, language appropriate interpreter training, and minority involvement in rehabilitation policy decisions.

Rehabilitation practitioners must be trained to evaluate culturally-biased content in assessment and testing procedures. Inappropriate testing norms may screen out individuals who otherwise may demonstrate aptitude or ability for the job, a job transfer, or for training or job upgrade. Case managers must learn to recognize and support the acculturalization process as well as a worker's desire to maintain his or her cultural identity. For the latter, counselors must be aware of means to overcome language and communication barriers and to incorporate cultural resources from the worker's community to assist in
rehabilitation and resolution of workplace labor issues.

TRENDS IN REHABILITATION PRACTICE

Rehabilitation is one of the fastest growing fields in the health care industry (Dellario, 1991). The application of rehabilitation services, technologies, legislation, and philosophy serves as a cornerstone of industrial rehabilitation and disability management practice. Recent trends in rehabilitation are uniquely applicable to industrial rehabilitation practice.

ECOLOGICAL APPROACH TO REHABILITATION

Traditional rehabilitation service models developed from a medically based conceptualization of disability and treatment. Within this framework, the individual was viewed as having an impairment that needed to be evaluated (diagnosed) in order for services to be provided to the individual (treatment) by trained professionals. Rehabilitation focus was on the individual and how services could be provided to the person to help overcome a disability in order to be productive in society.

Recently, rehabilitation has redefined disability, and the manner in which services are provided. The individual is viewed within the context of his or her environment and the requirements and supports that may or may not be present. This "ecological paradigm" may be better understood by examining how specific rehabilitation services are implemented.

Traditional evaluation utilizes a variety of tests, techniques, and activities to identify the individual's strengths, limitations, abilities, and aptitudes in order to establish a diagnosis, or to determine whether a person is eligible for programs or services. Once these factors are identified, rehabilitation services are provided to the individual to reduce or remove functional limitations, to build upon the individual's strengths, and to maximize vocational potential.

Recently, rehabilitation has recognized that the person's functional ability must be assessed within the context of the individual's working, living, social, and learning environments. This approach to assessment considers the functional capacities and functional limitations of the person in relation to the environmental demands, requirements, and supports that interact with the person and his or her abilities. Within this context, definitions of disability, functional limitation, functional capacity, and our approach to assessment and service delivery are dramatically altered.

Functional limitation results as much from the presence or absence of supports and resources, the attitudes and expectations of others, and physical barriers in the work environment, as from the presence or severity of a disability. Disability is not so much a function of the impairment or deficits in a person, but of rehabilitation's inability to meet the vocational needs of the person. Disability is not viewed as a deficiency on the part of the worker, but as a product of a disabling, unresponsive, or insensitive work environment (Hahn, 1991). The emphasis in not on the skill deficits or functional limitations of the worker, but on the disabling characteristics of the environment that limit the person access, participation, and performance.

The "ecological paradigm" has particular relevance to disability management practice.

The challenge to disability management shifts from considering the impairments of the person, to developing resources and increasing flexibility within the work environment that will respond to the injured workers' potential. An ecological approach to work-return planning identifies and implements services that the person may need, including the modifications, accommodations, and supports used to enhance independence, productivity, and integration in a specific work environment.

The ecological view of the person represents an evolution from a relatively circumscribed perspective of the person to a more systemic approach to rehabilitation. For the rehabilitation counselor this evolution signifies a different approach in the way services are delivered to the individual with a disability. For example, it is not sufficient to consider medical records and status, physical capacity, and functional ability and limitations of a person when determining employability, rehabilitation potential, or return-to-work options for a person with chromic low back pain. The rehabilitation counselor must also utilize information such as the range of work tasks available in a company, the type of modifications for the job and worksite, the accommodations that the employee will consider, economic incentives to encourage worker and employer participation, the impact of working and not working on the family, and the commitment of labor and management to minimizing work disruption and to providing a safe and satisfying work option.

In redefining the way disability is understood, the concept of functional limitations may not be appropriate for a worker who experiences injury or impairment. For example, a worker who has a restriction in lifting may not have a "functional limitation" for a work task that has been ergonomically redesigned or where assistive technologies are applied to modify lifting loads.

Work injury and work disruption become more manageable when resources are approached and coordinated from a systems rather than a deficit or disability perspective.

CONSUMERISM AND SELF-DETERMINATION TRENDS IN REHABILITATION

The individual's right to maximize his or her potential has long been a core principle in rehabilitation philosophy and practice. However, traditional rehabilitation practice has embodied this principle through a medical model service delivery approach where the range of diagnostic rehabilitation services and resources is provided to a relatively passive disabled client/patient by rehabilitation and physical medicine experts.

Increasingly, the field of rehabilitation has recognized that individuals have a right to assume responsibility in identifying services and in making decisions about rehabilitation goals that impact their lives.

Prompted by legislation such as the Rehabilitation Act of 1973 and the Americans with Disabilities Act of 1990, rehabilitation is shifting from a service provider or expert system to one that promotes a partnership relationship between the consumer and his or her counselor. The counselor's role is to work with the individual in identifying options, making decisions, choosing among alternatives, clarifying responsibilities, and becoming an advocate for the services and resources that are needed to promote quality of life as the individual defines it.

For the rehabilitation counselor, the change from an "expert system" approach to a counselor-consumer partnership approach requires a change in practice, as much as it represents a change in philosophy. In practice, the goal of rehabilitation efforts, the range of skills used by the rehabilitation counselor, and the process through which they are applied may be quite different than in a traditional rehabilitation approach.

The rehabilitation counselor assists the individual to choose appropriate goals and directions, to accept responsibility and risks that are inherent in any choice, to utilize resources and take control of available opportunities. Counseling and case management activities assist the individual to view himself or herself, not as a handicapped person, but as an individual who is empowered, has choices in his or her life, and is responsible for eventual outcomes. The rehabilitation counselor assists the individual with a disability to identify abilities and capacities in relation to the demands of vocational, educational, and social opportunities.

Employers. Employers often view any effort to "empower employees" as a potential threat to profits and efficient business practice. In reality, the philosophy and practice of empowerment and self-determination is as important to the employer as it is to the worker with a disability or injury.

For too long, employers have abrogated responsibility and control for the management of workplace injury to insurance claims managers, third-party administrators, and private rehabilitation providers. If they are to reverse the current trend of escalating disability costs, employers must become advocates for proven industrial rehabilitation and disability management practices and take responsibility for their own vested interests in maintaining productivity, reducing work disruption, providing safe work environments, and containing costs related to injury and rehabilitation.

Rehabilitation counselors must be able to help employers and labor to clarify their roles in managing disability and assume responsibility and accountability for disability management decisions. The rehabilitation counselor must be able to evaluate and demonstrate the economic and business benefits of on-site disability management strategies. The first step may be to develop a better understanding of the patterns of injury and disability within the work force, the patterns of current medical, health care, and rehabilitation service costs, and significant medical, claims, and labor relations barriers to work-return programs. For the employer who maintains a "Doubting Thomas" position, strategy to demonstrate success as well as to identify potential barriers to employer-based efforts is to implement a pilot disability management program within the interested industry.

Workers. Workers with disabilities traditionally have played a minor role in formulating their own return-to-work plans, deciding how their disability should be managed, maintaining identity and role as a worker, and participating in decisions that result in satisfying, safe, and productive work activity. Workers become dependent on a medical/legal/labor system that does not always function in the worker's best vocational interests. A great measure of the individual's responsibility and control for his or her ability to return to work is removed and the person is left idle subject to the action or inaction of a medical/legal/labor/management system.

The rehabilitation counselor must be able to understand the issues that confront the injured worker and help him or her to understand work-return options available, to assume responsibility for work-return planning, and to help the worker evaluate worksite modifications that minimize work disruption and increase productivity.

ESSENTIAL SKILLS IN INDUSTRIAL REHABILITATION AND DISABILITY MANAGEMENT: IMPLICATIONS FOR PROFESSIONAL PRACTICE AND COUNSELOR EDUCATION

Recent trends in rehabilitation, the economy, and the workplace clearly demonstrate that the rehabilitation counselor can play an integral role in the management of injury and disability in the workplace. Rehabilitation counselor educators have begun to identify the skills, competencies, and knowledge requirements of disability management practice and to examine how these abilities may be integrated within current rehabilitation counselor training programs.

From the previous discussion, it is evident that many of the skills and competencies are acquired through traditional curricula, while additional skills and specific knowledge areas need to be addressed through new courses and clinical experience.

The following discussion identifies four broad service areas that are relevant for disability management training in rehabilitation counselor education. These areas include:

- Applied disability management skills
- Case management procedures
- Administration, organization, and program development skills
- Disability-related knowledge and skills

Within each area, the specific knowledge, skill, and competencies needed by the disability manager are discussed. The disability management skills training curriculum offered at Boston University is detailed in Appendix A. In addition, case simulations, training exercises, and skill simulations are available from the author.

APPLIED DISABILITY MANAGEMENT SKILLS

A primary function of the rehabilitation counselor in employer-based disability management is to provide direct services to the injured worker and his or her family. These services include vocational counseling, vocational evaluation and assessment, application of occupational information to work-return planning, integration of multidisciplinary assessments in work-return planning, job analysis, utilization of job modification and reasonable accommodation strategies, application of rehabilitation technologies to work stations and the worksite, and job development and placement skills.

Vocational Counseling Function

The disability manager utilizes both personal adjustment and vocational counseling during work-return transition planning. The goal of counseling in industrial rehabilitation is to assist the injured worker to understand and adjust to the disability, to clarify work-return options, and to take responsibility for his or her part in the work-return process.

Counseling is utilized to address well-defined goals and specific problems that develop throughout rehabilitation interventions. The counseling process focuses on understanding work-return alternatives, establishing vocational goals, and delineating responsibilities for achieving specific objectives. While the structure is similar to outcome-oriented short-term counseling approaches that are highly counselor-directed, the emphasis with the injured worker is on identifying mutual goals and developing individual responsibilities for decision making, planning, and action. The counselor utilizes his or her skills to empower the injured worker and to solidify his or her role and responsibility in returning to work.

The disability manager must also be ready to address specific adjustment issues related to individuals who experience work injuries. These include issues of loss, feelings of abandonment by their employer and co-workers, of hostility toward employers, as well as the legal and medical systems; fears about re-injury when they return to work; loss of self-esteem related to injury; confusion and depression about being a family provider; issues about motivation and secondary gain; or confusion about career direction.

Very often the counselor is the target of the injured worker's anger, hostility, or rejection that may result from uncertainty about the injury, fears about loss of career, or frustration with individuals who may be associated with health care professionals or the employer. Failure to recognize that successful adjustment to a disability is a result of the interplay between factors such as disability characteristics and course, medical/legal influences, employer attitude and actions, and environmental supports and resources will dramatically reduce success the counselor will have in helping the worker.

There are also disability adjustment issues that distinct groups in the work force experience. For example, the older worker may experience depression at onset of vision or hearing loss, may fear termination if he or she reveals a disability, may have doubts about ability to learn high tech applications through retraining, or have concerns about retirement. Individuals from a minority group or different culture may be suspicious of a counselor who is not from the same background, or may resist participating in rehabilitation activities due to feeling uncomfortable about language and communication. Specific disabilities, such as chronic pain, stress disorders, AIDS, or psychiatric disability present unique adjustment issues that must be recognized and incorporated into vocational counseling.

The counseling function in disability management focuses on vocational adjustment and vocational planning, similar to traditional vocational counseling. However, characteristics of the disability, and influences of employment, legal, health care, and benefit systems require that the counselor be skilled in integrating multiple factors in the goal-oriented counseling process.

Vocational Evaluation and Assessments. Traditional assessment in rehabilitation has identified individual strengths, abilities, limitations, interests, and values related to vocational potential and identification of a viable vocational goal. In industrial rehabilitation the worker, and his or her ability to work, is explored within an environmental demand context. The goal of assessment is to identify how compatible the individual's abilities are with the requirements of the work activities and tasks. Vocational potential and ability to work is assessed by considering the capacity of the worker, the requirements of the work activity, and the characteristics of the work environment.

The counselor will use a variety of vocational evaluation approaches to assess the *worker's potential*, including paper-and-pencil tests, performance tests, and work samples. A primary strategy is to assess individual performance capacity in the worksite. Other evaluation procedures include physical and functional capacity evaluation to assess functional work performance capacities that are basic to performance output and sustained work activity.

To assess the *requirements and demands of the job*, the counselor will utilize job analysis procedures. Depending on the characteristics of the disability or injury and the demands of the job, the counselor may also utilize specific information from an ergonomic evaluation. The ergonomic evaluation examines the motion, movement, body mechanics, and effort requirements involved in the use of tools, equipment, and machinery (Shrey & Breslin, 1992).

The *worksite environment* is assessed using a worksite risk analysis process. Job activities and work environment demands, specific to the worker's functional capacity are assessed, incorporating job analysis and ergonomic evaluation information. Assessment is "environment specific" and considers the supports, resources, and worksite characteristics that will support and extend an individual's productivity.

The counselor utilizes information about the worker, work activity, and worksite to determine the degree of compatibility between the worker and the job, as well as recommendations for rehabilitation interventions to be included in an Individual Modified Reemployment Plan (IMRP).

Vocational evaluations and assessments have interdisciplinary applications (Lacerte & Wright, 1992). The counselor collaborates with the psychiatrist and interdisciplinary team members to integrate evaluations in the return-to-work plan.

In a separate, but related assessment role, the counselor is frequently required to serve as a vocational expert in forensic vocational rehabilitation. The vocational expert must be knowledgeable about current labor market trends, occupational information resources such as the *Dictionary of Occupational Titles*, (1991), *Complete Guide for Occupational Exploration*, (Farr, 1993), *Classification of Jobs*, (Field & Field, 1992), and the impact of disability on job performance and availability.

Job Analysis. Job analysis is a process that systematically identifies characteristics of a job that relate to worker requirements; work tasks; materials, tools, machines and equipment; and work environment characteristics. In work-return transition planning, job analysis provides information for a number of reasons, including vocational evaluation (functional capacity evaluation, ergonomic evaluation, worksite risk analysis), as a basis for medical approval for work return, for the development of job modifications and accommodations, and for developing functional job descriptions.

The Department of Labor has developed a formal approach to job analysis that is detailed in *The Revised Handbook for Analyzing Jobs* (1991). Understanding the purpose of the job analysis and how it will be used will guide how the counselor gathers job analysis information and formulates the analysis report. For example, job analysis information that is required to identify the essential functions of a job to be included in a functional job description will be substantially different from a job analysis used to develop a functional capacity evaluation. The counselor may also structure the analysis to be specific to a work setting or to specific functional disability characteristics.

Requirements for the Americans with Disabilities Act (ADA) and recent changes in the Department of Labor worker trait configuration require the counselor to be current in job analysis information, particularly if job analysis information may be used in litigation. (Specific steps to perform a job analysis are outlined in the appendices at the end of this chapter).

JOB MODIFICATION AND ACCOMMODATIONS

A key to successful prevention and worker-retention efforts is the effective and creative utilization of job modifications and accommodation intervention. The rehabilitation counselor applies information from assessment and job analysis as well as knowledge of rehabilitation technologies to modify or accommodate the worker, work tasks, or worksite. The counselor must be thoroughly versed in ADA regulations that specify use and application of "reasonable accommodations" in all employment practices. Modifications or accommodations may include:

- Job restructuring including reassigning nonessential job tasks, modifying work hours, or altering how work is accomplished;
- Provision of assistive devices/adaptation aids, including devices such as head sets, speaker phones, computer keyboard adaptations, or computer monitor screen enhancements;
- Work station modifications including customizing hand tools, raising/lowering work stations to accommodate lifting demands, modifying equipment, applying ergonomic modifications to work station heights, lifting and carrying devices, or structuring reaching demands; and
- Reassignment to vacant positions.

Job Development and Placement

While successful placement in a job is the goal of industrial rehabilitation, rehabilitation counselors often do not approach the process in the most effective manner (Shrey & Fraser, 1986). In industrial rehabilitation, counselors must understand the "corporate culture," be effective in marketing and networking, be skilled in industrial analysis, and be able to capitalize on underutilized placement resources such as local Chambers of Commerce, National Alliance of Businessmen, or Rotary Clubs.

Rehabilitation counselors must understand how financial disincentives associated with workers' compensation, SSDI, and LTD impact return-to-work planning, as well as how to use financial incentives such as targeted jobs tax credits and tax credits and deductions associated with accommodations to support the employer.

"Selective placement" techniques are more effective in industrial rehabilitation than are client-centered placement interventions. These interventions include active job-seeking skills training, marketing and networking, and direct employer contacts by the counselor.

An important job development skill is the ability to develop a labor market survey to identify where comparable jobs are in the local area. To complement this, a labor market trend analysis is developed to project outlook in the future for a particular region.

CASE MANAGEMENT PROCEDURES IN INDUSTRIAL REHABILITATION

Applied Skills in Disability Case Management

The emergence of efforts to manage health care service delivery more effectively (e.g. managed care and utilization review practices) dictates that vocational rehabilitation examine traditional approaches to case management service delivery. Case management has functioned, in theory if not in practice, as a rehabilitation service delivery process that is primarily structured to serve the client and to achieve client rehabilitation goals.

Case management in disability management is a proactive, integrated, and coordinated process that assesses injured worker needs; plans, negotiates, implements, and coordinates services; and evaluates services to determine outcome characteristics (National Coalition of Associations for the Advancement of Case Management, 1993). Case management in disability management has multiple outcomes, including delivery of quality services, cost containment, individual self determination, as well as coordination of planning and service delivery to meet the individual's disability management needs. As a disability management process, case management responds equally to the needs of the injured worker, the employer, and the various health care providers.

Case management is implemented through the application of several basic principles. The first principle is that case management should facilitate "*empowerment*" of the individual. As the injured worker develops a clear understanding of his or her medical status and return-to-work options, he or she will work more effectively toward identifying realistic work goals, and will be more involved in decision-making, service selection, and in establishing realistic time frames for intermediate objectives. Investment in and ownership of the disability management plan is strengthened.

The second principle recognizes that case management utilizes an *integrated approach* to planning and service delivery. The needs of an injured worker often encompass medical, vocational, emotional, and physical areas and involve the family, employers, the legal system, and other health care providers. Case management applies a holistic approach to the individual and utilizes multidisciplinary interventions to respond to these needs, thereby ensuring that these needs are addressed through a coordinated approach.

Case management also utilizes a *proactive approach* to disability management. Early identification of needs and early implementation of return to work planning protects the "occupational bond" between the worker and the employer, maintains the individual in productive work environments, and reduces costs.

Comprehensive planning is a process that defines case management as an *anticipatory process*. The disability case manager and interdisciplinary team identify available supports and resources, review and evaluate service provider performance, and consider financial or claims adjudication factors in coordinating services.

Structured and ongoing communication between the injured worker and his or her family, the disability case manager, and service providers results in a managed and cost effective approach to case management planning. Service delivery is driven by updated assessments, adjusted service plans, and revisions of time lines that reflect the worker's progress and the service provider's expertise.

Finally, effective case management is based on *skilled and knowledgeable professionals*. Disability case managers should demonstrate expertise in rehabilitation methods and procedures, medical and health care services, service costs, and claims adjudication procedures. Case management is performed within a framework of disability management principles and methods, ethical practice, laws and regulations, as well as an understanding of business, personnel, and rehabilitation practices.

The components of case management are identified as:

A. Understanding the individual's disability needs.
B. Determining readiness for return to work planning.
C. Developing individualized disability case management plans.
D. Negotiating, implementing, and coordinating internal and external services and service providers.
E. Monitoring quality and quantity of service delivery.
F. Documenting and evaluating service delivery and outcome characteristics.

Disability Analysis and Critical Case Review. Case management services require that rehabilitation counselors understand the factors that contribute to and also limit the implementation of effective disability management programs. Rehabilitation counselors must be proficient in conducting a formal *Disability Analysis* to identify policies, procedures, and protocols with respect to the employer's capacity to respond to work-disruptive injuries and disabilities, health care utilization patterns, current treatment trends, and subsequent work-return outcomes for injured and disabled workers. The analysis also assesses the labor relations impact on claims management and rehabilitation planning.

The rehabilitation counselor must also be able to perform a *Critical Case Review* to understand the chronology and pattern of interventions from outset of injury to current status of a worker. The goal of this analysis is to assess the employer's responsiveness to the needs of injured workers by focusing on: 1) past case management of injured workers, 2) work-return and work-performance barriers, 3) negative forces influencing rehabilitation failure, and 4) positive forces influencing rehabilitation success.

Through disability analysis and critical case analysis approaches, the rehabilitation counselor is able to identify financial, case management, and administrative obstacles to the successful management of work-related injuries. By identifying internal and external resources within the industry, the rehabilitation counselor is able to identify effective approaches to overcome disability management obstacles.

Development of the Individual Modified Reemployment Plan (IMRP). The rehabilitation counselor utilizes rehabilitation plans to structure service coordination and communication through clearly defined goals, objectives, and responsibilities. The IMRP functions as a key planning instrument in coordinating disability management activities, establishing time frames for evaluation of success of program components, and allowing the injured worker to monitor his or her own progress.

Development and implementation of the IMRP requires that the rehabilitation counselor utilize technical skills to work with industrial engineers, ergonomists, worksite supervisors, benefit managers, risk managers, health safety offices, and medical staff (Habeck, Leahy, Hunt, Chan, & Welch, 1991). The counselor must also respond to legal, medical, and labor interests that interact with work-return interventions.

The rehabilitation counselor will collaborate with the injured worker on developing the rehabilitation plan. An example of IMRP components is shown in Table 2.

Coordination of Disability Management Programs. Prevention, job retention, and early intervention programs are central to containing the cost of work-related injuries and reducing work disruption. Rehabilitation counselors should be knowledgeable about service components in each area and be able to develop or provide services ranging from proactive case management, education of co-workers and supervisors about safety and disability management, implementation of health screening efforts, coordination of worksite ergonomic evaluations, and marketing of EAP services that injured workers may access.

Counselors should utilize proven strategies related to job retention and early return-to-work programs, such as vocational and functional capacity evaluation, on-site transitional work, modified work options, job accommodations and rehabilitation engineering, and flexible work schedules.

Table 2
Key Variables and Critical Components of the Rehabilitation Plan

1. Specific impairments resulting in loss time or work disruptions
2. Impact the impairments may have on the worker's ability to perform the job
3. Services or interventions to be provided
4. Barriers to work return
5. Specific work return transition steps:
    A. Objectives
    B. Time frames
    C. Responsibilities of the claims supervisor, rehabilitation nurse, medical personnel, employee supervisor, injured worker and others
    D. Resources to be used
    E. Resources needed
6. Alternatives to work return if the employee is at high risk for not returning to work due to age, severity of injury, emotional or labor-relations problems
7. Monitoring schedule
8. Evaluation of overall rehabilitation activities and projected costs

Rehabilitation counselors in industry who develop, implement, and monitor employer-based transitional work programs should be familiar with Occupational Safety and Health Administration (OSHA) safety standards and National Institute of Occupational Safety and Health (NIOSH) guidelines. A goal of work return planning is the safe return to work in a position that does not promote re-injury.

ADMINISTRATION, ORGANIZATION, AND PROGRAM DEVELOPMENT SKILLS

Administration and organizational development skills are important elements of the rehabilitation counselor's skill repertoire and they are not typically trained in these areas. Nevertheless, specialized administrative knowledge and leadership skills are necessary to coordinate and manage disability management services within an employment setting.

Administration

Rehabilitation counselors must understand the varied laws, regulations, policies, and functions that impact employment practices of individuals with injuries or disabilities. These include income transfer and benefit programs such as long-term disability (LTD), short-term disability (STD), workers' compensation (WC), SSDI, and Early Retirement Incentive Planning (ERIP). These programs may differ across states (WC) or across employers (LTD, ERIP).

In addition, there are specific laws that promote employment opportunities at the work place and prevent discrimination of qualified workers with a disability. Representative of these laws are the Americans with Disabilities Act of 1990 (ADA) and the Civil Rights Act of 1991. These laws legislate specific services for individuals with disabilities and may have direct application to individuals who are injured on the job. Employers are often more receptive to creative disability management intervention for the injured worker. They are presented in the context of a relevant legislation (e.g., ADA). In addition to federal legislation promoting employment opportunities, the rehabilitation counselor should be familiar with state and federal affirmative action legislation that may apply to a particular employer.

The rehabilitation counselor must also understand the organizational structure of the company, the role of labor, the laws and regulations governing the collective bargaining process, how benefit systems are structured, and differences between self-insured companies and third-party administrators. Along with an understanding of the formal structure of the company is a careful assessment of the informal structure, including the "corporate culture," values and vested interests, and the protocols for formal and informal interactions between corporate, management, and labor personnel.

Leadership Skills

Disability management policies, programs, and benefits must be presented to and negotiated between management, labor, and health care staff. The rehabilitation counselor is often required to resolve disputes between labor and management, supervisor and worker, to encourage cooperation between groups, and to educate and train supervisors about disability management goals and benefits.

In developing the infrastructure of a disability management program the rehabilitation counselor utilizes a variety of program coordination skills needed for working with labor-management committees, developing communication networks between internal and external resources, coordinating community health care services, negotiating vendor agreements, and integrating rehabilitation vendors with on-site services. The leadership skills that are developed and demonstrated through these interactions are often considered to be developed through experience and exposure "in the trenches." However, internship experiences that gradually expose a student to these experiences develop confidence and skill in working with labor, management, and health care representatives. As the university training program develops a working relationship with an industry and it's labor representatives, the opportunity for expanded involvement in leadership activities is enhanced.

Disability-related Knowledge and Skills

Disabilities and disability characteristics found in the workplace are different than those typically found in public rehabilitation settings. The most common workplace disability is an orthopedic injury, including low back strain or injury resulting from trauma, such as a slip and fall, or from repetitive motion and cumulative trauma resulting from frequent and continuous lifting and carrying. The chapter has discussed a range of disabilities common to the workplace, including repetitive motion disorders, cardiac impairments, and AIDS. There are also other injuries, disabilities, and impairments that the rehabilitation counselor can expect to work with that are not frequently found in public rehabilitation practice and that should be included in rehabilitation counselor education curriculum.

Disabilities. Disabilities that represent unique case management challenges to the employer and counselor include occupational stress-related claims, cancer, and mental health and substance abuse problems.

Occupational stress is one of the ten leading work-related problems, involved in between 60 and 80% of all industrial accidents, according to the National Institute of Occupational Safety and Health (Sipkoff, 1993). White collar workers are involved in 70% of stress related claims, but only 20% of disabling injuries overall. Workers cite factors such as job pressures, harassment, discrimination, demotion, and job termination as reasons for stress related impairments. Stress is also expensive. The average occupational stress claim costs between $15,000 and $20,000 in benefit payments, about one half as much as other physical injuries (DeCarlo & Gruenfeld, 1989). Work place stress management is expected to be a $15 billion industry by the end of the 1990s (Miller, Springen, Gordon, Murr, Cohn, Drew, & Barrett, 1988), and the incidence and costs of occupational stress are expected to increase.

Approximately half a million people a year are diagnosed and treated successfully for cancer (American Cancer Society, 1992). Although cancer treatment has benefited from research and medical advances, the employment needs of people who have been successfully treated have been largely ignored. Research shows that cancer survivors are underrepresented in vocational rehabilitation programs (Conti, 1990). Individuals report that they are discriminated against because of fears and misunderstanding about cancer on the part of both coworkers and supervisors. Other barriers to successful return to work involve a lack of appropriate accommodation, inadequate insurance coverage, and supervisors who do not understand the disability or restrictions it may require. Counselors must be familiar with disability characteristics, course of treatment and treatment practices, adjustment reactions by the individual and family, characteristics of health care needs, and utilization of self help and advocacy groups.

Employer costs for mental health and substance abuse claims can be 2.5 times higher than any other disability. Costs related to mental health and substance abuse benefits increased 27% from 1987 to 1988 (Weiner & Siegel, 1989), with mental health claim expenditures ranging from 20-25% of overall employer health care costs (Kraman, 1988). In addition, mental health problems result in indirect costs and loss resulting from reduced productivity, increased absenteeism, short-term leave, accidents, property thefts, and costs associated with employee termination. It is no wonder that employers consider mental health and substance abuse as one of health cares most serious problems. Current treatment efforts range from EAP programs, short term counseling, outpatient therapy and utilization of inpatient treatment facilities.

Disability knowledge and skills. Rehabilitation education curriculum should emphasize impairment etiology and disability treatment patterns, physical system structures (e.g. musculoskeletal, nervous system, immune systems). The counselor needs to be familiar with diagnostic procedures, medical and physical rehabilitation interventions, typical courses of treatment, including medications, use of physical therapists, surgery, and home health care resources. Knowledge of medications should include antidepressants, pain medications, chemotherapy alternatives, and AIDS treatment such as AZT.

Counselors must be able to relate functional capacity impairment levels to the physical requirement of a job. The counselor must then work with the physician to plan eligibility for participation in transitional work activities. When little research has been reported on work return efforts with a disability, such as with cancer and cardiac impairment, research collaboration efforts may be initiated.

Counselors must understand how adjustment issues relate to a disability and the disability experience, especially when associated with the ageing process or with ethnic or cultural factors. Common adjustment issues in injured worker rehabilitation involve secondary gain, deconditioning process, symptom magnification, the "compensation syndrome," and medication dependency and abuse. Often times, adjustment issues are as closely related to chronic pain behaviors as are the objective impairment findings that are present in disabilities such as lo back pain.

Disability management is a multidisciplinary process and the counselor will utilize both internal and external experts in addressing work return efforts. Counselors must understand the expertise of diverse medical experts, as well as their potential lack of experience and knowledge of workplace modifications for the worker involved in a work transition plan.

Rehabilitation counselor education curriculum must present aspects of an impairment or disability, treatment course and intervention options, psychosocial adjustment issues related to the disability, the individual, and health care influences, and the integration of varied health care disciplines into disability management planning.

IMPLICATIONS FOR REHABILITATION EDUCATION

Rehabilitation counselor education (RCE) programs utilizing CORE training guidelines and standards are able to provide basic competencies and knowledge components that can be applied to employer-based disability management programs described in this chapter and throughout this book. However, RCE programs prepare rehabilitation counselors to work with individuals with a disability who receive services through the state-federal vocational rehabilitation system and do not provide the orientation, focus, skill training, and knowledge base that is necessary to deliver quality services to injured workers in today's industry/labor/legal/and health care environment.

Escalating health care costs and an inadequate health care delivery system has created a market demand on the part of employers for skilled and effective rehabilitation professionals who are able to provide quality services, reduce lost time due to disability, contain costs, and maintain productivity.

The question becomes whether rehabilitation educators are able to respond to the "market demands" and what the configuration of subsequent training efforts will look like. The concern is that RCE will maintain characteristics of a "rehabilitation model" and not orient a disability management training program from a true marketing approach, i.e. develop training from a market analysis of what the consumer needs. An effective training paradigm develops from a market analysis of the needs of the consumer (in this case the consumers include the injured worker, the labor/management system, and health care providers).

Following are proposals to promote more effective training of essential skills in disability management that can be offered in rehabilitation counselor education programs.

- Development of a *Best Practices* approach to disability management. There is currently sufficient documentation (Galvin, 1992; Habeck, et al., 1991; Schwartz, et al., 1989; Shrey, 1990) to establish accepted basic standards for disability management practice. While literature has documented the diversity of approaches that employers have utilized in delivering services to injured workers, common standards are evident and can be adopted by employers interested in establishing employer-based programs. *Best practices* approaches are found in detail throughout this book.

- Identification of *proficiency standards* for disability managers who practice in industry settings. Likewise, based on disability management literature over the past decade (Gilbride, Connolly, & Stensrud, 1990; Habeck & Ellien, 1986; Kilbury, Benshoff, & Riggar, 1990; Rasch, 1992; Matkin, 1987; Shrey, 1990) basic disability management roles, functions, skills, and competencies can be established. Many of these standards have been identified and discussed throughout this chapter.
- Development of *standards for training* in disability management. Training standards should identify core content areas, internship experience requirements, supervisor qualifications, ethical standards for practice, and objective proficiency levels. Minimum standards for concentration or specialization programs must be established. Options to be explored would include RCEP training, national training workshops, continuing education offerings, or Advanced Graduate Study degrees.
- Development of a *clearinghouse on technical assistance* in disability management. This effort would link resources such as the Job Accommodations Network, Project Enable, state Technology Assistance Programs, Regional Disability and Business Technical Assistance Centers, as well as share international efforts in disability management advances.
- Advocate for a *research and training center* in employer-based disability management models to solidify research efforts, advocate for training and training standards, and complement health care reform directions.

The challenge is for rehabilitation counselor educators to recognize and respond to the needs of workers who experience disability and potential job loss, employers who require a productive labor force, and health care providers who can provide coordinated and quality services. It is short sighted to limit rehabilitation training for a circumscribed number of individuals with a disability who are in the public sector rehabilitation system or to assume that workers who become disabled are best served through an insurance based rehabilitation system.

APPENDIX A

BOSTON UNIVERSITY
SPECIALIZATION IN INDUSTRIAL REHABILITATION & DISABILITY MANAGEMENT

DISABILITY MANAGEMENT SKILLS TRAINING ORIENTATION:

MODULE I: Introduction to Industrial Rehabilitation

Topics: History and development of industrial rehabilitation
Development and reform in insurance rehabilitation
Insurance rehabilitation and workers' compensation, LTD, STD, and personal injury
Development of proprietary rehabilitation
Differences and commonalities between public and private rehabilitation clientele and services
Determining eligibility for rehabilitation services
Legislation impacting injured worker rehabilitation:
  Americans with Disabilities Act of 1990
  Rehabilitation Act of 1973 and Amendments
  Civil Rights Act of 1991
Core concepts
Implications for employers and health care (Rehab)

MODULE II: Understanding Disability Management Issues

Topics: Principles of disability management
Barriers in managing disability in the workplace
Characteristics of disability in the workplace:
  Implications for rehabilitation counselors
Economic impact of injury and disability
Competing self-interests in managing disability

MODULE III: Medical Aspects of Injured Worker Rehabilitation

Topics: Interdisciplinary health care team
  Role & Function

Incidence of disability in the workplace
    Repetitive motion disorders
    Low back injury
    Orthopedic injury
    Stress related components, disorders
    AIDS
    Cardiac rehabilitation
    Cancer rehabilitation

Etiology, diagnostic procedures, interdisciplinary evaluations, treatment approaches, medical management
Medications, including signs of medication abuse
Managed care concepts

MODULE IV: Personnel & Business Management Practice

Topics: Hiring, training, promoting, and terminating employees
    Fiscal management and budgeting practices
    Benefit programs, including EAP services
    Management information systems
    Labor unions and collective bargaining regulations
    Labor/management interests
    Organizational development structures
    Principles in marketing

MODULE V: Vocational Evaluation & Assessment in Industrial Rehabilitation

Topics: The worksite approach to vocational evaluation
    Transferable skill analysis to match worker skills with job demands
    Physical and functional capacity assessment
    Ergonomic evaluation
    Job analysis: Identifying essential functions of the job and functional capacity
    Differential uses of job analysis
        Worksite risk analysis
        Occupational information resources: Utilization of
            DOT, GOE, OOH, COJ and local employment market resources;
        Impact of disability on worker trait profile
    Job accommodation and modification
        ADA and reasonable accommodation in all phases of employment practice

Rehabilitation engineering
Assistive and augmentative technology
Financial incentives for employers
Computer-aided vocational evaluation

MODULE VI: Vocational Counseling with the Injured Worker

Topics: Adjustment issues and injured worker counseling
Short-term and brief counseling approaches
Process vs. techniques in counseling the injured worker
Issues of chronic pain, secondary gain, "disability syndrome"
Self-esteem issues and worker/disability role identification
Counseling with families, aging workers, multicultural worker

MODULE VII: Corporate Health & Disability Analysis Process

Topics: Steps to performing a corporate disability analysis and injured worker case analysis procedures

Identify patterns of injury and illness
Identify patterns of medical and rehabilitation treatments and related costs
Describe linkages between employer and medical treatment facilities
Define employer characteristics, as they relate to illness and injury onset, health care utilization, and work return
Identify patterns of contract or benefit influence on health care, rehabilitation services and work return
Identify patterns of worksite and community influence on health care and rehabilitation services
Identify significant barriers to work return:
  Medical management problems
  Claims management problems
  Economic disincentives
  Psychological/social problems
  Labor relations/worksite problems
  Secondary disability/health problems

MODULE VIII: Case Management Strategies

Topics: Employee identification: Employees with potential for rehabilitation involvement

Program steps: Case management process, goals, and objectives;
Prevention and early return-to-work programs
Developing corporate policies and procedures
Identifying interventions and service areas
Management responsibilities: Roles and functions of labor and management in case management
Implementation plan: Developing and implementing an IMRP
Ethical issues in injured worker rehabilitation

Vocational expert testimony
    SSI-SSDI
    Personal injury
    Workers' compensation

MODULE IX: Selection & Utilization of Internal & External Disability Management and Rehabilitation Resources

Topics: Essential criteria for selecting community service providers
Identification and utilization of medical and rehabilitation providers
Procedures for evaluating service outcomes
Model work-adjustment and work-transition programs
Specific methods to facilitate work-return efforts

MODULE X: Job Development & Job Placement in Industrial Rehabilitation

Topics: Step-by-step procedure in industrial analysis
Job-seeking skills training
Labor market survey approach
Labor market trend analysis
Client-centered vs. selective placement approaches
Computer-aided job matching systems

MODULE XI: Disability Management Program Evaluation

Topics: Data collection procedures
Referral outcomes
Service outcomes
Cost/service assessments
Injured/disabled worker service satisfaction
Supervisor/manager satisfactoriness

MODULE XII: Americans with Disabilities Act: Labor & Management Compliance Strategies & Program Interventions

Topics: Labor/management involvement in the ADA Law:
  The Equal Employment Opportunity Commission
  Employer responses to ADA enactment and enforcement
  Employer incentives regarding ADA
  Technical assistance to employers
  Revisions of human resources policies and procedures
  "Essential" job functions
  "Qualified" individuals with disabilities
  Avoidance of employment discrimination
  Barrier removal and accommodation tax incentives
  Injured worker issues and interventions under ADA
  Assisting employers through development of compliance planning

DISABILITY MANAGEMENT TRAINING SEMINAR: RECOMMENDED READINGS

Brandt, B., & Rice, B. D. (1990). *The provision of assistive technology services in rehabilitation.* Hot Springs, AR: Arkansas Research and Training Center in Vocational Rehabilitation.

Devlin, P. (1989). *Work injury management: Advances in prevention, evaluation, and treatment.* Eugene, OR: Center for the Advancement of Industrial Rehabilitation and Evaluation.

Ethical issues in private sector rehabilitation. (1989). Athens, GA: Elliott and Fitzpatrick, Inc.

Farr, J. M. (1993). *The complete guide for occupational exploration.* Indianapolis, IN: JIST Works, Inc.

Field, J. A., & Field, T. F. (1992). *The classification of jobs* (4th revision). Athens, GA: Elliott & Fitzpatrick, Inc.

Grandjean, E. (1988). *Fitting the tasks to the man* (4th Ed.). New York, NY: Taylor and Frances, Ltd.

Hinds, K. (1988). *Workers' compensation cost control: A maverick approach.* Pensacola, FL: Ability Management Associates Publications.

Isernhagen, S. J. (1988). *Work injury: Management and prevention.* Gaithersburg, MD: Aspen Publications, Inc.

Matkin, R. E. (1985). *Insurance rehabilitation.* Austin, TX: Pro-Ed, Inc.

Perlman, L. (1983). *Rehabilitation in the public mind: Strategies of marketing.* (Mary E. Switzer Memorial Seminar, Monograph VIII). Alexandria, VA: National Rehabilitation Association.

Pope, M. H., Andersson, G. B. J., Frymoyer, J. W., & Chaffin, D. B. (1991). *Occupational low back pain: Assessment, treatment, and prevention.* St. Louis, MO: Mosby-Year Book, Inc.

Power, P. W. (1991). *A guide to vocational assessment,* (2nd Ed.). Austin, TX: Pro-Ed. Inc.

Roessler, R. T., & Rubin, S. E. (1992). *Case management and rehabilitation counseling: Procedures and techniques.* Austin, TX: Pro-Ed, Inc.

Scheer, S. J. (Ed.). (1991). *Medical perspectives in vocational assessment of impaired workers.* Gaithersburg, MD: Aspen Publishers, Inc.

Scheer, S. J. (Ed.). (1990). *Multidisciplinary perspectives in vocational assessment of impaired workers.* Gaithersburg, MD: Aspen Publishers, Inc.

Schwartz, G. E., Watson, S. D., Galvin, D. E., & Lipoff, S. (1989). *The disability management sourcebook.* Washington, DC: Washington Business Group on Health/Institute for Rehabilitation and Disability Management.

Shrey, D. (1991). Disability management, occupational bonding, and the industrially injured worker. In *Work injury management 1991: Industry and healthcare: Building a coalition (Proceedings),* Center for the Advancement of Industrial Rehabilitation and Evaluation.

Shrey, D. (1992). Employer-based work return transition programs and the deinstitutionalization of America's injured workers. *Work Injury Management, 1*(4), 4-6.

Shrey, D. (1993). Disability management. In A. Dell Orto & R. Marinelli (Eds.) *Encyclopedia of disability and rehabilitation.* New York: Macmillan.

Shrey, D. & Breslin, R. (1992). Disability management in industry: Accommodating workers with disabilities. *International Journal of Industrial Ergonomics, 9*(2), 183-190.

Shrey, D. & Breslin, R. (1992). The Americans with disabilities act, employer-based disability management strategies and work return transition programs. In B. McMahon & N. Hablutzel (Eds.) *The Americans with disabilities act: Access and accommodations.* Winter Park, FL: GR Press, Inc.

Shrey, D. & Hursh, N. (1993). Protecting the employability of the working elderly. In J. Felsenthal, F. Steinberg, & S. Garrison (Eds.) *Rehabilitation of the aging and older patient.* Williams & Wilkins Publishers.

Shrey, D. & McMahon, B. (1992). The Americans with disabilities act, disability management, and the injured worker. *Journal of Workers Compensation, 1*(4), 9-29.

Shrey, D. & Olshesky, J. (1992). Disability management & industry-based work return transition programs. In Caplan (Ed.) *Physical Medicine & Rehabilitation: State of the Art Review, 6*(2). Philadelphia: Hanley & Belfus, Inc.

Siefker, J. M. (Ed.). (1992). *Vocational evaluation in private sector rehabilitation.* Menomonie, WI: University of Wisconsin-Stout, Materials Development Center.

Taylor, L. J., Golter, M., Golter, G., & Backer, T. (1985). *Handbook of private sector rehabilitation.* New York, NY: Springer Publishing Co.

U.S. Department of Labor. (1991). *Dictionary of occupational titles.* (4th Ed., Rev.). Washington, DC: Author.

U.S. Department of Labor. (1991). *Revised handbook for analyzing jobs.* Washington, DC: Author.

Weaver, C. L. (Ed.). (1991). *Disability and work: Incentives, rights, and opportunities.* Lanham, MD: University Press of America, Inc.

Weed, R. O., & Field, T. F. (1990). *Rehabilitation consultant's handbook.* Athens, GA: Elliott and Fitzpatrick, Inc.

Winiarski, M. G. (1991). *AIDS-related psychotherapy.* New York, NY: Pergamon Press.

APPENDIX B

JOB ANALYSIS PROCEDURES AND APPLICATION: DEVELOPING FUNCTIONAL JOB DESCRIPTIONS

PLANNING

1. Determine purpose of Job Analysis.

    Outline Job Analysis procedures & activity.

    Estimate time frame for Job Analysis activity.

2. Obtain current list of job titles within the department and related job descriptions used by company, if available.

    Identify employment position and job description of position under analysis that is described within union agreement.

3. Tour facility to develop an overall understanding of the operations, procedures, and general flow of work performed.

PRELIMINARY INTERVIEW

4. Meet with department heads or supervisor to explain purpose of the analysis and how the information may be used.

    Identify who will be involved in providing or reviewing information.

    Review job description development steps and time frames.

OBSERVATION SCHEDULE

5. Orient workers to purpose and process of job analysis activity.

    Validate initial job description information.

Observe job being performed by trained and skilled employee. Work should be observed over more than one period and across more than one worker. Worker should perform a complete work cycle.

6. Develop observations within a job analysis format.*

   Modify job analysis format to comply with characteristics of the position and information needs of ADA.*

   Modify job analysis format to coordinate with utilization plan of the company.

7. Identify: Skills, activities performed;
   Equipment, tools, work devices utilized;
   Environmental conditions;
   Physical demand characteristics;
   Working conditions and job demands.*

   Establish both quantitative and qualitative characteristics of job functions.

   Identify basis for classifying job tasks as <u>essential</u> or <u>marginal</u>, to comply with ADA language.*

FORMATIVE INTERVIEW ACTIVITY

8. Review and adjust job tasks and activities through interview with qualified worker.

9. Review and confirm job analysis information with supervisor.

   Confirm essential and marginal job tasks.

   Identify experience and education levels, license and certification requirements of the position with the supervisor.*

DATA ANALYSIS

10. Synthesize job analysis data into Final Report format - format dictated by purpose, e.g. functional job description.*

11. Identify accommodation options that may be reasonable for the position (as needed).

FINAL REVIEW AND SUMMARY

12. Review and revise final job description with Human Resource Department personnel to authorize use for the work unit.

    Determine whether position description must be reviewed by union and comply.

    Obtain medical acknowledgement. (Optional)

13. Date review and update job description annually.

14. Send letter of acknowledgement and recognition. (If necessary.)

    * Job Analysis forms and protocols are available through the senior author.

REFERENCES

Acosta, F. X., Yamamoto, J., Evans L. A., Skilbeck, W. M. (1983). Effective psychotherapy for low-income and minority patients. *Journal of Clinical Psychology, 39,* 872-877.

American Cancer Society. (1992). *Annual report 1991.* Atlanta, GA: Author

American Heart Association. (1989). Heart and stroke facts. Dallas, TX: American Heart Association.

American Heart Association. (1990). *Heart and stroke facts.* Dallas, TX: American Heart Association.

Atwood, M. J., & Michalak, C. M. (1992). The occurrence of cumulative trauma in dental hygienists. *Work, 2,* 17-31.

Backer, T. E. (1987). *AIDS in the workplace: Challenges and responses.* Los Angeles, CA: Human Interaction Research Institute.

Benedict, R. C., & Ganikos, M. L. (1981). Coming to terms with ageism in rehabilitation. *Journal of Rehabilitation, 47*(4), 10-18.

Berkowitz, M. (1990). Should rehabilitation be mandatory in workers' compensation programs? *Journal of Disability Policy Studies, 1*(1), 63-80.

Berman, J. M., & Cosca, T. A. (1992). The job outlook in brief: 1990–2005. *Occupational Outlook Quarterly, 36*(1), 6-11.

Blake, R. (1981). Disabled older persons: Implications for rehabilitation, a demographic analysis. *Journal of Rehabilitation, 47*(4), 19-27.

Bogue, D. J. (1985). *The population of the United States: Historical trends and future directions.* New York: The Free Press.

Bollman, B. T., Ray, A. M., & Emener, W. G. (1990). On predicting populations for vocational rehabilitation services: Researching and educating our way into the future. *Rehabilitation Education, 4*(3), 171-176.

Brandt, B., & Rice, B. D. (1990). *The provision of assistive technology services in rehabilitation.* Hot Springs, AR: Arkansas Research and Training Center in Vocational Rehabilitation.

Brookmeyer, R. (1991). Reconstruction and future trends of the AIDS epidemic in the United States. *Science, 253,* 37-42.

Brown D. (1990). Facing the future: Readying rehabilitation for the year 2000. *Journal of Rehabilitation, 56,* 17-20.

California Workers' Compensation Institute. (1983). *A report to the industry: Vocational rehabilitation.* San Francisco: Author.

Carey, M. L., & Franklin J. C. (1992). In *Outlook 1990-2005. BLS Bulletin 2402.* Washington, DC: U.S. Department of Labor, Bureau of Labor Statistics.

Centers for Disease Control. (1992, June 30). *HIV AIDS survey report.* Atlanta, GA: Author.

Cohen, C. F., & Cohen M. E. (1989). AIDS in the workplace: Legal requirements and organizational responses. *Labor Law Journal, 40*(7), 411-418.

Conti, J. (1990). Cancer rehabilitation: Why can't we get out of first gear? *Journal of Rehabilitation,* October, 19-22.

Darling, E., & Lonnquist, J. (1988). AIDS, business, and the law. *EAP Digest, 8,* 46-49.

DeCarlo, D. T., & Gruenfeld, D. H. (1989). *Stress in the American workplace: Alternatives for the working wounded.* Ft. Washington, PA: LRP Publications.

Dellario, D. J. (1991). Rehabilitation doctorates: Evolution or extinction. *Rehabilitation Education, 5*(3), 161-166.

Dennis, C. (1991). Vocational capacity with cardiac impairment. In J. Scheer, (Ed.), *Medical perspectives in vocational assessment of impaired workers.* Aspen Publishers, Inc., Rockville, MD.

Douce, L. A. (1993). AIDS and HIV: Hopes and challenges for the 1990s. *Journal of Counseling and Development, 71*(3), 259-260.

Drury, D. (1991). Disability management in small firms. *Rehabilitation Counseling Bulletin, 34*(3), 243-256.

Dworkin, S. H., & Pincu, L. (1993). Counseling in the era of AIDS. *Journal of Counseling and Development, 71*(3), 275-281.

Ebener, D. J., & Wright, G. N. (1991). The emphasis of professional competencies in rehabilitation counselor education curricula. *Rehabilitation Education, 5*(2), 81-86.

Emener, W. G., & McFarlane, F. R. (1986). A futuristic model of rehabilitation education. In W. G. Emener (Ed.), *Rehabilitation counselor preparation and development.* Springfield, IL: C. C. Thomas.

Fagot-Diaz, J. G. (1988). Employment discrimination against AIDS victims: Rights and remedies available under the Federal Rehabilitation Act of 1973. *Labor Law Journal, 39*(3), 148-166.

Farr, M. (Ed.). (1993). *The complete guide for occupational exploration.* Indianapolis, IN: Just Works, Inc.

Field, J. E., & Field, T. F. (1992). *Classification of jobs.* Athens, GA: Elliott & Fitzpatrick, Inc.

Fitzgerald, M. H. (1992). Multicultural clinical interactions. *Journal of Rehabilitation,* 38-42.

Fullerton, H. N. (1992). Labor force projections: The baby boom moves on. In *Outlook 1990-2005. BLS Bulletin 2402.* Washington, DC: U.S. Department of Labor, Bureau of Labor Statistics.

Galvin, D. E. (1986). Employer-based disability management and rehabilitation programs. In E. L. Pan, S. S. Newman, T. E. Barker, & S. S. Newman (Eds.), *Annual review of rehabilitation (Volume V).* New York: Springer Publishing Company.

Galvin, E. E. (1992). Implementing a successful disability management program. In W. Zimmerman (Ed.), *Occupational disability management.* Point Alberni, B.C.: Disabled Forestry Workers Foundation of Canada.

Gapery, P. (1990). Whittling down workers' compensation lists. *Business and Health, 8*(8-9), 35-48.

General Accounting Office. (1987). *Social Security: Little success in rehabilitating disabled beneficiaries* (Report No. GA0/HRD 88-11). Washington, DC: Author.

Gilbride, D. D., Connolly, M., & Stensrud, R. (1990). Rehabilitation education for the private — for profit sector. *Rehabilitation Education, 4*(3), 155-162.

Greer, B. G., Jenkins, W. M., & Roberto, R. (1992). Carpal tunnel syndrome: A challenge for rehabilitation. *Journal of Rehabilitation,* 43-46.

Habeck, R. (1989). Implementing disability management programs in industry. In P. Devlin (Ed.), *Work injury management: Advances in prevention, evaluation, and treatment of work injuries.* Eugene, OR: Center for the Advancement of Industrial Rehabilitation.

Habeck, R., & Ellien, V. (1986). Implications of worksite practice for rehabilitation counselor education and training. *Journal of Applied Rehabilitation Counseling, 17*(3), 49-54.

Habeck, R. V., Leahy, M. J., Hunt, H. A., Chan, F., & Welch, E. M. (1991). Employer factors related to compensation claims and disability management. *Rehabilitation Counseling Bulletin, 34*(3)a, 210-226.

Hahn, H. (1991). Alternative views of empowerment: Social services and civil rights. *Journal of Rehabilitation, 57,* 17-19.

Hiatt, W. R., Nawaz, D., Regensteiner, J. G., & Hossack, M. B. (1988). The evaluation of exercise performance in patients with peripheral vascular disease. *Journal of Cardiopulmonary Rehabilitation, 8*(12), 525-532.

Hiatt, W. R., Regensteiner, J. G., Hagarten, M. E., Wolfel, E. E., & Brass, E. P. (1990). Benefit of exercise conditioning for patients with peripheral arterial disease. *Circulation, 81*(2), 602-609.

Hudson Institute. (1987). *Workforce 2000: Work and workers for the 21st century.* Indianapolis, IN: Author.

Joyce, M. (1988). Ergonomics offer solutions to numerous health complaints. *Occupational Health Safety,* 58-66.

Keeling, R. P. (1993). HIV disease: Current concepts. *Journal of Counseling and Development, 71*(3), 261-274.

Kelsey, J. L., & White A. A. (1980). Epidemiology and impact of low back pain. *Spine, 5*, 133-142.

Kemp, B., Brummel-Smith, K., & Ramsdell, J. (1990). *Geriatric rehabilitation.* Boston, MA: College-Hill Press.

Kilbury, R. F., Benshoff, J. J., & Riggar, T. F. (1990). The expansion of private sector rehabilitation: Will rehabilitation education respond? *Rehabilitation Education, 4*(3), 163-170.

Klein, B. P. Jensen, R. C., & Sanderson, L. M. (1984). Assessment of workers' compensation claims for back strains/sprains. *Journal of Occupational Medicine, 25,*(6), 443-448.

Kraman, G. (1988). Employers test new ways to shift risk on health costs. *New York Times*, June, 22, 1988.

Kutschur, R. E. (1990). Outlook 2000: The major trends. *Occupational Outlook Quarterly, 34*(1), 2-7.

Kutscher, R. E. (1992). Outlook 1990-2005: Major trends and issues. *Ocupational Outlook Quarterly, 36*(1), 2-5.

Lacerte, M., & Wright, G. P. (1992). Return to work determination. *Physical Medicine and Rehabilitation, 6*(2), 283-302.

Lawton, B. (1989). FAPs in the 1990s: challenges and support unities. *Health Values, 13*(1), 43-45.

Leong, F. T. L. (1986). Counseling and psychotherapy with Asian-Americans: Reviews of the literature. *Journal of Counseling Psychology, 33*, 196-206.

Leung, P. (1988). Robotics in rehabilitation. *Journal of Rehabilitation, 54*(4), 6-7.

Lewis, K. (1989). Persons with disabilities and the aging factor. *Journal of Rehabilitation, 55*(4), 12-13.

Lucos, S. (1987). Putting a lid on disability costs. *Management Solutions, 32*(4), 16-18.

MacKenzie, K. R. (1988). Recent developments in brief psychotherapy. *Hospital and Community Psychiatry, 39*, 742-752.

Mallory, M., & Bradford, H. (1989). An invisible workplace hazard gets harder to ignore. *Business Week*, 92-93.

Martin, G. E., McBride, M. C., & Jones, W. P. (1991). Theory congruency: A teaching model for rehabilitation counselor education. *Rehabilitation Education, 5,*(3), 199-207.

Martin, T. A. (1992). Cumulative trauma disorders come knocking: Repetitive stress injury on the rise. *Boston Computer Society Update*, 13-16.

Matkin, R. (1987). Content areas and recommended training sites of insurance rehabilitation: Identification and resolution. *Rehabilitation Education, 1*, 233-246.

McAbee, R. R., & Wilkinson, W. E. (1988). Back injuries and registered nurses. *AAOHN Journal, 36*(3), 106-112.

McCoy, J. L., & Weems, K. (1989). Disabled worker beneficiaries and disabled SSI recipients: A profile of demographics and program characteristics. *Social Security Bulletin, 52*(5), 16-28.

McCray, P. M. (1987). *The job accommodation handbook.* Verndale, MN: RPM Press, Inc.

McMahon, B. T., Shaw, L. R., & Mahaffey, D. P. (1988). Career opportunities and professional preparation in head injury rehabilitation. *Rehabilitation Counseling Bulletin, 31*(4), 344-352.

Miller, A., Springen, K., Gordon, J., Murr, A., Cohn, B., Drew, L., & Barrett, T. (1988). Stress on the job: What you and your boss can do about it. *Newsweek*, April 25, 40-45.

Millin, G., Jarvikoski, A., & Verkasalo, M. (1984). Treatment of patients with chronic low back pain: Comparison between rehabilitation in center and outpatient care. *Scandinavian Journal of Rehabilitation Medicine, 16*, 17-84.

Morris, A. (1984). Program compliance key to preventing low back injuries. *Occupational Health and Safety, 53*(3), 44-47.

Myers, J. E. (1983). Rehabilitation of older workers. *Rehab Brief.* Washington, DC: Department of Education, National Institute of Handicapped Research.

Nelson, W. J. (1990). Workers' compensation: Coverage, benefits, and costs, 1987. *Social Security Bulletin, 53*(4), 2-11.

Parker, R. M., & Szymanski, E. M. (1992). *Rehabilitation counseling: Basics and beyond* (2nd Ed.). Austin, TX: Pro-Ed, Inc.

Patenande, S. (1989). Promoting functional ability in industry. *Industrial Rehabilitation Quarterly, 2*(1), 34, 40-41.

Picard, M. H., Dennis, C., & Schwartz, R. G. (1989). Cost-benefit of early return to work after uncomplicated myocardial infarction. *American Journal of Cardiology, 63*, 1308.

Pope, M. H., Anderson, G. B., Frymazer, J. W., & Chaffin, D. B. (1991). *Occupational low back pain: Assessment, treatment, and prevention.* St. Louis, MO: Mosby-Year Book, Inc.

Rasch, J. D. (1992). RCE curriculum and insurance rehabilitation. *Rehabilitation Education, 6*(1), 33-99.

Reichert, D. A., & MacGuffie, R. A. (1988). AIDS: An overview for rehabilitation counselors. *Journal of Applied Rehabilitation Counseling, 19*(2), 34-3

Roessler, R. R. (1987). Work, disability, and the future: Promoting employment for people with disabilities. *Journal of Counseling and Development, 66*, 188-90.

Roessler, R. T., & Rubin, S. E. (1992). *Case management and rehabilitation counseling.* Austin, TX: Pro-Ed, Inc.

Schwartz, G. E., Watson, S. D., Galvin, D. E., & Lipoff, S. (1989). *The disability management sourcebook.* Washington, DC: Washington Business Group on Health/Institute for Rehabilitation and Disability Management.

Schiller-Myers, P., & Myers, D. W. (1987). AIDS: Tackling a tough problem through policy. *Personnel Administration, 4*, 95-108.

Shrey, D. E. (1990). Disability management: An employer-based rehabilitation concept. In S. Scheer (Ed.), *Assessing the vocational capacity of the impaired worker.* Rockville, MD: Aspen Publishers.

Shrey, D., & Breslin, R. (1992). Disability management in industry: Accommodating workers with disabilities. *International Journal of Industrial Ergonomics, 9*(2), 183-190.

Shrey, D., & Fraser, R. (1986). Perceived barriers to job placement revisited: Toward practical solution. *Journal of Rehabilitation*, Fall, 26-30.

Shrey, D. E., & Hursh, N. C. (1993). Protecting the employability of the working elderly. In J. Felsenthal, F. Steinberg, & S. Garrison (Eds.) *Rehabilitation of the aging and older patient*, Williams & Wilkins.

Siefher, J. M. (Ed.). (1992). *Vocational evaluation in private sector rehabilitation.* Menomonic, WI: University of Wisconsin-Stout, Materials Development Center.

Silvestri, G., & Lukasiewicz, J. (1992). In *Outlook 1990-2005. BLS Bulletin 2402.* Washington, DC: U.S. Department of Labor, Bureau of Labor Statistics.

Sipkoff, M. Z. (1993). Trends in stress-related workers' compensation claims. *EAP Digest, 5*(3), 28-30.

Smart, J. F., & Smart, D. W. (1992). Cultural issue in the rehabilitation of Hispanics. *Journal of Rehabilitation*, 29-37.

Smart, J. F., Smart, D. W. (1992). Curriculum changes in multicultural rehabilitation. *Rehabilitation Education, 6*(2), 105-122.

Smith, J. K., & Crisler, J. R. (1985). Chronic low back pain: The treatment dichotomy and implications for rehabilitation counselors. *Journal of Applied Rehabilitation Counseling, 16*, 28-31.

Social Security Administration. (1990). *Social Security Administration 1990 Annual report to congress.* Washington, DC: U.S. Department of Health and Human Services.

Stewart, M. J., & Gregor, F. M. (1984). Early discharge and return to work following myocardial infarction. *Social Science Medicine, 18*, 1027-1036.

Tabor, M. (1982). Reconstructing the scene: Back injury. *Occupational Health and Safety, 2*, 16-22.

Tate, D., Munrowd, D., Habeck, R., Karim, R., Adams, L., & Shepard, D. (1987). *Disability management and rehabilitation outcomes: The Buick-Oldsmobile-Cadillac Lansing Product Team Report.* East Lansing: Michigan State University School of Health Education, Counseling, Psychology, and Human Performance, Disability Management Project.

Thorn, K. (1990). *Applying medical case management: AIDS.* Canoga Park, CA: Thorn Publishing.

U.S. Department of Labor. (1990). Outlook 2000: The major trends. *Occupational Outlook Quarterly,* Spring, 3-7.

U.S. Department of Labor. (1991). *Dictionary of occupational titles* (4th Ed.). Washington, DC: Author.

U.S. Department of Labor. (1991). *Revised handbook of analyzing jobs.* Washington, DC: Author.

Victor, R. B. (1989). *Medical cost containment in workers' compensation: Innovative approaches.* Boston: Workers Compensation Research Institute.

Wakefield, R. K. (1985). Bad backs: Bad business. *Occupational health and safety practices.* Memphis, TN: Physicians Postgraduate Press, Inc.

Weiner, R. B., & Siegel, D. (1989). Managed mental health care issues and strategies. *Benefits Quarterly, 5*(3), 21-31.

White, A. (1982). Synopsis: Workshop on idiopathic low back pain. *Spine, 7*(2), 141-149.

Williams, T. F. (1986). The aging process: Biological and psychosocial considerations. In S. Brody & G. Ruff. *Aging and rehabilitation: Advances in the state of the art.* New York, NY: Springer Publishing Co.

Williams, W., & Rice, B. D. (1987). *The future workplace: Implications for rehabilitation.* Hot Springs, AK: Arkansas Research and Training Center in Vocational Rehabilitation.

Winiarski, M. G. (1991). *AIDS-related psychotherapy.* New York: Pergamon Press.

Zilig, R. (1989). AIDS: Implications for employment benefit plans and personnel policies. *Employment Relations Today, 15*(4), 229.

Section II

Disability Management Perspectives And Trends

—12—

HISTORICAL PERSPECTIVES ON THE REHABILITATION COUNSELING PROFESSION AND DISABILITY MANAGEMENT

Joseph E. Havranek, Ed.D., C.R.C.

INTRODUCTION

This chapter reviews and forecasts the growth and evolution of rehabilitation counseling from the years 1970 to 2000 in the areas of counseling strategies, disability benefit rehabilitation, medical treatment, changes in the workplace, and in the forensic area. Each of these topics are further subdivided and the trends in those subdivisions are reviewed and discussed. Finally, conclusions are drawn about a new paradigm in the rehabilitation counseling profession for the 1990s.

Rehabilitation counseling is one of the fastest changing professions. In 1970, virtually all rehabilitation counseling was performed within state-federal vocational rehabilitation agencies (McGowan & Porter, 1967; Wright, 1980). In the 1980s, private-for-profit rehabilitation expanded very quickly due to the perceived personal and economic benefits of rehabilitation (Thomas, 1991). Beginning with California workers' compensation reforms in the mid-1970s, other state workers' compensation laws were similarly amended to include rehabilitation services, often resulting in mandatory provision of rehabilitation services for both the insurance carrier and the injured worker. The full force of this legislation was felt in the 1980s. As insurance carriers and attorneys perceived the benefits of rehabilitation in workers' compensation, they also began to utilize rehabilitation counseling services in other types of disability claims (e.g., long-term disability, personal injury, product liability) (Rasch, 1985). Rehabilitation counselors, as expert witnesses, were also utilized with increasing frequency. The potential for higher salaries and the ability to structure one's own work activity led to an exodus of experienced and knowledgeable rehabilitationists from many state agencies into the private sector.

There are two trends this decade that will further change the concept of rehabilitation counseling. The first is the shift in location of many therapeutic vocational activities from the rehabilitation facility (Havranek, 1988) to the employment site (Swanbum, 1988). This helps sustain employee productivity as well as increase the effectiveness of rehabilitation services. At the employment site, the vocational rehabilitation counselor may serve as the coordinator among medical practitioners, allied medical providers, employers, unions, and others, providing expertise in the development, implementation, and evaluation of work return/worker retention plans for workers with disabilities.

Another trend for rehabilitation counseling is the broad application of assistive technology (Thomas, 1991). As scientific innovations become more practical and less expensive, and as the American workforce ages, the application of assistive technology will become a critical knowledge component for rehabilitation counselors.

COUNSELING STRATEGIES

The following section discusses the evolution of rehabilitation counseling, with respect to four areas: (1) the theoretical basis for counseling, (2) the service emphasis, (3) the role of the employer, and (4) the focus of treatment.

THEORETICAL BASIS FOR COUNSELING

The theoretical basis for counseling in the 1970s focused on three competing theories. "The Matching People and Jobs" approach emphasized that the psychological traits of individuals could be matched to the psychological requirements or demands of jobs to achieve maximum job satisfaction. "The Psychodynamics of Vocational Behavior" theory proposed that drives and desires were the salient issues in making career choices. "*The Vocational Development*" theory was based on the assumption of differential and dynamic psychology (Crites, 1969). The 1980s saw a shift away from a theoretical base to a more eclectic approach, marked by the integration of theories with practice (Riggar, Matkin, & Wolf, 1986). The result was an empirical model which emphasized practical aspects of case management, such as occupational information, report writing, and assessment of vocational potential (Field & Priaulx, 1984). Currently, a more personal style of counseling and case management is evolving whereby most theoretical bases and prescribed case management techniques are being synthesized into disability management systems. This approach is characterized by the rehabilitationist as the coordinator of services who has resources and knowledge of rehabilitation processes, in order to assist persons in achieving adjustment to disability, including employment (Field & Priaulux, 1984).

THE SERVICE EMPHASIS

A second shift in approach was from orientation toward work adjustment services in the 1970s, to work hardening during the 1980s, to rehabilitation at the workplace in the 1990s. Work adjustment services focused on behavior change utilizing specific behavioral outcomes as the criteria for success (Baker, 1983). Work hardening is a more global approach which prepares the individual to work through individualized job-specific work activities performed at a rehabilitation facility. Work hardening involves simulated work activity, musculoskeletal conditioning, work readiness, education classes, community re-integration outings, and group counseling (Havranek, 1988). Currently, a third shift toward a multidisciplinary model of rehabilitation at the workplace is underway (Shrey & Breslin, 1992). Industrial rehabilitation takes place at the worksite in this model with the expected result that it will reduce and/or eliminate most of the disincentives that result from the worker's lengthy separation from the worksite, thus creating more cost-effective services with better results.

ROLE OF THE EMPLOYER

The third major change in counseling strategies involves the role of the employer in the rehabilitation process. Before and during the 1970s, employers tended to become involved during the final phase of the rehabilitation process. Job development and placement were generally implemented only after the conclusion of all other rehabilitation services. The client was thus a product to be sold "as is." During the 1980s, employers, discouraged with rising costs of social security, workers' compensation, and other disability insurance policies, became more involved in the employment aspect of rehabilitation. However, this was largely a litigious involvement which drove up direct costs to the employers as well as premiums for the policies primarily due to increased legal costs. In the 1990s, employers are becoming active participants in rehabilitation efforts, particularly among supported employment and injured worker rehabilitation programs. This shift is due to a reduced labor pool, efforts to minimize costs of injured worker compensation, as well as the implementation of the Americans with Disabilities Act of 1990 (ADA), which mandates job modification and accommodation for persons with disabilities.

FOCUS OF TREATMENT

The final change in practice involved who would be included in the rehabilitation efforts. During the 1970s, the client was often the sole participant in the rehabilitation process. Little attention was given to other participants during the development of rehabilitation plans. During the 1980s, the roles of the family and other significant people were included (Power, 1988). The client's social, racial, and ethnic differences were also included in rehabilitation planning (Atkinson & Hackett, 1988). The 1990s will witness an ever-expanding circle of individuals involved in the rehabilitation process, including employers, unions, and the interdisciplinary rehabilitation team.

To demonstrate the magnitude of the changes in counseling strategies from 1970 through the 1990s, one only has to review the statuses at each end of the continuum. In 1970, rehabilitation counseling was characterized by a theoretical orientation, using work adjustment services that were limited in scope and application, with employment only considered at the end of the process, focusing solely on the client. In the 1990s there is a growing prevalence of (1) personal styles of counseling adapted from a wide variety of sources, (2) case services by a multidisciplinary treatment team at the workplace, (3) an emphasis on inclusion of the employer at the beginning of the rehabilitation process, and (4) the emergence of a wide variety of individuals and respective roles, which will be integrated in order to individualize rehabilitation services.

DISABILITY BENEFIT REHABILITATION

Rehabilitation in the early 1970s was almost entirely performed by state-federal vocational rehabilitation agencies. The Social Security Administration did have arrangements with many state agencies sponsoring rehabilitation for Social Security disability beneficiaries, but this was limited in both scope and impact. However, during the 1970s, benefit levels and costs related to workers' compensation and other disability benefit policies increased at an unprecedented level (Keane, 1985). Recognition of the costs of disability grew (Berkowitz & Hill, 1986; Havranek, 1991) and led to the implementation of private rehabilitation services (Matkin, 1985). These efforts were expanded by the organizations charged with reducing the costs of disability benefits (Rasch, 1985), and by the parallel growth of private sector rehabilitation during the 1980s. During the 1990s, efforts will be implemented to make these services more cost-effective (Welch, 1989). Given that employment is the objective of rehabilitation services, then it is a viable option to base rehabilitation at the employment site. This will enhance rehabilitation efforts to individualize services, as well as obviate the need for prolonged and expensive job search efforts.

MEDICAL TREATMENT

Medical treatment practice has also changed since 1970, especially as it relates to rehabilitation. The prevailing medical expenditure model in the 1970s was that of private hospital insurance, with major medical coverage as its basis. As costs began to escalate at rates in excess of inflation, employers began to contract with health maintenance organizations (HMO's), and individuals insured under those plans were required to obtain treatment from HMO member providers. This was done in an effort to reduce costs by contracting for services at discount group rates, and also to confine treatment to one establishment which would get no benefit from cross-referring patients between physicians and specialties. HMO's also had financial incentives to keep their patients healthy. The HMO approach had its limits, such as precluding the independent selection of one's physician, and that membership was required to get services. This, coupled with a diminishing proportion of the population with any type of coverage, led to increasing calls for substantial changes in providing national health care (Trieschmann, 1988), including national health insurance. These efforts to reform the medical care system are expected to continue throughout the decade.

The second treatment model to undergo significant revision was that of pain treatment. Despite technological advances in medicine and the proliferation of pain treatment programs, chronic pain syndrome remains one of the most difficult problems to treat (Aronoff & McAlary, 1990). During the 1970s, innovation and rapid expansion of inpatient multidisciplinary pain and stress centers was undertaken. The cost of these programs was prohibitive, and the programs often lost sight of work return goals because there was little resemblance between the treatment setting and work settings.

Therefore, a shift away from inpatient services and towards outpatient and self-help services (Charlesworth & Nathan, 1984; Sethi & Schuler, 1984) was implemented in the 1980s to reduce costs and keep patients in a real-world environment. In the 1990s it has been recognized that the single most important factor in managing chronic pain is a complete and accurate evaluation of the client (Shealy & Cady, 1990). To make the most reliable assessment on an ongoing basis, and to keep the client job focused, pain management services will be rendered increasingly at the worksite. The worksite is the primary impetus for pain as well as the place where pain must be dealt with in order to allow a return to full work status.

Substance abuse treatment is another practice to undergo substantial revision from 1970 to the 1990s. During the 1970s, substance abuse was generally either ignored (even when job performance was impaired) or dealt with through the criminal justice system. During the 1980s, substance abuse was recognized as a substantial impediment to job performance, costing industry around $100 billion each year (Nye, 1990). During this period the impaired individual was perceived as a "substance abuse victim" (Peele, 1989). This attitude, coupled with the implementation of Employee Assistance Programs (Gold, 1986; Lawton, 1988; Wallace, 1985), Student Assistance Programs (Grosshandler, 1990), and provision for treatment in many health insurance policies, led to a proliferation of inpatient treatment centers (Dickman, Challenger, Emener, & Hutchison, 1988). Additionally, there was a recognition of those with multidisabilities (i.e., substance abuse problems among persons with physical or mental disabilities) (Greer, 1986). However, treatment at those centers was costly and quality of treatment varied greatly. Therefore, treatment was re-focused toward outpatient services (Gold, 1986) and this trend will likely continue through the 1990s, as health care funds become less accessible. This change in perception has been codified in the ADA, which requires that reformed substance abusers be covered as disabled under the meaning of that statute, but that current abusers are not considered to be disabled.

The fourth treatment model to undergo substantial change was in the use of medical services and the roles of health care providers. During the 1970s, physicians were seen as the providers of health services and the physician tightly controlled and prescribed the medical treatment process. The 1980s reflected a progressive expansion of medical care providers and services, as more assertive health care providers emerged. Physical therapists, occupational therapists, and psychologists were now viable partners on the treatment team. Rehabilitation service providers entered the scene as case managers, whose role included the monitoring of medical services. Indeed, team treatment became standard practice, especially in rehabilitation hospitals and facilities. Many chiropractors became applied kinesiologists (Valentine, 1985), and aqua-therapy became an integral treatment device (McWaters, 1988). During the 1990s, health promotion and wellness became the primary components of preventative health care. These programs consist of self-responsibility, nutritional awareness, physical fitness, and stress management (Brandon, 1985), in which responsibility for one's health rests largely with the individual (Borysenko, 1987). Included in this new approach was the psychological necessity for responsibility, to make one complete and therefore healthy (Cusack, 1988).

One indicator of the radically changing nature of rehabilitation counseling is the services offered to people with AIDS. During the 1970s, there was no formal recognition of AIDS (Knapp & VandeCreek, 1990). During the 1980s, the disease was recognized, but little service was offered due to short life span anticipation, as well as the nature of the groups initially affected, leading to social ostracism for those infected. In the 1990s, as our culture and its people become increasingly accepting of people with AIDS, and as medical treatment improves with research programs around the world (Kurland, 1988), rehabilitation services will expand. Indeed, procedures for the provision of vocational rehabilitation services at the state-federal level to those with AIDS have already been established (Corthell & Oliverio, 1989). It is noteworthy that persons with AIDS were included for coverage under the ADA.

The final area of treatment to be revolutionized is that of traumatic brain injury (TBI) rehabilitation. During the 1970s, TBI was not generally recognized as a disability and there was no treatment specifically aimed at its remediation. The 1980s saw a recognition of the disability unto itself and advances in rehabilitation techniques were comprised of research and applications of therapeutic modalities consisting of pain management, neuropsychological and behavioral interventions, neural recovery, vocational rehabilitation, and community integration (Bach-y-Rita, 1989; Kreutzer & Wehman, 1990). Also included was a strong emphasis on the role of the family in the rehabilitation process (Esposito & Esposito, 1991; Sachs, 1991). Refinements of services and comprehensive treatment to include inpatient, outpatient, criteria for choosing appropriate treatment facilities, management of a wide variety of dysfunctions, family education, and skill training for the traumatically brain-injured are being implemented during the 1990s. Further evaluation of methodologies for cognitive (Calub, Burton, DeBoskey, & Hooker, 1990; Foster, 1988), behavioral, physical, psychosocial, and vocational rehabilitation strategies (Deutsch & Fralish, 1988) will be introduced to further define those areas that are viable and cost-effective. To summarize the shift in strategies for medical treatment, in 1970 a system prevailed which consisted of traditional private health insurance, utilizing inpatient pain treatment programs, in which substance abuse was not generally regarded as a disability, where almost all medical services were prescribed and tightly controlled by physicians, without any knowledge of AIDS as a disease, and no recognition of traumatic brain injury as a disability. At what is almost the other end of the spectrum in the 1990s, we are moving toward some form of national health insurance; pain is being dealt with at the workplace; substance abuse is now viewed as dichotomous in that recovering abusers are recognized as disabled while current abusers are regarded as criminals; wellness is increasingly seen as the responsibility of the individual; there is active research into the control and eradication of AIDS; traumatic brain injury is perceived as a disability; and treatment which has been developed is undergoing refinement.

WORKPLACE ISSUES

Many issues critical to the practice, nature, and shape of vocational rehabilitation counseling have also been substantially altered over the past three decades. These issues deal with the workplace. This section examines several issues which comprise a major change, including: ergonomics, pre-employment screening, job analysis, assistive technology, attitudes toward inclusion of those with disabilities in the workforce, and access to the work environment.

During the 1970s, ergonomics was recognized by state rehabilitation agencies as a service to be offered to only a few (i.e., to individually match a client and the work station, using new, expensive, high technology engineering applications, to be generated by a limited number of rehabilitation engineering centers) (Antenucci & Corthell, 1979). Ergonomics was also recognized by organized labor as a means to prevent work-related injuries (Goldsmith & Kerr, 1982). Realization of the importance of ergonomics grew in the 1980s, as its potential as a rehabilitation tool was more widely disseminated (Pati & Adkins, 1981), and as it was implemented by employers as a means of establishing a job-worker match (Matheson, 1987), and as a means to reduce cumulative trauma (Chaffin & Anderson, 1991; Isernhagen, 1988). With the implementation of ADA in the 1990s, ergonomics will achieve even greater utilization as rehabilitation engineering moves into the private sector to assess job modifications and adaptations of work settings, as well as public accommodation accessibility. Evidence for this contention is the increased attention being given to the subject of ergonomics among schools of engineering (Enderle, 1990). Also notable is the change away from on-site job evaluations strictly as evaluation sites and towards rehabilitation at the job site (Kell, 1989). Another workplace practice to undergo significant development was pre-employment screening. There was very little standardization of selection instruments and less predictive studies on which to base such screening in the 1970s. During the 1980s, pre-employment screening was utilized primarily to screen individuals out of jobs, whether it be on a physical basis (Fleeson, 1988; Morris & Anderson, 1988) or for psychological reasons (Lowman, 1989). In the 1990s, pre-employment screening, per se, is not permissible under ADA. Instead, evaluations will be undertaken to determine if an individual can perform a job, given reasonable accommodation. Thus in the 1990s, the on-site vocational rehabilitation specialist may be well-qualified to coordinate job placement efforts on the part of employers. Note: ADA permits pre-employment screening if it is validated against essential job functions and if it is performed for everyone being screened for that particular job (Hablutzel & McMahon, 1992).

Dovetailed with the change in pre-employment screening is a concomitant change in the nature and role of job analysis in the placement process. Although resources for conducting job analyses were available in the 1970s (Pati & Adkins, 1981; U.S. Department of Labor, 1972), rehabilitation counselors generally had little knowledge of the techniques and applications involved. During the 1980s, the application of job analysis became common, by both employers (Gael, 1983; Ivancevich, & Glueck, 1986) and rehabilitation professionals (Chaffin & Anderson, 1991; Deneen & Hessellund, 1981; Lytel & Botterbusch, 1981; U.S. Department of Labor, 1983). However, job analysis, like pre-employment screening, was used primarily to screen out applicants during the 1980s. The 1990s will demand a different emphasis on job analysis, whereby job analysis will be used to determine ways in which persons with disabilities can do work (screening in).

The fourth workplace issue to be revolutionized is assistive technology. During the 1970s, assistive technology was rarely identified and sparsely used by persons with disabilities (Pati & Adkins, 1981). With the advent of the minicomputer in the 1980s, individual applications requiring extensive development and programming were undertaken as case services (IEEE Computer Society, 1981). In the 1990s, access is becoming more routine and relatively inexpensive software packages are emerging to assist persons with disabilities in independent living, education, work, recreation and leisure, personal mobility, communication, controls of environment, and transportation (Enders & Hall, 1990). Additionally, considerable research and applications are being implemented specifically for children with disabilities (Enders & Hall, 1990; Frankoff & Alexander, 1987). Also of significance is the Technology-Related Assistance for Individuals with Disabilities Act of 1988, which is to develop consumer-responsive, statewide systems of assistive technology services (Enders & Hall, 1990; Sowers & Powers, 1991).

Another workplace issue to undergo substantial change is attitudes toward persons with disabilities (Havranek, 1991). During the 1970s, persons with disabilities were often regarded as subhuman, reflecting a history of discrimination dating back to Biblical times. This attitude was one of pity, and disability benefits were seen as the appropriate societal response. The 1980s was a time of recognition of the value of persons with disabilities, accompanied by implementation of the Rehabilitation Act of 1973, mainstreaming of children with disabilities, and more accessible facilities to encourage interaction among persons with and without disabilities. This led to the dispelling of those myths, as individual potential became recognized. With implementation of the ADA's mandate for employment and accommodation, further supported by the Civil Rights Act of 1991, persons with disabilities will finally have opportunities to demonstrate those potentials at the workplace.

Initial efforts towards workplace accessibility were addressed by the Architectural Barriers Act of 1968 and the Rehabilitation Act of 1973 (Hopf & Raeber, 1984). These efforts were of limited impact because of their application to a select set of facilities, with little enforcement. During the 1980s, building codes began to reflect minimal accessibility requirements, spurred by the 1978 independent living amendments to the Rehabilitation Act of 1973 (Geist & Calzaretta, 1982), the revised regulations adopted by the American National Standards Institute published in 1981 (Hopf & Raeber, 1984), and the Education for All Handicapped Children Act, P.L. 94-142 (Wielkiewicz & Calvert, 1989). Implementation of Supported Employment programs furthered accessibility to both the workplace and to work itself (Bellamy, Rhodes, Mank, & Albin, 1988; Morris, 1989; Wehman & Moon, 1988). Indeed, many strategies for integration of the disabled and the nondisabled are already being implemented successfully (Brown, 1982; Mulick & Antonak, 1987; Sowers & Powers, 1991). The ADA requires accessibility to most employment, public accommodations, transportation, and communication facilities. Increasing exposure of the nondisabled population to people with disabilities will continue to diminish the impact of negative attitudes toward persons with disabilities. Concurrently, innovation in constructing and organizing the workplace will provide persons with disabilities more opportunity to become employed in the competitive labor market (Mueller, 1990).

In summary, there have been many significant changes in workplace issues. In 1970, employers were characterized as giving very little attention to ergonomics. Pre-employment screening was not standardized, there was sparse knowledge of procedures and applications of job analysis, and assistive technology was rarely considered as a rehabilitation service. Attitudes toward persons with disabilities resulted in their exclusion from most community activities, and there were no accommodations to allow persons with disabilities access to work. Conversely, in the 1990s, rehabilitation practices will increasingly reflect the priorities established by the ADA (e.g., job modifications and adaptations to the workplace, rehabilitation at the job site, job placement, and job analysis aimed at reasonable accommodation using assistive technology), in which persons with disabilities will be recognized for their tangible contributions to employment and other activities, and in which every aspect of society will be accessible for persons with disabilities.

FORENSIC REHABILITATION

The rehabilitation counselor as "Vocational Expert" is a field which is expanding to new vistas never before anticipated. The term "Vocational Expert" has been defined as one who is very skilled, highly trained, and knowledgeable in the field of trades, professions, and occupations, with intent to be involved in assessment and/or testimony (in any form) in a litigious forum (Havranek, 1988). The term "forensic rehabilitation" has been consistently used to describe the services provided by Vocational Experts since the late 1980s.

In 1970, Vocational Experts were predominately used by Administrative Law Judges in the Social Security Administration's Office of Hearings and Appeals to assist in the determination of eligibility for disability insurance benefits. The 1980s was a time of dramatic expansion in the utilization of Vocational Experts. They became involved in workers' compensation hearings as well as in suits for personal injury, medical malpractice, product liability, intentional torts, divorce, and long-term disability, for both plaintiff and defense (Deutsch, 1990). Rehabilitationists also began to prepare Life Care Plans to facilitate award settlements among catastrophic disability cases (Deutsch, Weed, Kitchen, & Sluis, 1989). For example, Vocational Experts became involved in determining increments of disability and quantifying those increments into dollar amounts for court consideration (Field, Weed, & Grimes, 1986; Gamboa, Holland, & Tierney, 1988).

The role of the Vocational Expert will continue to expand in the 1990s. The ADA will require an integration of ergonomic analyses, accessibility studies, recommendations for job accommodations and modifications, and job analyses into a comprehensive assessment followed by expert testimony. Other new arenas for the Vocational Expert include wrongful termination, sexual harassment, railroad workers' injury claims (FELA), toxic torts, damages to the integrity of the family, and civil-criminal interface (Lees-Haley, 1990), as well as mental health practitioner malpractice (Woody, 1988).

One measure of the importance of the Vocational Expert is that, in almost every jurisdiction, it is the expert who testifies at the request of either plaintiff or defense and is responsible for integrating medical, psychological, social, educational, and vocational information into the legal arena. Rendering this service requires specialized knowledge as well as a personality that is not easily intimidated by the adversarial nature of the litigious system. As such, Forensic Rehabilitation may be a career expansion area for a limited number of rehabilitationists to pursue.

CONCLUSIONS

A paradigm involves the models upon which a discipline bases its perceptions of itself and its relationship to the world around it (Guba, 1990; Kuhn, 1970). From the 1970s through the 1990s, rehabilitation counseling has undergone such a conceptual and practical transformation that a new paradigm has emerged. This paradigm affects the foundational structure of rehabilitation practice. Social and political changes, as well as innovations in rehabilitation practice constitute a virtual revolution in rehabilitation services and their applications.

In the introduction to this chapter two trends were identified. The first was the shift in location of rehabilitation services away from the facility and into the workplace. This has been shown to be true in the areas of: counseling strategies, involving a multidisciplinary model of rehabilitation at the workplace; pain treatment, re-oriented to services directed at on-job tasks; pre-employment screening and job analysis, to be inclusive rather than exclusive in function; assistive technology, implemented to enhance both independent living and work activities; access to the workplace, so that persons with disabilities can become full participants in the workforce; and, forensic services, increasingly utilized for individual work situations.

The second trend is the utilization of assistive technology. Already modern culture has become an "orthotic society," in that such technology as eyeglasses, athletic equipment, power tools, and computers, are common. The goal of this process is to make living easier. The logical extension is to construct devices and architecture which will facilitate accommodations for persons with disabilities. The costs of this process will continue to diminish over time as development costs are covered and only production costs must be included in the prices for these products. In addition, further cost enhancements will be realized for our entire society as productivity for persons with disabilities is more fully realized.

This new paradigm of rehabilitation counseling will be of benefit to all. Persons with disabilities will be served by ensuring equal opportunities for employment. Employers will be able to use more of the abilities previously ignored, while reducing disability costs. Society will benefit by a more efficient utilization of its members, as well as a diversion of resources away from disability benefits and toward productive habilitation and rehabilitation endeavors. Additionally, the individualized treatment of people with disabilities should enhance productivity by employing those whose interests and abilities more nearly match those required of each job, as well as reducing employee grievances and turnover and thus producing increased benefit to employers.

Two driving forces will cause rehabilitation counseling to continue to follow the new paradigm. First is the full implementation of the Americans with Disabilities Act of 1990. This act mandates the individualization of opportunities and services. The second force is the increasing amount of resources being allocated to nonproductive disability benefits. With the diversion of some of those resources into employing or making life more independent for persons with disabilities, the net social benefit will be more productive utilization of assets. Therefore, the expanding roles and functions of the rehabilitation counselor regarding implementation of ADA is crucial. Case law will ultimately determine the impact of the act. Therefore, it is critical that rehabilitationists undertake their responsibilities with the knowledge that what they do in the present could have far-reaching consequences for many people with disabilities into the future.

REFERENCES

Americans with Disabilities Act of 1990, P.L. 101-338 (1990).

Antenucci, B., & Corthell, D. (1979). *Rehabilitation engineering: A counselor's guide.* Menomonie, WI: Stout Vocational Rehabilitation Institute.

Aronoff, G. M., & McAlary, P. W. (1990). Multidisciplinary treatment of intractable pain. In S. Lipton, E. Tunks, & M. Zoppi (Eds.), *Advances in pain research and therapy, Volume 13: The pain clinic* (pp. 267-278). New York: Raven Press.

Atkinson, D. R., & Hackett, G. (1988). *Counseling non-ethnic American minorities.* Springfield, IL: Charles C. Thomas.

Bach-y-Rita, P. (1989). *Traumatic brain injury.* New York: Demos Publications.

Baker, R. J. (1983). From evaluation to adjustment: Programmatic and client centered considerations. In R. A. Lassiter, M. H. Lassiter, R. E. Hardy, J. W. Underwood, & J. G. Cull (Eds.), *Vocational evaluation, work adjustment, and independent living for severely disabled people* (pp. 126-134). Springfield, IL: Charles C. Thomas.

Bellamy, G. T., Rhodes, L. E., Mank, D. M., & Albin, J. M. (1988). *Supported employment: A community implementation guide.* Baltimore: Paul H. Brookes Publishing Co.

Berkowitz, M., & Hill, M. A. (Eds.). (1986). *Disability and the labor market: Economic problems, policies, and programs.* Ithaca, NY: Cornell University Press.

Borysenko, J. (1987). *Minding the body, mending the mind.* New York: Bantam Books.

Brandon, J. E. (1985). Health promotion and wellness in rehabilitation services. *Journal of Rehabilitation, 51*(4), 54-58.

Brown, P. L. (1982) *Managing behavior on the job.* New York: John W. Wiley & Sons.

Calub, C., Burton, J. T., DeBoskey, D. S., & Hooker, C. (1990). *A cognitive rehabilitation system: Evaluation, treatment & generalization.* Tampa, FL: DeBoskey & Associates.

Chaffin, D. B., & Anderson, G. B. (1991). *Occupational biomechanics: Second edition.* New York: John Wiley & Sons.

Charlesworth, E. A., & Nathan, R. G. (1984). *Stress management: A comprehensive guide to wellness.* New York: Atheneum.

Corthell, D. W., & Oliverio, M. (1989). *Vocational rehabilitation services to persons with H.I.V. (AIDS).* Menomonie, WI: University of Wisconsin-Stout.

Crites, J. S. (1969). *Vocational psychology: The study of vocational behavior and development.* New York: McGraw-Hill.

Cusack, O. (1988). *Pets and mental health.* New York: The Haworth Press.

Deneen, L. J., & Hessellund, T. A. (1981). *Vocational rehabilitation of the injured worker.* San Francisco: Rehab Publications.

De Point, B. (Ed.). (1990). *Tools of the trade: A hands-on training program for supported employment personnel.* Minneapolis: Rise, Inc.

Deutsch, P. M. (1990). *A guide to rehabilitation testimony: The expert's role as educator.* Winter Park, FL: GR Press, Inc.

Deutsch, P. M., & Fralish, K. B. (1988). *Innovations in head injury rehabilitation.* New York: Matthew Bender.

Deutsch, P. M., Weed, R. O., Kitchen, J. A., & Sluis, A. (1989). *Life care planning for the head injured: A step by step guide.* Winter Park, FL: GR Press, Inc.

Dickman, F., Challenger, B. R., Emener, W. G., & Hutchison, W. S. (Eds.). (1988). *Employee assistance programs: A basic text.* Springfield, IL: Charles C. Thomas.

Enderle, J. D. (Ed.). (1990). *National science foundation 1990 engineering senior design projects to aid the disabled.* Fargo, ND: NDSU Press.

Enders, A., & Hall, M. (Eds.). (1990). *Assistive technology sourcebook.* Washington, DC: RESNA Press.

Esposito, E. F., & Esposito, F. W. (1991). A family perspective. In P. Wehman, & J. S. Kreutzer (Eds.), *Vocational rehabilitation for persons with traumatic brain injury.* (pp. 323-334). Rockville, MD: Aspen Publications, Inc.

Field, T. F., & Priaulux, C. K. (1984). The professional work of the rehabilitation counselor. In W.G. Emener, A. Patrick & D.K. Hollingsworth (Eds.), *Critical issues in rehabilitation counseling.* (pp. 173-188). Springfield, IL: Charles C. Thomas.

Field, T. F., Weed, R. O., & Grimes, J. W. (1986). *The vocational expert handbook.* Tuscon: VALPAR, Inc.

Fleeson, W. P. (1988). Preplacement physical examinations. In S .J. Isernhagen (Ed.), *Work injury: Management and prevention.* (pp. 106-112). Rockville, MD: Aspen Publications, Inc.

Foster, M. B. (1988). Work hardening with the head injured survivor: Special considerations. In J. E. Havranek (Ed.), *Physical capacity assessment and work hardening therapy: Procedures and applications.* (pp. 105-115). Athens, GA: E & F, Inc.

Frankoff, D. J., & Alexander, M. A. (1987). The child and technology. In M. G. Eisenberg, & R. C. Grzesiak (Eds.), *Advances in clinical rehabilitation: Volume 1.* (pp. 77-114). New York: Springer Publishing Co.

Gael, S. (1983). *Job analysis: A guide to assessing work activities.* San Francisco: Jossey-Bass Publishers.

Gamboa, A. M., Holland, G. H., & Tierney, J. P. (1988). Assessing work and earning capacity. In M. G. Eisenberg, & R. C. Grzesiak (Eds.), *Advances in clinical rehabilitation: Volume 2.* (pp. 6-36). New York: Springer Publishing Co.

Geist, C. S., & Calzaretta, W. A. (1982). *Placement handbook for counseling disabled people.* Springfield, IL: Charles C. Thomas.

Gold, M. S. (1986). *The facts about drugs and alcohol.* New York: Bantam Books.

Goldsmith, F., & Kerr, L. E. (1982). *Occupational safety and health: The prevention and control of work related hazards.* New York: Human Sciences Press.

Greer, B. G. (1986). Substance abuse among people with disabilities: A problem of too much accessibility. *Journal of Rehabilitation, 52*(1), 34-38.

Grosshandler, J. (1990). *Coping with alcohol abuse.* New York: Rosen Publishing Group.

Guba, E. G. (1990). *The paradigm dialogue.* Newbury Park, CA: Sage Publications.

Hablutzel, J. D., & McMahon, B. T. (1992). *The Americans with Disabilities Act: Access and accommodations.* Winter Park, FL: GR Press, Inc.

Havranek, J. E. (Ed.). (1988). *Physical capacity assessment and work hardening therapy: Procedures and applications.* Athens, GA: Elliott & Fitzpatrick, Inc.

Havranek, J. E. (1991). The social and individual costs of negative attitudes toward persons with physical disabilities. *Journal of Applied Rehabilitation Counseling, 22*(1), 15-22.

Havranek, J. E. (1992). Methods and uses of job analysis: Implications for implementation of the Americans with Disabilities Act of 1990. *NARPPS Journal & News, 7*(3), 113-118.

Hopf, P. F., & Raeber, J. A. (1984). *Access for the handicapped: The barrier-free regulations for design and construction in all 50 states.* New York: Van Nostrand Reinhold Co.

IEEE Computer Society. (1981). *Proceedings of the Johns Hopkins first national search for applications of personal computers to aid the handicapped: October 31, 1981.* Los Angeles: Author.

Isernhagen, S. J. (1988). *Work injury: Management and prevention.* Rockville, MD: Aspen Publishers, Inc.

Invancevich, I. M., & Glueck, W.,F. (1986). *Foundations of personnel management.* Plano, TX: Business Publications, Inc.

Keane, R. M. (1985). Providing rehabilitation services to the insurance industry. In L. J. Taylor, M. Golter, G. Golter, & T. E. Backer (Eds.), *Handbook of private sector rehabilitation* (pp. 22-54). New York: Springer Publishing Co.

Knapp, S., & VandeCreek, L. (1990). *What every therapist should know about AIDS*. Sarasota, FL: Professional Resource Exchange.

Kreutzer, J. S., & Wehmen, P. (Eds.). (1990). *Community integration following traumatic brain injury*. Baltimore: Paul H. Brooks Publishing Co.

Kuhn, T. S. (1970). *The structure of scientific revolutions: Second edition*. Chicago: University of Chicago Press.

Kurland, M. L. (1988). *Coping with AIDS: Facts & fears*. New York: The Rosen Publishing Group.

Lawton, B. (1988). The EAP and workplace psychiatric injury. In R. C. Larson, & J. S. Felton (Eds.), *Psychiatric injury in the workplace*. (pp.695-706). Philadelphia: Hanley & Belfus, Inc.

Lees-Haley, P. R. (199). Opportunities for a personal injury practice. In P. A. Keller, & S. R. Heyman (Eds.), *Innovations in clinical practice: Volume 9* (pp. 221-227). Sarasota, FL: Professional Resource Exchange.

Lowman, R. L. (1989). *Pre-employment screening for psychopathology: A guide to professional practice*. Sarasota, FL: Professional Resource Exchange.

Lytel, R. B., & Botterbusch, K. F. (1981). *Physical demands job analysis: A new approach*. Menomonie, WI: University of Wisconsin-Stout.

Matheson, L. N. (1987). *Work capacity evaluation 1987: Systematic approach to industrial rehabilitation*. Anaheim, CA: E.R.I.C.

Matkin, R. E. (1985). *Insurance rehabilitation*. Austin, TX: pro-ed.

McGown, J. F., & Porter, T. L. (1967). *An introduction to the vocational rehabilitation process*. Washington, DC: U.S. Government Printing Office.

McWaters, J. L. (1988). *Deep water exercise for health and fitness*. Laguna Beach, CA: Publitec Editions.

Morris, A. W., & Anderson, C. K. (1988). Pre-employment screening: The physical perspective. In S. J. Isernhagen (Ed.), *Work injury: Management and prevention* (pp. 92-105). Rockville, MD: Aspen Publishers, Inc.

Morris, K. C. (1989). *A job trainer's manual: Supported employment for low functioning rehabilitation clients and disabled secondary students*. Springfield, IL: Charles C. Thomas.

Mueller, J. (1990). *The workplace workbook: An illustrated guide to job accommodation and assistive technology*. Washington, DC: The Dole Foundation.

Mulick, J. A., & Antonak, R. F. (1987). *Transitions in mental retardation, volume 2: Issues in therapeutic intervention*. Norwood, NJ: Ablex Publishing Corporation. Nye,

Nye, S. G. (1990). *Employee assistance law answer book*. New York: Panel Publishers.

Pati, G. C., & Adkins, J .I. (1981). *Managing and employing the handicapped: The untapped potential*. Lake Forest, IL: Brace-Park.

Peele, S. (1989). *Diseasing of America*. Lexington, MA: D.C. Heath.

Power, P. J. (1988). The family & the rehab process: Counselor roles and functions. In S. E. Rubin, & N.M. Rubin (Eds.), *Contemporary challenges to the rehabilitation counseling profession* (pp. 243-258). Baltimore: Paul H. Brookes.

Rasch, J. D. (1985). *Workers compensation insurance and law practice: The next generation*. Springfield, IL: Charles C. Thomas.

Riggar, T. F., Matkin, D. R., & Wolf, A. W. (Eds.). (1986). *Applied rehabilitation counseling*. New York: Springer Publishing Co.

Sachs, P. R. (1991). *Treating families of brain-injured survivors*. New York: Springer Publishing Co.

Sethi, A. S., & Schuler, R. S. (1984). *Handbook of organizational stress coping strategies*. Cambridge: Ballinger Publishing Co.

Shealy, C. N., & Cady, R. K. (1990). Multidisciplinary pain clinics. In R. S. Weiner (Ed.), *Innovations in pain management: A practical guide for clinicians, Volume 1* (pp. 2-3 - 2-21). Winter Park, FL: GR Press, Inc.

Shrey, D., & Breslin, R. (1992). Disability management in industry: Accommodating workers with disabilities. *International Journal of Industrial Ergonomics, 9*(2), 183-190.

Sowers, J., & Powers, L. (1991). *Vocational preparation and employment of students with physical and multiple disabilities.* Baltimore: Paul H. Brookes Publishing Co.

Swanbum, N. E. (1988). Employer point of view. In S. J. Isernhagen (Ed.), *Work injury* (pp. 331-337). Rockville, MD: Aspen Publishers, Inc.

Thomas, K. R. (1991). *Rehabilitation counseling: A profession in transition.* Athens, GA: Elliot & Fitzpatrick, Inc.

Trieschmann, R. B. (1988). *Spinal cord injury: 2nd edition.* New York: Demos.

U.S. Department of Labor. (1983). *A guide to job analysis.* Menomonie, WI: University of Wisconsin-Stout.

U.S. Department of Labor. (1972). *Handbook for analyzing jobs.* Washington, DC: Superintendent of Documents.

Valentine, T. (1985). *Applied kinesiology: Muscle response in diagnosis, therapy & preventive medicine.* Rochester, VT: Healing Arts Press.

Wallace, J. (1985). *Alcoholism: New light on the disease.* Newport, RI: Edgehill Publications.

Wehman, P., & Moon, M. S. (1988). *Vocational rehabilitation and supported employment.* Baltimore: Paul H. Brookes Publishing Co.

Welch, E. M. (Ed.). (1989). *Workers compensation: Strategies for lowering costs and reducing workers' suffering.* Fort Washington, PA: LRP

Wielkiewicz, R. M., & Calvert, C. R. (1989). *Training and habilitating developmentally disabled people: An introduction.* Newbury Park, CA: Sage Publications.

Woody, R. H. (1988). *Fifty ways to avoid malpractice: A guide for mental health professionals.* Sarasota, FL: Professional Resource Exchange.

Wright, G. N. (1980). *Total rehabilitation.* Boston: Little, Brown & Co.

—13—

OCCUPATIONAL STRESS: A DISABILITY MANAGEMENT PERSPECTIVE

Robert G. Lasky, Ph.D.

INTRODUCTION

Perhaps the one word that best reflects the current state of American business and industry is *change*. This is evidenced by many factors, including technological advances, the complexities of a rapidly changing global economy, and the need for identifying and implementing new ways to manage change in the workplace. In his book *Future Shock*, Toffler (1970) predicted an age of rapid change in the American economy and the difficulties associated with such change. More recently, business and industry is being challenged to change the entire ecosystem of management practice and philosophy or risk becoming obsolete (e.g., Drucker, 1992; Peters, 1992). It is not uncommon to be reminded daily of the demise of large and small companies, employee layoffs, and the loss of employment benefits once thought to be sacrosanct. Along with the many changes that the American economy is experiencing, and is expected to experience into the 21st century, the increasing demands on workers, coupled with diminishing coping resources, are leaving the workforce with increasing health problems and employers with escalating health care costs. If the American economy and its workforce are expected to survive, business and industry must be responsive to the occupational stress that accompanies workplace change. Either business and industry learns to control occupational stress, or risk the likely consequences of stress eroding American industrial vitality.

The purposes of this chapter are to (1) present an overview of the impact of occupational stress on worker health and business and industry losses; (2) provide an understanding of the complex nature of occupational stress; (3) identify specific sources of occupational stress; (4) discuss several important preliminary issues related to controlling occupational stress; and (5) present strategies for the prevention and control of occupational stress. In this chapter, the term *occupational stress* is defined as an imbalance between workplace demands (e.g., job knowledge and skills needed, supervisory relationships, ergonomic factors, safety considerations, management policies), and the worker's ability to cope with these demands, experienced as mental or physical strain and dysfunction.

Occupational stress may be adaptive, in that stress is a natural and necessary fact of life, needed to perform the ordinary demands of working and living. However, when work demands exceed worker coping skills, workers have a greater likelihood of experiencing an unhealthy response, or distress, shown by physical, emotional, interpersonal, cognitive, or behavioral problems. During the past 10 years, numerous studies have shown that workplace stress contributes greatly to worker health problems, including illness, accidents, and cumulative trauma.

OCCUPATIONAL STRESS AND HEALTH

Workplace stress plays a critical role in worker health and well-being. A recent national survey of 1,299 workers found that workers reporting high job stress were three times more likely than workers reporting low job stress to suffer from frequent illness (Northwestern National Life Insurance Company, 1992). Specific stress-related areas of emotional and physical discomfort reported by workers experiencing high stress jobs included fatigue or exhaustion, tight neck or shoulder muscles, feelings of anger, anxiety, headaches, insomnia, and depression. Job stress has also been associated with higher risks for numerous illnesses, disorders, and injuries, including cardiovascular disease (Johnson & Hall, 1988; Karasek, Baker, Marxer, Ahlbom, & Theorell, 1981; LaCroix & Haynes, 1987; National Center for Health Statistics, 1989; Tyroler et al., 1987), visual problems (Hedge, Erickson, & Rubin, 1991), musculoskeletal disability (Fitzgerald, 1992; Spitzer, LeBlanc, & Dupuis, 1987), back pain (Waddell, Morris, DiPaola, Bircher, & Finlayson, 1986), and a variety of other disorders including coronary heart disease, headaches, sleep disorders, and other somatic problems that affect job performance (Cooper & Marshal, 1976; Friend, 1982; Quick & Quick, 1984; Spector, Dwyer, & Jex, 1988). An overview of various potential personal and organizational consequences from distressful experiences is shown in Figure 1.

Stress has also been related to infectious diseases associated with the onset and growth of bacteria and viruses. Cohen and Williamson (1991) conducted an extensive review of the research literature related to stress and infectious disease in humans. They found substantial evidence for an association between stress and increased illness behavior (i.e., symptoms and the use of health services), with less convincing but provocative evidence for a similar association between stress and infectious pathology. Frankenhauser (1991) examined the psychophysiology of workload, stress, and health vis-a-vis men and women, finding that sex differences relating to stress have decreased markedly. An increasing number of women are experiencing the physiological impact of stress via catecholamine reactivity often

PERSONAL

A. Physical

- High Blood Pressure
- Muscle Tension
- Tension Headaches
- Nervous Tics
- Cumulative Trauma Injuries
- Constipation
- Stomach Cramps
- Shortness of Breath
- Dizziness
- Back Injuries

B. Emotional

- Anxiety
- Frustration
- Anger/Hostility
- Depression
- Lowered Self-esteem
- Feeling Self-conscious
- Feeling Restless
- Feeling Hopeless
- Feeling Guilty
- Feeling Helpless

C. Behavioral

- Problem Drinking
- Increased Smoking
- Violence
- Illicit Drug Use
- Irresponsibility
- Social Isolation
- Poor Eating Habits
- Lack of Exercising

D. Cognitive

- Poor Memory
- Poor Decision-making
- Excessive Worrying
- Catastrophizing
- Racing Thoughts
- Daydreaming
- Poor Judgement
- Preoccupation

E. Interpersonal

- Feeling Inferior to Others
- Feeling Superior to Others
- Feeling Alone
- Feeling Unlovable
- Sexual Difficulties
- Avoiding Others
- People Phobic
- Being Passive with Others

ORGANIZATIONAL

- Thefts
- Sabotage
- Increased Healthcare Costs
- Absenteeism
- Accidents
- High Turnover
- Low Productivity
- Disloyalty

Figure 1. Examples of the Potential Effects of Workplace Distress

triggered by achievement demands and workloads higher than those experienced 20 or more years ago. Frankenhauser found an increasing risk for adverse health consequences brought about by women's multiple roles and difficulty leaving the strains of work when returning home.

The impact of psychosocial stress factors was also shown in a recent report by the National Institute for Occupational Safety and Health, (NIOSH), (cited in Bureau of National Affairs, 1992, August), related to the use of video display terminals (VDTs) and musculoskeletal disorders and symptoms. In this report, conducted at a major telephone company, U.S. West Communications, NIOSH found that directory assistance operators and other workers using VDTs had a "high prevalence" of upper extremity disorders, associated with prior medical conditions, work practices, psychosocial aspects of the workplace, and electronic monitoring of employees. An initial focus in this study was on the ergonomic factors associated with VDTs. However, even after ergonomic changes were made, there was little change in worker-reported musculoskeletal problems. Pressures from electronic monitoring and supervision increased worker stress to the point where physical distress was experienced. When such monitoring was terminated, worker symptoms began decreasing. An important finding from this study was that the psychosocial work environment, including factors such as fear and being replaced by computers, increasing work pressure, and surges in workload, are related to the occurrence of work-related upper extremity musculoskeletal disorder and symptoms.

Psychological stress in the workplace is thought to contribute to cumulative trauma disorders (CTDs), given that the risk of CTDs is increased two to three times under stressful conditions, given equal exposure to other physical factors that pose risk, with traditional management being partially to blame (Bureau of National Affairs, 1992, April). The relationship between workplace stress and CTDs is not yet clear, with much anecdotal information and little hard evidence to date. "A number of studies link work organization issues and psychological stress to CTDs, but do not allow a conclusion to be drawn as to which is the cause and which is the effect, or if there is some other factor causing both," according to MacLeod (cited in Bureau of National Affairs, 1992, April).

The impact of environmental conditions and health has also been a focus of study in recent years. What has been referred to as the "sick building syndrome" (SBS) involves reports of common symptoms, such as headaches, fatigue, and eye irritation, from workers in the same office environment. Poor air quality, "closed" environments, and the use of air conditioning, have been a primary focus of such office symptoms, but Hedge and his associates (Hedge, 1989; Hedge, Burge, Robertson, Wilson, & Harris-Bass, 1989; Hedge et al., 1991) found that these and related physical symptoms were also related to job stress, feelings of low job satisfaction, and video display terminal use. Sick building symptoms were reported more often by workers who rated their job as stressful or were actively involved with the use of VDTs. These, and related problems found to be associated with job stress, not only impaired worker physical and emotional health, but have a serious financial impact.

OCCUPATIONAL STRESS IS EXPENSIVE

Although it is difficult to estimate accurately, job stress is costing American industry billions of dollars in workers' compensation, health care costs, long-term disability costs, and unproductive worker hours. The impact of occupational stress on health and industry productivity on the American economy has been estimated as high as $150 billion per year, with some business leaders estimating that trying to manage workplace stress might become a $15 billion industry within the 1990s (Miller, et al., 1988). The California Workers' Compensation Institute (1990) reported that during the 10-year period between 1979 and 1988, mental stress claims for California workers increased 540%. This trend has continued, with mental stress claims having increased over 700% in the past 10 years (Courtney, 1992). Up to 85% of all industrial accidents are caused by an inability to cope with job stress, according to Jones (1984), citing research derived from the National Safety Council, the College of Insurance, and the National Institute for Occupational Safety and Health. Psychological or psychosomatic problems contribute to more that 60% of long-term disability claims, and $26 billion is spent annually on associated disability payments and medical bills. According to McGrath (cited in Bureau of National Affairs, 1991), lost productivity traceable to depression has an estimated price tag of $20 billion annually, with physical symptoms including sleepiness, inability to concentrate, and carelessness. The total cost of workplace accidents in 1990 was $63.8 billion, or $540 per worker (National Safety Council, 1991). Losses such as these have had tremendous impact on the economy, as well as creating significant legal implications of workplace stress.

In California, workers' compensation mental stress claims may currently be made by workers who perceive that their job has contributed to emotional distress and related symptomatology. The only stipulations for filing such claims, at this time, are that the worker must have worked for a company for at least six months, and must prove that at least 10% of his or her stress was due to job-related problems. Litigation in the job stress arena is becoming commonplace, threatening already precarious industry-based health care system. AIDS in the workplace is rapidly becoming another source of occupational stress for workers fearing contact with co-workers who are HIV-positive, according to Lieber (cited in Staff, 1992). Workers' compensation may even be sought by HIV-positive workers claiming that job stress has exacerbated their debilitation (Kendig, 1992). Donnelly (cited in Staff, 1992, pp. 1-2), indicated that stress in general has been proven to hasten disease's progress, and "It is pretty clear that stress has a direct effect on the immune system and as such, a traumatic life circumstance, such as the breaking up of a marriage or a death, can bring on some extreme AIDS symptoms. But as far as stress in the workplace, this is a new field and one that, as yet, has not come up in the legal clinics."

Occupational stress is rapidly becoming a major concern for the insurance industry, particularly in the area of workers' compensation. Occupational stress workers' compensation claims are usually classified as one or more of three types (DeVader & Ciampetro-Meyer, 1991):

- Physical-mental: A mental disability resulting from a physical event such as a fall or motor vehicle accident.
- Mental-physical: A physical disability such as a heart attack resulting from a stressful work environment.
- Mental-mental: A mental disability resulting from a stressful work environment, such as anxiety after witnessing another worker's death.

Courts are more inclined to rule in favor of the first two because it is easier to establish the extent of something physical, according to DeVader and Giampetro-Meyer (1991). The most dramatic increase in occupational stress claims has been in the mental-mental area, which may be alleged as a specific incident or as the result of repetitive or cumulative trauma (Courtney, 1992). Mental-mental stress claims, Courtney reported, are (1) most often related to alleged harassment by a supervisor or manager, (2) commonly filed post-termination from employment, (3) difficult to disprove due to the subjective nature of the alleged job stress, (4) higher in medical-legal costs than other types of claims, and (5) potentially more prone to fraud than other claims.

CHARACTERISTICS OF OCCUPATIONAL STRESS

The term *stress* is often used in different ways, making it difficult to define precisely. In a recent study, Jex, Beehr, Terry, and Roberts (1992) tested the effect of using the word *stress* in the measurement of occupational stressors and strains. Workers from two organizations were asked to complete a questionnaire that included specific occupational stressors, strains, and 16 items where the word *stress* was used. The word *stress* was interpreted by respondents as both employee's strains or reactions to the work environment (i.e., stress as a response) and to job stressors or aspects of the environment itself (i.e., stress as stimulus).

As a stimulus, the term *stressor* is used to define any stimulus that the individual perceives as a threat (Asteria, 1985). Stressors may be physical or psychosocial, emanating from internal or external sources. As a response, stress may be considered as the impact of a stimulus, be it favorable or unfavorable, on the individual. The term *distress* is often used to indicate a negative impact of a perceived stressful situation.

Lazarus & Folkman (1984) suggested that stress may be defined a particular relationship between the person and the environment that is appraised by the person as taxing or exceeding his or her resources and endangering his or her wellbeing. Matteson & Ivancevich (1987) regard stress as an adaptive response, moderated by individual differences, that is the consequence of any action, situation, or event that places special demands upon a person. The term *occupational stress* is an application of these stress concept to the workplace.

Occupational stress may be thought of as job-related discomfort or illness that people experience because of their work situations (Beehr, 1991). Price (1992) also stated that, according to a large body of research, job stress is a consequence of two key ingredients: a high level of job demands and little control over one's work. While these approaches to occupational stress identify specific aspects of a stress response, they do not take into consideration the importance of workers' individual appraisals of workplace situations. Certain workplace situations may be generally agreed to contribute to worker distress, but may not actually be distressful to a worker who is able to cope effectively with a given job stressor. For example, most workers might agree that having too much work to do with too little time to complete the work is stressful and react accordingly. This same situation may be perceived by other workers as challenging or enjoyable because the time passes by more quickly. Given the above understandings, occupational stress may best be considered as job-related experience(s) perceived by a worker as taxing or exceeding his or her ability to cope effectively, often leading to increased susceptibility to physical, emotional behavioral, cognitive, or interpersonal distress. Figure 2 presents a model of occupational stress to illustrate the worker-job relationship and its consequences.

The Occupational Stress Syndrome shown in Figure 2 represents the relationship between workers and their jobs. Workers are influenced by physical and psychosocial stressors both at work and outside of work. Occupational stress occurs when there is an imbalance between *relevant* worker-job physical or psychosocial attributes and the worker's ability to copy. It is important to note that worker job attributes must be relevant in that the primary impact of the specified characteristic(s) should be on the worker-job relationship. For example, worker physical pain may be an important stressor in certain aspects of the job but not in others. If worker pain is not a relevant stressor in certain aspects of the job, workers should be able to continue working at the tasks that they are able to do without pain and eliminate tasks that contribute to pain and dysfunction.

Cognitive appraisal refers to an evaluative cognitive process that mediates the relationship between the worker-job relationship and worker response potential.

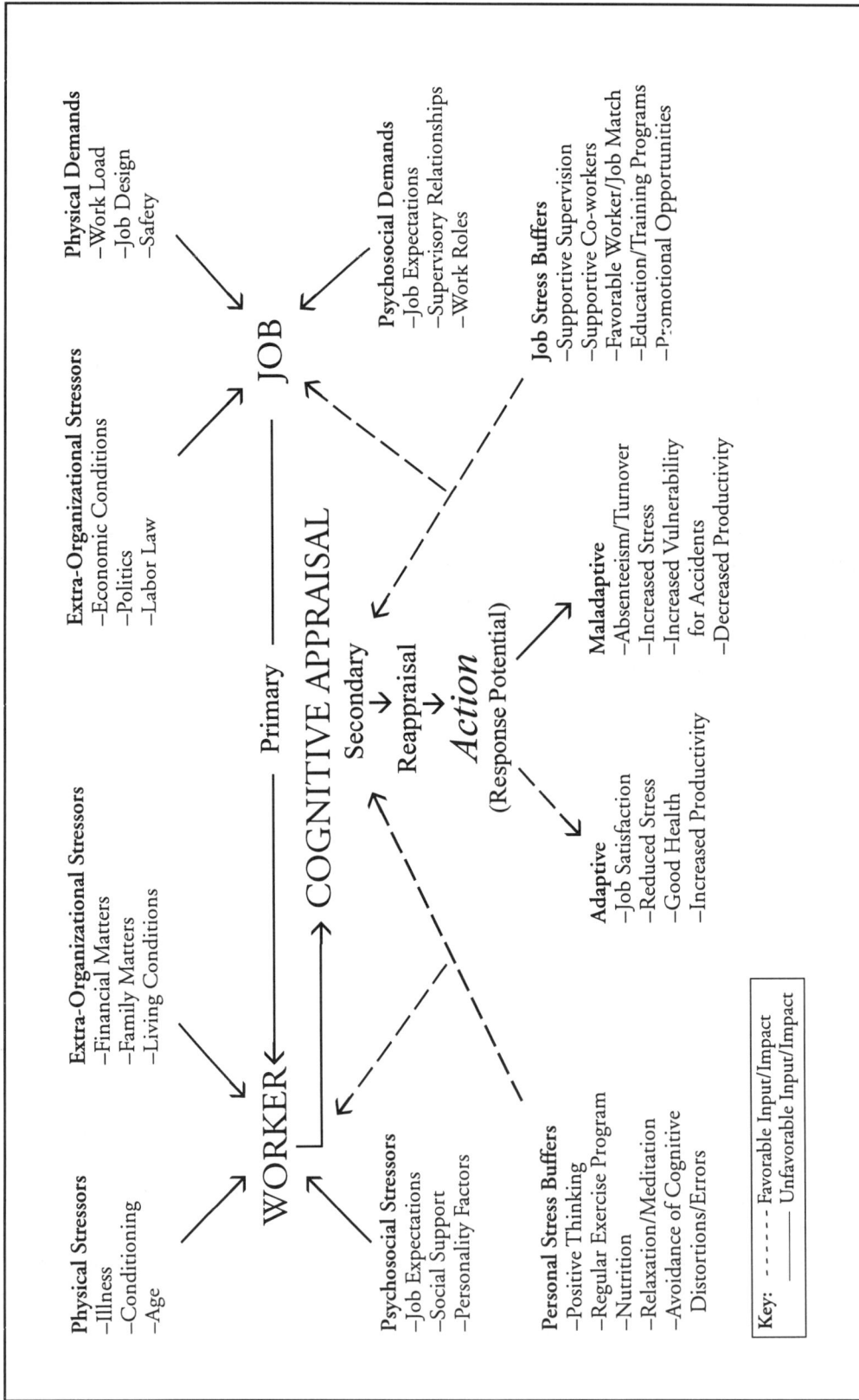

Figure 2. Occupational Stress Syndrome: Influence of Worker and Job Stressor on Worker Health and Well-being

Lazarus and Folkman (1984) identified three types of cognitive appraisal: (1) primary appraisal — the judgment that a stimulus or situation is either irrelevant, benign (or positive), or stressful; (2) secondary appraisal — the evaluation of what coping strategies are available; and (3) reappraisal — a changed appraisal usually based on new information from the environment and/or the person. These cognitive evaluative processes help to determine whether the worker's response potential will be adaptive or maladaptive. Adaptive responses tend to reduce or minimize stressful consequences, while maladaptive responses increase the worker's vulnerability to impaired health and personal functioning.

If the worker is able to cope with job stressors, worker distress will likely be minimized or absent in the short run. However, job stressors may be cumulative and lead to worker dysfunction in time. Major life events (e.g., being terminated from work, getting a new boss) may not always lead to job stress and dysfunction. Rather, it is daily hassles that, in combination with more major stressors, may be attributable to life and occupational distress and health status (Kanner, Coyne, Schaeffer, & Lazarus, 1981; Weinberger, Hiner, & Tierney, 1987). Major stressors may lead to many other secondary stressors, or hassles, that actually increase vulnerability to significant health problems (Dohwenrend & Dohwenrend, 1981; Dohwenrend & Shrout, 1985). While hassles likely increase stress-related health risks, other factors may protect people from such risks.

Kobasa and her associates (Kobasa, 1979; Kobasa, Maddi, & Kahn, 1982) found that certain people have developed what is referred to as "hardiness," a personality characteristic manifested by a strong commitment to self, an attitude of vigorousness toward the environment, a sense of meaningfulness, and a sense of internal control. Hardiness is thought to be a source of resistance to the potentially harmful effects of stress (Antonovsky, 1982). Three important characteristics of hardiness are commitment, control, and challenge. The more of these qualities people have, the more they are stress resistant. Also, the way people perceive their surroundings may help or hinder their reactions to various sources of stress. As shown in Figure 2, workers may become aware of physical or psychosocial stressors originating from themselves or their jobs. Many kinds of stressors affect individuals and their relationship to their jobs. The characteristics of both the workers and their jobs present the potential for physical or psychosocial stressors.

WORKER PHYSICAL STRESSORS

Sources of worker physical stress include pain, fatigue, illness, the effects of alcohol and drug, and other internal physical factors. When such distress is experienced while on the job, workers have an increased likelihood to not pay attention to their work placing them at greater risk for adverse consequences. Contributors to internal physical stress may include the absence of positive lifestyle behaviors (e.g., physical exercise, good nutrition), leaving the individual vulnerable to lower thresholds of internal physical stress buffers.

JOB PHYSICAL STRESSORS

The work environment may also contribute in many ways to worker stress reactions. Cooper and Davidson (1987) identified several work-related factors contributing to organizational stress, including job fit and satisfaction, equipment and training, shift work, work overload, work underload, physical danger, work-related self-esteem, the worker's role in the organization including present and future role ambiguity and conflict), responsibility for people, organizational boundaries, career development, over- and under-promotion, status congruency, remuneration, relationships with colleagues (including supervisors and subordinates), organizational structure and climate, politics, consultation communication, participation in decision-making, restriction on behavior, and rigidity of departmental policies. MacLennan (1992) identified several external stressors related to the condition of the work environment: (1) sensory and perceptual factors (e.g., outlook, light, noise, special proportions, temperature, humidity); and (2) safety considerations (e.g., clean air, toxic exposure, equipment design, appropriateness). Mace (1992) identified additional external sources of stress, including odor, exposure to the elements, visual impact (e.g., CRTs), and the encumbrances of protective equipment. Mace also reported that the nature of the work performed constituted sources of external stress, including physical demands (e.g., strength, posture), physical risk, repetitiveness, time pressures, tolerance for error, intellectual demands, interpersonal demands, and psychological demands.

WORKER PSYCHOSOCIAL STRESSORS

The individual's inner psychological states that contribute to stress overload may be regarded as cognitive errors and distortions. Specifically, cognitive theoreticians and clinicians (e.g., Beck, 1976; Burns, 1980; Ellis, 1962; McKay, Davis, & Fanning, 1981) have postulated a variety of distinct cognitive errors and distortions that contribute to personal distress and problem behaviors. Examples of how workers may use selected cognitive errors and distortions include:

Overgeneralization: Reaching a general defeatist conclusion based on a single negative incident or piece of evidence.
    Incident: One aspect of a performance appraisal is negative.
    Thought: "His criticism of my productivity was unwarranted. He's trying to get rid of me because of this recession."

Extremist Thinking: Using dichotomous reasoning, such as seeing things as either right or wrong, good or bad, black or white, if you are not perfect you're a failure.
  Incident: Taking too much time to complete a basic work task.
  Thought: "It's important for me not to make a mistake, I must get this job done perfectly or they'll see me as a failure."

Magnification/Catastrophizing & Minimization: One overestimates the importance of things or expects disasters; conversely, one shrinks any positive aspects of events or achievements.
  Incident: A company in town lays off 100 employees.
  Thought: "The ABC company is laying people off. Our town is caught up in this recession. I just know I'll be the next person to lose my job...and probably my marriage and children too." (Magnification)
  "These layoffs are just temporary and won't effect me. I'm too small a fish to be noticed here anyway." (Minimization)

Blaming: Holding others responsible for your pain or discomfort (external); or holding oneself responsible for the pain and discomfort of others (internal).
  Incident: Supervisor requests to stay after work to complete the work.
  Thought: My husband will never believe that I had to stay late for work. Because of my supervisor, my marriage is doomed." (External)
  "I know that I'm a slow worker and that I will probably lose my job...I deserve to stay after work, anyway." (Internal)

Shoulds: Having an iron-clad set of rules that you and others should act. People who break the rules anger you, or you feel guilty if you violate the rules.
  Incident: Fellow workers not keeping up with productivity demands.
  Thought: "It makes me so angry that I'm the only one who is able to make the daily quota of widgets. My co-workers are sluggards who should be fired...so should management!"

The emotional consequences of the above cognitive errors and distortions are not difficult to imagine. Maintaining such thinking is likely to create significant personal distress, loss of productivity, and potential long-term disability-related losses as suggested earlier in this chapter.

JOB PSYCHOSOCIAL STRESSORS

External sources of psychosocial stress include aspects of supervisory style and overall organizational climate. MacLennan (1992) identified a variety of external sources of psychological stress, including: (1) clarity of role functions and promotional policies; (2) opportunities for staff development; (3) rate of work flow and pace; (4) availability and functionality of human and physical resources; (5) quality of benefits and leave policies; (6) flexibility of hours of work; and (7) fairness of salary scales. MacLennan also identified the impact of interpersonal relationships and organizational style climate as psychological sources of stress: (1) atmosphere; (2) management; (3) supervisory and peer relations; (4) toleration of discrimination and harassment; (5) prestige of the occupation and organization. Additional potential sources of external psychological stress are identified by Mace (1992):

Supervisory Style

- Opportunity for participation in decision-making, especially when it affects the individual
- Emphasis on criticism and punishment vs. emphasis on recognition and rewards
- Overly rigid or overly loose organizational structure
- Unclear or negative policies about employees or about the work performed
- Unclear or rigid lines of communication

Organizational Climate

- Perception of differences between stated philosophy and actions
- Openness to ideas from the rank and file
- Autonomy of departments and individuals
- Emphasis on methods vs. emphasis on results and outcomes
- Feeling of support and concern for the individual employee.

Perhaps one of the most significant job psychosocial stressors is supervisor attitude. Many supervisors, when thrust into the role of management, feel that they must keep a close eye on workers because they cannot be trusted. For supervisors and managers to take the role of punitive overseer of workers is often expected by both workers and supervisors. Unfortunately, this situation brings with it much unnecessary stress for both worker and supervisor alike. McGregor (1960) identified supervisory attitude as being Theory X or Theory Y. McGregor cited the 1923 "scientific management" approach of Frederick Taylor as being Theory X. Theory X, a term coined by McGregor, was very much like Taylor's scientific management approach, which argued that to speed up productivity, employers must have standardized work routines, stress careful planning, use time-and-motion studies, task analysis, and the like. Theory X also assumes that workers must be goaded or guided to be productive because they are not to be trusted to be self-motivated to do good work. Conversely, McGregor argued that workers are not like machines, as Taylor, an engineer, believed, and psychological efficiency was important in the workplace, too. McGregor argued that Theory Y managers believe that workers needs and goals can be consistent with company goals. Also, Theory Y managers tend to assume that workers are industrious, creative, and reinforced by challenging work. Thus, manager or supervisor attitude plays a critical role in relation to job psychosocial stress.

As discussed above, the potential impact of job psychosocial stressors are related to workers' perceptions. Workers' thoughts and feelings about various aspects of their jobs affect their work and personal behaviors. Examples of how job psychosocial stressors may affect worker responses include the following:

Work Overload

Potential Thoughts and Feelings

- Perception of too much to do (e.g., overwhelmed)
- Feeling unable to perform up to expected standards or lacking the ability to do the job
- Lack of control
- Anger
- Anxiety, Depression

Potential Behaviors

- Frantic attempts to keep up with demands
- Displacing frustration onto co-workers, family, friends
- Venting anger towards management
- Increased likelihood of burnout
- Decreased productivity

Work Underload

Potential Thoughts and Feelings

- They don't like the quality of my work
- We're going to downsize and I'll lose my job
- My knowledge and skills are not respected
- I'm not trusted
- I'm a failure

Potential Behaviors

- Absenteeism
- Anxiety/Depression
- Social isolation/withdrawal

Role Ambiguity

Potential Thoughts and Feelings

- Unsure of what is expected on the job
- Confusion
- Personalizing failure for not being able to perform job well
- Torn between conflicting demands

Potential Behaviors

- Disorganized
- Panic attacks
- Fear and avoidance of supervisors and managers
- Continual requests for supervision and guidance

Inadequate Career Advancement Opportunities

Potential Thoughts and Feelings

- Frustration with perception of a "dead-end" job
- No one cares about performance
- Lack of incentive to achieve, burnout
- Apathy
- Cynicism/Anger

Potential Behaviors

- Underachieving (i.e., doing the least possible to get by)
- Griping, complaining
- Sabotage, theft
- Seeking employment elsewhere

EXTRA-ORGANIZATIONAL STRESSOR

There are additional sources of external occupational stress that Matteson & Ivancevich (1987) referred to as *extraorganizational stressors*. Included in this category are: (1) family; (2) relocation; (3) economic and financial; and (4) residential. Family stressors (e.g., marital discord, child-rearing pressures, dual career families) may affect workers' functioning on the job. For example, if a worker is unable to refrain from dwelling on a stressful family situation, the worker may be at risk for injury from not attending to safety aspects of the job. Conversely, work pressures may disrupt family life, increasing stress and strain in marital or other aspects of family functioning. During periods of company downsizing, relocation often upsets family stability, creating problems for both workers and family members. Economic and financial matters, especially during periods of economic recession, also place burdens on workers and their families, as the threat of a loss of financial stability may create sufficient anxiety to lead to one or more of the debilitating consequences of such stress as discussed earlier in this chapter. Lastly, residential stressors, or aspects of the community one lives in, may be yet another source of distress. When workers' hours, salary and benefits, and standard of living are eroded, they are often forced to live in less expensive, and often significantly more dangerous, surroundings. Thus, such extra-organizational stressors are, indeed, an important part of occupational stress.

The reality of multiple influences affecting stress responses is often disheartening to employers. They may appreciate the relevance of occupational stress from an organizational or workplace perspective, but believe that extra-organizational sources of stress are not deserving of consideration or workplace intervention. Such a dualistic perspective continues to be shared by even contemporary healthcare professionals who, for example, believe that individuals' problems are either mental or medical, valid or fraudulent, compensable or noncompensable, and similar polarized constructs. The reality is that workers, and people in general, are influenced by the stressors in all aspects of their lives.

COMPLEX NATURE OF OCCUPATIONAL STRESS

The impact of stress on personal health and well-being is complex and not easily predictable. It is important to note that not all stress is distressful. Healthy stress, referred to by Selye (1956) as *eustress*, may be regarded as necessary to cope with the ordinary demands of life and living. The important difference between what constitutes eustress rather than distress is the impact on the individual and performance. As performance demands, stress remains a positive, energizing force until the demands are too great for coping ability. At this point, as stress increases, there is an increased susceptibility for distress (i.e., a maladaptive response). In the workplace, this situation occurs when workers are challenged to perform to an appropriate productivity standard. If productivity demands are increased further, beyond the ability of the worker to respond or keep up, health is theoretically compromised incrementally, and the likelihood of a physical or emotional breakdown increases. When performance demands are too low, coupled with low job stress, personal health and well-being may also be compromised for the worse. Such a situation may occur when a worker is under-challenged to a point where work becomes uninteresting, monotonous, or boring. Such a condition is related to job burnout, occurring after prolonged periods of high stress. Burnout is characterized by feelings of hopelessness, thoughts of leaving and withdrawing from work, feeling demoralized, and work losing meaning for workers (Price, 1992).

Although this chapter focuses on occupational stress, in reality, stress has few territorial boundaries. Work-related situations that are perceived as stressful for some workers may not affect others similarly. Also, external stressors (e.g., family, finances, relationships) or personal lifestyle habits (e.g., lack of exercise, poor nutritional habits, cigarette smoking) may have a cumulative affect that results in one or several health problems. The effects of stress are complicated further by the individual's genetic composition, one that will protect for certain disorders yet produce vulnerability in others. Thus, it is difficult to predict how stressors will affect a given worker. Workers experiencing the same occupational pressures may be expected to respond in vastly different ways, from successful coping to a systems breakdown, be it physical or emotional.

There are multiple influences on individual experiences. For example, in a work environment, the worker may be strongly influenced by the physical aspects of her job, including the work setting, temperature, and other physical aspects of her job, including the work setting, temperature, and other physical aspects of the immediate external environment. She may also be aware of having internal physical experiences as well, including low back pain and a headache. Cognitively, she may be thinking that, despite the pain, she needs to stay at work rather than lose a day's pay. She may also be thinking about her sick child who stayed home this morning rather than going to school. Given these influences, her mood may be somewhat anxious, and she is prone to be emotional and distant from her job. Her work behavior is likely to be impaired, given her concerns, leading to lowered productivity and angry remarks from her supervisor, which, in turn, increases her stress. Given this scenario, one may predict that a variety of internal and external factors, influenced by job demands, personal health, economic matters, and family issues, may place this individual in a vulnerable position that contributes to a stress-related physical, emotional, behavioral, cognitive, or interpersonal problem as described in Figure 1.

CONTROLLING OCCUPATIONAL STRESS: PRELIMINARY ISSUES

Prior to initiating any occupational stress reduction program, management must be aware of issues that may, in large part, determine the outcome of such efforts. These issues include:

- Organizational readiness for actively engaging in a stress reduction program
- Preferred methods for detecting work stressors
- Impact of stress reduction program on the organizational climate

ORGANIZATIONAL READINESS FOR STRESS REDUCTION PROGRAMMING

Despite years of research and articles regarding occupational stress and its impact on worker productivity, workers' compensation losses, long-term disability claims, absenteeism, and the like, many employers appear reluctant to invest in identifying or initiating programs to reduce stress in the workplace. Evidence for this belief is difficult to document given the multifaceted nature of the workplace stress problems. The Northwestern National Life Insurance Company (1992) survey of workplace stress invited 195 private sector worksites to participate in their study, with 37 to 19% agreeing to participate. Of those companies that participated, only 50% returned completed questionnaires. No mention is made of why over 80% of those contacted chose not to participate, or why the response rate was 50%. Although it may be argued that this level of participation and response are favorable for this type of research, this may also represent a belief that occupational stress research will not have any favorable results. That this belief is the operating factor is a reasonable assumption given diminished resources related to economic recession, employers' perceptions that stress-related disorders – especially mental disorders – are fraudulent, and doubts that anything can be done to control job stress.

For those employers realizing that occupational stress is a serious matter affecting worker health and productivity, employee programs aimed at reducing workplace stress commonly include one to several "stress management" sessions for employees, as long as such sessions do not take up too much valuable work time. Paradoxically, many employers express much enthusiasm for identifying ways to reduce occupational stress claims, such as those cited earlier relative to California where occupational mental stress claims are commonplace. However, on closer examination, a majority of employers are interested more in learning about reducing fraud in stress-related claims than in implementing programs to reduce stress. Such beliefs about the nature of occupational stress serve as deterrents to reducing occupational stress, as employers' belief systems tend to rule out the existence of legitimate occupational stress employee problems.

Changing employers beliefs about worker motivation is not easy. Many employers and managers believe that their workers are not to be trusted and must be closely supervised to assure compliance with productivity standards and product quality. Such a management belief system is difficult to change given that there will be occasions when such beliefs are reinforced by worker behaviors. Unfortunately, incidental verifications of such beliefs are reinforced by worker behaviors. Unfortunately, incidental verifications of negative management beliefs are easily generalized to most, if not all workers. Such beliefs also bring suspicious or hostile actions towards workers who are seen as untrustworthy and ever-vigilant to take advantage of their employer. Conversely, there are managers who see their workers in a most favorable light and value their support and contribution to company goals and objectives. When this occurs workers are more likely to be valued, respected, and highly regarded. Such beliefs are likely to lead to management trusting workers and rewarding employees more often. In effect, workers may be watched, but in an effort to catch them doing something well.

DETECTING WORKPLACE STRESS

It is critical that employers, especially at a senior management level, take an active role in alleviating workplace stress if they wish to minimize their productivity and worker losses. Disability management emphasizes a proactive approach that progressive employers need to take to minimize such losses. A variety of options available for employers for identifying workplace stress problems, including both informal and formal procedures (Mace, 1992). Information identification of worker stress takes place through observation of behavior, including job performance evaluations, interactions with supervisors, interactions with peers, interactions with subordinates, and observed mood, especially when marked changes occur from previously observed mood or behavior. Matteson & Ivancevich (1987) identified several formal ways to identify worker stress, including: (1) the use of self-report questionnaires; (2) biochemical measures (measurement of stress-related hormones, such as corticosteroids, catecholamines, and cholesterol); (3) psychophysiological measures (e.g., heart rate, blood pressure); and (4) performance measures.

Mace (1992) reported that both informal and formal methods of stress detection have a variety of strengths and limitations, as shown in Figure 3:

I. Informal Methods:

   A. Strengths:
      (1) they are immediate, here and now happenings
      (2) measurement is ongoing
      (3) quick intervention methods may be used to lessen worker stress

   B. Limitation:
      (1) they tend to be unstructured
      (2) they are usually subjective and open to interpretation
      (3) and they are often difficult to measure

II. Formal Methods

   A. Strengths:
      (1) they are quantifiable
      (2) conducive to research and structured interventions

   B. Limitation:
      (1) potentially intrusive and difficult (e.g., biochemical, psychophysiological)
      (2) nonspecific unless carefully structured
      (3) may only questionably be related to worker experiences

Figure 3. Strengths and Limitations of Informal and Formal Workplace Stress Measures

Which method managers choose depends on a variety of factors, including availability of fiscal resources, internal personnel resources (e.g., human relations, organizational development specialists), availability of external consultants (e.g., psychologists, employee assistance counselors, wellness specialists), and management needs.

Once workplace stress has identified workplace stress as a concern to be addressed, it needs to consider identifying resources available to respond. Some companies have internal resources, such as organizational development specialists, usually located in human resource departments. External consultants may also be considered, including organizational stress experts such as clinical psychologists, employee assistance program counselors, occupational medicine specialists, organizational psychologists, and stress treatment specialists (Northwestern National Life Insurance Company, 1992). After the need for stress management intervention is determined, a useful first step is an anonymous survey of workers identified as being in need of stress management services. These workers are asked to complete, one or several, self-report questionnaires (e.g., Organizational Climate Survey, Lasky, 1992; SCL-90 R, Derogatis & Towson, 1990) aimed at identifying organizational stressors and workers' responses to workplace stress. Results from such measures provide a base of understanding of the need and emphasis for stress management training interventions. Depending upon identified needs, management may negotiate interventions, from a one-hour presentation to workers on relaxation or assertiveness to an ongoing program workshop encompassing a wide range of stress management intervention.

IMPACT OF STRESS REDUCTION EFFORTS ON THE ORGANIZATIONAL CLIMATE

Management must be prepared to respond to findings in a manner that will show workers that efforts to reduce stress are sincere and management is committed to make recommended changes. Unless such a commitment can be given by management, up front, there may be even greater stress generated by exploring and acting on stress-related findings in a half-hearted fashion. The adage "Be careful what you wish for, because you may get your wish" is especially true regarding organizational stress reduction efforts.

Expectations play an important role in organizational stress reduction programs. Management expects that investment in a stress reduction program should lead to identifiable outcomes (e.g., increased productivity, reduced absenteeism, or increased employee morale). Employees may have different expectations from management concerning their involvement in a stress reduction program (e.g., increased input in decision-making, job design changes, improved employee-management communication). Unless both management and employee expectations, are taken into account prior to any organizational stress reduction efforts, expectations discrepancies are likely to increase organizational stress. This risk may be minimized by assessing and clarifying expectations of any stress reduction efforts prior to conducting stress reduction training. Unfortunately, this is seldom done, resulting in expectation discrepancies for management and employees making matters worse than they were prior to stress reduction efforts.

One way to minimize organizational climate problems evolving after stress reduction efforts is to consider the outcome of such efforts prior to conducting training in stress reduction. For example, a stress reduction task force may be convened in the early stages of organizational stress reduction planning to identify possible goals and outcomes for the organizations. Such a task force may include management alone or management and employees together. Hypothetical outcomes may be generated by the task force in an effort to determine the impact on the organization from such outcomes, for better and for worse. Such planning would help to prepare the organization for any changes suggested by stress reduction programming. By considering the potential impact on the organization, management and employee expectation discrepancies, contributing to increased organizational stress, could be minimized.

CONTROLLING STRESS IN THE WORKPLACE

A well-known phrase that is applicable to controlling workplace stress is "an ounce of prevention is worth a pound of cure." Indeed, disability management concepts emphasize prevention and early intervention to reduce disability and related costs (Fruen, 1992). In this regard, there are three levels of prevention available to business and industry to help manage occupational stress: primary, secondary, and tertiary prevention (Quick, Murphy, Hurrell, & Orman, 1992). *Primary prevention* is concerned with the reduction of new cases of occupational stress and aims to reduce risk factors or change the nature of stressors. *Secondary prevention* attempts to alter the ways in which individuals respond to existing risks and stressors. *Tertiary prevention* tries to heal those who have been traumatized or distressed at work. Tertiary prevention or treatment has been the most common response to occupational distress, in the forms of therapeutic interventions from various medical or mental health practitioners. However, all three levels of prevention are closely related and no clear boundaries separate them. Each of these occupational stress prevention levels will be discussed with a focus on interventions and outcomes utilized by management.

PRIMARY PREVENTION

Primary prevention is often considered as the most preferred focus for reducing or eliminating occupational stress. It is designed to identify and target the sources of occupational stress and develop strategies to improve the situation. There is a wealth of information available to management on helping to make the workplace less stressful. This information is seldom packaged as "stress management" or similar terms relating to stress reduction, but the primary goals of progressive management systems include empowering employees, do-hassling the workplace, improving worker morale, and developing similar job-enhancing improvements. Most current strategies have been designed to help business and industry cope better with rapid changes in the national and world economy that demand new ways to adjust, not only in thinking and actions, but philosophy, belief systems, and management principles. For business and industry not to take needed changes seriously is to risk everything. With this in mind, progressive companies are rapidly changing to adapt to the demands and needs of workers and customers.

These areas of primary prevention that management has used directly or indirectly to reduce occupational stress and increase worker productivity, morale, and health are: (1) job design; (2) total quality management; and (3) worker-job matching systems. Each of these areas will be discussed with a focus on their impact in reducing occupational stress.

Job Design

Concerns related to job design may be physical or psychosocial. Physical occupational stressors include worker exposure to injury, exposure to neurotoxic agents, and ergonomic aspects of the job and workplace. The National Institute for Occupational Safety and Health (1988) has been a strong force in identifying exposure risks and helping industry to reduce or eliminate worker risks to neurotoxic disorders. Ergonomic issues concerning worker stress have been discussed at length elsewhere (e.g., Feuerstein, 1991; Luczak, 1992) and will not be reviewed in this chapter. Psychosocial stress related to job design will be discussed as a principal focus of primary prevention. Following an extensive review of the literature, Sauter, Murphy, and Hurrell (1990) proposed a variety of strategies to reduce workplace stress related to job design:

1. **Work Load and Work Place**

    Findings:
    a. Control over work load is more critical than work load per se when determining health consequences.
    b. Workers on machine-paced work are more vulnerable to adverse health effects, such as depression, anxiety, and somatic effects.

    Recommendations:
    a. Work loads should be commensurate with worker capabilities and resources.
    b. Workers should be provided with increased control over the pace of their work.

2. **Work Schedule**

    Findings:
    a. Rotating shifts and permanent night work have been linked to physical, emotional, and behavioral disturbances.

Recommendations:
a. Work schedules should take into account demands and responsibilities outside the job.
b. When shifts rotate, rotations should be stable and predictable, and should be in a forward (day-to-night) direction.

3. **Role Stressors:**

Finding:
a. Role ambiguity and conflict have been linked to emotional distress and high blood pressure.

Recommendation:
a. Roles and responsibilities at work should be well defined and clearly explained to reduce expectation discrepancies and related stress.

4. **Career Security Factors:**

Findings:
a. Lack of job security has been related to adverse psychological effects.

Recommendations:
a. Workers should be informed of promotional opportunities and avenues for growth within the organization.
b. Organizations should inform workers about developments that may affect their employment.

5. **Interpersonal Relations**

Findings:
a. Poor relationships with supervisors, fellow workers, and subordinates are important risk factors.
b. Social support at work or off work can buffer other adverse work effects.

Recommendation:
a. Jobs should provide opportunities for personal interaction for both emotional support and to help accomplish work tasks.

6. **Job Content**

    Findings:
    a. Jobs that allow better use of skills, provide little stimulation and have little intrinsic meaning, are associated with job dissatisfaction and poor mental health.

    Recommendation:
    a. Design jobs to provide meaning, stimulation, and opportunity to use skills.

Several important worker considerations are warranted given the above. First, it is clear that worker-perceived control over job tasks and the work environment is critical to avoid stress in the workplace. Also, many in the workforce are involved with shift work, rotating shifts, and night shifts. This appears to be a source of concern that, if not monitored carefully has great potential for added worker stress. Regarding role ambiguity there are many areas of business and industry that either do not have adequate job descriptions or have such descriptions written in vague and ambiguous terminology. If ambiguity and related stress are to be avoided, job descriptions should be criteria-based, meaning that job duties are objective and measurable. Too often the subjective negative evaluation of a supervisor contributes greatly to increased worker distress.

The recent study mentioned earlier in this chapter by Northwestern National Life Insurance Company (1992) clearly identified the recession, downsizing, "rightsizing," streamlining, and similar terms as contributors to worker stress. Many workers may fear the potential loss of their jobs when this is not a realistic threat. Employers would reduce worker stress by keeping workers informed about company status at all times, especially when the economy is suffering. Interpersonal relationships in the workplace are critical. Employers need to find ways to get workers involved with each other at the worksite as well as reinforcing a positive identity with the company after work hours (e.g., sporting events, picnics). There may also be many ways that boring, or dead-end jobs might be changed for the better. Actively seeking worker input regarding such changes is critical and directly related to the next section on total quality management.

Total Quality Management (TQM)

American industry is experiencing extensive change requiring innovative change strategies in order to survive and flourish (Peters, 1992). According to Hurrell, the "diseases of adaptation" resulting from the stress reaction are many and varied, including anxiety, depression, accidents on the job, and chronic illnesses like alcoholism and cardiac disease (cited in Bureau of National Affairs, 1992). Total quality management (TQM), and related quality-oriented approaches (e.g., continuous quality improvement, minor change to quality improvement), are rapidly becoming necessary for business and industry to compete on national and international levels. TQM is currently at the forefront of innovative management strategies aimed at (1) helping workers to reduce or eliminate stress and hassles in the workplace and (2) valuing worker input regarding constructive changes to help the company become more efficient, profitable, and hassle-free, while meeting customer needs.

Total quality management is an extension of the pioneering efforts of W. Edwards Deming and Joseph Juran who, during World War II, helped to develop a quality-based manufacturing system referred to as Statistical Quality Control (SQC). People working in manufacturing usually know SQC as a rigorous scientific method of identifying the quality and productivity that can be expected from a given production process (Drucker, 1992). As a process, SQC was effective in helping to identify malfunctions quickly, showing where they occurred, and encouraging workers to correct the problem immediately. The Japanese embraced this system following WWII with its focus on process and quality improvement. This was a move that, in large part, turned the Japanese economy into the world economic power it is today. According to Drucker (1992), "Japan's major productivity gains are the result of social changes brought about by SQC" (p. 303). American industry has not been as enthusiastic about making the many changes inherent in SQC thinking and action during the past 40 years. Only within the past 10 years has American industry, from manufacturing to service industries such as health care, taken steps toward change emphasizing quality. Interestingly, Henry Ford (1926), in his book, *Today and Tomorrow*, offered a variety of ideas that endure today (e.g., consider your customer's needs first; use continuous improvement in design and manufacturing; create new markets by lowering your cost) that are very much in line with TQM thinking. Such ideas, however, have until recently, been largely ignored by American companies.

Total Quality Management embraces a way of thinking that is different from conventional management thinking. Peters, (1991) identified various ways in which TQM thinking differs from conventional management thinking: (1) In conventional management (CM) thinking quality improvement costs money and time; in TQM thinking, quality improvement saves money and time; (2) In CM thinking, quality is as important as quality; in TQM, without quality, quantity is irrelevant; (3) in CM thinking, work is a series of events; in TQM, work is an integrated process; (4) in CM thinking, quality is the result of better inspection; in TQM, quality is built in from the start; and (5) in CM thinking, to achieve quality, we need more and better people; in TQM thinking, quality can be achieved with the people you have right now, simply by leading and training them differently. Unfortunately, it is not easy to change from CM thinking to TQM thinking, prompting many companies trying to make such changes to not only fail in TQM, but to revert to a more recalcitrant form of conventional management. Lasky & Mace (1993) elaborated on the many ways management can fail at TQM, despite the best of efforts to implement TQM practices and principles.

Numerous American companies have reported significant favorable changes by embracing TQM concepts. For example, Peters (1992) reported that circa 1988 Titeflex, a Springfield, MA company manufacturing flexible hoses, was bogged down in paperwork and bureaucracy adversely affecting workers and productivity. By implementing management changes in line with TQM thinking, smaller teams of workers were empowered to make changes as necessary to make systems function more effectively; business was significantly improved. One recent approach described by the Japan Human Relations Association (1992), in their book *Kaizen Teian 2*, presents a way of thinking to enhance worker morale and productivity. *Kaizen* refers to the "continuous incremental improvement of standard work practices." A *Teian* is a proposal or suggestions, so *Kaizen Teian* is a company-wide system for formulating, evaluating, and implementing continuous quality improvement proposals from workers. When workers are valued for their input, no matter how small, reduced occupational stress is a predicted by-product. Numerous such examples of the positive impact of empowering workers and using TQM thinking, beyond the scope of this chapter, have been documented (e.g., Berry & Parasuraman, 1992; Peters, 1992; Townsend & Gebhardt, 1990; Walton, 1990).

Worker-Job Matching

In recent years there has been a renewed interest in matching workers with their jobs on the basis of psychosocial factors. An outgrowth of the personality and vocational testing movement in the 1950s, known as the trait-factor approach (Guilford, 1959; Williamson, 1965), assumes that traits are the properties of persons, not of behavior; traits are inferred from behavior. Holland (1959) proposed that job choice is related to personality and identified six orientations, or personality styles that have counterparts in the workplace: Realistic, Investigative, Social, Conventional, Enterprising, Artistic. For example, a person having an "investigative" orientation would likely have a preference for thinking rather than acting, associability rather than sociability, and would prefer occupations that mirror these characteristics in terms of job category, such as occupations in the technical and scientific fields. The vocational matching system developed by Holland has found widespread research support (e.g., Cole & Hanson, 1971; Edwards & Whitney, 1972) and is a key component in many currently used vocational interests inventories (Campbell & Hansen, 1981; Johansson, 1986).

There are a variety of approaches used that are related to trait-factor and personality characteristics associated with vocational choice and psychosocial aspects of occupations (e.g., Carlson Learning's Personal Profile System [PPS]; Wilson

Learning's Social Styles Inventory; and the Myers-Briggs Type Indicator). Typically, such approaches use paper-and-pencil instruments designed to determine the person's style vis-a-vis four personal factors that purportedly correlate with certain aspects of work, such as leadership style, preferred work environments, and strengths and limitations regarding interpersonal functioning.

In the Carlson Personal Profile System, for example, a brief questionnaire yields interpretive information that reveals a profile pattern of four factors – Dominance, Influencing, Steadiness, and Cautiousness. A person scoring high in "Dominance" is reported to have tendencies such as wanting immediate results, initiating action, and finding challenges reinforcing. The dominant style is also related to needing work environments that include power and authority and provide the opportunity to accomplish result. Another primary style, the "Cautious" style, reflects tendencies including having preferences for tasks requiring attention to details and working under strict guidelines. "Cautious" style workers have a preference for secure and stable work environments. The PAS approach also describes how people with differing styles are likely to relate to one another – for better or for worse. An important assumption for the PAS and other four-factor systems, is that each style has limitations that may be supported by other styles' strengths. Essentially, there is no one best personal style, although there are some assumptions made that personal styles are suited to different types of work. Thus, all things considered, the "Dominant" style may be expected to prefer and function better on jobs such as manager, politician, or senior administrator. The worker with the "Cautious" style would likely do better in job areas such as accounting, engineering, or quality control testing.

Reviews concerning the efficacy of personality systems such as those above have been inconclusive. Lee (1991) provided a review of various instruments designed to reveal personal profiles related to work demands. In this review, the appeal of such instruments to helping identify worker-job matches was noted. However, the potential for abuse was also presented, as "the enthusiasm for trainers greatly exceeding the validity evidence of some of these instruments." Indeed, on the surface, four-factor personality instruments are enticing given their apparent implicity, but there is little regard for the complexity that permeates worker-job matching within complex work environments. This leaves the door open for potential error or abuse in determining worker-job compatibility. Additionally, those who administer such testing are not often required to have professional credentials related to counseling or testing. An enthusiastic marketer of such worker-job matching instruments is in a position to oversell instruments promising to efficiently place the right person with the right job; let the buyer beware.

SECONDARY PREVENTION

Secondary occupational stress prevention may be regarded as the implementation of worksite stress management interventions that aim to prevent or reduce the duration, intensity, and impairment of existing stress-related physical, emotional, cognitive, or behavioral problems. Many companies recognize the potential losses that workplace stress contributes in the form of worker health problems, lowered productivity, and injured worker compensation plans. This awareness has prompted many companies to provide stress management interventions for workers. One of the earliest attempts to reduce workers stress, conducted at the Converse Rubber Company in Boston, was a relaxation/meditation program to reduce worker blood pressure (Peters, Benson & Porter, 1977). After a 12-week relaxation/meditation program, workers demonstrated a statistically significant reduction of blood pressure, albeit the reduction was considered too small to be of clinical significance. Another study, using a variety of psychological treatment strategies (e.g., relaxation, biofeedback, psychotherapy) aimed at reducing worker headaches and general anxiety resulted in a significant reduction of symptoms and a significant cost-benefit to the company, evidenced by $5.50 saved for every $1 invested in the program over a three-year period (Manuso, 1983).

A variety of stress management programs have been offered to workers, generally with favorable outcomes reported. Meditation and relaxation training sessions were provided to New York Telephone workers. These sessions were found to reduce workers' anxiety, hostility, and depression, while increasing stress coping skills (Carrington et al., 1980; Collings, 1984). In another study, workers were provided with relaxation exercises and increased participation in the workplace, leading to an increase in worker job satisfaction, increased quality of job performance, and a reduction of malpractice risk (Jones & Hall, 1988). After an extensive review of stress management intervention programs in the workplace, Ivancevich, Matteson, Freedman, and Phillips (1990) concluded that there is a need for more rigorous research designs, better controls, and more representative worker samples, Furthermore, the research to date on the use of stress management interventions in the workplace has been encouraging but still replete with anecdotes, testimonials, and methodologically weak research designs.

TERTIARY PREVENTION

Workers who succumb to problems related to workplace stress often find help coping and overcoming their difficulties by using corporate employee assistance programs (EAPs). In this chapter, a review of industry-based stress management tertiary prevention interventions will focus on an overview of EAPs, with logistical concerns germane to EAPs in the workplace.

The EAP is an important resource for many American workers experiencing occupational stress. For many companies, troubled workers are referred to EAP counselors to evaluate, treat, and make referrals to external human service resources. A primary aim of most EAPs is to respond quickly and efficiently to worker problems that may be interfering with worker productivity. Many companies also have EAPs that provide programs and information pertaining to worker wellness. Since the early 1950s, EAPs have evolved from "traditional" programs, focused on helping workers with alcohol programs, to "broad brush" programs that help workers with a wide range of problems (e.g., alcohol and substance abuse, personal and family problems, occupational stress). The growth of EAPs is shown by the change from 25% of Fortune 500 companies having EAPs in the early 1970s, to 80% of these companies currently having EAP programs (Bureau of National Affairs, 1987). There has also been a dramatic increase in the number of EAPs in the last 40 years, from an estimated 100 programs in the United States in 1950, to more than 10,000 such programs currently (Feldman, 1991).

Many EAP programs embrace the traditional model of helping workers impaired by alcohol abuse. There are a number of advantages of traditional alcohol abuse-oriented EAP programs. Alcohol continues to be the drug of choice for many workers who seek to find relief from the stress of everyday living. It is not uncommon for people to have a drink or two following a stressful day at the office, and alcohol may even be expected in certain stress-related business transactions. It has been estimated that 12% of any workforce has alcohol- or drug-related problems (Kiernan, 1992). Once the substance abuse problem has been treated, work and other problems often disappear. Substance abuse is often related to many other serious physical and emotional illnesses and even mortality. These, and related, advantages of traditional alcohol-oriented EAPs help to reverse many of the direct and indirect problems associated with occupational stress. However, there are problems associated with traditional programs. Many traditional EAP program counselor are continuing to work on their own recovery from alcoholism. Although "having been there" has certain advantages, traditional EAP counselors may feel that the only treatment that works is what has worked for them, and this is often expensive inpatient care. Also, many workers may feel the need for help but deny that their problems are alcohol-related, and thus avoid going to the traditional EAP counselor who may be perceived as a recovering alcoholic.

Broad brush EAPs typically provide counseling and referral for a wide variety of psychosocial and work-related problems. Problems other than alcohol and drug abuse are seen as just as real and debilitating. Often problems in the workplace are related to difficulties with family members and significant others, leading to problems such as codependency and any of the stress-related symptoms identified earlier in this chapter. For many workers, broad brush programs do not have the stigma associated with traditional programs that focus on alcohol and drug abuse. There are, however, several problems with broad brush EAPs that may compromise their effectiveness. First, companies may not wish to foster a sense of paternalism or dependent relationships with employees by being perceived as a provider of many expanded services. Rather, companies may wish to increase employee responsibility for issues that are seen as being beyond the workplace. Also, broad brush programs may become a dumping ground for problems workers versus finding improved strategies for managing employees. Another difficulty with broad brush programs is in identifying and treating the major, secondary, and additional problems affecting workers. In this regard, broad brush EAPs may be charged to any and all worker problems, when change in the workplace environment or management practices may be a more attractive alternative.

An additional concern regarding EAPs is whether they should be within or external to the company. Internal EAPs are those that provide in-house staff for assessment, treatment, referral and follow-up services. Internal EAPs have the advantage of a greater knowledge of the dynamics and managerial style affecting the organizational climate. Managers and workers can also be easily informed about the advantages of using the internal EAP, although an external EAP can easily provide in-house training in response to worker or management needs. There is also a greater likelihood that management will regard the internal EAP more favorably, as if it is seen as a branch of the corporate family. There are several potential disadvantages of internal EAPs. Undoubtedly, the greatest difficulty is perceived confidentiality. Even if strong safeguards are in place, workers are often reluctant to use internal EAPs because of the perceived threat that information will be provided to management, with severe consequences. Also, there is often a staffing problem, with management being unwilling to provide significant staff and counseling services for the internal EAP to function effectively.

External EAPs are programs contracted with agencies outside the company. One obvious advantage or the external EAP is a reduced expense to smaller companies that often cannot afford the staffing of an internal EAP. Another advantage is location being independent and external to the company; this also enhances workers' perceptions of greater confidentiality. External EAPs also may utilize additional counseling agencies where indicated. There are disadvantages in using external EAPs. An external EAP is less likely to be truly aware of the organizational culture and management style that affects workers well-being. Companies with external EAPs may feel removed from such external programs aimed at reducing worker distress. Lastly, companies may not feel the need to involve external EAPs with internal company matters, such as management training and worker stress management programs.

Management has a variety of options open regarding the use of EAPs as discussed above. EAPs are designed to provide timely interventions to problems that, if ignored, might lead to more costly and long-term care. Employers must examine their current practices in responding to worker distress to determine if an EAP will best meet their needs, and what kind will be most appropriate.

PRACTICAL ISSUES IN PROVIDING WORKPLACE STRESS REDUCTION SERVICES

Disability management practitioners, and employers, recognizing the need for reducing worker stress, are often faced with important practical issues about implementing workplace stress reduction services. Several important areas of concern about implementing such services include: (1) level of management concern; (2) service providers; (3) timing of intended service; (4) identified worker groups; and (5) programs evaluation.

SERVICE PROVIDERS

An important initial consideration is who is best equipped to provide workplace stress reduction services. The recommendation of the Northwest National Life Insurance Company (1991) report addressed this issue, recommending the following as organizational stress experts:

- clinical psychologists
- employee assistance program counselor
- occupational medicine specialist
- organizational psychologists
- stress treatment specialists
- wellness specialists

Certainly any of these practitioners is potentially able to provide stress reduction training to workers. Whoever does provide services is encouraged to find out, as precisely as possible, what the need for services is in a given company, what has been done in the past to address identified, or related needs, the outcome of prior intervention services, management involvement (e.g., policies and practices) in promoting organizational stressors, and openness of management to make organizational changes, where indicated, to reduce worker stress.

LEVEL OF MANAGEMENT CONCERN

Your friend Harry is a supervisor at the ADT Valve Company. He mentions to you his concern about stress that he's experiencing, as are other supervisors, due to layoffs and increased workloads. He would like to have someone come into his plant to provide a stress management seminar for supervisors. He asks for your advice, since you have done this for other companies. Of course, Harry will have to discuss this with senior management for approval. It may help if he has some specific information about your services, such as what you have done with other companies, outcome data, etc. Also, it helps if there is a documented need for services. Upper management may be unaware, or even deny, that workplace stress is contributing to company losses. There may be hope that their becoming informed about the scope of the problem may be persuasive enough to go to the level of considering what to do next. Sometimes, only the CEO must be convinced that examining the issue of workplace stress is warranted. One way or another, upper management must believe that there is a problem that affects more than one or a few workers, and that stress management interventions will help to resolve the problem. Towards these ends, the provider of services must have a good understanding of issues relevant to the specific company, including who is in the position to make decisions about providing stress reduction services in the workplace, whether or not such programs have been conducted previously, outcome of such services, etc. Such preparation in the preliminary stages of providing workplace stress reduction services is critical if one is to be considered favorably as a service provider.

TIMING OF WORKPLACE STRESS INTERVENTIONS

In health care, early intervention is generally agreed to be desirable. Some employers are using pre-employment psychological tests in an effort to reduce losses. Borofsky (1993) presented a case study comparing lost time due to accidents, lost time due to unauthorized absences, and turnover rates for two groups of workers in a medium-sized manufacturing company. A group of employees hired prior to using psychological screening was compared to a second group who was pre-screened on psychological tests. It was found that twice as many employees from the unscreened group were involved in accidents that from the second, screened (tested) group. Also, during the 1989 period, workers in the unscreened group accounted for lost time totaling almost 8% of total scheduled hours, whereas the test group lost time totaling 1.75%. During 1991, the company experienced 104 OSHA recordable injuries and illnesses, 94% of which involved the untested group with only 6% attributable to the tested employees. It is important to note that there may be legal or ethical issues regarding the use of pre-employment psychological testing, and such matters should be carefully examined prior to using psychological questionnaires for employment purposes.

Balzer and Kocher (1993) argue that preventing disability is a primary goal, especially when dealing with workers' compensation losses. More specifically, they encourage the use of psychological intervention for work injuries, combined with physical rehabilitation to avoid work injuries becoming chronic and costly for employers. Corey and Wolf (1992) also argue for the use of an integrated therapeutic approach, including psychological intervention, with a focus not only on the injured worker, but supervisors and peers, the relationship of the worker to significant others at work, and the work environment. Such a systems-oriented focus helps to provide a better understanding of all aspects that might be contributing to worker distress. Bigos, Battie, and Spengler, (1991) found that emotional distress, existing prior to the injury and not necessarily related to work, may raise the likelihood of reporting low back pain at work, while reducing coping capabilities and leading to longer convalescence. Frymoyer (1992) also reviewed conditions affecting length of disability in low back pain, finding that psychosocial and environmental factors are much more predictive of disability than are the physical aspects of the job. He found that there are three predictors of disability: (1) work environment (e.g., quality of supervisory and co-worker relationships, physical condition of the job, repetitive or menial tasks); (2) perception of compensability; and (3) the duration of the current episode. Frymoyer recommends early and aggressive interdisciplinary rehabilitation, combining physical and psychosocial therapy intervention. Thus, regarding secondary and tertiary prevention, especially with back injuries, early psychosocial interventions appears warranted, yet is seldom supported by insurers who are disinclined to use such services during initial phases of evaluation or treatment for fear of driving up costs.

TARGETED WORKER GROUPS

The information provided in this chapter suggests that all workers can benefit from all levels of workplace stress prevention. Unfortunately, blue collar workers are often the last to receive any formal stress reduction training, yet the greatest risks in a given business or industry may lie with these workers. One way to determine which worker to target for stress reduction intervention is asking employees directly through structured interviews, or asking workers to respond to a brief questionnaire, such as the Organizational Climate Survey developed by Lasky (1992), or the Northwestern National Life Insurance Company (1992) NWNL Workplace Stress Test, both designed to assess the presence and impact of occupational stress. Information from such questionnaires helps to determine worker perceptions of the extent, severity, and specificity of workplace stress problems. This information may then form a base from which any stress reduction interventions are negotiated within a given company.

PROGRAM EVALUATION

It is critical for any workplace stress reduction program to monitor the effectiveness of the proposed program. Ideally, a well-designed study will take into account matters pertaining to internal and external validity, as well as other issues addressed in most resources pertaining to research design (e.g., Anastasi, 1982; Kazdin, 1980). Without such an evaluative component, there may be no way of telling what effect, if any, even the best of interventions had with the worker population studied. If group designs are not feasible, well-designed single-case studies may be applicable, such as a multiple baseline design (Barlow & Hersen, 1984). Stress reduction trainers are strongly encouraged to be data driven, not only to verify their training, but as a source of providing data to use in marketing their services to other prospective companies.

CONCLUSIONS

Despite the semantic issues relating to the term *stress* presented in this chapter, it is clear that workplace stress adversely affects workers' physical, emotional, and behavioral well-being. Efforts are being made by progressive business and industry to de-hassle the workplace, with Total Quality Management and related strategies aimed to increase worker empowerment, prevent workplace inefficiency, and increase productivity. Other systems of controlling stress on the job, including physical and psychosocial job design changes, matching workers and jobs on relevant psychosocial characteristics, employee assistance programs, and stress management programs at the workplace certainly appear to be responsive to helping workers to reduce distress. However, there remains a need for research support of these efforts if there is to be a favorable cost-benefit accounting.

The existing literature relating to workplace stress interventions remains deficient in the area of well-designed research substantiating the impact of stress reduction interventions on any number of important outcome variables (e.g., worker health, disability costs, productivity, morale). Much of the current documentation concerning workplace stress control remains anecdotal, with well-intended effective stress reduction interventions for workers that often present favorable outcomes. However, this is not sufficient. Increasingly, employers are remiss in entertaining any form of human service intervention without assurance that this will have some "bottom-line" impact, especially in terms of revenue saved. In this regard, researchers and clinicians must be ready to provide data supporting their intentions to reduce worker stress and document the value this has to employers in concrete terms. This is the era of management care in the health care industry. For better or for worse, the need for workplace stress interventions must be well documented, as must proposed services aiming to make significant reductions in worker stress.

Unfortunately, workplace stress is not always easy to document, many managers continue to adhere to Theory X beliefs and actions, and some companies may even regard workplace stress-related problems as a write-off, or the cost of doing business. For such persons, even reams of the most thorough research support showing the favorable impact of workplace stress management programs will have little effect. Hopefully, the information presented in this chapter refutes such thinking, and provides an impetus for disability management services to view workplace stress as a primary need for both workers and management.

REFERENCES

Anastasi, A. (1982). *Psychological testing.* New York: Macmillan.

Antonovsky, A. (1982). *Health, stress, and coping.* San Francisco, CA: Jossey-Bass.

Asteria, M. F. (1985). *The physiology of stress.* New York: Human Sciences Press.

Balzer, D., & Kocher, B. (1993). Early psychological intervention limits chronic claims costs. *Work Injury Management, 2*(1), 1-4.

Barlow, D. H., & Hersen, M. (1984). *Single case experimental designs: Strategies of studying behavior change.* Elmsford, NY: Pergamon Press.

Beck, A. T. (1976). *Cognitive therapy and the emotional disorders.* New York: Times-Mirror.

Beehr, T. A. (1991). Stress in the workplace: An overview. In J. W. Jones, B. D. Steffy, & D. W. Bray (Eds.), *Applying psychology in business: The handbook for managers and human resource professionals* (pp. 709-714). Lexington, MA: Lexington Books.

Berry, L., & Parasuraman, A. (1992). *Marketing services: Competing through quality.* New York: Free Press.

Bigos, S. J., Battie, M. C., & Spengler, D. M. (1991). A prospective study of work perceptions and psychosocial factors affecting the report of back injury. *Spine, 16,* 1-6.

Bureau of National Affairs. (1987). *Employee assistance programs: Benefits, problems, and prospects.* Washington, DC: Bureau of National Affairs Response Center.

Bureau of National Affairs. (1992, April). *Workers' Compensation Report, 3*(8), 178-179.

Bureau of National Affairs. (1992, August). *Workers' Compensation Report, 3*(16), 352-353.

Burns, D. D. (1980). *Feeling good.* New York: New American Library.

California Workers' Compensation Institute. (1990, June). *Mental stress claims in California workers' compensation: Incidence, costs and trends.* CWCI Research notes. (Available from CWCI, 120 Montgomery Street, Suite 1300, San Francisco).

Campbell, D. P., & Hansen, J. C. (1981). *Manual for the SVIB-SCII* (3rd Ed.), Palo Alto, CA: Stanford University Press.

Carrington, P., Collings, C. H., Benson, H., Robinson, H., Word, L. W., Lehrer, P. M., Woolfolk, R., & Cole, J. W. (1980). The use of medication — relaxation techniques for the management of stress in a working population. *Journal of Occupational Medicine, 22,* 221-231.

Cohen, S., & Williamson, G. M. (1991). Stress and infectious disease in humans. *Psychological Bulletin, 109*(1), 5-24.

Cole, N. S., & Hanson, G. (1971). *An analysis of the structure of interests* (ACT Research Report No. 40). Iowa City: American College Testing Program.

Collings, C. H. (1984). Stress and the workplace. In S. M. Weiss, J. A. Herd, N. E. Millers, & S. Weiss (Eds.), *Psychological factors at work: Their relation to health* (pp. 99-108). Geneva, Switzerland: World Health Organization.

Cooper, C. L., & Marshall, J. (1976). Occupational sources of stress: A review of the literature relating to coronary heart disease and mental health. *Journal of Occupational Psychology, 9,* 11-28.

Corey, D. M., & Wolf, G. D. (1992). An integrated approach to reducing stress injuries. In J. Quirk, L. Murphy, & J. Hurrell (Eds.), *Stress and well-being at work.* Washington, DC: American Psychological Association.

Courtney, J. (1992, October). *Current perspectives on stress related disability claims.* Paper presented at the Occupational Stress Institute, sponsored by Liberty Mutual Insurance Company, Orange, CA.

Derogatis, L. R. & Towson, M. D. (1990). *SCL-90-R.* Minneapolis, MN: National Computer Systems.

DeVader, C. L., & Giampetro-Meyer, A. (1991). Reducing managerial distress about stress: An analysis and evaluation of alternatives for reducing stress-based workers' compensation claims. *Santa Clara Law Review, 31*(1).

Dohrenwend, B. S., & Dohrenwend, B. P. (1981). Life stress and illness: Formulation of the issues. In B. S. Dohrenwend & B. P. Dohrenwend (Eds.), *Stressful life events and their contexts* (pp. 1-27), Canton, MA: Neale Watson.

Dohrenwend, B. S., & Shrout, P. E. (1985). Hassles in the conceptualization and measurement of life stress variables. *American Psychologist, 40*, 780-785.

Drucker, P. F. (1992). *Managing for the future: The 1990s and beyond.* New York: Truman Talley Books.

Edwards, K. J. & Whitney, D. R. (1972). A structural analysis of Holland's personality types using factor and configural analysis. *Journal of Counseling Psychology, 19*, 136-145.

Ellis, A. (1962). *Reason and emotion in psychotherapy.* Secaucus, NJ: Citadel Press.

Feldman, S. (1991). Today's EAPs make the grade. *Personal, 68*, 4.

Feuerstein, M. (1991). A multidisciplinary approach to the prevention, evaluation, and management of work disability. *Journal of Occupational Rehabilitation, 1*, 5-12.

Fitzgerald, T. E. (1992). Psychosocial aspects of work-related musculoskeletal disability. In J. C. Quick, L. R. Murphy, & J. J. Hurrell (Eds.), *Stress and well-being at work.* Washington: American Psychological Association.

Ford, H. (1926). *Yesterday, today, and tomorrow.* New York: Doubleday.

Frankenhauser, M. (1991). The psychophysiology of workload, stress, and health: Comparison between the sexes. *Annals of Behavioral Medicine, 13*, (4), 197-204.

Friend, K. E. (1982). Stress and performance: Effects of subjective work load and time urgency. *Personnel Psychology, 35*, 623-633.

Fruen, M. (1992). Disability management focuses on prevention. *Business and Health*, October, 24-28.

Frymoyer, J. W. (1992). Predicting disability from low back pain. *Clinical Orthopaedics and Related Research, 279*, 101-109.

Guilford, J. P. (1959). *Personality.* New York: McGraw-Hill.

Hedge, A. (1989). Environmental conditions and health in offices. *International Review of Ergonomics, 3*, 87-110.

Hedge, A., Burge, P. S., Robertson, A. S., Wilson, S., & Harris-Bass, J. (1989). Work-related illness in offices: A proposed model of the "sick building syndrome. *Environmental International, 15*, 143-158.

Hedge, A., Erickson, W. A., & Rubin, G. (1991). *The effects of smoking policy on indoor air quality and sick building syndrome in 18 air-conditioned offices.* In Proceedings: Healthy buildings-IAQ '91 ASHRAE Conference (pp. 151-159). Atlanta, GA: American Society of Hating, Refrigeration, and Air Conditioning Engineers.

Holland, J. (1959). A theory of vocational choice. *Journal of Counseling Psychology, 6*, 35-45.

Ivancevich, J. M., Matteson, M. T., Freedman, S. M., & Phillips, J. S. (1990). Worksite stress management interventions. *American Psychologist, 45*, 252-261.

Japan Human Relations Association. (1992). *Kaizen Teian 2.* Cambridge, MA: Productivity Press.

Jex, S. M., Beehr, T. A., Terry, A., & Roberts, C. (1992). The meaning of occupational stress items to survey responses. *Journal of Applied Psychology, 5*(77), 623-628.

Johansson, C. B. (1986). *Career Assessment inventory manual.* Minneapolis: National Computer Systems.

Johnson, J. V., & Hall, E. M. (1988), Job strain, workplace social support, and cardiovascular disease: A cross-sectional study of a random sample of the Swedish working population. *American Journal of Public Health, 78*, 1336-1342.

Jones J. W. (1984). A cost evaluation for stress management. *EAP Digest, 1*, 34-39.

Jones J. W., Barge, B. N., Steffy, B. D., Fay, L. M., Kuntz, L. K., & Webber, L. J. (1988). Stress and medical malpractice: Organizational risk assessment and intervention. *Journal of Applied Psychology, 73*, 727-735.

Kanner, A. D., Coyne, J. C., Schaeffer, C., & Lazarus, R. S. (1981). Comparison of two modes of stress measurement: Daily hassles and uplifts versus major life events. *Journal of Behavioral Medicine, 4*, 1-39.

Karasek, R., Baker, D., Marxer, F., Ahlbom, A., & theorell, T. (1981). Job decision latitude, job demands, and cardiovascular disease: A prospective study of Swedish men. *American Journal of Public Health, 71*, 694-705.

Kazdin, A. E. (1980). *Research design in clinical psychology.* New York: Harper & Row.

Kendig, E. (1992). *Legal perspectives on stress-related losses.* Presentation at the Occupational Stress Institute, sponsored by Liberty Mutual Insurance Company, Orange, CA.

Kiernan, T. (1992, October). *Employee assistance programs and occupational stress.* Paper presented at the Occupational Stress Institute, sponsored by Liberty Mutual Insurance Company, Orange, CA.

Kobasa, S. C. (1979). Stressful life events, personality and health: An inquiry into hardiness. *Journal of Personality and Social Psychology, 37*, 1-11.

Kobasa, S. C., Maddi, S. R., & Kahn, S. (1982). Hardiness and health: A prospective study. *Journal of Personality and Social Psychology, 42*(1), 168-177.

LaCroix, A. Z., & Haynes, S. G. (1987). Gender differences in the genderness of workplace roles: A focus on work and health. In R. Barnett, G. Baruch, & L. Biener (Eds.), *Gender and stress* (pp. 96-121). New York: Free Press.

Lasky, R. (1992). *Organizational climate survey.* Unpublished Manuscript.

Lazarus, R., & Folkman, S. (1984). *Stress, appraisal, and coping.* New York: Springer.

Lee, C. (1991). What's your style? *Training*, May, 27-31.

Luczak, H. (1992). Good work design: An ergonomic, industrial engineering perspective. In J. C. Quick, L. R. Murphy, and J. J. Hurrell (Eds.), *Stress & well-being at work.* Washington: American Psychological Association.

Mace, D. L. (1992, October). *Controlling stress on the job: What management can do.* Paper presented at the Occupational Stress Institute, sponsored by Liberty Mutual Insurance Company, Orange, CA.

MacLennan, B. (1992). Stressor reduction: An organizational alternative to individual stress management. In J. C. Quick, L. R Murphy, & J. J. Hurrell (Eds.), *Stress and well-being at work.* Washington, DC: American Psychological Association.

Miller, A., Springen, K., Gordon, J., Murr, A., Cohn, B., Drew, L., & Barrett, T. (1988, April). Stress on the job. *Newsweek.*

National Center for Health Statistics. (1989). *Viral and health statistics: Health characteristics by occupation and industry, United States, 1983-85* (PHS No. 90-1598). Washington, DC: Author.

National Institute for Occupational Safety and Health. (1988). A national strategy for the prevention of psychological disorders. In *Proposed national strategies for the prevention of leading work-related diseases and injuries, Part 2,* NTIS Publication No. PB89-130348, Cincinnati, OH: Author.

National Safety Council. (1991). *Accident facts.* Chicago: Author.

Northwestern National Life Insurance Company. (1991). *Employee burnout: America's newest epidemic.* Minneapolis, MN: Author.

Northwestern National Life Insurance Company. (1992). *Employee burnout: Causes and cures.* Minneapolis, MN: Author.

Peters, R., Benson, H., & Porter, D. (1977). Daily relaxation breaks in a working population: Effects on self-reported measures of health, performance, and well-being. *American Journal of Public Health, 67,* 946-953.

Peters, T. (1991). *Tom Peters live.* Boulder, CO: CareerTrack Publications.

Peters, T. 91992). *Liberation management.* New York: Knopf.

Price, R. H. (1992). Employee stress levels. In Northwestern National Life, *Employee burnout: Causes and cures.* Minneapolis, MN.

Quick, J. C., & Quick, J. D. (1984). *Organizational stress and preventative management.* New York: McGraw-Hill.

Quick, J. C., Murphy, L. R., Hurrell, J. J., & Orman, D. (1992). The value of work, the risk of distress, and the power of prevention. In J. Quick, L. Murphy, and J. Hurrell (Eds.), *Stress and well-being at work.* Washington, DC: American Psychological Association.

Sauter, S. L., Murphy, L. R., and Hurrell, J. J. (1990). Prevention of work-related psychological disorders: A national strategy proposed by the National Institute for Occupational Safety and Health. *American Psychologist, 45*(10), 1146-1158.

Selye, H. (1956). *The stress of life.* New York: McGraw-Hill.

Spector, P. E., Dwyer, D. J., & Jex, S. M. (1988). Relation of job stressors to effective, health, and performance outcomes: A comparison of multiple data sources. *Journal of Applied Psychology, 73,* 11-19.

Spitzer, W. O., LeBlanc, F. E., & Dupuis, M. (1987) Scientific approach to the assessment, and management of activity-related spinal disorders: A monograph for clinicians. Report of the Quebec task force on spinal disorders. *Spine, 75,* (Suppl.), 3-59.

Staff. (1992, March). AIDS in the workplace will increase job stress. *Stress Management Advisor,* p. 1.

Toffler, A. (1970). *Future shock.* New York: Random House.

Townsend, P., & Gebhardt, J. (1990). *Commit to quality.* New York: John Wiley & Sons.

Tyroler, A., Haynes, S. G., Cobb, L. A., Irvin, C. W., James, S. A., Kuller, L. S., Miller, R. E., Schumacher, S. A., Syme, S., & Wolf, S. (1987). Environmental risk factors in coronary heart disease. *Circulation, 76* (Supple. I), 139-144.

Waddell, G., Morris, E. W., DiPaola, M., Bircher, M., & Finlayson, D., (1986). A concept of illness tested as an improved basis for surgical decisions in low-back disorders. *Spine, 11,* 712-719.

Walton, M. (1990). *Deming management at work.* New York: G. P. Putman's Sons.

Williamson, E. G. (1965). *Vocational counseling: Some historical, philosophical, and theoretical perspectives.* New York: McGraw-Hill.

Weinberger, M., Hiner, S. L., & Tierney, W. M. (1987). In support of hassles as a measure of stress predicting health outcomes. *Journal of Behavioral Medicine, 10,* 19-31.

—14—

Disability Management: A Family Perspective

Paul W. Power, Sc.D., C.R.C.
Arthur E. Dell Orto, Ph. D., C.R.C.

INTRODUCTION

The United States has recently witnessed an unprecedented increase in the cost of health care and work-related disability (Shrey & Breslin, 1992). Each year about one-half of one percent of employed persons in the United States experience work disruptions lasting at least five months because of a disabling injury or illness (Hester & Decelles, 1985). According to the National Institute for Occupational Safety and Health, half the work force will suffer some type of occupational disorder by the year 2000 (Jacobs, 1992). Consequently, employers can expect an average of 75 lost work days per year per 100 full-time workers due to work-related disabilities (Gapen, 1990). With this rising incidence and magnitude of disability in the workplace is the added realization that a large segment of employed persons are at risk for unemployment due to disability. This segment includes older workers, employees engaged in substance abuse, and individuals with stress and mental impairments (Habeck, Shrey, & Growick, 1991).

All of these factors have stimulated legislative and programmatic responses to the problems of work-related disability. The development of industry-based disability management programs, the passage of the Americans With Disabilities Act, and the continued growth of private sector rehabilitation services reflect the importance of disability management at the work site. For example, the Michigan Disability Management Final Report (1988) explains that the key premise of any disability management program is focused on employer responsibility:

    a. To promote the general safety and health of workers by providing a work environment that minimizes risks.

b. To support workers who, due to illness, injury or disability, experience difficulty in maintaining a productive role in employment.
c. To access medical and/or vocational rehabilitation services for workers whose injuries, illnesses or disabilities result in a substantial interruption of productive service.

Consequently, disability management is a pro-active process, requiring interdisciplinary approaches and creative interventions in the rehabilitation of injured workers.

A review of the literature indicates several definitions for disability management programs, such as (1) a collaborative approach between industry/management and the individual workers that includes preparatory education, policy development, prevention, and early identification at the workplace with a focus on the total impact of disabling events (Tate, Habeck, & Galvin, 1986); (2) a program that organizes the industry's response to disability in a way that reduces the impact of injury on the person's ability to function within a vocational role (Mitchell, 1982); (3) efforts directed towards individuals with chronic or permanent functional limitation or disability, or an individual with symptoms indicating a risk of disability (Jarvikoski & Lahelma, 1980); and (4) a continuum of actions aimed not only at minimizing the impact of disability, but also preventing disability and therefore maintaining a healthy work force (Schwartz, 1984).

Most definitions of disability management reflect a diversity of themes which include: health promotion, job site accommodation, early intervention, work-return transitioning, and worker retention. Numerous disability management interventions and strategies include variations and combinations of these themes in actual practice. However, one major area within disability management programs appears to be missing; namely, the family of the injured worker. It is important to involve the family in the disability management process because the attitudes and role of the family can be a powerful force in facilitating the worker's adjustment to illness and disability as well as supporting work-return transition goals (Tate, 1992).

Traditionally, rehabilitation and disability management programs have focused on the injured worker without considering the family. The commonly accepted definition of disability has focused on individual limitations and not on environmental/familial/contextual influences that may significantly contribute to the person's limitations. Shrey and Olsheski (1992) state that the "complex problems associated with work-related disabilities have been analyzed in a somewhat unilateral fashion. Most of the emphasis has been placed on identifying characteristics of workers with disabilities as factors that hinder vocational rehabilitation and work return" (p. 234). Traditional case management approaches have, therefore, failed to address family issues such as environmental influences, that can impact the worker's potential return to work or the ability to maintain a quality of life that makes life worth living and not worthless.

Disability management interventions need to address the multifaceted nature of disability and the importance of the person, the ongoing, long-term needs of the family, and the responsibility of the employer. A primary goal of disability management programs should be to contain the powerful and intergenerational impact of disability. This is an important point because the disability experience will influence how children perceive life and living as well as their attitudes toward loss and the disability management experience.

It should also facilitate the worker's safe return to productive employment, but not at the family's emotional or physical expense. Programmatic efforts directed to the worker's return to work should be based on an understanding of the dynamic interplay among diverse personal-environmental factors, including the family, rather than on analyses that exclusively target medical, legal, or financial factors. Often these considerations are based on the interests of others rather than the interests of the family.

However, an understanding of the family also implies an understanding of the industrial family. The industrial family may be burdened by functional or dysfunctional behaviors similar to those experienced by the families of injured workers.

The functional industrial family has had a history of engaging in open communication with its employees, who are, in a sense, "family members." It also has demonstrated its concern by support of workers who are injured. In comparison, the dysfunctional industrial family is limited in its vision, and sees workers as expendable entities that are to be tolerated and not compensated beyond minimum level. The dysfunctional industrial family is not interested in mutual gain, but sustained profit for the company at large.

If the workplace functions like a healthy family system, then the disability of a worker can be perceived as an opportunity to care rather than a burden to be avoided at any legal, emotional, or financial cost. In a healthy industrial family, disability is not an aberrant event, but rather part of the life, living, and working experience.

The purpose of this chapter is to discuss and explore the role of the family in disability management. Within this context, this chapter addresses how the family can contribute to the containment of the effects of a disability, and explores the role of the family as a mutual partner in the disability management process.

Also discussed is the experience of the injured worker in adapting to a disability, and the often life-long and intergenerational impact of the disability experience on the family. An important point stressed in this chapter is that the family can influence the outcome of the disability management process. Though labor and management in many industries are relatively uninvolved with injured workers and their families (Bruyere & Shrey, 1991), where disability management programs do exist, the additional involvement of the family may facilitate prevention of disability occurrence, enhance the possibility of early return to work, and reduce secondary trauma. In this instance, secondary trauma is defined as those direct and indirect consequences to self or others that result from a disability. An example of a secondary trauma is the situation where the family is overwhelmed by a work-related injury and is not vigilant regarding the supervision of a child. Consequently, if the child is injured the result is more stress for the family.

ADAPTING TO THE DISABILITY EXPERIENCE BY THE INJURED WORKER AND FAMILY

The sudden onset of a disability resulting from an industrial injury, or the unexpected diagnosis of an illness that implies a reduction in work productivity, usually brings a serious disruption to the worker's and family's lives. Depending on the circumstances of the injury or illness, this change in the worker's everyday life brings feelings of anger, anxiety, loss, and even guilt. Shrey and Olsheski (1992) report that many injured workers have what is described as the "workers' disability syndrome." This is characterized by such behaviors as the tendency to exaggerate the effects of their injuries or illnesses, valuing the secondary gains associated with an injury, preferring the status of receiving financial compensation benefits, tending to hire attorneys to maximize their financial settlements, and typically disliking the job and lacking sufficient motivation to return to work.

A key point in understanding the injured worker is being aware of what has been lost by the worker as well as the family and what can be gained as a result of the injury. The worker with a disability often experiences a transition from self-perception as a productive worker to one who may have lost or may be losing the capacity to earn a living, as well as maintain personal and familial integrity. Medical treatment associated with injury or illness, rehabilitation interventions that focus on living with limitations, and the legal issues emerging from the litigation activity frequently exacerbate the worker's sense of loss and create an expectation of financial reward based on hope and driven by desperation.

Depending on the worker's age, the nature of the injury or illness, and the extent of loss caused by the trauma, the disability experience results in uncertainty for the worker and vulnerability for the family. Workers in the stage of post-injury transition are living in two worlds: one world invites the worker to consider many life options that exclude the possibility of returning to work; the other world is filled with hopes that eventual return to work is possible. The emotional processes that result from exploring these opportunities, and from the realities of loss related to disability and potential gain related to compensation, are often characterized by conflict, ambiguity, fear of the unknown, hope, anger, and desperation. Within this context, it is no surprise that the illness and disability experience not only affects the worker; it also has a powerful impact on the family. The disability of a family member challenges the core values and resources of the family system. Not only must the family adapt to the emerging needs of the person with a disability but also it must continue to maintain a sense of unity by regrouping its members, refocussing its resources, and redefining its functions.

The worker's own emotional reaction can affect everyday family functioning, and, in turn, the family's perception of the disability/illness event can impact on the worker's adjustment. If family members perceive that the individual's sudden unemployment results in a decided decrease in financial resources, added family stress can occur (Kephart-Sulit, 1992). Also economically dependent family members may also lose confidence in the worker's ability to provide for daily or long-term needs. This loss may influence them to enter the labor force to compensate for the reduced wages of the primary earner. Conversely, if compensation benefits provide wage replacement income comparable to or exceeding the worker's base salary, then these monetary benefits may become a significant disincentive to return to work (Hester & Decelles, 1985).

The family's reaction to the disability situation may depend on the worker's reaction to the disability or illness, circumstances of the injury, cultural considerations, benefit opportunities, the age and the number of years the worker was in the labor force, employer attitudes, timeliness of disability management interventions, and how the family has dealt with previous crises. When previous crises have identified family resources and helped to establish coping patterns, then the impact of the disability may be less devastating, especially when the employer has been understanding, concerned, and supportive. A family that has weathered the experience of having a "breadwinner" out of work for many months due to severe illness, for example, has had an opportunity to assess its resources as well as its support system. If coping patterns have been effective in the past, then these will usually be adopted again in the new crisis. However, past success should be considered in the context of families not being able to deal with a new stressor, such as a catastrophic injury, because their resources have not been replenished or the new disability may represent the reality of a job or career loss, as often is the case with a severe stroke or traumatic brain injury.

The family's reaction may also be expressed by anger or hostility toward the employer, denial of long-term implications to family life, bonding with lawyers, and perhaps an eventual acknowledgment and acceptance of the injury situation. Family members, for example, who deny the reality of a disability or its complexity, are not going to effectively assist the injured worker during the treatment and rehabilitation process. At the same time, a family that has adapted to the implications and reality of disability could be a constructive force in the return-to-work process. Many families never reach this acceptance "phase" because of their continued anger and denial precipitated by factors occurring around the time of disability onset. These factors may include misinformation about the worker's residual capacities, inattention to family needs by the worker's employer, or dashed expectations and hopes for the family's future. However, since each family is unique and changing, so are the family reactions to the life- or work-related illness or disability of a family member. The complexity of the family's life-long reaction to a work-related disability is presented in the following case example:

Remember Us

Ray was a 49-year-old truck driver. He was happily married, had three children, and was a central figure in his family and community. Known for his generous spirit and hard work, Ray was always there for his family, friends, and co-workers.

One day a crane malfunctioned due to improper maintenance and reckless operation by a co-worker and Ray sustained multiple injuries resulting in quadriplegia and other complications. Since the accident occurred out-of-state, Ray's wife, Kathy, and his three children moved into a nearby motel for three months. During the time they were there, they were robbed and assaulted by an intruder which left them traumatized and terrorized. While there was some initial contact from family and friends, Ray was not visited by anyone from his company, and only received flowers and a fruit basket.

When Ray was discharged from the hospital, Kathy became the primary caregiver. This caregiving process was complicated by an unresponsive bed sore which delayed rehabilitation and caused great frustration.

During this time, Kathy's mother moved in because she needed to be supervised as a result of Alzheimer's Disease which made her incapable of living alone. Although Kathy had two brothers and two sisters, they refused to become involved and felt that Kathy was home anyway so why not take care of her mother. While Kathy was a very competent caregiver, the ongoing demands took their toll. She realized that she could not manage her mother and Ray and was forced to place her mother in a nursing home where she soon died. Kathy felt guilty and distressed, and felt that she had abandoned her mother.

During the next three years, support was limited. Family and friends stayed away because they could not relate to Ray as a person with a disability. While medical needs were being met by health care insurance, workers' compensation benefits, and a substantial settlement, emotional needs were not being met. Ray was very upset because only one friend from his job visited. He felt abandoned, isolated, and betrayed because he had worked at the company for 22 years. He also felt his bosses were angry because he "won" his case.

Because Kathy had financial resources, some people felt that she had become "rich" as a result of her husband's injury. Kathy's perspective, however, was that she bought a new car and clothes to make herself feel better so that she could take better care of her husband whom she loved.

Three and one-half years after the injury, their 16-year-old daughter attempted suicide, and a few months later, their 18-year-old son was arrested for selling drugs. At this point, desperation clouded the family and problems abounded. Kathy also had a back injury which prevented her from doing any physical care, and kept her in constant pain.

At this time, a sustaining force for the family was their personal injury lawyer who was always available and who guided the family's hope to expect an additional settlement. In anticipation of another windfall, large sums of money were invested by Ray and Kathy, but were lost in poor real estate and venture capital investments.

The situation became more complicated when Ray aspirated on food and died while he was being fed by an inexperienced home health care aide. Kathy felt guilty and responsible because she was out food shopping and felt that if she was home he would have lived.

Five years after the injury:

- Ray is dead.
- Kathy is an out-patient being treated for depression in addition to chronic back pain.
- Her son is in jail for selling drugs.
- One of her daughters is a single parent coping with ongoing emotional problems related to the loss of her father.
- Her other daughter is very successful in college and a positive force in the family.

The complexity of this case created barriers to functional communication between the employer and co-workers since there was a question of improper maintenance of equipment as well as reckless operation of a crane by a co-worker. As a result co-workers became very defensive and were fearful for their jobs. When co-workers and the employer avoided Ray, both he and his family felt more anger and resentment, and relied more on the services of their personal injury lawyer who met their needs by creating an adversarial relationship with the employer by focusing on Ray and the family as victims. These needs could have become a focus for disability management intervention. Often needs consequent to a disability emerge not only from the event itself, but from the context in which the disability event occurs. This context includes the employer's policies and attitudes toward injured workers, the existence or nonexistence of rehabilitation resources, and a family environment that may be a source of encouragement or discouragement to the worker's return to paid employment.

In the case of Ray, many opportunities were lost due to the inadequacy of proactive disability management. In retrospect, if the company and union representatives had visited Ray in the hospital and supported the family, the intensity of initial trauma would have been contained. Granted, being 400 miles from family and employer during his initial hospitalization is not conducive to frequent visitation, it does, however, create an opportunity for a disability manager to be a representative of former support systems.

Another critical point illustrated in this case is the awareness that the primary caregiver and other family members are often at great risk for and vulnerable to secondary trauma which could result in the family situation going from bad to worse. This is where the disability manager can involve the spouse, caregiver, and significant others in educational and self-help support groups that focus on the long-term issues related to the disability experience and successful rehabilitation.

Unfortunately, few companies sponsor and support in-house self-help groups for injured workers and their families. One reason that such programs are limited is that industry does not want to empower injured workers and consequently have to deal with a consumer group that may create more "problems." The result is often increased isolation which creates an atmosphere of alienation not conducive to mutual interests and goals.

Also, if a disability manager had been involved with Ray, in his home, it would have been apparent that Kathy and the children were at risk. It is important to realize that the most ideal disability management plan can falter when the injured worker is more preoccupied with familial distress rather than focusing on the worker's return to work.

Although Ray was severely injured, he was cognitively intact and wanted to return to work. While re-employment was possible, the family was so angry, protective, and traumatized that they could not realize that Ray had an option to redefine himself as a worker with a disability. As a result, Ray lived an optionless lifestyle until his death. The harsh reality is that the disability experience took a great toll on all involved.

Responsive and responsible disability management services could not have changed the reality of this case, but they could have made the experience more bearable. This case example portrays the complexities of emotions and issues that can result from a serious disability experience. These issues can become a focus for disability management when the family is considered as a factor in the rehabilitation process.

During the disability management process, the family has ongoing and changing needs. The communication of information about the injured family member's job potential, the identification of resources within the community, exposure to role models, and ongoing communication and expressed concern from the employer to the injured worker and the family are a few needs that arise from a work-related injury that can influence the disability management process. Interacting with these needs are factors that specifically pertain to the individual worker. Living with a disability demands the development of a wide array of coping mechanisms. Some of these mechanisms include the development of support systems and, constructive outlets for anger and frustration, as well as cognitive reframing of the disability experience into a functional perspective. A functional perspective is one that enables the family to meet life's challenges based on skills and hope, as compared to being victimized by liabilities and desperation.

There are several issues to consider when planning a disability management program that is committed to the worker and the worker's family.

PROGRAMMATIC EFFORTS FOR FAMILY INTERVENTIONS

One of the goals of rehabilitation is to encourage and facilitate the worker's transition to work by understanding his or her assets and limitations. An awareness of these factors generates an understanding of how the family can be an effective, collaborative partner in the disability management process. The assumption is that disability management has as a goal the containment of the impact of injury and the prevention of other serious disabilities which may be a result of secondary trauma. Since family members can have an integral role in this process, this family involvement can include:

1. **Developing realistic expectations for the injured worker that may include return to work.** A number of factors are important in this process such as: (a) the family's perception of the disability; (b) its impact on family life; (c) the family's access to individual and environmental resources: (d) the information the family has gained about the worker's potential for employment; and (e) the impact that litigation and attorney involvement have on the family's outlook for the worker. If family members can "see beyond" the conflict that litigation engenders, then they might appreciate the benefits of an appropriate return to early, pre-injury family functioning. However, all workers will not return to work and some disabilities are all-consuming for the person as well as the family.
2. **Providing reinforcements, where appropriate, to the worker for eventual return to work.** Once the family is convinced that it is of considerable benefit both to the worker and to family members to attempt to return to

work, then the family can provide support for this goal. Reinforcements flow from the pattern of family functioning and are distinctive to each family and may simply be the return to pre-injury activities or the expression of support and understanding. An occurrence of a disability usually disrupts this aspect of family functioning, and timely disability management can result in many of these activities being regained.

3. **Becoming a resource for the employee-employer relationship.** If an employer is genuinely interested in the worker's re-employment, then family members who understand this concern can assist management in the sharing of information with the worker, and conveying the organization's positive expectations for the worker. Company benefits, planned job site modifications, and resources for disability adjustments may be information communicated by the employer as well as the family, especially if the worker believes that the employer is not benevolent and may be more concerned about cutting losses than the family's well-being. In this situation, the role of family support groups can be most helpful in providing support and a perspective on an often complicated situation.

4. **Stabilizing family life after the disability trauma.** Eventual return to work implies that family life as well as the worker's post-injury trauma has stabilized following the injury. However, there are many factors which can inhibit this re-orientation of family life, such as continued litigation, uncertainty about residual work capacities, and the negative behavioral patterns resulting among family members from the disability events. These patterns may include avoidance of the worker, anger at the individual because of perceived loss of benefits, or an exacerbation of substance abuse problems. However, if family life has gradually returned to a level of productive functioning that, while it may be different than pre-injury, still brings satisfaction to family members, then this environment is more conducive to the worker's rehabilitation. Such a restoration may be quite difficult, for frequently the obstacles outweigh the advantages. Compensation benefits, for example, can be very attractive to families when they perceive that these benefits bring new rewards. Some families may conclude that they are more financially secure following disability or chronic illness onset.

Awareness of family dynamics can be of invaluable assistance to the disability manager in facilitating the injured worker's re-employment process. These dynamics include how family members interact with the person who has been injured and how they involve the person in family life. For example, many injured workers may have continued guilt because of the circumstances of disability onset, such as an accident resulting from drinking or carelessness. The family member with a disability may withdraw from family life or harbor the conviction that everyone is angry at him or her. Yet when other family members are accepting of this individual and are eager to dismiss the past and assist the person to a more productive future, then this support may facilitate the worker's own awareness that one should "get on" with the business of living and contributing to the family.

In combination with this family acceptance is the flexibility that members have for shifting their responsibilities to adjust to the disability-related situation. This flexibility may even include the injured person's spouse assuming paid employment, or temporarily giving up accustomed activities. When family members consider and then undertake any necessary role modifications, then these are important steps to providing a supportive family environment within which the worker can plan for reasonable and realistic life options. Consequently, the worker may consider an option of either return or nonreturn to work. A supportive family environment may enhance and facilitate the option of "return" and enable a decision to be made from strength—not confusion, fear, and intimidation.

With an understanding of the different ways that available families can assist their member's return to work, what then are specific programmatic efforts which could be developed to enlist and then implement this assistance? In the context of disability management, the family is not viewed as a target for change, but as a collaborative resource both to the injured worker and to the employer. Yet this collaboration implies certain assumptions for effective work return or life return planning. These assumptions include:

1. **Family commitment to the injured worker's return to employment.** As stated earlier in this chapter, the family may have ambivalent feelings about job re-entry. Family members may feel alienated because of the employer's lack of concern for the injured worker, or the litigation process over workers' compensation may have stimulated conflicting beliefs about the worker's employability or the hope for a financial settlement. Or, the family may be quite eager for eventual employment. Family income may have diminished considerably; family roles may have been seriously disrupted because of the injury, and members are anxious for a return to pre-injury family life functioning. The worker may be enthusiastic for job return, and is able to look beyond any inactivity, possible employer rejection, or litigation to a return of satisfactions gained from employment. This enthusiasm may mobilize family members to collectively work toward re-employment goals. Family commitment, moreover, may emerge from different family needs, such as continued income, more varied options for the future, and control of any stigma evolving from unemployment of the primary wage-earner. When these needs are strong, family members may be seeking involvement in a program directed to re-employment goals.

2. **Employer commitment to the injured employee's return to work.** Employer policies often prohibit the injured worker's early return to work, and "these policies perpetuate the attitude that workers should not return to work following an accident or illness unless they return at 100% capacity" (Shrey & Olsheski, 1992, p. 235). However, the enactment of the Americans with Disabilities Act provides new challenges for both industry and families because workers will have new opportunities for employment Employers must now accommodate workers with a disability in their performance of essential job functions.

   However, problems can occur because the employer may not show any interest in the worker or the worker's family early in or during the disability process. Consequently, a message is conveyed that the family must "go it alone" in any efforts for job restoration, and that the employer will assume little responsibility in the worker's rehabilitation or the family's security and quality of life. Frequently, an employer is prevented from initiating direct family involvement because of impending or ongoing litigation. Yet the employer is a key player for the worker's eventual job return, and avoiding early attention to the worker and the family could be self-defeating. Disability management interventions can recognize, however, the importance of the employer's responsibility and active involvement in the return to work process (Shrey & Olsheski, 1992). Rehabilitation interventions with the family can be directed and supported through corporate disability management policy and through joint labor-management efforts (Bruyere & Shrey, 1991). These efforts could also be enhanced by company-supported disability management groups for injured workers and their families.

3. **The opportunity for early worker and family participation in the return-to-work process.** Successful programming in this employment area necessitates that the employer and related service providers recognize the importance of early intervention and early return to work after the injury or disability onset. This may occur during hospitalization, or immediately after hospitalization discharge. Early contact with the worker and the available family represents a first step and initiates a bonding process. Circumstances of the injury may inhibit the contact, such as worker carelessness or the employer's inattention to safety procedures. But if the employer is at all interested in the employee's return to work, then such attitudes may be put aside. Any latent hostility over injury-related issues that perpetuate communication delays may increase negative feelings within the family. A phonecall, or a visit to the family by an employer's representative may lay the groundwork for eventual family collaboration. This early employer-initiated contact may assist the family to incorporate hopefulness in their understanding of the disability event. The family members' perception of the

disability, as it affects family roles and plans, is a pivotal component for family adjustment and the employee's work return process.

Yet initial communication is not the sole responsibility of the employer, for the sharing of appropriate information by those providers involved in the worker's rehabilitation establishes a foundation for effective programming. This information may include the identification of the worker's residual capacities, an understanding of the compensation system, and an awareness of vocational and life options. The coordinated utilization of this knowledge can assist both the worker and family to appreciate realistic rehabilitation possibilities and that perhaps a more positive understanding of all the implications of what has happened can eventually contribute to the family's adjustment. Following a disability event the family, at some point, wishes to perceive what the future will be like, and even harbors the question, "Will the worker's eventual attempt to enter the labor force be penalized with loss of benefits, a loss that will affect family functioning?" The family's understanding of important disability facts can minimize anxiety, assist in the development of efforts, and become an incentive for any willingness to share in programming sponsored by the worker's employer.

4. **An understanding of the conflict arising from such competing forces as lawyers, doctors, employers, and workers, and the impact of this conflict on any family participation in the return-to-work process.** The worker's post-injury experience is often characterized by uncertainty and unresolved anxieties. There are also ambiguous messages from providers who are intervening for, supposedly, the worker's welfare, but who may be more concerned about their own financial gain and self-interest. Family members are not only concerned about the life adjustment of their injured family members; they must also deal with persons who are involved in the worker's rehabilitation process. The input from all these providers will usually produce conflict, for each person may have different expectations and unique frames of reference, and the family's welfare may be a secondary or a nonexisting consideration. Often the conflict has as its source the competing interests of providers, and attention to family concerns and to the possibility of utilizing the family for rehabilitation goals, may be lost. While this conflict is expected, it will have to be minimized if optimal disability management is going to occur.

5. **An awareness of how the family can contribute to the disability management process.** Underlying this awareness is the conviction that the family has a vital role in the disability management and rehabilitation process. One of the reasons traditional vocational rehabilitation approaches are not effective in getting injured workers back on the job has been the lack of attention to the injured worker's total life environment (Shrey & Olsheski,

1992). A major component of this "total life environment" is the family which should be included in the injured worker's rehabilitation plan. During the disability management process, this awareness creates an understanding of the many obstacles that may prevent re-employment or worker retention, such as negative family expectations, related to the family member's return to work, and the possible incongruence between the job demands initially planned by the employer and the worker's functional capacities. These assumptions can, therefore, guide the program planner to develop appropriate disability management and work return interventions. The family, the worker, and the employer are the key ingredients in this process. The challenge for program planning is facilitating cooperation and collaboration among these parties and establishing a common ground.

A PROPOSED PROGRAM

1. **Background and Goals**

Many employer resources include disability management programs and services that provide financial support, primary prevention activities, and post-disability services (Gottlieb, Vandergoot, & Lutsky, 1991). These programs generally emerge because of a concern for employee welfare, and offer such return-to-work alternatives as light duty, alternative or modified jobs in the company, flexible/shorter hours, physical accommodations, transitional jobs, and trial work. Though some employers typically inform the employee about such options only at the time of injury, others make no effort to inform injured or ill workers about the disability management program at the time of disability onset (Gottlieb et al., 1991).

For employers having disability management services, it is helpful to have a programming dimension that includes attention to the worker's family. Underlying this suggestion is the belief that the worker's return to employment occurs in a context of psychological and social variables that influence the development and maintenance of the disability (Jacobs, 1992). The worker's emotional reaction to the disability and the family's and employer's responses to the disability experience are decided factors that must be incorporated into disability management programming. The following are goals for programs that are committed to utilizing the family as a resource in their intervention efforts:

   a. **Establish procedures to protect and foster the employability of workers.** Workers can send signals long before their withdrawal from the labor force. The onset of disability can be a gradual process and such signs as increased absenteeism, excessive use of sick days, physical and emotional complaints, and work performance problems are symptomatic

of employees at high risk for lengthy and costly work disruptions. These signals can often be understood by or caused by family members, and if a cooperative relationship has been established with an employer, often the family can work with the employee to seek needed assistance.
   b. **Develop plans designed to ensure a timely return to employment.** This goal includes planning with the family to reduce long-term disability effects, such as inactivity, job avoidance, exaggeration of injuries or illnesses, blaming the employer for the injury, and only thinking about a financial settlement. Though compensation factors may introduce conflicting interests during programming efforts, and represent influential secondary gains for the worker, this goal implies that the employer offers attractive options to long-term compensation benefits. These options often must appear quite reinforcing to the worker if they are to become compelling work return incentives.

Goals that include the family can be developed to utilize existing resources within the industrial organization, and build on the employer's demonstrated commitment to the injured employee's well being. The approach, focusing on the perspectives of prevention and minimization of disability effects, should be primarily educational and implemented as early as possible in the worker's original employment for the organization, and/or when the worker has been injured or diagnosed with a serious illness. Demonstrated concern, such as historical and present treatment of other injured workers and their families, greatly enhances the credibility factor in the disability management program.

2. **Prevention**

In employment settings, prevention and health promotion programs are important elements of employee support services (Bruyere & Shrey, 1991). While disability prevention programs are typically designed for employees at high risk for lengthy and costly work disruptions due to physical and emotional problems (Boschen, 1989), this proposed prevention program would be developed for all workers at the initial time of their employment, and integrated with the standard orientation to company benefits, policies, and work procedures. An effort would be made to include the worker's family and to introduce them to the varied aspects of the work environment. If the family member were to have a work-related accident and accruing disability, then a bonding between employer and the worker and one's family can minimize the long-term effects of a disability. This bonding should really begin as the worker is hired, for this early connection to the family conveys the message that the employer cares, has certain worker expectations, and also possesses specific needs, such as worker productivity and a sharing of information by family members when they become aware of deteriorating work performance or of the signs of disability onset. In today's workforce, many jobs are quite stressful and the way the employee handles the stress might eventually become self-destructive (e.g., the use of alcohol or drugs). The family might be the first "point" of awareness of these behaviors and their potential on-the-job consequences.

This orientation session with the family can also include information regarding company personnel who have the responsibility for work-related problems and the resources the company uses to alleviate these problems. Any information conveyed to family members carries the implication that the organization respects and values their contribution to the worker's welfare, and that, when work-related difficulties arise, the family can be viewed as a source of support. Evidence suggests that family support can help to prevent more severe consequences from harmful or threatening experiences (Jamison & Virts, 1990).

3. **Minimization of Long-Term Disability Effects**

As stated earlier in this chapter, disability management through prevention programs has been offered in industry to deal with employees in the acute phase of work disruption, or in the sub-acute phase. Included in this group are those injured workers with sufficient lost time to qualify for temporary total workers' compensation benefits due to medical restrictions, or those workers in the chronic phase of disability, namely, employees undergoing surgery, those with severe impairments expected to cause work disruptions in excess of 30 days, those receiving long-term disability benefits, and employees having catastrophic injuries. In these phases, the worker's available family can be included in disability management programmatic efforts. If corporate procedures and policies reflect a commitment to the successful implementation of prevention and rehabilitation programs, then effective programs will include and require both early and ongoing attention to the worker's family, and a focus on educating family members in certain areas which will assist them to become an invaluable resource in the minimization of the negative effects of long-term disability. Early intervention can take the form of contact with the family and sharing information about company-related resources to deal with the disability (e.g., ongoing injured worker support groups).

To be effective and relevant while working with the family challenged by a disability, the disability manager should understand the dynamics that are unique to each family. The following assessment approach explores this information, and focuses on the unique characteristics of the family. It can identify those areas of family life that may be negatively influencing the patient's adjustment, and, in turn, indicate those factors in the family constellation that could promote the adaptation of family members.

The following information represents suggested family assessment guidelines which can serve as an outline when taking a family history. This format is similar to one used with families coping with disability in general (Power & Dell Orto, 1980; Power, Dell Orto, & Gibbons, 1988).

An Assessment Approach: Areas to Explore

I. **Family Demographic Information**
   A. Age and gender of family members
   B. Occupation of spouse and family
   C. Educational background of parents and siblings
   D. Ethnicity
   E. Religion
   F. How long in present location
   G. Family members contributing to family income
   H. People available in time of crisis
   I. Adequate medical insurance coverage
   J. Previous family psychopathology
   K. Family role of injured worker
   L. Serious family problems? Any previous serious illness/disabilities?

II. **Communications Issues**
   A. Who is family spokesperson?
   B. What are the family activities and the nature of communication?
   C. Who dominates family discussion?
   D. Quality of communication with the family member who is injured?

III. **Division of Labor in Family**
   A. Roles of family members before and after injury onset?
   B. Expectations by family members for family tasks?
   C. Who is responsible for transportation?
   D. Is family work done willingly or under duress?

IV. **Characteristics of the Disability**
   A. What was the cause of injury and circumstances?
   B. How is the person limited emotionally, physically, and intellectually?
   C. Understanding by family members of the nature and implications of disability?
   D. Attitudes by others toward the disability?
   E. Family members' perception of and expectations for the future?

V. **Impact of Disability on the Family**
   A. On regular performance of home duties
   B. On outside family activities
   C. Any identification of continued adjustment and problems
   D. Is employer involved and providing adequate support?
   E. Expectations of family members for each other toward household duties, maintaining social contacts, and vocational goals
   F. How have the family members accepted the financial restrictions, if any, imposed by the disability?
   G. What is the perception of family members about their resources in dealing with the disability?
   H. How does each family member describe how they are dealing with the presence of a disability in the family?
   I. How have family members in previous family generations handled disability situations?
   J. Who do family members believe is the best person to care for the injured worker?
   K. Has there been a realignment of family goals?
   L. Has there been a change in the social needs of family members?
   M. Do family members' refer to past areas of satisfaction, including previous successful experiences with crises?
   N. Does the family have a stronger relationship with a personal injury lawyer than with the disability manager?
   O. Does the worker and his/her family want to return to work or be compensated for the loss?

Relevant family assessment enables the disability manager to become aware of the amount of burden, resulting from the disability, experienced by the family, the needs and expectations resulting from this burden, and the family members' interpretations of their new situation. The family usually attempts to make sense out of the traumatic event. Each family member's feeling of control are challenged by the trauma, and the family's perception of the experience will influence their adjustment. This adjustment is characterized by how the family decides to "live with" the disability experience, and how the family responds to the needs of both the worker and employer. If the employer, for example, is committed to the employee's eventual return to work, even though modifications may have to be made, then the family's positive adjustment is expressed through their efforts to be a helpful partner to this goal achievement.

An educational component for the family in disability management programming will emphasize the communication of information on how family members can assist the worker to eventual re-employment. Also, it can address how they can take care of themselves, what are effective coping skills to handle the unexpected situations emerging from an industrial injury, and what are problem solving skills that might be necessary both to maintain family life and to pursue options that will lead to worker, employer, and family member satisfaction. Specifically, information can indicate the many ways of involving the injured worker in family life, and this involvement can convey the message that one can still be productive and worthwhile as a family member. Work-related injuries are often powerful threats to a person's self-esteem, identity, and life goals. A new appreciation of self-esteem following an injury could be a facilitative step to re-employment. This is when exposure to other injured workers who are positive role models can be helpful in the disability management process.

Further, if family members are to become useful partners in the worker's job return process, then they must be aware that taking good care of themselves provides strength to meet the everyday demands accruing from living with a person with a chronic illness or disability. Families often have to be given permission to seek their own enrichment and pleasures. Yet legitimate social and/or recreational outlets are not the only approaches to family enhancement. The acquisition of stress management skills and learning effective coping styles can help the family feel that they are more in control.

An awareness of problem-solving skills for minimizing disability-related issues is an important area in programming for the injured worker. Family members often have to be assisted to evaluate the different options presented by an attending physician, a lawyer, and an interested employer, and view each option through the lens of perceived long-term satisfactions, family values, quality of life, and what is ultimately best for the worker and his/her family. Educational information can show the family that there may be many more options for the injured worker than remaining permanently unemployed or unnecessarily delaying return to work.

With an understanding of family dynamics, the disability manager can also encourage family involvement in support groups. Themes for these groups could include employer expectations and identification of the obstacles injured workers will encounter in returning to a job. Other themes could include an awareness of the potential conflict arising from the competing influences of doctors, lawyers, and the employer. An ongoing group process may prepare the worker and family to deal eventually with these conflicts and reach a resolution that is in their best interest. Yet early intervention and effective programming may not eliminate the problems or obstacles encountered by workers in the process of returning to a job. While appropriate programming may energize the former employee's return, this effort still relies on employer commitment to worker productivity, medical coordination, a willingness for family involvement in rehabilitation planning, worker cooperation, and a key person within the worker's organization to make all of these goals possible.

THE ON-SITE DISABILITY MANAGER

Effective programs require strong leadership, and often the most likely person to direct a program that includes family members is an on-site disability manager. Since disability managers are accustomed to dealing primarily with employer-employee relations, working with the worker's family may be a new frontier and, hence, requires additional training and preparation to work with the family. But successful programming will also require further coordination among employers, labor organizations, attorneys, and health care/allied health professionals in the community. Historically, there has been limited labor union contact in disability management programs (Bruyere & Shrey, 1991), but the union can provide feedback to the worker and the available family on many issues, such as job expectations and possible benefit arrangements.

Within industry, the roles for family-focused on-site disability management are multidimensional. Some of these potential roles are: (1) case manager, (2) educator, (3) facilitator, (4) consultant on implementation of The Americans with Disabilities Act (ADA), (5) group leader, (6) advocate, and (7) support person. These roles become unique when issues, problems, and interventions are based on a family perspective. Building on the realization that the family can make a difference for the return-to-work process, the on-site disability manager assumes the roles of educator and support person. Since programming with families involves the communication of information and presentation of role models, the disability manager will need to be acquainted with family needs, such as support, acceptance, information, and structure. Most families want to know where they stand in practical, nonjargonistic terms so they can understand and deal with the problem, as well as timely, detailed, and realistic information about all the aspects of the return to work or return to life process. The need for structure implies that the family has concrete information about company officials who have decision-making roles, the company's return-to-work expectations, and perhaps information on how to deal with specific company staff and even attorneys. A response to these needs demands a professional who is knowledgeable about company policies and family dynamics and comfortable with disability issues.

CONCLUSION

The utilization of the family as a resource to enhance the potential for the injured worker's return to work is based on the employer's commitment to understanding family and worker needs.

While no company wants to deal with high cost related to industrial injury and disability, all employers must realize that they are entrusted with the safety and well-being of workers who want to work and do not want to lose their ability to work in the process. Disability management is a way of thinking that recognizes the multidimensionality of the disability process and emphasizes the mutual responsibility of the employer toward the worker and the worker toward the employer.

An alliance between the family, the worker, and the employer can often reduce life-long consequences that emerge from an injury on the job. A solid family-company collaboration is not only an opportunity for industry, it is a moral responsibility.

REFERENCES

Boschen, K. (1989). Early intervention in vocational rehabilitation. *Rehabilitation Counseling Bulletin, 32*, 254-265.

Bruyere, S. M., & Shrey, D. E. (1991). Disability management in industry: A joint labor-management process. *Rehabilitation Counseling Bulletin, 4*, 227-242.

Gapen, P. (1990). Whittling down workers' compensation costs. *Business and Health*, 8-9, 35-48.

Gottlieb, A., Vandergoot, D., & Lutsky, L. (1991). The role of the rehabilitation professional in corporate disability management. *Journal of Rehabilitation*, April/May/June, 23-28.

Habeck, R. V., Shrey, D. E., & Growick, B. S. (1991). Preface. *Rehabilitation Counseling Bulletin, 34*, 178-180.

Hester, E. J., & Decelles, P. G. (1985). *The worker who becomes physically disabled: A handbook of incidence and outcomes.* Topeka, KS: The Menninger Foundation.

Jamison, R. N., & Virts, K. L. (1990). The influence of family support on chronic pain. *Behavior Research and Therapy, 28*, 283-287.

Jacobs, K. (1992). Work practice for the new millennium. *Rehabilitation Management*, February/March, 71-72.

Jarvikoski, A., & Lahelma, E. (1980). *Early rehabilitation at the workplace.* New York: World Rehabilitation Fund.

Kephart-Sulit, B. (1992). Peace of mind. *Risk and Insurance, 7*, 22-24.

Michigan Disability Management Final Report. (1988). In *Disability management in the workplace*. Sixteenth Institute on Rehabilitation Issues. Arkansas Research and Training Center, University of Arkansas, Fayetteville.

Mitchell, K. (1982). *The self-insured employer and rehabilitation: A disability management model.* Industrial Commission of Ohio. A paper presented to the Ohio Self-Insurers Seminar, April.

Power, P., & Dell Orto, A. (1980). *Role of the family in the rehabilitation of the physically disabled.* Austin, TX: Pro-Ed.

Power, P., Dell Orto, A., & Gibbons, M. (1988). *Family interventions throughout chronic illness and disability.* New York: Springer.

Schwartz, G. (1984). Disability costs: The impending crisis. *Business Health, 1*, 25-28.

Shrey, D. E., & Breslin, R. E. (1992). Disability management in industry: A multidisciplinary model for the accommodation of workers with disabilities. *International Journal of Ergonomics, 9*, 1-8.

Shrey, D. E., & Olsheski, J. D.. (1992). Disability management and industry-based work return transition programs. *Physical Medicine and Rehabilitation, 6*, 233-244.

Tate, D. (1992). Factors influencing injured employees return to work. *Journal of Applied Rehabilitation Counseling, 23*, 2, 17-20.

Tate, D., Habeck, R. V., & Galvin, D. E.. (1986). Disability management: Origins, concepts, and principles for practice. *Journal of Applied Rehabilitation Counseling, 17*, 5-12.

Legal Perspectives On Disability Resolution And Industrial Rehabilitation

Luca E. Conte, Ph.D., C.R.C.
Mary K. Van Antwerp, J.D.

As workers' compensation laws continue to change and expand, both in levels of complexity and sophistication, the roles of attorneys and professional experts has expanded as well. Historically, many states relied upon simple tables of "scheduled loss" (i.e., a flat listing of the compensation paid for a specific injury) to resolve permanent disability claims arising from work injuries. Today, a fact-finding process to establish the extent of future "occupational disability" is more frequently utilized (Field & Weed, 1987; Osborne v. Johnson, KY., 432 S.W 2d 800, 1968).

The current disability resolution process suffers from four major flaws, which may negatively affect both the determination of a final settlement agreement and the ultimate rehabilitation and reemployment of the injured worker. These are: 1) a reactive, rather than proactive, approach to disability resolution; 2) a strong litigation orientation; 3) a tendency to maximize (plaintiff) or minimize (defense) the impact of disability; and 4) the failure to utilize disability management and/or prevention strategies (see Chart 1).

The disability settlement process has become quite similar to civil lawsuit procedures (Weed & Field, 1990). The aggrieved party (in this case, the injured worker), contacts an attorney to file an action against the defendant (i.e., the employer), to recover compensation for perceived losses (e.g., loss of job, earning capacity, or future occupational access). Some states still provide for a jury trial of workers' compensation claims. In most states, the trial is heard by an administrative law judge who typically has ultimate authority for determination of the extent of actual losses, as well as the awarding of damages or compensation.

Once an injured worker initiates the filing of a disability claim, it is highly likely that the claimant has become frustrated, depressed, and angry over the dis-

Chart 1
Disability Management Problem Resolution Strategies

Problem	Consequence	Solution	Intervention
Reactive approach to disability resolution	Extended treatment/lost time Decreased likelihood of RTW Greater likelihood of litigation Greater costs for TTD, medical, attorneys, and settlements	Become proactive and manage disability issues	Establish corporate disability program with accountable individual/dept.; assign medical surveillance staff; develop corps of physicians for efficient medical services
Strong litigation orientation	Polarizes worker/management Increases development of "disabled" attitude and behaviors Decreases likelihood of success for rehab and medical therapy programs	Use litigation as last resort and/or in cases of clear abuse/fraud	Utilize corporate attorney as advisor in management team, especially during early phase of claims
Tendency to maximize (employee) or minimize (employer) disability	Reification of disability in employee's mind Confusion of facts Makes "fairness" secondary to "winning" Contributes to polarization of workers	Avoid litigation and use only at final steps of claims resolution if all other steps have failed	Minimize use of expert opinions, especially in early phases of claim Concentrate on RTW planning and the worker's residual abilities
Absence of disability management strategies	Uncontrolled medical and disability-related costs Strong worker/management distrust	Manage disability with the same emphasis medical/labor relation issues are managed	Utilize in-house or contracted disability management providers, managers and/or planners Develop preventative and restorative health programs

ability experience and the increasing likelihood of residual physical or mental impairments (Vander Kolk & Stewart, 1988). Statements such as "someone has got to pay" are frequently heard at this stage, and reflect the claimant's outrage over being injured in the first place, as well as the perceived loss. These emotions often set the stage for an awkward and often fruitless stand-off between employee and employer: two parties, neither of whom feels totally responsible for the unfortunate work accident or injury, bracing themselves for an inevitable conflict over "what is fair compensation."

The consequences of this litigation-orientation are profound. For employers, it typically results in increased costs, including defense attorney fees, increased medical costs (associated with prolonged or unnecessary treatment), increased personnel costs (associated with lost time, replacement labor, retraining, and administration), and settlement awards/payments. Employers may also be affected in immeasurable ways, such as decreases in employee morale and adverse labor relations problems (see Chart 2).

Chart 2
Possible Solutions to Common Employer Omissions

Problem	Consequence	Solution	Intervention
No contact occurs with employees off on W. C./S & A	Medical costs are uncontrolled, due to delayed and/or inappropriate treatment, extending lost time costs and impeding recovery	Establish a program of medical surveillance of injured workers	Identify a specific point of responsibility (e.g., company nurse, rehab company) to monitor and coordinate services
Supervisors do not support return to work efforts of injured workers	Employees remain off work longer, and/or go on to file expensive legal actions	Establish "top down" commitment to reemployment of disabled employees	Develop affirmative policy; initiate training of managers; establish transitional work programs
Injured employees become angry with perceived reluctance of employer to deal "fairly" with them	Increase likelihood of attorney involvement; decreased plant morale due to employee "grapevine"	Make rehabilitation efforts as visible and publicized as possible	Conduct physical therapy and transitional work programs at the plant; if possible, provide rehabilitation services as a benefit

For the plaintiff, the beginning of litigation usually signals the transformation of a physical impairment into a life-altering disability. In the worst-case scenario, the injured worker sets out to prove the existence of a disability. The claimant's behaviors may be manifested in marginal compliance or rejection of professional recommendations (e.g., home exercise or physical therapy programs, job placement assistance, offers of retraining); a search for validation of disability status through other authoritative sources (e.g., physician "hopping," applications for long-term disability or Social Security benefits); a subtle withdrawal from friends and family; a decrease in activity level, even for those activities which are still within the person's physical capacity; an increased preoccupation with pain and somatic complaints, often marginally related to the specific injury; and the avoidance of involvement in many life activities which may lead to a more normative lifestyle.

A second consequence of the litigation-orientation concerns the reification of disability as part of the injured worker's self-concept. Central to the issue is the understanding that most non-disabled persons have had little or no experience with disability and thus do not know how to view or respond to the advent of their own physical impairment.

The litigation process, which necessarily involves the accumulation of "facts" and opinions from physicians and other experts, puts the injured worker at the center of intense scrutiny and conjecture concerning the **potential** consequences of the injury. In an effort to assist their clients, many physicians and other plaintiff experts may tend to exaggerate or offer a more pessimistic view of the future in their testimonies, a practice which contributes to the viewpoint that the injury is, in fact, life-defining, potentially unstable, and at-risk of further deterioration, and serious enough to involve significant permanent restrictions in overall activities.

These messages, conveyed to the injured worker in attorney and/or hearing offices rather than physician examination rooms, have an air of finality about them. They negate the equally plausible likelihood that the body will continue to heal, pain will subside over time, and that physical activity may increase with gradual challenges and the judicious use of physician guidelines.

Once the collection of data is completed and the judge makes a ruling, the injured worker is left with a series of conflicting opinions and messages, such as, "You have suffered a permanent impairment, it will impact upon you in serious ways specified by the experts, but you will have to make up your own mind as to how this is going to affect you for the rest of your life." It would indeed be a rare individual who could ignore the prognostications of all of the experts and would not be strongly influenced to avoid any further risks, challenges/opportunities, or changes because of his or her injury, which has by now been firmly transformed into a **dis-abling** condition. Disability management strategies (see below) are designed to reduce or prevent this potentially devastating dynamic from becoming predominant, since once the adversarial process begins, it most likely will not be reversed.

CAUSES OF LITIGATION

Workers' compensation costs have increased by more than 75% nationally during the five-year period from 1984 to 1989 (Burton & Schmilde, 1992). In an increasingly litigious society, with economic downturns and workers' compensation premiums continuing to rise, it is no wonder that both injured employees and employers feel they have nothing to lose by fighting claims through active litigation. The purpose of this section is to identify some of the specific reasons such claims end in litigation and to suggest alternatives for earlier claims resolution.

There are many potential causes of litigation, derived both from employer and employee actions or errors (see Tables 1 & 2). The causes of litigation range from easily corrected problems, such as failure to take a report of injury seriously or failure to maintain contact with an employee during recovery, to much more complex issues involving controversial medical treatments, subrogated claims or legal technicalities. For example, the injured employee may try to assert that the workplace was unsafe, or that the employer's safety procedures were flawed, thus trying to insert an element of fault into the workers' compensation system, which is intended to be a no-fault system. Since some states provide for a penalty against the employer if the employee can prove that the employer violated a safety guideline, such claims immediately place the employer in a defensive position, thus increasing levels of suspicion. Other areas where employers have experienced dubious workers' compensation claims include: 1) false claims for fictitious injuries; 2) claims for injuries incurred in nonwork-related activities; and 3) claims involving exaggerated physical impairments or claims based on subjective report only (e.g., pain, psychological stress).

Employers who may have had negative experiences in the past (e.g., an employee who faked an injury, an extreme award made by a judge), may adopt the attitude that, if the claim is ignored, it will go away. Oftentimes the injured worker is ignored as well, particularly when the injury appears relatively minor. Employers who have had first-hand experience with a fictitious injury also tend to believe that most individuals who claim a workers' compensation injury are, to some extent, malingerers. Finally, the employer may negatively view the employee as "damaged goods," as a result of a work-related injury, or based on information obtained after the worker was hired. For example, the employer may not discover until after a new injury that the employee already had a pre-existing disability, and that this disability was not disclosed at the time of initial employment.

Several examples may assist in illustrating how employers may develop negative biases towards injured workers. These examples are derived from actual injured workers with whom the authors have had contact.

1. Employee A is injured lifting a 50-gallon drum of liquid. He sustains a herniated disc, and already had a prior back disability. The employee is off work for six months and is pursuing a total disability award. Surveillance is conducted by a private investigator hired by the insurance carrier. The employee is observed riding roller coasters and bumper cars at an amusement park, carrying shingles up and down a ladder while helping a friend shingle a roof, and carrying small children. All of this activity was occurring while the employer was holding a light-duty job open for the claimant and the claimant was collecting workers' compensation benefits.
2. Employee B claims to have sustained a cumulative trauma injury from working as a receptionist, resulting in a diagnosis of carpal tunnel syndrome. The employee self-refers to a doctor known for early surgery, and subsequently undergoes two carpal tunnel releases within two weeks after the "injury" is reported. The claimant's mother and sister have both had the same surgery and collected workers' compensation settlements. The medical records show no objective evidence of any nerve impingement on nerve conduction or electromyogram testing. The claimant had only worked for the employer for two weeks when she reported the injury. An investigation is conducted by the insurance carrier and three witnesses are located, to whom the claimant admitted that she was perfectly healthy but that she wanted a "nest egg" like her mom and sister got from workers' compensation. The claimant's sister, who currently has carpal tunnel syndrome, indicates that the claimant asked her what symptoms she had suffered with the condition and what she should tell the doctor. The sister is willing to testify against the claimant, if necessary.
3. Employee C sustains an inguinal hernia and reports that he sustained it on the job while lifting a drum of liquid. The employer disputes the claim as the drums involved weigh over 1,000 lbs. each and, while the employee does lift them, he does so with a forklift. However, the medical histories all indicate that the injury occurred at work. The employer insists that the insurance carrier deny the claim. A denial letter is sent to the employee and the next day he comes in to show the company nurse the denial letter and says, "Oh, well, it was worth a try. I never did feel right lying. My wife put me up to it."

It is important that the employer maintain objectivity and treat each claimant professionally and consistently at the outset. Written and enforced policies and procedures on claims reporting and disability resolution, are essential to maintaining objectivity (Carbine, Schwartz, & Watson, 1988). Employer concerns regarding the legitimacy of a particular claim should be promptly communicated to the claims adjuster, who is in the best position to evaluate and perhaps investigate a questionable claim.

Delays in claims administration are another common cause of litigation. Although timely investigation and payment is usually mandated by statute, delays often occur in the initial stages of filing. Such delays are often characterized by the failure by employers or employees to file formal reports of injury. There may also be delays in investigating questionable claims, and administrative delays in issuing temporary total disability or medical payments. Many insurance carriers will initiate payments even if the claim appears questionable. However, payments may later be terminated if, after investigation, it is determined that the claim is not compensable. Such investigations usually require the insurance carrier to obtain all of the claimant's medical records, which the claimant may consider an invasion of privacy. Many claimants who have come to expect workers' compensation benefits become angry when benefits cease for any reason, and often use this as their primary reason for obtaining legal counsel.

Disagreements over the expert opinions of medical providers can also lead to litigation. Some states allow for the employer or the insurance carrier to select the medical provider, while other states allow that the choice be made by the employee (e.g., K.R.S. 342.020; Ind. Code 22-3-3-4). In either case, the employer is generally entitled to an independent medical examination by a physician of choice. If that physician feels the claimant has reached maximum medical improvement or can be assigned a permanent impairment rating, most states allow termination of the initial (temporary total) benefits. When the employee's physician offers a different opinion from that of the physician chosen by the employer, temporary total disability benefits may be terminated. This will typically lead to heightened adversarial relationships between the employee and the employer, with increased attorney involvement. At this point, the ultimate decision regarding termination of temporary total disability benefits will be made by an independent judge, if the parties cannot agree to a mutually satisfactory resolution.

One possible solution to this costly and time-consuming litigation process would be the involvement of a rehabilitation coordinator (Gottlieb, Vandergoot, & Lutsky, 1991). Assistance could be offered to the claimant in returning to work in the same job, perhaps with accommodations, a new job with the same employer, or a new job with a different employer. If an individual is enabled to return to work, despite the disability, the motivation to pursue litigation is greatly reduced, especially when the worker's job, wages, and fringe benefits have been secured.

The rehabilitation coordinator who is initiating a return-to-work effort for a recovering worker needs to examine certain key issues during this process, including the claimant's legal representation. The earlier the retention of counsel, the more likely the claimant has been told that returning to work may affect the size of a potential settlement. Factors associated with "secondary gain" can have a determinative outcome on the success of vocational services, and must be identified immediately if the prospects for return to work are to be properly evaluated (Albrink, 1992).

The question arises as to who will pay for a rehabilitation coordinator's involvement. Some states, such as California, mandate the involvement of a rehabilitation counselor at the employer/carrier's request, with penalties if a rehabilitation counselor is not retained. Other states have no requirement or a requirement with no penalties for noncompliance. The cost can be significant to the employer/carrier and the rehabilitation counselor needs to work closely with the contracting party to control costs.

Another potential source of litigation concerns disagreements over the type and duration of medical care. Certain medical modalities have proven controversial and often are subsequently denied by insurance carriers, particularly if the employee is in an employer choice-of-doctor state. For instance, the employee prefers to go to a chiropractor while the insurance carrier has referred the worker to an orthopaedic surgeon, indicating that no further payments will be made for chiropractic treatments. If the employee continues chiropractic treatment, this in and of itself, could lead to litigation, since the insurance carrier may (rightfully) refuse to pay for treatment for someone other than the designated treating physician. Similarly, insurance carriers may also refuse to pay what they may deem as unreasonably protracted treatments. For example, many orthopedic physician groups now own physical therapy centers and may influence extended or inappropriate use of these services for their patients. Likewise, a chiropractor may recommend manipulation on a weekly basis for multiple-year periods.

Other potential causes of litigation are listed in Tables 1 and 2. The rehabilitation professional can serve a useful function in resolving disability cases, but can play an even greater role in assisting injured employees, employers, and attorneys in preventing claims from reaching litigation. For example, it is well recognized that workers having extended periods of work disruption often develop signs of depression or other psychosocial problems (Hannah, Hannah, Hosher, & Vardy, 1988; Kiernan & McGaughey, 1992). The rehabilitation coordinator may provide support, guidance, and counseling to such individuals, helping them through what may be a critical period of recovery. Occasionally, the worker's psychological condition may deteriorate or there may be evidence of pre-existing psychological pathology which can greatly complicate the recovery from a seemingly insignificant work injury. By communicating these observations and their implications to all involved parties, the likelihood of litigation may be further reduced, as appropriate services can be established from the appropriate payor to the benefit of the claimant, without the confrontation and adversity that often accompanies litigation.

The rehabilitation coordinator can help both the defense and plaintiff attorneys to quickly focus on the pertinent issues whenever the claim reaches litigation.

The attorneys will want to identify attempts made at job placement, if the claimant cooperated, and the subsequent outcomes. At the point of litigation, both the defense and plaintiff attorneys will have identified expert medical witnesses, with divergent opinions regarding work disability. The claimant's attorney may try to find a physician who will impose significant functional restrictions, while the physician selected by the defense attorney may provide an opinion that minimizes disability. The rehabilitation professional may be asked to serve as an expert witness to interpret these two opposing sets of restrictions, providing reasons why one medical opinion appears more reasonable than the other. For instance, one physician may maintain that the claimant should be able to tolerate sitting six hours out of an eight-hour work day. Concurrently, the rehabilitation professional may have administered testing during which the claimant could not sit for more than one hour. Therefore, the rehabilitation professional may question the physician's sitting restrictions and/or advise the plaintiff's attorney to obtain a more detailed functional capacity evaluation to objectively substantiate such restrictions. Conversely, the plaintiff attorney's medical witness may testify that the claimant cannot use his right hand to write, when the claimant has successfully completed manual dexterity and written tests with the counselor, using only the right hand for two continuous hours. Such observations and clinical insights can greatly enhance the understanding of all parties regarding the extent and nature of an individual's disability status. The results may ultimately bring a swift resolution to what may otherwise be an unnecessarily lengthy litigation process.

PREVENTIVE LITIGATION STRATEGIES

The following case studies are presented and analyzed in an effort to illustrate how the likelihood of litigation might be avoided or eliminated.

EXAMPLE 1

Joe Allen filed a claim for workers' compensation benefits alleging an injury to his low back sometime between 6/26/93 and 6/30/93. He admitted that he did not notify his employer of the injury until 8/23/93, but justified this delay by maintaining that he had continued to work until notice was given. Joe took a vacation for two weeks in July, and first sought medical treatment on 8/22/93.

Joe's co-workers testified that he never mentioned an injury to anyone at work until 8/16/93 and that, as a union steward, Joe knew the policies of reporting injuries. The judge ruled in favor of the employer and dismissed Joe's claim based upon a lack of timely notice of injury.

Analysis

Most states require that an injured employee report injuries to the employer in a timely fashion (e.g., Ind. Code 22-3-3-1; K.R.S.342.185). Some states require written notice, but most will accept verbal notice. However, Joe's example might just as easily have been decided in Joe's favor, given that the delay in notice was only two months. There are published cases wherein such a delay has been excused for good cause shown.

What could have been done to avoid this litigation? Would a compromise have been appropriate? Joe had back surgery and, therefore, the employer's potential liability was substantial. First, the employer should have a clear policy, as this one apparently did, regarding the reporting of injuries. The policy should include to whom injuries are reported, procedures for reporting, and a contingency plan if the proper person is not available. Second, the employer might have obtained a rehabilitation coordinator to assist Joe in the negotiation of medical services, regardless of whether the costs of his surgery would eventually be paid by workers' compensation or health care insurance. This is particularly true of self-insured companies, where all medical costs are ultimately borne by the company. By allowing a third party to work with and assist the employee, the likelihood of litigation would be reduced, while concurrently increasing the probability that Joe would return to work after treatment with a positive work attitude.

EXAMPLE 2

Sarah Wirtz sustained a fracture injury to her wrist during the course and scope of her employment at ABC Company. Sarah is 31 years old with a high school education. As a result of the injury, Sarah was off work for 10 weeks and her wrist was placed in a cast which was removed after six weeks. Ten weeks after the injury, Sarah was released by her physician to return to work. She received a raise shortly after returning to work, and she continued to work at her regular job. Sarah's physician reported that she had sustained a 15% impairment to the arm below the elbow. Sarah works in a state where "occupational disability" is the basis for compensatory benefits, rather than percentage of impairment.

The employer thus takes the position that Sarah has sustained no occupational disability, as the physician has placed no restrictions on her activity, despite the impairment rating. Additionally, the employer argues that Sarah has returned to work earning the same or a higher wage as she had prior to the injury. The judge agrees and dismisses Sarah's claim for permanent disability.

Analysis

This scenario arises frequently in fracture claims where the injury is perceived to be particularly traumatic and the injured employee feels entitled to a settlement. The decision to dispute permanency was in all probability made by the insurance carrier rather than the employer, although the employer may have agreed with the decision. How could this litigation have been avoided? The most obvious possibility for avoiding this type of litigation is a compromise settlement. Presumably, the insurance carrier paid an attorney $2,000 or more to defend this claim. By negotiating a compromise settlement, the carrier/employer can reduce settlement costs, improve employee morale, and at the same time limit exposure to a potentially significant award. However, caution is advised, as such settlements should be negotiated judiciously to avoid setting a precedent for making awards in all similar cases.

EXAMPLE 3

Pete Welder, after being on the job for six weeks, begins to experience numbness in his index, middle, and ring fingers on his right dominant hand. His job involves welding joints in awkward spaces at a construction site. Pete maintains that he has never had these symptoms previously. Off the job, Pete is a part-time professional pianist with a local band and has recently become active in a bi-weekly bowling league, where he is captain of his team.

Pete's physician diagnoses his problem as carpal tunnel syndrome and relates it to Pete's job activities. Pete neglects to inform this physician about his hobbies; nor does this physician inquire about Pete's avocational activities. Pete then reports the injury to his employer. The insurance carrier investigates Pete's disability claim, sends Pete to an independent examiner who is informed of his hobbies, and subsequently denies the claim based upon the independent examiner's opinion that Pete's condition is related to his hobbies, not to his work.

Pete seeks legal counsel and the claim is litigated. The insurance carrier films Pete's job and secures the opinions of two additional independent examiners who, like the first, determine Pete's condition is not work-related. Pete's attorney does not inform the treating physician about the hobbies and on cross-examination by the insurance carrier's attorney, that physician admits that piano playing and bowling can also cause symptoms of carpal tunnel syndrome. The judge rules in favor of the employer and dismisses Pete's claim.

Analysis

This claim could have been avoided by more active involvement of an employer representative (e.g., adjuster, case manager, rehabilitation counselor) with the original treating physician. The employer knew about Pete's hobbies and knew he was seeking medical care for his complaints of numbness. However, the employer did not follow up with the physician to explore what information he was given and how he reached his conclusion.

Some employers send a company representative with injured employees to the examining physician. Many companies are developing banks of job videotapes, which are of assistance not only in workers' compensation claims, but also when the employer needs to defend a claim under the Americans with Disabilities Act, where the "essential functions" of the job are critical to determine.

DISABILITY MANAGEMENT STRATEGIES INVOLVING ATTORNEYS

Given the potentially serious negative consequences that can result from litigation, an expanded role for attorneys is clearly indicated in order to minimize the likelihood and magnitude of disability. This expanded role would involve movement from simply a compensation/litigation mediator, to a return-to-work strategist. The new role would then involve: 1) assisting in prevention of litigation, 2) assisting in the management of recovery efforts for injured workers, and 3) modifying the litigation process to minimize disability reification.

Prevention of litigation can best be accomplished by eliminating or minimizing the myriad of controllable sources of litigation discussed previously. These include establishing and maintaining effective communication with injured workers, adhering to policies designed to maximize return-to-work efforts post-injury, and extending reasonable rehabilitation services to those employees who are motivated to return to the work force in a timely fashion, but may not be able to return to their former job.

CHECKLIST FOR AVOIDING LITIGATION

1. Maintain and enforce a detailed policy for reporting injuries.
    * include proper personnel (and back up personnel) to whom injuries are to be reported.
    * treat each employee consistently and require reporting of all injuries, no matter how minor.
    * submit "first report of injury" forms to appropriate parties (e.g., State workers' compensation office, insurance carrier, home office) as required as soon as possible. In questionable claims, maintain above procedures

but notify the insurance carrier in a separate letter of specific concerns/questions about the legitimacy of a particular claim.

2. Establish and maintain a vigorous case management program to follow injured workers through all phases of treatment and rehabilitation. This can be done by utilizing existing staff as disability managers (e.g. personnel managers, affirmative action staff, employee assistance coordinators, medical staff), or by contracting with outside organizations (Shrey, 1990). The key issue is to <u>maintain communication</u> with injured workers and all treatment providers throughout the entire rehabilitation process.

3. Create and maintain a bank of job descriptions and, if feasible, accompanying videotapes for each job. Then, <u>communicate</u> this information to the employee's medical treatment providers. Even in an employee choice-of-doctor state, the employer is not prohibited from making a job videotape available to the physician. This can be used for questions on causation and for return to work. For example, the employee may erroneously tell the physician that there is no sit-down work available, or may be unaware of other lighter-duty work that may be available. If the employer can send the physician a video showing the physical demands of available alternative work, the employee may be released by the physician to the job shown on the video. Returning the employee to work may prevent the worker from developing the "disability" personality described previously.

4. Create transitional work options. Transitional work options, as opposed to light-duty programs that often become permanent by default, are specifically <u>time-limited</u> and targeted for temporary work activities (Habeck, 1991). By providing on-site therapeutic conditioning and monitoring services to injured workers, the opportunities for a safe and timely return to full employment is optimized.

5. Keep the insurance carrier/rehabilitation professional informed. If the employer becomes aware that the employee is changing physicians, the carrier should be notified immediately. In an employer choice-of-doctor state, the carrier may want to intervene and select a different physician, or require the employee to continue treatment with the initial treating physician. Even in employee choice-of-doctor states, "doctor shopping" is discouraged and should be brought to the carrier's attention.

6. Maintain accurate and complete records. Not only are wage records important, but so is the employee's medical history, if known by the employer. Most employers require doctor excuses when an employee is off sick. These should be retained and made available to the carrier as evidence of prior medical treatment, as appropriate.

VOCATIONAL EXPERTS

The use of vocational experts has become more common over the past decade (Marlin, 1988). Vocational experts have long been under contract by the Social Security Administration's Office of Hearings and Appeals. They participate as objective expert witnesses to assist administrative law judges in determining work disability during the appeals process. However, vocational experts are increasingly called upon to testify in catastrophic cases of death and/or severe injury, and personal actions including divorce and palimony suits. More recently, there has been a dramatic increase in the use of vocational experts in the area of workers' compensation claims to assess the degree and magnitude of occupational loss (Weed & Field, 1990). Not only has the use of these experts increased, but there has also been a proliferation of proprietary tools (e.g., vocational tests, computer programs) to assist these experts in reaching their conclusions. As the use of vocational experts becomes more widely accepted, there is a need for other professionals to understand the principles that establish their credibility and the subsequent validity and objectivity of their tools.

Currently, there exists a wide diversity in background and experience among vocational experts. Many possess impressive educational credentials, including degrees in counseling, psychology, and vocational rehabilitation. However, it is important that the expert has demonstrated successful clinical experience in the vocational rehabilitation of persons compromised by a disability. Otherwise, the prediction and assessment of an impaired individual's future employment prospects may be less than accurate. This issue is central to the selection of a vocational expert. Individuals without this knowledge and experience in providing vocational rehabilitation services may overstate or understate the limitations (occupational disability) imposed on a person by an impairment.

The current professional activities of the vocational expert draws attention to another critical issue. When experts become involved full-time in providing testimony, their clinical activities become severely compromised. In effect, they often lose touch with local labor market developments and service provision trends. Thus, to be a true expert, the professional must maintain a balance of clinical involvement and related activities — all of which established the expert's credibility in the first place.

The use of proprietary tools by vocational experts deserves a word of caution. Many of these tools include sophisticated computer analyses to search volumes of government data on census information, job titles, industrial codes, and wage rates (e.g. Gamboa, 1987). While this information may be impressive to the layperson, there are some serious limitations to using "homogenized" approaches to determining work disability and subsequent occupational wage loss. Computerized approaches have to rely on the principle of homogeneity (i.e., all disabled persons are essentially the same). In other words, the mythical concept of "the average disabled person" displaces the reality of "individuality" among each and every person whose work activities are compromised by a disability. Thus, for example, disabled individuals who utilize wheelchairs are counted in the same disability statistics as persons with low back strain, those with cardiac conditions, and/or those with mild mental retardation. Each of these conditions has very different implications regarding ability to earn a wage, but counted together provide very little useful information on the vocational potential of the so-called "disabled population."

Computerized approaches need to be used in conjunction with individualized clinical insight when rendering an accurate objective opinion of work ability or disability. Moreover, computerized approaches that utilize national data bases too often yield over-generalized opinions, which may have marginal applicability in the local labor market. Therefore, the vocational expert would be well advised to review the reliability and validity of available tools and instruments, and to challenge the applicability of specific data sources which may, otherwise, be utilized inappropriately.

Vocational experts can be vital resources when clarifying the degree of loss sustained by an individual with personal injury or tort claims. However, when their focus is narrow and overly reliant on generalized data, much can be sacrificed with respect to an individual's real potential for future vocational participation and subsequent earnings.

Table 1
Employer Errors Which Contribute To Litigation

1. Failure to take employee's injury seriously (including supervisor comments, delays in submitting first report of injury, comments about medical treatment, etc.).
2. Failure to maintain contact with employee during recovery.
3. Failure to pay for reasonable and necessary medical treatment.
4. Delay in authorizing treatment/services.
5. Delay in making temporary total disability or sickness and accident benefit payments.
6. Premature termination of benefits.
7. Failure to pay for voluntary services which may be crucial to return-to-work efforts (e.g., job accommodations/aids).
8. Failure to participate in return-to-work efforts (e.g., light duty programs, transitional work schedules/job tasks).

Table 2
Employee Actions Which Contribute to Litigation

1. Retaining counsel prematurely.
2. Resistance to medical monitoring/coordination.
3. Resistance to requests for information.
4. Failure to maintain communication with the employer.
5. Filing unwarranted complaints or grievances with union representatives.
6. Pursuit of controversial medical services (e.g., chiropractic, pain clinics, nontraditional psychiatric/psychological treatments).
7. Inappropriate medical services (e.g., use of generalists rather than specialists, multiple physicians, use of emergency room rather than treating physician).
8. Failure to follow medical advice (e.g., therapy programs, weight loss, exercise regimens).
9. Delay in giving notice of injury.
10. Filing of dual claims involving workers' compensation and another insurer/payor (e.g., product liability, automobile no-fault, disability insurance).
11. Failure to participate in return-to-work efforts.

REFERENCES

Albrink, J. S. (1992). Professional ethics: Serving the higher good. *CRC: The Counselor,* Winter, 3-4.

Burton, J. E., & Schmilde, T. P. (1992). Employers' cost of workers' compensation insurance; 1984-1989. *John Burton's Workers' Compensation Monitor.*

Carbine, M., Schwartz, G., & Watson, S. (1988). *Disability intervention and cost management strategies for the 1990s.* Washington, DC: Washington Business Group on Health.

Field, T. F., & Weed, R. O. (1987). Determining disability: A labor market approach. *Journal of Applied Rehabilitation Counseling, 18*(1), 3-5.

Gamboa, A. (1987). Assessing capacity to perform work and earn money. *Journal of Applied Rehabilitation Counseling, 18*(3), 49-51.

Gottlieb, A., Vandergoot, D., & Lutsky, L. (1991). The role of the rehabilitation professional in corporate disability management. *The Journal of Rehabilitation, 57*(2), 23-28.

Habeck, R. V. (1991). Managing disability in industry. *NARRPS Journal & News, 6*(4), 141-146.

Hannah, T., Hannah, E., Mosher, D., & Vardy, L. (1988). Fitness benefits of a lifestyles program for the rehabilitation of workers' compensation recipients. *The Journal of Rehabilitation, 54*(4),37-41.

Kiernan, W. E., & McGaughey, M. (1992). A support mechanism for the worker with a disability. *The Journal of Rehabilitation, 58*(2), 56-62.

Marlin, J. (1988). Estimating monetary loss doe to personal injury. *Journal of Forensic Economics,* May, 1-18.

Shrey, D. (1990). Disability management: An employer-based rehabilitation concept. In S. Scheer (Ed.), *Multidisciplinary perspectives in vocational assessment of impaired workers.* Aspen, CO: Aspen Publications.

Weed, R., & Field, T. (1990). *Rehabilitation consultant's handbook.* Athens, GA: Elliott & Fitzpatrick.

Integrated Disability Management And Claims Management: An Employer-Centered Alternative To Costly Litigation

Steven Cantlon

The only solution to lengthy workers' compensation claims that is acceptable to both the claimant and the employer is the substitution of a paycheck for the compensation check. The central challenge is how to get back to that paycheck in the shortest possible time. Unfortunately, the accepted solutions to this challenge have tended to remain in the realm of traditional claims management and rehabilitation.

Traditional claims management is defined as the gathering, recording, and reporting of claims information that is either factual, medical, or actuarial. "Factual" claims information includes the specific detailed information which defines the injury or occupational disease, provided by both the claimant and the employer. Included in this information are the details of the claim form and identification of the industry classification. "Medical" claims information includes the actual medical documents used to define and justify the diagnosis, the extent of disability and its relationship to the injury or disease, and the appropriateness of the payment of fees. "Actuarial" claims information includes the compensation paid, medical fees paid, reserves assigned or assessed by the state, explanations of applied rate-making formulas, trends, and projections.

Traditional rehabilitation has been characterized as the concerted attempt to lessen the impact of the injury/disease on the ability to work and to reduce the resulting length of disability. This traditional approach is characterized as "reactive," since it usually assumes post-injury involvement in an established and lengthy disability claim. Traditional rehabilitation services and skills are brought to bear on a structured plan of substantial duration (e.g., several months or longer). Such plans are usually carried out off the worksite, and often within rehabilitation facilities.

Neither traditional claims management nor rehabilitation, alone, is fully effective in reducing workers' compensation costs or minimizing residual disability. However, the integration of these two services facilitates effective disability management. For this process to be effective, one additional key element needs to be added — proactive early intervention in the injury or disease process. This crucial concept will be discussed in more detail later in this chapter.

ADMINISTRATIVE CLAIMS SERVICES

To establish the appropriate context for analysis, a brief summary of the tasks and activities required to carry out administrative claims services are listed below:

- Proper claims completion
- Payment of compensation and medical benefits
- Reserving, record keeping, auditing, reporting management information, loss information, loss analysis, and trend information
- Administrative hearings, and/or legal representation
- Independent medical examinations
- Medical utilization reviews
- Identification and pursuit of second injury fund opportunities
- Access to and monitoring of rehabilitation services
- Access to and representation before the workers' compensation bureaucracy

The management reports dealing with these services should include the measurement of their effectiveness since the aim of all of these services is cost control. Most of these services are well understood in today's workers' compensation environment, but only three aspects will be dealt with here: (1) information gathering, (2) investigation and litigation, and (3) rehabilitation.

INFORMATION GATHERING

If a claimant insists that his or her medical problem is work-related, and the employer insists that it is not, it may be appropriate that the issue be aggressively litigated. Many such disagreements, however, turn out to be a matter of detail, perception, and diagnosis.

Consider the case of a hypothetical worker named Joe. On a particular day at work when Joe was handling boxes on the line, he said that he hurt his back and wanted to file a claim. The employer, when responding to this information, recalled that Joe had been complaining about back pain for months. The employer, therefore, thought it reasonable to contest Joe's specific claim. Joe's reaction then became emotional — "The company is trying to cheat me out of my claim."

The next step was to get an appropriate diagnosis of Joe's condition. Often the diagnosis of "back strain" is expressed in reports only as a diagnostic code number. This was clearly not adequate to sort out the differences in perception between Joe and his employer. A further request was made to Joe's doctor to provide a specific diagnosis as well as information concerning any pre-existing problems involving Joe's back.

The doctor's report revealed that Joe was indeed suffering from back strain from two sources — a lumbosacral strain due to lifting his child at home; and a thoracic strain due to a recent industrial injury. A check with Joe confirmed the doctor's information. Joe and the employer then agreed that the industrial claim should be allowed for the thoracic strain.

As a result, the employer avoided costly litigation and the corrosive effect of Joe's sour attitude in the shop. Joe got his full benefits immediately, and also avoided the cost of litigation.

Though this example seems somewhat simplified, it is based on an actual claim that proceeded to a hearing. The relevant point is that effective information gathering and clarification can avoid, rectify, or minimize many problems that are more a matter of perception than reality. Often these incorrect perceptions by either the claimant or the employer misdirect the claim at the beginning and thus lead to major cost implications.

LITIGATION

One line of defense against the rising cost of workers' compensation is to successfully contest, or in the alternative, successfully limit the initial claim. As will be explained later, extensive litigation is not only counter-productive, it actually maximizes the cost to the employer. Where there is a clear basis for a legal challenge, however, the claim should be contested.

The claim should be investigated as soon as the employer becomes aware of it, while the details are still fresh.

- What actually happened, and what part or parts of the body were allegedly injured?
- Were there witnesses?
- Does the diagnosis support the injury?
- Was there a pre-existing condition, and if so, does it matter?

- Should affidavits be prepared?
- Should a defense medical examination be scheduled?
- Should the employer attend a formal allowance hearing?

However, few questions are more important than the following: Is there a realistic alternative explanation for the diagnosis? If not, a hearing officer or judge is likely to give the claimant the benefit of the doubt. Since physicians are obliged to be advocates for their patients, they tend to accept their patients' explanations of the injury and the circumstances under which it occurred, and will support their patient's pursuit of a claim. For much of the claim's history, the patient may be the physician's only source of information. In addition, most experienced workers' compensation physicians know that workers' compensation insurance often pays more fully and over a longer period than other forms of insurance.

The answers to all these questions and the assembling of the resulting documents is only useful to the extent that they address concisely and accurately the concerns of the judge or hearing officer. Without this critical focus, the entire investigative process is likely a waste of time and money. The individual responsible for the litigation, whether in-house, from a law firm or within a service company, should be consulted at the beginning of this investigative process, and in some cases, should maintain control of the process.

The gathering of information needs to be conducted in the context of an administrative process that is systematic and organized. It must have an effective recall component so that the individual documents and reports are timely. All of this information then needs to be reviewed by an experienced litigant for accuracy and completeness, so that it can be organized and presented in the most effective manner.

Private investigations, activities checks, video-taping, surveillance, and other investigative strategies can be effective if they are carefully managed and properly focused. The litigant should definitely be consulted before such activities are contracted so that only the information and evidence that matters is gathered. Too often these reports contain information that is extraneous, obviously biased, or even harmful.

For example, documenting that a disabled claimant is able to mow a small plot of grass, with frequent rest breaks, does not equate to the demands of a continuous eight-hour-a-day job. In addition, when surveillance is discovered by the claimant and discussed on the shop floor, it often causes bitter resentment and is viewed as an intrusion into an individual's private life. Conversely, the discovery and documentation of an income or the disabled claimant's repeated and sustained engagement in activities clearly inconsistent with the claimed disability can be quite effective, and may terminate a claim even in the absence of supporting medical documentation.

The litigation process, including its organization, completeness, built-in expertise, and recall component, needs to be emphasized. A significant number of cases lost or in which the results are delayed are due to missing or incomplete information. An effective claims management program must include this process whether it exists in-house or is provided by a contract service. Formal requests to expand an accepted claim that are challenged by the employer may need to go through all or part of this same process.

The most frequently asked question by employers, as they attempt to judge the success of their efforts at litigation, is "How many did we win and how many did we lose?" This is understandable, but it is the wrong question. The workers' compensation statutes in most jurisdictions are construed liberally and ever more so when viewed historically. Frequently, litigating new claims as a cost-control measure is unsuccessful by the time appeals are exhausted and, as mentioned earlier, it is expensive and destructive in a variety of ways. The defining question is, "How many decisions were favorable and how many were unfavorable?"

Limiting the diagnoses in a claim that is otherwise going to be allowed is favorable. Limiting the length of compensation, though ordered paid, can be very favorable. Converting a new claim to the reactivation of an old, less expensive claim is favorable. Actively assisting a claimant to reopen an old claim can be very cost-effective, particularly if there is a limited experience period. Though compensation is not stopped immediately, steering claimants towards rehabilitation and return to work and away from open-ended compensation is favorable. If claimants refuse rehabilitation, a powerful argument can be made that compensation should not continue. Doctors, judges, and hearing officers all become more conservative when made aware of that refusal.

If the employer's in-house compensation manager or service company is thinking and acting with this perspective, the employer's workers' compensation program probably is effective. If not, it is fair to ask in who's interest these decisions are being made and these actions taken. A clear distinction needs to be made between intentions and results. Intentions are essentially meaningless. It's the **results** that count. Expressed differently, is the employer viewed as a narrowly focused, self-serving adversary, or as part of an organization interested in acceptable problem resolution on a timely basis? The reader is invited to ponder which perception is likely to be the more effective in achieving mutually satisfying outcomes.

THE ISSUE OF LITIGATION COSTS

Workers' compensation is, and emphatically should be, a no-fault benefit delivery system. Asking a lawyer or other litigant when to litigate is no different than asking any other professional who wants to sell his or her services if they are necessary. However competent these professionals are, engaging in a dispute may be the most costly solution to the problem. Since workers' compensation is no-fault, success is defined in terms of promptness of solution and acceptability to both the claimant and the employer. In addition, since they are the payor, cost-effectiveness is a major concern for the employer.

Most people know instinctively that conservative solutions to medical problems should be tried first (e.g., lifestyle management and medications before the option of surgery is considered). Surgery, if it **is** required at this point, has then been more clearly and objectively indicated and is a last resort. Litigation, likewise, should be a last resort that is used only when there is a clear dispute and when other attempted solutions have failed. Litigation is by definition expensive, produces enormous delays, and like surgery, can leave its own residual problems.

Litigation too often offers the appearance of an easy solution. If the problem is simply handed to an advocate, the claims manager, service company, or union representative no longer has to deal with it. However, at the same time they can appear to their boss or client to be aggressively handling the problem.

Litigation is often characterized as an adversarial process through which a workers' compensation claimant's and employer's disputes are argued by the worker's advocate and an employer representative. Human nature being what it is, this perspective is nearly always biased. For the practitioner, litigating is comfortable, even enjoyable. For the parties, the injured claimant and his or her employer, the dispute is personal and adversarial, and as a result can be stressful and damaging. Permanent harm may result from the strong emotions engendered by engaging in a battle which only leads to hardened attitudes resulting from the length of the battle, and a lingering distrust in each other's goodwill.

Claimants are often financially devastated by the very long delays litigation produces. Employers are often struggling under the collective weight of compensation paid well beyond what is reasonable. The cooperative atmosphere required for effective rehabilitation is destroyed. The interest on the part of the parties to re-establish the employer-employee relationship may be nonexistent. The simple perception of fairness may be badly damaged. At the end of this resource-consuming adversarial process, most claimants feel they got too little; most employers feel the claimant got too much.

There is one more seldom-perceived destructive effect of litigation. Claimants' representatives use the most liberal doctors they can discover; employers use the most conservative physicians. In effect, the worst get rewarded in the medical profession; and by extension, the more objective and reasonable physicians get penalized by not being consulted, as neither defense nor plaintiff attorneys tend to value their unbiased opinions. Worse yet, each side tends to believe "their" doctor, which all but guarantees a loss of objectivity.

When an employer attempts to stop compensation by initiating litigation, the claimant's reaction is usually anger. If an advocate has not been hired by the claimant, one now will be. The advocate's entire focus, in turn, will be the guarantee of continued compensation until an administrative or judicial order is received terminating it. Unfortunately, the adversarial process used to secure this order of termination is so lengthy, and so often involves multiple examinations, investigations, and hearings, that the effect is often to actually delay the termination of compensation. The employer is, at this point, paying for both the compensation and the litigation.

Throughout this entire process, the claimant has been trying to prove how disabled he or she is. The employer has been trying to prove how disabled the worker is not. Neither polarized perspective is likely to reflect the accurate reality of the injury and its impact on both employee and employer.

Claimants who discover a link between the use of medical services and their compensation are motivated to use those services, sometimes to the point of excess. Claimants who are involved in litigation are yet more powerfully motivated to use and abuse those services. Claimants who are actively involved in rehabilitation tend to gradually use medical services less often. Claimants who are working use them little or not at all.

The effects of litigation on structuring reserves for claims is sometimes dramatic as well. Claims in which compensation is being paid and in which its continuation is being aggressively pursued, are typically viewed as having a high cost potential. The assigned reserve tends to reflect that perception. By comparison, claimants actively pursuing rehabilitation are so much more likely to return to work that the reserves can usually be reduced, sometimes dramatically. In Ohio, independent actuarial studies (Ohio Bureau of Workers' Compensation, 1993) found that difference so dramatic that the reserves for state-funded claims are reduced by as much as one half. Currently, the maximum reserve in Ohio is $250,000. In short, the presence of rehabilitation in just one such claim can substantially improve the premium rate of a state-funded employer or the funding level for the self-insured employer.

WHEN THE CLAIMANT REFUSES REHABILITATION

If it is true that claimants pursuing rehabilitation and return to work should get the benefit of the doubt and all the help that is available, it is equally true that claimants who refuse rehabilitation require a different approach. Their demand for continued compensation should be challenged. They may yet recognize the personal benefits of rehabilitation, but at this point it is time to litigate aggressively. As noted earlier, doctors, judges, and hearing officers all tend to become more conservative when made aware that a claimant has refused to take any responsibility for his or her own condition.

PAYMENT OF BENEFITS

Once the claim has been ordered paid, or otherwise accepted, the broader problem exists of paying compensation and medical expenses accurately and in a timely fashion. Many claimants visit an attorney for the first time because they have not received their money and do not know why. Most jurisdictions have established criteria for this process (e.g., within 30 days for medical bills and within 21 days for compensation).

The in-house compensation manager or service company should be able to easily demonstrate timeliness. Accuracy, however, requires a substantial level of knowledge by the claims examiner or claims manager. If usual, customary, and reasonable standards for medical fees exist, they must be known, systematized, and used. The same principle applies to commonly used diagnostic codings. If treatment parameters and prior authorization requirements exist, they must be consistently applied, in part to reinforce the accountability of the medical community, and in part, to protect the employer's cost.

The computer reporting that must accompany this program should demonstrate the program's effectiveness to the employer. If these reports are not reader-friendly, they should be suspect, and a better reporting method should be pursued.

Other chapters in this book address the rapid increase in national health care costs. Employers pay most of this cost in the form of workers' compensation and group insurance benefits. In workers' compensation at least, the only way employers can reverse this trend is to initiate control and responsibility for their injured and disabled workers. To do this, they must have current, accurate, and readable information. Management reports that meet this test take a fair degree of computer capacity and sophistication in terms of both hardware, software, and trained personnel.

To avoid the substantial cost of this equipment and the personnel needed to operate it, most employers today utilize the professional expertise of a third-party administrator or claims management service. These professionals, in turn, may be part of an insurance package, or they may work directly for the employer. Nearly all the reports generated by these professionals, no matter how well or badly formatted or overloaded with excessive information, can identify what has been paid in compensation and medical benefits and assigned reserves. To be genuinely useful, however, the report must be well-written and it must demonstrate clearly to its reader the location of costs by specific claim. Today's employer must use limited resources wisely and, therefore, needs to know by division, department, and job classification, the location of losses as they are generated.

The reports must analyze the losses, and in particular, provide trend information. Armed with such a report, the employer can accurately evaluate its established claims management program and the accumulating effects of new claims. When effectively prepared, such reports are quite useful and contain important decision-making information for management. Nothing pleases businesses more than to be satisfied that the money approved for the workers' compensation program is now paying off and improving the bottom line.

THE DISABILITY MANAGEMENT APPROACH

Waiting to return the claimant to full or transitional work upon being released by the attending physician is expensive and ineffective. Unnecessary extended lost time often leads to permanent and total disability claims for injured workers who, otherwise, may have experienced a timely return to work. Physicians are notorious for their conservatism in releasing claimants to work, and identifying unjustified work restrictions. They are often vulnerable to manipulation by patients who choose to perceive themselves as disabled. Most physicians have, after all, gone from academia to medical school to professional practice and are unfamiliar with the blue collar working environment. Additionally, for the physician to develop an effective relationship with the patient, he or she needs to trust that patient, who is all too often the physician's only source of information.

Traditional rehabilitation services (e.g., occupational and physical therapy, work hardening, pain and stress management, and vocational counseling) are generally well known in today's claims environment, and will not be dealt with at length in this chapter. However, there are at least two critical elements to any consistently successful rehabilitation effort. The first is proactive early intervention. The second is the preservation of the claimant's self-image as a wage earning employee versus the perception of being a disabled victim. These two elements further suggest that rehabilitation services that are delivered at the worksite are likely to be the most effective.

The series of early intervention techniques and timely return-to-work strategies are generally manifested through transitional work programs at the worksite. Transitional work techniques include work trials, where the injured employee is essentially brought back to work for the purpose of evaluation, safe work practices education, and coaching to determine if the employee is capable of productive work. If the injured employee can work, but there is a significant decrease in productivity, on-site conditioning and gradual return-to-work programming may be initiated. If the employee can effectively perform the work tasks, but not for a full eight hours a day, a structured gradual return to work plan may be implemented with accommodations and/or temporary modified duty assignments. A comprehensive overview of transitional work options is included in the chapter entitled "Disability Management Practice at the Worksite: Developing, Implementing and Evaluating Transitional Work Programs."

No one can better facilitate access and accommodations at the worksite than the employer. Usually, early in the claim, no one knows the claimant's abilities better than the injured worker. The goal is to reconcile the perceptual differences between the two. If an objective third party, a trained professional, evaluates both perceptions early in the injury process, an acceptable solution is nearly always possible. If the third party's intervention is both early and focused on the shortest possible separation of the claimant from the job site, the probability of success from transitional work strategies increases dramatically. However, the success of transitional work also requires the coordination of a disability management team, consisting of the employer and the injured worker, a union representative (if relevant), a claims representative, and disability management professionals. As much as possible, the disability management team's activities should include the coordination of return-to-work interventions at the worksite.

Initially, the creation of a disability management team may require additional effort and time. However, once the team becomes operational, the work load and time demands will steadily decline. The claims among injured workers involved in transitional work are generally of shorter duration, since many issues leading to traditional disputes and hassles have been eliminated early in the claims process. There is a refreshing sense of stress reduction for all concerned.

Promoting a structured rehabilitation program to the claimant often requires the special skills and knowledge of a rehabilitation case manager. Successfully promoting the same program with the employer often requires the special skills and knowledge of a service company, as well as a rehabilitation case manager.

The case manager's training and experience often permits a neutral, objective, and personalized relationship with the claimant that may be difficult to achieve by others, including the attending physician. The difference is often the time and personal attention given the claimant. This may be the claimant's first experience with an individual whose contribution to the conversation does not begin and end with compensation, but rather with the reinstatement of a paycheck.

The single greatest advantage offered by transitional work for the claimant is the fact that the work habit is not lost. The claimant maintains a critical self-perception as a productive worker. The injured employee also maintains contact with and reinforcement from the peer group in the workplace. Disputes, the adversarial relationship, high costs, lengthy delays, and the destructive effects of litigation are avoided. The claimant tends not to be focused on the extent of disability, but rather on how and when to return to work. The actual length of disability is shortened, sometimes dramatically. A paycheck has been substituted for the compensation check.

The most rewarding benefit for the employer may be the improvement of the bottom line. The most notable effect for the supervisor, shop manager, or compensation manager, is the retention of control by the employer over the recovery and reintroduction of the injured employee to the work process. The personnel director is likely to notice the retention of trained and experienced employees.

The training and experience of an effective service company often permits the rehabilitation professional to identify "problem" claims even before the attending physician begins to make written observations about the lack of progress. The service company's skills at identifying and projecting the cost of the claim, with and without effective management, permits the employer to clearly identify the long-term financial value of its initial commitment of resources. Often the likelihood of success can be projected as well.

Combining the skills of a case manager with those of the claims manager at the beginning of the claim definitively permits a proactive, integrated, cost-effective workers' compensation program for both the employer and the injured employee. Applying either skill independently reduces clarity and commitment at the beginning of a claim and limits results at the end. The employer should expect from their service company communication with and coordination among disability management team members, as well as the tracking and reporting of both the medical and compensation progress of the cooperative effort. The service company, in short, should be able to translate effective disability management strategies into savings for the employer.

QUESTIONS AN EMPLOYER SHOULD ASK

Assuming a new Chief Financial Officer or Benefits Director at the Widget Company were considering proposals from a workers' compensation service company or third-party administrator, what questions should be asked? Since the workers' compensation process begins with the claim, the first question might be "Can the service company identify those claims which can be successfully challenged? Additional questions of importance may include the following:

- If the basic claim is valid, have the opportunities to limit its scope been identified?
- If the claim is becoming expensive, does the employer have to ask what to do or does the service company offer suggestions?
- If contact is not that frequent, can the service company demonstrate that they are "on top of" the claims?

- Since most of the cost is in a relatively few claims, is there continuity in the management of those claims?
- Is the claims professional personally responsible for managing claims, making decisions in them with the employer's input, and attending administrative or legal hearings in all or most of the claims?
- Who is responsible for training the employer's Account Manager or Account Executive
- Is the service company's internal recall process sophisticated and systematized enough to prompt the asking and answering of the right claims management questions at the right time?
- Does the service company have a process for systematically identifying and pursuing second injury fund opportunities?
- Are there significant hidden costs? In other words, is some of the proposed service subcontracted and billed "in addition to" other contracted services?
- Is there an overall focus to the service proposal? If so, is it focused on litigation or return to work? Some reflection is required here since many companies offer both skills.
- Are the computer reports reader-friendly? After reading them, will the reader feel comfortable? Will the reader understand the information well enough to make decisions? Will any questions remain unanswered? Will the employer understand where the costs are? Have the trends been identified?
- Are the cost-control methods proactive? If the range of skills needed to put them into effect are not all in- house, is there a well-established and available network of professionals, including doctors, attorneys, and in particular, rehabilitation experts?
- Is the general approach to cost control a fight with the injured employee or a pay check for the injured employee? If the latter is claimed, is there a well defined and measureable process to achieve that end?
- If rehabilitation and return to work fail, will the claim be promptly challenged?

Beyond these important questions, the employer exploring a relationship with a service provider should understand how the providers's procedures will affect the employer's injured workers. The employer should also feel comfortable regarding advanced communications from the service provider, with respect to unanticipated developments and the employer's desired level of involvement in the claims management process.

A FUTURE MODEL THAT CAN DELIVER RESULTS

There is a high level of national concern and a growing national debate associated with the rapid increase in health costs. Virtually, all interested parties agree that it simply cannot continue. Much of that cost is in the area of workers' compensation. The high cost and destructive effect of litigation has been discussed. State legislatures that are willing to dramatically reduce benefits are not in evidence, and are not likely to be. The remaining option is for employers to initiate a cooperative nonadversarial claims and disability management program that, if successful, would by definition substantially reduce both the medical and compensation costs in workers' compensation. Employer-centered disability management and transitional work programs could, in many respects, serve as important models for the larger health care issue. It is, after all, employers who pay most of the tab for workers' compensation and group health insurance in this country. It may be that they, more than any other group, have the motivation and resources to change direction and avert the coming crisis.

REFERENCES

Ohio Bureau of Workers' Compensation. (1993). *Rate reserve table.* pp. 6, 8

A Canadian Perspective On Disability Management

Wolfgang Zimmermann

Gainful employment is viewed by most individuals as a primary method of achieving independence and self-respect. Conversely, the loss of employment through injury or illness often represents the loss of independence and self-worth. The purpose of this chapter is to discuss the need to protect the employability among Canadian workers with disabilities through effective disability management strategies.

There are multiple barriers to the full occupational integration of persons with disabilities in all societies. Forces preventing work participation may include social stereotyping of persons with disabilities as less than fully capable of producing goods and services. Social policy and laws that fail to promote the equal participation of persons with disabilities also impede social and occupational integration. The personal and economic consequences of workplace disability and the failure to accommodate the needs of workers is costly.

According to McMahon and Hablutzel (1992), summaries of the U.S. Senate hearings on the Americans with Disabilities Act of 1990 reflected that:

> Historically, society has tended to isolate individuals with disabilities and despite some improvements, such forms of discrimination against individuals with disabilities continue to be serious and pervasive social problems.
>
> Census data, national polls and other studies have documented that people with disabilities, as a group, occupy an inferior status in our society and are severely disadvantaged socially, vocationally, economically and educationally.

> Individuals with disabilities are a discrete and insular minority who have been faced with restrictions and limitations, subjected to a history of purposeful unequal treatment and relegated to a position of political powerlessness in our society, based on characteristics that are beyond the control of such individuals and resulting from stereotyped assumptions not truly indicative of the individual ability of such individuals to participate in, and/or contribute to society.

There has been a growing public awareness in Canada regarding the need for strategies to integrate persons with disabilities into the workplace. As a society, Canadians are beginning to recognize the economic impact of lost productivity among an escalating portion of the population that is becoming tax recipients rather than producers and tax payers. Likewise, Canadian employers are discovering the importance of disability management and workplace reintegration strategies, in light of exorbitant workers' compensation, short-term disability and long-term disability insurance premiums. In Canada, there is a growing trend for labor unions and management to jointly accept greater responsibility for workers who experience work disabilities, lost time, and lost wages.

Much of the current awareness of disability issues in Canada has been fueled by legislative changes, political developments, and court rulings. For example, several recent Canadian Supreme Court decisions have held both employers and labor unions liable for the failure to accommodate workers with disabilities. Other legislative developments have included the federal Employment Equity legislation, such as provincial Human Rights codes, and Workers' Compensation Board statutes that mandate rehabilitation services among injured workers and the right to return to work. Also, activities associated with the International Year of the Disabled and the Decade of the Disabled, initiated in Canada in 1981, have significantly heightened public awareness of disabled worker issues.

Despite promising trends in disability awareness and legislation, significant gaps continue to exist between public awareness and disability management practice. While corporate and social policies are being scrutinized and reformed, the workforce participation rates among persons with disabilities has not significantly changed. For example, the 1992 review of the Canadian Human Rights Commission, presented to Parliament in 1993, indicated that labor force availability of people with disabilities was 5.4%, while the actual labor force participation was 2.5%. These figures translate to an unemployment rate of more than 50% among those individuals with disabilities who are capable of working (Report of the Canadian Human Rights Commission to Parliament, 1992).

THE EXPERIENCE OF DISABLED WORKER GROUPS AND ASSOCIATIONS IN CANADA

Over the past few decades, numerous "injured worker groups" have been initiated in Canada to promote the legal, financial, and political interests of persons with disabilities. Historically, the formation of such groups has been strongly based on specific types of disabilities (e.g., visual impairment, spinal cord injury, amputation). Most groups offer member support services, solidarity in mutual experiences and concerns, and political action strategies to unify the groups' missions.

Those organizations that represent the interests of workers' compensation beneficiaries tend to direct their economic and political interests towards policy changes among Canada's various Workers' Compensation Boards (WCBs). Workers' compensation in Canada is a compulsory social insurance scheme, similar to the workers' compensation laws and statutes in many American states. In English Canada, the system was originated in Ontario by Chief Justice William Meredith in 1913, as reflected in *The Final Report of Laws Relating to the Liability of Employers* (Strategic Plan: Canadian Injured Workers' Alliance, 1991). Chief Justice Meredith recommended that workers receive benefits for injuries, regardless of worker or employer fault. Workers gave up the right to sue the employer in exchange for the "no-fault" system.

Despite the good intentions of the "no-fault" workers' compensation system in Canada, the actual administration of workers' compensation programs has not been without problems. Today's workers' compensation issues are more complex, and the activities of disability rights groups are focused on the following:

- Human rights legislation and committees
- Employment Equity legislation and initiatives
- The Canada Assistance Plan
- The Vocational Rehabilitation of Disabled Persons Act
- The Canadian Jobs Strategy and the Labor Force Development Strategy
- Employability Enhancement Agreements for Social Assistance Recipients
- Workers' Compensation legislation
- Provincial/Territorial legislation and programs for education, training, support services, and management of the labor market

Disabled worker advocacy groups appeared to have gained momentum during the early 1980s, as economic conditions deteriorated. A shrinking labor force, coupled with fewer financial resources, forced many disabled workers into economic hardship. The failure to coordinate social programs and agency services among injured workers caused undue frustration which, in turn, set the stage for an adversarial relationship between injured employees and the Workers' Compensation Boards. This frustration further stimulated growth among organizations representing the interests of injured workers. The Canadian Injured Workers' Alliance relates the common process involved in the formation of injured workers' groups:

> ...if a worker has a problem [and] gets frustrated in his dealings with the board, puts an ad in his local paper...if anybody else has a problem with the WCB, gets some responses, forms a small group, develops a constitution, then lobbies the board on individual issues, often without training and without understanding of how the Act reads or that there's a board policy manual...Sometimes going off half-cocked and sometimes right on, but winning cases, more by chance than by design. And then, if the founding member's claim gets resolved, sometimes then [he says] "I'm going to get on with my life," and the group may fold. Conversely, when claims are being rejected, people just give up and leave (Canadian Injured Workers' Alliance, 1992, p.3).

Local injured workers' groups exist in several Canadian provinces with provincial coalitions in Quebec, Ontario, Manitoba, and Saskatchewan. Over time, specialized service organizations have evolved, such as Workers' Compensation legal clinics in Ontario and Workers' Advisor offices under the jurisdiction of provincial governments.

The organization and activities of injured workers' groups range from loose, informal networks providing mutual reinforcement and support, to highly structured, registered societies with defined missions and strategies. The more sophisticated groups may offer claims appeal services for injured workers, circulate informational newsletters, sponsor training seminars and conferences, provide individual counseling and other support services for disabled workers and their families, and provide political advocacy services.

The growth of injured worker groups and organizations has stimulated a national network of such groups, which was initiated at a national conference on the re-employment of disabled workers. As a formal network, the conference participants met and passed the following resolutions, which express the sentiments of many injured worker groups across Canada, as reflected in the Proceedings of the First National Conference on the Reintegration of Disabled Workers (1990):

That injured workers have the right to re-employment without economic loss and to receive full compensation until re-employment.

The right to re-employment shall include full reinstatement with the original employer, if the worker chooses.

That the wage loss system now in effect in several jurisdictions in Canada is detrimental to the physical, mental and financial well-being of injured workers.

That injured workers be actively involved in the restructuring of the Workers' Compensation Acts.

Given that the right to return to work at the present time is deceiving, and given that the employer is under no obligation, it is proposed:

- that the right to re-employment not be subjected to any time limits;
- that the loss of income and the costs incurred in the rehabilitation of injured workers be borne by the pre-accident employer for as long as it takes to return the victim to work;
- when re-employment occurs, that it be according to the considered opinion of the physician treating the worker in order to avoid the intervention of physicians defending the interests of the employers and the Board and who would prematurely return the injured worker to work.

All workers are not protected by Workers' Compensation and whereas many find the premiums for coverage too expensive, be it resolved that there be universal coverage by WCB for all.

THE ROLE OF WORKERS' COMPENSATION BOARDS

The roles and functions of Canadian Workers' Compensation Boards, including vocational rehabilitation services provided to injured workers, is well documented (Workers' Compensation Board of Ontario, 1992). The following discussion is briefly summarized from that document:

Each Canadian province/territory has its own Workers' Compensation Board, which is mandated by provincial legislation. All Canadian Workers' Compensation Boards are exclusive, which means that the law requires certain industries to insure in a monopolistic provincial fund. Each Board has a

Chairperson and at least two other members. Many Canadian Boards have changed from having all-purpose boards to having appeal boards and corporate boards of directors. Each Canadian board has the power to examine, hear, and determine all matters and questions arising under the Workers' Compensation Act. For example, the boards are guided by provincial Acts, which provide only basic guidelines for the boards to follow. Each provincial board formulates its own rules, decisions, and orders. The Courts do not play a significant role in the day-to-day operations of a board.

In 1990, there were over one million work-related injuries in Canada. Over 619,000 of these required time off from work. The costs of claims was about $4.3 billion. The injured worker's claim is against the fund, not against the employer. The amount employers pay is determined by the type of industry they do business in, the dollar amount of their payroll, and by their past experience with workplace injuries. Experience rating further rewards or penalizes individual employers. Employers also benefit from the no-fault insurance system, which was described earlier in this chapter. When a workplace accident occurs, the board pays out benefits regardless of the fault of the accident. As such, workers cannot sue their employers or their co-workers, even if they directly caused the accident.

Many of the principles regarding benefits to workers are similar in both the Canadian and United States Workers' Compensation systems. Canada, however, has managed to arrange broad health insurance coverage of its entire population, to deliver, in general, adequate care, and to pay about 9% of GNP compared to 11% of GNP in the U.S., where 25% have inadequate coverage.

Many of the Canadian provinces appear to have used the Ontario Workers' Compensation Board as a general model, with certain differences and modifications. For example, the Vocational Rehabilitation Department at the British Columbia Workers' Compensation Board has the same hierarchy of objectives as Ontario and is committed to early intervention. Rehabilitation allowances cover the cost of retraining or education programs if those programs are considered necessary to overcome the effects of a residual disability. Discretionary payments can be made when wage loss benefits have been terminated for workers seeking employment or awaiting training. However, programs offered by the Canada Employment and Immigration Commission are considered before providing allowances. Typically, services provided to clients within most provinces include vocational assessment and planning, job readiness and placement assistance, counseling, skill development, and employability assessment.

Most provinces have services for injured workers that feature an active case management system, functional evaluation units, a vocational/work evaluation program, a worksite and job modification program, a job search assistance program, a vocational rehabilitation program, a training program, and specialized services (e.g., spinal cord or other severe injuries; industrial diseases; assistance for surviving spouses and dependents of deceased workers).

In Alberta, a Rehabilitation Centre specializes in work hardening, a program designed to facilitate early intervention and early re-employment of injured workers. Alberta's case management strategy was adopted in 1989, whereby a case manager coordinates various Board services and helps ensure early intervention in physical, medical, and vocational rehabilitation in cases involving more than 30 days lost time from work. The case manager establishes a rehabilitation/work-return plan with the participation of the worker.

Saskatchewan offers specialized services, which include supportive counseling, technical aids, modification to the home/workplace, and personal care. Its Job Readiness Program, Employer Liaison Program, and Employment and Skills Development Workshop are directed towards jointly established and clearly focused employment opportunities for injured/disabled workers.

Manitoba features an Adjustment Program for injured workers, which addresses the personal, social, or emotional difficulties that result from the injury. Specific services include social, supportive, financial, and vocational counseling. Manitoba has a strong focus on vocational assessment and employment services, including a Job Finding Club, Individualized Marketing Service, Worksite Modification Services, and On-the-job Training Services. Manitoba's Information Systems Project measures key variables such as time between injury and vocational rehabilitation intervention, duration and cost of vocational rehabilitation involvement, types of vocational rehabilitation intervention, and employment status at time of case closure and in subsequent years. The Disability Prevention and Management Program in Manitoba is a model for other provinces for technical assistance and information dissemination to employers to address safety hazards at the workplace.

Quebec's Commission de la santé et de la sécurité du travail de Québec [for the health and security of work of Quebec] has programs quite similar to the other provinces. However, the Ergonomic Analysis Worksheet is a unique approach, which facilitates the return-to-work process among those with permanent functional limitations. The worksheet approach allows for the creation of a worker profile, company profile, comparison of worker capacities and job task demands, and selection of corrective measures.

Newfoundland's program includes the unique Self-employment Assistance Program. This program is designed for workers unable to benefit from conventional rehabilitation services due to lack of education, lack of skills, age, limitations due to the injury, or the failure of conventional programs.

THE ROLE OF LEGISLATION

Federal and provincial governments play a major role in the successful reintegration of workers with disabilities. While fair and equitable employment opportunities are a social responsibility, governments in other countries have demonstrated the initiative, leadership, and commitment to injured worker reintegration. For example, Germany developed an enforced quota/grant-levy system. Australia recently enacted COMCARE legislation to enforce employer responsibility in workplace-based disability management systems. The United States recently enacted the Americans with Disabilities Act, extending mandatory affirmative action among an estimated 93% of American businesses.

Canadian government intervention at the federal and provincial levels is critical to ensure broad-based implementation of effective reintegration measures. In Canada, this will require a variety of approaches. For example, legislated employment equity, such as that which currently covers all federally regulated workplaces, will need to be strengthened, enforced, and broadened through federal-provincial cooperation. Contract compliance, similar to U.S. legislation requiring minimum minority group representation for all federal contracts, should be enacted in Canada. A national standard on mandatory rehabilitation for all long-term disability insurance carriers and a tax incentive system are clearly desirable alternatives. While vocational training cannot guarantee permanent reintegration into workplaces, it is essential for persons with disabilities to be able to compete equitably in the labor market with persons without disabilities. There is also a need for the support of private sector leadership, both financially and technically.

THE ROLE OF JOINT LABOR-MANAGEMENT INITIATIVES

Joint labor-management commitments and initiatives offer the greatest prospect for immediate reintegration. At the national level, the Canadian labor movement has not sufficiently demonstrated a leadership role in support of full and fair employment opportunities for persons with disabilities. Labor unions have been inhibited by a lack of understanding and awareness of the needs of disabled workers.

Likewise, Canadian employers have traditionally focused on hiring only the physically fit, regardless of the position to be filled. The pervasive attitude among employers has been to compensate injured workers for their losses, and to let the workers' compensation system take care of the injured workers' needs.

One model approach to enhance labor-management sensitivity to injured workers' needs is Germany's national Rehabilitation Councils. Germany's Rehabilitation Councils were established following the implementation of the 1974 Severely Disabled Persons Act, which required employers with more than 100 workers to fill six percent of their positions with workers with severe disabilities. Rehabilitation Councils are comprised of equal representation from employers, unions, consumers, and government. Councils are designed to provide a permanent forum for discussion, information dissemination, and the development of disability management strategies.

Examples of labor-management initiatives include the use of collective agreements between employers and unions to structurally address disabled workers' issues; the development of an employer-based disabled workers' omsbudsman system (as in Germany); the designation and training of operationally based case managers to coordinate results-oriented reintegration (as in Australia); and the development of training/education awareness programs for all employers, employees, and union members.

OCCUPATIONAL DISABILITY MANAGEMENT

The most effective reintegration strategies for injured workers are characterized as workplace-based disability management programs. Disability management programs at the workplace are typically designed to meet the expectations of injured workers, while reducing the social and economic costs. Occupational disability management is defined as:

> A return-to-work process for workers with disabilities using services, people, and materials designed to minimize the impact and economic cost of disability to workers, employers, and society. The process is workplace-based, managed, and directed in consultation and cooperation with injured workers, employers, labor unions, and rehabilitation professionals.

Depending on the occupational group, at any given time, approximately eight to 12% of the Canadian workforce experiences lost time and receives benefits from Weekly Indemnity (WI), Workers' Compensation (WCB), or Long-term Disability (LTD). Current hiring practices suggest that skill, training, and work experience constitute about 30% of the desired characteristics in the employee selection process. Another 70% of the desired characteristics and qualities are based on compatibility between potential workers and corporate cultures (Zimmermann, 1992). Therefore, it is in the employer's best interests to retain experienced and skilled workers, even when they become injured and require accommodations. An effective disability management program in industry enables employers to retain skilled and qualified workers, based on the following principles:

Efficiency: increased organizational productivity

Economy: coordination of return to work programs that minimize the personal and economic costs of injury and disability.

Social Responsibility: concern with employee welfare and reflection of positive organizational values.

Legislative Obligations: Employment equity, human rights, affirmative action, and legislative statutes.

CASE MANAGEMENT AND OCCUPATIONAL DISABILITY MANAGEMENT

Employer-based disability management programs are emerging in Canada, as a result of the increased costs of workers' compensation, short-term disability, and long-term disability insurance. The Disabled Forestry Workers' Foundation of Canada has implemented a disability management program at a sawmill in British Columbia, as a joint labor-management initiative. MacMillan Bloedel, one of Canada's largest forestry products companies and IWA-CANADA, a large forest industry union, initiated this program to serve as a model for other Canadian employers.

The disability management committee has ultimate authority for the program and consists of the company's human resources manager, a senior staff supervisor, the union camp committee chairman, and the committee vice-chairman. Aside from directing the operations of the disability management program, the committee is responsible for formulating the program's policies and procedures. An initial responsibility of the committee was the selection of an on-site disability case manager, an individual who had been an employee at the sawmill. This individual was selected because of his familiarity with other employees, work processes, labor-relations issues, and the prevailing corporate culture.

The case manager's role is to achieve the cooperation and support from labor and management in the drafting of individualized case management plans. The case manager maintains contact with the injured worker's physician and other health care professionals, and serves as a liaison with work supervisors, co-workers, and union members. Most important, the case manager is the first point of contact for the injured worker, and an ongoing source of support and guidance. The case manager works jointly with the disability management committee in identifying transitional work options and in identifying job site accommodations.

The ultimate priority in this program is for the injured worker to receive the earliest possible interventions that will facilitate a safe and timely return to work. No distinction is made among workers who are injured on the job and those with nonwork-related injuries. The goal is to protect the employability of the worker, and to coordinate services that will minimize personal and economic losses for the worker and the employer.

When a return to work is not possible for the injured worker, the disability manager coordinates services with external agencies and service providers in the community, in order to achieve the best possible social and economic outcome for the worker and his or her family. This typically requires the case manager's resourcefulness in accessing specialty services, which may include physiotherapy, occupational therapy, nursing, psychology, vocational counseling, and ergonomics.

The cooperation among various insurance providers, including the Workers' Compensation Board of British Columbia, the long-term disability carrier, and weekly indemnity insurance carrier, is essential to the success of this program. MacMillan Bloedel has recognized that the key to success is having easy access to information related to the disability management program's operations. This program features a comprehensive computerized database, which is used to measure the success of the program. The support of first-line supervisors and shop stewards has been particularly critical to this program's operations, especially when active participation is required to create work-return options. MacMillan Bloedel has learned to more efficiently utilize internal technical and ergonomic resources when designing creative and productive alternative jobs for workers during their transitional work experience.

According to the Workers' Compensation Board of Ontario (1992), Cuddy Food Products in Ontario also developed a disability management program which relies on both internal and external expertise, such as workplace safety and personnel training, health care professionals, worksite designers, ergonomists and engineers, and union representatives. Injured workers are brought back onto the line, either in a gradual return-to-work situation or in an alternative position. A teamwork approach reduces the chances of repetitive strain injuries by permitting the worker to move around the plant and perform an array of tasks that utilize different muscle groups. A company ergonomist addresses the needs of injured workers and assesses potential work station changes which prevent injuries from occurring.

THE NATIONAL INSTITUTE OF DISABILITY MANAGEMENT AND RESEARCH

In order to replicate and expand model disability programs throughout Canada, the National Institute of Disability Management and Research was founded and supported by the Disabled Forestry Workers' Foundation of Canada, in partnership with North Island College of British Columbia. This unique labor-management initiative is one of the most exceptional developments in disability management in North America. The Institute's mandate is to develop appropriate resources and research to support the introduction and implementation of workplace-based disability management programs. The goal is to identify the most cost-effective approach towards maintaining the employability of disabled workers, while reducing the economic costs of disability to employers.

The Institute offers a variety of training and educational programs for labor and management personnel. Programs include:

- A six-week disability management/coordination course for workplace-based case managers
- A three-day orientation to disability management principles and practices for labor/management reintegration committees
- A three-day course for line managers, supervisors, and shop stewards

The research component of the Institute is developing a databank which will focus on:

- Best practices research in disability management
- Information needed for employers to comply with statutory and employment equity requirements
- International collaboration on database development (formal networking with Germany, Australia, New Zealand, and the United States)
- Strategies to reduce the human, social, and economic cost of disability in industry

Another goal of the Institute is to achieve long-term partnerships among employers, labor unions, and government, to meet the challenges of job reintegration.

CONCLUSION

The failure to occupationally reintegrate workers with disabilities represents an inordinate waste of expertise, resources, and potential productivity. Many corporate and government representatives have claimed that it is difficult to substantiate evidence for the savings which will result from reintegration. However, managed return-to-work programs have consistently demonstrated economic advantages over social welfare and workers' compensation benefit programs.

During times of rapidly shifting economic conditions and the challenges of participating in a global economy, disability management programs will be subject to the same scrutiny as other cost-reduction programs in industry. However, employers, labor organizations, and government leaders are rapidly learning that social responsibility and reducing corporate disability costs are not mutually exclusive concepts. In tomorrow's workplace, the corporate survivors will surely be those who have taken control and responsibility for their own disability problems, while creatively utilizing the skills, work experiences, and abilities that disabled workers bring to the worksite.

REFERENCES

Canadian Human Rights Commission. (1992). *1992 Report of the Canadian human rights commission to Parliament.* Ottawa: Author.

Canadian Injured Workers' Alliance. (1991). *Strategic plan.* Thunder Bay, Ontario: Author.

McMahon, B., & Hablutzel, N. (1992). *The Americans with disabilities act: Access and accommodations* (Implications for Human Resources, Rehabilitation, and Legal Professionals). Winter Park, Florida: GR Press, Inc.

Proceedings of the First National Conference on the Reintegration of Disabled Workers. (1990). Ottawa: Author.

Workers' Compensation Board of Ontario. (March 20, 1992). Chapter 1: *North America's workers' compensation-based vocational rehabilitation programs,* in the companion document to Strengthening vocational rehabilitation: A vocational rehabilitation program review — Discussion paper for consultation (pp. 11-38).

Zimmermann, W. (1992). *Industrial disability management: An effective economic and human resource strategy.* Port Alberni, BC: Disabled Forestry Workers Foundation of Canada.

18

HEALTH INSURANCE, WORKERS' COMPENSATION, AND THE AMERICANS WITH DISABILITIES ACT

Brian T. McMahon, Ph.D., C.R.C.[*]

The purpose of this chapter is to provide a brief overview of the Americans with Disabilities Act (ADA, PL101-336) and describe its implications for two specific aspects of Human Resources Management: the administration of health insurance benefits and the management of injured worker issues. In addition to the statute itself, which was signed into law on July 26, 1990, Regulations and Interpretive Guidelines for implementing ADA Title I (the Employment Provisions) appeared in the *Federal Register* on July 26, 1991. A more readable presentation of this material is available in the *Americans with Disabilities Act Handbook,* published by the Equal Employment Opportunity Commission (EEOC, 1992a). Further clarification regarding specific expectations for employers is also available in the *Technical Assistance Manual on the Employment Provisions (Title I) of the Americans with Disabilities Act* (EEOC, 1992b). The reader is encouraged to become familiar with these documents to achieve a full appreciation of this chapter.

INTRODUCTION

It has been said that the ADA will change the way we live and do business in America. To many observers the ADA is "...unequivocally the most momentous piece of civil rights legislation since 1964. No single event or law has had a greater effect upon the employment of persons with disabilities" (McMahon & Shrey, 1992, p. 9).

---

[*] Appreciation is extended to David P. Mahaffey for assistance with manuscript preparation.

There are significant financial reasons why the ADA was enacted, including the wasting of $100 billion annually to subsidize approximately 10 million Americans with disabilities who are employable and eager to work. The woeful labor force participation of working-age adults with disabilities plummeted in the past 20 years (from 41% to 32%) in spite of state antidiscrimination statutes and the Rehabilitation Act of 1973 which required affirmative action efforts by federal contractors (International Center for the Disabled, 1986). Additional motives for the ADA's passage include the containment of runaway workers' compensation costs, the demonstrable affordability of accommodations, and the proven cost-benefit of accommodating individuals when necessary (Bowe, 1992; McMahon & Shaw, 1992; Shaw & Linder, 1992).

The Employment Provisions of the ADA (Title I) became effective on July 26, 1992, for employers with 25 or more employees. This number was reduced to 15 or more employees on July 26, 1994. Covered entities include private employers, state and local governments, employment agencies, labor unions, and joint labor-management committees.

Not all individuals with disabilities are protected by the Employment Provisions; these apply only to "qualified individuals with a disability "...who meet the skill, experience, education, and other job-related requirements of a position and can perform the essential functions of a job" (29 CFR, 1630.2). Certain individuals are not protected by the ADA Title I including persons who currently use illegal drugs; persons who use prescription drugs illegally; persons of varying sexual orientations without disabilities; persons who represent a direct threat; persons who are not qualified to perform a job's essential functions with accommodation; and persons with selected behavior disorders.

Title I of the ADA prohibits employment discrimination in all employment activities. This prohibition applies not only to hiring but to all aspects of the employment process including testing, work assignments, evaluation, disciplinary action, training, promotion, medical examination, layoff/recall, termination, compensation, leave, and benefits administration. As such, the ADA is much more than a "Hire the Handicapped" law. Nothing in the ADA is intended to challenge or lower an employer's evenly applied productivity requirements or qualification standards which are job-related and consistent with business necessity.

One form of discrimination involves refusing to make a reasonable accommodation to the known physical or mental limitations of a qualified individual with a disability. Refusal to accommodate on the basis of unreasonableness, or undue hardship, has become increasingly difficult to justify. First, Title I Regulations have clarified that if the hardship is financial, only the final net cost of the accommodation to the employer (after employee, insurer, service provider, or consumer group contributions; tax credits and deductions; etc.) provide the basis for hardship. Second, because most individuals with disabilities require no job accommodation, and

90% of accommodations cost less than $2,000 prior to such offsets, claims of "undue hardship" do not typically represent a strong defense. Finally, reasonable accommodations apply to all personnel actions, not just those which facilitate job performance (McMahon, Dancer, & Jaet, 1993; McMahon & Shaw, 1992).

Less publicized are the six other forms of the ADA Title I discrimination which include the following (29 CFR, 1630.5-12):

1. limiting, classifying, or segregating an employee because of his/her disability;
2. participating in a contractual relationship which subjects a qualified individual with a disability to discrimination;
3. denying employment opportunities to a worker who has a known relationship or association with a person with a disability;
4. using qualification standards, employment tests, or other selection criteria which are not job-related and necessary for the business and which tend to screen out an individual with a disability;
5. failure to use employment tests in the most effective manner to measure actual abilities in relationship to persons with sensory, manual, or speaking impairments; and
6. discriminating against an individual who has sought redress or attempted to enforce the provisions of the ADA.

Some employers have questioned whether ADA will be rigorously enforced. There exist several reasons why aggressive enforcement appears likely. These include strong public and Congressional support, the timeliness and thoroughness of federal regulations and technical assistance, unprecedented levels of consumer awareness and involvement, the modest cost of job accommodations, and expanded penalties for discrimination in the 1991 Civil Rights Act (McMahon et al., 1993; McMahon & Shrey, 1992). Depending upon their size, employers have had either two years (more than 25 workers) or four years (15 to 25 workers) between the enactment and effective dates to begin the ADA Title I implementation, thus minimizing the excuse of insufficient preparation time.

ADMINISTRATION OF HEALTH INSURANCE BENEFITS[1]

A compelling disability perspective on health insurance was published by the National Council on Disability (NCD, 1993), which estimates that "...three million persons with disabilities — 15% of the population with disabilities — lack any form of health insurance. Millions more lack access to adequate health insurance" (p. 2). Of the numerous findings contained in this report, the following are excerpted as relevant to this chapter (NCD, 1993, pp. 2-6, parentheses and numbers added):

1. Private insurance often seeks to minimize the risk of serious illness and, as a result, may exclude persons with disabilities from coverage.
2. Medical underwriting and preexisting condition exclusions restrict access to private insurance for persons with disabilities and may constitute a discriminatory practice.
3. While being employed typically facilitates access to private insurance, it does not guarantee it. Some employers, especially in small firms, do not offer coverage. Individuals with disabilities employed in small businesses that do offer insurance may find that they are excluded from their employer's insurance policy based on their health status.
4. The public health insurance system in the United States fosters dependence rather than independence and isolation rather than integration.
5. People with disabilities often forego employment opportunities in order to maintain public health insurance. Despite recent legislation to reduce this work disincentive, the link between income and access induces many persons with disabilities to (continue this practice).
6. Persons with disabilities feel that their employment choices are limited by the availability and adequacy of health insurance. The spirit of the Americans with Disabilities Act is diluted by the lack of adequate insurance protection.
7. The emphasis on acute and episodic care rather than on prevention and wellness runs counter to the needs and objectives of many persons with disabilities.
8. The range of services covered by insurance is typically limited and often restricts or excludes coverage of many services (e.g., assistive devices, personal assistance, preventive care) that are important for persons with disabilities to achieve independence.

---

[1] Prior to discussing ADA implications for the administration of health insurance plans, it is worth noting that 2.5 million people work in the insurance industry. Therefore, although they may be consulted for ADA guidance by employers/policy holders, insurance companies might do well to first pay equal attention to their ADA obligations as employers under Title I.

In the legislative development of the ADA, lawmakers were made aware that access to insurance benefits (particularly group health insurance) has long been a serious sticking point in the effective job placement of qualified individuals with disabilities. Rather than undertake health insurance reform as part of the ADA legislative effort, however, lawmakers addressed this issue in the Miscellaneous Provisions (Title V) of the ADA.

ADA INSURANCE PROVISIONS OF TITLE V

Generally, the language of Title I may be regarded as descriptive of the protections afforded to individuals with disabilities. Title V, however, offers certain protections to employers. Title V states that an employer may establish, sponsor, observe, or administer a bona fide plan of benefits which is based upon sound actuarial practices and is consistent with the requirements of state law as long as such a plan is not used as a subterfuge to evade the purposes of the ADA. Currently, however, subterfuge is undefined.[2] While the Title V requirements appear brief and concise, volumes may be written about their significance. For example, the entire plan for health insurance reform in at least one state (Oregon) was put on hold due to its inconsistency with these few lines (Hanson & Watson, 1993; McMahon & Carlson, 1992; McMahon et al., 1993).

The nondiscrimination requirements of the ADA apply to all employment practices and activities including the provision and administration of health insurance and other benefit programs (e.g., life insurance and pension plans). According to the *Technical Assistance Manual on the Employment Provisions (Title I) of the Americans with Disabilities Act* (EEOC, 1992b, Chapter 7.7) this means that:

1. If an employer provides insurance or other benefit plans to its employees, it must provide the same coverage to its employees with disabilities. Employees with disabilities must be given equal access to whatever insurance or benefit plans the employer provides.
2. An employer cannot deny insurance to an individual with a disability or subject an individual with a disability to different terms or conditions of insurance, based on disability alone, if the disability does not pose increased insurance risks.[3] Nor may the employer enter into any contract or agreement with an insurance company or other entity that has such effect.

---

[2] Some have quipped that "subterfuge" means not following the written examples provided in the EEOC's guidance.
[3] Regrettably, it is not clear as yet whether this means increased risk of occurrence or risk of cost; the relationship of risk to cost is as yet unspecified.

3. An employer cannot fire or refuse to hire an individual with a disability because the employer's current health insurance plan does not cover the individual's disability, or because the individual may increase the employer's future health care costs.[4]
4. An employer cannot refuse to hire an individual (whether or not that individual has a disability) because the individual has a family member or dependent with a disability that is not covered by the employer's current health insurance plan, or that may increase the employer's future health care costs.

In brief, the ADA will continue to permit differentiation in insurance risk classification; preexisting condition clauses; and discretionary limits on certain procedures, treatments, and drugs as long as such provisions are evenly applied. McMahon et al. (1993) summarized the implications of Title V provisions this way (p. 63):

a. It is now unlawful for an employer to refuse to hire an individual on the basis of insurability, or because health insurance premiums might escalate, whether such escalation is real or perceived. (It is more often a misperception).
b. Contractually established limitations on treatments, procedures, the number of reimbursable treatments or procedures, or prescription drugs, while legal, must apply to all employees—not just those with a disabling condition.
c. Contractually established pre-existing conditions exclusions, while legal, must apply to all conditions — not just isolated impairments such as AIDS.

REVIEWING EXISTING DOCUMENTS AND PRACTICES

In a world where self-insurance is common practice, insurance issues usually involve employers, third party administrators, and/or insurers. Recent court cases indicate that all three parties can be held responsible for making a prudent response to the intent of the ADA. It is therefore recommended that each requests from the other a systematic and appropriate response to the ADA in policy, procedure, and action (McMahon & Carlson, 1992). For example, insurance companies have been advised to initiate this process by providing written reminders to their policyholders to

---

[4] Concerns regarding this point may be overstated, because typically health status is used as an underwriting criteria only for employers with ten or fewer workers, and such small employers are not covered by ADA (Hammond, 1992).

be aware of the ADA effective dates, requirements, and penalties. Mention of the insurer's availability to offer balanced and positive assistance toward compliance is also helpful (Kessler, 1992).

Actuaries, underwriters, and insurers are encouraged to review current policies and practices to verify that even the appearance of adverse impact is eliminated. Such a review will involve administrative and transaction costs (time and money) which may be significant. A recent survey indicated that such a review was a relatively high area of both employer concern and activity compared to other ADA implementation issues (McMahon et al., 1993).

INSTITUTING COST-CONTAINMENT MEASURES

Given the current need to contain the costs of insuring employees, how does one reduce insurance expenses without at least appearing to evade the spirit and intent of the ADA? Insurers in the near future are likely to become more sensitive to the possibility that changes in benefit structures or coverages might have an adverse impact, or could be perceived as unfair. The ADA may portend a slowing down of cost-containment or benefits restructuring activity (Hammond, 1992).

A conservative approach to reducing benefits as a cost-containment measure may prove cost-effective if it is carefully monitored to ensure appropriate utilization. Until case law or additional regulations provide further clarification, the following steps are recommended when instituting new cost-containment strategies (Sampson, 1992):

1. State in writing that the requirements of the ADA law, regulations, requirements, and obligations have been read and understood.
2. State in writing that the written guidance provided by the EEOC has been reviewed and considered.
3. State in writing the business purpose and rationale for the changes.
4. Describe the changes themselves, which ideally will:
    a. focus upon changes in co-payments or deductibles which are across-the-board;
    b. address changes in across-the-board benefits involving restrictions to procedures, treatments, drugs, or their quantities; (such restrictions should never be triggered by a particular diagnosis); and
    c. ensure that pre-existing condition clauses apply to all conditions, not just a select impairment or group of impairments.
5. State that the changes described are believed to be lawful, and are not intended in any way to discriminate against individuals with disabilities, or any group of individuals with disabilities.

PROPOSED HEALTH INSURANCE REFORM MEASURES

Several authors have speculated upon the implications of various healthcare reform approaches for rehabilitation, ADA implementation, and people with disabilities in general (Griss & Hanson, 1990; Hanson & Watson, 1993; Watson, 1993). The most current and specific agenda for reform, from a disability perspective, was put forth in March 1993 by the National Council on Disability (1993). NCD has developed 22 recommendations to increase adequacy of health insurance coverage for persons with disabilities. Those which are relevant to this chapter would require the Congress and/or Administration to:

1. ensure that any healthcare reform plan adequately meets the needs of persons with disabilities, including full portability of coverage and a broad scope of benefits.
2. enact legislation mandating community rating for all health insurance plans as a means of spreading the health insurance risk and reducing the cost of coverage for persons with disabilities.
3. enact legislation mandating the elimination of preexisting condition exclusions and waiting periods to increase the availability of private insurance coverage for persons with disabilities.
4. enact legislation prohibiting underwriting that excludes individuals from groups on the basis of their health status.
5. enact legislation mandating that insurance be guaranteed for small groups and individuals....prohibiting insurers from dropping persons from coverage because of deteriorating health and...promoting portability of coverage.
6. enact legislation that regulates annual insurance premium increases in order to stabilize health insurance costs.
7. amend the Internal Revenue Code to permit greater deductions for health care, personal assistance, and assistive technology expenses for persons with disabilities.
8. amend the Social Security Act to eliminate the 24-month waiting period for Medicare benefits to ensure continuity of coverage for qualified persons with disabilities.
9. mandate a Medicaid buy-in for persons with disabilities to reduce employment disincentives.
10. expand Section 1619 work incentive provisions of the Social Security Act to Medicare.
11. expand access to personal assistance services and assistive devices.

It is clear that despite the hesitation of the ADA lawmakers to enter into the health insurance arena with more than the few, high-impact lines of Title V, the national agenda for health insurance reform as it affects persons with disabilities is far more ambitious than what the ADA currently requires.

MANAGEMENT OF INJURED WORKER ISSUES

In the first 12 months since the Title I effective date, the EEOC received precisely 12,677 complaints against employers (Bell, 1993a, Bell, 1993b). An additional 7,200 complaints were filed under various state antidiscrimination statutes. Referring to the EEOC data as presented in Figure 1, approximately 80% of these involve currently employed workers with disabilities. This number is striking when one considers that for all matters of employment discrimination (e.g., race, gender,

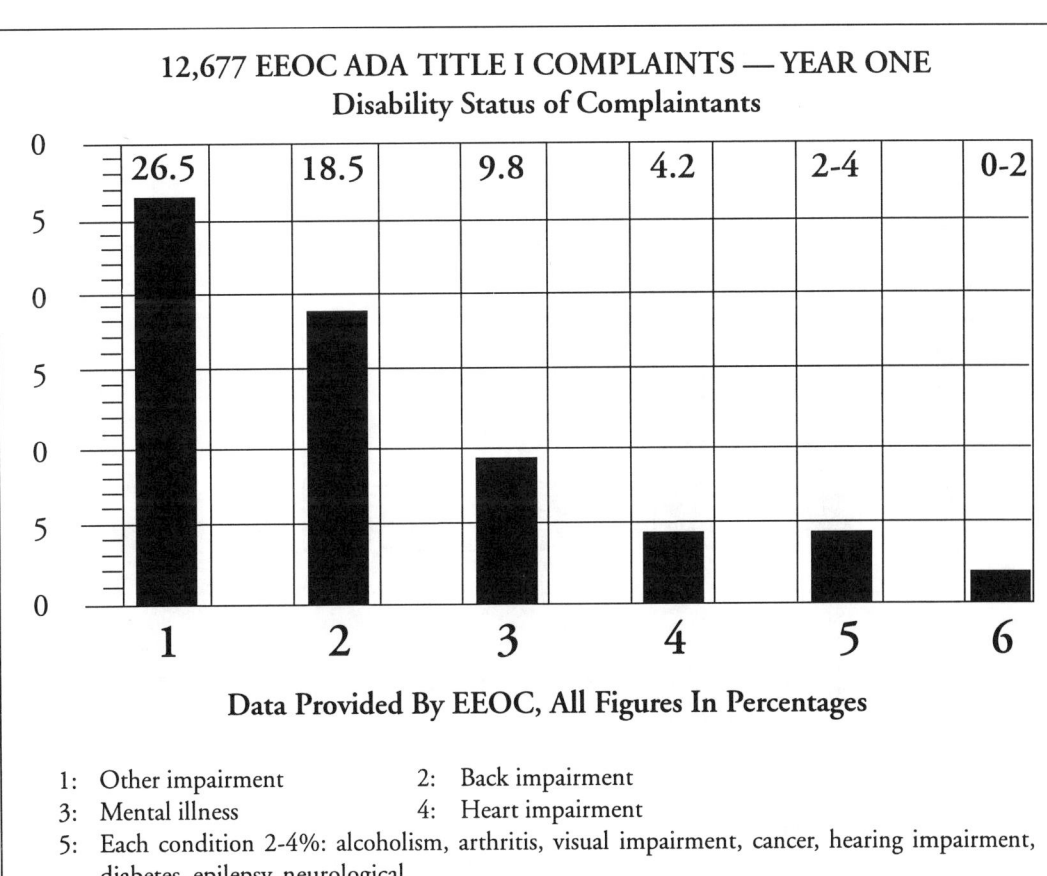

Figure 1. Disability Status of Complainants

age), the figure is 60%, and the labor force participation rate for working-age adults with disabilities is only 32%. However, the reporting period did coincide with an economic depression in which hiring activity was well below average.

Figure 1 indicates that the single largest definable impairment involved in the 12,677 complaints is back impairment (18.5%), which is the leading consequence of work-related injury. This is followed by mental illness (9.8%), with every other impairment lagging behind at 4% or less. Figure 2 depicts the same 12,677 complaints according to the nature of the alleged discriminatory behavior. The largest category of alleged violations involves wrongful discharge (48.7%), followed (at a considerable distance) by failure to provide reasonable accommodation (22.2%).

One conclusion which might be drawn from these data is that the nature of disabling conditions associated with employment complaints does not mirror the relative prevalence of those same conditions in the general population. A second

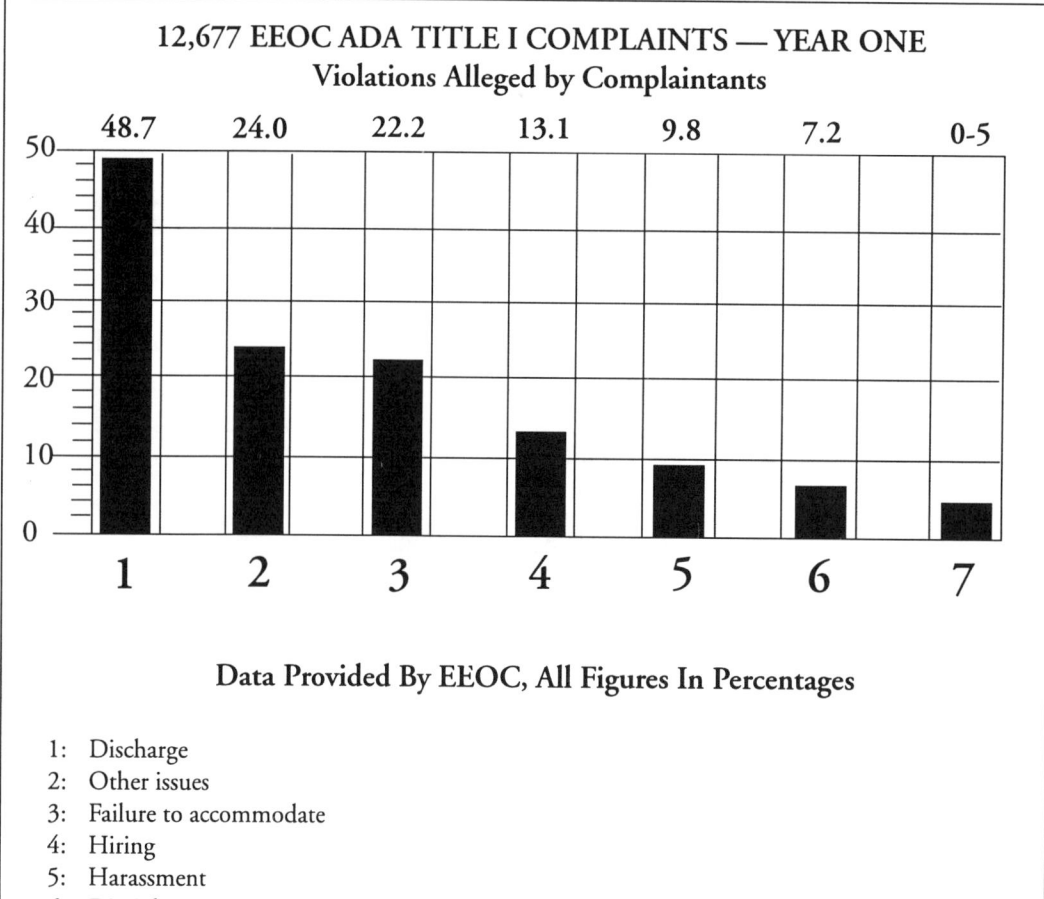

Figure 2. Violations Alleged By Complaintants

conclusion is that a surprising amount of the ADA legal activity is centered around injured worker issues, particularly the termination of individuals with back impairment who are seeking reinstatement and/or accommodation. The EEOC estimates that the level of the ADA litigation involving injured worker issues is in the area of 30% (Bell, 1993a, Bell 1993b).

Small wonder, then, that Gilbride and Stensrud (1993) discovered that the single largest increase in employer concern over a 12-month period regarding 10 distinct ADA issues was in the area of "Impact on Workers' Compensation Claims," which cost more than $53 billion in 1990. These concerns are so widespread that in some circles ADA liability insurance is being made available. Home Insurance of New York, for example, in conjunction with Wisenberg Insurance and Risk Management in Houston, has developed a policy to provide protection for businesses against ADA-related litigation (Thompson Publishing Group, 1992). This is hardly what the architects of the ADA intended. Rather their efforts were focused upon increasing access to the labor force for the 68% of working-age adults with severe disabilities who were chronically unemployed.

The lack of foresight and naiveté of the ADA lawmakers regarding workers' compensation is further illustrated by provisions of the Title I Regulations which, for example, require employers to consult first with individuals with disabilities regarding accommodation issues. Regrettably, if that individual is an industrially injured union member who is involved in an adversarial workers' compensation resolution process, which often operates outside the Human Resources Management system, such collaboration is unwieldy, at best. Nonetheless, the applicability of the ADA to all personnel activities and to all terms, conditions, and privileges of employment, (including the overall management of workers' compensation issues) requires further clarification of the ADA-workers' compensation interface, however unanticipated or difficult this might become (Blumenthal, 1992).

McMahon and Shrey (1992) published the first refereed article on the ADA-workers' compensation interface, the highlights of which are summarized below with the benefit of more recent developments and insights (Hanson & Watson, 1993; McMahon et al., 1993).

THE STANDING OF INJURED WORKERS AS AMERICANS WITH DISABILITIES

The implications of the ADA for injured workers appear to be misunderstood or, at a minimum, understated. First, Title I of the ADA does not necessarily apply to all injured workers. Only injured workers who meet the ADA's definition of "qualified individual with a disability" will be considered disabled under the ADA, even if they satisfy criteria for receiving benefits under workers' compensation or other disability systems (e.g., long-term disability, veterans, social security). Thus many, but not all, injured workers will meet the ADA definition of disability; i.e., "...a physical or mental impairment which substantially limits one or more major life activities; or a record of such impairment; or being regarded as having such an impairment" (29CFR, 1630.2, emphasis added).[5]

Employers have been cautioned that anything less than a thorough familiarity with the key concepts of the definition of disability could be very expensive (McMahon et al.; McMahon & Shrey, 1992). While the definition is very generous when it comes to impairment, the pool of protected individuals narrows quickly when the following stipulations are considered (McMahon et al., 1993, p. 60):

a. the impairment must be substantially limiting;
b. the substantial limitation must be a result of the impairment;
c. the substantial limitation must be to a major life area;
d. even when these conditions are met, the individual must be qualified for the position in question;
e. the individual may not be a current user of drugs or represent a direct threat; and
f. the individual's impairment cannot be one of a number of impairments explicitly excluded from ADA protections.

Clearly, then, all injured workers are not Americans with disabilities. However, by mistakenly regarding a minor impairment, such as a routine work injury, as a substantially limiting event, the employer may be conferring the protections of the ADA upon an individual whose medical impairment alone does not deserve such protection. Thus, the proclivity of some employers to pay inordinate attention to the etiology of an impairment (e.g., work-related injury) may have the unintended effect of providing ADA protections to injured workers who would not otherwise deserve them. McMahon and Shrey speculated (1992), "The precise number of injured workers who will meet ADA's definition of disability is impossible to estimate. Such statistics will likely be affected by the attitude employers of the future will assume toward this population" (p. 14).

RESTRICTED INQUIRY REGARDING WORKERS' COMPENSATION HISTORIES

The ADA does not permit employers to make any health-related inquiries before making a job offer to an employment candidate. Many employers are concerned about their ability to obtain information which they deem important to

---

[5] For a detailed discussion of the vague vs. flexible ADA definitions and their potential for frivolous litigation, see McMahon, Dancer, & Jaet (1993, p 60) and Hablutzel & McMahon (1992).

making an informed hiring decision. Employers are equally concerned that higher workers' compensation costs and premiums will result from the new restrictions upon pre-job-offer inquiry. This is particularly true in those states which hold an employer responsible for pre-employment, pre-existing conditions. Although some states have a second injury fund mechanism designed to counterbalance such an occurrence, many of these are not operational and many other states have no such fund. Presently, portions of the employer community regard these issues as discouraging in their efforts to fully comply with the ADA Title I (Commerce Clearing House, 1993a, p. 4).

Restrictions on inquiry regarding health status also extend to questions about applicants' workers' compensation history. The EEOC showed some flexibility in the *Technical Assistance Manual on the Employment Provisions (Title I) of the Americans with Disabilities Act* (EEOC, 1992b), which allows limited inquiry into previous claims of work-related illness or injury. As expected, such inquiry may occur only after a conditional offer of employment, preferably as part of a medical screening. A conditional offer of employment may be rescinded, however, only if a fraudulent workers' compensation history is discovered, which means a history of repeated (more than two), unsuccessful claims (claims denied) in a short time (probably less than six months). This very restrictive definition of "fraudulent workers' compensation history" is likely to apply to very few individuals.

THE "WHEN" OF REEMPLOYMENT AS A MEDICAL DETERMINATION

Historically, injured workers seeking reinstatement might be denied this opportunity because an employer requires medical verification that they have reached "maximum medical improvement," or are "free of medical restrictions," or have "fully recovered." Employers are no longer allowed to require that an injured worker (who meets the ADA definition of disability) be 100% recovered and able to perform all job duties before returning to the job (Commerce Clearing House, 1993b). These obsolete workers' compensation terms and the personnel policies and practices which rely on them have little to do with the point in time at which the injured worker is "qualified" for employment, which is the only ADA-relevant consideration. The individual is qualified at that moment in which he/she can perform the essential functions of the job (and only the essential functions) with reasonable accommodation. This is not solely a medical determination, as the individual with a disability is regarded by the ADA as the disability expert.

By providing that the employer assist (accommodate) qualified injured workers, the ADA architects intend to facilitate a timely return to work with the same employer, which has long been the job placement priority of rehabilitation professionals (Dent, 1990; Siefker, 1992). Should the ADA, which improves the "placeability" of persons with disabilities, be considered in fixing a level of wage impairment and indemnity payments in workers' compensation cases? Should the ADA be a consideration in estimating the placement potential for Social Security Disability Income (SSDI) or long-term disability (LTD) recipients? In speculating upon such profound effects, Ronca (1993, p. 9) summarized it this way:

> ADA is a law with a laudable purpose. Nevertheless, it has entered the web of existing laws of social insurance with unforeseen consequences to all. The appearance of ADA may, however, prove to be a useful stimulus. A reexamination of fundamental definitions of disability and a much-needed study of the coordination of the entire scheme of social insurance are themselves welcome programs for the balance of the decade.

SCREENING FOR "DIRECT THREAT"

Injured workers seeking reinstatement may be denied this opportunity because a physician has identified a "safety issue," which may well become the most litigated issue in the ADA-workers' compensation interface (Hablutzel & McMahon, 1992). McMahon and Shrey (1992) and McMahon et al. (1993) have written extensively to caution employers about the vulnerability of the "direct threat" defense (McMahon et al. 1993, p. 63):

It is also true that employees who represent a direct threat are excluded from Title I protections. But the standard for direct threat in the ADA is significantly more rigorous than in most state workers' compensation statutes. Direct threat must involve a significant risk of substantial harm which cannot be eliminated or reduced to an acceptable level by reasonable accommodation. Furthermore, the specific risk factors and harm must be specified, their probabilities of occurrence calculated, and their imminence established. This is not a light burden of proof for employers. The rigorous direct threat standard is reflective of the influence of the empowerment movement throughout the ADA, which (consistent with its history) has the clear intention of reducing the role of medical "experts" on employment decision-making.

ADA AND THE NATIONAL LABOR RELATIONS ACT

The role of organized labor has not been overlooked by the architects of the ADA. First, Title I responsibilities, requirements, and penalties for discrimination apply equally to both unions and employers. Second, collective bargaining agreements are mentioned as examples of contracts which, should they have a discriminatory effect against qualified persons with disabilities, would be unlawful. Third, collective bargaining agreements are identified as one of several forms of partial evidence to defend an employer's judgment as to which job functions are essential.

The National Labor Relations Act (NLRA) is intended to ensure that "labor peace" is maintained via good-faith collective bargaining efforts. Title I of the ADA is intended to eliminate discrimination in all aspects of employment which are related to the existence or consequence of disability. Here we have an example of two major federal laws with completely different purposes which have several areas of potential conflict. While it has been established that the ADA will prevail in conflicts with state workers' compensation statutes and the less restrictive aspects of state antidiscrimination laws, it is not clear that the ADA would rule the day in a conflict with the NLRA. And such conflicts do exist.

For example, ADA obligates employers "...to engage in an interactive exchange with employees with disabilities to try to reach reasonable accommodations. But it is a violation of the NLRA to deal directly with employees where a collective bargaining agreement is in effect, even in instances when an employee initiates the exchange" (Commerce Clearinghouse, 1993c, p. 4). General counsel for the National Labor Relations Board (NLRB), Mr. J. Hunter maintains that an employer is required to involve the union only if the reasonable accommodation being considered "...changes the job or working conditions in material, substantial, or significant ways" (Commerce Clearinghouse, 1993c, p. 4). It is obvious that the requirement of employers to consider reasonable accommodations; the recommended, interactive process for identifying accommodations; the bargaining unit's refusal to accept or approve an accommodation; and the historical prohibition against modifying a union contract during its current term are all potentially conflicting facets of ADA implementation in an organized environment.

Another area of potential conflict may involve the ADA requirement that an employer treat as confidential that information which is obtained from post-offer medical examinations or similar legally conducted inquiries. The NLRA describes the duty of an employer to provide "relevant" information requested by a union so that the bargaining unit might negotiate in an informed manner. However, both the NLRB and the courts have traditionally recognized that confidentiality and privacy are factors that must be weighed before ordering an employer to turn over information to a union (Commerce Clearinghouse, 1993c, pp. 4-5). This issue may represent minimal conflict, if any.

Without question, the most negative rhetoric involving the interface of the ADA and NLRA has centered around the EEOC's position that reassignment to a vacant position may be a reasonable accommodation and thus legally required. This was immediately interpreted by unions as an assault on seniority rights which are contractually established in the collective bargaining agreement and guaranteed by the NLRA. Seniority rights are perceived as the cement of the structure of organized labor, often providing the opportunity for longer term members to move into less physically demanding positions or more preferred work schedules as a reward for consistent union membership and service to the employer over time.

Regrettably, some labor leaders have condemned the ADA in its entirety because of this singular issue.

Organized labor appears to be caught between fulfilling its own ADA obligations by championing the rights of members with disabilities to reasonable accommodations vs. the integrity of the collective bargaining agreement. As one respected legal publication states, "...employees with disabilities could allege hiring hall discrimination if they are not accommodated, while employees without disabilities can argue that accommodations for employees with disabilities violate seniority rights" (Commerce Clearinghouse, 1993c, p. 4-5).

The final resolution of this conflict between contractually established seniority rights and the rights of qualified, current employees with disabilities to this particular form of reasonable accommodation will likely occur in the courts in the near future. In the interim, these considerations are recommended to obviate or at least minimize potential conflicts on a case-by-case basis:

1. When collective bargaining agreements are negotiated or renegotiated, an explicit provision should be included which permits both the employer and the union to take all steps necessary to comply with the ADA.
2. Reassignment to a vacant position applies only to currently employed, qualified individuals with disabilities, including injured workers with substantially limiting impairments who are seeking reinstatement with the same employer.
3. "Vacant position" refers to currently vacant openings. There is no legal requirement to hold or "freeze" a vacant position which might resolve an accommodation problem, nor to consider the candidate for future vacancies.
4. Reassignment to a vacant position is an accommodation consideration of last resort. Job modification, job restructuring, alternative work schedules, and other potentially effective solutions (even personal assistance) should be contemplated prior to reassignment.
5. There is no obligation to create "light duty" jobs where none exist. Where they do exist, it is helpful to identify these as time-limited, "transitional employment" experiences which do not convey the same privileges and benefits as would accrue to an occupant with the usual levels of seniority.
6. In evaluating the individual's ability to perform in the vacant position, only essential functions can be considered and all of the issues of reasonable accommodation must once again be brought to bear.
7. In nonunion environments, the right of a currently employed, qualified individual with disability to a vacant position (if this is the only reasonable accommodation available) is noncompetitive.

8. Compensation for performance in the vacant position is unrelated to previous levels of employee compensation. For purposes of ADA compliance, such compensation may be higher or lower than the previous job as long as it is consistent with the pay classification for the vacant position. In brief, there is no "wage-loss" provision in the ADA, although pertinent aspects of the local workers' compensation statute would apply.

THE PROMINENCE OF THE ADA OVER STATE WORKERS' COMPENSATION LAWS

The EEOC states clearly that the ADA requirements supersede any conflicting state workers' compensation laws. *The Technical Assistance Manual on the Employment Provisions (Title I) of the Americans with Disabilities Act* (EEOC, 1992b, Chapter 9) offers this example:

> Some state workers' compensation statutes make an employer liable for paying additional benefits if an injury occurs because the employer assigned a person to a position likely to jeopardize the person's health or safety, or exacerbate an earlier workers' compensation injury. Some of these laws may permit or require an employer to exclude a disabled individual from employment in cases where the ADA would not permit such exclusion. In these cases, the ADA takes precedence over the state law. An employer could not assert, as a valid defense to a charge of discrimination, that it failed to hire or return to work an individual with a disability because doing so would violate a state workers' compensation law that required exclusion of this individual.

FILING BOTH WORKERS' COMPENSATION AND ADA CLAIMS

In most workers' compensation statutes, exclusivity provisions limit the remedies available to an injured worker to medical, dollar compensation, and rehabilitation benefits. But employment discrimination is a separate offense, and filing a workers' compensation claim in no way prevents an injured worker from filing a separate charge of discrimination under the ADA. "Exclusivity" clauses do not prohibit a qualified individual with a disability from filing a discrimination charge with the EEOC, or from filing a suit under the ADA if the EEOC issues a "right to sue" letter. Similarly, no injured worker can be made to sign an agreement which prohibits his/her right to apply for subsequent employment with the same employer as part of a permanent partial disability (PPD) settlement or other legal agreement. One's civil rights cannot be bought away or waived by any such contract.

CONCLUSION

Health insurance reform, particularly if it lays to rest the impediment of pre-existing conditions, has enormous potential to improve the initial hiring of qualified persons with disabilities who have been chronically unemployed for so long. Disability management programming, with its emphasis on worksite rehabilitation and transitional employment, is clearly the ultimate cost-containment solution for injured worker issues. Both the health insurance reform movement and the disability management movement have been given enormous impetus by the Americans with Disabilities Act. Conversely, if careful planning for ADA consistency results in their long-term success, each movement has the potential to deliver on the promise of the Americans with Disabilities Act for both employers and qualified workers with disabilities.

REFERENCES

Bell, C. (1993a). *What can we learn from ADA litigation?* Presentation at First Annual ADA Milestones Conference, Milwaukee, Wisconsin.

Bell, C. (1993b). The Americans with Disabilities Act and injured workers: Implications for rehabilitation professionals in the workers' compensation system. *Rehabilitation Psychology, 38*(2), 103-116.

Blumenthal, S. (1992). Impact of the ADA on the vocational rehabilitation of industrially injured workers under workers' compensation. *In the Mainstream, 17*(1), 19-22.

Bowe, F. G. (1992). Development of the ADA. In N. Hablutzel & B. T. McMahon (Eds.), *The Americans with Disabilities Act: Access and accommodations*. Winter Park, FL: GR Press, Inc.

Commerce Clearing House. (1993a). ADA vs. workers' compensation. *Accommodating Disabilities, 15*, 4.

Commerce Clearing House. (1993b). Can full duty releases still be required? *Accommodating Disabilities, 18*, p.9.

Commerce Clearing House. (1993c). Employer dilemma: ADA conflict with federal law. *Accommodating Disabilities, 15*, 4-5.

Dent, G. L. (1990). *Return to work by design*. Stockton, California: Martin-Dennison Press.

Equal Employment Opportunity Commission. (1992a). *Americans with Disabilities Act handbook*. Washington, DC: Government Printing Office.

Equal Employment Opportunity Commission. (1992b). *Technical assistance manual on the employment provisions (Title I) of the Americans with Disabilities Act*. Washington, DC: Government Printing Office.

Gilbride, D. D., & Stensrud, R. (1993). Challenges and opportunities for rehabilitation counselors in the Americans with Disabilities Act era. *NARPPS Journal, 8*(2), 67-74.

Griss, R., & Hanson, S. (1990). *Accessibility, adequacy, and affordability of health insurance for persons with disabilities and chronic illness*. Oakland, CA: Berkeley Planning Associates.

Hablutzel, N., & McMahon, B. T. (Eds.) (1992). *The Americans with Disabilities Act: Access and Accommodation*. Winter Park, FL: GR Press, Inc.

Hammond, P. (1992). Health insurance issues and the ADA. *In the Mainstream, 17*(1), 23-30.

Hanson, S. P., & Watson, S. D. (1993). The Americans with Disabilities Act, health and workers compensation insurance, and health care reform: Implications for private sector rehabilitation. *NARPPS Journal, 8*(2), 83-90.

International Center for the Disabled. (1986). *Survey of disabled Americans: Bringing disabled Americans into the mainstream*. New York: International Center for the Disabled.

Kessler, L. (1992). *Americans with Disabilities Act: Focus on insurers*. Presented at Alliance of American Insurers Symposium, Washington, DC

McMahon, B. T., & Carlson, J. G. (1992). Disabilities Act: What employers need to know. *National Underwriter, 13*(10), 69-71.

McMahon, B. T., Dancer, S., & Jaet, D. N. (1993). Providers of technical assistance and employers: Myths, concerns, and compliance behaviors regarding the Americans with Disabilities Act. *NARPPS Journal, 8*(2), 53-66.

McMahon, B. T., & Shaw, L. R. (1992). Considerations for the rehabilitation consultant. In N. Hablutzel & B. T. McMahon (Eds.), *The Americans with Disabilities Act: Access and accommodations*. Winter Park, FL: GR Press, Inc.

McMahon, B. T., & Shrey, D.E. (1992). The Americans with Disabilities Act, disability management and injured worker issues. *Journal of Workers Compensation, 1*(4), 9-28.

National Council on Disability. (1993). *Sharing the risk and ensuring independence: A Disability perspective on access to health insurance and health-related services*. Washington, DC: Author.

Ronca, T. J. (1993). ADA v. workers' compensation: A definitional crisis? *Cost Containment and Reform Activity Report, 2*(1), 8-9. Boca Raton, FL: National Council on Compensation Insurance.

Sampson, R. (1992). *Americans with Disabilities Act: Focus on insurers.* Presented at Alliance of American Insurers Symposium, Washington, DC.

Shaw, L. R., & Linder, G. (1992). Resources for job accommodation. In N. Hablutzel & B. T. McMahon (Eds.), The Americans with Disabilities Act: Access and accommodations. Winter Park, FL: GR Press, Inc.

Siefker, J. M. (Ed.). (1992). *Vocational evaluation in private sector rehabilitation.* Menomonie, Wisconsin: University of Wisconsin—Stout Materials Development Center.

Thompson Publishing Group. (1992). Insurance company offers ADA liability protection. *ADA Compliance Guide, 3*(12).

Watson, S. (1993). An alliance at risk: The disability movement and health care reform. *The American Prospect, 12,* 60-67.

Ziemba, T., & McMahon, B. T. (1992). Reinforcing the need for progressive human resources practices. In N. Hablutzel & B. T. McMahon (Eds). The Americans with Disabilities Act: Access and accommodations. Winter Park, FL: GR Press, Inc.

Protecting The Employability Of The Working Elderly

Donald E. Shrey, Ph.D., C.R.C.
Norman C. Hursh, Sc.D., C.R.C., C.V.E.

INTRODUCTION

The escalating number of older workers in the work force signals a clear need for industry to examine the relationship between the aging process, disability incidence, productivity, and health care costs. While demographic trends of the aging population are well documented, the impact of an aging work force on business and industry is highly complex and far less understood. Older workers represent the fastest growing segment of the nation's work force and with fewer individuals entering the work force over the next decade, older workers represent a potentially valuable resource in an expanding economy. However, the aging process is often accompanied by functional losses and increasing incidence of impairment and disability that results in work disruption, loss of productivity, and escalating health care costs.

This chapter discusses the following questions related to the older worker who experiences an impairment or disability:

- How is the work potential of older workers impacted by aging, impairment, and disability?
- How can industry reduce the personal and economic costs of work-related injury and disability?

Note: From *Rehabilitation of the Aging and Elderly Patient* (Chapter 41) by Donald Shrey, Ph.D., C.R.C. and Norman C. Hursh, Sc.D., C.R.C. (Eds.) Gerald Felsenthal, M.D., Susan J. Garison, M.D., and Franz U. Steinberg, M.D. Williams and Wilkens. Reprinted by permission.

♦ What are the disability management interventions available to industry to reduce work disruption, sustain productivity, and enhance quality of work life for older workers with injury or disability?

THE AGING WORKER: DEMOGRAPHICS AND STATISTICS

Older individuals represent the fastest growing segment of the general population and the work force. In 1984, there were 28 million elderly persons in the United States, representing 12% of the population. Older individuals are expected to represent 13% of the U. S. population by the year 2000, and 21 % of the population by 2030, representing over 51 million people (Lewis, 1989). This dramatic increase is a result of several factors, including increased life expectancy, an aging baby boom population, improved medical care available to increasing numbers of people, and an increased adherence to fitness and healthy lifestyles.

While the number of individuals entering the work force is decreasing, due to a lower birth rate, the number of older workers in the work force, proportionately, is increasing. Between the years 1982 and 2000, the number of workers between 18 and 34 years of age will decrease 12%. However, individuals between 35 and 54 years of age will increase 53% (Bauman, Anderson, & Morrison, 1986; Fullerton, 1992). The significance for industry is that a projected economic expansion will result in 23.3 million new jobs by the year 2005, with older workers representing a valuable labor pool resource (Carey & Franlin, 1992).

The correlation between aging and disability prevalence is significantly high (Sax & Bauman, 1987). Older individuals have a disability rate eight times that of individuals under 45 years of age (Kemp, Brummel-Smith, & Ramsdell, 1990). In addition, the older person is more likely to experience multiple and chronic impairments, as well as a higher degree of disability (Myers, 1987). The annual number of days of restricted activity due to illness increases from 16 for individuals between 25 and 44 years of age, to 26 for individuals between 45 and 64 years of age. In addition, 35% of older workers have a disability serious enough to limit working, housework, or involvement in a major life activity (Myers, 1987).

According to Blake (1981), two-thirds of individuals with work disability are over 40. The frequency and rate of secondary work limitations, occupational disability, and total disability are greater after 55 years of age than for any other work group (Holland & Falvo, 1990). This has significant implications for employers concerned with work disruption and productivity loss, health care utilization and cost containment, and escalating workers' compensation costs (Shrey & Bruyere, 1991).

Illnesses and disabilities with the greatest impact on work and day-to-day functioning are chronic disabilities (e.g., hypertension, hearing and visual impairment, heart disease, diabetes, arteriosclerosis) (Robinson, 1986). Aging is also accompanied by increases in progressive and cumulative disability (e.g., degenerative disc disease, carpal tunnel disorders, arthritis). Cumulative trauma disorders impact work through fluctuating and cyclical periods of work disruption, and progressively greater use of sick time and other health care benefit utilization.

The aging process for older workers is also associated with physical, emotional, and sensory developmental losses in areas such as memory, judgment, reaction time, and intellectual or cognitive ability. The functional losses experienced by older persons are typically viewed as an accepted and expected part of the aging process. The reality is that developmental losses are highly selective, variable, and gradual across individuals and the aging process itself. Jobs requiring physical strength, endurance, and rapid work pace realize greatest decline in performance with aging (Robinson, 1986). However, physical effort, ability, and performance, even across age groups, are highly individualized factors. Additionally, the impact of functional losses for the older worker is dependent on the work activity of the individual. Management, service, or information technology positions are less affected by developmental loss or physical decline than jobs which are physically labor-intensive.

Older workers are often viewed as more accident-prone and susceptible to injury. While accidents, injury, and acute impairments are often associated with the aging process, they actually decrease with age (Myers, 1983; Robinson, 1986). Hester (1987) found that injuries account for 35% of disabilities between 45 and 54 years of age, but only 20% of disabilities between 55 and 64 years. More important to employers and industry is that older workers are less resilient, take longer to recuperate, and therefore experience longer periods of work disruption when injured or disabled. For the employer, older worker injury and impairment results in loss of productivity, uncertainty about worker availability, potential for extended leave, and costs associated with recruiting, selecting, hiring, and supervising new workers.

Older workers and individuals with a disability are often conceptualized as the "aged" or the "disabled" and viewed as a homogeneous group with similar and stereotypical characteristics (Bozarth, 1981). The older worker is portrayed as having reduced reaction time, slower in learning new tasks or keeping up with technological advances, unable to adjust, reacting poorly to stress, losing memory, intelligence, and so forth. In reality, the older worker, as well as the elderly in general, represent a highly heterogeneous group (Lewis, 1989). The functional losses associated with aging are highly variable in terms of individual performance differences and, for many, functional abilities may be as well maintained as in younger workers (Williams, 1986).

Losses and impairment do occur with increasing incidence, but the development is over a span of time. The variability between individuals actually increases with age (Bozarth, 1981). The heterogeneity of the aging work force dictates that assessment and development of vocational potential be individualized to best determine how available work return options and health care resources may be tailored to the individual.

CURRENT ISSUES

Disability Costs

Management of escalating health care costs is becoming an increasing concern for all employers. Older workers represent a segment of the work force with escalating health care cost liability due to the higher incidence of illness and chronic disability. It has been estimated that between $98 and $362 billion are spent annually on overall health care services, with 50% spent on older individuals (Nash, 1987; Williams & Jones, 1985).

Work-related injuries related to the aging process, including cumulative trauma disorders, represent a large percentage of medical claims. For example, degenerative disc disease, common to individuals between 40 and 60 years of age, costs industry between $10 and $14 billion annually in lost production, employee turnover, and medical reimbursement (McAbee & Wilkinson, 1988). The average cost of a workers' compensation claim rose from $8,811 in 1988 to $9,225 in 1989 (Fuchsberg, 1990).

Once out of work due to injury or illness, older workers stay out longer than younger workers (U.S. Dept. of Labor, 1989) and develop increased dependence on public and private health care systems. If they receive income maintenance benefits, such as Social Security Disability Insurance (SSDI) or Long-Term Disability (LTD), there is little financial incentive to return to work. Studies consistently document that less than 1% of individuals receiving SSDI benefits return to work and leave the benefit roles. Reliance on income transfer benefit systems such as SSDI or LTD is very costly, with approximately $22.7 billion in 1989 and $24 billion in 1990 paid in SSDI benefits alone (Social Security Administration, 1990).

With increasing numbers of older workers with disability or impairment, demand on both income and medical benefit programs (e.g., SSDI, LTD, Medicare, and Medicaid), will increase sharply. As the work force ages, it becomes imperative to manage rapidly escalating costs (Nash, 1987).

Economic and Employment Market Characteristics

Between 1990 and 2005, the U.S. economy is expected to grow by 20% (Silvestri & Lukasiewicz, 1992). While this statistic represents continued economic growth, trends are not as dynamic as in previous decades. Currently, the labor force is experiencing lower retirement ages among workers, fewer people entering the work force, and a greater proportion of older individuals in the work force.

Over the next decade, the labor market will shift from a strong manufacturing and industrial market to a service and information technology market (Kutscher, 1992). It is projected that by the year 2000, the service field will provide 90% of all new jobs, with business service and health service industries accounting for the greatest increase in countable jobs (Carey & Franlin, 1992).

A shift to service industries will reduce the need for workers to be involved in work that has a high physical demand and a corresponding high risk for injury and cumulative trauma. The emphasis and expansion in the service and information technology area will require a work force armed with a range of new skills and specialized abilities. Workers must take advantage of training and retraining opportunities to remain marketable to employers. This presents a challenge to older workers, who are often reluctant to participate in retraining, or who view themselves as unable to profit from training. The challenge, however, is placed equally on the employer to orient workers to the economic changes, and to identify training and retraining methods responsive to the workers' learning styles, while providing incentives for workers to take advantage of the training opportunities.

Technological Impact

The economy is also shaped by rapid technological developments. For the older worker, technology represents both challenge and opportunity. Technological applications rapidly displace old jobs with new ones, with skill obsolescence occurring as jobs become outdated. Older workers must be receptive to exploring how their skills transfer to new jobs, and how to utilize existing training resources to keep pace with technological advances.

Technology also creates opportunities for individuals who experience impairment or decline in functional capacities. Jobs and worksites can be "engineered" to reduce ergonomic barriers to performance, or modified to accommodate functional deficits. Technology has developed assistive devices that accommodate disability and augment functional abilities. Examples include adapted computer keyboards to accommodate physical disabilities and enhanced keyboards to prevent carpal tunnel syndrome for data entry personnel.

Older workers with impairments and disabilities will need to be flexible in adapting to new jobs and retraining, and receptive to technological accommodations that enhance performance and promote work retention. As the need for workers increases, it will become more feasible for employers to retrain older workers who are physically unable to perform former jobs. Employers must integrate reasonable accommodations, work retention strategies, and training and retraining as the normal course of doing business.

Vocational Rehabilitation Practice

The philosophy of rehabilitation is congruent with the needs of older workers with disabilities. Unfortunately, the practice of rehabilitation has not been responsive to the need (Bozarth, 1981). Persons over 45 represent only 23% of state vocational rehabilitation caseloads, compared to 50 to 60% of the population with impairments (Bauman et al., 1986; Myers, 1983). Vocational rehabilitation services needed for the elderly disabled are presently limited or nonexistent (Salmon, 1981), and older workers (over 45 years of age) with a disability have not been served when otherwise eligible. Sax and Bauman (1987) cite the lack of adequate information about aging and disability available to vocational rehabilitation counselors, and incorrect conclusions about work capacity and potential for employment, as critical deterrents for vocational rehabilitation's involvement with older workers. Rehabilitation and health care professionals categorically accept functional loss, physical decline, injury, and dependence as part of the aging process.

Older workers with disabilities represent a group for whom disability is a common experience and for whom services are least provided (Blake, 1981). It is clear that clarification is needed, with respect to the roles, responsibilities and policies of vocational rehabilitation, health care systems, and labor and industry. Rehabilitation services for disabled and impaired workers appear to be cost-effective over time and employers should view rehabilitation as a viable cost-containment effort with older workers (Becker & Kaufman, 1988).

ATTITUDINAL BARRIERS TO WORK RETENTION

Although chronic disability, cumulative trauma, and developmental losses result in work disruption and jeopardize ongoing employability for older workers, there are several barriers that play a far more significant role in successful and sustained work performance for older workers with impairments or disability. These barriers include stereotypical attitudes about the older person, public policy decisions that reflect disincentives for the individual to attempt work, and barriers in the work environment itself.

Employer Attitudes

The attitude of employers, health care professionals, and the older worker toward aging and disability represents the most significant and pervasive barrier confronting the older worker with a disability. Older workers face systematic stereotyping and discrimination based solely on chronological age, a bias identified as "ageism" (Benedict & Ganikos, 1981). Ageism is not a benign or static concept, but an active and instrumental belief system that impacts social interaction, employment practice, health care management, and public policy (Barry, 1981).

Employer attitudes toward the older worker affect hiring and promotion decisions as well as efforts to develop realistic work return options when faced with progressive disabilities. Employers view the older worker with a disability as less capable, inflexible, unwilling to be retrained, lacking physical skills, and as a factor contributing to increased health care costs (Nash, 1987). Decisions about hiring older workers are based on judgments about productivity, injury risk, adaptability, potential health care and insurance costs, memory and judgement, and age-related employment costs (Becker & Kaufman, 1988; Myers, 1987). Additionally, when an individual is considered for employment, employers often view the older worker as having fewer years of future employment and, subsequently, of less worth to the company (Nash, 1987).

Bauman et al. (1986) reported findings of an employment age discrimination study, which indicated that eight of ten Americans believe most employers discriminate against older worker. Six of ten employers believe older workers are discriminated against in the work force. Age discrimination was found to be the most frequently cited case brought to the Equal Employment Opportunity Commission (EEOC) board (Bauman et al., 1986).

Attitudes of Health Care Professionals

Ageism is particularly limiting when it affects the level and type of services offered by rehabilitation professionals, health care providers, and health benefit systems. Although rehabilitation philosophy is well-suited to working with the older person with a disability, vocational rehabilitation counselors demonstrate a high degree of age bias and tend to view older persons more negatively than younger individuals (Benedict & Gantos, 1981; Myers, 1983). Younger persons are viewed as more likely to have significant years of work life ahead of them; older individuals are faced with increasing functional loss, illness, and withdrawal from vocationally productive activity (Benedict & Gantos, 1981). The potential for return to normalcy, independence, and self-sufficiency for an older worker with an impairment is considered unlikely. Moreover, it is viewed as acceptable and expected that the older person will have an inability to perform up to previous standards or levels of functioning after rehabilitation (Myers, 1987).

When the functional disability or impairment that is present in older workers requires a worksite modification or negotiations with union and management representatives, counselors often resist contacting employers to develop labor/employer relationships (Dunn, 1981). The full range of vocational rehabilitation services is not made available to the older worker who may desire to continue work.

Attitudes of Older Workers with a Disability

The relevance of negative attitudes, stereotypes, and ageism among medical and rehabilitation professionals, and society as a whole, is that the attitudes and values are transmitted to the older worker (Benedict & Gankos, 1981). Older workers, in turn, internalize the negative social judgments and conclusions about their own worth, productivity, and potential (Myers, 1987) and develop a lower self-concept. They may perceive their role as a worker as being incapable, unproductive, and less desirable.

Older persons with impairments or disabilities are often placed in "double jeopardy" according to Rubenfeld (1986), since they are faced with multiple stereotypes. There is a similarity of attitude toward older individuals and those who have a disability. Each are seen as dependent, having problems with coping, and unable to adjust. The impaired aged are seen as sick or disabled. The stereotypes associated with aging are compounded with the experience of a disability. The perception of illness further restricts employment practice and health care efforts (Becker & Kaufman, 1988).

In effect, attitudinal barriers become more overwhelming and restricting than the developmental losses and chronic and progressive impairments experienced by the older worker. Ageism masks the reality that a wide range of individual differences exist, and that the older worker with an impairment experiences adaptive skills as well as losses. It further conceals the fact that the individual requires individual planning skills if capacities and potentials are to be maximized (Brody & Ruff, 1986).

Despite the social implications of disability, many older workers who experience functional loss, cumulative trauma, or injury want to work. Work serves an important economic, social, and psychological function at a time in life when the individual experiences other losses.

Lower expectations about adaptive capabilities, level of functioning, and future potential, are instrumental in shaping health benefit structure and health care system response: the response to the older worker with an injury or impairment is viewed in medical and economic terms, rather than through rehabilitation or disability management efforts. Societal response to the elderly has been a result of ageism: provide social security, medical insurance, income maintenance, and support, rather than rehabilitation needed to promote independence, productivity, and self-sufficiency.

DISABILITY MANAGEMENT PROGRAMS IN INDUSTRY

As individuals live and work longer, the health care problems associated with aging are expected to increase (Williams, 1986). Although business and industry will rely on older workers to fill new jobs, they must recognize and take responsibility for the disability, impairment, and performance characteristics that accompany aging. Several employers have developed responsive programs that utilize the potential that the older worker brings to the work force and that must be considered as the individual works and ages.

Recent literature has described several creative work retention programs for older workers. Coberly (1985) described industrial policy and programs that emphasize work retention up to and beyond normal retirement age, as alternatives to lay-offs and costly early retirement incentives. Atlantic Richfield and Northern Natural Gas Company utilize job-sharing and part-time work variations, where two workers may share the same job or have specified responsibilities for half a job. This allows a person to transition to lesser hours while retaining benefits and continuing contributions to the pension fund (and tax base).

Several companies have formal or informal programs directly responsive to injury or disability through job modification, job transfer, or retraining programs as alternatives to disability retirement (Coberly, 1985; Sax & Baumann, 1987). The U.S. Postal Service was able to return workers to modified jobs, despite their having "retired" on disability. Stouffers, General Dynamics, and Xerox, recognizing the high physical demand impact of certain work activities, have formal programs of evaluation and job transfer of older workers to less physically demanding jobs. Such programs reduce the impact of injury, prolong the working life of the employee, and continue worker productivity in a position commensurate with functional abilities (Sax & Baumann, 1987). Similarly, General Electric found it cost-effective to retrain older workers whose skills have become obsolete through technological advances, rather than hire and retrain younger workers (Coberly, 1985). While the programs and policies cited above respond to the aging worker in general, there are also more comprehensive disability management programs in industry that respond to injury, disability, and illness on the job.

Disability management programs in industry represent a proactive, comprehensive, and multidisciplinary approach to resolving work disability and subsequent costs. They often include prevention, rehabilitation, and treatment interventions to control personal and economic costs of injury and disability. Employer control and responsibility in the planning and coordination of interventions and services seems to be the key to successful disability management programs. Model disability management programs have been implemented in such industries as 3M (Davidson, 1985), Kimberly-Clark Corporation, Control Data Corporation, and Volvo Corporation (Galvin, 1983). Shrey (1988, 1989, 1990a, 1990b) described the coordinated and structured methods for controlling worker injury and reducing work disruption through use of prevention, education, labor and management collaboration, early return to work planning, and related processes. Significant cost savings have been reported in studies by Sears-Roebuck and Company, Aluminum Company of America (ALCOA), and E. I. duPont (Hinds, 1988).

Industry-based disability management programs have the capacity to assess individual vocational potential and design work return programs to maximize functional abilities (Shrey, 1990a). The increasing numbers of older workers experiencing chronic and progressive disability are often denied the benefits of such programs. As a result, many will never attain their employment potential.

DISABILITY MANAGEMENT: STRATEGIES AND INTERVENTIONS

A variety of strategies, programs and interventions exist for reducing the impact of disability on the older worker's capacity to perform work. The primary components of a disability management system discussed in this section include the following: Assessment, Disability Case Management, Medical Management, Disability Resolution Process, Rehabilitation Plan Development, and Work Return Transition/Worker Retention Programs. These primary program components are highly relevant to a multidisciplinary service systems concept, targeting employer obligations under the Americans with Disabilities Act.

ASSESSMENT WITH THE OLDER WORKER

Assessment, as a generic process, has traditionally been used with older individuals as a diagnostic tool to identify the presence and extent of a disability. There has been little recognition, and less application, of assessment methods in prevention, planning, and rehabilitation of older workers who experience functional loss, cumulative or progressive disability, or acute traumatic injury. Medical and health care planners are often unaware of the multiple evaluation functions that can assist older workers and, subsequently, assessment has been more a medical intervention than an ongoing rehabilitation option.

To be effective in evaluating older workers, assessment must recognize that work disruption or declining productivity is a function of the kinds of work performed, the characteristics of the work setting, and the changing functional abilities of the worker. There are several assessment strategies that can be used instrumentally with older workers to enhance vocational potential. These methods include transferability of skills analysis, worksite risk analysis, and vocational evaluation.

TRANSFERABLE SKILL ANALYSIS

The analysis of transferable skills is a formal process that considers the individual's education and work experience to identify a range of jobs in which same or lesser skills are required; similar tools, equipment, or machinery are used; and the same materials, procedures, subject matter, or services are involved. The objective of a transferable skills analysis is to identify jobs that are compatible with the individual's present or expected functional capacity.

For many older workers there is gradual loss of specific functional abilities due to functional loss or cumulative trauma which is experienced over an extended time. Analysis of transferable skills during this time identifies performance abilities not affected by impairment. The skill transfer analysis process specifies skills, knowledge, and abilities that may transfer to jobs and job tasks, equipment, machines, or work fields that are within the individual's residual functional capacity.

Assessment of transferable skills is also important when technological change, or a changing labor market, results in job skills or entire jobs becoming obsolete. The prospect of change or participating in retraining can be traumatic for the older worker, who may have little confidence in his or her ability to learn or profit from retraining. Analysis of transferable skills facilitates the older worker's smooth transition to related jobs, demonstrates that older individuals may presently be able to perform the essential job tasks within the new job, and utilizes the retraining approach that complements the individual's preferred learning style.

WORKSITE RISK ANALYSIS

In addition to evaluating worker skills, information about the job and worksite must be analyzed. Using job and task analysis and ergonomic evaluation techniques, worksite risk analysis assesses the degree of compatibility between the job activities and work environment demands and the individual's functional capacities.

Ergonomic evaluation examines the motion, movement, body mechanics, and effort requirements involved in the use of tools, equipment, and machinery within the specific work setting. Job analysis is a more comprehensive description of the job activities, including functions, methods, techniques, and procedures used in performing the job; the worker characteristics (skills, knowledge, and abilities) needed; and a description of the results of the work effort in terms of goods, service, or products.

The goal of worksite risk analysis is to identify and reduce/remove elements that constitute work hazards for the worker. The analysis includes recommendations regarding job accommodations and job or worksite modifications or adaptations to machines or tools. Worksite risk analysis also delineates the use of assistive or augmentative devices to enhance productivity, and includes recommendations for technological modifications required to substitute mechanical or electronic adaptations for physical effort requirements of the job.

Little consideration is given to the "reasonable accommodations" that can be made to respond to the older worker's impairment. Employers often view accommodations or modifications as too expensive (Nash, 1987), although studies have demonstrated that over 50% of accommodations cost under $100. Technology is available to provide assistive and augmentative devices, modify job and worksite equipment, and "engineer" worksite barriers to accommodate declining abilities. However, existing technology to respond to work disruption related to disability and impairment has not been systematically applied in industry.

VOCATIONAL EVALUATION

Vocational evaluation is a comprehensive, systematic process designed to identify and explore vocational alternatives, and maximize the vocational potential of the individual. For the older worker with a disability, vocational evaluation provides multiple functions as outlined in Table 1.

Table 1 Vocational Evaluation Individual—Environmental Factors		
INDIVIDUAL		**ENVIRONMENTAL**
Residual Skills	— IDENTIFY —	Job Requirements
Abilities		Job Experience Levels
Aptitudes		Required Training/Education
Adjustment to Aging Process	— ASSESS —	Work Return Barriers
Residual Functional Capacities		Physical Job Demands
Accommodation Needs		Accommodation Options
Individual's Expectations	— CLARIFY —	Employer's Intentions
	Return to Previous Job Reasonable Accommodations Transitional Work Alternative Jobs Retraining Options Retirement	

Vocational evaluation is particularly useful for older workers who may experience a period of work disruption due to injury and discover that their previous job becomes unavailable or unrealistic. Other workers may benefit from vocational evaluation when productivity is decreasing, and accommodations, job transfer, or other adjustments are needed. The function of evaluation for both individuals is to delineate the multiple options available, identify the services needed to promote work retention, and develop an industrial rehabilitation plan resulting in sustained employment.

The evaluation process results in an Individualized Modified Reemployment Plan (IMRP) to reduce work disruption, return the worker to suitable work activity, and promote sustained employment in a satisfying job.

ADA: IMPLICATIONS FOR OLDER PERSONS WITH DISABILITIES, EMPLOYERS AND REHABILITATION SERVICE PROVIDERS

The ADA has important implications for older workers with disabilities. The employment-related provisions of the act, under Title I, currently covers all employers with 15 or more employees. The Act utilizes the definition of "individual with a disability" originally put forth in the Rehabilitation Act of 1973.

Specifically, Title I of the ADA prohibits discrimination against a "qualified" individual with a disability in making an employment decision. A "qualified" individual under the act is one who meets the definition of disability and can perform the "essential functions" of the job with or without reasonable accommodation. The ADA does not define the term "essential functions," but this same language was utilized in the Rehabilitation Act of 1973 to avoid individuals being disqualified as a result of their inability to perform functions which were considered of marginal importance to overall job function.

Given these provisions of the law, employers are required to be very specific in regard to the essential tasks and functions required of a "qualified" applicant for any position for which they hire. Moreover, employers need to enumerate those qualifications in writing prior to advertising, interviewing, or hiring. There is a legal incentive for employers to consider job restructuring and job modifications which could both eliminate marginal tasks from the job description and enable otherwise "qualified" individuals with specific limitations to perform the "essential" functions of a job.

The United States has recently witnessed an unprecedented increase in the cost of health care in general and work-related disability and illness in particular. In the American health care system this has translated into direct costs to business, industry, and government which have significant implications for the stability of the U.S. economy. Additionally, the passage of the ADA, prohibiting discrimination in employment practices toward individuals with disabilities, requires that employers prepare to demonstrate compliance. In this environment, it is increasingly obvious that employers need to establish policies and procedures for the management of disability and illness among workers when employability is threatened. Employer-based programs utilizing interdisciplinary collaboration to intervene with both workers with disabilities and their work environments will characterize companies that successfully respond to the challenges of this changing business environment.

DISABILITY CASE MANAGEMENT

Disability Case Management may be considered an alternative management support system for controlling injury and disability problems. Within the context of disability management services, the defined duties of the case manager are based on the specific interventions, programs, and services required to facilitate the employer's management of workers with disabilities. Tasks performed by the case manager typically focus on resolving barriers to safe and productive work performance. For example, the case manager may be responsible for obtaining multidisciplinary evaluations of older workers with impairments to identify specific work disability and job handicap problems (e.g., job analysis, independent medical examination, functional capacity evaluation, vocational evaluation, psychological assessment) to identify the relationship between job demands and older workers' mental and physical capacities.

Work disability involves medical, legal, ergonomic, vocational, psychosocial, and labor relations issues. Resolving issues of work disability requires a high level of coordination, decision-making, and planning. Therefore, interdisciplinary collaboration among labor-management resources and community-based services is an essential component of effective case management. The case manager functions as a liaison among managers, physicians, safety personnel, labor organizations, insurance carriers, and others, while carefully orchestrating work return and worker retention planning activities for older persons with disabilities.

MEDICAL MANAGEMENT

Many case managers provide medical management services for impaired employees to ensure quality rehabilitation and treatment outcomes. Typically, medical management involves the close monitoring of employees with prolonged work disruptions, such as those having greater than three months projected time loss, or injured workers experiencing excessively lengthy hospitalizations. The case manager is often responsible for making visits to physicians and treatment programs, functioning as a liaison between the employer, other community treatment providers, and the impaired worker. The case manager may accompany injured workers to physician office visits for examinations or for independent medical evaluations. Likewise, the case manager may be required to make visits to "home-bound" impaired workers to monitor the recovery process and to facilitate planning activities for return to work.

DISABILITY RESOLUTION PROCESS

The Disability Resolution Process is a key component of industrial rehabilitation and disability management. This multidisciplinary process involves the coordination of objective medical, functional capacity, psychological, and vocational evaluations for older workers with disabilities. Ideally, the case manager arranges and coordinates multiple evaluations, as dictated by the older worker's specific needs. Once the worker's capabilities, motivations, and work qualifications have been comprehensively assessed, work environment information must be obtained through a formal job analysis.

As previously discussed, there are a variety of job analysis approaches, some of which are rather basic and informal, and others which are relatively complex. Generally, the Disability Resolution Process requires a formal analysis of tasks associated with a specific job or group of jobs, in order to identify what the older worker does; the purpose of performing each job task; the tools, equipment, and processes used in the performance of the job; physical demands required of the older worker performing the job; knowledge, skill, and experience level required to safely and accurately perform the job; and other measurable and descriptive information.

The written job analysis report serves as an accurate, objective functional job description. Accommodations cannot be made in the absence of this information. Job analysis information may be made available to treating physicians when projecting safe work return dates among older workers with injuries. The job analysis report may also be used when developing on-site work return transition and modified duty options for older workers with disabilities.

The purpose of the Disability Resolution Process is to resolve any questions or issues involving the relationship between the older employee's physical/mental job demands and the worker's capacities to successfully perform competitive employment. Both overestimation and underestimation of the worker's capabilities can result in unnecessary prolongation of disability and subsequent costs. If the physician overestimates the worker's physical capabilities, premature return to work may result in re-injury. More commonly, the physician conservatively sets return to work restrictions which greatly underestimate a patient's physical capabilities, thus delaying the restoration of function. Consolidation of information from the functional capacity evaluation, medical/psychological impairment evaluation, and vocational assessment helps substantiate the older worker's medical impairment, disability, and job handicap.

The outcome of the Disability Resolution Process is the identification of realistic, attainable options for resolving questionable or unknown disability and work performance problems. Such options may include job-site redesign, reasonable accommodations, rehabilitation engineering, ergonomic job restructuring, assignment of temporary modified duty, or referral to treatment or rehabilitation programs.

REHABILITATION PLAN DEVELOPMENT

Rehabilitation plans enhance communication and service coordination through clearly defined goals, objectives, and responsibilities. The rehabilitation plan also serves as a tool to evaluate the progress of the worker, as well as the quality of services provided by insurance, medical, and rehabilitation providers.

In formulating rehabilitation plans for older workers with disabilities, three important tasks are accomplished. The first is to determine what obstacles prevent employment or worker retention, and what must be done to remove these barriers. To make this determination, knowledge of the older worker's capabilities, physical job demands, and the relationship between these two factors is identified (i.e., the Disability Resolution Process). Second, the older worker with a disability and the employer must be made aware of any incongruence between job demands and worker functional capacities, and available options for remediating these differences. The third step involves development of a schedule that provides for evaluation of success at definite points. This helps the older worker to pace his or her own progress, making adjustments as needed. The Rehabilitation Plan serves as the key instrument in the coordination of disability management activities for older persons with disabilities.

WORK RETURN TRANSITION/WORKER RETENTION PROGRAMS

Some of the most effective disability management systems in industry promote the development of on-site work return transition/worker retention (WRT) programs. It is highly desirable for employers to develop and implement such programs, in order to: prevent work disruptions among older employees with medical impairments that effect work performance; promote a safe and timely return to work among impaired workers on medical leave, workers' compensation, or long-term disability, and accommodate older workers in alternative jobs.

The success of WRT programs is not only dependent upon their actual design, but also corporate policy, labor relations issues, and a host of other conditions. Once these critical factors are considered, the degree of success in a WRT program is only limited by available resources and the employer's creativity, flexibility, and imagination.

The development of a successful worker-job "fit" is a function of both the capabilities of the older worker and the requirements of the job. In a significant number of cases, job modifications such as tool redesign, utilization of aids or adaptive devices or job site restructuring are effective methods for enabling an older individual with a disability to perform essential job tasks. These same interventions can be utilized in a preventive manner to identify and redesign jobs which are likely to result in work-related injuries and disabilities. The participation of ergonomists, allied health professionals, and vocational rehabilitation specialists in the development of disability management programs and individual accommodation interventions is imperative. Such a multidisciplinary effort is required to avoid an over-reliance on medical model interventions which seek to remove the older individual's symptoms without regard to the possibilities for accommodation which may exist in the work environment.

On-site work return transition and worker retention programs, when properly designed, are far superior to clinic-based work hardening services. The goal of these programs is to promote worker retention among employees with work performance problems resulting from a physical impairment, or an earlier return to work among employees with physical restrictions. WRT programs are designed to provide a therapeutic work environment that identifies the older worker's restructured skills, accommodates for functional loss or impairment, or restructures the job to match the person's capabilities. The case manager may coordinate and manage the work return transition and worker retention program in collaboration with vocational rehabilitation specialists, physical therapists, ergonomists, managers, and supervisors.

The Americans with Disabilities Act signed into law by President Bush in July 1990, affects over 40 million persons with disabilities. This law is considered by many to be the most important U.S. civil rights legislation in recent history. When considered in the context of injury and disability trends among older workers, this act will have important implications for rehabilitation professionals, employers, and others, as new legal incentives for employers to develop disability management programs emerge. The law is intended to extend civil rights protection similar to that found in other civil rights legislation related to race, sex, age, and ethnicity to individuals with disabilities. Regulations have been developed by the federal Equal Employment Opportunity Commission (EEOC), which is also responsible for disseminating information to employers regarding their responsibilities under the ADA.

CONCLUSION

Health care and demographic trends indicate a compelling need to protect the employability of the working elderly. Despite the myths and misperceptions of older workers' capacity to perform competitive employment, the aging process does not necessarily pose an economic burden to employers. Proven disability management strategies and interventions have important implications to controlling the personal and economic costs of injury and disability in the workplace. This chapter described many essential features of proactive disability management systems that have profound implications for employers, health care providers, and the millions of working elderly. The future implementation of disability management concepts in industry will facilitate the retention of older workers and the years of skills and experience they bring to the U.S. labor force.

REFERENCES

Barry, J. R. (1981). Challenges of the future. *Journal of Rehabilitation, 47*(4), 94-95.

Bauman, N. J., Anderson, J. C., & Morrison, M. H. (1986). Employment of the older disabled person: Current environment, outlook, and research needs. In S. Brody, & G. Ruff. *Aging and rehabilitation: Advances in the state of the art.* New York, NY: Springer Publishing Company.

Becker, G., & Kaufman, S. (1988). Old age, rehabilitation, and research: A review of the issues. *The Gerontologist, 28*(4), 459-468.

Benedict, R. C., & Ganikos, M. L. (1981). Coming to terms with ageism in rehabilitation. *Journal of Rehabilitation, 47*(4), 10-18.

Blake, R. (1981). Disabled older persons: A demographic analysis. *Journal of Rehabilitation, 47*(4), 19-27.

Bozarth, J. D. (1981). The rehabilitation process and older people. *Journal of Rehabilitation, 47*(4), 28-32.

Brody, S., & Ruff, G. (1986). *Aging and rehabilitation: Advances in the state of the art.* New York, NY: Springer Publishing Company.

Carey, M. L., & Franklin, J. C. (1992). In *Outlook 1990-2005. BLS Bulletin 2402.* Washington, DC: U. S. Department of Labor, Bureau of Labor Statistics.

Coberly, S. (1985). Keeping older workers on the job. *Aging, 349,* 23-36.

Davidson, G. (1985, April). *Private sector efforts to control disability-related health costs.* Paper presented at the Meeting on Economics of Disability, U.S. Department of Education, National Institute of Handicapped Research, Washington, DC.

Dunn, D. J. (1981). Vocational rehabilitation of the older disabled worker. *Journal of Rehabilitation, 47,* (4), 76-81.

Fuchsberg, G. (1990, July 16). Employers' use of accident records raises specter of blacklisted workers. *The Wall Street Journal,* pp. B1, B3.

Fullerton, H. N. (1992). Labor force projections: The baby boom moves on. In *Outlook 1990-2005. BLS Bulletin 2402.* Washington, DC: U. S. Department of Labor, Bureau of Labor Statistics.

Galvin, D. (1983). Health promotion, disability management, and rehabilitation at the workplace. *The Interconnector, 6,* (2), 1-6.

Hester, E. J. (1987). The need for rehabilitation services among older workers. In L. G. Perlman, & G. F. Austin (Eds.), *The aging workforce: Implications for rehabilitation.* Alexandria, VA: National Rehabilitation Association.

Hinds, K. F. (1988). *Workers' compensation cost control: A maverick approach.* Pensacola, FL: Ability Management Associates Publications.

Holland, B. E., & Falvo, D. R. (1990). Forgotten: Elderly persons with disability — A consequence of policy. *Journal of Rehabilitation, 56*(2), 32-35.

Kemp, B., Brummel-Smith, K., & Ramsdell, J. (1990). *Geriatric rehabilitation.* Boston, MA: College-Hill Press.

Kutscher, R. E. (1992). Outlook 1990-2005: Major trends and issues. *Occupational Outlook Quarterly, 36*(1), 2-5.

Lewis, K. (1989). Persons with disabilities and the aging factor. *Journal of Rehabilitation, 55*(4), 12-13.

McAbee, R. R., & Wilkinson, W. E. (1988). Back injuries and registered nurses. *AAOHN Journal, 36*(3), 106-112.

Myers, J. E. (1983). Rehabilitation of older workers. *Rehab Brief.* Washington, DC: Department of Education, National Institute of Handicapped Research.

Myers, J. E. (1987). Challenges for the older worker in the rehabilitation process. In L.G. Perlman, & G. F. Austin (Eds.), *The aging workforce: Implications for rehabilitation*. Alexandria, VA: National Rehabilitation Association.

Nash, B. E. (1987). The state of the art: An overview of the world of work. In L. G. Perlman, G. F. Austin (Eds.), *The aging workforce: Implications for rehabilitation*. Alexandria, VA: National Rehabilitation Association.

Robinson, P. K. (1986). Age, health, and job performance. In J. E. Birren, P. K. Robinson, & J. E. Livingston (Eds.), *Age, Health, and Employment*. Englewood Cliffs, NJ: Prentice-Hall, Inc.

Rubenfeld, P. (1986). Ageism and disability: Double jeopardy. In S. J. Brody, & G. F. Ruff (Eds.). *Aging and rehabilitation: Advances in the state of the art*. New York, NY: Springer Publishing Company.

Salmon, H. E. (1981). Theories of aging, disability and loss. *Journal of Rehabilitation, 47*(4), 44-50.

Sax, E. B., & Baumann, N. J. (1987). Options for equality of services for the older worker with a disability. In L. G. Perlman, & G. F. Austin (Eds.), *The aging workforce: Implications for rehabilitation*. Alexandria, VA: National Rehabilitation Association.

Shrey, D. E. (1988). The employer: A key force in managing disability. *The Disability Manager, 1*(2), 3-5.

Shrey, D. E. (1989). Managing disability in the work place. *The disability manager, 2*(2), 2-3.

Shrey, D. E. (1990a). Disability management: An employer-based rehabilitation concept. In S. Scheer (Ed.), *Assessing the vocational capacity of the impaired worker*. Baltimore, MD: Aspen Publications.

Shrey, D. E. (1990b). Managing disability hinges on strong labor relations. *The Greater Cincinnati Business Record*, July, 2-8.

Shrey, D. E., & Bruyere, S. M. (1991). Disability management in industry: A Joint labor-management process. *Rehabilitation Counseling Bulletin, 35*(3), 227-242.

Silvestri, G., & Lukasiewicz, J. (1992). In *Outlook 1990-2005. BLS Bulletin 2402*. Washington, DC: U. S. Department of Labor, Bureau of Labor Statistics.

Social Security Administration. (1990). *SSA/90 - Annual report to the congress*. Washington, DC: United States Department of Health and Human Services.

U. S. Department of Labor. (1990). Outlook 2000: The major trends. *Occupational Outlook Quarterly*, Spring, 3-7.

U. S. Department of Labor. (1989). *Labor market problems of older workers*. Washington, DC: United States Department of Labor.

Williams, T. F. (1986). The aging process: Biological and psychosocial considerations. In S. Brody, & G. Ruff. *Aging and rehabilitation: Advances in the state of the art*. New York, NY: Springer Publishing Company.

Williams, T. F., & Jones, P. W. (1985). Rehabilitation in our aging society. *Aging, 350*, 2-3.

Williams, W., & Rice, B. D. (1987). *The future workplace: Implications for rehabilitation*. Hot Springs, AK: Arkansas Research & Training Center in Vocational Rehabilitation.

Managed Care Concepts In The Delivery Of Disability Management Services To Industry

William J. DeMarco, C.M.C.
Karen Wolfe, R.N., M.A., M.B.A.

AN OVERVIEW OF MANAGED CARE DELIVERY PRODUCTS AND SYSTEMS

Managed care is the fastest growing segment of the national health care economy. The term *managed care* has been used to describe everything from health maintenance organizations (HMOs) to discount arrangements with insurers. However, confusion over terminology has not prevented government and business from turning to managed care techniques, methods, and processes to contain rising health care costs.

According to the Workers' Compensation Research Institute (1992), a number of cost-containment strategies have been implemented that were specifically authorized by state statutes or regulations affecting workers' compensation. As a result, employers have the opportunity to influence the choice of an injured worker's treating physician in nine of the 48 jurisdictions included in the report.

A new program in Michigan, for example, promotes utilization review by requiring payors to review certain cases and encouraging them to institute reviews for others as needed. At this writing, Florida and New Hampshire are launching pilot programs to implement state-prescribed managed care and workers' compensation programs, and five states — Kansas, Louisiana, Michigan, Ohio, and Rhode Island — specifically authorize selective contracting. Oregon recently amended its laws to encourage employers and insurers to contract with managed care companies.

Limiting the employee's choice of provider is the most common cost-containment strategy, used in 21 of the 48 jurisdictions studied in the Research Institute's report (Workers' Compensation Research Institute, 1992). Fee schedules are used in 26 states, capping reimbursement levels for procedures performed by physicians and therapists. Although 32 states have laws allowing them to regulate hospital charges, only 18 states currently do so; another five plan to start.

Because of the inherent confusion over terminology, any discussion of applied managed care concepts must start with a look at the lexicon. In this section, the definitions will be unbundled to clarify terms, while providing a historical perspective of the intertwined relationship between managed care models and occupational medicine. Several future models will be described in anticipation of the market trend toward increased use of managed care techniques, methods, and processes.

THE BEGINNINGS OF THE HEALTH MAINTENANCE ORGANIZATION

The relationship between managed care and occupational medicine began with the health maintenance organization (HMO), from which the managed care industry has borrowed nearly all of its technology. Interestingly, HMOs started by caring for injured workers at the turn of the century. Consequently, the industries participating in health care contracting during the early 1900s are still some of HMOs' biggest clients today.

In the Pacific Northwest, lumber companies needed to provide immediate treatment to a scattered work force exposed to hazardous occupations. These companies began using service bureaus to receive and review claims, and to direct workers to various hospitals or physicians' offices. By using a service bureau, a lumber company could keep good workers healthy, treat injured workers, and prevent long-term disability claims. The resulting quasi-union trust funds were forerunners to the Taft-Hartley trust funds popular today with trade and labor organizations. Several HMOs, including Group Health Cooperative of Puget Sound, still rely heavily on joint labor-management support within the lumber industry for occupational medicine services.

Additional examples of HMOs reflect cooperative efforts among school districts, city governments, garment workers (Rhode Island Group Health), government workers (Group Health Association, Washington, DC) and construction projects funded by the government (Kaiser Permanente). All of these organizations needed to protect the employability of their workers before, during, and after an injury by providing care on an ongoing basis for a predictable cost.

THE GROWTH OF IPAs AND OTHER HMO MODELS

Pioneering HMOs were distinguished from one another by the type of delivery system they chose to use. Railroads used a hospital network, while the lumber industry generally used group practices. In certain areas, independent networks of physicians became "company doctors" that contracted with the service bureaus.

These networks of independent physicians are called *independent practice associations* (IPAs). Clackamas County, Oregon still operates one of the nation's most effective IPAs (Group Health Association of America).

The IPA approach to constructing a delivery system, as developed during the 1950s, fell into two categories. In a *closed panel* IPA, the physicians all worked together in a group practice, usually as staff. *Open panels* were more broadly distributed physician associations, made up of solo practitioners or those practicing in small groups. Now called "clinics without walls," open panel IPAs began the delivery of health care based on capitation, the payment to the physician of fixed amounts per month per employee. Capitation tied physician income to patient volume and not necessarily to procedural costs.

Various managed care organizations emerged from the open and closed panel plans, spurred in part by the growth of the insurance industry, which became prevalent following World War II. Returning GIs expected full-time employment and comprehensive medical care for themselves and their families as part of the good life. Because worker disability benefits and related compensation for death benefits and insurance were tied to security and retirement, they were insured by different corporations under different arrangements than health care.

Additionally, in some states, laws designed to protect injured workers during the recession of the early 1920s were still prevalent, creating an entirely separate industry than the traditional health organization of the 1950s. As currently recognized, insurance organizations split into two divisions — *property-casuality*, and *personal lines and life*. This is similar to the Canadian experience and continues to be the method by which most health plans are operated today.

In the 1960s, Blue Cross became a leader among insurance organizations specializing in health care. Accompanied by Blue Shield in some states, this highly visible insurer/health service organization created unique legislation for itself on a state-by-state basis and found its first client base to be school districts and employee cooperatives.

By tying the various open or closed panel delivery systems with programs offered by the insurers, providers found that they could receive full reimbursement for treating injured workers. They could also be reimbursed directly by the insurer for basic office visits and, in some cases, preventive care services. This simplified the claims process by eliminating the need for providers to collect payments from patients for services rendered.

Some of these provider organizations combined the delivery and financing of care and actually became the insurer, calling themselves HMOs or IPAs. Other nondelivery system corporations and groups were reimbursed separately by one or more payors after the patient was seen. The separation of reimbursement and delivery of service made the management of receivables a new function, but an essential science in most doctors' offices.

By the mid-1960s, the federal government took an active role in the growth of managed care services by creating Medicare retiree coverage and using both the integrated delivery and reimbursement system (HMOs), as well as the nonintegrated fee-for-service approach.

Through the HMO Act of 1973, the federal government tried to change provider incentives by encouraging more integration of financing and delivery systems to create local delivery systems. Government officials thought that salaried physicians working in a group atmosphere would be able to provide more cost-effective treatment. At the same time, it was believed that physicians would be able to provide more preventive services, reducing the large claims cost resulting from catastrophic problems. The providers had the incentive to be cost-effective and prevention-minded because they were at risk financially.

Government officials were particularly concerned about the Medicare and Medicaid populations, because expanding needs and costs would force the government to either raise Medicare taxes or decrease services. The planned "traditional HMO" group of providers would compete with fee-for-service clinics to deliver care to employers using Section 1310 of the HMO Act of 1973 (National Industry Council for HMO Development, 1984). The statute required employers to offer either open or closed panel plans, or both, if these plans operated in the service area where a number of the employees resided.

In 1976, HMO enrollment nationwide stood at three million enrollees. By 1993, the enrollment had been projected to exceed 40 million. This is despite the fact that more than half of the states have passed anti-HMO and antimanaged care legislation and that, up until 1991, any physician who became a full-time contractor for an HMO risked the potential loss of American Medical Association membership.

PPOs AND OTHER FINANCING MECHANISMS

When HMOs became popular in the late 1970s, the insurance industry took action against the competitive threat. By 1980, every major insurer owned or operated, at least in part, a health care plan somewhere in the United States. Because the insurers could not integrate care and financing, they were subject to using the 80th percentile of a market-driven fee schedule. This allowed the insurer's policyholders to seek care from virtually any physician without facing major restrictions. However, it also put the insurance company in the awkward position of being subject to premium competition while still being forced to offer more services to keep employer groups satisfied. Competition with HMOs and IPAs became a disadvantage over time because managed care organizations traditionally sought a lower-than-usual fee schedule or some form of capitation or at-risk dollars to be set aside for those performing the most services for the lowest cost.

Managed Care Concepts

Since the early 1980s, insurance companies have offered what they call HMOs, IPAs, point-of-service, and other arrangements. Many insurers characterize preferred provider organizations (PPOs), employer provider organizations (EPOs) or some variation as the delivery system of the future, when, in fact, these are not delivery systems at all. They are financing mechanisms designed to create a specific access point for specific benefits. The insurer's product is the policy sold to its beneficiary or subscriber. This is different from the product sold by health plans, which is the actual care provided.

A preferred provider organization can be defined in many ways. The most recent and broad-based definition can be found in the *Managed Health Care Handbook* (Kongstvedt, 1989):

> PPOs are entities through which employer health benefit plans and health insurance carriers contract to purchase health care services for covered beneficiaries from a selected group of participating providers.

This does not sound like a delivery system but rather a financing mechanism. In fact, it may be the model for a function in which the insurance broker places the benefits needs of its clients with a service bureau similar to those used at the turn of the century. As a result, some industry experts have replaced "PPO" with the term *preferred provider arrangement* (PPA) because it more accurately describes an arrangement between buyer and seller.

Some provider organizations have negotiated with industry for preferred access to the work force. The American Association of Preferred Provider Organizations (AAPPO) has set some basic standards for members to follow to be sure their group is, in fact, becoming an organized delivery system. But PPOs do not finance care or go at risk for providing care like most HMOs do.

COMPONENTS OF A MANAGED CARE SYSTEM

The Managed Care Cost/Control Matrix (see Fig. 1) may clarify the differences among types of managed care by showing the relationship between case management and the cost of management for various types of programs and services. The matrix shows considerable variation in both the degree of case management and the cost of management. In catastrophic case management, the PPO and the HMO provide the strongest case management, with the HMO at the highest cost. Claims processing, underwriting, provider bill audit, data profiling, and even discharge planning probably offer some relief for health care costs. However, by themselves, they are traditional insurance functions that offer limited management and control.

As health care costs continue to increase, employers are increasingly considering HMOs a cost-effective investment in care for their employees. Catastrophic case management, for example, is relatively inexpensive but offers strong case man-

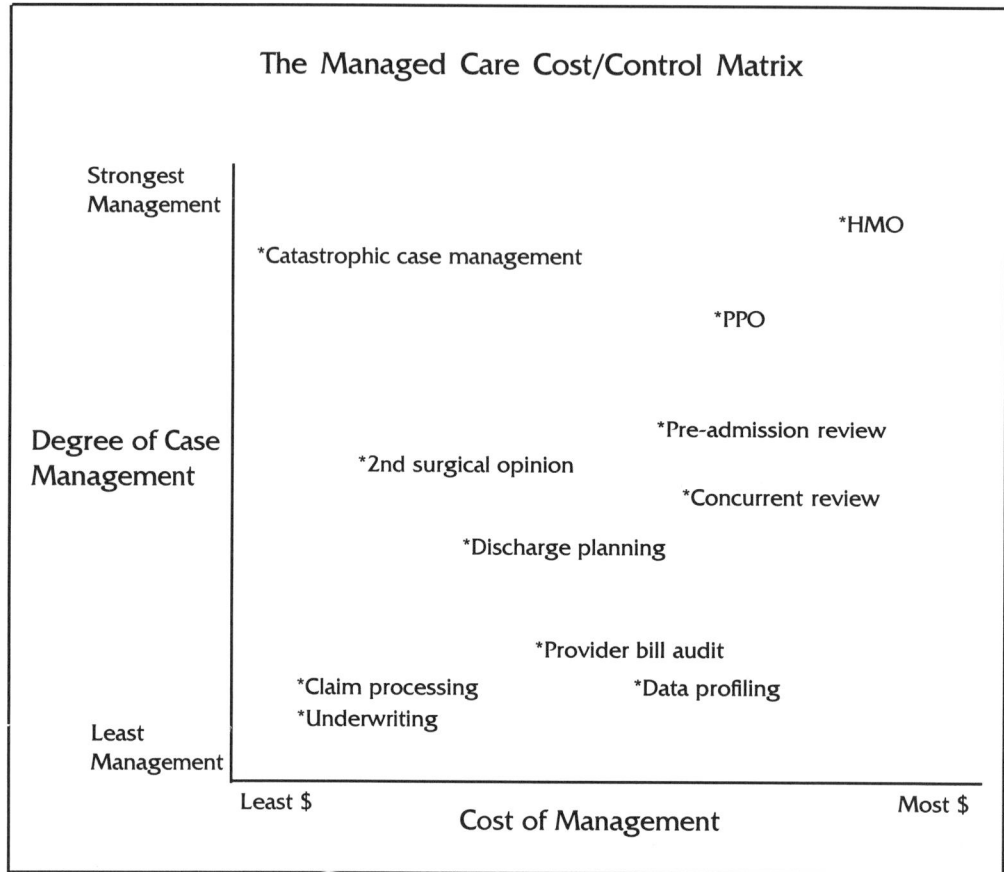

Figure 1. The Managed Care Cost/Control Matrix

agement, based on the matrix. It is becoming one of the key methods for measuring outcomes and maintaining accountability for both traditional fee-for-service plans and HMOs.

Figure 2 delineates several managed care components more clearly by showing these key operational elements:

- The *data profile* shows physician or hospital performance based upon a combination of claims information and the provider's general background according to a historical cost index for Medicare.
- *Concurrent review* examines claims information in the hospital or the physician office at the time services are being provided. In contrast, retrospective review often informs the employer and/or the insurer after the fact that a cost has been incurred. The concurrent review process is intended to keep claims current and to forestall unnecessarily large claims or costly admissions for unnecessary purposes.

- The *bill audit* has become familiar for most people in the workers' compensation arena. The audit reviews the complexity of the bill to determine whether services were, in fact, offered.
- The *PPO* offers an opportunity to negotiate in advance for services. Fee schedules and other issues are handled before a perspective enrollee enters the delivery system.
- *Second surgical opinion,* the seeking of a second physician opinion before surgery, is a review process that has been encouraged and required in most health plans.
- *Pre-admission review* is exactly as it sounds. Before hospital admission occurs, specific review criteria are internalized and the medical director makes judgments on nonroutine admissions

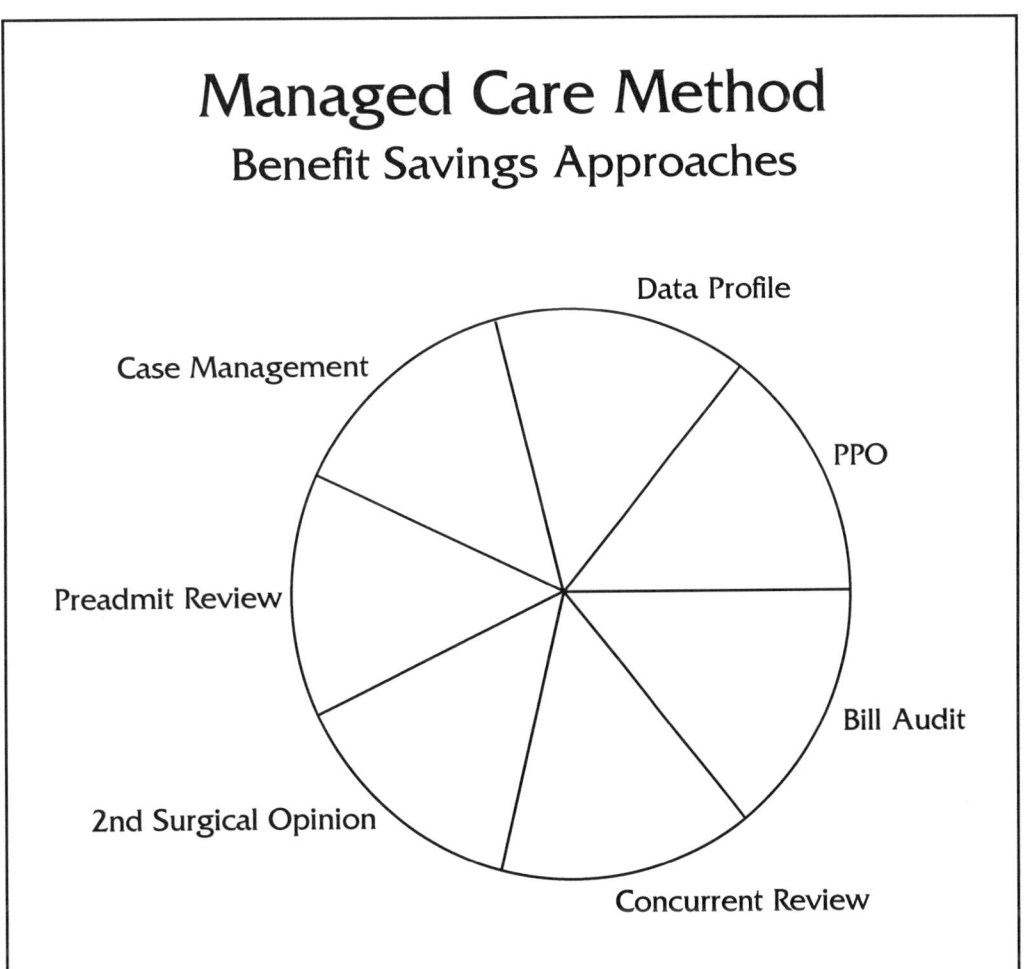

Figure 2. Managed Care Method

* *Case management,* which has become a complex area, refers to the use of a database to track and evaluate care provided and the delivery system's ability to expand upon its organizational barriers to make use of alternative methods for outpatient and inpatient care.

Of course, managed care does not simply consist of one or two of these segmented activities. Instead, by meshing them together, it has the capability to change behavior in the delivery system, to expand beyond the organization's normal boundaries in delivering care, and to bring together a continuity of patient care that lowers actual costs over time by assuring quality, and by changing the overall patient health status.

MANAGED CARE AND OCCUPATIONAL MEDICINE

Workers' compensation IPAs and PPOs operate nationwide. Some states require special regulations or licensure, but most of these organizations are strictly delivery systems. In several parts of the United States, HMOs now offer a workers' compensation component to their comprehensive package of services for employers (Workers' Compensation Research Institute, 1992). In addition, some insurers tie workers' compensation with traditional insurance, severing the line between "income security issues" and treatment management issues. Employers also bind the workers' compensation portion of their health care costs together and manage it internally with select physicians and hospitals in an abridged, managed care direction.

At this writing, managed care has not significantly expanded within the workers' compensation area, possibly due to legislation in many states designed to protect employees' choice of provider. It is argued by some (Workers' Compensation Research Institute, 1992) that removing this choice would create a "company doctor" image and reduce access to care for necessary services (Swedlow, Johnson, Smithline, & Milstein, 1992). The opposing viewpoint argues for licensure and certification of occupational medicine, the renaming of the Occupational Environmental Association, and the focus on workplace risks associated with lifestyle that create a predisposition for industrial accidents.

As occupational medicine becomes more widely recognized as an industry-centered specialty, whose medical standards and outcomes are governed by industrial organizations, the ability of these providers to work with managed care companies will improve. This will happen because the occupational medicine provider will not be viewed as an insurance company or employer-owned specialist, but rather as the industrial specialist they want to become.

The continued specialization of medicine is guided by technology and consumer demand for immediate gratification. Concurrently, work force characteristics are shifting towards a less individualized, more service-oriented environment. Therefore occupational medicine practitioners need to redefine their services in relation to disability patterns, legislative trends, and disability management principles and practices. For example, such legislation as the Americans with Disabilities Act of 1990 may tell us to look to the regulations for more options in offering specialty services.

Social trends, such as a greater need for long-term care and the increasing number of AIDS patients and work-related stress claims, are indications that employers and managed care companies need a disability management delivery system, not just a traditional treatment system for injured workers. Reimbursement is also changing. Soon the resource-based relative value schedule (RBRVS), used by Medicare to reimburse for physician services and hospital global budgets, will be in use by managed care companies and self-funded employers who suffer from fee schedule inflation (Physician Payment Review Commission, 1993). Packages of inpatient/outpatient services, ambulatory procedure groupings (APGs), and, ultimately, patient treatment methods measured on a performance basis will be the preferred method of payment in the very near future.

DISABILITY MANAGEMENT MODELS

Several chapters in this text consider model programs from an industrial viewpoint as well as from a family viewpoint. The purpose of this chapter is to provide a more "nuts and bolts" approach to how disability management in managed care systems works. Knowing how to fit the pieces together is as important as examining each one individually. In this and the following sections, a practical approach is taken, by addressing concerns of physicians who want to apply managed care principles to disability management — or to adapt to the managed care provisions being thrust upon them by employers and insurers in the disability area.

Most physicians become frustrated with managed care because it adds a layer of administration due to the *transactional* nature of the reimbursement system. In all areas of medicine, and especially rehabilitative medicine, trends suggest a departure from having each claim examined by a third-party managed care administrator to determine its appropriateness and payment level. Instead, evaluation is being performed on a case-by-case basis, with payment tied to outcomes and the physician's overall performance.

This is why several states require licensed case managers to serve as intermediaries, ensuring that the assessment of the illness, the expected outcome, and the pay process are linked. If not, the case manager, on behalf of the government compensation pool, will question the provider's fee or performance. Private employers who hire case managers to review compensation claims will need to have the same standards.

ADMINISTRATIVE AND REIMBURSEMENT COMPONENTS OF A DELIVERY SYSTEM

In considering need for technology to follow patients through the system on a case-by-case basis, almost every physician office spends considerable time tracking patients, referrals, and charges. Staff time spent searching for files to submit billings on a case-by-case basis is becoming increasingly expensive. This points to the need for a computerized system that can handle these needs efficiently.

Any physician considering increased involvement in managed care should ask: "Does our office use a relative value reimbursement methodology? If so, how well are we tracking resource costs vs. proposed resource costs on volume related to managed care contracts?" If the practice's resource costs exceed those proposed under the contract, the services offered should be re-evaluated. For example, if physicians are losing money by conducting independent medical evaluations and would rather perform some other procedure, it may be best to refer IMEs to a fellow practitioner who will, in exchange, agree to refer musculoskeletal patients, acute care cases, or another preferable service. This sort of exchange is how a network starts. The issue, however, is whether the physician has adequate administrative capability to create a case profile and know in advance whether he or she will be paid for providing it. This advance work and tracking represents a departure from the traditional fee-for-service environment.

MARKETING AND PRODUCT DEVELOPMENT STRATEGIES

Working in proportion to the expected gain, a physician could rely exclusively on third parties for market share and face the option of having fees discounted on a case-by-case basis. Or the physician could develop packages of disability management services that could be presented directly to industry, either individually or among a group of colleagues. This approach gives the physician multiple pricing options and also greater control. For example, if a link-up with a large employer does not increase business as much as expected, the physician can stimulate referrals through discussion or offer to visit the plant and hold meetings with employees.

Occupational medicine has always been associated with "dark hallways and slippery floors" in a manufacturing atmosphere. Traditionally, the biggest claims have occurred in the manufacturing environment, where problems with machinery and carelessness lead to time loss and expensive medical bills. Most employers fear this loss of productivity and associated costs.

Despite this perception, business and industry in the United States now operates largely in a service economy. This means that no one, including physicians, can expect to market the same products as those marketed at the peak of the manufacturing boom. The lesson for those involved in disability management is that they need to develop products to be marketed to industry in areas like ergonomics, stress reduction, fitness testing, repetitive injury, and perhaps sports medicine, to help the "weekend warriors" make it to Monday morning after a long weekend.

DIVERSIFICATION FROM EXISTING MANAGED CARE COMPANIES

Managed care will change the functions and responsibilities of business managers and medical office staff, who may need to "get smart" about managed care and the business-to-business process of negotiating with industry. One promising approach to providing disability management services is to negotiate a joint effort with a managed care company that wants to add disability management products. For example, suppose that a managed care company has suddenly announced plans to "roll out" a workers' compensation division. The company's strategy is to take an existing book of employer business and resell these employers on an additional product, creating more administrative income and broadening the company's attractiveness over competitors in the area who lack this capability.

The managed care company can bring employees into its workers' compensation program, through formal contracting channels in states where channeling is permitted. Referrals may also be accessed through informal channeling processes by anticipating injured workers' willingness to follow the direction of their union or employer out of loyalty to the company or fear of a complex system. Unless they take the first step, physicians who now provide occupational medicine to those employees may see them being channeled away by the managed care company. The logical recourse is for the physician to establish a mutually agreeable contract with the managed care company.

The physician can demonstrate a serious intent to collaborate with a managed care company by researching the company's strengths, size, and success record with entrances into other markets, as well as obtaining a list of employers in the area with which both the physician and the managed care company have mutual business dealings.

If interested in pursuing collaboration, the managed care company most likely will send the physician a credentialing form. At this point, based on the research, the physician should contemplate these considerations regarding the nature of the contract:

- Am I signing with a managed care company that is strictly an administrative or reimbursement conduit for an area employer?
- Am I signing with a provider network that delivers disability management services and then will negotiate on my behalf with the third-party managed care company?

♦ Or am I signing with an employer who has formulated a managed care relationship with a third party who then wants to work directly with my organization?

If the physician simply signs on with a list of participating providers, it is important to know how many other providers are on the list. This indicates the number of providers that can be chosen in the physician's specific community. From that, the physician can extrapolate the number of added visits or procedures to be gained by taking part. This also will be a factor in assessing whether fee schedules are acceptable, because most older managed care companies expect a fee schedule 8% to 10% lower than the usual and customary rates of most insurance companies.

Although capitation for workers' compensation may seem a long way off, all employers and insurers will want price in advance of service within the next several years. The reason has to do with the large variations in charges, nationally and locally, as shown in Figure 3.

START-UP OF A MANAGED CARE DISABILITY NETWORK

Another option for physicians is to start their own managed care disability network. Note, however, that the opportunity to start a network of preferred pro-

Procedures	11 States	Median Range of Fees
Neurolysis at Carpal Tunnel	$694	$400-1,028
Lumbar Laminectomy	$2,250	$1,040-3,400
Knee arthroscopy w/ Meniscectomy	$1,464	$979-2,147
Inguinal Hernia Repair Unilateral	$795	$575-1,152
Office Visit Intermediate Patient	$40	$25-63
Emergency, Initial Visit	$76	$36-130

Source: Workers' Compensation Research Institute, 1990 Study.

Figure 3. Range of Fees and Median for Six Common Procedures

viders only lasts a short while — until two or more contracting companies have earned the faith and trust of the majority of employers. Then, it is usually a matter of waiting for three years until the managed care contract runs out of creativity in developing new products or until employees start looking for local area providers to augment their existing relationships.

The place to start in developing a network is with a market assessment of what employers need and are willing to buy. Consider the public official in California who analyzed his constituency's preferences on key issues and found significant support for public transportation. He ran twice on the platform favoring the use of public taxes to pay for public transportation — and was defeated both times. He didn't know why until his strategists conducted an exit poll interview. They found that, while most people wanted public transportation, they did not want to pay for it (Levitt, 1983).

This shows the importance of designing an interview questionnaire that asks about desired services and also affirms the payment method for each preferred service. Phone interviews produce little accurate response, resulting only in discussions with lower level managers who have the time to answer the phone. They know the problems but cannot make the decision to buy. The mail-out survey method is redundant, because the response will favor a specific, self-select group.

The face-to-face interview with employers with existing relationships and with other employers is the most valuable. Timing is key. The physician who responds to a mass mailing from a managed care company, will appear to be on the defensive. Conducting all of the interviews before a managed care company comes in is a better strategy. It makes the physician look like a leader in the market because the willingness to do whatever it takes to retain local business has been demonstrated.

STRATEGIC ALLIANCES WITH MANAGED CARE COMPANIES

Another option for the physician disability management network is a strategic alliance between the network and a managed care company. An alliance can be by handshake or contract. It does not have to be a formal corporation or joint venture. For example, a physician may be successful in forging a network of colleagues to form a disability management network. The network functions as the negotiator for the group and also does marketing and nonmedical consulting. If the physicians do not want to raise the capital to build a full-blown administrative and reimbursement company, the strategic alliance may be the answer. A well-organized delivery system is attractive to a managed care administrative and reimbursement company, which would negotiate with insurers, HMOs, and large employers whose workers are scattered nationally. The physician network could contract with several of these administrative organizations by sending each a request for proposal stating that the network wanted to have an alliance with this third party, but that the physicians had conditions concerning the evaluation of care and case management decision making. Some national networks would pay a local management entity or foundation case management and provider management fees, which they would pass back to their employer or insurer as a management fee.

MAKEUP OF A NETWORK: DELIVERY SYSTEM AND ADMINISTRATION

The services that a disability management network can provide depend on the size of the market and the network's core strengths. For example, the network may want to provide acute care for work-related injuries but also may be open to serving as an ambulatory care center for other patients who need traditional outpatient care.

Level 1 Sophistication is at the simplest level, whereby individual primary care physicians in the network could become the point of entry for other specialists who would agree to refer initial visits or after-hour care of their patients. This basic health service, is a high-demand specialty that can provide an alternative to excessive emergency room costs for most employers and their injured workers. The physician also might want to provide limited on-site services as a corporate medical advisor.

Level 2 Sophistication requires more specialization in occupational medicine. Physicians in the network who are trained in this area might treat patients fitting specific procedure codes or ICD-9 diagnoses that have been identified with the case manager in advance of service. The physician's "other" occupation would be to consult with industry or to evaluate issues of concern to the employer or third-party contractor (e.g., the ergonomic design of the work environment, environmental toxins). Clients might include not only manufacturers, but also other businesses, such as retail stores, computer companies, and nursing homes. Some practitioners at this level have a physical therapist on staff or build a referral network of occupational and physical therapy specialists for follow-up care. At Level 2, the physician also refers major surgical patients to a specific hospital or surgeon under contract with the network.

Level 3 Sophistication is the tertiary care, surgery, and inpatient link to the network. Between Levels 2 and 3 are specialized outpatient pulmonary, laboratory, and x-ray capabilities, as well as other services that are more procedurally driven.

Level 4 Sophistication is the quaternary care level. This is the exclusive domain of the highest credentialed professional in the network. In some cases, network physicians may need to seek out an agreement with an out-of-town specialist. They also may need to contract with a hospital for short-term rehabilitation or convince a nursing home to set aside a handful of beds or an area on a prearranged basis for short-term rehabilitation therapy.

MANAGEMENT ISSUES

The local delivery system needs to have a *small* team of professional managers to conduct negotiations with industry and other third parties and to deal with the service needs of physicians, office managers, and the hospital support team. These providers are going to have questions or need authorization to admit and release patients, update medical records, and verify patient management plans through the case manager. How the local delivery system is governed will dictate whether the local delivery system needs to hire full-time staff up front or gradually move into this role once the market can be expanded to produce this need.

If the network chooses not to hire full-time staff, several other options exist:

- Rent — Some physician networks have rented management and sales capabilities by using temporary consulting to negotiate contracts and set up operations while training an existing staff member to become a full-time person and manage the operation.
- Lease — In some cases, physician networks have leased two full-time staff people part-time, or equal to one full-time person, from a local hospital. The leased employees conduct negotiations and provider relations through their hospital staff subordinates. This alliance can be structured as a separate entity from the hospital and the physician network to comply with federal joint venture guidelines. It should have written contracts concerning administrative services to the local delivery system in exchange for other services from physicians.
- Start-up management team — This is the method used by several physicians interested in remaining an independent, physician-owned network. Under this example, a full-time executive director of the local delivery system is hired to represent a physician board elected by the network. The executive director reviews all agreements from various purchasers and proposes needed services to industry. Usually a full-time registered nurse or case manager, the director has a secretary trained on medical records or a part-time nurse on staff. This staffer covers for the director when he or she is in the field answer-

ing provider questions or gathering case management data from homebound patients recovering from catastrophic accidents and injuries. A part-time medical director reviews cases questioned by insurers and authorizes the use of any non-network services and referrals that may need to be recommended.

PHYSICIAN MOTIVATION VS. CONTROL

The best article for physicians to review when thinking about placing "adequate" controls in the delivery system without sending negative messages to participating physicians is *A Physician's View of Managed Care* (Berenson, 1991). It summarizes several issues concerning physicians' skepticism towards market competition, contracting and credentialing, physician payment, gatekeepers, and utilization review.

Berenson (1991) compares how managed care is practiced versus how it is intended to be. Managed care companies have been so slow to truly manage care, he says, because they have been able to make money easily by selling transactional services — claims management, physician discounts, and "regulatory approaches" to managing costs. Physicians dread managed care because they view this approach as an intrusion and a threat to patient/physician relationships.

If employers, consumers, government, and managed care companies really want managed care to work, physicians need a common ground that allows them to benefit from their relationship with managed care. These benefits need not be always financial, although the reward mechanisms most managed care companies have are contradictory to the purpose of managing care. Quality of incentives, patient satisfaction, and professional recognition for superior performance all become motivating factors because they permanently change behavior and set managed care as a process, not a goal.

The real goal of the managed care process is to obtain superior performance, measurable in terms of improving the patient's health status, rather than just treating a specific illness or injury. Performance also must be measurable in terms of overall cost of care per patient or group of patients, based on performing the right services for the right patient at the right time. If high-quality care is encouraged, the cost per managed care enrollee will go down. If the cost side of the equation is affected first, quality reduction, in addition to having inexpensive care, may result.

An HMO's goal is to improve the patient's health status by paying physicians a fixed compensation and then focusing on quality outcomes, not regulatory controls, to lower overall costs. HMOs pride themselves on their collaborative development process for group standards and strive to treat the correctly diagnosed patient at the right time in their treatment path and under the correct location in the delivery system, either outpatient or inpatient. If physicians succeed in doing this, they are rewarded with a combination of incentives and praise, not further production quotas, requirements, and discounts.

MAKEUP OF A NETWORK: MARKETING, PRODUCT DEVELOPMENT, AND STRATEGY

The health care delivery system is truly the "product" being sold to third parties. The conceptual dimensions of this product are the boundaries within which the third party will see the benefits. This means that selling a total solution to the health care problem in this country is outside the boundaries of what a disability management delivery system can promise. To set expectations means to set some limits on what will or will not be a product and will assist the strategic formation as well as the product development sequence for the medical group.

Product development is a process, just like marketing is a process. Marketing, in its classic definition, focuses upon the needs of the buyer — in this case, the employer, the HMO, or the insurer. Sales focuses exclusively on the needs of the seller — in this case, the physician or the hospital. In health care, the words are used interchangeably, because health care management has always survived without formal "patient accrual" strategies. Many business people who are not focused on the particular needs of this market fail. Their failure comes from not adapting to the market and not having the capital to carry product improvements to the market long enough to sustain a competitive edge.

CRAFTING A COMPETITIVE STRATEGY

Market-based Strategic Planning (MSP) is a different concept than the traditional planning process in which lists of tasks and deadlines comprise the marketing plan. The concept of strategic planning began early in World War II, when the use of multiple variables in planning and the science of logistics gave rise to the discipline of operations research. Studies of the efficiencies of moving materials, supplies, personnel, and resources soon were impacted by the technology of automation (DeMarco & Garvey, 1986). During the 1950s, systems analysis and programming were applied to everything from accounting to management, and a systems approach to operations research was the precursor to the 1960s concept of research and development. Out of these beginnings emerged strategic planning, the "catch-all" for any activities related to assessing an organization's future needs/resources.

Although *strategic planning* and *market-based planning* are used synonymously, the terms have contradictory objectives. Strategic planning focuses on the needs of the organization, while marketing strategy focuses upon the needs of the marketplace. Marketing strategy, as related to medical groups and HMOs, can be defined as the "method used to focus, target, and attract the most desirable enrollees from an overall marketplace, bearing in mind the realities of the competitive position of one's product and its strengths and weaknesses as perceived by the purchasing public."

Market-based strategic planning brings together the concepts of management's needs and the needs of the marketplace. Dr. Theodore Levitt (1983), a Harvard University professor of marketing, points out that management strategy must be market based to be successful in a competitive environment. Market-based strategic planning embodies the external and environmental research activities with the internal management activities of program development and research. Health care executives need to concentrate on objectives tied to realistic expectations available in the marketplace. This process includes financial and operational considerations to implement strategy, but the basic assumptions must be market based. Without a well-documented answer to "why we need to do this," a plan of "how to do something" will fail.

Figure 4 depicts the strategic planning process, which can be used by medical networks, groups, physician-hospital joint ventures, and others to create a local delivery system attractive to third-party organizations. The environmental or external assessment examines the events, forces, or trends outside the health care organization that are most likely to influence its future. These include such factors as population demographics, changing reimbursement patterns, and competition with other area health care organizations and providers. Because of the importance of the external assessment, it is discussed in more detail later.

The environmental and internal assessments are blended into a strategic issues analysis and an evaluation of the present situation. External assessment leads to recognition of the need for market share retention and growth, while internal assessments focuses on the feasibility on diversification through various workers' compensation and disability management products.

These considerations, plus deciding on strategic positioning in the marketplace, leads to the development of a strategic plan to become involved with various third parties. It is important to note the strategic planning is an intra-active process, which may involve several successive versions before a workable plan is reached. Each revision produces results that approximate the desired plan more closely, until a final plan is evolved. Even then, flexibility should be a prime consideration.

An implementation plan is comprised of the facility plan, a financial plan, a human resource plan, and a marketing plan, all of which map out the physical and financial requirements, human resource and management skills needed for the health care organizations to successfully enter this disability management marketplace.

Market-based strategic planning works because it *creates opportunities.* A consistent approach to implementing the decision-making process grows out of what at first is a confusing mass of variables and logistics — including development options, systems applications, market planning, and organizational ambitions. Management without opportunities is a static process. Unnoticed opportunities leave the unfulfilled promises of the management process open to competitors capable of building on them through market-based strategic planning.

Managed Care Concepts

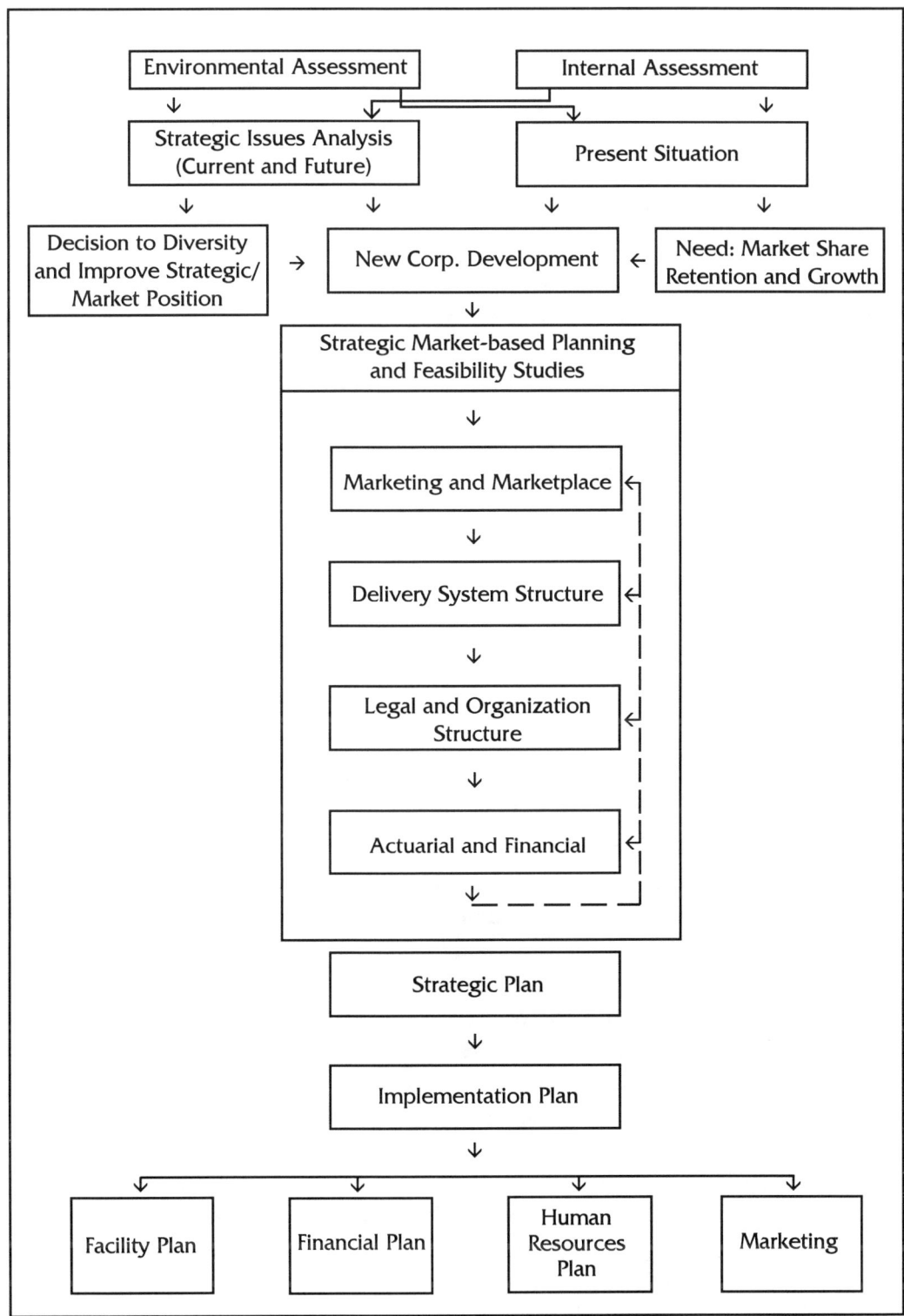

Figure 4. Strategic Planning Process

BUILDING A DEFENDABLE POSITION

The "acid" test of a plan's defendability is from a standpoint of durability. That means a clear product diversification process with a specific delivery system and the flexibility to retain current patients, thereby positioning the network for growth and maintaining the satisfied patient base on a long-term basis.

The flow of considerations from marketing through financial impact for each new product are the questions of durability to be asked as part of the market-based strategic planning process. The best way to illustrate the elements of competitive strategy and defendable positioning is to study what has not worked:

1. Consider, for example, a physician who dreams up products and services without looking at the depth and scope of the market potential. Time and effort may be spent printing brochures, selling to employers and third parties, and following through on awareness and education programs, only to find that the competition will benefit from the long-term durable product need that has been identified.
2. Another example includes physicians and hospitals who generally believe discounts will support product entry. Instead, discounts assure that the product will be devalued by implying unlimited elasticity in price. They also destroy steady income from current patients by discounting the rate they are paying. In a competitive market, some price concessions are necessary, but in a product entry situation, this is neither a long-term durable or defendable position. The hospital that goes through its emergency room address listings to find its clients is only fooling itself.
3. A network or agreement will only succeed if its partners are loyal. Securing the loyalty of employers and third parties requires mutual commitment. Commitment is not mutual unless a written agreement offered to the provider describes specific service in exchange for specific volume or specific methods by which patients enter the system of care. The alternative is to risk being dumped upon by every third party who demands an employer receive treatment after they have been home 90 days on disability. Results are difficult to achieve after the patient has developed coping behaviors that do not necessarily include returning to work.
4. Provider-run organizations that have not created or funded a business-to-business strategy often fail because they lack experience. Consider the complexity involved in hiring and motivating a full-time marketing director and overseeing program development process, a public relations initiative, and related sales and marketing activity. Led by a person with no understanding of managed care and limited experience with a delivery system, the venture is bound to fail. In addition, undercapitalizing a semivariable

commitment to a complex product sold to an unsophisticated audience invites failure.
5. Other organizations fail because they do not anticipate legislative change. Many providers view workers' compensation laws as the last bastion of free enterprise and fee-for-service billing. However, state governments are already setting in motion fee schedules, utilization review, licensed case managers, and other regulatory approaches to managed care. Providers who anticipate an increase in questioned procedures and other "standards of care" issues in traditional care will have the advantage in the new delivery system.

MAKEUP OF A NETWORK: EXPANDING INFORMATION SYSTEM USE

The notion of using information in disability management is not new. Employers, insurers, insurance administrators, and others have long understood the value of using computers to track disabilities. In fact, the use of computers to help manage disabilities of all kinds is widely accepted and has been implemented in several ways. What is not generally understood, however, is how to reframe and reconceptualize the computer as an information management tool which will positively influence the disability management process itself, serve as a platform for accountability and decision making, and act as a tool for behavioral change.

Merely computerizing information is not the same as information management, which implies far more than data capture, storage, and reporting, the common uses for computers. Information management must be understood in new terms. This requires entering a new paradigm of disability management in which computerized information is used to change behavior, to effect disability prevention, and to target an array of positive outcomes.

Whether a disability arises out of the work setting and is compensable through the workers' compensation system, or is associated with a benefit plan in the form of short- or long-term disability or other absence benefits, the need to monitor is certain. The key questions are, what is the potential of computerized monitoring and how can disability managers move into the next paradigm of information management to achieve more powerful and positive results for quality care and cost management?

Insurers and insurance administrators were the leaders in recognizing how computerization could increase accuracy and speed the claims adjudication process. Checks are processed and payment reports written in a never-ending cycle. Insurers have implemented computerized bill audit systems as part of their cost-containment efforts. The computer is essential to these efforts because it does not forget the events it records.

Computers in disability management have been helpful for other applications, as well. Operations managers who want to know when a disabled worker is expected to return can find out immediately after the information is entered. Computerization can also greatly alleviate the burden of required workers' compensation and OSHA documentation and reporting of disabilities. Those reports are data rich. When entered into a computerized base, they are an excellent platform for the next paradigm of information management.

Monitoring the medical course of a disability is a more recent use of computer technology. Occupational health providers are particularly concerned about demonstrating their cost-effectiveness to employers and insurers. Unfortunately, most only monitor their own participation in the disability case, forgetting to monitor other influences such as medical utilization outside their purview. Workers' compensation is particularly fragmented, so these efforts sometimes perpetuate the problem rather than contributing to the solution.

USING INFORMATION TO DEVELOP NORMATIVE DATA

Many people involved in disability management today recognize the potential of Day 1 case management in disability management. Many also recognize a need for disability duration and medical services utilization guideline data. In other words, they want computerized normative data suggesting appropriate disability durations that can be used as criteria in case management.

Normative data are not available, even though insurers and insurance administrators have been computerized for years, because standards were not used. Professional medical input into insurance computer systems was minimal, if existent at all, so diagnostic codes were not used. Broad injury type categories and body parts were, and frequently still are, the only descriptive criteria. In many cases, left and right body parts were not distinguished.

Attempting to interpolate standard disability duration for a given injury type from such data is impossible. Indications of severity are nonexistent. Happily, available systems now monitor disability and return to work by ICD-9 code. However, insurers are not always keen about these systems because the users are not medically oriented professionals. Nevertheless, when coded appropriately with ICD-9 codes and recorded for a statistically representative population, normative data will be readily available.

Stated differently, in the case of disability duration, normative data are unavailable because the information opportunity was missed. Computerization was available, but information was not. Historically, part of the reason was technology constraint. Systems could not accommodate so many data fields, but also the narrow focus was on cutting checks and printing reports, the task at hand. System designers did not analyze information potential.

Similarly, medical utilization normative data is not available. If insurers had kept data about treatments and procedures with return-to-work outcomes by ICD-9 code, clear guidelines would be available. Imagine the possibilities. Of course, the data is available in the final analysis. Unfortunately, it is only available item by item in medical and claims records. The cost of retrieving data from manual systems is unapproachable.

USING INFORMATION TO TRACK TRENDS

The concept of trending data is widely supported, but not widely implemented as an internal management tool. Trending analysis provides a platform of information from which problems can be identified early and decisions made. Making those decisions is relevant only in the present. When decisions are based on old data, several additional risks ensue. One is that the information is no longer valid or is not valid for the same group. Acting on invalid or inaccurate data is risky because it causes anger and resentment among the affected persons or groups.

Trending should occur as concurrently as possible with the events being monitored. Only then is the data a valuable management tool. For instance, insurance loss runs, while dated the most recent month, actually contain data that is several months old. Many reasons account for this, and insurers are not singularly responsible. For example, many employers and employees are delinquent in giving insurers their accident information. Nevertheless, caution should prevail in using insurance loss runs to create action items for intervention. Concurrent information is the only credible information for the new paradigm of information management.

Concurrent information is created as nearly simultaneously to the event as possible. When data is viewed as an important management tool, resources are allocated to key the data immediately. This is a must. Reports can be run reflecting events keyed moments before. The implication is, of course, that the employer must get involved in the disability management process. Relying on the insurer or insurance administrator alone does not contribute to effective solutions for quality control and cost management.

USING INFORMATION TO CHANGE BEHAVIOR

Using information to change behavior is the power potential in the new information paradigm. It is really simple. Concurrent information is distributed to the people who can influence it, such as supervisors and managers.

Many people now acknowledge that workplace accidents are not caused so much by dark hallways, slippery floors, and malfunctioning equipment as by attitudes and relationships affected by management, especially direct supervisory management. When supervisors receive concurrent information about the incidence in their departments, specifically the elements they can influence, and when their managers also receive that information (it is public information), the supervisors change their behavior. Their leadership style improves.

Using information in this way has a powerful sentinel effect. People perform differently when the spotlight is on them. Not only that, but never before have they had useful benchmarks to follow. Frequently, supervisors are given cost information only, which can have a punitive effect. More comprehensive information, which might include financial information, offers facts such as what occurred, when, who was involved, and the number of lost or modified work days associated with the disability. The information has characteristics that can be acted upon.

The accountability is still there, but supervisors also have the opportunity to appreciate a broader scope and to act accordingly. Including work days lost and modified days portrays actual modified work program utilization and guides the supervisor toward more efficient implementation. In other words, immediate feedback, just as in any learning situation, is key to performance.

The same methodology can be used with providers. Elaborate plans have been devised under the heading of *cost-containment* to "manage" providers. Once again, the use of information and its powerful sentinel effect can have astounding results. Providers — not only physicians, but chiropractors, physical therapists, rehabilitation counselors, and others — benefit from the concurrent feedback and benchmarking. Especially when coupled with performance figures of similar providers and grouped by ICD-9 codes, concurrent information has a profoundly positive impact. Providers are expected to perform in certain ways, but too often are not offered feedback. Concurrent performance information is the basis for guidelines and, eventually, normative guidelines.

The power of information to influence behavior or performance cannot be underrated. It is objective and factual, not skewed by personal and territorial issues, and therefore, more easily accepted and acted upon. Individuals, whether supervisors, managers, or providers can make rational decisions on its basis.

USING INFORMATION FOR CONTINUOUS QUALITY IMPROVEMENT

Continuous quality improvement through information can be applied to the provider community. In jurisdictions where employers have no "control" over provider selection, information acts as the juror in provider performance. Providers also generally want to be viewed as doing a good job for all concerned. The information makes performance public, and continuous information perpetuates it. As the number of cases increases in the database, valid normative data is made available.

The new paradigm of information management is simple, yet powerful. Post-occurrence concurrent data collection results in prevention. Of course, it requires careful system and report design with thoughtful distribution. There are verifiable cases where this plan has been implemented, resulting in 50% to 60% reduction in case frequency and severity. It is clearly a matter of approach.

In this information management approach, supervisors, managers, and providers are viewed as competent persons to be supported with helpful information to guide them. Upper management communicates the importance by allocating resources for data input and processes for information gathering and distribution.

COMBINING INFORMATION MANAGEMENT WITH CASE MANAGEMENT

The most effective way to implement an information management process is to implement an information-based case management approach. A case manager, tooled with a computerized information system designed to monitor and coordinate cases from Day 1 will naturally and automatically produce the appropriate data, which can be formatted into information for distribution to supervisors, managers, and providers.

An available individual to undertake this task within a company is an occupational health nurse. Corporations can redirect nurse functionality from first aid care to case management for powerful disability management results. By leveraging nurses' knowledge of health and health systems for disability management and using their expertise in coordinating the process, huge gains can be made in quality and cost management. Upper management can make this happen by tooling them with an appropriate information system and thereby enjoy the revenue conservation that results.

INFORMATION SYSTEM DESIGN

If managing behavior with information is so simple, why has it not been widely implemented? The reason is widespread organizational and system fragmentation. Many persons are involved in most disability cases. When many competent persons are involved, each working in their discrete domains, when participants protect territories and disciplines, when persons with the power to design systems do not have adequate knowledge of health and human behavior, system design is fragmented like the system itself.

Organizations are similarly fragmented. American industry has evolved a peculiar internal fragmentation. Health, safety, and workers' compensation are not allied with benefits administration. Risk management is not closely allied with human resources.

Operational (line) management is not involved with health and safety. Management information services are mandated to support the main product line, and appropriately so. If the product line is manufacturing a product, for instance, resources are limited for human resources information. While these are generalizations, they are true more often than not.

Information system design for disability management must combine expertise of computer systems, health and safety, insurance and loss control, as well as knowledge of human behavior and organizational psychology, a rare combination in one person but available with a team approach. Information systems for disability management as described here have been designed and are available on the market. Purchasing such a system is quicker and more economical than system development.

REDEFINING THE ROLES OF BUYER AND SELLER TO IMPROVE OUTCOMES

There are no secret methods in selling to employers or insurers, but employers' skepticism over dealing with providers on a direct basis cannot be overcome unless "sellers" of care adopt the marketing approach of focusing upon the needs of the employer as a buyer, not just a payor. This acceptance of the employer as a buyer extends throughout the marketing process to accept providers as a delivery system that works together. This group of caregivers is held accountable for making improvements in the delivery system and also in assisting buyers to understand that the patients or customers who use this system actually drive the cost upwards if they use the system incorrectly.

The legal and disorganized relationships among providers place the user of the workers' compensation system in the awkward position of abusing the system unintentionally. After that, the user finds it is more convenient to abuse the system, which drives costs up for buyers and caregivers. This vicious circle of abuse usually adds another layer of regulatory "protections" to fend off abuse but still protect the employee. The employee, or user of care, will continue to drive legislation until caregivers and buyers get together on not just cost containment — which again carries the connotation of restrictions, rules, and discounted payments — but rather on what drives the cost. The cost comes from the worker being off work, his or her productivity being interrupted, and the company's replacement cost to get the idle worker's manufacturing machine back to full production.

SHIFT FROM "COST-CONTAINMENT" TO PRODUCTIVE HEALTHY EMPLOYEES

Finding common ground to make workers productive is essential. This cannot be done by simple utilization review and quality assurance that looks at isolated incidents along the treatment path. This cannot be done by claims management or underwriters. Claims management looks at paid claims experience, not the worker who decided to avoid the compensation route and be treated by the HMO or family medical plan for a work-related injury. Underwriters look at probabilities of illness and disease and can predict lost work days but cannot measure the impact of changing a company policy to, for instance, require seat belts to avoid head injuries. They cannot predict the improvements of operating in a smoke-free environment.

The real issue becomes: Did we get the person back to work, or improve their health status through better treatment until they could return to work? In other words, from the time the patient entered the health care system until they were discharged or given a reassigned work status and went through a recovery program, what were the costs and the possible alternative treatments available? Was the caregiver the right person for the right patient at the right time?

COORDINATING CARE THROUGH CASE MANAGEMENT

Managing care, when redefined as a positive nonrestrictive collaborative environment for decision making, is really coordinated care. Intercepting patients before they get in over their heads, abusing the system they did not understand, or following bad advice concerning how to "game" the system and avoid returning to work, are all matters in a coordinated care environment.

The service bureau worker who worked for the lumber mills in the Pacific Northwest coordinated care case-by-case by matching the caregiver with a specific employee and then paying the caregiver, the specialist, the hospital or the affiliated rehabilitation specialist with a fee as part of the continuing care process.

Today, case management is used for large, catastrophic cases, such as head injuries and trauma. True coordinated care treatment plans have not been organized for small- and medium-sized cases because of the cost. Most insurers, employers, and HMOs saw case management as a compliance check after care was administered. The new definition of case management is to coordinate, from beginning to end, all the facets of the treatment plan. As workers' compensation costs triple every 10 years, the future will call for more case management. A broader definition of case management will emerge because its ability to not only curb costs but also improve worker productivity is being measured more frequently.

The National Council on Compensation Insurance has recommended managed care solutions for immediate implementation. These solutions included utilization review, case management, bill audits, and fee schedules for provider networks. A national employer coalition and clearinghouse on medical expense management for industry, the Washington Business Group on Health, published a book in conjunction with the Institute for Rehabilitative and Disability Management, and stated, "Every company, including several businesses, should adopt certain foundation strategies as the first step in developing a disability management program. Strategies should include:

1. Build a human resource philosophy that values employees.
2. Gain senior management approval.
3. Intervene early and regularly.
4. Develop case management capabilities.
5. Create modified duty jobs to allow early return to work.
6. Cultivate supervisors who allow and encourage early return to work.

THE FUTURE OF MANAGED DISABILITY

The market potential for managed disability, and specifically the coordinated care aspects of case management, extend far beyond traditional boundaries. The clients, or buyers of services from caregivers, can include workers' compensation carriers and third-party PPO networks that need local case management and related services to cover clients' needs. Hospitals entering into direct contracts with indemnity insurance companies or private industry for traditional care can benefit from disability management products and services, and employers who are self-funded and self-insured for their workers' compensation need a medical partner to assist in answering many questions concerning quality of care and continuity of service.

The following examples show how managed disability can work in the following markets: long-term care HMOs, mental health care, and industry. All of these markets need a specific product/delivery system, and all need marketing to gather a continuous flow of visits or bed days to meet their corporate objectives.

EXAMPLE 1: LONG-TERM CARE HMOs

For the past five years, the Carondolet St. Mary's Nursing Program in Tucson, Arizona, has had a Social HMO program guided by professional nurse care management (Ethridge, 1991). The Social HMO is one of a handful of pilot projects funded by Medicare to address all-encompassing needs of the elderly in various inpatient and outpatient settings. Services are capitated and paid to the hospital for a specific predefined set of services.

The professional nurse care management is provided by a formalized group practice of credentialed nurses who are governed and self-managed by peer review. They evaluate their own performance based on outcomes and have successfully guided patients through a continuum of care within and outside of the hospital. As part of a four-year study, the group analyzed several key indicators of performance: decreased length of stay, reduction in the acuity of admissions, and overall reduction in the number of admissions through brokering care to outpatient alternative delivery systems when admission criteria were not met.

The secret to their success is that patients tell the nurses about warning signs of illnesses early enough so that unnecessary care is avoided and patient health status improved. Using this effective yet economical care, the group has approached a third-party payor as a "Nursing HMO" and continues to look for methods to manage critical care patients and measure outcomes for the continuum of care.

To this writer's knowledge, this is the first time a hospital nursing group has been permitted to operate a network of relationships outside the hospital, as well as inside. By breaking down barriers to care and constructively moving towards becoming a self-reliant team of professionals, this model is a successful pilot project for other health care facilities and comprehensive disability management services.

EXAMPLE 2: MENTAL HEALTH

The redefinition of disability services encompasses mental disability, as well as physical disability. Claims for employer-induced stress in the workplace are being upheld in California, and several other states are revamping laws to include employee assistance program coverage for employees who can prove their stress or psychiatric impairments are, in fact, work-related. Michigan, West Virginia, Hawaii, Kentucky, and New Jersey are all undergoing these changes at the writing of this book.

In *The Law of Workmen's Compensation* (1990), Duke University professor Arthur Larson divided mental-related injuries into three categories.

- Physical trauma that produces a mental disorder.
- Mental stimulus that produces a physical disability.
- Mental stimulus that produces a mental disorder.

Between 1979 and 1988, workers' compensation claims for mental stress rose 700% in California, according to a June 1990 report of the California Workers' Compensation Institute. Characteristics of the population submitting these disability claims may refute conventional assumptions or wisdom.

- Women accounted for 55% of mental health care stress claims. This is double the percentage for all disabled injuries.
- Stress claimants' average age was 40.
- The average income being paid to the claimants at the point of injury was $410 a week. This is 12% higher than the amount paid to the average California disabled worker.
- Forty percent of stress claims were filed by sales and clerical services workers.

Employers will watch these developments closely as employees and local attorneys begin to win precedent-setting cases. California insurers estimated the average stress-related claims cost at $11,389 for cases closed in 1985. Cases still open as of 1990 averaged $18,500. These are definitely higher than average compensation care costs, so disability management may provide a solution.

In 1987, New York introduced an intensive case management program to test the capacity of the mental health care system to respond to the needs of individuals who were not well served by the current system (Surles et al., 1992). As of early 1992, almost 600 intensive case managers had been hired, and a full statewide effort has emerged.

On average, each New York case manager handles 10 persons and, for the most part, are residents of the community where their clients reside. The case manager acts as an advocate by assisting clients to access dental, medical, and psychiatric care, as well as housing, community support, and rehabilitation. Services go beyond normal client/manager contact to include friends, relatives, and extended family. Individuals enter the system at the nomination of medical or behavioral specialists. The population is normally comprised of people who cannot or will not receive this care in any other manner, so policy implications are more the goal than cost containment, per se. However, the theoretical framework is coordination of care using outcomes-based case management. The success of case management is determined by judging the outcomes of the services provided. Therefore, these are not "services and treatment" models of case management. Rather, they are "person and environment" models, since the outcomes are measured in terms of environmental changes as well as changes in the status of the person being served (Surles et al., 1992).

The principal means of evaluation is a client-founded outcome evaluation. Every six months, a detailed protocol is conducted. The intent is to match pre- and post-test findings of a noncase management group of individuals with similar characteristics to the "managed" group. Some 4,296 case management clients were monitored alongside a general population of individuals classified as "seriously and persistently mentally ill" in a study reported in *Health Affairs* (Surles et al., 1992). The findings are unique, in that the program recruited a population disproportionate to the common population with these types of diseases.

"The typical case management client for this study is young (62% under 40), male (61%), unemployed (87%), single (93%), and a nonminority group member (61%). With the exception of dental services, significant declines in unmet needs occurred in the first six months," according to the published results of the study (Surles et al., 1992). (see Fig. 5.)

Managed Care Concepts

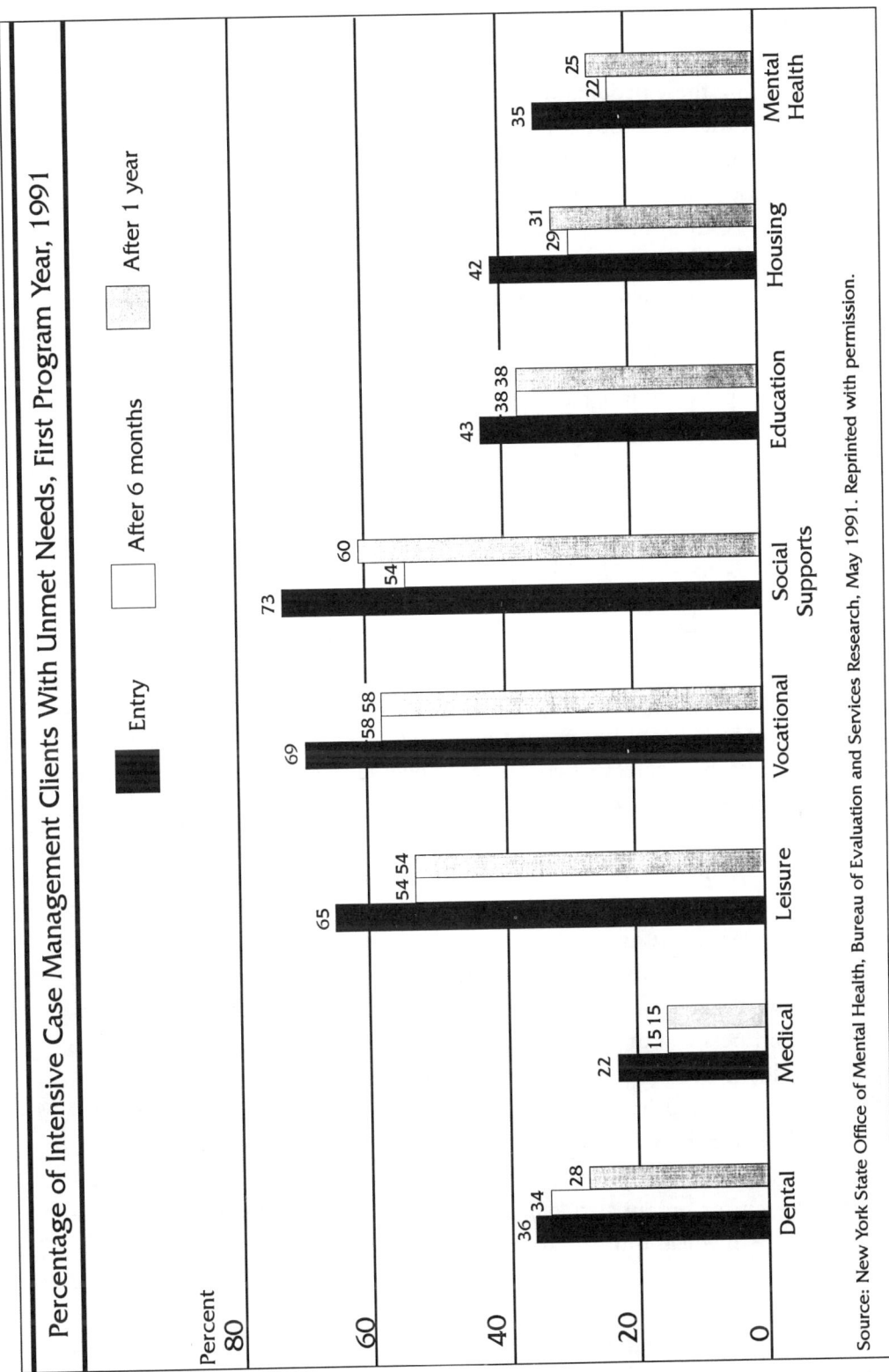

Figure 5. Percentage of Intensive Case Management Clients with Unmet Needs, First Program Year, 1991

The program successfully met its objective of meeting unmet needs for a population of highly needy individuals. The traditional health care delivery system had failed or was failing these people, many of whom were tested as either a danger to themselves or to others. According to conclusions based on the study, the probable indications for improved health status were present partly because of self-reliance and partly because of *access to the system* when guided by a trained case manager.

Similar to the Carondolet St. Mary's experience (Ethridge, 1991), case managers were instructed to work outside traditional boundaries of state government mental health departments and encouraged to rely on community resources as an alternative to expensive inpatient treatment, prescriptions, or therapy.

The crossover to workers' compensation mental health is that many who file claims will be people who have failed to enter a traditional health care system and are now going to enter the system as an injured worker.

EXAMPLE 3: PRIVATE INDUSTRY

An employer representing 6,200 eligible employees in three Midwestern states found that its claims for workers' compensation had increased 62% in 10 years. In addition, the employer's projected increases were expected to place it in the state pool by year end. After attempting claims management research, the employer recognized that managing the problems were within the company's control, but that the company's corporate culture needed to change. As a result, the company enacted a "whole system" strategy of encouraging people to stay healthy through incentives. A program applying corrective action to lifestyle-related and, therefore, preventable illnesses, was instituted after a study showed the potential adjustable costs and cost per employee related to these illnesses (see Fig. 6).

When its claims costs were compared to a national database, the employer found a high diagnosis rate for lung and heart disease, as well as head injuries. The employer added a seatbelt requirement to the insurance policy. Workers were told that their benefits would be revoked immediately if they were involved in an automobile accident, on personal or company business, and not wearing a seat belt. The company also instituted a smoke-free environment at work.

The positive method used to communicate the smoke-free environment included incentives for those employees who *voluntarily* stopped smoking. In addition, employees were given physical exams and lifestyle questionnaires to determine what current or potential risk factors were the greatest issues for their personal lifestyles. A medical director and two nurses were hired to work with local primary care physicians to follow exam protocols by age cohort and administer the lifestyles tests.

Employees without primary care physicians were given the names of three available doctors in their area. Employees who quit smoking, lost weight, increased

	Adjustable Costs	Cost per Employee
Mental Health	$2,100,762	$123.58
Smoking	1,014,326	59.66
Hypertension	810,073	47.65
Seat Belt Use	351,018	20.65
Alcohol Use	280,651	16.51
Diet	210,358	12.37
	$4,767,188	$280.42

Source: University of Michigan, National Center for Health Promotion, Ann Arbor, MI.

Figure 6. One Company's Expenditures for Lifestyle-related Illnesses

exercising, or sought counseling voluntarily received a $10 per month reduction in their monthly premium.

Workplace accidents decreased. The remaining incidents were managed under a contract with a case management company affiliated with a local rehabilitation company. The local rehabilitation company agreed in advance of service to a fee schedule for specific services and groups of services. Case managers were paid based upon length-of-stay requirements and/or the ability to assess protocols for follow-up care in a timely manner. The company's third-party administrator was told to contract with several regional medical specialists for high-cost claims over a specific dollar amount or if a specific expected length of stay was to exceed the norms for any particular reason.

The next step was to inform primary care physicians that they would have to be credentialed and agree to use a resource-based relative value schedule method of payment and billing. The company increased the conversion factor for these procedures from the $31.01 RBRVS reimbursement for Medicare patients under RB.RVS to $46.83, with the provision that no employee would be balance billed beyond these company-reimbursed levels.

The final step will be to initiate negotiations with specific hospitals for specific groupings of service by severity, once the third-party administrator has collected more detailed data.

The savings to date are impressive, in both workers' compensation and traditional medical costs. Under the system, there is no reason to cheat. The union has enforced a strong back-to-work program, managed under the direction of the rehabilitation clinic. The corporation reports ongoing case management savings of approximately $4 for every dollar invested in that particular service.

This, again, is an example of an outside group — in this case, a local rehabilitation company — agreeing to provide managed care disability services, although in this case the impetus for improved management came from within the company.

CONCLUSION

The managed care evolution will reach its saturation point when all hospitals and physicians can sell satisfactory, low-cost, high-quality services independently to employers and employees who use the delivery system correctly. This anticipates a broad number of opportunities for disability managed care.

A number of misconceptions about the managed care delivery system bear repeating. First, the concept of health care delivery systems is in contrast to that of the financing systems. Financing systems merely represent variations on the traditional insurance arrangement that connects with the delivery system.

Second, some delivery systems are run by insurance companies and others who have defined managed care in a regulatory and, therefore, negative light, in an attempt to create positive behavior. The managed care concept, as it was originally practiced in the HMO setting, was more collaborative. It relied more on physicians to manage one another through consensus and clinical determination of medical standards, which, in turn, created cost savings. This is opposed to the claims management approach, which attempts to assess in advance of service which specific claims should or should not be appropriate.

Third, strategic market-based planning, as described earlier here, is different from traditional strategic planning. Providers can understand the difference between marketing and sales if they understand the needs of the employer and the consumer.

Parallels were also drawn between various managed care delivery systems and the use of case management, which seems to be the thread tying all of the various systems together. Unlike the traditional utilization review, quality assurance and *transactional* methods employed by various managed care entities, the transformational delivery system methodology that links incidents together into case-by-case evaluations provides a much more dramatic picture and therefore a much more effective tool for case management.

The term *coordinated care* was reviewed in light of case management applied to long-term care, to mental health, and to industry. Coordinated care can best be defined as the ability to seek, within and outside the boundaries of the health care delivery system, those solutions that would provide the best opportunity to improve the health status of enrollees with the most reasonable use of resources.

No one direction has consistently proven to be most successful in the design of managed care strategies. However, providers have dealt most successfully with managed care by understanding the rules of managed care and then developing a local delivery system that includes standards for case evaluation and clinical determination. This requires that more physicians be involved with coordinating care from the standpoint of improving worker productivity, instead of just cost containment.

The health care delivery system of the future will include a greater dimension of home care and outpatient services and procedures. This is evidenced by the changing reimbursement environment for public programs such as Medicare and Medicaid and the number of employers who have continued to restrict hospital inpatient services, including use of the emergency room.

Outpatient services for home health care therapy and the ability to make full use of telemetry and other technology are in their infancy. For those in the rehabilitative medicine area — whether dealing with long-term care, mental health, or traditional occupational-related injury — these technological advances will represent a greater economic and political opportunity than that which currently exists.

It is then the responsibility of physicians, hospitals, and other providers engaged in the delivery system to formulate their own strategy and develop some common sense of purpose and direction in the face of these changes. It is not enough to be passive and receive reimbursement from a third party, nor is it enough to practice medicine without building a constituency over the long term. Certainly health care has founded itself on broader principles of quality and access but has constructed a reimbursement system that is contradictory in both the minds of the physician and the patient. Perhaps the correction of that system must start with the physician and the patient — and the ability to coordinate disability management services in a contemporary health care delivery system.

REFERENCES

Berenson, R. A. (Winter, 1991). A physician's view of managed care. *Health Affairs, 10*(04), 106-119.

DeMarco, W. J. & Garvey, T. J. (1986). *Going prepaid, a strategic buying decision.* Denver: Center for Research in Ambulatory Health Care Administration.

Ethridge, P. (July, 1991). A nursing HMO: Carondelet St. Mary's experience. *Nursing Management,*

Group Health Association of America. 624 9th St., N. W., Washington, DC 20001.

Kongstvedt, M. D. (1989). *Managed health care handbook,* Chapter 2, p. 2. Aspen Publications.

Larson, A. *Law of workmen's compensation.* Duke University.

Levitt, T. (1983). *Marketing imagination.* New York: Free Press.

National Industry Council for HMO Development. (1984). *The health maintenance organization industry 10-year report 1973-1983,* 1984 update. Author.

OMB's logic: Less protection saves lives: *A letter blocking health standards for 6 million workers shocks officials at Labor Department.* Washington Post, 1990.

Physician Payment Review Commission. (1993). *Physician payment review commission annual report 1993.* Washington, DC: Author.

Surles, R. C., Blanch, A. K., Shern, D. L., & Donahue, S. A. (Spring, 1992). Case management as a strategy for systems change. *Health Affairs, 11*(1), 151-163.

Swedlow, A., Johnson, G., Smithline, N,. & Milstein, A. (1992). Increased costs and rates of use in the California Workers' Compensation system as a result of self-referral by physicians. *The New England Journal of Medicine, 327*(21), 1502-1506.

Workers' Compensation Research Institute. (1992). *1992 Annual Report.* Boston, MA: Author.

An International View Of Older Workers And Work Disability: Trends And Implications For Occupational Rehabilitation

Andrew G. Remenyi, M.A., A.I.E.

PEOPLE WITH DISABILITIES AND THE LABOR FORCE

While policies often exist relating to the support of people who are disabled and individuals who are chronically ill, no country can assert that it has a completely planned, rational rehabilitation policy. Instead, what is found at the policy level, especially in countries where the work ethic and economic growth are still major determining ideologies of social interaction, are a range of initiatives which either contradict each other, or operate together in splendid disharmony.

Employment and unemployment policies, social welfare and income support programs, disability legislation and rehabilitation programs, retirement programs, and job creation programs are often at odds in terms of their goals, implementation, and outcomes. Nash (1987) observed that "Unstable, inconsistent, or fragmented public policies regarding disabled workers could benefit from a review by professionals in this field. For example, there are currently 22 separate, unrelated public programs to assist displaced workers. Could the resources of each be better used if these programs were linked?"(p. 10). Hearne (1991) described Vocational Rehabilitation (VR) in the U.S. as having "... insufficient linkages to programs and services that promote employment skills and goals for youths with disabilities, inadequate linkages between Vocational Rehabilitation offices and the business community, and poor coordination with voluntary and private agencies providing rehabilitation services."(p. 119). Kuehn (1991), drawing heavily on Berkowitz's (1987) and Stone's (1984) formulations, made the point that welfare system programs in the U.S. (e.g., SSI-Supplemental Security Income, SSDI-Social Security Disability

Income) which provide income maintenance or medical assistance, are part of the United States' "... need-based distribution system as opposed to the work-based distribution system." The work-based programs are in the special education and rehabilitation system and "... their purpose is legally protective or vocationally corrective," as distinct from the workers' compensation and income support systems which are basically ameliorative responses to disability. Berkowitz (1987) and Kuehn (1991) have identified the core of U.S. public policy towards disability to be overwhelmingly in the sector of ameliorative programs. Different systems are doing different things, unequally, and apparently without mutual referencing.

Further evidence of this is provided by Mirkin (1987) who examined the employment policies across 12 West European countries, and found that excess labor supply in these countries was driving the use of disability transfer programs to encourage older workers to retire at increasingly earlier ages. The employment problem was being solved by using income-support programs (pensions), a pseudo-solution in the long run because of increasing costs, both human and economic, associated with an increasing older population.

This uneasy fact is perhaps best exemplified in the outcomes of policy operations for particular groups in society. Bowe (1993) quoted figures from the U.S. Bureau of the Census (1992) which show that fewer working-age adults (16-64 years) with disabilities are working now than 20 years ago, despite national laws aimed at increasing the employment levels of people with disabilities. Yelin (1991) drew earlier attention to this: "The employment picture for persons with disabilities has worsened dramatically over the last two decades, despite the presence of section 504 of the Rehabilitation Act and a huge expansion of the laborforce during the 1980s" (p. 130).

Bowe (1993) has also cited figures (see Table 1) to show that in 1990, of 12.8 million people with work disabilities, over half considered themselves prevented from working because of their disabilities. This is proportionately more than in 1970. He laments that people with disabilities experience an inherent conflict between wanting to work and wanting to qualify for welfare (Medicaid) and income-support programs such as SSDI (Social Security Disability Income) and SSI (Supplemental Security Income), which define disability as inability to engage in work.

This conflictual systemic interaction between the goals and outcomes of various social policies is most readily seen in times of high unemployment. As can be expected in adverse economic times, particular programs of income support vary in their generosity and number; governments become more directly involved in the labor market to create jobs; and the eligibility for income support becomes more restrictive. Burkhauser and Hirvonen (1989) made a detailed comparison of disability policy in times of economic crisis in the U.S., Sweden, and the Federal Republic of Germany.

Table 1
Laborforce Participation of Working-Age Adults with Work Disabilities, 1990

Category	No.	%
All (16-64)	12,826,449	100
In Laborforce	5,043,990	39
Not In Laborforce	7,782,459	61
Not Prevented From Working	1,188,459	15
Prevented From Working	6,594,000	85

Source: 1990 Census of Population And Housing. From: Bowe, F. G. (1993). Statistics, politics, and employment of people with disabilities. *Journal Of Disability Policy Studies*, 4(2), 83-91.

Table 2 reflects the disability recipient ratios by age, of labor force participants in each of these countries. Eligibility for disability benefits in the U.S. is substantially more restricted than in Sweden or Germany. For the total population, the disability recipient ratios for the U.S. increased between 1970 and 1975. Burkhauser and Hirvonen (1989) explain this was because vocational characteristics (e.g., the possibility of early retirement) were factored into disability eligibility decisions, a practice terminated during the Carter and Reagan administrations with a resulting steady state thereafter. By contrast, the Swedish and German disability recipient ratios, for their total populations, have increased steadily since 1970 and are substantially higher than the U.S. figures. Burkhauser and Hirvonen explain that the reason for this is that health eligibility criteria for disability pensions have been tempered by labor market conditions, and Germany, in particular, has operated with an explicit eligibility of handicapped workers for special early retirement (as reflected in Table 2, in the 60-64 years row, for year 1985). For the 15-44 year group, Germany's disability recipient ratio is much lower than that of Sweden or the U.S. (20 vs. 20 vs. 6 for 1985), with the probable explanation for this lying in the use of employment quotas and medical and vocational rehabilitation measures.

The highest number, proportionately, of disability transfer recipients, for each of the three countries, is in the 60-64 year age group. Burkhauser and Hirvonen (1989) explain this as "... the result of increases in the size and accessibility of disability income transfers and of the relative shift away from the job supported work programs for men in this age group." Increased generosity of retirement pensions, benefits, and (in Sweden) lowering of the retirement age, are other explanations. It is important to moderate the view that generous disability pensions are the sole cause of declining labor force participation (in all countries, at any rate) be-

Table 2
Transfer Recipients per Thousand Active Laborforce Participants, by Age, 1970 - 1985

	1970	1975	1980	1983	1985
Age					
15-44 years					
U.S.A.	11	17	16	16	20
Germany	n.a.	n.a.	n.a.	n.a.	6
Sweden	18	20	19	20	20
45-59 years					
U.S.A.	33	68	83	71	71
Germany	n.a.	n.a.	n.a.	n.a.	91
Sweden	66	95	99	112	108
60-64 years					
U.S.A.	154	265	285	273	254
Germany	n.a.	n.a.	n.a.	n.a.	1,284
Sweden	229	382	382	453	512
Total population					
U.S.A.	27	42	41	39	41
Germany	61	68	77	93	97
Sweden	49	67	68	73	74
Unemployment rates					
U.S.A.	4.8	8.3	7.0	9.5	7.1
Germany	0.7	4.7	3.8	9.1	9.3
Sweden	1.5	1.6	2.0	3.5	2.8

Sources: Population data for Sweden and the United States are from International Labour Organization 1970-1986. Population data for Germany are from Statistisches Bundesamt: Statistisches Jahrbuch fur die Bundesrepublik Deutschland 1987.

cause recently though the real value of benefits has been reduced, the rate of work disability has risen (Yelin, 1991).

The point illustrated by such data is that the policies adopted in any key sphere of societal operation (labor market, health, welfare) have both practical and philosophical ramifications for the policies and programs in other spheres. It would be unrealistic (perhaps even undesirable) to expect total integration and harmony between them, but some monitored alignment appears to be necessary to ensure consistent and congruent national policies. Income support programs which vitiate employment and independent living goals, are a case in point.

A CASE IN POINT: AUSTRALIAN REACTIONS

Unemployment is a huge problem, to the point where even very fast economic growth over several years will not quickly reduce the number of long-term unemployed. The Australian government recently released a paper in which it determined that it would work on maximizing sustainable economic growth and take direct specific action to reduce the number of unemployed people, both courses of action being seen as mutually reinforcing.

Over the last 15 years, the number of people unemployed for more than a year has risen with each downturn in the economy, and with 350,000 Australians, or 40% of all unemployed people, in this category. The largest group of long-term unemployed are in the 20-24 year group, but, people aged 50-plus years are more likely than young people to be out of work for long periods, once unemployed.

As in other countries, Australia is impacted by the devastating consequences of unemployment. The longer one is out of a job, the harder it is to re-enter the labor market; one's skills deteriorate and one's confidence and self-esteem diminishes (Dew, Penkower, & Bromet, 1991; Harris, Merrett, & Radford, 1986; Smith & Crisler, 1985; Studnicka, Studnicka-Benke, Wogerbauer, & Rastetter, 1989; Winefield, Tiggemann, & Winefield, 1991). Employers regard long-term employed persons as unemployable. Subsequently, such persons are alienated from mainstream society, and faced with risks of poorer health. They often become dependent on welfare and community health services (Wilson & Walker, 1993; Yuen & Balarajan, 1989) which becomes an economic burden to government because of reliance on unemployment benefits, and not being a tax-contributor.

Also, as in other countries, there have been very significant changes in employment patterns in Australia. The majority of women without young children are in the workforce. Part-time jobs make up one-quarter of all jobs, with three-quarters of these being held by women. The number of manufacturing jobs has decreased markedly, but service sector jobs (e.g., retail industry, tourism) have increased. Most job growth (7% between 1990 and 1992) has been in small- and medium-sized enterprises with the number of jobs in enterprises with 100 or more employees falling by the same amount over the same period. Employment is growing most rapidly in high- and low-paid jobs, with middle-level jobs declining.

In the face of these challenges, the government has determined to:

- achieve much more rapid and sustained economic growth;
- remove impediments to labor market and industry efficiency;

- reform labor market programs and services, doing more to meet individual and industry needs; and,
- restructure the social security systems so it reflects the job opportunities and work patterns of the 1990s and beyond. (Committee on Employment Opportunities [CEO], 1993, p. 5).

Insightfully, the Australian government further considers that, "A major challenge is to integrate economic, environmental and social objectives. To a large extent, these objectives can be mutually reinforcing. Indeed they must be." (p. 5).

To achieve this integration, the government has proposed a Job Compact to provide temporary but worthwhile jobs for people who have been unemployed for a long time. The jobs, which would be between six and nine months in duration, in the main, would emanate from the private and public sectors "on condition that they provide substantial benefit to society."

Table 3
Australia
Unemployment by Age, August 1993

Age	Total Unemployment ('000)	Rate	Long-term Unemployment ('000)	Rate
15 to 19	153	23.1	26	4.0
20 to 24	188	16.1	68	5.9
25 to 29	127	11.6	41	3.7
30 to 34	102	8.9	38	3.3
35 to 39	100	9.0	33	3.0
40 to 44	71	6.5	31	2.9
45 to 49	66	6.9	34	3.5
50 to 54	46	7.0	24	3.6
55 to 59	42	10.2	24	5.8
60 to 64	29	13.3	17	8.0
TOTAL	924	10.7	338	3.9

Source: ABS, Labour Force, Australia, Cat. no. 6203.0 and unpublished data. Committee on Employment Opportunities. (1993). *Restoring full employment*. Canberra, ACT: Australian Government Publishing Service.

Job Compact participants would have their progress "case-managed," and, as unemployment duration increases, have more intense contact with the Commonwealth Employment Service (CES) case manager. They would be required to undertake an "activity test" to progress to other job and market programs (including voluntary work) while on income support; and they would be required to accept reasonable job offers or program opportunities or risk losing income support entitlements.

Consequently, the Australian government is reviewing income support provisions for unemployed people to ensure that they are responsive to changes in the labor market (e.g., more women in the workforce; the increase in part-time jobs; the fall in the real value of wages) and to address disincentives to job-seeking while persons are on income support. At present, the social security income test discourages unemployed people from part-time jobs. It treats married couples as a joint income unit, one being a job-seeker and the other a dependent spouse, and thus discourages both spouses from seeking and obtaining employment.

Though these initiatives appear well intentional, the cursory treatment of people with disabilities is a disquieting feature which illustrates the incongruence among different policy jurisdictions. The market initiatives to combat unemployment in Australia appear to have overlooked fundamental circumstances among people with disabilities in Australia:

i. People with disabilities constitute around 11% of the workforce and 15% of the working-age population (Australian Bureau of Statistics [ABS], 1993);
ii. The workforce participation rates of disabled persons aged 15-64 years are much lower (54.9%) than those of people without a disability (76.9%);
iii. People with disabilities face higher unemployment rates (the unemployment rate of people with disabilities was 17.8% in 1993, compared to 12% for those without a disability); and,
iv. they are more likely to be long-term unemployed than those without disabilities (CES data show that in October 1993, 61% of people with disabilities who are unemployed had been so for more than one year, compared with 47% of the total population); (Australian Bureau of Statistics [ABS], 1993).

These figures are echoed in other countries and in the U.S., where, according to Hahn (1993), more than two-thirds of disabled adults of working age do not have jobs. What is disquieting in Australia is that long-term unemployed persons with disabilities are rarely mentioned in the Government discussion paper; they are considered to be people who "may have severe difficulties obtaining employment," and "...that some specially disadvantaged people could be able to receive income support (Special Benefit) without the need to comply with the usual activity test requirements for unemployed people" (Committee on Employment Opportunities [CEO], 1993, p. 177).

One interpretation of the scant coverage of persons with disabilities is that they have been completely normalized, and require no special treatment outside the normal provisions for the unemployed population. Another is that, if they are a problem, the income support provisions is all that they require. Neither interpretation seems adequate on either utilitarian or humanitarian grounds. As Hudson (1993) argued about public policy on aging: "...disability benefits assume that the recipient is entering an extended period outside the labor force analogous to retirement and accord little formal attention to rehabilitation potential..." (p. 254). Once again, there may be a conflict or imbalance between social policies aimed at general market imperatives and those which would be aimed at the human rights of disadvantaged people.

One key, but perhaps cynical question to be asked is: Who is to be chosen for the Job Compact program? On its own admissions, the Committee on Employment Opportunities (CEO) has said that it will be selective: "The Job Compact would be prohibitively costly if it were provided to all unemployed people" (p. 126). But it goes on to say that "... the Job Compact should be applied to those with the least chance of getting a job, that is those who have been out of work the longest" (p. 126). The CEO has not stipulated with whom it will begin the scheme; the danger in it not doing so is that it will choose a group or be pressured to choose a group with whom its success rate is likely to be high (often called "creaming"). Disadvantaged persons (e.g., persons with disabilities and older workers) may therefore have less chance of being included in this program.

These "fringe workers," as they are sometimes called, are assumed to benefit automatically from an improved economy and from mainstream market and income support programs of assistance. But, this has not been statistically supported. In the meantime, their disability status is too easily translated into one of unemployability.

General population policies and programs can miss groups with equal rights but special needs. What appears to be a worldwide approach to resolving this problem has been called "targeting within universalism" (Skocpol, 1991). Another expression of this dichotomy is "separate services versus mainstreaming" (DeJong, Batavia, & Griss, 1989). An approach such as this requires acknowledgment of the special needs of disadvantaged groups rather than avoidance or exclusion, based on the needs of others. Australia appears to be adopting such an approach explicitly, at least for people with disabilities, and this is exemplified in the relatively new Commonwealth Government initiative commenced on November 12, 1991, called the Disability Reform Package. The aims of the Package are:

- to improve the participation of people with disabilities in employment, education and training activities;
- to make it easier for people with disabilities to participate in, and contribute to the community; and,
- to make sure those people who have severe disabilities and who have limited job prospects get adequate and secure income support.

This package addresses the special employment needs of people with disabilities. It is a coordinated and integrated program delivered through three different government departments (Social Security; Employment, Education and Training; and, Health, Housing and Community Services). In many countries, the needs of specific populations (e.g., older persons, people with disabilities, unemployed persons) have spawned separate networks or jurisdictions of operation. But these sectors seldom collaborate to identify common needs, to function in a unified fashion maximizing the strengths and resources of their separate territories, or to deliver services in an integrated and mutually supporting way. There are signs of an increasing awareness of this problem. Sheets, Wray, and Torres-Gil (1993) discuss how public policies might be reformed to integrate the separate domains of aging, health, and disability to provide a focus for the rehabilitation of older persons based on independent living and rehabilitation principles which are consistent with the Rehabilitation Act of 1973, the updated Older Americans Act of 1992, and the Americans with Disabilities Act of 1990. Beedon (1993) has also argued for a coalition of aging and disability groups to effect change in general and to move disability policy into the twenty-first century.

The Australian government's policy response to unemployment, as outlined in its discussion paper *Restoring Full Employment* (1993), recognizes that the long-term unemployed need special assistance. Also acknowledged is that they are not a homogeneous group, that the group with the highest incidence of long-term unemployment is 20-24 year olds, with around 40% of the long-term unemployed being below 30 years old, and that older age groups suffer the greatest disadvantage in terms of duration of unemployment (Committee on Employment Opportunities [CEO], 1993, p. 20). However, the general labor market policy and programs it has adopted to combat unemployment fail to target the most disadvantaged group, and in so doing it leaves unaddressed extensive and compelling data on laborforce participation rates. Consideration of laborforce participation rates unearths another worldwide issue which once again illustrates the frequent problem, observed in many countries, of the mismatch between the goals of different policy jurisdictions and the difficulty of providing solutions to national problems.

LABOR-FORCE PARTICIPATION AND THE OLDER MALE WORKER

POPULATION AGING

General statistics on population show that in many industrialized and developing countries there has been an increase in the numbers and proportions of older persons in the population. The reasons for this vary from country to country. The age structure of Australia's population, for example, has been shaped by (i) declining fertility, which results in the young becoming a smaller proportion of the population relative to older age groups; (ii) declining mortality which results in a growth in the average life span and in increasing numbers at older ages; and, (iii) immigration. The median age for immigrants in 1988-89 was 26.7 years, five years younger than the median age of the total Australian population (Bureau of Immigration Research, 1990). Hence, migration has tended to retard aging of the Australian population and has increased the numbers in the laborforce; but later, the addition of these persons has served to increase the numbers at old age.

By world standards, Australia has an age structure that is younger than many other aging populations. In 1985, Sweden's elderly comprised 16.9%, the UK's 15.5%, and Denmark's 15.1% (Torrey, Kinsella, & Taeuber, 1987). Torrey et al. (1987) estimated that, in 2025, Australia's elderly will be 16% of the population compared to 19.5% in the U.S., 22.2% in Sweden, and 20.3% in Japan.

Such demographics often lead to ominous economic projections that there will be a decrease in the workforce numbers and an increase in the unemployed who will need to be supported by the employed. This crude measure of the balance between those of working age and the aged is called the "age dependency ratio," and various commentators have expressed fears that the number of those in the active workforce (between 15 and 64 years) will not provide a large enough tax base to support those not in the workforce who constitute the dependent age groups, especially the elderly. Some commentators (Schulz, Borowski, & Crown, 1991) countered that the estimations of rises in the age dependency ratio will probably be offset by a decline in the youth dependency ratio (with population growth tendencies being towards zero). Schulz et al. (1991) have stated:

> ... an important conclusion remains unchanged: Total dependency ratios will be lower when members of the baby boom retire than they were when the baby boomers were children in the 1950s and 1960s (p. 338).

Others (Kendig & McCallum, 1986) further cautioned that this offset may not be enough, as current government spending (including pensions and medical services) on the aged is roughly twice or thrice (Kendig & McCallum, 1986; Schulz et al., 1991) that spent on youth. A key area of spending on the aged is on pensions, the costs of which are rising. Also, with greater numbers of older persons comes, inevitably, more health problems and disability, and escalating health costs. However, another moderator of dependency ratio and disparate governmental spending is argued by some to be shifts in productivity and increases in per capita expenditure. Shultz et al. (1991) argued in a note of hope that:

> ... the future dependency burden will be manageable.... In fact when we examined the effects of real economic potential on the ability of Australia, Japan, and the United States to afford population aging, we found that demographic impacts were swamped by economic growth effects (page 338).

LABOR-FORCE PARTICIPATION DATA

Older workers are retiring younger and being retrenched in preference to younger workers. In the U.S. in 1950, nearly one-half of all men aged 65 and over were in the workforce; today the figure is about 17% (Quinn & Burkhauser, 1990). In Australia, in 1947, about one-third of men aged 65 and over were in the workforce, but in 1984, only one-tenth of this group were employed, (Kendig & McCallum, 1986). Workforce participation rates have declined significantly in Australia for men aged 50-59 years and 65 years and over, and dramatically for men aged 60-64 years. In 1970, the laborforce participation rate for men aged 55-59 years was 91.2%. By 1989, this rate had fallen to 75.5%. Similarly, between 1970 and 1989, laborforce participation of men aged 60-64 years had decreased by over a third while participation rates for men aged 65 years and over had fallen by over one-half, from 22.1% (1970) to 9.0% (Office on Aging, 1990).

The workforce participation rates for males aged 55-64 years, between the years of 1974 and 1981 were 15% in Australia, 2% in Japan, and 6% in the U.S. (Kendig & McCallum, 1986). The trends for older women are far less dramatic, and other factors (e.g., the increase in part-time work availability) may explain why the workforce participation of women in general is on the increase. The following tables provide laborforce participation rates for men aged 55-59 years, 60-64 years, and 65 years and over, in 10 industrialized countries.

Table 4
Laborforce Participation Rates for Men Aged 55-59 in 10 Industrialized Countries, 1960-1988/89

	1960	1970	1980	1988	1989
Belgium	85.1[a]	-	74.0[b]	-	-
Finland	90.4	76.6	67.7	59.1	59.7
France	82.4[c]	-	80.9	67.3[f]	70.2
Germany	88.7[a]	89.2	82.3	79.8	78.6
Italy	83.7[a]	81.0	74.8	-	67.8
Japan	91.2[d]	-	-	91.3	91.6
Nether.	-	86.9[e]	74.2	66.6	65.3
Sweden	-	90.0[e]	87.7	-	87.0
U. K.	-	93.1	90.1	80.3[g]	-
U. S.	88.9	89.5	81.9	78.9	78.8
Average	87.2	86.7	79.3	-	75.5[h]

[a]1961; [b]1979; [c]1968; [d]1971; [e]1971; [f]1987; [g]1986; [h]Simple arithmetic average of rates for 9 countries (incl. UK 1986). Data from ILO Year Book of Labour Statistics, Copyright © International Labour Organization (1962, 1970, 1989-90); Mirkin (1987). Davies, Matthews, & Wong. (1991). Ageing and work. *International Review of Industrial and Organizational Psychology, 6,* 149-211.

Table 5
Laborforce Participation Rates for Men Aged 60-64 in 10 Industrialized Countries, 1960-1988/89

	1960	1970	1980	1988	1989
Belgium	70.8[a]	-	40.1[b]	-	-
Finland	79.1	65.0	43.0	29.5	27.8
France	-	68.0	47.6	25.7[e]	23.1
Germany	-	74.9	44.2	34.5	34.2
Italy	53.6[a]	-	39.6	-	35.2
Japan	83.7[c]	-	-	71.1	71.4
Netherlands	-	73.9[d]	50.1	26.8	24.5
Sweden	-	78.7[d]	69.0	-	62.9
U. K.	-	87.0	71.2	53.4[f]	-
U. S.	77.1	71.7	61.0	53.6	54.1
Average	72.9	74.2	51.7	-	43.0[g]

[a]1961; [b]1979; [c]1965; [d]1971; [e]1987; [f]1986; [g]Simple arithmetic average of rates for 9 countries (incl. UK 1986).
Data from Davies and Sparrow (1985); Mirkin (1987); ILO Year Book of Labour Statistics, Copyright © International Labour Organization (1989-90); Davies, Matthews, & Wong, (1991). Ageing and work. *International Review of Industrial and Organizational Psychology, 6,* 149-211

Table 6
Laborforce Participation Rates for Men Aged 65 and over in 10 Industrialised Countries, 1950-1988/89

	1950	1960	1970	1980	1988	1989
Belgium	24.7	9.8[a]	-	8.8	-	-
Finland	56.7	39.7	19.0	17.0	9.7[f]	8.8[f]
France	38.0	30.5	15.1	6.0	4.7[a]	3.5
Germany	26.6	22.6	19.9	7.4	4.9	4.5
Italy	43.7[b]	23.6[c]	12.9	12.6	-	7.9
Japan	51.7	56.0	48.9	45.5	36.0	35.8
Netherlands	35.5[d]	-	11.4	4.8	-	-
Sweden	36.1	27.1	19.2	14.2	-	-
U. K.	32.5	25.4	19.9	10.8	7.5[h]	-
U. S.	42.1	30.3	25.7	17.7[e]	15.9	16.0
Average	38.8	29.4	21.3	14.5	-	12.0[i]

[a]1961; [b]1951; [c]1961; [d]1947; [e]1981; [f]65-74 years old; [g]1987; [h]1986; [i]Simple arithmetic average of rates for 7 countries (incl. Uk 1986). Data from Davies & Sparrow (1985); Mirkin (1987); ILO Year Book of Labour Statistics, Copyright © International Labour Organisation (1989-90); Davies, Matthews, & Wong, (1991). Ageing and work. International Review of Industrial and Organizational Psychology, 6, 149-211.

EXPLANATIONS OF LABORFORCE PARTICIPATION TRENDS FOR OLDER MALES

There are several explanations for these trends; while details are peculiar to particular countries, there are also common elements:

i. *Economic development away from an agriculture base* to a service sector and manufacturing base, hallmarks of industrialization, has been associated with a decrease in the laborforce participation rate of older workers who have often not had the skills to keep pace, or have found their skills to be obsolete.

ii. *Mandatory retirement ages* of 65 years for men and 60 years for women in many industrialized countries, linked to public pension schemes, have forced the retirement of those 65 years and over, especially in conditions of high unemployment. As (Habib, 1990) said:

> Population with aging has the most serious implications when it emerges simultaneously with macroeconomic conditions of high unemployment, a high rate of inflation and a slow productivity growth (p. 341).

Social pressures arise at these times such as the argument that an older person's early retirement would make way for younger workers.

iii. *The use of early retirement policies* have become attractive when benefits do not accrue in the event of a worker continuing to work until compulsory retirement age. Mirkin (1987) has given evidence to show that the problem of rising unemployment was often tackled (implicitly if not explicitly) by governments and employers through the development of early retirement schemes. Age also appears to be an important criterion in the selection of employees for redundancy (Jolly, Creigh, & Mingay, 1980), a tendency encouraged by the availability of early retirement schemes (Casey & Laczko, 1989). In Australia, the availability of increased wealth in the form of lump sum superannuation payments and retrenchment benefits has been a common reason for quitting the workforce (Foster, 1988).

iv. *Poor health has been posited as another cause of early withdrawal from the workforce*, and this is based mainly on self-reports of those who have retired early. Older persons are more likely than younger persons to experience disability and multiple and chronic impairments, and about two-thirds of persons with work disability are over the age of 40 (Shrey & Hursh, 1994). In a general review of workers who withdrew from the workforce prior to retirement, Kingson (1982) found that disability and health problems were the major reasons for them ceasing work, with older workers who had chronic unmanaged health problems being at high risk of early involuntary retirement and subsequent economic hardship. Kingson also reviewed the social and personal costs of early retirement. He differentiated between workers who were retired and disabled, retired healthy workers, and unhealthy workers not working. He found that disabled workers were most likely to exit the workforce precipitously and that retired unhealthy workers had a higher mortality rate than retired disabled workers. More recently, Chirikos and Nestel (1989) pointed out, "... there is still little agreement at the moment about how much poor health really matters." They also pointed out that work incapacity must be distinguished from the desire for leisure and that, "...work incapacity is not synonymous with the presence of health problems, since many individuals continue to work even with impaired physical conditions" (p. 177). However, in a complex empirical analysis following these observations, they nonetheless concluded:

> ...that health-related physical conditions play an important role in determining the ability of male workers to delay retirement and, correspondingly, in increasing the potential of some unintended toll in advancing the age of retirement (p. 197).

v. *The experience of long-term unemployment appears also to have served to discourage older workers from continuing to seek employment,* and instead, they have accepted early retirement. Studies in most industrialized countries show that the duration of male unemployment rises with age and that the long-term unemployed are more likely to be 55 years and older. Love and Torrence (1989), in their study of over 2,000 U.S. workers who had lost their jobs due to plant closures and relocations, reported that the median duration of unemployment for workers 55 years and over was 27 weeks, while that for workers 45 years and under was 13 weeks. Rones (1983) reported that the older unemployed are far less likely to gain new employment than younger workers and are less likely to spend time looking for work. Not surprisingly, early retirement may come as a welcome relief from disappointment in the market (Walker, 1985). More generally, the connection between unemployment and health is also well researched. Wilson and Walker (1993), in a comprehensive review of unemployment and health, concluded that unemployed men and their families have increased mortality experience particularly from suicide and lung cancer. They have a reduction in psychological well-being and are more likely to use general practitioner and hospital services and receive more prescribed medicines. This effect is still demonstrable with adjustments for social class, poverty, age, and preexisting morbidity. Frese and Mohr (1987) showed that prolonged unemployment or re-unemployment leads to depression, reduced hope, and financial problems, while being employed or retired leads to a reduction of depression and financial problems. Rife and Kilty (1989) provide evidence indicating that older discouraged workers who had stopped job searching were more vulnerable than active searching workers in their financial, emotional, and social functioning. McCallum (1989) provided preliminary evidence to suggest that a syndrome of under-use exists which limits the opportunities for older Australians to engage in activity and to be involved in the community.

Some commentators (Casey & Laczko, 1989) have pointed out that many persons who lose their jobs do not retire early, and should be counted among the long-term unemployed. In Australia, this has been called "hidden unemployment" and the study conducted by the Bureau of Labour Market Research (Stretton & Williams, 1985, pp. 35-36) came to the alarming conclusion that the numbers of such persons may be equal the level of recorded unemployment. Drury (1993) has drawn attention to "the 'forgotten' unemployed for whom long-term unemployment for three or more years is common." (p. 12). Quinn and Burkhauser (1990) made a similar point in distinguishing between involuntary and voluntary retirement. They cited early studies which showed that people retired only because they had to (Stecker, 1951), and more recent ones (Reno & Grad, 1985) which showed that financial considerations were of principal importance in the decision to retire.

Australian data also shows a clear trend towards longer duration of unemployment as age increases. In Australia, the average duration of unemployment for a person 45 to 65 years of age is 81 weeks, and 29% of unemployed people over 45 years of age have been unemployed for over two years.

Now, focusing on the decreasing laborforce participation rates of older male workers may lead us to concentrating on aging workers as if they were a homogenous group. This would miss the point that it is not older workers, *per se,* who are the problem, it is the fact that they are retiring early. As Schulz, Borowski, and Crown (1991) stated, "It is the growing numbers of managed persons retiring before age 65 that should be a major concern." (p. 339).

The solutions to the problem of premature retirement have come in the form of attempts to increase and prolong employment among older persons, thus achieving three socio-economic goals: First, increasing the workforce size and the number of taxpayers who can help finance other dependent persons; second, controlling public pension and income maintenance costs; and, third, providing opportunities for meaningful and dignified independent living for aging persons without undue reliance on health and social welfare systems.

Table 7
Average Duration in Weeks of Unemployment by Age, August 1993

Age	Males	Females	Persons
15 To 19	27.6	28.1	27.9
20 To 24	47.9	52.2	49.6
25 To 34	56.8	48.3	53.7
35 To 44	64.4	56.3	61.0
45 To 54	82.3	84.3	83.1
55 To 59	102.6	66.7	94.9
60 To 64	106.2	119.5	109.0
Total (A)	60.2	52.0	57.1

(A) Includes persons aged 65 and over, details of whom are not shown separately.
Source: ABS, Labour Force, Australia, Cat. No. 6203.0 and unpublished data. Committee On Unemployment Opportunities. (1993). *Restoring full employment.* Canberra, Act: Australian Government Publishing Service.

Undercutting the achievement of these goals and underpinning many of the above explanations for the decreasing participation of older males in the labor force is the phenomenon of age discrimination. It has been given great prominence in the U.S. and in some European countries (e.g., France) and is becoming increasingly important in Australia as an issue to be confronted directly in order to increase older worker participation in the workforce and to ensure equity and justice.

AGE DISCRIMINATION

TOWARDS A BALANCED RIGHTS PERSPECTIVE

Chronological age has long been used as a discriminative criterion in many areas of human behavior. Thus, eligibility to drink, vote, obtain contraceptives, go to school, leave school, begin and leave working life, gain the pension, and receive student or pension concessions are examples of eligibility to behave, take on responsibilities' or gain advantages, based on age. Examples of age discrimination, such as those cited, may be viewed as legitimate discrimination, for they have usually been sanctioned by the community in some clear way (often for the protection of the age groups concerned), or have been given the status of rights by laws.

Other examples of discrimination based on age appear to depend on discretionary judgments, as for example, when employers hirer younger versus older workers, landlords rent premises to older in preference to younger tenants, or restaurateurs refuse bookings to patrons with young babies. The notion of age discrimination can also operate in two-edged, paradoxical ways, as noted by Robinson (1993) and Zola (1989). Thus, it is often argued that a certain group in the community (e.g., older unemployed males) have special needs and require special services. Yet, when it comes to unemployment, it is argued that their age should not be considered by employers. In comparison, since workforce participation rates are effected by the premature retirement of older workers, it is argued that workplaces should give special consideration to the training and support needs of this group. As Robinson (1993) has argued so eloquently:

> Approached pragmatically, what we are talking about often comes down to what is called 'interest group politics' in which individuals and groups compete for their 'share of the pie' which seems to be getting smaller (p.1).

This issue has its equivalents in other discrimination corridors. With respect to people with disabilities, for example, Zola (1989) has opined that an oppressed minority perspective which utilizes civil rights strategies to achieve goals, has its limitations, and that a more powerful approach may be to acknowledge "the near universality of disability." In a similar vein, Halper (1993) argued that, in the U.S., aged lobby groups have been very successful in legitimizing age as a basis for accruing a wide range of benefits, from Medicare to discounts in stores. While this strategy has attracted to those over 65 years per capita health expenditures six times that for Americans under 18 years of age, he argues that it has been at the cost of strengthening images of older persons as dependent, needy, and impaired, thus weakening arguments against ageism.

In the area of Australian unemployment, it is not only difficult but dangerous to argue for the preeminence of the needs of one age group over the other. Youth, older men, older migrant women, are all badly off and focus on one group cannot be at the expense of the others. The art and challenge of politics is how to spread finite resources as fairly as possible.

This does not mean that unfavorable discrimination on the basis of age does not occur often enough to be problematic. It does and it occurs both blatantly and subtly. Sometimes, chronological age cannot easily be pointed to as the sole or main reason for an older worker being made redundant over a younger worker; it may be that the older worker's skills have become obsolete, or that the company will save more money and retain more workers if they get rid of the more highly paid, older workers. Cases of dismissal have been recorded where discrimination on the basis of age has been acknowledged while the dismissal has been at the same time justified on reasonable factors other than age (Snyder & Barrett, 1988).

Discrimination has also stood the test of time. Take for example, this passage (Kossoris, 1940):

> During the last 20 years, workers have repeatedly voiced their objections to discrimination against older workers in management's hiring policies. One of the reasons cited in justification for this policy is that the older worker is more of an accident risk than is the younger worker. In substantiation, it has been contended, first, that the physiological changes which accompany age decrease the speed of the older worker's reaction to danger, thus increasing his chances of getting hurt; and second, that once injured, his chances of recovery without permanent impairment are less, and that his period of recovery is longer than for the younger worker.
>
> The present article is an attempt to evaluate these contentions. It shows that older workers were injured less frequently than younger workers; but once injured they experience proportionately more deaths and permanent impairments than the younger workers. Similarly, their healing periods in temporary disability were, on average, longer.

This abstract by Max Kossoris in the Monthly Labour Review, October, 1940 began an article on the relation of age to industrial injuries.

COMMUNITY EXPECTATIONS AND STEREOTYPES OF OLD AGE

Age discrimination, being treated unfavorably because of chronological age, occurs generally in public attitudes and stereotypes. In many societies it is expected that, as people age, they will become more problematic in terms of failing health. This is particularly so among service-welfare of Western-Europe (e.g., the Netherlands, Germany) and North America, including the U.K. and Australia (Moss, 1992). It is expected that as persons age, they will move from a condition of independence, characterized by youthful images of beauty, strength, wealth, and health, to various conditions of dependence, characterized by ugliness, frailty, poverty, and chronic illness. Correll (1993), writing about Australian care for the aged warned that these images often serve to reinforce traditional policies based on notions of institutional care and dependency. Innovative services aimed at prevention of disease through early intervention, and monitoring of disability progression through case management, rely on different images of aging which stress autonomy, independent living, self-management, and community care support.

The media also appears to reinforce ageist stereotypes (e.g., senility) by focussing on high-profile diseases, such as Alzheimer's disease or Parkinsonism, which actually affects very few of those 65 years and older. Heller (1993) called for the development of prevention programs for older adults that reverse ageist images and encourage the maintenance of useful social roles. Much of the literature construes the consequences of aging as a modern crisis: (i) in epidemiological terms, because of their increasing numbers of older persons; (ii) in biological terms, because of their decline in health and physical status; (iii) in economic utility terms, because of their decreased energy, earning capacity, reduced memory, skills, and learning capacity; and, (iv) in social welfare terms, because they are seen as a burden to families, hospitals, and other care institutions.

THE OLDER WORKER AND PERFORMANCE

Community images of old age generalize to every aspect of life, especially to working life. Thus, powerful myths about the aging worker still influence employer personnel practices (Stagner, 1985; Shafer, Choppa, & Siefker, 1993). For example:

i. Older workers are slower than younger workers and do not have the physical capacities to perform the job. Research (Harwood, 1988) shows that there are some very small average age-related declines for workers over 45 years in reaction time and in physical strength. Concurrently, research suggests that, where declines occur, they are often compensated for by experience (Salthouse, 1988) and greater job involvement and organizational commitment (Rabinowitz & Hall, 1977; Arnold & Feldman, 1982). Further, an underlying and erroneous assumption about loss of capacity with age is that jobs always require peak performance (Robinson, 1986).
ii. Older workers have high absenteeism rates, more accidents, and more job changes. Research reflects that older workers have fewer accidents in the workplace, display less absenteeism, and are more reliable in their jobs (Rosen & Jerdee, 1976).
iii. Sheppard (1986) cited in Shafer et al. (1993) has also dispelled myths that older workers are opinionated, hard to get along with, and less serious, committed, and ambitious than younger workers.

Davies, Matthews, and Wong (1991) provided a comprehensive review of the relationship between performance and age in empirical, production records, and performance ratings studies. Overall, research has shown that individuals vary greatly across performance indicators and that it is not possible to generalize with respect to performance and age (Habib, 1990; Rhodes, 1983; Welford, 1985).

AGE DISCRIMINATION IN THE WORLD OF WORK

Problems of age discrimination in the world of work may be summarized as follows:

1. *The long-term decline in the workforce participation rates of older workers.* Many see this as a human rights issue in that older workers have a right to participate equally in the community and are clearly disadvantaged in financial, social, and human fulfillment terms in not being able to do so. Drury (1993) reported on the findings of Eurolink Age that: "...age discrimination against older workers exists in various forms in all twelve European Community (EC) countries." Drury argued that the majority of older workers across the EC who lose their jobs do not enter early retirement but become unemployed. They suffer financial hardship, some waiting during the time of unemployment and relying on unemployment benefits until these run out. Then some wait many more years before they become eligible for pension benefits.
2. *The duration of unemployment is longer for older workers than for others.* The guiding motive for action on this front is that older workers are carrying an unfair burden of the general workforce unemployment problem. Even worse, as Drury (1993) explained, in seven EC countries, the older unemployed are not even recorded on unemployment statistics as they have been put on social benefits, resulting in a significant reduction in income from employment. In Belgium, Denmark, Ireland, France, and the Netherlands, this occurs at age 55, in Germany at 58, and in the U.K. at 60. Their duration of unemployment on social benefits can be up to 10 years until they are eligible for pension benefits. Not surprisingly, the Eurolink Age Report has recommended that, in order to give a truer account of unemployment rates for those over 55 years, the numbers of older workers on automatic social benefits should be recorded in official unemployment figures.
3. *The practices of employers in key employment areas (recruitment and selection; training; disability management; retrenchment and dismissal) discriminate against the older worker.* Specifically:
    i. Many employers encourage older workers to leave the workforce early (to accept voluntary redundancies and to retire early). Many studies show repeatedly that people like retirement especially in countries where early retirement schemes are generous (e.g., France, Germany, the Netherlands), and it is not surprising, therefore, that many workers see early retirement,

as a right. Those who would rather work beyond the age of 50 years, or who are not covered by generous schemes in early retirement see the practice of early retirement as a discriminatory scheme to get rid of them. Drury (1993) and Godlee (1993), in their separate analyses of the Eurolink Age (age discrimination in employment in the EC) study, reported that workers over age 50 are being deliberately targeted by employers for job losses in all EC countries. "Almost all countries report that older workers are over represented in redundancies although no systematic age related figures exist" (Drury, 1993, p. 14).

In Australia, a survey of retirees conducted in late 1986 (ABS, 1987) indicated that 22% reported that their reason for leaving was "voluntary retirement." But in a later analysis, Foster (1988) attributed these retirements to, among other reasons, attractive early retirement packages where benefits are not substantially increased should the worker continue to work until compulsory retirement age; and, to the availability of and the increased real value of pensions. In Canada also, as reported by David (1993) there exist for older employees strong incentives for "voluntary early retirement," including, "...strong pressure from various sources to vacate their position" (p. 23).

ii. Many employers discourage older workers from returning to work following unemployment and absences for whatever reason. Age discrimination in hiring is evident in the EC countries (except in France where it is outlawed) through age limits set in job advertizements (Drury, 1993; Godlee, 1993). In Australia, survey results of unemployed workers noted that, when seeking employment, over half of those aged 45 years and over stated that the main impediment to being hired was that they were considered too old by the employers (ABS, 1988). At the time of this survey, the Office on Ageing in New South Wales (1990) undertook a survey of a leading newspaper's (*Sydney Morning Herald*) job advertizements on July 8, 1989. It indicated that 29% of private employment advertizements had age restrictions, and that 85% of these stipulated age criteria that were under 24 years of age. David (1993) characterized Canada's market as one in which "older workers need not apply." It is one in which employers seek flexible management opportunities in order to control wages, resulting in what she called a "dualization and casualization of the laborforce." This, in turn, results in long-term jobs being available for only the highly skilled, with less skilled jobs being taken up by contingent casual. Older workers whose skills have become obsolete and who have not had training opportunities, are easy casualties in this dual system.

iii. Many employers set exclusory eligibility criteria (quotas and age limits) for training schemes available to all workers. Drury (1993) and Godlee

(1993) reported that "No EC country provides targeted training programs for older workers," and some (Denmark, Greece, Ireland, Italy, and the U.K.) exclude older workers by setting maximum age limits for training programs. In Australia, training is less likely to be given to older workers because employers assume that there will be a limited return on their training investment (New South Wales Office on Ageing, 1990, p. 27). The whole subject of training programs for older workers has recently been underscored in a report of the Australia Council on the Ageing (1993). It made four recommendations for retraining the older unemployed:

R1.7: The Department of Employment, Education and Training (DEET) offer retraining and counselling opportunities specifically designed for older workers. R1.8: Federal resources be allocated to the publication and promotion of training programs targeted to older people. R1.9: Vocational retraining for potentially long term unemployed start immediately after unemployment and specifically after retrenchment. R1.10: Vocational counselling be expanded to ensure that appropriate retraining is suggested and newly unemployed be given the resources to access retraining programs.

Taylor and Walker (1993) in the U.K. have quoted figures from the Department of Employment survey of 3.5 million economically active people of working age who had received some kind of educational training. Only 4.5% were of age 50-59 years and 3.3%, 60-69 years. "This compared to 45.9% for the 16-19 age group, falling sharply to 18.3% for those 20-24 and declining thereafter" (p. 38).

iv. Through their employment and unemployment practices, employers perpetuate the myths that workers 45 years and over are less productive, less adaptable, and just too old. Yet it is clear from the above discussion that the criteria for "old" shifts with the purposes of employment practices. Who then is old? Ashbaugh and Fay (1987) analyzed 105 studies in which "older worker" was operationalized using some chronological age as a threshold. The study showed little agreement on when a worker becomes an older worker and mainly arbitrary methods were used in setting threshold age. This appears to be standard practice. In the U.S., the Age Discrimination in Employment Act (ADEA) sets 40 as the beginning of old age; in Australia, the Department of Social Security sets this at 45 years. A more interesting question is why such age thresholds are set at all. In themselves, are they not also examples of age discrimination? Why has it been necessary to single out older workers for special consideration, indeed for protection?

4. *Older workers receive less attention in the occupational rehabilitation system and the system is often not suited to their needs.* Bauer (1979) compared Vocational

Rehabilitation agency (VR) disability data with Social Security data and found that "the proportion of the disabled and severely disabled population increases with age, but that the proportion of VR clients declines by age" (p. 177). Blake (1981) presented data to show that, as the incidence of disabilities increases, service by rehabilitation agencies decreases. Thomas, Browning, and Greenwood (in press) argued that older workers need different attention in occupational rehabilitation (Dunn, 1981; Myers, 1985) because they sustain more serious (although fewer) injuries than younger workers and because (Root, 1981) they take longer to recover owing to biological aging effects (Brown, 1992). Many retired workers reported that they withdrew from the workforce for ill-health and injury reasons. The implications for workplace injury and disability management programs are profound. In addition, if attempts to maintain older persons at work longer are successful, there is every likelihood that workplaces will need to cope with another consequence of this success, that is, a higher number of impairments and disabilities as older workers stay longer on the job. Current projections view this problem as becoming more severe (Zedlewski & McBride, 1992) for the general population, not just the working population.

5. *Older worker self-evaluations: The nondiscriminative weight of cumulative experience.* Persistent negative messages can become internalized attitudes which severely influence feelings of self-efficacy, self-worth, and handicap. Negative attitudes toward older persons are very pervasive in the media, in popular humor, and in professional and personal interactions. Attempts to encourage increased participation of older workers in the workforce and in training programs, which many are currently reluctant to enter, will therefore entail not only improving the public image of older workers, but older persons generally (Myers, 1987).

INITIATIVES TO COMBAT THESE PROBLEMS

These problems, which are of concern in differing degrees in most countries, suggest three major areas of need in terms of deliberate action. First, there is a need to correct and reverse practices and attitudes which discriminate against the older worker. Some initiatives may be educational and some legislative, such as eliminating mandatory retirement and protecting older workers against premature dismissal or retirement. The effect of legislative measures is immediate in securing rights and curbing blatant discriminative practices, but probably long-term in changing community attitudes. Second, there is a need for society to devise plans and policies which provide monetary and in-kind incentives for continuing at work and which mutually reinforce other income support schemes (e.g., pensions, superannuations). Partial pension schemes, tapered or phased retirement schemes will not work if what they offer by way of income and other incentives is inferior to normal retirement entitlements. Third, there is a need to develop schemes designed to encourage continued employment of older persons following disablement and after official retirement age.

Education vs. Legislation

Broadly speaking, deliberate measures addressing these needs have either been educational or legislative in nature (with the U.S. being far ahead of many countries in legislative measures). There is always some debate as to whether legislation, for example against age discrimination, is desirable and likely to be effective. Taylor and Walker (1993) found in their U.K. survey that while 53% of employers were in favor of legislation, 36% felt that legislation would actually increase the numbers of older persons in employment, while 58% said it would make no difference at all. The U.S. experience with the Age Discrimination in Employment Act (ADEA) of 1967, which legislates for individuals to be judged on ability, not age, has been that it does make a difference. Ventrell-Monsees (1993) reported that blatant discrimination has disappeared, that job advertizements and training and promotion opportunities are not closed to older workers. In addition, mandatory retirement policies have become unlawful (since 1986 amendments) and early retirement policies cannot be used to force people into retirement. Conversely, Ventrell-Monsees noted that age discrimination has become "more subtle" and has "gone underground" (p. 43). Older workers can be given reasons other than their age (e.g., "you're too qualified") for not being successful; early retirement schemes have replaced mandatory retirement policies in the U.S., but still constitute a way to evict older workers. A further example of subtle ageism allocates blame to populations over events. In what Day (1993) and Binstock (1990) have called "new stereotypes," older people are depicted as affluent and burdensome to society. Day (1993) found that there was more resentment against old-age benefits within generations than between them, but perhaps the major concern here is that stereotypes such as the old being "greedy-geezers" (Longman, 1987), exist at all. However, Ventrell-Monsees (1993) expressed the belief that legislation is changing ageist attitudes over time as workers become more aware of their rights in the workplace. In comparison, Quadagno and Hardy (1991) argued that the ADEA has actually reduced the flexibility and efficiency of early retirement programs as a management mechanism. They have warned that if early retirement pensions become less attractive to employers, workers may have to rely on Social Security for income in later life.

In considering the issue of which approach to combating ageism works best, the question is one of empirical research. Palmore (1982) argued that for ageism to be reduced, it is important to know which methods are most efficient and effective. This is based on being able to specify what determines discriminations and stereotypes against older people. In this view, Riley and Riley's (1991) call for more social science research on the effect of the ADEA (and perhaps all other relevant legislation) is apt.

The Workplace as the Target

If age itself is not a key disincentive to work, but rather obsolescence of skills; injury, ill-health and disablement (Chirikos & Nestel, 1989); discrimination; and, employer practices, then programs to combat these phenomena are the real requirements. Thus, retraining schemes for older workers and wage subsidy schemes to employers who recruit and retain older workers are clear avenues for employer-based development. Special employment programs for older persons, and disability management programs, geared to the needs of older workers, are also required. As a very practical solution to the needs outlined above, one can see how salient and important are workplace disability and injury management programs, which are directly targeted to assisting workers to return to and maintain their work. They are a singularly powerful laborforce participation enhancer because accommodations made at the workplace (e.g., attendance flexibility, ergonomic changes, exercise and health promotion, monitoring of progress and well-being, clearly integrated communication practices) may encourage the continuance of many workers who might otherwise withdraw. Disability management programs need to be operating for both employees and employers to meet social and vocational rehabilitation goals. The benefits to the worker of effective workplace rehabilitation programs are clear. The benefits to the employer are also clear in that the employer is complying with regulations to provide rehabilitation, is managing human resources humanely and cost-effectively, is saving on the costs of recruiting, processing, and training replacement workers, and is retaining a stable, skilled, and experienced workforce. Disability management programs are thus a working example of employer-incentive-driven programs which could provide the model needed to encourage employers to hire, train, and maintain older workers in the workforce.

Many public programs aimed at the unemployed have a common problem. They are programs meant to rectify a damage already done. Further, there is always the problem of people affected by unemployment not being aware, or taking a long time to become aware of programs that are available to them. Workplace support paradigms (e.g., occupational rehabilitation and disability management programs) may be among the best investments to increase laborforce participation, because they can prevent unemployment, which is the current prelude to long-term unemployment for people with disabilities and for older workers.

Given that so many workers give ill-heath or injury as their reason for early retirement (Kingson, 1982) rehabilitation at the workplace becomes even more crucial as both restorative and apreventative measures. Rehabilitation has long contained the notion of restoration of health or, if this is not possible, alteration to an improved form of functioning. It also contains the notion of reinstatement of rights, status, and privileges, and the provision of services which enable resumption and pursuit of normal activities. These notions are totally compatible with rights to work and equal participation on the part of all who wish to, and with meeting the needs of persons (e.g., through education and training) to enable them to do so.

However, incentives and skilled assistance must be provided for employers to establish and conduct effective occupational rehabilitation programs at the workplace. This sentiment has been expressed before, somewhat pessimistically, by Nash (1987): "Employers must be assisted in developing ways to make work competitive with retirement or unemployment as a life-style choice. Whether incentives can be found that will motivate both employers and workers to alter current trends is highly problematic, however" (p.11). His pessimism may have had some basis for, six years later, Drury (1993) has repeated the warning: "In the end, however, employers will make decisions based on their financial interests. The challenge therefore is to ensure that older workers represent an economic investment to employers in the future." This idea would also apply to the contribution of people with disabilities. It is obviously not easy to represent older workers and persons with disabilities as economic investments to many employers. We are forced to acknowledge that the question of incentives, of what will make it worthwhile for employers to make accommodations for older persons and those with disabilities, is inherently difficult. For example, employees with disabilities (Greenwald, Dirks, Borgatta, McCorkle, Nevitt, & Yelin, 1989; Yelin, Greenblatt, Hollander, & McMaster, 1991; Yelin, Henke, & Epstein, 1987) who can control the pace and scheduling of their work activities are less likely to stop working than those who have no such control and who, therefore, cannot satisfy the inflexible conditions (e.g., start times) of their work. But, is this knowledge sufficient to make employers change working conditions to make them more flexible? The impediments to this may be that the current inflexible system has worked efficiently and profitably for the employer and reasonably for most employees. It may also be that the current working conditions have been the subject of hard-won resolutions agreed to by unions and employers, and have become entrenched in award conditions. So, what will make it worthwhile for employers to disturb the universe? Punitive or harnessing legislation and the pressure of attitude change measures, will, of course, provide some impetus for change, even if only to comply. In Australia, many large employers are able to incorporate the demands of legislation and to provide assistive services for their employees. This is because they are making large profits, have an image to maintain as a good employer, believe that their investment in employees is good business sense in terms of staff morale, turnover, absenteeism, etc., or, feel that they have a social responsibility to fulfill. However, many small employers, struggling to remain in business, find it difficult to make serious efforts for their employees, especially for their minority employees, unless they have incentives to do so. In

Australia, positive incentives in the form of government assistance, (e.g., subsidized training, tax incentives or wage subsidies to hire disadvantaged persons, specialized advice to effect workplace modifications, professional support for employee problems) is clearly a good beginning.

RELATED ISSUES

REHABILITATION AND THE DISABILITY DEBATE

Rehabilitation concepts such as impairment, disability, and handicap have been given some stability in common usage by definitions such as those proposed by the World Health Organization (W.H.O.) in 1980. Concepts are of course general, living notions, which have a habit of breaking out of their straight-jacketing definitions, in response to pressure group interests, changing ideologies and understandings, and economic and political circumstances. Because concepts continue to be amenable to various definitions of them, it is not surprising that they will be used to achieve the particular and several purposes of those employing them, and that their definitions will from time to time be criticized for being too restrictive, too expansive, too specialized, discriminatory, inflexible, economics-biased, humanitarianly idealistic, etc. Now this reviewing of our bread-and-butter concepts is of course a developmentally healthy process. We have all gained from the expansion of the rehabilitation concept from a narrow medical restoration view to one incorporating social-environmental factors and rights to independent living. It is also possible to envisage that the concepts we are now using will no longer be useful, will die forever, or later be resurrected. "In a minute there is time /For decisions and revisions which a minute will reverse" (Eliot, 1963).

Our concepts, it really goes without saying, can create communication possibilities and communication problems for us. If we share the same meanings, the former is likely to result. If we do not, the latter may not result. A case in point is the concept of disability, over which there is currently very lively debate in the literature.

Some (e.g., Pfeiffer, 1993) have argued that the W.H.O. definition of disability, coming as it does in a trio of definitions conceptually parasitic on one another (impairment, disability, handicap), is offensive because it implies causal progression and places the problem in the person rather than in society. Others (Chirikos, 1989) have argued that the term implicitly treats impairment status as permanent, fixed and dichotomous, rather than as fluid and continuous. Reisine and Fifield (1992), Zola (1993), Hahn (1993), Brown (1993), and Kuehn (1991) have argued in different ways that our data on disability is a function of how we define it for research and policy purposes. Some definitions may include most people some of the time, and others include only some of the people but most of the time.

As well as discussing issues and reporting findings particular to rheumatoid arthritis and disability, Reisine and Fifield (1992) conducted a study (N=998) using four different definitions of disability, depending on source (The Social Security work disability definitions, the NHIS definition, four American College of Rheumatology definitions, and three Arthritis Research definitions). Their research revealed that: (1) Rates of disability varied widely depending upon how disability is defined; (2) Current measures underestimate disability in women; (3) Using NHIS data, many more people are disabled than receive income replacement benefits. Pfeiffer (1993) characterized disability data as "soft data" because it is based on differing definitions. Chirikos (1989) lamented the difficulty for policymakers who, especially in an era of limited resources, "... need to know which rehabilitation investments yield the highest returns." He concluded about the U.S., rather starkly: "Put simply, available national data on the size and composition of the disabled population are not altogether adequate for policy purposes." He advocated longitudinal studies of the effects of disability because the "... empirical literature on disability is mostly cross-sectional in nature, and implicitly treats disability status as permanent." (p. 87).

Hahn (1993) has argued that disability policy has been based on two different paradigms. One is the *functional-limitations* paradigm which has been supported by medical and economic understandings of disability resulting in placing limits on a person's major life activities or restricting the amount and kind of work that a person can perform. Hahn argued that this kind of thinking has formed the basis of programs of vocational rehabilitation, and SSDI (Social Security Disability Income) and SSI (Supplemental Security Income) programs where the focus has been on medical causation, prevention, and clinical focus on eradicating the disability trait(s) within the individual.

Public policy has also adopted, most frequently and widely, an economic viewpoint which has resulted in rehabilitation legislation and vocational rehabilitation programs designed to encourage the employment of persons with disabilities, and which has perpetuated a clinical focus of matching job requirements to skills and interests of the disabled worker. Australia appears to be facing, with the Job Compact program, a similar economic and utilitarian policy guided by a person-job matching process in a case-management model of service delivery.

The second paradigm is the *minority-group* paradigm based on a socio-political definition of disability focusing on interaction between individuals and their environments and highlighting that people with disabilities are a minority group who "... have been subjected to prejudice and discrimination on the basis of visible or labelled physical differences." Hahn (1993) may argue that this perspective forms the basis of U.S. antidiscrimination laws such as Section 504 of the Rehabilitation

Act of 1973, the Civil Rights Restoration Act, and the Americans with Disabilities Act of 1990.

Brown (1993), in a provocative article, examined how the four (abbreviated) goals (equality of opportunity, full participation, independent living, economic self-sufficiency) of the Americans with Disabilities Act (ADA) and extant W.H.O. definitions of impairment, disability, and handicap relate to each other. He has argued for revitalizing the concept of handicap for monitoring implementation of the ADA. Handicap points to the interaction between the individual and the environment, and as such, interactive situations and indicators of them which demonstrate the ADA goals in action, are the appropriate targets of evaluation, not individuals with disabilities.

Zola (1989) argued that the meaning of disability data will vary along a number of dimensions. The *prevalence* of disability will vary considerably depending on the definition/measure used. Thus, we will have different numbers if we gather data on the basis of how many persons have *chronic conditions or impairments* (these may be single or multiple, fluctuating or permanent, etc.); how many have *functional limitations* (these are behavioral correlates such as mobility or sensory limitations); and how many have *activity limitations* (these are major roles considered normative for specific age groups).

This breakdown of interpretational measures of disability is not unlike Berkowitz's (1985) five-level model of analysis of disability comprising (1) Classification (based on an etiology of work injury, congenital dysfunction, or chronic disease); (2) Impairment, (3) Activity limitation; (4) Job activity limitation; and, (5) Disability.

Disability data will also vary because of *trends in prevalence*. In all countries the number of people with disabilities has risen steadily. It has risen because of (1) methods used (e.g., self-report questionnaires vs. records) and definitions of success (e.g., number of years of living following a cancer diagnosis); (2) advances in care (e.g., diabetics, AIDS sufferers, spinal-cord and head-injured persons now live longer); (3) demographics (while people are living longer, they also have more disabilities). Associated to this is *temporality*, that is the length of time that people will have disabilities is steadily increasing, because they are living longer.

Finally, disability data will vary because of the *spread* phenomenon. That is, new manifestations of old diseases (e.g., post-polio syndrome; post-traumatic stress disorders), and co-morbidity (having more than one disability is more likely with increasing age).

Zola's (1989) arguments encounter an even more challenging set of conclusions:

1. That since disability is not something one has, but is a set of characteristics most people share to some degree at some time (e.g., like having the flu), the search for a definition of disability in terms of which numbers of disabled per-

sons are counted, may be misdirected, unless we have a *valid* purpose. In some circumstances, it may be valid and advantageous to "special" needs as a minority group (Zola says in cases where "high economic costs are involved, such as in mass transportation and long-term care..."), or when there is clear evidence of discrimination or oppression. DeJong et al. (1989) also argued for the sometime usefulness of characterizing persons with disabilities as "health minorities" with the caution that this is undesirable if it leads to "segregated solutions" (p. 345). In an article describing the facets involved in "the disablement process," Verbrugge and Jette (1994) defined disability as "...difficulty doing activities in any domain of life...due to a health or physical problem." As such, they claim that disability is not a personal characteristic but represents rather a gap between personal capability and environmental demand which many of us can experience.

2. As disability is not a fixed status pathology but a changing set of characteristics or phenomenon, acceptance and adaptation to it at the level of the individual will not be once-off, but will be an ongoing life process of development, setbacks, self-management, and self-fulfilment. A full-blown form of this perspective may perhaps be seen in persons with hearing impairments who are asserting their right to choose whether they will have cochlear implants because they value their hearing-impaired culture, as one wherein they are able to transfer and receive meaning through sign language, more than they value the ability to speak in our language. And, they reject the assumptions of remedial hearing technology that they need to be normalized into a hearing world.

Disability has generally been viewed as a subconcept of rehabilitation, and many of the criticisms of disability as a concept can be equally applied to rehabilitation. It has had, in the past, a narrow medical focus; it has come to have wider reference to social, political, and environmental deficits and to individual rights. It has recognized its dependence on other fields and networks and has assisted other causes, by association, to gain legitimacy: medical rehabilitation; vocational rehabilitation; geriatric rehabilitation; workplace rehabilitation; compensation rehabilitation; psychiatric rehabilitation, etc. It has shepherded mutually reinforcing movements such as normalization and independent living. It underpins common conversation, policy discussions, and programs of many other "new morbidities" and human causes of today: AIDS sufferers; oppressed ethnic minorities; civilian war and disaster casualties; disadvantaged women; thalidomide victims; incest and sexual abuse victims; the homeless; the long-term unemployed; the working poor; persons with learning disabilities; disabled older workers when Mary Switzer became (in 1967) Commissioner of the Social and Rehabilitation Service within the Department of Health, Education and Welfare, rehabilitation was being geared to be the cornerstone of national health, education, and welfare policy (Hughes, 1986). The income support programs for needy Americans, rehabilitative services for Americans with disabilities, and specialized services for mothers and children, youth, and older persons, were all designed under Switzer on rehabilitation principles.

Clearly, it has been a most elastic concept, but not unassailable by competing legitimate ideologies and vested interests. When it was being used to describe what professionals do in the process of assisting individuals with disabilities to adjust it was seen as reinforcing the prevailing "clinical" model of service delivery. This was encumbered by assumptions (1) that the individual is dependent on the professional (attacked by the empowerment ideology); (2) that the problem for rehabilitation services to solve was located in the individual (exposed by the victim-blaming ideology); (3) that the solution to problems of persons with disabilities lay in the empirical, positivistic approach of findings of scientific methods of inquiry (regaled by the socio-political activist ideology). Disability rights activists in particular have eschewed traditional rehabilitation approaches which focused on professional endeavors to effect individual client change, in favor of approaches which mobilized persons with disabilities to change social-environmental circumstances which obstruct the self-management and independent living of persons with disabilities.

The shift here was really from individual rehabilitation to environmental or social rehabilitation, a concept applying to all of society. Its currency as a general concept applying to all, not just special groups, is perhaps not yet totally devalued. Almost anyone can become unemployed, contract AIDS, be the victim of disasters both natural and man-made, become old, mentally disturbed, etc. The Disability Rights movement has coined the acronym TAB, Temporarily Able-Bodied, to refer to this transitory state of ours (although the author prefers TA, Temporarily-Able, to reflect mental and emotional conditions also).

As a singular but complex and over-arching concept, the term "rehabilitation" and its subconcepts, will always be assailable, and fall in and out of favor. If we are to deal with the empirical world more effectively we need a coherent theory of rehabilitation, an abstract system of ideas describing and explaining individual and environmental intervention principles where recovery and independent functioning, regardless of cause, are required on the part of members of society. What would such a theory require? At the risk of putting too simplistically a complex and daunting undertaking, it would require at minimum:

1. A clarification of the concept of rehabilitation, all its related concepts, and extant definitions; a rigorous analysis of fundamental assumptions underlying various practical approaches and ideological positions; and, a summary of existing knowledge.

2. A set of propositions or axioms, and related corollaries, concerning the rationale, purposes and methods of rehabilitation, national and international, from which a large number of empirical observations can be deduced.
3. A statement of the relationship between these axioms and possible courses of implementation and action, prediction, and fruitful lines of experimental inquiry.
4. A statement of ways of evaluating and testing the axioms, and of improving their usefulness over time.

PROFESSIONAL MEDIATING ROLES

The system, with its structures, institutions, and policies will always require some translation to those affected by it, especially as it is complex and not necessarily consistent or coherent in its messages. Professionals and other care-givers have a de facto clear mediating role between the system and those who operate within it. In the compensation and rehabilitation systems of many countries, physicians have the legal role of determining whether a person's injury or condition prevents working. This fact alone places physicians in a unique gatekeeping system-mediating role. There has, of course, been some serious questioning of the simple relationship assumed between impairment determination and employability. More poignantly as many have noted (Crewe & Athelstan, 1981; Kuehn, 1991) and as Berkowitz (1985) has stated: "There are many examples where medical illness would be irrelevant in explaining employability and earnings" (p. 364). Further, medical conditions have often been minimized not through clinical treatment but through environmental manipulation, as urged by the independent living movement. The validity of medical estimates of residual function has also been questioned. Recommendations for "light work," and the absence of advice on accommodating to the patient's work conditions further testify to the fact that many physicians have little direct experience of work settings outside medicine.

In the area of occupational rehabilitation in particular, physicians have been inappropriately cast in the role of determining occupational disability. Bowe (1993) presented figures based on the 1990 U.S. Census of Population and Housing to the effect that of 12.8 million with work disabilities, over half considered themselves prevented from working because of their disabilities. Bowe expressed disbelief that so many adults with disabilities think they cannot work "... because with the appropriate education, training, adaptive equipment, and placement assistance, nearly all individuals with disabilities probably can perform at least some jobs" (p. 87). As Bowe reluctantly opined, pure self-interest is one explanation for these perceptions (they say they can't work because they are getting or hope to get disability benefits). Another explanation is that some clients have genuinely developed the expectation of not working through the social networks, including professionals, with whom they have come into contact. In this view, we can easily invoke sociological explanations of sick-role acquisition, and psychological explanations of the development of chronic pain syndromes. It is also reasonable to surmise that "significant persons" such as physicians, who have early contact with their patients, and whose society-deemed role it is to diagnose impairment, assess functional capacity, prescribe treatment and make prognoses, will have primary influence on the enduring perceptions and expectations their clients develop about their disabilities and the consequences of them for life, work, and security. Discussion between the doctor and the patient of the options available to the patient assists him or her to assign value to them and to construct a meaning of the disability. The role of the doctor is therefore not a neutral one, and it is coming to be seen as a formal mediating one rather than an informal side-effect role. The mediating, gate-keeping role of doctors can perhaps best be seen in operation in organizations which employ doctors. Companies (usually middle-sized to large) in many countries often employ doctors to manage their occupational health and safety, occupational rehabilitation, or disability management programs. In the U.S. too, prepaid care organizations such as Health Maintenance Organizations (HMOs) are expanding and they employ doctors to provide health care within predetermined cost-boundaries. In these settings, it is reported that doctors are experiencing pressure to change "their role from serving as agent for the patient's welfare to balancing the patient's needs against the need for cost control" (Iglehart, 1992). In company disability management and occupational health and safety programs, the physician is sometimes seen to be the agent of the organization, rather than the employee advocate, and the professional operations of the physician are seen to be harnessed, controlled, and directed by the work organization. This trend of work organizations dictating the work of occupational groups and professions (thus challenging autonomy of professional decision-making) is not confined to physicians, as Abbott (1988) noted.

While the gate-keeper role of physicians can be seen to be explicitly operating in companies which have them, it has always been an informal role in forceful operation since physicians have provided medical certificates to validate compensation claims and to justify time off work. However, the magnitude of this gate-keeping role has not been reflected in medical training curricula and the subject of assessment of fitness for work has mostly been treated summarily. In carrying out their gate-keeping role, which goes beyond the traditional treatment-giver role to a higher plane entailing partnership and advocacy (Greenwald & Groat, 1993), there is a clear need for physicians:

1. to become more familiar with work environments;
2. to be able to discuss with their clients the return-to-work and income support options available to them, including the economic disincentives to work among injured workers;

3. to be able to provide their services in a framework compatible with the basic principles of occupational rehabilitation and disability management. Thus they must understand the impact of early intervention; their concurrent role in an interdisciplinary, co-ordinated program for disability management and return to work, their role in enhancing the process of "bonding" between the worker and the employer (Shrey, 1993; Shrey & Olsheski, 1992); and their role in providing expert medical assessment information for use in designating appropriate jobs in transitional work programs.

Much of this relies on the goodwill and understanding of the physician and on the assumption that, providing good service either directly to the patient or indirectly through advocacy on behalf of the patient, is its own reward. This is surely so in many instances. But it is also true that many physicians are not familiar with work environments, with regulations, policies, and programs affecting the welfare of workers, and with principles of rehabilitation. Some, reflecting general population attitudes and stereotypes, also hold negative attitudes to older people (Butler & Lewis, 1982) and to persons with disabilities. The question arises as to incentives for doctors to give special attention to their disadvantaged clients. In the U.K., general practitioners are being provided financial incentives to provide prevention rather than treatment services in order to facilitate early detection, education about, and treatment of high-risk groups within the community. This is the result of radical reforms introduced into the National Health Service (NHS) in 1990 (Hughes, 1993b). In many countries, laws and regulations constitute a social stimulus to force compliance. Of their nature, many are also general in their application and removed from the immediate and intimate interactions of people *in situ*. They may or may not have impact. For example, going through a red traffic light does not always guarantee a fine or a sentence for the offender. Similarly, many who have been retired early do not invoke legislation against age discrimination for their dismissal. Yelin (1991) warned in relation to the ADA and enforcement of its regulations against discrimination in employment "...only a fraction of the hundreds of thousands – perhaps millions – of individuals who will suffer discrimination subsequent to the passage of the ADA will ever file such a claim" (p. 145). Other social stimuli to discourage discrimination, in the case of employers, sometimes hurt more and are more accurately targeted such as loss of community regard as a reputable employer, cost of recruitment, absenteeism, job turnover, retraining, loss of experienced and skilled staff, etc. But such social enforcements are usually disincentives to inappropriate behavior, rather than incentives to appropriate behavior. Like most forms of punishment, they have undesirable side effects (e.g., evasion schemes, inaction, revenge or cost-response measures). A more constructive path, therefore, is to discover and offer "carrots" which, as any good behaviorist knows, have the effect of reinforcing appropriate, desirable behavior. Have we discovered enough of the right carrots for employers and physicians to do the right thing by their employees and patients? Disabled and older persons need special attention because they have particular needs. What's in it for employers and physicians to provide this? The intrinsic rewards associated with having dealt well with an employee, or having provided good service to a patient are certainly important. But are they enough? Behavior reliant on noble sentiments or principles, or on goodwill, is often as short-lived as it is rare.

A related issue is whether personnel at the workplace are able to deliver appropriate services and develop sound occupational rehabilitation programs. In Australia, with the new workers' compensation and rehabilitation legislation requiring workplaces to provide rehabilitation to injured workers, there has been widespread use of personnel in positions such as Rehabilitation Coordinator, Case Manager, etc. Many have no training in rehabilitation and disability management and are therefore ill-equipped to deal with the work and disability needs of workers. This appears also to be true for many who are professionally trained in rehabilitation but who have a narrow clinical focus and experience (Remenyi, 1989). Vocational rehabilitation requires the ability to network across community services, to operate across and within the boundaries of different organizational and social systems, to provide clients with vocational counseling and assessment and job placement services informed by sophisticated market information, to provide counseling to assist people to adjust to and cope with their disabilities, to advise as to modifications to the workplace, to liaise with workplace personnel at different levels in the organization and so on. Rehabilitation counseling for older displaced workers who wish to work is advocated by Shafer et al. (1993). They have outlined how the techniques of rehabilitation counseling practice may be adapted to address the special concerns of older workers. These techniques would include vocational counseling; goal selection following an assessment of transferable skills and available job sources; training or retraining; job placement; assessment of physical capacities; and, educating employers about the advantages of hiring and retaining older workers.

In a recent nationwide survey in Australia, Remenyi (in press) asked a wide range of rehabilitation service delivery staff what they thought of rehabilitation counseling activities. Specifically, respondents were asked how important they thought the activities to be and how well they were being carried out in their agencies. In Australia, the rehabilitation counseling profession is only beginning to be established, but the overwhelming evidence from this research is that rehabilitation counseling activities are sanctioned by all other rehabilitation practitioners in the field and they see these activities as best undertaken by those specifically trained in rehabilitation counseling.

Rehabilitation counselors, because of their skills and training, are qualified to provide services to people with employment and disability problems. But, all professionals who deal with people with these problems have a role in giving realistic advice, in dismantling entrenched stereotypes which perpetuate myths and negative attitudes towards disadvantaged groups, and in fostering communication across separate boundaries of behavior and service delivery.

SERVICE DELIVERY VIA CASE MANAGEMENT

In almost all countries, there is concern for how to meet increasing demands on health care systems while budgets tighten. Cost-benefit and cost efficiency drives have resulted in rationalization of programs in order to encourage, rather than the expansion of services, the integration of services for all needy people within established health and welfare services.

The case management model has reemerged (from its traditional, limited sense of coordinating treatment services) as a paradigm for service delivery skills. These skills emphasize the utilization of efficient community resources, linking client needs with extant primary health care systems, coordinating professional and care-giver efforts, and networking across different community sectors such as health, welfare, employment, and education. Case management represents a client-support model, popular in decentralized systems of health care, which aims to meet client needs within the framework of service agency policies and resources. Akabas, Gates and Galvin (1992) have defined case management as "... a method of coordinating and integrating a range of social, health and rehabilitation services to enhance the functioning and quality of life of the individual, improve the quality of care, and conserve costs" (p. 125). It is a model which has become popular in many areas of service delivery. In Australia, the Commonwealth Rehabilitation Service (CRS) has adopted this model and all service delivery staff, from whatever professional or discipline background, undergo generic training in it. In the State WorkCover system, employers who conduct their own in-house rehabilitation, injury or disability management systems appoint rehabilitation coordinators to conduct case management within the workplace. Rehabilitation providers who enter workplaces as contractors also provide their services along individual case management lines. In the Compensation and Rehabilitation scheme conducted for the federal government, employees, and agencies (Comcare), case managers (usually nonprofessional) are trained on-the-job and appointed to provide services.

In the Job Compact scheme of the federal government in Australia, described earlier, the delivery of market assistance to individuals will be through a case-management model, culminating in an action plan monitored by a CES case manager or a small team of case managers in concert with the job seeker (Committee on Employment Opportunities [CEO], 1993, p. 147).

The case management model has many guises and operates in many settings. In the U.K., a program of community care is in operation, that is "...providing the services and support which people who are affected by problems such as aging, mental illness, mental handicap, or physical or sensory disability need to be able to live as independently as possible in their own homes, or in 'homely' settings in the community" (HMSO & Secretaries of State for Health, 1989). Case Managers have been utilized to ensure "... that resources are managed effectively, that individuals' needs are reviewed regularly and that each service has a single point of contact" (Hughes, 1993a).

It could also be argued that the 1990 initiatives of the U.K. NHS to encourage General Practitioners to provide prevention rather than treatment services, is really a community case management role being given to doctors to facilitate early detection, education about, and treatment of high-risk diseases for high-risk groups within the community. Similarly, the ubiquity and centrality of the case-management model is seen also in HMOs. They use case managers called "utilization managers" (Hurley & Bannick, 1993) who monitor and influence quality and service usage across key players in the HMO system; in fact, these utilization managers have a role similar to case managers in some Australian occupational rehabilitation agencies, and in insurance companies.

Psychiatric care is another subsystem of health which has employed varieties of case management models.

ISSUES IN CASE MANAGEMENT

The Case Management model would appear to have some obvious general advantages, though they vary considerably across settings:

1. Deliberate tailoring of client needs and services;
2. Agency or system goals can be clearly communicated;
3. Monitoring of case progress leads to efficiencies in terms of time and costs;
4. The contribution of service providers outside the immediate agency can be integrated into the service plan, and evaluated;
5. In work-site, or other on-site services, case managers can (a) refer clients directly after injury or disablement; (b) recommend on a discretionary basis, that assistance be given at-risk clients even before paperwork or a claim has been presented, to prevent disability occurrence; and (c) can develop close working relationships with key agency personnel, thus being of direct support to them in their role as human resource managers.

Many would claim that the case management model has much to recommend it. However, it requires sophisticated administrative, recording, and monitoring procedures, and highly developed professional and personal skills on the part of the case manager. In addition, it is not a model which is immune to the operation of professional barriers and rivalries. This is made worse when case managers are not themselves professionally trained, and they report difficulties in being accepted by professionals whose activities they often need to coordinate. This is the case in the compensation and rehabilitation systems in Australia (Remenyi, 1989). Other problems stem from case managers in a particular system or organization having to deal with external personnel; goal, managerial style, service regime, administration and accountability differences across different organizations increase the possibilities of misunderstandings, poor communication, and fragmentation of service delivery (Berlman, Hunter & McMahon, 1990; Glendenning, 1982; Hudson, 1991). The case management model also places special strains on the case manager who is as much the agent of the system as of the individuals in it. Approving services tailored to individual needs, which are also acceptably cost-efficient to the organization, raises problems of role allegiance and confidentiality, and problems consistent with the nature of gate-keeping, and boundary spanning positions (Budrys, 1993; Katz & Kahn, 1978).

One area of service delivery which has employed the case management model extensively is that of chronic mental illness. This is of particular interest in Australia because some rehabilitation services have been specifically directed at assisting psychiatric clients to live more independently and to seek employment in the open market. The Commonwealth Rehabilitation Service has embarked on this endeavor, and it uses an intensive case management model of service delivery. At the same time, the Report of the National Inquiry into the Human Rights of People with Mental Illness (the Burdekin Report) was released at the end of 1993. Its general conclusions and findings point to a national disgrace, to a system that has not been able to respond to the needs of people affected by mental illness when the philosophies of normalization, de-institutionalization and community reintegration were introduced. The author quotes: "People affected by mental illness are among the most vulnerable and disadvantaged in our community. They suffer from widespread, systemic discrimination and are consistently denied the rights and services to which they are entitled." While there is trenchant criticism of the entire system, the role of general practitioners and psychiatrists in psychiatric rehabilitation in Australia, because of their positional status in the system, is highlighted. Thus, the author quotes: "General practitioners fail to identify mental illness in a significant proportion of patients .... However, they have a profound influence over the use of other health services. They initiate referrals to specialists and allied health professionals and they can directly influence treatment options." (pp.192-3).

The report recommends more effective integration of general practitioners into the health system (i.e., liaison with community-based mental health professionals), and that they should receive more comprehensive mental health education. Psychiatrists were also seen to be deficient in current psychiatric knowledge, and in interpersonal skills. Many left employment in the public sector to treat easier clients in more lucrative private practices (Burdekin, 1993).

In the U.S., the recidivism or "revolving door" pattern of psychiatric hospital use has been a recurring issue in mental health policy. As in many countries, the experience is that services to these clients are difficult to provide. Various types of intensive and focused case management programs offer long-term commitment, attention to daily living needs, home contact, assertive advocacy, and small client caseloads.

Dietzen and Bond (1993) claim that while there are many examples in the literature of case management programs which have resulted in reduced hospital use by clients (the index of success) some studies actually show an increase in hospital use among clients who receive case management services. In their study they compared seven assertive community treatment programs in order to examine changes in hospital use and client satisfaction under each program. They found no significant correlation between change in hospital use and frequency of services provided, regardless of the type of program. They also found surprisingly few associations between the intensity of services and client satisfaction, although very low frequencies of service were ineffective in reducing hospital use. Basically, this amounts to more services not meaning better, although very few services means worse. Dietzen and Bond have drawn attention to shortcomings of the study; for example, they might have obtained different results had they compared the effect of the different case management programs on levels of functioning and needs satisfaction, and had they factored in the quality of contact and helping skills level of case managers. But their findings are nonetheless important for case management. Wasylenki, Goering, Lemire, Lindsey, and Lancee (1993) argued that assertive case management is an effective means of serving difficult-to-engage client groups provided trained personnel are available. They describe assertive casework as normal casework with the addition of aggressive outreach and provision of direct services. This study, conducted in Toronto, of 59 psychiatrically disturbed homeless persons, is impressive in its details about subjects and measures; they do caution about significant methodological limitations (e.g., no control group), but they are optimistic about the effectiveness of assertive case management.

Hornstra, Bruce-Wolfe, Sagduyu, and Riffle (1993) matched (by age, number of previous hospitalizations, and days spent in the hospital) 112 schizophrenic patients involved in an intensive case management community-based psychiatric rehabilitation program with 112 schizophrenic patients who received only medication services and minimal case management. The patients in the intensive case management group used significantly more services during the study period than did the patients in the minimal case management group. But, no significant differences were found between the two groups in number of hospitalizations and days in hospital. They concluded that intensive case management was no more effective than medication services and minimal case management.

One strength of this study was that Hornstra *et al.* (1993) operationalized case management in terms of measurable events. They note in their review that many studies of the effect of intensive case management (Stein & Test, 1980; Mulder, 1985; Curtis, Millman, Struening *et al.*, 1992) fail to provide operational definitions of case management, a necessity as it is not a unitary concept with many instances of case management differing widely in their program elements. Further, some studies did not match patients' or pre-study level of service use, on symptom level or on diagnosis.

In the context of disability management, Akabas et al. (1992) reiterated that although case management is both widespread and popular, its effectiveness is not based on cost-benefit evaluative studies. The reasons for this, they argued, are that such studies are basically difficult to conduct, that existent studies in companies have been driven by vested interests, or have demonstrated only particular benefits for particular companies, and that it is difficult to compare different case management programs because they contain so many different, situation-specific elements (Austin & O'Connor, 1989). How effective the case management model is, remains an empirical question; some results are encouraging, but it is probably wise to heed Dietzen and Bond's (1993) conclusion: "We are a long way from having the assessment technology to predict which service packages are best suited to which clients."

REFERENCES

Abbott, A. (1988). *The system of professions: An essay on the division of expert labor.* Chicago: University of Chicago Press.

Akabas, S., Gates, L. B., & Galvin, D. (1992). *Disability management.* New York: AMACOM.

Arnold, H. J., & Feldman, D. C. (1982). A multivariate analysis of the determinants of job turnover. *Journal of Applied Psychology, 67,* 350-360.

Ashbaugh, D. L., & Fay, C. H. (1987). The threshold for aging in the workplace. *Research on Aging, 9*(3), 417-427.

Austin, C., & O'Connor, M. (1989). Case management: Components and program contexts. In M. Petersen & D. White (Eds.), *Health care of the elderly* London: Sage Publications.

Australian Bureau of Statistics. (1987). *Retirement and retirement intentions, Australia (Government Report No. Catalogue No. 6238.0).* Canberra: ABS.

Australian Bureau of Statistics. (1988). *Job search experience of unemployed persons, Australia No. (Catalogue No. 6222.0).* Canberra, A.C.T.: ABS.

Australian Bureau of Statistics. (1993). *Labour force, Australia.* Canberra, A.C.T.: ABS.

Bauer, D. (1979). *Economic development and the older worker.* Washington, D.C.: The National Council on the Aging, Inc.

Beedon, L. (1993). Moving disability policy into the 21st century. *Topics in Geriatric Rehabilitation, 9*(2), 18-28.

Berkowitz, E. D. (1987). *Disabled policy: America's programs for the handicapped.* New York: Cambridge University Press.

Berkowitz, M. (1985). *Analysis of costs and benefits in rehabilitation.* (Contract No. 300-84-0259). New Brunswick, NJ: Rutgers, The State University of New Jersey, Bureau of Economic Research.

Berlman, P., Hunter, D., & McMahon, L. (1990). Keep it integrated. *Health Service Journal* (5 July), 996-997.

Binstock, R. H. (1990). The politics and economics of aging and diversity. In S. A. Bass, E. A. Kutza, F. M. Torres-Gil (Eds.), *Diversity in aging.* Glenview, IL: Scott, Foresman.

Blake, R. (1981). Disabled older persons: A demographic analysis. *Journal of Rehabilitation,* October/November/December, 19-27.

Bowe, F. (1993). Statistics, politics, and employment of people with disabilities. *Journal of Disability Policy Studies, 4*(2), 83-91.

Brown, E. (1992). Biological aspects of ageing. In Minichiello et. al. (Eds.), *An introduction to gerontology: A multidisciplinary perspective* (pp. 17-71). Sydney, Australia: Prentice-Hall.

Brown, S. C. (1993). Revitalizing "handicap" for disability research. *Journal of Disability Policy Studies, 4*(2), 57-76.

Budrys, G. (1993). Coping with change: Physicians in prepaid practice. *Sociology of Health and Illness, 15*(3), 353-374.

Burdekin, B. (1993). *Report of the national inquiry into the human rights of people with mental illness.* A.C.T., Canberra: Australian Government Publishing Service.

Bureau of Immigration Research. (1990). *Australia's population trends and prospects 1989.* Canberra, A.C.T.: Australian Government Publishing Service.

Burkhauser, R. V., & Hirvonen, P. (1989). United States disability policy in a time of economic crisis: A comparison with Sweden and the federal republic of Germany. *The Milbank Quarterly, 67*(Supplement 2, Part 1), 166-194.

Butler, R., & Lewis, M. (1982). *Aging and mental health.* St. Louis: C.V. Mosby.

Campbell, J. Kermit (1993). United States trends in disability management. In *Proceedings of the Australian Society of Rehabilitation Counsellors, 2nd National Conference* (November 30, 1993). Sydney, NSW: ASORC.

Casey, B., & Laczko, F. (1989). Early retired or long-term unemployed? The situation of non-working men aged 55-64 from 1979 to 1986. *Work, Employment and Society, 3*(4), 509-526.

Chirikos, T. N. (1989). Aggregate economic losses from disability in the United States: A preliminary essay. *The Milbank Quarterly, 67*(2), 59-91.

Chirikos, T. N., & Nestel, G. (1989). Occupation, impaired health, and the functional capacity of men to continue working. *Research on Aging, 11*(2), 174-205.

Committee on Employment Opportunities (CEO). (1993). *Restoring full employment.* ACT, Canberra: AGPS.

Correll, D. (1993). Aging and care for the aged: Misguided concepts lead to poor practices. *Ageing International, XX*(2), 60-63.

Council on the Ageing (COTA, Aust.) (1993). *Federal budget submission for 1993.* Melbourne: COTA (Aust).

Crewe, N. M., & Athelstan, G. T. (1981). Functional assessment in vocational rehabilitation: A systematic approach to diagnosis and goal setting. *Archives of Physical and Medical Rehabilitation, 62,* 299-305.

Curtis, J., Millman, E., Struening, E., et al. (1992). Effect of case management on rehospitalization and utilization of ambulatory care services. *Hospital and Community Psychiatry, 43,* 895-899.

Day, C. L. (1993). Public opinion toward costs and benefits of social security and medicare. *Research on Aging, 15*(3), 279-298.

David, H. (1993). Canada's labor market: Older workers need not apply. *Ageing International, XX*(3), 21-25.

Davies, D. R., Matthews, G., & Wong, C. S. K. (1991). Ageing and work. *International Review of Industrial and Organizational Psychology, 6,* 149-211.

DeJong, G., Batavia, A. I., & Griss, R. (1989). America's neglected health minority: Working-age persons with disabilities. *The Milbank Quarterly, 67*(Supplement 2, Pt. 2), 311-351.

Dew, M. A., Penkower, L., & Bromet, E. J. (1991). Effects of unemployment on mental health in the contemporary family. *Behavioral Modification, 15*(4), 501-544.

Dietzen, L. L., & Bond, G. R. (1993). Relationship between case manager contact and outcome for frequently hospitalized psychiatric clients. *Hospital and Community Psychiatry, 44*(9), 839-843.

Drury, E. (1993). Older workers in the European Community: Pervasive discrimination, little awareness. *Ageing International, XX*(3), 15-16.

Dunn, D. S. (1981). Vocational rehabilitation of the older disabled worker. *Journal of Rehabilitation, 47*(4), 76-81.

Eliot, T. S. (1963). The love song of J. Alfred Prufrock. In *Collected poems 1909-1962.* London: Faber and Faber Limited.

Foster, C. (1988). *Towards a national retirement incomes policy* (Social Security Review, Issues Paper No. 6). Canberra: Department of Social Security.

Frese, M., & Mohr, G. (1987). Prolonged unemployment and depression in older workers: A longitudinal study of intervening variables. *Social Science and Medicine, 25*(2), 173-178.

Glendenning, F. (Ed.). (1982). *Care in the community: Recent research and current projects.* Stoke: Beth Johnson Foundation.

Godlee, F. (1993). EC discriminates against older workers. *British Medical Journal, 307,* 757-758.

Greenwald, H., Dirks, S., Borgatta, E., McCorkle, R., Nevitt, M., & Yelin, E. (1989). Work disability among cancer patients. *Social Science and Medicine, 29,* 11.

Greenwald, N. F., & Groat, B. A. (1993). Advocacy roles and responsibilities for health care practitioners. *Topics in Geriatric Rehabilitation, 9*(2), 74-83.

Habib, J. (1990). Population aging and the economy. In R. H. Binstock & L. K. George (Eds.), *Handbook of aging and the social sciences* (pp. 328-345). San Diego: Academic Press, Inc.

Hahn, H. (1993). The political implications of disability definitions and data. *Journal of Disability Policy Studies, 4*(2), 41-52.

Halper, T. (1993). Rationing health care on the basis of age: Is this the future of American health care? *Ageing International, XX*(3-6).

Harris, R., Merrett, S., & Radford, A. (1986). *The effects of unemployment on physical and psychological health.* Adelaide, South Australia: Department of Primary Care and Community Medicine, Flinders University.

Harwood, E. (1988). Retirement of operation retirement. In *Australian Association of Gerontology.* Brisbane, Queensland: Australian Association of Gerontology.

Hearne, P. G. (1991). Employment strategies for people with disabilities: A prescription for change. *The Milbank Quarterly, 69*(Supplements 1/2), 111-128.

Heller, K. (1993). Prevention activities for older adults: Social structures and personal competencies that maintain useful social roles. *Journal of Counseling & Development, 72*(2), 124-130.

HMSO, & Secretaries of State for Health, S. S., Wales and Scotland (1989). *Caring for people: Community care in the next decade and beyond.* London: HMSO.

Hornstra, R. K., Bruce-Wolfe, V., Sagduyu, K., & Riffle, D. W. (1993). The effect of intensive case management on hospitalization of patients with schizophrenia. *Hospital and Community Psychiatry, 44*(9), 844-847.

Hudson, R. (1991). Thrown back into troubled waters. *Health Service Journal (30* May), 24-25.

Hudson, R. B. (1993). Social contingencies, the aged, and public policy. *The Milbank Quarterly, 71*(2), 253-278.

Hughes, D. (1993a). Caring for people efficiently. *Health Policy, 25*(1,2), 81-94.

Hughes, D. (1993b). General practitioners and the new contract: Promoting better health through financial incentives. *Health Policy, 25*(1,2), 39-50.

Hughes, J. (1986). *The vital few.* New York: Oxford University Press.

Hurley, R. E., & Bannick, R. R. (1993). Utilization managers in medical risk contract HMOs: From control to collaboration. *Quality Review Bulletin, 19*(4), 131-137.

Iglehart, J. (1992). Health policy report, the American health care system, managed care. *The New England Journal of Medicine, 327,* 742-747.

International Exchange of Experts and Information in Rehabilitation (IEEIR) (1994). *Developing awareness of disability in the world* (Monograph #54). New Hampshire: IEEIR.

Jolly, T., Creigh, S., & Mingay, A. (1980). *Age as a factor in employment.* (Research paper No. 11). London: Department of Employment.

Katz, D., & Kahn, R. L. (1978). *The social psychology of organizations.* New York: Wiley.

Kendig, H., & McCallum, J. (1986). *Greying Australia. Future impacts of population ageing.* A.C.T., Canberra: Australian Government Publishing Service.

Kingson, E. R. (1982). The health of very early retirees. *Social Security Bulletin, 45*(9), 3-9.

Kossoris, M. D. (1940). Relation of age to industrial injuries. *Monthly Labor Review,* October, 789-806.

Kuehn, M. D. (1991). An agenda for professional practice in the 1990s. *Journal of Applied Rehabilitation Counseling, 22*(3), 6-15.

Longman, P. (1987). *Born to pay: The new politics of aging in America.* Boston: Houghton Mifflin.

Love, D. O., & Torrence, W. D. (1989). The impact of worker age on unemployment and earnings after plant closings. *Journal of Gerontology, 44,* 190-195.

McCallum, J. (1989). *The dynamics of community involvement in old age: The syndrome of underuse* (No. 9). National Centre for Epidemiology and Population Health.

Mirkin, B. A. (1987). Early retirement as a labor force policy: An international overview. *Monthly Labor Review, 110*(3), 19-33.

Moss, S. (Ed.) (1992). *Aging and developmental disabilities: Perspectives from nine countries.* New Hampshire: International Exchange of Experts and Information in Rehabilitation (IEEIR).

Mulder, R. (1985). *Evaluation of the Harbinger Program.* Lansing, Michigan: Department of Mental Health.

Myers, J. E. (1985). Rehabilitation of older people. *Annual Review of Rehabilitation, 4,* 1-54.

Myers, J. E. (1987). Challenges for the older worker in the rehabilitation process. In L. G. Perlman & G. F. Austin (Eds.), *The Eleventh Mary E. Switzer Memorial Seminar* (pp. 31-37). Washington, DC: National Rehabilitation Association.

Nash, B. E. (1987). The state of the art: An overview of the world of work. In L. G. Perlman & G. F. Austin (Eds.), *The Eleventh Mary E. Switzer Memorial Seminar.* Washington, DC: National Rehabilitation Association.

Office on Ageing (1990). *Directions on ageing in New South Wales-employment.* Sydney: Office on Ageing, NSW.

Palmore, E. B. (1982). Attitudes toward the aged: What we know and need to know. *Research on Aging, 4*(3), 333-348.

Pfeiffer, D. (1993). The problem of disability definition. *Journal of Disability Policy Studies, 4*(2), 77-82.

Quadagno, J. S., & Hardy, M. (1991). Regulating retirement through the age discrimination in employment act. *Research on Ageing, 13*(4), 470-475.

Quinn, J. F., & Burkhauser, R. V. (1990). Work and retirement. In R. H. Binstock & L. K. George (Eds.), *Handbook of aging and the social sciences.* San Diego: Academic Press, Inc.

Rabinowitz, S., & Hall, D. T. (1977). Organizational research on job involvement. *Psychological Bulletin, 84,* 265-288.

Reisine, S., & Fifield, J. (1992). Expanding the definition of disability: Implications for planning, policy, and research. *The Milbank Quarterly, 70*(3), 491-508.

Remenyi, A. G. (1989). The training of rehabilitation professionals in Victoria, Australia. *Rehabilitation Education* (Special Issue), 3/4, 281-292.

Remenyi, A. G. (in press). *The rehabilitation counselling front in Australia.*

Reno, V. P., & Grad, S. (1985). Economic security, 1935-85. *Social Security Bulletin, 48*(12), 5-20.

Rhodes (1983). Age-related differences in work attitudes and behavior: A review and conceptual analysis. *Psychological Bulletin, 93,* 328-367.

Rife, R., & Kilty, K. (1989). Job search discouragement and the older worker: Implications for social work practice. *The Journal of Applied Social Science, 14*(1), 71-94.

Riley, J. W., & Riley, M. W. (1991). Social science and the ADEA. *Research on the Ageing, 13*(4), 458-462.

Robinson, P. K. (1986). Age, health and job performance. In J. E. Birren, P. K. Robinson, & J. E. Livingston (Eds.), *Age, health and employment.* New York: Prentice-Hall.

Robinson, B. (1993). When should age matter? *Ageing International, XX*(3), 1-2.

Rones, P. L. (1983). The labour market problems of older workers. *Monthly Labour Review,* May, 3-19.

Root, N. (1981). Injuries at work are fewer among older employees. *Monthly Labour Review, 104*(3), 30-34.

Rosen, B., & Jerdee, T. H. (1976). The nature of age-related job stereotypes. *Journal of Applied Psychology, 59,* 511-512.

Salthouse, T. (1988). Aging and skilled performance. In A. Colley & J. Beech (Eds.), *The acquisition and performance of cognitive skills.* Chichester: Wiley.

Schulz, J. H., Borowski, A., & Crown, W. H. (1991). *Economics of population aging.* New York: Auburn House.

Shafer, K., Choppa, A. J., & Siefker, J. M. (1993). Vocational rehabilitation of older displaced workers. *Journal of Rehabilitation,* July/August/September, 35-39.

Sheets, D. J., Wray, L. A., & Torres-Gil, F. M. (1993). Geriatric rehabilitation: Linking aging, health, and disability policy. *Topics in Geriatric Rehabilitation, 9*(2), 1-17.

Sheppard, H. L. (1986). Work and aging. In *Invitational conference on work, aging and vision.* Washington, DC:

Shrey, D. (1993). Workplace-based disability management: Challenges & opportunities for joint employer-rehabilitation professional initiatives. In *Australian Society of Rehabilitation Counsellors Second National Conference Proceedings.* Sydney, New South Wales: ASORC.

Shrey, D., & Hursh, N. (1994). Protecting the employability of the working elderly. In G. Felsenthal, S. J. Garrison, & F. U. Steinberg (Eds.). *Rehabilitation of the aging and elderly patient.* Baltimore: Williams & Wilkins.

Shrey, D., & Olsheski, J. (1992). Disability management and industry-based work return transition programs. *Physical Medicine & Rehabilitation: State of the art review, 6*(2), 303-314.

Skocpol, T. (1991). Targeting within universalism: Politically viable policies to combat poverty in the United States. In C. Jencks & P. E. Peterson (Eds.), *The urban underclass* (pp. 253-277). Washington, DC: Brookings Institute.

Smith, J. K., & Crisler, J. R. (1985). Variables associated with the vocational rehabilitation outcome of chronic low back pain individuals. *Journal of Applied Rehabilitation Counseling, 16*(4), 22-24.

Snyder, C. J., & Barrett, G. V. (1988). The Age Discrimination in Employment Act: A review of court decisions. *Experimental Aging Research, 14,* 3-47.

Stagner, R. (1985). Aging in industry. In J. E. Birren & K. W. Schaie (Eds.), *Handbook of the psychology of aging* New York: Van Nostrand Reinhold.

Stecker, M. L. (1951). Beneficiaries prefer to work. *Social Security Bulletin, 14*(1), 15-17.

Stein, L. I., & Test, M. A. (1980). Alternative to mental hospital treatment, 1: Conceptual model, treatment program, and clinical evaluation. *Archives of General Psychiatry, 37,* 392-397.

Sterns, H. L. (1987-88). Education and training of the older worker: Special issue: Late-life learning. *Generations, 12*(2), 22-25.

Stone, D. (1984). *The disabled state.* Philadelphia: Temple University Press.

Stretton, A., & Williams, L. (1985). *Labour force participation at higher ages: Policy implications from the BLMR research work* (Economic Paper No. 4(1)). BLMR.

Studnicka, M., Studnicka-Benke, A., Wogerbauer, G., & Rastetter, D. (1989). Psychological health, self-reported physical health and health service use. Risk differential observed after one year of unemployment. *Social Psychiatry and Psychiatric Epidemiology, 26*(2), 86-91.

Taylor, P., & Walker, A. (1993). Dealing with age discrimination in England: The merits of education vs. legislation. *Ageing International, September,* 36-40.

Thomas, S. A., Browning, C. J., & Greenwood, K. M. (in press). Rehabilitation of older injured workers.

Torrey, B. B., Kinsella, K., & Taeuber, C. M. (1987). *An aging world* (International Population Reports Series P-95 No. 78). Bureau of the Census U.S. Department of Commerce.

U.S. Bureau Of The Census. (1992). *Selected and social characteristics: 1990.* CPH-L-80, Table 1. Washington, D.C.: Author.

Ventrell-Monsees, C. (1993). How useful are legislative remedies: America's experience with the ADEA. *Ageing International, September,* 41-45.

Verbrugge, L. M., & Jette, A. M. (1994). The disablement process. *Social Science and Medicine, 38*(1), 1-14.

Walker, A. (1985). Early retirement: Release or refuge from the market. *Quarterly Journal of Social Affairs, 1,* 211-229.

Wasylenki, D. A., Goering, P. N., Lemire, D., Lindsey, S., & Lancee, W. (1993). The hostel outreach program: Assertive case management for homeless mentally ill persons. *Hospital and Community Psychiatry, 44*(9), 848-853.

Welford, A. T. (1985). Changes of performance with age: An overview. In N. Charness (Ed.), *Aging and human performance*. Chichester: Wiley.

Wilson, S. H., & Walker, G. M. (1993). Unemployment and health: A review. *Public Health, 107*(3), 153-162.

Winefield, A. H., Tiggemann, M., & Winefield, H. R. (1991). The psychological impact of unemployment and unsatisfactory employment in young men and women: longitudinal and cross-sectional data. *British Journal of Psychology, 82*(4), 473-486.

World Health Organization (W.H.O.) (1980). *International classification of impairments, disabilities, and handicaps*. Geneva: World Health Organization.

Yelin, E., Greenblatt, R., Hollander, H., & McMaster, J. (1991). The impact of HIV-related illness on employment. *American Journal of Public Health, 81*(1), 79-84.

Yelin, E., Henke, C., & Epstein, W. (1987). The work dynamics of the person with Rheuamtoid Arthritis. *Arthritis and Rheumatism, 30*, 5.

Yelin, E. H. (1991). The recent history and immediate future of employment among persons with disabilities. *The Milbank Quarterly, 69*(Supplements 1/2), 129-149.

Yuen, P., & Balarajan, R. (1989). Unemployment and patterns of consultation with the general practitioner. *British Medical Journal, 298*, 1212-1214.

Zedlewski, S., & McBride, T. (1992). The changing profile of the elderly: Effects on future long-term care needs and financing. *The Milbank Quarterly, 70*, 247-276.

Zola, I. K. (1989). Toward the necessary universalizing of the disability policy. *The Milbank Quarterly, 67*, Suppl. 2, Pt. 2, 401-429.

Zola, I. K. (1993). Disability statistics, what we count and what it tells us. *Journal of Disability Policy Studies, 4*(2), 9-39.

Glossary Of Terms

Access: An individual's ability to obtain medical services on a timely and financially acceptable basis.

Account: Stems from the term used in receivables management; in the sales field, denotes a customer or client that purchases (or potentially may purchase) specific services or products. An employer or union is called an "account" by the HMO. When an HMO sales representative finalizes a contract with an account, the expression "the HMO closed the account" is generally used. (see **Subscriber**).

Account number: A number which identifies an account used for accounts receivable or other processing. The account (or item) is used to identify a specific person or category for which data will be accumulated and reported.

Account receivable: An amount unpaid by a customer or patient arising from sales or services rendered; not necessarily due or past due. It is often said that a sale is not finalized until the customer pays the billing (i.e., account receivable).

Actuarial: Having to do with probabilities. Actuarial studies performed for HMOs normally consist of projections of utilization and costs of specific benefits for a defined population.

Actuary: A professional trained in the science of loss contingencies, investments, accounting, statistics, and subjects relating to insurance programs and systems.

Acute restrictions: Work restrictions which are imposed when the worker's condition is readily apparent, extent of work restrictions is fairly obvious, physical limitations are easily ascertained by the attending physician, and the duration of the work restriction is expected to be less than 14 days before the worker can return to normal duties with or without restrictions.

Administrative claims services: The administrative tasks and activities required among claims administrators, which may include: proper claims completion; payment of compensation and medical benefits; reserving; record keeping, auditing, reporting, management information; assessing and reporting loss information; performing a loss analysis, and trend information reporting; representation of administrative hearings and/or legal representation; coordination of independent medical examinations; conducting medical utilization reviews; identifying and pursuing second injury fund opportunities; accessing and monitoring rehabilitation services: and providing employer representation before the workers' compensation bureaucracy.

Administrative law judge: An administrative official charged with the responsibility of rendering a final decision on the cause, nature, and consequences of an alleged work-related injury. This decision typically includes a disability settlement.

Administrative loading: Or retention as in insurance. The amount added to the prospective actuarial cost of the health care services (pure premium) for expenses of administration, marketing, and profit.

Adverse Selection: Disproportionate enrollment of adverse risks, like an impaired or older population, with a potential for higher health care utilization than budgeted for an average population.

Alternative Delivery System (ADS): A method of providing health care benefits that departs from traditional indemnity methods. An HMO, for example, can be said to be an alternative delivery system.

Anniversary: The beginning of a subscriber group's benefit year. A subscriber group with a year coinciding with the calendar year would be said to have a January 1st anniversary.

Annual report: A report of operating results and financial state of an organization prepared and released once a year that includes a balance sheet, an income statement, a statement of changes in financial position, the auditor's opinion, charts, graphs, and comments from management about the year's performance.

Attrition rate: Disenrollment expressed as a percentage of total membership. An HMO with 50,000 members experiencing a 2% monthly attrition rate would need to gain 1,000 members per month in order to retain its 50,000-member level.

Auxiliary storage: A storage device in addition to the "core" or main storage of the computer. Auxiliary storage is used for the permanent storage of information and includes magnetic tape, cassette tape, cartridge tape, hard disks, and floppy disks. Auxiliary storage cannot be accessed as rapidly as main storage.

Glossary of Terms

Backup: Duplicate data files, redundant equipment, or procedures used in the event of failure of a component or storage media.

Bad debts: Uncollectible accounts receivable.

Balance sheet: A statement of financial position at a given time that shows the assets, liabilities, and net worth (equity) of the organization.

Basic health services: Benefits that all federally qualified HMOs must offer; defined under Subpart A, 110.102 of the Federal HMO Regulations.

Beneficiary: A person covered by a specific health care plan; usually refers to participants in the Medicare or Medicaid programs.

Benefit package: A collection of specific services or benefits that the HMO is obligated to provide under terms of its contracts with subscriber groups.

Benefit year: A 12-month period that a group uses to administer its employee fringe benefits program. A majority of subscribers use a January through December benefit year. A benefit year, however, may not match the fiscal year used by a group.

Break-even point: The HMO membership level at which total revenues and total costs are equal and that produces neither a net gain nor loss from operations.

Bubble memory: A new form of computer memory that uses magnetized "bubbles" to store information. A major advantage is that information stored in a bubble memory is retained when electrical power is turned off.

Budget: A financial plan used to estimate, guide, and control future operations.

Burnout: A condition that occurs after prolonged periods of stress and hassles with reduced capacity of personal control. Burnout, usually used in reference to work (e.g., job burnout), is characterized by feelings of helplessness, hopelessness, and thoughts of leaving work. Workers who are burned out have lowered productivity, are demoralized, and feel that work no longer has meaning.

Capitation: The per capita dollar value of providing a specific menu of health services to a defined population over a set period of time. FFS/PPD medical groups usually receive, in advance, a negotiated monthly payment from the HMO.

Case analysis: As an importation component of the Disability Management Analysis, the case analysis is a retrospective review of information within the records of individual injured/disabled workers. Information obtained from the case analysis is helpful in assessing the level of employer involvement and respective outcomes in response to work disruptions caused by illness or injury. Case analysis information is supplemented by gathering additional details from treating physicians, the worker's supervisor, and others. The purpose of the case analysis is to review the chronology of events which occurred from the worker's disability onset to the present. The goals of this process are: (1) to evaluate the effectiveness of the employer and/or other third-parties (e.g., insurance claims adjuster, private rehabilitation provider, medical and allied health providers) in resolving work disruptions due to illness or injury; (2) to distinguish between those impaired workers having little or no potential for work return, and those who may benefit from aggressive case management and work return planning activities; (3) to evaluate the quality of information available to the employer to facilitate effective disability management planning for individuals with disabilities; and (4) to assess the existence and quality of communications between external service providers and the employer, as relates to implementing effective strategies to resolve work disabilities.

Case coordinator: A member of the disability management team whose responsibility is to ensure that parties work together to plan, design, and carry out the disability management plan and to assure that information exchange between all parties is complete and relevant.

Cash indemnity benefits: Sums that are paid to insureds for covered services and that require submission of a filed claim. Insureds may assign such payments directly to providers of services (hospitals, physicians, etc.). Payments may or may not fully reimburse insureds for costs incurred.

Cathode Ray Tube (CRT): A screen similar to a television screen which is used for computer terminals. The terminal itself is often called a CRT.

Causality: Attribution of work activity as a primary cause for an aggravation of a bodily injury.

Central Processing Unit (CPU): The portion of a computer containing the arithmetic, logic, central, and in some cases, main storage units.

Chronic conditions: Those conditions in which the extent of the worker's functional capacities are not readily apparent, the worker may not be medically stable, and physical limitations are not functionally defined in relation to the worker's job demands (e.g., the worker's work restrictions are unknown or unclear). Such workers are not expected to return to work with or without restrictions in less than 14 days. Workers classified as having a chronic condition will require services which may include a functional capacity evaluation, job analysis, case management, and therapeutic monitoring by the on-site therapist.

Claims management: The gathering, recording, and reporting of claims information that is either factual, medical, or actuarial. "Factual" claims information includes the specific detailed information which defines the injury or occupational disease, provided by both the claimant and the employer. Included in this information are the details of the claim form and identification of the industry classification. "Medical" claims information includes the actual medical documents used to define and justify the diagnosis, the extent of disability and its relationship to the injury or disease, and the appropriateness of the payment of fees. "Actuarial" claims information includes the compensation paid, medical fees paid, reserves assigned or assessed by the state, explanations of applied rate-making formulas, trends, and projections.

Coefficient of Variation (CV): A statistical procedure to determine the variability of the set of scores or values, derived by dividing the standard deviation for the set of values by the average, expressed as a percentage.

Cognitive appraisal: Term that applies to an individual's perception of events, internal or external, for better or for worse. A cognitive appraisal mediates, or intervenes, between an event and reactions to the event (e.g., a worker reprimanded by his supervisor believes that he will be fired). Cognitive appraisals may be logical, erroneous, or distorted. Logical, or rational appraisals usually minimize negative outcomes. Cognitive errors and distortions often increase adverse emotional or behavioral outcomes (e.g., a worker reprimanded by his supervisor for a mistake feels that he is worthless as a person. This cognitive appraisal contains two primary cognitive errors or distortions; (1) *overgeneralization* from one incident, and (2) *catastrophizing* in that such a self-appraisal disproportionately devalues the worth of the worker).

Coinsurance: That portion of the cost of receiving covered care for which the insured is financially responsible; usually according to a fixed percentage, as in major medical coverage. Often coinsurance applies after a stated deductible has been met.

Commission: A form of incentive payment used by HMOs to remunerate sales representatives, usually in addition to applicable base salaries; computed and paid on a fixed sum per subscribers or enrollee or a percentage of premium basis.

Community rating: A method of determining an HMO premium structure that is not influenced by the expected level of benefit utilization by specific groups. Expected utilization of the community as a whole is considered.

Community rating by class: A modification of established community-rating principles, whereby individual groups can have different rates depending on the composition by age, sex, marital status, and industry. The changes were included in the 1981 amendments to the Federal HMO act affecting qualified plans.

Compiler: A program designed to accept a source program which is the programming language and convert it, instruction by instruction, into machine language understandable to the computer.

Compliance: The act of a federally qualified HMO's fulfilling and continuing to fulfill all requirements for federal qualification.

Complete method: A method of determining outstanding claim liabilities whereby the claims already paid are divided by a factor indicating the percentage of estimated claims paid to date.

Composite rate: A uniform premium applicable to all eligibles in a subscriber group regardless of number of claimed dependents. This rate is quite commonplace among labor unions and large employer groups and usually does not require any contribution by the union member or employee.

Compositing: A term used for combining a multiple-tiered rate structure into a tier structure with fewer tiers. For example, combining a rating system using two-person contracts and three-or more-person contracts, into a premium structure which includes all families of two or more.

Computer: A tool or machine for managing data/information.

Concurrent review: A method of monitoring/controlling utilization; the evaluation of medical need for a service at the time the patient is initially seen, diagnosed, or admitted.

Configuration: A term used by computer people in referring to the equipment that will be assembled to work as a unit for a business. It includes the options chosen, as well as peripheral devices.

Continuous Quality Improvement (CQI): A system of management that encourages attention to customer needs and employee participation and empowerment in organizational decision making. CQI and *Total Quality Management (TQM)* are often used interchangeably.

Contract: An HMO agreement executed by a subscriber group (see group contract). The term may be used in lieu of "subscriber" when referencing penetration within a given subscriber group. Also used to designate an enrollee's coverage (see single, double, and family contract). Also, designates the FFS/PPD medical group's contractual agreement with the HMO.

Contract Mix: The distribution of enrollees according to contacts classified by dependency categories, for example, the number or percentage of singles, doubles, or families. Contract mix is used to determine average contract size.

Contract type: Classification of employees into categories usually based on enrolled dependent status. Typical would be a single employee, an employee with one dependent, or an employee with two or more dependents.

Conversion factor: An arithmetic number which is multiplied by the HMO capitation rate to produce a rate for single employees.

Coordination of Benefits (COB): A typical insurance provision whereby responsibility for primary payment for medical services is allocated between carriers where a person is covered by more than one employer-sponsored health benefit program. This coordination avoids a person being reimbursed twice for the same medical services.

Copayment: A modest payment made by an HMO enrollee at the time that selected services are rendered. Some HMOs require a $2.00 copayment for each doctor's office call. Some impose a fixed dollar amount for inpatient hospitalization. Copayments are subject to limitation as defined in Subpart A, 110.105 of the Federal HMO Regulations.

Cumulative Trauma Disorder: A disorder, usually musculoskeletal in nature, which is precipitated by repeated or prolonged exposure to physical stressors. When these physical stressors exceed the body's ability to provide nutrient support to the affected tissues, an accumulation of minor injuries eventually cause pain which, left unaddressed, may lead to disability. CTD's are frequently aggravated by the psychological climate as well as the physical environment in which the individual lives and works.

Data: Basic elements of information–facts, numbers, letters, and symbols–that can be processed by a computer or a person.

Data base management: A storage and retrieval system that allows easy access to stored information and efficient compilation of special reports. In data base management, a complete item of data (that is, a CTP-4 procedure number and the description associated with that number) is stored in the data base only once and can be referred to by one or more short names or code numbers, rather than having to be described in full each time it is needed.

Data base system: Data stored on disks that are directly accessible through an on-line terminal and that can be changed through direct input from the terminal. A data base system can also be updated through batch processing of data entered into the system.

Data collection: The act of bringing data from one or more sources to a central point.

Data entry: The act of entering data into a system via a terminal or in some other manner which provides data elements used and processed by a system to provide information.

Data processing: A series of planned actions and operations using data elements in storage to achieve a desired result.

Data sets: Within a data base system, sets of related data are established to maintain data which will be used by programs, both on-line and for other processing. For

Deductibles: Amounts required to be paid by insureds as stipulated by contract. For example, all Medicare beneficiaries must satisfy the annual deductible for Part B. Medical Insurance, before entitlement to coverage of 80% of reasonable medical charges incurred thereafter. The amount paid out-of-pocket is considered a deductible while the remaining 20% of reasonable medical charges is deemed to be the beneficiary's coinsurance level.

Dependents: Those persons designated in writing by the HMO enrollee meeting the dependency tests as stipulated in the contract with the subscriber group. Dependency requirements may vary somewhat among contracting subscriber groups of an HMO.

Demographics: The statistical characteristics of a defined population (age, sex, income level, race, education, dwellings, employment status, etc.), that aid in assessing marketability within that population.

Glossary of Terms

Differential: The out-of-pocket (or payroll deduction) difference that an eligible who opts for HMO coverage may have to pay.

Disability: Any restriction or lack (resulting from an impairment) of ability to perform an activity in the manner or within the range considered normal for a human being.

Disability management: The proactive employer-centered process of coordinating the activities of labor, management, insurance carriers, health care providers, and vocational rehabilitation professionals for the purpose of minimizing the impact of injury, disability, or disease on a worker's capacity to successfully perform his or her job.

Disability management analysis: An auditing tool for examining the patterns of influence that contribute to work disruptions and unacceptable costs related to worker injuries and impairments. The analysis involves the collection of information from a variety of sources, in order to diagnose both positive forces and negative disability management influences.

Disability Management Intervention Team (DMIT): An interdisciplinary team that derives, coordinates, and resolves individualized disability management programs for workers based on collective information established from occupational handicap assessments. Team members include a worker, union representative, direct supervisor, case coordinator, physician(s) and other health care professionals.

Disability settlement: A cash award paid by an employer or his insurance representative to compensate an injured worker for a permanent disabling condition.

Distress: A biopsychosocial or behavioral condition, or response, that exists when environmental demands are perceived as exceeding one's coping resources and threatening personal well-being.

Double contract: Two-person coverage as designated on the HMO enrollment card by the enrollee; includes the enrollee and one dependent.

Dual choice: A health benefit offered by an employment group permitting eligibles of the group a voluntary choice of health plans; usually the employer's primary insurer plus an HMO.

Emergency: In the Federal Employees Health Benefits (FEHB) program, emergency is defined as: "The sudden and unexpected onset of a condition requiring medical or surgical care which the member secures immediately after the onset (or as soon, thereafter, as the care can be made available, but in any case, no later than 24 hours after the onset). Heart attacks, cardiovascular accidents, loss of consciousness or respiration, and convulsions are "medical emergencies." However, the Plan may determine that other similar acute conditions are "medical emergencies." The latter allows latitude for claims adjudication.

Employee Assistance Program (EAP): A program established to help workers overcome psychosocial or behavioral problems that undermine work performance.

Enrollment: The process of converting subscribers group eligibles into HMO members; or the aggregate count of HMO enrollees as of a given time.

Enrollment meeting: A meeting designed to allow the HMO representatives to present their prepaid healthcare plans to the eligibles of a subscriber group. The meeting can be mandatory as prescribed by the group, formal or informal, and conducted at worksites or off the premises. It provides an opportunity for eligibles to obtain answers to their specific questions.

Ergonomics: An interdisciplinary science concerned with the application of natural laws governing human work. It is the application of technology to assist the human element in manual work.

Ergonomic job evaluation: An evaluation of the work environment that identifies hazards, evaluates risks, and recommends possible modifications in predicting interactions arising between people, processes, and environments.

ERISA: Employee Retirement Income Security Act of 1974, Public Law 93-406. HMOs that contract with firms subject to ERISA compliance can be expected to provide certain annual information to these firms in order to meet federal reporting requirements.

Essential job tasks: Tasks absolutely necessary to produce the required job outcome.

Experience rating: A method of determining an HMO premium structure based on actual utilization of individual subscriber groups; not a permissible rating method under federal qualification requirements. Age, sex, and utilization experience are the principal determinants in rate setting using this method. Outside the HMO setting, experience rating is the most prevalent method used.

Glossary of Terms

Family contract: An enrollment arrangement by which the HMO member designates eligible dependents as enrollees. The term may have a different interpretation based on the prevailing rate structure for different subscriber groups.

FEHB: Federal Employees Health Benefits program, administered through the U.S. Office of Personnel Management.

Fee-for-service (FFS): Fees charged by a medical group for each procedure or treatment performed. Such fees may be based on prevailing competition in the immediate marketplace or know what the market will bear.

Feasibility analysis: Study to gather and analyze information and financial data or forecasts to assess criteria, to enumerate influences and deterrents, advantages and disadvantages of a task, project, program, or action. The feasibility study presents conclusions and strategies or recommendations accordingly.

Firmware: An electronic circuitry board which allows a computer to perform a certain type of processing. (see ROM).

Fixed cost (expense): An expenditure or expense that does not vary with volume of activity, such as level of membership fluctuation for an HMO.

Functional Capacity Assessment (FCA): A battery of tasks designed to measure an individual's objective and subjective functional ability and tolerance to do physical work.

Functional capacity evaluation: A one- to- two-day assessment by a physical therapist to specifically determine a disabled person's residual physical abilities.

Group contract: An agreement entered into between the HMO and a subscribing group containing rates, performance covenants, relationships among parties, schedule of benefits, and other conditions. The term is generally limited to a 12-month period and may be renewed after that.

Handicap: A disadvantage for an individual resulting from an impairment or a disability that limits or prevents the fulfillment of a role that is normal for that individual.

Hardware: The electronic, magnetic, and electromechanical equipment or devices which comprise a computer and associated data processing equipment.

Hassles: The irritating, frustrating, distressing demands of life events that are experienced in everyday life and living.

HCFA: Health Care Financing Administration, part of the U.S. Department of Health and Human Services. In addition to its many other functions, HCFA is the contracting agency for HMOs who seek direct contractor/provider status for provision of the Medicare benefit package.

Health Maintenance Organization (HMO): An organization of healthcare personnel and facilities that provides a comprehensive range of health services to an enrolled population for a fixed sum of money paid in advance. These health services include a wide variety of medical treatments and counsel, inpatient and outpatient hospitalization, home health service, ambulance service, and sometimes dental and pharmacy services. HMOs are organized into four types: group practice model, individual proactice association (IPA) model, staff model, and network model.

Health services analyst (HSA): A position in the FFS/PPD medical group and/or at the HMO level. The HSA is concerned with such functions as demographic/epidemiological research, planning, coordinating, monitoring, and budgeting.

HMO Regulatory Agency: A state agency empowered to grant or rescind an HOM's authority to transact business, to license its solicitors, and to regulate its affairs in the best interest of the consuming public. In nearly all states, these powers are vested in insurance departments. In California, the regulator agency is the state's corporations commission.

Impairment: Any loss or abnormality of psychological, physiological, or anatomical structure or function.

Impairment rating: Numerical assessment of anatomic or physiologic dysfunction generally performed by a physician in association with settlement of permanent partial or total disability cases.

Impartial Medical Evaluation (I.M.E.): A formal assessment by an expert practitioner asked to determine a person's work capacity, residual impairment, or rehabilitation needs.

Incentives: As related to medical care delivery, this term refers to economic incentives for providers to motivate efficiency in patient care management.

Glossary of Terms

Indemnity carrier: Usually an insurance company or benevolent association that offers select coverages within a framework of fee schedules, limitations, and exclusions as negotiated with subscriber groups. Insureds are reimbursed after carriers review and process filed claims. Aetna, Connecticut General, and Prudential are examples of indemnity carriers.

Indemnity insurance: Indemnity insurance typically means coverage offered by insurance companies and Blue Cross plans, whereby individual persons insured are indemnified through reimbursement by the carriers for their medical expenses. Payments may be made through reimbursement by the carriers for their medical expenses. Payments may be made to the individual incurring the expense, or in many cases, directly to providers. The important point is that the indemnity relates only to a specific loss incurred by the insured person after the fact.

Independent medical examination: A second opinion by a qualified physician to determine the extent of permanent impairment resulting from an injury and to secure recommendations regarding physical restrictions, future treatment, medication., etc.

Individualized Disability Management Program: A written plan defining the terms, conditions, rights and remedies under which services will be provided in attempting to return an individual to work. The program is derived by the disability management intervention team through a critical and comprehensive review of information gained by the occupational handicap assessment.

Injured worker rehabilitation: The concerted attempt to lessen the impact of the injury/disease on the ability to work and to reduce the resulting length of disability. This traditional approach is characterized as "reactive," since it usually assumes post-injury involvement in an established and lengthy disability claim. Traditional rehabilitation services and skills are brought to bear on a structured plan of substantial duration (e.g., several months or longer). Such plans are usually carried out off the worksite, and often within rehabilitation facilities.

Injury management: A broad term meant to include the processes of injury prevention, injury control, injury-related cost containment, and integration of persons with disabilities in the workplace through ergonomics.

Intensity factor: A multiplier or weighting element used in computations to allow for the quantitative influence of a specific variable.

Interactive system: As compared with a batch system, an interactive system gives the user immediate results and allows for an interchange of information between user and machine. For a manager, this is a particularly useful aid to decision making, because one can gain a desired piece of information (for example, the impact of a 10% increase in fees), enter a new command based on that information, and gain the next piece of information, all in a few seconds.

Interdisciplinary approach: The utilization of a variety of resources across a multitude of information domains.

Isoinertial: Muscle contraction against the constant force of gravity.

Isokinetic: A muscle contraction resulting in joint movement at a constant velocity.

Isometric: A muscle contraction without any joint movement.

Job Analysis: A process that generally involves a formal analysis of tasks associated with a specific job or group of jobs, which identifies specifically what the worker does. A job analysis often includes: the purpose of performing each job task; the tools, equipment, and processes used in the performance of the job; physical demands required of the worker performing essential job functions; knowledge, skill, and experience level required to safely and accurately perform the job; and other measurable and descriptive information. The job analysis report serves as an accurate written job description to be made available to treating physicians when determining work return dates. Also, the analysis may be used when developing on-site transitional work and modified duty options for disabled workers, as well as for ADA compliance or other disability management purposes.

Job description: A document that outlines in broad terms the purpose, scope, duties, and responsibilities of a position. Also known as a position guide.

Lag factor: Lag factor is a general term indicating a percentage of claims incurred in a given accounting period but received, processed, and paid by specific months following the close of the accounting period.

Language: Language or computer language refers to a group of symbols, numbers, letters, works, or a combination of these that can be used to communicate with the computer and cause it to perform desired operations for processing data. Most application systems are written in higher level languages, for instance COBOL, BASIC, FORTRAN, etc., and then translated by the computer's compiler into machine language.

Glossary of Terms

Loss ratio: The ratio between costs incurrece for health care services and premiums.

Mainframe: Computers which are referred to as "mainframe" are the largest and most powerful machines manufactured. These computers can handle the largest files, largest number of records, and can process at high speeds with more multiple users than minicomputers.

Marginal cost: Change in the total cost of producing services that results from unit of change in the quantity of services being produced. Marginal cost in health economics is the appropriate cost concept to consider when contemplating expansion or contraction of services and personnel.

Market area: The targeted geographic area or areas in which the principal market potential is deemed to be; it may be the same as an HMO's defined service area, but not necessarily. Frequently, market areas overlap service areas. (see Service Area.)

Market share: That part of the market potential that an HMO or a FFS/PPD medical group has captured; usually market share is expressed as a percentage of the market potential.

Marketing: Process of understanding the needs and wants of a target market. Its purpose is to provide a viewpoint from which to integrate the analysis, planning, implementation, and control of the health care delivery system.

Maximum medical improvement: The point during recovery, designated by a physician, where maximum recovery has occurred.

Maximum medical rehabilitation: A level of rehabilitation when there is unlikely to be any further significant improvement in the worker's medical condition.

Medical disability evaluation: A comprehensive clinical assessment utilized to evaluate the presence of a medical condition, establish a diagnosis and medical treatment plan, evaluate residual work abilities, restrictions and precautions, and to establish the extent and anticipated consequences of the impairment to determine disability.

Medical group practice: "Provision of healthcare services by a group of at least three licensed physicians engaged in a formally organized and legally recognized entity; sharing equipment, facilities, common records, and personnel involved in both patient care and business management" is the definition of medical group practice approved by the American Group Practice Association, the American Medical Association, and the Medical Group Management Association.

Member: Anyone enrolled in an HMO and entitled to receive benefits; used synonymously with the term "enrollee."

Member month: A unit of volume measurement. A member month is equal to one member enrolled in an HMO for one month, whether or not the member actually receives any services during the period. Two member months are equal to one member enrolled for two months or two members enrolled for one month. Many internal operating statistics for HMOs are expressed in terms of member months.

Mental-mental disability: A mental disability resulting from a stressful work environment, such as anxiety after witnessing another worker's death.

Mental-physical disability: A physical disability, such as a heart attack, resulting from a stressful work environment.

Microcomputer: A very small computer that can sit on a desk and is usually devoted to one user. The computer system is built using an integrated-circuit (IC) microprocessor. Can also refer to the microprocessor circuit alone.

Minicomputer: Originally a computer significantly smaller in size, capacity, and software capability than its larger mainframe counterparts. Technological advances have blurred these distinctions.

MIS: Management information system; either an automated or manual system that produces timely reports on various aspects of the HMO and the medical group in order to facilitate effective decision making.

Modem: A device that modulates and demodulates signals transmitted over communication facilities, creating types of data that can be handled better over phone lines and then retranslated to the form of data needed for computer processing.

Network model: An organizational form in which the HMO contracts for medical services within a "network" of medical groups. Health Net, a Blue Cross-sponsored HMO serving southern California, is an example of a network model. For federal qualification purposes, such models are designated as IPAs.

Nonphysical Factors Assessment: The assessment of nonphysical worker characteristics and factors such as job satisfaction, worker attitude toward employer, compromised psychosocial functioning, manifestations of the aging process, worker personality factors, substance abuse, and factors associated with secondary gains, to determine their impact on the worker's success in a transitional work program and to facilitate planning of the work-return process.

Occupational ability: Ability to perform (to standards), all essential tasks of a job without safety or health hazards to self or others.

Occupational bonding: The concept of maintaining a mutually positive relationship between the worker and the work environment. Workers who derive intrinsic satisfaction from relationships with supervisors, co-workers, work processes, and organizational environments tend to value their roles as workers. Employers that promote positive labor relations that support workers' safety, health, and employability tend to strengthen the worker-employer bond. Occupational bonding is an important concept in on-site transitional work programs for injured workers, since workplace-based programs reduce unnecessary lost time, thus enabling the worker-employer bond to be maintained. Conversely, community-based therapeutic programs for injured workers often extend lost time from work, resulting in a gradual weakening of the employer-worker bond. Occupational bonding maintains the injured worker's self-concept as a worker, rather than as a patient, when the worker is enabled to maintain work productivity and psychosocial relationships with supervisors and co-workers.

Occupational fitness: Degree by which an individual's work capacity matches the demands of a job.

Occupational handicap: Ability to perform work within a given work environment.

Occupational handicap assessment: A set of evaluations to assess an individual's ability to perform within a given work environment. The evaluations consist of a medical disability evaluation, an ergonomic job analysis, a work capacity evaluation, and a vocational evaluation.

Occupational Health Nurse – Certified (COHN): One who is recognized for professional experience and expertise by the American Board of Occupational Health Nurses. Certification requires a minimum of five years experience in occupational health nursing, successful completion of a comprehensive examination, and maintenance of proficiency through continuing education.

Occupational stress: A detrimental physical, emotional, cognitive, or behavioral consequence occurring when environmental demands exceed coping resources in the workplace. Also refer to *stress* and *distress*.

Off-line: Pertains to equipment or devices not in direct communication with the central processing unit of a computer. The term is also used to refer to a listing of a file which is done on the printer rather than on the terminal from which the listing is requested.

On-line: Pertaining to equipment or devices directly connected to the central processing unit (CPU).

Operating system: The collection of programs for operating the computer, acting as an intermediary between the software and the computer. Different operating systems will prevent software from being run on different computers.

OHMO: Office of Health Maintenance Organizations, with headquarters in Rockville, MD; a component of the U.S. Department of Health and Human Services, charged with responsibility for directing the federal HMO program.

Open enrollment period: The period of time stipulated in a group contract in which eligibles of the group can choose a health plan alternative for the coming benefit year; in the FEHB setting, this period is called "open season." There is also an open enrollment period as defined in the Federal HMO Regulations requiring HMOs who meet certain criteria to conduct annual open enrollments for periods of not less than 30 days; refer to 110.107 of the Federal HMO Regulations. This federally required "open enrollment" of individuals should not be confused with enrollment of individuals many HMOs pursue as a normal part of their marketing strategies.

OPM: Office of Personnel Management, with headquarters in Washington, DC. This agency administers and directs the Federal Employees Health Benefits programs. It is the contracting source for HMOs wishing to become FEHB carriers.

Out-of-area benefits: The scope of emergency benefits (and related limitations) available to HMO members while temporarily outside their defined services areas. Some HMOs offer unlimited out-of-area emergency coverage. Others impose a stated maximum annual dollar benefit. Emergency coverage is usually the only HMO benefit in the total benefit package for which members may need to file claim forms for reimbursement of their out-of-pocket expenditures for care.

Paradigm: The models upon which a discipline bases its perceptions of itself and its relationship to the world around it.

Peer review: Evaluation of a physician's performance by other physicians, usually within the same geographic area and medical specialty.

Glossary of Terms

Penetration: The percentage of business that an HMO is able to capture in a particular subscriber group or in the market area as a whole. For example, signing up 10 enrollees or members out of 100 eligibles yields a 10% penetration.

Peripheral device: Any device connected to the computer but not part of the computer itself, for example, disk drives and printers.

Physical-mental disability: A mental disability resulting from a physical event such as a fall or motor vehicle accident.

Physician extender: A specially trained and licensed (when necessary) individual who performs tasks, which might otherwise be performed by physicians themselves, under the direction of a supervising physician.

Premium: Used interchangeably with the term "rate;" an expression of the price charged for each class of coverage within a given rate structure. In a broader sense, premium is often the used to express the dollar volume contributed by a subscriber group, for example, "That group generated $50,000 in premium last year."

Primary appraisal: The initial judgment that a stimulus or situation is either irrelevant, benign (or positive), challenging, or threatening.

Primary occupational stress prevention: Events designed to identify and target the sources of stress and develop strategies to reduce and manage risks and improve the situation. Examples of primary stress prevention include improved job design to prevent worker injuries, worker control over work load, and increased worker empowerment for work-related decisions.

Prior authorization: A method of monitoring/controlling utilization; the evaluation of need and the approval for medical service prior to its being performed, particularly using outside resources.

Progressive rates: A method employed by some HMOs in which they implement new rates either monthly, quarterly, or semiannually. Any new or renewal subscriber groups with anniversaries falling within such periods would automatically be subject to prevailing rates in effect during those periods, and these rates are generally guaranteed for the full 12-month benefit year. This method is said to offer greater rate parity than a fixed rate throughout the HMO's fiscal year; consequently, it has the effect of containing rate changes on a group-to-group basis each benefit year.

Proprietary: Operated for the purpose of gaining a profit.

Providers: Those institutions and individuals who are licensed to provide healthcare services (for example, hospitals, skilled nursing facilities, physicians, pharmacists, etc.). Providers in a defined service area are principally owned by, affiliated with, employed by, or under contract to an HMO.

Qualified: Meeting HMO program standards defined by the federal HMO law.

Quality assurance: Activities and programs intended to assure the quality of care in a defined medical setting. Such programs must include peer or utilization review components to identify and remedy deficiencies in quality. The program must also have a mechanism for assessing its effectiveness.

RAM: Random-Access Memory. The semiconductor chips within the computer that serve as a "scratch pad." The CPU enters and retrieves information from RAM almost instantaneously, but unlike data in external storage or in the new bubble memories, the contents of RAM are lost when electrical power to the computer is turned off.

Rate: See **Premium**.

Rate structure: A classification of dependency options and related premiums applicable to a given subscriber group. Most groups employ one of the following rate structures in their health benefit programs: 1) a composite or one-tier rate, 2) a two-tier rate, 3) a three-tier rate, or 4) a four-tier rate.

Reappraisal: The changed appraisal of an event or situation based on new information from the environment and/or the individual's perception of coping resources.

Record: A group of related facts or fields of information treated as a unit. For example, one account is a record in a file containing many patient accounts.

Regulations: Usually refers to the Federal HMO Regulations as promulgated by the Secretary, U.S. Department of Health and Human Services. These regulations attempt to incorporate the spirit of congressional legislation into practical, working rules of conduct.

Reinsurance: A type of protection purchased by HMOs from insurance companies specializing in underwriting specific risks for a stipulated premium. This becomes a cost of doing business for HMOs. Typical reinsurance risk coverages are: 1) individual stop-loss, 2) aggregate stop-loss, 3) out-of-area, and 4) insolvency protection. As HMOs grow in membership, they usually reduce their reinsurance coverage (and related direct costs), being in a financial position to assume such risks themselves).

Repetitive strain injuries: see Cumulative Trauma Disorders.

Reserves: Restricted cash investments or highly liquid investments intended to protect the HMO membership against insolvency or bankruptcy. Regulatory agencies may mandate reserve requirements; also, some HMOs establish voluntary reserves by systematically setting aside a small portion of each month's realized revenues.

Responsibility costing: An accounting method that identifies costs with persons, departments, or "centers" that have responsibility for the costs (as contrasted to identifying costs with services or functions).

Retrospective review: A method of monitoring/controlling utilization; the evaluation of medical need for a service after the service has been performed.

Risk: The chance or possibility of loss. For example, physicians may be held at risk if hospitalization rates exceed agreed-upon thresholds. The sharing of risk is often employed as a utilization control mechanism within the HMO setting. Risk is also defined in insurance terms as the probability of loss associated with a given population.

Risk retention: A description of the limitations of financial liability remaining with a major entity to the HMO program. For example, the HMO may accept all risk to guarantee provision of services to its enrolled population. This risk may be limited by arrangements with reinsurers. Also, the fee-for-service/prepaid medical group may take full risk, or limit its risk by contractual arrangements with the HMO corporation.

ROM: Read-Only Memory. If RAM is like a scratch pad, then ROM is like a printed book whose pages cannot be erased. System software is often stored in ROM. ROM-based software is called firmware.

Saturation: A condition that occurs when an HMO achieves its maximum penetration either in a subscriber group or in the marketplace itself. When this condition becomes evident, an HMO's first goal is to retain its saturation level while assessing how to make further inroads for an increase in market share or how to expand its service or market area.

Secondary appraisal: The determination of what coping resource are available.

Secondary occupational stress prevention: The implementation of worksite stress management interventions that aim to prevent or reduce the duration, intensity, and impairment of existing stress-related problems at work.

Self-insured: An employer who elects to provide workers' compensation benefits directly to injured employees rather than through an insurance company.

Semivariable costs: Costs that do not increase in a consistent linear progression with activity. For example, commissions of 2% of revenues are variable, but commissions of 2% of revenues up to a ceiling of $2,500 are semivariable.

Service area: The territory within certain boundaries that an HMO designates for providing services to members. Since easy access into the health delivery system is a primary HMO tenet, it is generally believed that a member should not have to drive longer than 30 minutes in order to gain access to the system. Some HMOs establish a mileage radius from their medical delivery sites; some rely on zip codes; others use county boundaries in defining services areas.

Shared risk: In the context of an HMO, an arrangement in which financial liabilities are apportioned between two or more entities. For example, the HMO and the medical group may each agree to share the risk of excessive hospital cost over budgeted amounts on a 50-50 basis.

Single contract: Coverage for one person as designated on the enrollment or enrollment change card by the enrollee.

Small subscriber group aggregate: A combination of small businesses, professional associations, or other entities formed for the purpose of being considered a single, large subscriber group.

Software: All programs and routines necessary to direct the hardware of a computer system and used to extend the capabilities of computers, such as assemblers, compilers, subroutines, and application systems, such as accounts receivable, etc.

Solvency: A financial condition in which an HMO, a medical group, or another organization is able to pay or retire its debts when due.

Standardization: The uniformity of the assessment procedure. All procedures, including instruction, demonstrations, subject placement, and data collection, are the same each time the assessment is administered.

Stop-loss: An arrangement between an HMO (including the FFS/PPD medical group) and a reinsurer whereby absorption of prepaid patient expenses are limited, either in terms of overall expenditures and deficit, or by limiting losses on an individual expensive hospital and/or professional services claim.

Stress: A term used as either a *stimulus* or a *response*. As a stimulus, stress is best regarded as a stressor, meaning a threatening event, perceived by an individual, that challenges or demands a response (e.g., a supervisor berates an employee for making a mistake). As a response, stress refers to distress, or adverse effects following exposure to a stressor (e.g., an employee whose supervisor berates him for a mistake becomes tense and irritable). Distress may be regarded as the physical, behavioral, emotional, cognitive, or interpersonal consequence of a situation that challenges or threatens personal well-being. Stress is mediated by individual differences and perceptions of events and conditions.

Stress management training: The application of behavioral and psychological strategies to reduce stress and improve coping skills.

Stressor: Any condition, event, or stimulus that challenges, or threatens an individual.

Student dependency: An allowance extending the age limit for dependent children beyond that initially established by a subscriber group or an HMO. For example, full-time postsecondary student dependents may be carried by a subscriber to age 23, while the normal age limit for dependent children may be 18.

Subrogation: Seeking, by legal or administrative means, reimbursement from others responsible for certain categories of medical expenses such as workers' compensation, third-party negligence liability, or no-fault auto medical coverage.

Subscriber: An employer, union, or association that contracts with an HMO for its prepaid health care plan, which is offered to eligible enrollees.

Supplemental health services: The benefits of HMO offers that exceed their basic health service requirements, as defined in Subpart A, 110.101(c) and 110.102 of the Federal HMO Regulations.

System: A set or group of entities, operations, or procedures combined to achieve a given purpose. The work "system" has several uses in data processing.
- **Application system:** A set of programs that performs a specific task, such as the processing of an accounts receivable system.

- System failure: The malfunction of one or more components involved in a computer system and its operation, brining processing to a halt.
- System hardware: A configuration of machinery that constitutes the computer and related equipment.
- System manager: An individual who deals with computer system problems, diagnosing them and taking action to resolve them.
- System software: The programs that run the computer.

Table: A collection of data in a form usable by the computer as a reference or source of data used in processing, for instance, a physician table used to verify that a physician and other information that could be used in processing rather than requiring the information be input with every transaction. A table may also be a data set in a data base system.

Temporary total disability benefits: A statutorily mandated weekly payment to an injured worker designed to replace lost wages during the recovery period following a work-related injury.

Tertiary occupational stress prevention: Providing direct treatment strategics (e.g., stress management, employee assistance programs) to help physically, emotionally, behaviorally, or cognitively impaired workers to improve their health and return to productive work.

Time sharing: It is possible to buy an application package and rent time from a company to process data for a system. In some cases, the user must furnish its own operator. Some companies may furnish the operator as part of time-sharing charges.

Title XVIII: Commonly refers to the Medicare program.

Title XIX: Commonly refers to the Medicaid program.

Total quality management (TQM): A system of management that encourages attention to customer needs and employee participation and empowerment in organizational decision making. TQM and *Continuous Quality Improvement (CQI)* are often used interchangeably.

Transaction: A set of data elements which, as a unit, describe a specific action or procedure, for example, one lab test, an office visit, a payment, sending a recall notice, etc.

Transferable skills: Skills assessed by a vocational rehabilitation evaluation that may be utilized in various work environments or jobs.

Transitional work: Any job or combination of tasks and functions that may be performed safely and with renumberation by a worker whose physical capacity to perform functional job demands has been compromised.

Transitional work program: An individualized program facilitating an injured worker's gradual transition from disability, to modified work, to the eventual vocational objective.

Triage: Commonly used to describe the sorting out and screening of patients seeking care to determine needed services and establish priority. A classification of patients in accordance with the nature or degree of injury or illness. In battle or disasters, victims are classified according to a priority system to maximize the number of survivors.

Turnkey system: When a computer is purchased along with application software, the company that sells the system will contract to install the computer and the application system and to have all parts of the system and related devices running before it is turned over to the purchaser. This approach is called a turnkey system. The purchaser does not have to begin paying for the system until the seller's commitments have been made unless the contract specifies otherwise.

User groups: Those who have purchased a given brand of computer have organized into groups to interface with the manufacturers to solve problems and improve the hardware or related software. They also exchange information and may sell or exchange application software.

Utilization: The frequency with which a benefit is used, for example, 3,200 physician's office visits per 1,000 HMO members per year. Utilization experience multiplied by the average cost per unit of service delivered equals capitated costs.

Utilization review: A process that measures use and/or consumption of available resources (including professional staff, facilities, and services) to determine medical necessity, cost effectiveness, and conformity to criteria for optional use.

Variable costs: Costs that increase or decrease in direct proportion to volume (for example, reinsurance premiums calculated on a per member month basis). Thus, as membership rises, so does the cost (in direct proportion).

Venture capital: Private capital offered in return for a large share of ownership in a new business venture, where the chance of failure may be high, but success will produce extreme financial gain.

Vocational expert: One who is very skilled, highly trained and knowledgeable in the field of trades, professions, and occupations, with intent to be involved in assessment and/or testimony (in any form) in litigious forum.

Vocational rehabilitation evaluation: An evaluation to identify an individual's vocational aptitudes, interests, skills, abilities, values and psychosocial barriers impeding return to work.

Wash of premium: A practice designed for administrative ease in subscriber groups where HMO enrollment or disenrollment occurs at various times throughout a given month. Based on negotiation with such a group, there may be agreement to waive the partial month premium going in while charging a full month premium on the backside. This arrangement is conceded to "wash" any differences over time, but in reality, this result might never happen, depending on the dynamics of the work force in question.

Work ability box: An evaluative and organizational concept used to assess occupational handicap. It is used to develop and facilitate individualized disability management programs by integrating environmental work factors with information obtained from the medical disability evaluation, work capacity evaluation, ergonomic job analysis and vocational evaluation.

Work capacity evaluation: An evaluation measuring an individual's capacity to dependably perform the work demands specific to the job.

Worksite analysis: The gathering and analysis of comprehensive information from the worker, the employer, and the worksite, in order to identify the employer's functions, work schedules, work pace, work postures/methods, physical demands, required vocational training/certification, utilization of equipment/vehicles/tools, environmental conditions, vision, and hearing demands, psychological demands, physiological demands, essential job functions, reasonable accommodations, marginal job functions, and critical job demands.

INDEX

A

Access, defined, 603
Account, defined, 603
Account number, defined, 603
Accounts receivable, defined, 603
Acquired immunodeficiency syndrome, 316-318
Actuarial, defined, 603
Actuary, defined, 603
Acute restrictions, defined, 603
ADA. *See* Americans with Disabilities Act
Adjustments, to transitional work program, after testing of, 96-102
Administration
    health insurance benefit, Americans with Disabilities Act, 482-487
    managed care, 528, 532-534
    skills, in industrial rehabilitation, 334
Administrative claims service, 452
    defined, 603-604
Administrative law judge, defined, 604
Administrative loading, defined, 604
Advancement opportunities, inadequate, as psychosocial stressor, 384
Adverse selection, defined, 604
Age discrimination, 572-583
Aging worker
    age discrimination, 572-583
    Americans with Disabilities Act, 511-515
    assessment, 508
    attitudinal barriers, 504-506
    case management, 512, 592-596
    costs of disability, 502
    demographics, 500-501
    with disability, attitude of, 505-506
    disability management, 11, 506-511
    disability resolution process, 513-514
    discrimination against, 572-583, 576-579

combatting, 579-583
economic characteristics, 502-503
employer attitude, 504-505
employment characteristics, 502-503
health care professional attitude, 505
international view, 555-602
intervention, 508
males, 564-572
mediation with, 588-592
medical management, 512-513
performance level of, 575-576
rehabilitation, 583-588
  development of plan, 514
statistical analysis, 500-501, 557
stereotypes, 574-575
technology and, 503
transferable skill analysis, 508-509
trends, 318-319
vocational evaluation, 510-511
vocational rehabilitation practice, 503-504
work return transition program, 514-515
worksite risk, 509

AIDS. *See* Acquired immunodeficiency syndrome
Alternative delivery system, defined, 604
Americans with Disabilities Act, 112
  aging worker, 511-515
  claim, and workers' compensation claim, filing both, 495
  compliance with, 11-13
    as advantage of transitional work program, 119
  cost-containment, 485
  "direct threat," screening for, 492
  ergonomics and, 168-169
  health insurance benefit, administration of, 482-487
  management issues, 487-495
  medical determination regarding reemployment, 491-492
  and National Labor Relations Act, 492-495
  overview, 479-481
  reform measures, 486-487
  standing of injured workers, as Americans with disabilities, 489-490
  Title I complaint statistics, 487-488
  Title V provisions, 483-484
  workers' compensation prior history, inquiry restriction, 490-491
Analysis, disability management, 56-67
  community influence, 64-67
  cost analysis, 62-63

Index

    interviews, 56-58
    patterns of disability, 60-61
    policy, 63-64
    procedures, 63-64
Anniversary, defined, 604
Annual report, defined, 604
Assessment
    aging worker, 508
    functional capacity. *See also* Functional capacity assessment
        as component of physical therapy program, 114-115
    of handicap, 209-210
    nonphysical factors, as component of physical therapy program, 116
Assistive technology, 363
Associations, experiences of, in Canada, 467-469
Attitude Survey, National Workers' Compensation, 10
Attitudinal barriers, aging worker, 504-506
Attorney, disability management strategy, 444
Attrition rate, defined, 604
Auxiliary storage, defined, 604
Availability, of jobs, importance of in occupational health nursing, 151

B

Back injury, ergonomics, 161
Backup, defined, 605
Bad debt, defined, 605
Balance sheet, defined, 605
Bank of job tasks, development of, 98
Basic health service, defined, 605
Beneficiary, defined, 605
Benefit package, defined, 605
Benefit payment, 458-459
Benefit year, defined, 605
Break-even point, defined, 605
Bubble memory, defined, 605
Budget, defined, 605
Burnout, defined, 605
Business trends, in industrial rehabilitation, 308-309

C

Canada
    associations, experiences of, 467-469
    case management, 474-475

disability management, 465-478
    joint labor-management initiatives, 472-473
    legislation, 13, 472
    National Institute of Disability Management and Research, 475-476
    workers' compensation boards, role of, 469-471
    workers' groups, experiences of, 467-469
Capacity, for work, evaluation of, 213
Capitation, defined, 605
Cardiac disabilities, 314-318
    rehabilitation, job-simulated, 315
Cardiovascular endurance, in functional capacity assessment, 286
Case analysis, 58-59
    defined, 606
Case coordinator, defined, 606
Case history, of physical therapist, 122-127
Case management
    aging worker, 512, 592-596
    managed care, 543, 545-546
    procedures, in industrial rehabilitation, 330-333
    resource
        assessment, 73-78
        rehabilitation plan development, 74-77
    services, as a key principle of disability management, 28
Cash indemnity benefits, defined, 606
Cathode ray tube, defined, 606
Causality
    defined, 606
    and workers' compensation insurance, 180-182
Central processing unit, defined, 606
Challenges, in occupational health nursing, 150-152
Chronic conditions, defined, 606-607
Claims management
    administrative, 452
        defined, 603-604
    defined, 607
    disability management, integration of, 451-464
        administrative claims service, 452
        benefit payment, 458-459
        information gathering, 452-453
        litigation, 453-455
        costs of, 455-457
        model, 463
        potential workers' compensation service, questions to ask of, 461-462
        refusal of rehabilitation, 457-458
Coefficient of variation, defined, 607

Index 633

Cognitive appraisal, defined, 607
Coinsurance, defined, 607
Collective agreement provisions, samples, 244-245
Commission, defined, 607
Community influence
    insurance carrier, 65
    medical profession, 65-66
    workers' compensation attorney, 65-66
Community occupational health services, linkage with, 97
Community rating, defined, 608
Competition, and managed care, 535-537
Compiler, defined, 608
Complete method, defined, 608
Compliance, defined, 608
Composite rate, defined, 608
Compositing, defined, 608
Computer, defined, 608
Concurrent review, defined, 608
Configuration, defined, 608
Conflict, in labor-management initiatives, 229-230
Consumerism, and rehabilitation, 323-325
Continuous quality improvement (CQI), defined, 609
Contract
    defined, 609
    mix, defined, 609
    for services, for disability management, 35-39
        job analysis services, 36-37
    type, defined, 609
Conversion factor, defined, 609
Coordination of benefits, defined, 609
Coordination of treatment/rehabilitation, in occupational health nursing, 151-152
Copayment, defined, 609
Cost
    analysis, disability management, 62-63
    containment
        Americans with Disabilities Act, 485
        ergonomics, role in, 160-162
        with managed care, 524
    of disability, of aging worker, 502
    of disability management, 8-10
    -effectiveness, of promptness of intervention, 22-24
    of health care, 8-10
    of insurance coverage, 8-10
Counseling
    employer, role of, 357

service, emphasis on, 357
strategies of, 356-358
theoretical basis of, 356-357
vocational, 326-329
Counselor. *See* Rehabilitation counselor
Court testimony, by physician, 194-196
Credibility issues, of performance, in functional capacity assessment, 278-282
Cross-cultural rehabilitation counselor, 320-321
Cumulative trauma disorder, defined, 609

D

Data
    base management, defined, 610
    base system, defined, 610
    collection, defined, 610
    defined, 610
    entry, defined, 610
    processing, defined, 610
    sets, defined, 610
    system, for evaluation of transitional work program, 99
Decision-making functions, plan approval/funding, separation of issues, 44-45
Deductible, defined, 610
Demographics, defined, 610
Dependency, student, defined, 624
Dependents, defined, 610
Development of program, 56-78. *See also* Program development
Diagnosis of medical condition, 211
Dictionary of Occupational Titles, 111
    strength demands of work defined in, 289
Differential, defined, 611
Dignity, in disability management, importance of, 46-47
"Direct threat," screening for, under Americans with Disabilities Act, 492
Disability. *See also* Work disruption
    defined, 5, 178, 209, 611
    evaluation of, 210-213
    settlement, defined, 611
Disability management. *See also* Rehabilitation; Transitional work program; Worksite disability management
    accessibility, 46
    aging worker, 499-506, 555-602. *See also* Aging worker
    Americans with Disabilities Act, 479-497, 479-498
    analysis, defined, 611
    assistive technology, 363

Index

Canada, experience of, 465-478
case management services, as a key principle of disability management, 28
claims management, integration of, 451-464
concepts of, 4-13
contractual services, 35-39
counselor. *See* Rehabilitation counselor
definitions, 4-13, 611
development of program, 56-78
dignity, importance of, 46-47
disability, defined, 5
disability resolution services, 36-37
early return to work, as a key principle of disability management, 26-27
economics of, 8-10
educators, 311
employer-based transitional work program, as a key principle of disability management, 28-29
enhancement of program, 96-102
ergonomics, 157-174, 362. *See also* Ergonomics
family issues, 411-432. *See also* Family issues
forensic rehabilitation, 364-365
handicap, defined, 5
history of, 355-370
impairment, defined, 5
implementation of program, 78-95. *See also* Program implementation
injury prevention, 162-168. *See also* Injury prevention
intervention
    promptness of, 22-24
    team, defined, 611
introduction to, 3-4
job analysis, 362-363
joint labor-management initiatives, 32-35
    disability management committee, 38
    as a key principle of disability management, 26
key organizational concepts in
    decision-making functions, plan approval/funding, separation of issues, 44-45
    goal-orientation rehabilitation plan, 44-45
    partnerships, 43-44
labor relations, 13-20
    positive, promotion of, 18-20
legal issues, 434-449. *See also* Legal issues
managed care concept, 519-554. *See also* Managed care
medical management, 39
medical treatment, historical perspective, 359-361
models, 29-32
    using managed care, 522-532

objectives of, 6-7
occupational bonding, as a key principle of disability management, 28
occupational health, 131-155. *See also* Occupational health
in occupational health nursing, application of, 141-150
    General Electric, 141-144
    Honeywell, 144-146
    Marriott Corporation, 146-148
    Quaker Oats, 148-150
older worker, 11
physical therapist, 107-129. *See also* Physical therapist
predictor, work disruption/disability, 16-18
proactive intervention, 46
as a key principle of disability management, 27
program objectives, 77
quality assurance, 47-48
rehabilitation, historical perspective, 358-359
resolution process, aging worker, 513-514
resolution services, contractual, 36-37
respect, importance of, 46-47
responsible employer, 18
skills, 325-338, 326-329
stress, occupational, 371-409. *See also* Stress, occupational
team, 28
timeliness, 46
trends, 310-311, 312-313
    acquired immunodeficiency syndrome, 316-318
    cardiac disabilities, 314-318
    repetitive motion disorders, 312-313
vocational counseling, 38-39, 326-329
work-return transition/worker retention program, 38
Discharge summary, as component of physical therapy program, 118
    sample of, 127
Discrimination
    against aging worker, 572-583, 576-579
        combatting, 579-583
    against person with disability, legislation against. *See* Americans with Disabilities Act
Dispute resolution
    with labor-management initiatives, 237-238
    taskforce, 97
Distress, defined, 611
Diversification, in managed care, 529-530
Double contract, defined, 611
Dual choice, defined, 611
Duty statement for in-house rehabilitation counselor, 40

E

Ecological approach to rehabilitation, 322-323
Economic characteristics of aging worker, 502-503
Economics
    of health care, 8-10
    in industrial rehabilitation, 305-309
    of insurance coverage, 8-10
    with promptness of intervention, 22-24
Education
    of rehabilitation counselor, 325-338
    of worker, stress-reduction, in trauma-related disability management, 261-262
Educators, in disability management, 311
EEOC. *See* Equal Employment Opportunity Commission
Eligibility criteria, disability management program, labor-management committee on transitional work, 83-85
Emergency, defined, 611-612
Employee actions, contributing to litigation, 448
Employee assistance program
    defined, 612
    use of, 99-100
Employer
    attitude, regarding aging worker, 504-505
    -based transitional work program, as a key principle of disability management, 28-29
    errors, contributing to litigation, 447
    omissions, solutions to, 435
    questions to ask, potential workers' compensation service, 461-462
    responsible, 18
    role of, 228-229, 357
    study, of transitional work program, 92-93
Employment characteristics, aging worker, 502-503
Employment Retirement Income Security Act, overview of, 612
Employment trends
    growth projections, 307
    in industrial rehabilitation, 305-309
    rehabilitation counselor, 309
Enhancements, to transitional work program, after testing of, 96-102
Enrollment, defined, 612
Epidemiology of injury/disease in workplace, 178-180
Equipment, functional capacity assessment, 290-292
Ergonomics, 173, 362
    Americans with Disabilities Act, 168-169
    back injury, 161
    cost control, 160-162

defined, 157, 612
evolution of, 158-159
Human Factors and Ergonomics Society, 172
injury prevention, 160-162
    model for, 162-168
International Foundation for Industrial Ergonomics and Safety Research, 172
International Labour Organization, 172
job analysis, 214
model, for report on occupationally-related pain, 251-253
National Safety Council, 172
scope of, 159-162
upper extremity, 161-162
usage of term, 158
World Health Organization, 172
ERISA. *See* Employment Retirement Income Security Act
Essential job task, defined, 612
Evaluation
    after lengthy treatment, physician, role of, 188
    of physical therapy program, 114, 118
        sample of, 122-123, 127
    of transitional work program, data system for, 99
    of worker, transitional work, 85-86
Examination, pre-employment, 187
Exercise program, independent, as component of physical therapy program, 117
    sample of, 126
Exertion, reporting of, in functional capacity assessment, 281-282
Expansion, of transitional work program, 97
Experience rating, defined, 612
Extremity, upper, ergonomics, 161-162

F

Family contract, defined, 613
Family issues
    adaptation by family, to disability, 414-419
    case study, 416-419
    disability manager, 430
    intervention programs, 419-429
    overview, 411-414
Feasibility analysis, defined, 613
Federal agencies, publications by, for physical therapist, 110-112
Fee-for-service, defined, 613
Firmware, defined, 613
Fixed cost, defined, 613

Index

Forensic rehabilitation, 364-365
Functional capacity assessment
    ability, perceived, rating of, 283
    cardiovascular endurance, 286
    case study, 292-297
    data, objectivity/subjectivity of, 276
    defined, 613
    equipment, 290-291
    exertion, reporting of, 281-282
    future of, 297-298
    genetic risk factors, 272
    goal of, 269-270
    grip strength assessment, 283-284
    indications for, 270-271
    job analysis, 271-275
        compatibility analysis, physician's role, 182-187
    mobility tasks, 287-288
    on-site, equipment for, 291-292
    order of tasks, 289
    pain level scale, subjective reporting of, 280
    performance credibility, 278-282
    physical therapy program, 114-115
        sample of, 123
    posture tasks, 287-288
    reliability of, 277-278
    safety issues, 275
    standardization, 276
    strength
        assessment, 284-286
        demands of work defined in *Dictionary of Occupational Titles,* 289
    validity of, 276-277
    work recommendations, 288
Funding issues, decision-making function issues, separation of, 44-45

G

General Electric, disability management program, 141-144
Genetic risk factors, in functional capacity assessment, 272
Getting to Yes; Negotiating Agreements Without Giving In, 234
Goal setting, as component of physical therapy program, 116
    sample of, 124
Goal-orientation rehabilitation plan, 44-45
Grip strength assessment, in functional capacity assessment, 283-284
Group contract, defined, 613

Group practice, medical, defined, 617-618
Guide for Occupational Exploration, 111

H

Handicap
    assessment of, 209-210
    defined, 5, 178, 209, 613
    diagnosis, 211
    ergonomic job analysis, 214
    external resources, 216-217
    individualized program, 215-217
        case example, 217-219
    medical condition, presence of, 211
    medical disability, evaluation of, 210-213
    medical treatment plan, 211
    methodology for assessment of, 210-217
    residual work ability assessment, 211-212
    vocational rehabilitation evaluation, 214-215
    work capacity evaluation, 213
    work precautions, 212
    work restrictions, 212
Hardware, defined, 613
HCFA. *See* Health Care Financing Administration
Health care, cost of, 8-10
Health Care Financing Administration, overview of, 614
Health care professional, attitude regarding aging worker, 505
Health insurance benefit, administration of, Americans with Disabilities Act, 482-487
Health maintenance organization
    beginning of, 520
    defined, 614
    long-term care, future trends, 546-547
Health promotion resources, use of, 99-100
Health services analysis, defined, 614
History, worker
    as component of physical therapy program, 114
    physical therapist, 122-127
Honeywell, disability management program, 144-146
Human Factors and Ergonomics Society, 172

I

Impairment
    defined, 5, 178, 209, 614
    rating, by physician, 190

Index

Incentive, defined, 614
Indemnity carrier, defined, 615
Indemnity insurance, defined, 615
Independent exercise program, as component of physical therapy program, 117
    sample of, 126
Independent medical evaluation, by physician, 193-194
Independent practice association, 520-522
Individualized program, of disability management, development of, 215-217
Industrial health publications, 113
Industrial rehabilitation. *See also* Rehabilitation
    administration skills, 334
    case management procedures, 330-333
    education, 303-338
    job modification/development, 329-330
    job placement, 329-330
    knowledge, disability-related, 335-337
    leadership skills, 334-335
    organizational skills, 333-337
    program development skills, 333-337
    rehabilitation plan, key variables, 333
    skills, applied, 326-329
    training orientation, sample, 339-343
    vocational counseling in, 326-329
Information gathering, in disability management, 452-453
Information system design, in managed care, 543-544
Injury management, defined, 615
Injury prevention. *See also* Ergonomics
    model for, 162-168
    in occupational health nursing, 136
Insurance, workers' compensation, 180-182
    causality and, 180-182
Insurance carrier, influence of on disability management, 65
Insurance coverage, costs of, 8-10
Intensity factor, defined, 615
Interactive system, defined, 616
Interdisciplinary approach, defined, 616
Interdisciplinary factors in trauma-related disability management
    disability model, 265
    fatigue to disability continuum, 256
    intervention strategies, 249-251
    management
        early return to work, facilitation of, 264
        role of, 254-255
    medical care, appropriateness of, 262-263
    pain

organizational responsiveness to, 259-261
report, ergonomic model, 251-253
proactive *vs.* reactive approach, 255-258
stress-reduction, education of worker and, 261-262
theoretical support, 253-254
time factor in disability prevention, 259
workers' compensation system, and disability prevention, overview of, 258-259

International Classification of Impairments, Disabilities, and Handicaps, 177-178

International Foundation for Industrial Ergonomics and Safety Research, 172

International Labour Organization, 172

Intervention
proactive, as a key principle of disability management, 27
prompt
as advantage of transitional work program, 119
importance of, 20-26
as a key principle of disability management, 26-27
psycho-social impact of, 24-26
strategies, trauma-related disability, 249-251

Interviews, disability management, 56-58

IPA. *See* Independent practice association

Isoinertial, defined, 616

Isokinetic, defined, 616

Isometric, defined, 616

J

Job analysis
defined, 616
in functional capacity assessment, 271-275
services, 36-37

Job availability, in occupational health nursing, 151

Job description, defined, 616

Job development, 329-330

Job placement, 329-330
appropriate, as advantage of transitional work program, 119

Job task bank, development of, 98

K

Key organizational concepts in disability management, 43-48
decision-making functions, plan approval/funding, separation of issues, 44-45
goal-orientation rehabilitation plan, 44-45
partnerships, 43-44

Knowledge required, for worksite disability management, 42-43

L

Labor market trends, in industrial rehabilitation, 305-308
Labor relations
 and disability management, 13-20
 positive, promotion of, 18-20
Labor union, role of, 226
Labor-management committee, 93
 meeting frequency, 81-82
 mission statement, 82-83
 policy/procedure, 82-85
 program eligibility criteria, 83-85
 referral process, 83
 transitional work, 80-81
Labor-management initiatives, 32-35, 225-247
 Canadian, 472-473
 collective agreement provisions, samples, 244-245
 conflict, 229-230
 dispute resolution, 237-238
 employer, role of, 228-229
 establishment of program, 241-242
 history of, 32-33
 labor union, role of, 226
 partnership between, importance of, 235-237
 preparation for, 238
 process overview, 238-241
 responsibility, 230-233
 return to work pact, 234-235
  negotiated, sample guidelines for, 245-247
 trends in, 33-35
 workers with disabilities, 226-227
Lag factor, defined, 616
Language, defined, 616
Leadership skills, in industrial rehabilitation, 334-335
Legal issues
 attorney, disability management strategy, 444
 employee actions, contributing to litigation, 448
 employer errors, contributing to litigation, 447
 employer omissions, solutions to, 435
 litigation
  avoidance of, checklist for, 444-445
  causes of, 437-441
 process overview, 436
 preventive strategies, 441-444
 problem resolution strategies, 434-435

vocational experts, 446-448
Letter, return-to-work, and physician, role of, 188
Lifestyle-related illness, company expenditures for, 551
Light duty, *vs.* transitional work program, 79-80
Litigation, 453-455
    avoidance of, checklist for, 444-445
    causes of, 437-441
    costs of, 455-457
    employee actions contributing to, 448
    employer errors contributing to, 447
    preventive strategies, 441-444
    process overview, 436
Long-term care HMO, future trends, 546-547
Loss ratio, defined, 617

M

Mainframe, defined, 617
Male population, aging worker, 564-572
Managed care
    administration, 528, 532-534
    alliance with, 531-532
    case management, 543, 545-546
    competition and, 535-537
    components of, 523-526
    cost control, 524
    delivery system, 532-534
    disability management models, 522-532
    disability network, start-up of, 530-531
    diversification, 529-530
    future trends in, 546-552
    health maintenance organization, beginning of, 520
    health of employees, *vs.* cost-containment, as focus, 544-545
    independent practice association, 520-522
    information system
        design, 543-544
        expansion, 539-544
    and lifestyle-related illness, 551
    long-term care HMO, future trends, 546-547
    management, 535-534
    marketing, 528-529
    mental health, future trends, 547-550
    normative data, 540-541
    and occupational medicine, 526-527

Index

    overview, 519-527
    physician view of, 534
    preferred provider organization, 522-523
    private industry, future trends, 550-552
    product development, 528-529
    reimbursement system, 528
    strategic planning process, 537
    trend tracking, 541
Management
    facilitation of early return to work, 264
    orientation of, labor/management outline, 70-72
    training topics, 69
Management-labor committee. *See* Labor-management committee
Marginal cost, defined, 617
Market area, defined, 617
Market share, defined, 617
Marketing
    defined, 617
    managed care, 528-529
Marriott Corporation, disability management program, 146-148
Meaning, attainment of through work, 177
Mediation, with aging worker, 588-592
Medical care, appropriateness of, in trauma-related disability management, 262-263
Medical determination, regarding reemployment, under Americans with Disabilities Act, 491-492
Medical evaluation, independent, by physician, 193-194
Medical management, 39
    aging worker, 512-513
Medical profession, influence of on disability management, 65-66
Medical surveillance, and role of physician, 189-190
Medical testimony, 194-196
Medical treatment
    historical perspective, 359-361
    plan, 211
Member month, defined, 618
Mental health, managed care, future trends, 547-550
Mental-mental disability, defined, 618
Mental-physical disability, defined, 618
Methods-time measurement standards, 113
Microcomputer, defined, 618
Mission statement
    labor-management committee on transitional work, 82-83
    transitional work program, 82-83
        key principles, 93-94
Mobility tasks, in functional capacity assessment, 287-288

Model programs, for disability management, 29-32
Modem, defined, 618
Modification of job, 329-330
    permanent, placement of worker in, 87
Monitoring, on-site, of transitional workers, 86
Multicultural issues, in workplace participation, 319-321

N

National Institute for Occupational Safety and Health, publications of, 110-111
National Institute of Disability Management and Research, 475-476
National Labor Relations Act, and Americans with Disabilities Act, 492-495
National Safety Council, 172
National Workers' Compensation Attitude Survey, 10
Network model, defined, 618
Nonphysical factors assessment, as component of physical therapy program, 116
    sample of, 124
Nontraditional jobs, development of, 98
Nurse. *See also* Occupational health, nursing
    certified occupational health nurse, defined, 619
    interaction with client, overview of, 139

O

Objectives, of disability management, 6-7
Occupational ability, defined, 208
Occupational bonding
    defined, 7, 619
    as a key principle of disability management, 28
Occupational fitness, defined, 209
Occupational handicap. *See* Handicap
Occupational health, nursing, 131-155
    certified (COHN), defined, 619
    disability management, 135-150
        application of, 141-150
            General Electric, 141-144
            Honeywell, 144-146
            Marriott Corporation, 146-148
            Quaker Oats, 148-150
        challenges, 150-152
    job availability, 151
    perspective, 132-133
        contemporary, 132-133
        historical, 132

planning issues, 137
prevention issues, 136
process issues, 137-138
productivity, 138-140
treatment/rehabilitation, coordination of, 151-152
Occupational medicine, managed care and, 526-527
Occupational Safety and Health Act, 111
Off-line, defined, 620
Older worker, disability management, 11
On-line, defined, 620
Open enrollment period, defined, 620
Operating system, defined, 620
Order of tasks, and functional capacity assessment, 289
Organizational climate
    as psychosocial stressors, 382-383
    stress reduction efforts, effect on, 390-391
Organizational skills, in industrial rehabilitation, 333-337
Out-of-area benefits, defined, 620

P

Pain
    level scale, subjective reporting of, 280
    occupationally-related, report on, ergonomic model, 251-253
    of worker, organizational responsiveness to, 259-261
Partnership, 43-44
    between labor and management, importance of, 235-237. *See also* Labor-management initiatives
Pathophysiology of injury/disease in workplace, 178-180
Patterns of disability, 60-61
Payment, of benefits, 458-459
Peer review, defined, 620
Performance credibility, functional capacity assessment, 278-282
Physical therapist, 107-129
    case closure by, 120
    case history, 114, 122-127
        example of, 122
    customized program, 120
    discharge summary, 118
        sample of, 127
    evaluation
        of program, 118
        sample of, 122-123
    functional work capacities assessment, 114-115

sample of, 123
goal setting, 116
    sample of, 124
independent exercise program, 117
    sample of, 126
industrial health publications, 113
methods-time measurement standards, 113
nonphysical factors assessment, 116
    sample of, 124
physical therapy evaluation, 114
program components, 113-118
program development, 116-117
    sample of, 126
program evaluation, sample of, 127
program updates, sample of, 126-127
publications for
    Dictionary of Occupational Titles, 111
    Guide for Occupational Exploration, 111
    Work Practices Guide for Manual Lifting, 110
qualifications, 110-113
records review, 114
scheduling, 119-120
travel, 119
updates, 117-118
vehicle, 120
worker profile, 116
    sample of, 124
worksite analysis, 115-116
    sample of, 123-124
worksite environment, 120
Physical-mental disability, defined, 621
Physician
    managed care, perspective on, 534
    role of, 182-187, 212-213
        case study, 198-200
        disability, defined, 178
        epidemiology of injury/disease in workplace, 178-180
        evaluation, after lengthy treatment, 188
        functional capacity/job requirement, compatibility analysis, 182-187
        handicap, defined, 178
        impairment, defined, 178
        impairment rating, 190
        in independent medical evaluation, 193-194
        insurance, workers' compensation, 180-182
            causality and, 180-182

Index

International Classification of Impairments, Disabilities, and Handicaps, 177-178
    participation of, and return-to-work outcome, 196-198
    pathophysiology of injury/disease in workplace, 178-180
    pre-employment examination, 187
    return-to-work letter, 188
    screening, 189-190
    Social Security disability evaluation, 191-193
    surveillance, medical, 189-190
    testimony, medical, 194-196
    training in disability management, 177-182
    work, attainment of meaning through, 177
Physician extender, defined, 621
Physician worksite tour, 96
Pilot program, transitional work program, 94-95
Pilot testing, of transitional work program, 89-91
Placement mechanism, transitional work program as, 98
Plan approval, decision-making functions, separation of issues, 44-45
Planning issues, in occupational health nursing, 137
Policy, disability management, 63-64
Posture tasks, in functional capacity assessment, 287-288
PPO. *See* Preferred provider organization
Precautions, for work, 212
Predictor, of work disruption/disability, 16-18
Pre-employment examination, 187
Preferred provider organization, 522-523
Premium, defined, 621
Prevention. *See* Injury prevention
Primary appraisal, defined, 621
Principles of, disability management, overview, 26-29
Prior authorization, defined, 621
Private industry, managed care, future trends, 550-552
Proactive intervention, 27, 46
Procedures
    disability management, 63-64
    transitional work program, 90-91
Process issues, in occupational health nursing, 137-138
Product development, managed care, 528-529
Productivity, in occupational health nursing, 138-140
Profile, of worker, as component of physical therapy program, 116
    sample of, 124, 125
Program development
    analysis, disability management, 56-67
        case analysis, 58-59
        community influence, 64-67
        cost analysis, 62-63

>   interviews, 56-58
>   patterns of disability, 60-61
>   policy, 63-64
>   procedures, 63-64
>   case management resources, 73-78
>   rehabilitation plan development, 74-77
>   as component of physical therapy program, 116-117
>   sample of, 126
>   management
>   awareness of, 67-72
>   orientation of, 67-72
>   labor/management outline, 70-72
>   training topics, 69
>   planning for, 77
>   skills, in industrial rehabilitation, 333-337
> Program implementation, transitional work
>   defined, 78
>   labor-management committee on, 80-81
>   therapeutic advantages of, 78-79
>   *vs.* light duty, 79-80
> Program updates, as component of physical therapy program, sample of, 126-127
> Promptness of intervention, 22-24
>   cost-effectiveness, 22-24
>   economic savings, 22-24
>   importance of, 20-26, 22
>   as a key principle of disability management, 26-27
>   psycho-social impact of, 24-26
> Proprietary, defined, 622
> Psychiatric disability, options for, 99
> Psychosocial impact, of early intervention, 24-26
> Psychosocial stressor, 380-384
>   advancement opportunities, inadequate, 384
>   organizational climate, 382-383
>   role ambiguity, 384
>   and supervisory style, 382
>   work overload, 383
>   work underload, 383-384
> Publications
>   *Dictionary of Occupational Titles,* 111
>   by federal agencies, for physical therapist, 110-112
>   *Guide for Occupational Exploration,* 111
>   in industrial health, 113
>   by U.S. Department of Labor, 111-112
>   *Work Practices Guide for Manual Lifting,* 110

Q

Quaker Oats, disability management program, 148-150
Qualifications, physical therapist, 110-113
Quality assurance, 47-48
    defined, 622

R

Rate structure, defined, 622
Rating of impairment, by physician, 190
Reappraisal, defined, 622
Records review, as component of physical therapy program, 114
    sample of, 122
Referral process, labor-management committee on transitional work, 83
Refusal of rehabilitation, by claimant, 457-458
Rehabilitation. *See also* Disability management
    of aging worker, 583-588
    consumerism and, 323-325
    ecological approach to, 322-323
    forensic, 364-365
    historical perspective, 358-359
    needs, response to, promptness, importance of, 22
    overview, 3-53
    plan
        development, 74-77
            for aging worker, 514
        transitional work, 86
    refusal of, by claimant, 457-458
    self-determination trends, 323-325
    skills needed for, 325-338
Rehabilitation counselor
    cross-cultural, 320-321
    duty statement for in-house, 40
    education, 325-338
    employment trends, 309
Reimbursement system, managed care, 528
Reinsurance, defined, 622
Reintegration into community, model of transitional work program establishment for, 100
Reliability of functional capacity assessment, 277-278
Repetitive motion disorders, 312-313
Reserves, defined, 623
Resources, external, use of in individualized program development, 216-217
Respect, in disability management, importance of, 46-47

Response to rehabilitation needs, promptness, importance of, 22
Responsibility, of workers, in transitional work program, 87
Responsibility costing, defined, 623
Responsiveness, of organization, to pain of worker, 259-261
Restrictions, for work, 212
Return to work
    early, as a key principle of disability management, 26-27
    letter, 188
    pact, 234-235
    program, negotiated, sample guidelines for, 245-247
Role ambiguity, as psychosocial stressor, 384

S

Safety issues, in functional capacity assessment, 275
Saturation, defined, 623
Scheduling, for physical therapist, 119-120
Screening, and role of physician, 189-190
Self-determination trends in rehabilitation, 323-325
Self-insured, defined, 624
Semivariable cost, defined, 624
Service area, defined, 624
Shared risk, defined, 624
Single contract, defined, 624
Skills required, for worksite disability management, 42-43
Social Security disability evaluation, physician role, 191-193
Software, defined, 624
Standardization
    defined, 624
    of functional capacity assessment, 276
Standing of injured workers, as Americans with disabilities, under Americans with
    Disabilities Act, 489-490
Stereotypes of aging worker, 574-575
Stop-loss, defined, 624
Strategic planning process, in managed care, 537
Strength
    assessment, 284-286
        in functional capacity assessment, 284-286
    demands of work defined in Dictionary of Occupational Titles, 289
    grip, assessment, in functional capacity assessment, 283-284
Stress
    characteristics of, 376-386
    complexity of, 385-386
    control of, 387-401

cost of, 375-376
defined, 619, 624
detection of, 388-390
effects of, overview, 373
extraorganizational, 385
and health, 372-375
intervention, 401-404
    evaluation, 404
    impact on organizational climate, 390-391
    management concern, 401-402
    primary, 391-392
        job design, 392-394
        total quality management, 394-396
        worker-job matching, 396-397
    secondary, 398
    service providers, 401
    tertiary, 398-401
    timing of, 402-403
occupational, 371-409
physical stressors, 379-380
psychosocial stressors, 380-384
reduction, education of worker and, 261-262
syndrome of, 377-378
target worker groups, 403
Student dependency, defined, 624
Subrogation, defined, 624
Supervisor of worker, responsibility of, 89
Supervisory style, as psychosocial stressors, 382
Surveillance, medical, and role of physician, 189-190

T

Task bank, development of, 98
Team concept, as a key principle of disability management, 28
Technology, and aging worker, 503
Tertiary occupational stress prevention, defined, 624
Testimony, in court proceedings, by physician, 194-196
Testing, of transitional work program, 89-91
Time factor, in disability prevention, 259
Time parameters, transitional work, 86-87
Time sharing, defined, 624
Timeliness, of disability management, 46
Total quality management (TQM)
    defined, 626

and prompt intervention, 25
and stress prevention, 394-396
TQM. *See* Total quality management
Training
    in disability management, for physician, 177-182
    model, 303-352
    orientation, in industrial rehabilitation, sample, 339-343
    topics, for management training, 69
Transferable skill
    analysis, aging worker, 508-509
    defined, 627
Transitional work program. *See also* Disability management; Worksite disability management
    adjustments to, after testing, 96-102
    advantages of, 118-119
        Americans with Disabilities Act compliance, 119
        early intervention, 119
        employee benefit, 119
        job placement, appropriate, 119
        team members, 119
        worksite "clinic," 119
    case manager, responsibilities of, 87
    community occupational health services, linkage with, 97
    data system, for evaluation, 99
    defined, 78
    dispute resolution taskforce, 97
    employee assistance program, use of, 99-100
    employer
        -based, as a key principle of disability management, 28-29
        study, 92-93
        trends in use of, 101
    evaluation, 89
        of worker, 85-86
    expansion to all workers with restrictions, 97
    health promotion resources, use of, 99-100
    job task bank, development of, 98
    labor-management committee, 80-81, 93
        meeting frequency, 81-82
    mission statement, 82-83
        key principles, 93-94
    model of, for reintegration into community, 100
    monitoring, on-site, 86
    nontraditional jobs, development of, 98
    to permanent modified duty work, placement of worker in, 87
    physician worksite tour, 96
    pilot program, 94-95

pilot testing, 89-91
as placement mechanism, 98
policy/procedure, 82-85
procedural steps, 90-91
program eligibility criteria, 83-85
psychiatric disability, 99
referral process, 83
rehabilitation planning, 86
responsibilities of workers, 87
therapeutic advantages of, 78-79
time parameters, 86-87
trends in, 100-102
vs. light duty, 79-80
worker unable to transition , procedures for, 92

Trauma-related disability
disability model, 265
fatigue to disability continuum, 256
intervention strategies, 249-251
management
early return to work, facilitation of, 264
role of, 254-255
medical care, appropriateness of, 262-263
pain
report, ergonomic model, 251-253
of worker, organizational responsiveness to, 259-261
proactive *vs.* reactive approach, 255-258
stress-reduction, education of worker and, 261-262
theoretical support, 253-254
time factor in disability prevention, 259
workers' compensation system, and disability prevention, overview of, 258-259

Travel, physical therapist, 119
Trends, in use of transitional work program, 100-102
Triage, defined, 627
Turnkey system, defined, 627

U

Updates, as component of physical therapy program, 117-118
Upper extremity, ergonomics, 161-162
U.S. Department of Labor, publications of, 111-112
U.S. Equal Employment Opportunity Commission, 12

V

Validity of functional capacity assessment, 276-277
Variable costs, defined, 627
Vehicle, for physical therapist, 120
Venture capital, defined, 627
Vocational counseling, 326-329
Vocational evaluation, 38-39
    aging worker, 510-511
Vocational expert, 446-448
    defined, 628
Vocational rehabilitation, 38-39
    aging worker, 503-504
    counseling. *See* Counseling
    evaluation, 214-215

W

Wash of premium, defined, 628
Work
    ability
        box, defined, 628
        report, sample form, 84
        residual, assessment, 211-212
    attainment of meaning through, 177
    disruption. *See also* Disability
    disruption/disability, prediction of, 16-18
    environment, therapeutic, 7-8
    overload, as psychosocial stressor, 383
    recommendations, and functional capacity assessment, 288
    underload, as psychosocial stressor, 383-384
Worker
    aging. *See* Aging worker
    defined, 208
    with disabilities, joint labor-management initiatives, 226-227
    disability, defined, 209
    handicap
        assessment of, 209-210
        defined, 209
        methodology for assessment of, 210-217
            diagnosis, 211
            ergonomic job analysis, 214
            external resources, 216-217
            individualized program, 215-217

Index

        case example, 217-219
        medical condition, presence of, 211
        medical disability evaluation, 210-213
        medical treatment plan, 211
        residual work ability assessment, 211-212
        vocational rehabilitation evaluation, 214-215
        work capacity evaluation, 213
        work precautions, 212
        work restrictions, 212
    history, 122-127
    impairment, defined, 209
    occupational ability, defined, 208
    occupational fitness, defined, 209
    occupational stress and, 371-409
    profile, as component of physical therapy program, 116
        sample of, 124, 125
    responsibilities of, 88-89
    unable to transition to, transitional work program, procedures for, 92
Worker retention program, aging worker, 514-515
Worker-job matching, and stress prevention, 396-397
Workers' compensation
    attorney, influence of on disability management, 65-66
    boards, role of, in Canada, 469-471
    claim, and Americans with Disabilities Act claim, filing both, 495
    complexity of, 10
    prior history, inquiry restriction, under Americans with Disabilities Act, 490-491
Workers' groups, experiences of, in Canada, 467-469
Workplace
    disability, trends in, 309-311
    injury, trends in, 309-311
Work-return transition/worker retention program, 38
Worksite
    analysis, as component of physical therapy program, 115-116
        sample of, 123-124
    development of program, 56-78
    disability management. *See also* Disability management; Transitional work program
    duty statement for in-house rehabilitation counselor, 40
    enhancement of program, 96-102
    ergonomics, 157-174. *See also* Ergonomics
    evaluation of program
    functional capacity assessment, 269-300, 290. *See also* Functional capacity assessment
    implementation of program, 78-95. *See also* Program implementation
    interdisciplinary factors in trauma-related disability, 249-267. *See also* Trauma-related disability
    joint labor-management initiatives, 225-247. *See also* Labor-management initiatives

knowledge required, 42-43
manager, role/function of, 39-43
occupational health nurse, role of, 131-155. *See also* Occupational health, nursing
physical therapist, role of, 107-129. *See also* Physical therapist
physician, role of, 175-205. *See also* Physician, role of
risk, aging worker, 509
skills required, 42-43
training model, 303-352. *See also* Training model
worker, perspective of, 207-223. *See also* Worker

World Health Organization, 172